AF903099

MATLAB APPLICATIONS FOR THE PRACTICAL ENGINEER

Edited by **Kelly Bennett**

MATLAB Applications for the Practical Engineer
http://dx.doi.org/10.5772/57070
Edited by Kelly Bennett

Contributors

Mostefa Ghassoul, Antonio Gauchía, Beatriz Lopez Boada, Maria Jesus Boada, Vicente Diaz Lopez, Milton Macedo, Abdul-Ganiyu Adisa Jimoh, Edward Kofi Appiah, Ayodeji S.O. Ogunjuyigbe, Aduwati Sali, Jit Mandeep, Alyani Ismail, Abdulmajeed Aljumaily, Chandima Gomes, Ali M. Al-Saegh, Gasta M'Boungui, Betty Semail, Frederic Giraud, Kelly Bennett, James Robertson, Teodor Lucian Grigorie, Ruxandra Botez, Marian Gaiceanu, Roger Chiu, Francisco J. Casillas, Francisco G. Peña-Lecona, Miguel Mora-González, Didier López-Mancilla, Jesús Muñoz-Maciel, Ramón Silva-Ortigoza, Celso Márquez-Sánchez, Victor Manuel Hernández-Guzmán, Fernando Carrizosa-Corral, Magdalena Marciano-Melchor, Jesús Antonio Álvarez-Cedillo, Hind Taud, José Rafael García-Sánchez, Drago Strle, Dusan Raic, Tiago Almeida, Alexandre César Rodrigues da Silva, Ian Andrew Grout, Mayra Antonio-Cruz, Mariana Marcelino-Aranda, Carlos Alejandro Merlo-Zapata, Griselda Saldaña-González, Patricia Pérez-Romero, Antonis Georgantzoglou, Joakim Da Silva, Rajesh Jena, Mato Miskovic, Ivan Miskovic, Marina Mirošević, Cristina-Maria DABU, Rafael Cuerda Monzani, Afonso José Do Prado, Leonardo Lessa, Luiz Fernando Bovolato, Viliam Fedak, Pavel Záskalický, Zoltan Gelvanič, František Ďurovský, Robert Uveges, Wael Al-Tabey, Hassan Al-Haj Ibrahim

Published by InTech

Janeza Trdine 9, 51000 Rijeka, Croatia

Copyright © 2014 InTech

Individual chapters are under their authors' copyright and distributed under the Creative Commons Attribution 3.0 license, which allows users to download, copy and build upon published chapters provided that the authors and publisher are properly credited, which ensures maximum dissemination and a wider impact of the authors' work. Any republication, referencing or personal use of the individual chapters or any of their contents must explicitly identify the original source.

Permission for commercial use of the book as a whole, such as (but not limited to) reprint rights, republication, distribution, sales, translation, and reproduction in any and all forms of media, must always be obtained from InTech.

Notice

Statements and opinions expressed in the chapters are these of the individual contributors and not necessarily those of the editors or publisher. No responsibility is accepted for the accuracy of information contained in the published chapters. The publisher assumes no responsibility for any damage or injury to persons or property arising out of the use of any materials, instructions, methods or ideas contained in the book.

Publishing Process Manager Iva Lipovic

Technical Editor InTech DTP team

Cover InTech Design team

MATLAB® (Matlab logo and Simulink) is a registered trademark of The MathWorks, Inc.

First published August, 2014
Printed in Croatia

Additional hard copies can be obtained from orders@intechopen.com

MATLAB Applications for the Practical Engineer, Edited by Kelly Bennett
p. cm.
ISBN 978-953-51-1719-3

We are IntechOpen, the world's leading publisher of Open Access books

Built by scientists, for scientists

4,200+
Open access books available

116,000+
International authors and editors

125M+
Downloads

151
Countries delivered to

Our authors are among the
Top 1%
most cited scientists

12.2%
Contributors from top 500 universities

BOOK CITATION INDEX
CLARIVATE ANALYTICS
INDEXED

WEB OF SCIENCE™

Selection of our books indexed in the Book Citation Index
in Web of Science™ Core Collection (BKCI)

Interested in publishing with us?
Contact book.department@intechopen.com

Numbers displayed above are based on latest data collected.
For more information visit www.intechopen.com

For EU product safety concerns:
IN TECH d.o.o., Prolaz Marije Krucifikse Kozulić 3, 51000 Rijeka, Croatia,
info@intechopen.com or visit our website at intechopen.com.

Meet the editor

Kelly Bennett is currently a research engineer at the Army Research Laboratory. His diverse background includes semiconductor processing and design, RF circuit design, Ferroelectric thin film basic research for non-volatile memory applications, radiation hardening of electronics, acousto-optics research in spectroscopy and imaging applications, and database design and development. He has worked for the Army Research Laboratory for over 29 years as a research engineer and scientist and has over 40 professional publications in the open literature, many of which focus on the performance issues of big data in computational environments such as MATLAB. His expertise as an IT professional includes professional certification in JAVA development and enterprise development as well as fluency in many object-based, object-orientated, and SQL languages.

Contents

Preface

Being an automotive enthusiast and hobbyist, there is a saying around the race track that speed isn't everything, it's just most everything. Similar sentiments can be said about MATLAB. MATLAB isn't everything to a practicing engineer, it's just most everything. MATLAB is an indispensable asset for scientists, researchers, and engineers. The richness of the MATLAB computational environment combined with an integrated development environment (IDE) and straightforward interface, toolkits, and simulation and modeling capabilities, creates a research and development tool that has no equal. The book is written for a wide range of users including students, practicing engineers, researchers, and scientists. The diversity of the applications throughout the book shows the wide-ranging capability of MATLAB to perform technical computational efforts in support of research, development and engineering.

The common, central theme amongst all the book chapters contained in this book is MATLAB. As you will notice, MATLAB is used by vast array of researchers, engineers, and students from many different types of organizations ranging from academia, government, and industry. The book chapters range on a variety of topics including:

- Applied Mathematics
- Database Development
- Control Applications
- Modeling, Identification, and Simulation
- Image Processing

From quick code prototyping to full blown deployable applications, MATLAB stands as a de facto development language and environment serving the technical needs of a wide range of users. This is clearly demonstrated throughout the book and in some instances the results may not have been possible without the use of MATLAB.

As a collection of diverse applications, each book chapter presents a novel application and use of MATLAB for a specific result. I am thankful to each author for their diligence and high-level of technical effort presented in each book chapter. It has been my pleasure to serve as your book editor.

Although open access publishing is not fully accepted by the scientific community as a whole, I believe great benefit is provided by providing a great opportunity for researchers and engineers to share their technical efforts within the technical community without some of the hindrances presented by more traditional publishing avenues.

Finally, I want to take this opportunity to thank InTech for their patience in working with me on this project and on many of occasions, patiently leading me though the various steps of the development process of this book. It is with great pleasure, that I present to you a book on MATLAB applications that I believe you will find very interesting and helpful to your research efforts.

Kelly Bennett
Research Engineer
U.S. Army Research Laboratory,Sensors and Electron Devices Directorate,
Adelphi, MD, USA

Section 1

Social Networking Applications

Chapter 1

Knowledge Discovery and Information Extraction on the Open Internet Using MATLAB and Amazon Web Services (AWS)

Kelly Bennett and James Robertson

Additional information is available at the end of the chapter

http://dx.doi.org/10.5772/58895

1. Introduction

The popularity of social networking has allowed access to staggering amounts of unique data, which has created new possibilities for data analysis and exploitation. Such data has proven useful in marketing, decision making, destabilizing terrorist networks, behavior evolution, and determining future social trends [1].

Increased usage of social networking sites has also been observed during events related to natural disasters; significant political, sporting, and social events; and other crises. Twitter users provide status updates through tweets. Since tweets are typically short and always less than 140 characters, they may need to undergo additional analysis to provide contextual clues. Applying traditional natural language processing algorithms on such data is challenging. Before making use of this data, it must first be extracted, processed and analyzed appropriately using certain algorithms and theories.

According to a 2011 study from the International Data Corporation (IDC)–a marketing firm specializing in information technology and other consumer technologies–unstructured data, that is, data that does not have a pre-defined data model or is not organized in a pre-defined manner, is growing at a faster rate than structured data. Within the next decade, unstructured data will account for 90 percent of all data created.

A large driving factor in the increase in unstructured data is social networking data, such as tweets. It is estimated that more than 80 percent of all potentially useful data is unstructured [2].

INTECH
open science | open minds

© 2014 The Author(s). Licensee InTech. This chapter is distributed under the terms of the Creative Commons Attribution License (http://creativecommons.org/licenses/by/3.0), which permits unrestricted use, distribution, and reproduction in any medium, provided the original work is properly cited.

The success of businesses in the coming decade will likely rely on their ability to successfully analyze data from social networks.

In addition to the increase in social networking, cloud computing technologies continue to increase in popularity and provide end users the ability to quickly spin up powerful servers with analytical capabilities, making analysis of large amounts of data more affordable and practical than in previous decades.

Main topics addressed in this chapter include:

- Explore viable approaches for extracting social networking data sets using tools compatible with MATLAB[1] and cloud technologies and infrastructures.
- Use existing data mining and statistical tools within MATLAB to conduct analysis on social networking site data.
- Discuss potential cost savings and document approaches for implementing social networking site data analysis via the cloud through vendors such as Amazon Web Services (AWS).
- Provide a tutorial on the use of MATLAB tools to analyze unstructured data with an emphasis on social networking data.
- Provide an overview and example on the use of MATLAB in a commercial cloud environment, such as AWS.

2. Previous work

Muhammad Mahbubur Rahman, author of "Mining Social Data to Extract Intellectual Knowledge," was able to extract data from Facebook using various data mining techniques. He first determined the most frequent terms that were being used, such as birthday, about me, gender, and music, and then created a database using these terms and the appropriate data types. [1] From the "about me" information, he was able to use an Euclidian distance formula to put each user into a certain "class", for example, aggressive, dishonest, romantic, eager to learn, or lazy. Grouping classes by age and gender creates a method of comparing various attributes by age and gender. This type of research demonstrates the ability to use data mining techniques to provide intellectual knowledge that can be used to possibility predict human behavior, provide insight into human decision making, or provide a method of determining anomalous events.

Data mining has proven useful in Twitter as well, with much research performed into detecting trends and bursty keywords. One has to pay attention to some abnormalities with Twitter, such as many people use smart phones to tweet and it is common for people to make mistakes while typing on smart phones. One would have to account for misspellings and merge them

1 Registered trademark of Mathworks Corporation.

into one variable so they are not separated and lost. In addition, some phrases are commonly abbreviated, such as "NYC" for "New York City," or reduced, such as "Vegas" for "Las Vegas." A study, using algorithms to account for these abnormalities, was performed that determined trendy and bursty keywords on Twitter with 92% accuracy when compared with Google trends [3].

Karandikar [4] described an approach to determine the most suitable topic model to cluster tweets by analyzing the effect of change in topic model parameters such as training data size and type and the number of topics on its clustering performance. The model was able to cluster tweets, using this approach, with an accuracy of greater than 64 percent for the two specific events.

Perera [5] developed a software architecture using a Twitter application program interface (API) to collect tweets sent to specific users. The extracted data were processed to characterize the inter-arrival times between tweets and the number of re-tweets. Analysis revealed that the arrival process of new tweets to a user can be modeled as a Poisson process while the number of retweets follows a geometric distribution.

Turner and Malleson [6] presented an exploratory geographical analysis of a sample of Twitter post data from June 2011 to March 2012 in the city of Leeds, England. Geographical cluster detection methods were used in combination with text mining techniques to identify patterns. Preliminary results suggested that the data could be used as a means of exploring daily spatial-temporal behavior.

The following presents insight in to the MATLAB toolboxes that can be used in detecting anomalies, that is, deviation from the normal pattern of life.

3. MATLAB toolboxes and classes for anomaly detection

MATLAB™ is a high-level language and interactive environment for numerical computation, visualization, and programming. MATLAB's product family includes numerous toolboxes for parallel computing, math, statistics and optimization, control system design and analysis, signal processing and communication, image processing and computer vision, test and measurement, and other areas [7]. A key feature of these products is the ability to research a number of algorithms quickly without having to design and code the algorithm.

MATLAB's interactive environment allows end users to quickly prototype their own algorithms if existing toolboxes do not provide the desired functionality. A well-established community of users supports the exchange of algorithms for those wishing to share their research and prototypes.

This research took advantage of the MATLAB community and the existing toolboxes. From the file exchange, Vladimir Bondarenko's contribution of the class to the Twitter REST API v1.1 was used to interface with Twitter to search for and extract tweets for specific topics and geographic regions [8]. Existing MATLAB Statistics and Neural Network Toolboxes were also used in this research to provide statistical algorithms and unsupervised learning methods, such as cluster analysis, for exploring data to discover hidden patterns and groupings in the data.

3.1. TWITTY — Twitter REST API interface

Twitty is a useful interface that runs within MATLAB for communicating with Twitter. Methods used in Twitty are essentially wrapper functions that call the Twitter API [9]. The API caller function, callTwitterAPI(), does the main work.

Key steps to successfully using the Twitter API include obtaining Twitter credentials and using JavaScript Object Notation (JSON) parsers. The MATLAB file exchange provides a JSON parser developed by Joel Feenstra [10]. The JSON parser parses a JSON string and returns a MATLAB cell array with the parsed data. JSON objects are converted to structures and JSON arrays are converted to cell arrays. Twitter credentials are easily created by registering at the Twitter site, creating an application, and retrieving consumer and access keys. These keys are required for running Twitty and include specific values for:

- ConsumerKey
- ConsumerSecret
- AccessToken
- AccessTokenSecret

To use these keys in a MATLAB script, users assign the values to their credential structure. Then, a twitty instance can be created and methods, such as search, can be called as shown in Figure 1.

```
% Create credentials
credentials.ConsumerKey = 'YourConsumerKey’
credentials.ConsumerSecret = 'YourConsumerSecret'
credentials.AccessToken = 'YourAccessToken'
credentials.AccessTokenSecret = 'YourAccessTokenSecret'
% Create Twitty Instance
tw = twitty(credentials);
% Search for World Series Related Tweets
tw.search(‘World Series’);
```

Figure 1. Twitty search method example.

Twitty provides a number of useful methods for interacting with the Twitter API. Example calls, along with a brief description, are shown in Table 1. Additional methods and detailed descriptions are found by typing *twitty.API* at the MATLAB prompt.

http://dx.doi.org/10.5772/58895

Method	Example Call	Description
search(text string)	tw.search('World Series')	Search all public tweets containing the words "World Series"
search(multiple parameters)	tw.search('NFL', 'count',20, 'include_entities','true', 'geocode','39.051300,-95.724660,1700mi','since_id',LastID)	Search public tweets having a identifier greater than LastID within 1700 miles of Topeka, Kansas containing the word "NFL" . Return entity data also (e.g., hashtags, URL mentions)
updateStatus()	tw.updateStatus('Watching the World Series tonight')	Twit the text "Watching the World Series tonight" from your account to the public
sampleStatuses()	tw.sampleStatuses()	Return a continuous stream of random public tweets

Table 1. Twitty method examples.

3.2. MATLAB — Statistics TOOLBOX™

The Statistics Toolbox™ provides statistical and machine learning algorithms and tools for organizing, analyzing, and modeling data. Key features include data organization and management via data set arrays and categorical arrays, exploratory data analysis with the use of interactive graphics and multivariate statistics, and regression or classification for predictive modeling [11]. The toolbox also includes functions that allow users to test hypotheses more effectively by checking for autocorrelation and randomness as well as other tests, for example, t-tests, one-sample tests, and distribution tests such as Chi-square and Kolmogorov-Smirnov.

Clustering algorithms available within MATLAB's Statistical Toolbox include *k*-means and hierarchical approaches. Clustering algorithms are particularly useful for analyzing social networking data as they help identify natural groupings that can then be further analyzed to determine similarities or differences and make business, marketing, or other decisions.

A *k*-means clustering algorithm forms *k* clusters by minimizing the mean between all cluster members. Clusters are defined by the centroid or center of each cluster. The algorithm works by moving data between clusters until the sum of the distances between each member and the centroid is minimized.

MATLAB allows different distance measures to be selected. Table 2 lists the available distance measures and a brief description and example call.

Distance Measure	Description	Example call
Squared Euclidean	Each centroid is the mean of the points in that cluster.	kmeans(meas,3,'dist','sqeuclidean');
City Block	Sum of absolute differences. Each centroid is the component-wise median of the points in that cluster.	kmeans(meas,3,'dist','cityblock');
Cosine	One minus the cosine of the included angle between. Each centroid is the mean of the points in that cluster.	kmeans(meas,3,'dist','cosine');
Correlation	One minus the sample correlation between points. Each centroid is the component-wise mean of the points in that cluster.	kmeans(meas,3,'dist','correlation');
Hamming	Percentage of bits that differ in binary data. Each centroid is the component-wise median of points in that cluster.	kmeans(meas,3,'dist','hamming');

Table 2. MATLAB *k*-means clustering distance measures.

Visually displaying the results for multidimensional data can be challenging. However; the silhouette plot, available within the MATLAB Statistics Toolbox, displays a measure between 0 and 1, representing how close each point in one cluster is to the points in the neighboring clusters. Values close to 1 indicate points are distant from neighboring clusters whereas values close to 0 indicate points are not distinctly different from one cluster or another. Negative values indicate points that are most likely assigned to the wrong cluster.

In the following example, cidx2 represents the cluster index for each given sample of data. Assuming cidx2 was returned from the call to the *k*-means function, an example call of the silhouette function is:

```
silhouette(meas,cidx2,'sqeuclidean');
```

Hierarchical clustering groups data to create a tree structure consisting of multiple levels. Users can prune parts of the tree depending upon the application and level of detail required. The links between data are represented as upside-down U-shaped lines with the height of each line indicating the distance between the data. This height is known as the cophenetic correlation distance between the two objects. MATLAB has a function that measures this distance.

http://dx.doi.org/10.5772/58895

The closer the value of the cophenetic correlation coefficient is to 1, the more accurately the clustering solution reflects your data.

Distance measures, similar to the *k*-means clustering, need to be selected to generate the linkages of the tree. Figure 2 shows the code to create a tree based on the Euclidean distance for a matrix named 'meas' and displays the results in a tree and then calculates the cophenetic correlation.

```
eucD = pdist(meas,'euclidean');
clustTreeEuc = linkage(eucD,'average');
[h,nodes] = dendrogram(clustTreeEuc,0);
measCophenet = cophenet(clustTreeEuc,eucD);
```

Figure 2. MATLAB code to calculate cophenetic correlation.

3.3. MATLAB – Neural Network TOOLBOX™

The Neural Network Toolbox™ provides functions and apps for modeling complex nonlinear systems that are not easily modeled with a closed-form equation. Primary features include data fitting, clustering, and pattern recognition to forecast future events, both supervised and unsupervised network architectures, and training algorithms, such as gradient descent and conjugate gradient methods, to help automatically adjust the network's weights and biases [12]. Also included are preprocessing and post-processing functions that improve the efficiency of neural network training and enable detailed analysis of network performance by reducing the dimensions of the input vectors using principal component analysis and normalizing the mean and standard deviation of the training set.

MATLAB's Neural Network Toolbox provides self-organizing maps for both unsupervised and supervised clustering. Self-organizing maps retain topological information for similar classes and provide reasonable classifiers. Self-organizing maps can be used for multidimensional data with complex features, making them attractive for analysis of social networking data. The self-organizing maps functionality within MATLAB can be used to cluster tweets based on the Twitter-extracted fields.

Self-organizing maps learn to classify input vectors according to how they are grouped in the input space. The neurons in a self-organizing map can be arranged based on specific topologies. Within MATLAB, topologies for gridtop, hextop and random are possible. Results are not affected by the choice of topology used; however, visual inspection of the data space is best achieved by use of a hexagonal grid (hextop) [13]. A gridtop topology has neurons evenly spaced in matrix of specific dimensions. For example, an 80-neuron self-organizing map may be arranged in an 8 × 10 gridtop topology. A hextop topology is similar, but the shape of the grid can best be described as a hexagon. A random topology has the neurons randomly located. Figure 3 illustrates gridtop, hextop and random topologies for a 3 × 4 set of neurons.

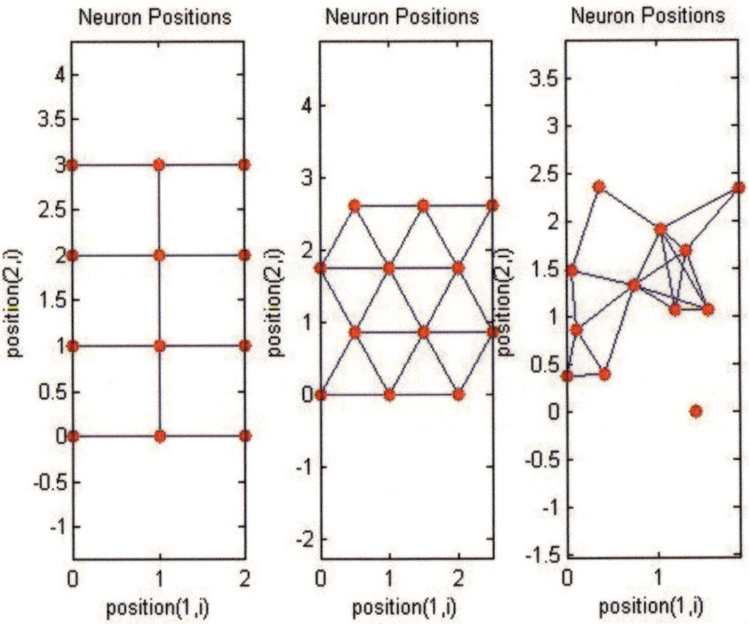

Figure 3. Gridtop, hextop, and randtop self-organizing map topologies.

The self-organization map routine can be run in MATLAB by calling the selforgmap function. Once a map is set up, it can be trained using specific input, and results can be displayed visually. Figure 4 shows a code example to generate a 3 × 4 neuron self-organizing map, conduct training, and display the results.

```
net = selforgmap([3 4]);
net = train(net,meas);
view(net);
y = net(meas);
classes = vec2ind(y);
```

Figure 4. MATLAB code example to generate a 3 × 4 neuron self-organizing map, conduct training, and display the results.

The Neural Network Toolbox also contains the nnstart tool, which provides an interactive tool for loading data and selecting algorithms and training iterations. As shown in Figure 5, the interactive tool allows the user to select run options and then train for a specific number of epochs.

http://dx.doi.org/10.5772/58895

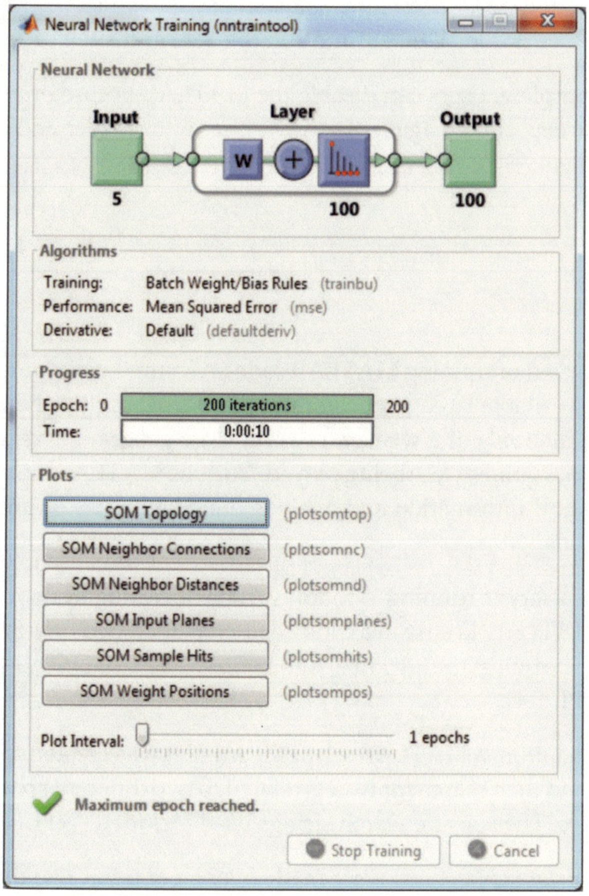

Figure 5. MATLAB's nnstart interactive interface.

The addition of the MATLAB's Parallel Computing Toolbox™ allows the user to speed up training and handle large data sets by distributing computations and data across multiple processors and graphic processing units (GPUs). The ability to spin up multiple central processing units (CPUs) and GPUs from cloud services such as AWS makes this toolbox attractive. The user may be limited by the availability of MATLAB licenses for this option. MATLAB and AWS are currently working out a process to make this more feasible with a pay-as-you-go license feature that could be quite attractive for businesses that do not have the resources to purchase hardware and software.

3.4. Deploying MATLAB on AWS

Cloud service providers such as AWS can significantly reduce the startup and maintenance costs for high-performance computers needed for efficient running of complex math, statistics, and optimization algorithms. AWS has free and pay tier options that will fit most budgets. Previous research has shown the cost of running multiple high-performance servers for many hours was just a few dollars [14]. As long as users have a valid MATLAB license, they can install MATLAB on the AWS machine(s) and run the data and analysis.

Once the runs are complete, users can disable the MATLAB license on the AWS machine. If users need to run the experiment again, they can spin up the server and enable the license to continue the experiment.

4. Experiment

The experiment consisted of running MATLAB code on commercial cloud architecture (AWS) to collect publically available tweets on common keywords, such as NFL and World Series, during specific time intervals of a weekend over a large geographic region when both NFL games and World Series games were being played. Various MATLAB tools and functions were used to gather statistical information and analyze the data by use of unsupervised learning and clustering methods.

For this experiment, a server running Windows[2] 2008 operating system was spun up in the AWS free tier. A MATLAB license was installed that included the Statistics and Neural Network toolboxes. The twitty.m and parse_json.m files were also uploaded to allow MATLAB to call the Twitter API.

After successful installation, a MATLAB script file (m file) was created to provide the proper Twitter credentials, and then search for tweets related to two different sports events, the World Series and NFL games. The specific search strings used included "NFL" and "World Series".

Four different 3-hour data collections were made over a period of two days. Collection times included Saturday from 5 PM to 8 PM and 8 PM to 11 PM and Sunday from 1 PM to 4 PM and 5 PM to 8 PM during the weekend of the 2013 World Series. During this time frame, a World Series event took place on both Saturday and Sunday evenings, and a series of NFL games occurred on Sunday afternoon and evening.

A large geographic collection area, centered over a 1700 mile radius about Topeka, Kansas, was used for this experiment. This geographic radius included most of the continental United States and parts of Canada and Mexico. The search parameters included the Twitter entities for storing User-, URL-, and hashtag-mentions. Sampling occurred every 60 seconds over the 3-hour window with Twitter ID information being used to eliminate duplicate tweets in the time frame. A sample call for the search is as follows:

```
S=tw.search('NFL',        'count',20,        'include_entities','true','geoco-
de','39.051300,-95.724660,1700mi', 'since_id',LastID);
```

In this call, Twitter is being searched for up to 20 tweets that include the text "NFL" that originated within 1700 miles of Topeka, Kansas. The LastID variable was updated after each

2 Registered trademark of Microsoft Corporation.

http://dx.doi.org/10.5772/58895

iteration to gather only recent tweets beyond a specific ID. Appendix A shows the MATLAB m file that was run for the experiment.

Statistics and analysis were run at the end of the data collection using existing MATLAB tools and functions provided in the Statistics and Neural Network Toolboxes. Within the Statistics Toolbox, the *k*-means and hierarchical clustering approaches and associated visual displays were used.

The distance measure used for all *k*-means calculations was the default selection of Squared Euclidian. An example call used for three clusters with Squared Euclidian distance is as follows:

```
kmeans(meas,3,'dist','sqeuclidean');
```

The self-organizing map functions within the Neural Network Toolbox were used to cluster the Twitter collected data.

In addition to the existing Statistical and Neural Network functions, some simple data manipulation algorithms were used to extract the time between tweets. As shown in Figure 6, the following code example determines and stores the time between tweets found in MATLAB cell array named DatesQ2.

```
for i=1:length(DatesQ2)-1

 time1 = [str2num(DatesQ2{i}(26:30)) 10 str2num(DatesQ2{i}(9:10)) str2num(DatesQ2{i}(12:13))
str2num(DatesQ2{i}(15:16)) str2num(DatesQ2{i}(18:19))];

 time2 = [str2num(DatesQ2{i+1}(26:30)) 10 str2num(DatesQ2{i+1}(9:10)) str2num(DatesQ2{i+1}(12:13))
str2num(DatesQ2{i+1}(15:16)) str2num(DatesQ2{i+1}(18:19))];

 deltaWorldSeries(i) = abs(etime(time1,time2));

end
```

Figure 6. MATLAB code to determine time between tweets.

In this code, time {i} and time {i+1} values are constructed using the default time structure of the Twitter collection and converted to a MATLAB time structure. The dates are then differenced using MATLAB's built-in elapsed time function (etime). This process continues to calculate the time delta for all consecutive tweets for all search queries.

Appendix B shows the Data analysis m file used for this experiment.

5. Initial results and discussion

Results were provided using MATLAB's visual and plotting functions. To better understand the frequency, or popularity, of the two search terms for each time period during the experiment, some baseline descriptive statistics were calculated.

5.1. Boxplots

Boxplots are a convenient way for visualizing the interquartile range, average and outlier data. Figures 7–10 represent boxplots for the 3-hour experiment windows from Saturday 5 PM to 8 PM, Saturday 8 PM to 11 PM, Sunday 1 PM to 4 PM, and Sunday 5 PM to 8 PM, respectively.

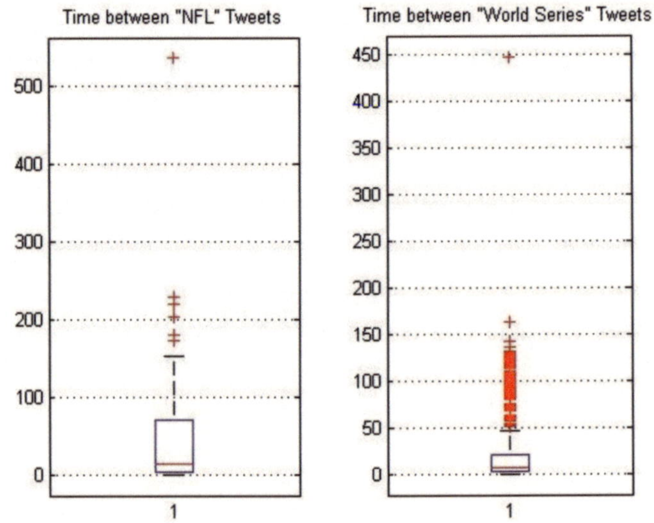

Figure 7. Boxplot for NFL versus World Series time between tweets, Saturday 5 PM to 8 PM.

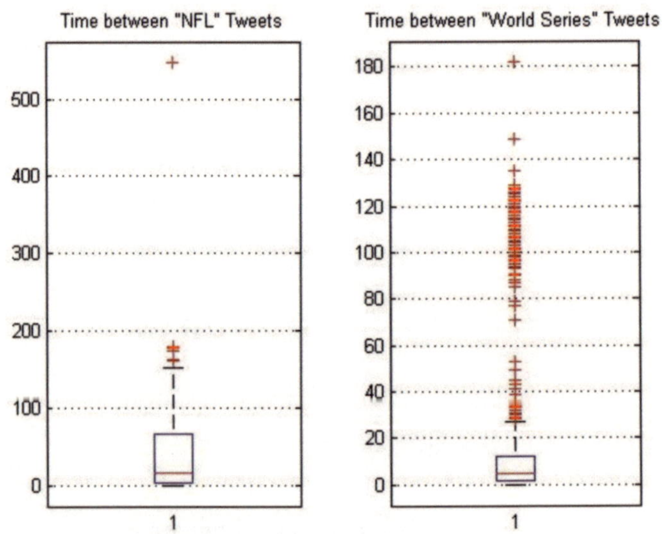

Figure 8. Boxplot for NFL versus World Series time between tweets, Saturday 8 PM to 11 PM.

http://dx.doi.org/10.5772/58895

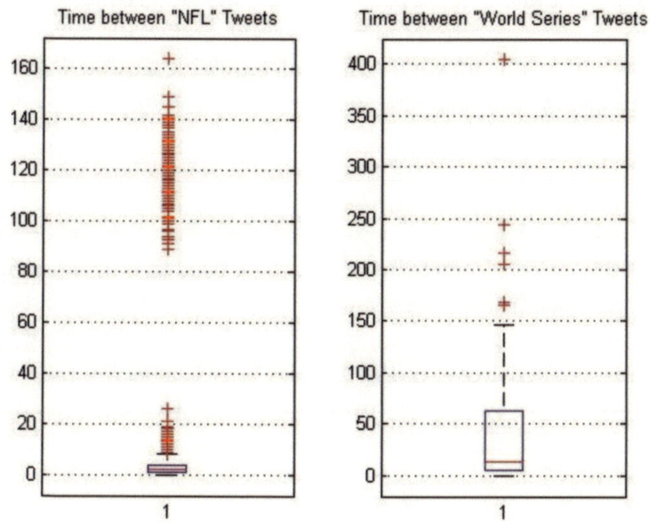

Figure 9. Boxplot for NFL versus World Series time between tweets, Sunday 1 PM to 4 PM.

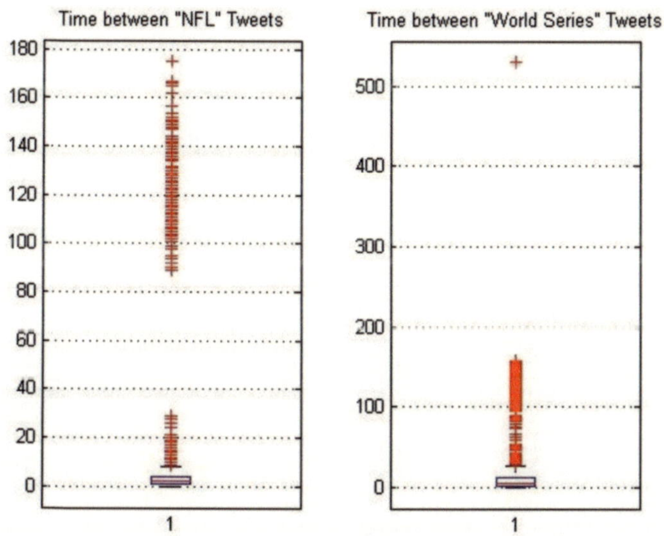

Figure 10. Boxplot for NFL versus World Series time between tweets, Sunday, 5 PM to 8 PM.

Reviewing the boxplots in Figures 7–10 reveals a couple of interesting trends. In most cases, outliers outside of the interquartile ranges exist; however, as a sporting event gets closer to start time, the frequency of tweets increase. Note the narrowing of the boxes for both the NFL and World Series plots during or approaching the actual game events. By Sunday late afternoon, there was significant activity in both the NFL and World Series tweets in terms of frequency. The descriptive statistics were very similar, making it difficult to see any difference, in terms of tweet frequency between NFL and World Series fans.

5.2. XY plots

MATLAB was also used to plot the time between tweets for each collection period and search query. This view, although somewhat cluttered, can be used to quickly compare the number of tweets and any other patterns obvious in an xy plot. The time between tweets is plotted in Figures 11–14, for each of the four collection periods. The most revealing information from these plots is the noticeable increase in the number of tweets as the events draw closer. On Saturday, the number of tweets related to the World Series was higher than NFL tweets. This seems reasonable since a World Series game took place on Saturday but no NFL games occurred until Sunday.

On Sunday, with multiple NFL games taking place, the number of NFL tweets was larger than World Series-related tweets. However, the number and frequency of World Series tweets was also high due to the Sunday evening World Series event, but not as significant as the NFL-related tweet activity.

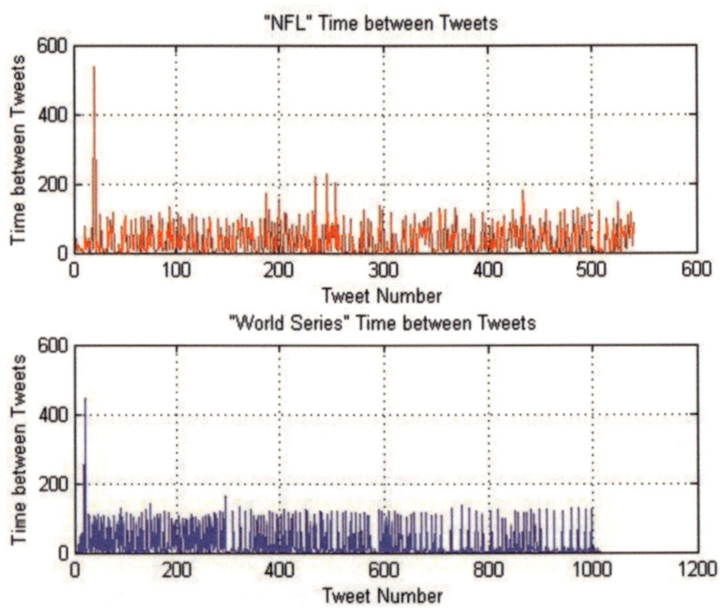

Figure 11. XY plot for NFL versus World Series time between tweets, Saturday 5 PM to 8 PM.

http://dx.doi.org/10.5772/58895

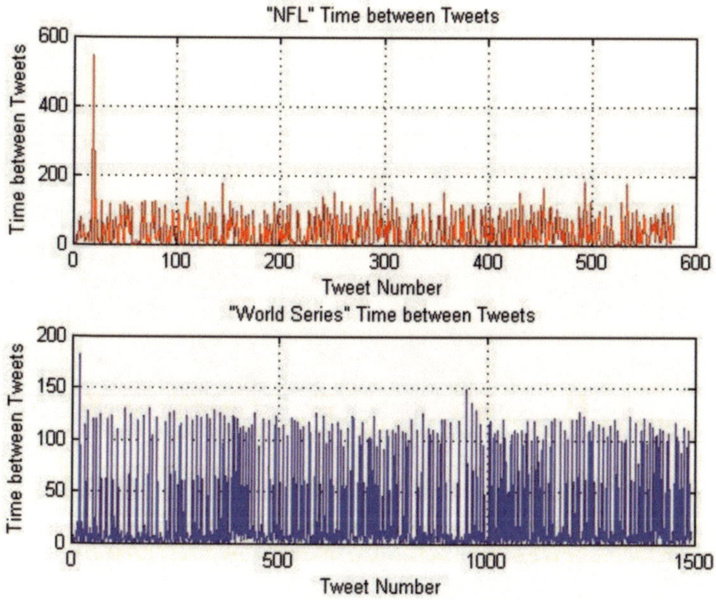

Figure 12. XY plot for NFL versus World Series time between tweets, Saturday 8 PM to 11 PM.

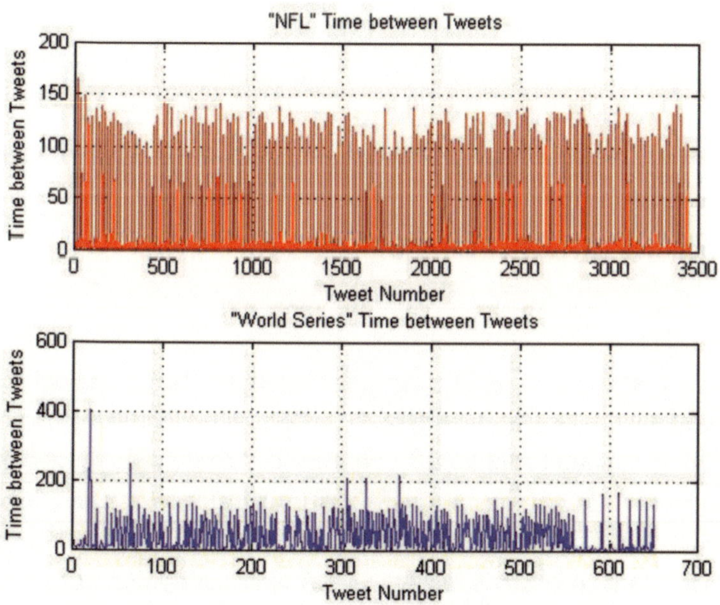

Figure 13. XY plot for NFL versus World Series time between tweets, Sunday 1 PM to 4PM.

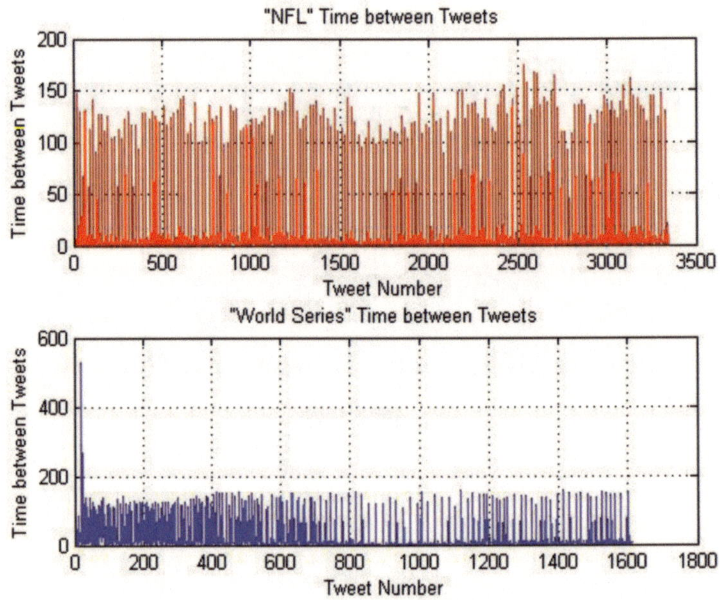

Figure 14. XY plot for NFL versus World Series Time between tweets, Sunday 5 PM to 8 PM.

5.3. Histograms

The histogram functionality within MATLAB was used to get a better idea of the quantity and length of the time between tweets for each of the collection periods. As shown in Figures 15 and 16, on Saturday, the number of tweets with time difference values less than 10 seconds was much greater for World Series than NFL tweets. In all histograms, a handful of tweets had a time between tweets of greater than 100 seconds. The shift to NFL interest is very visible on Sunday in the histograms shown in Figures 17 and 18. Note the significant increase in the both the number and quantity of tweets occurring in less than 10 second intervals for NFL tweets. However, in Figure 18, the histograms for Sunday late afternoon and evening reveal similar results for the time between tweets for both NFL and World Series texts.

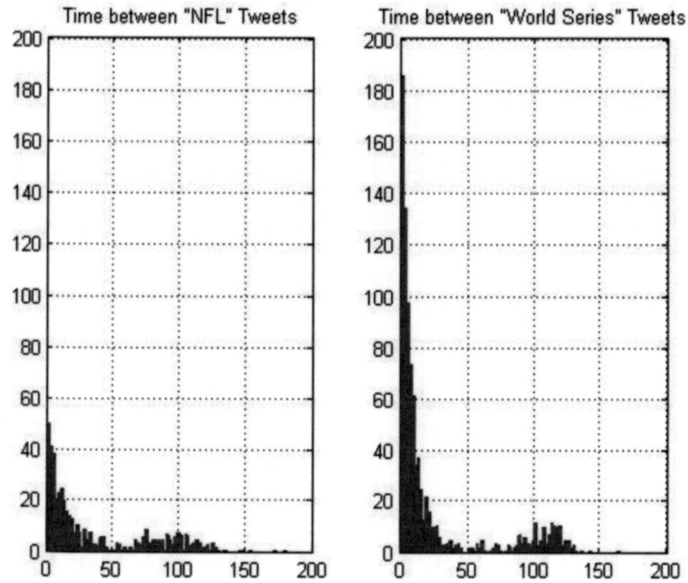

Figure 15. Histogram plot for NFL versus World Series time between tweets, Saturday 5 PM to 8 PM.

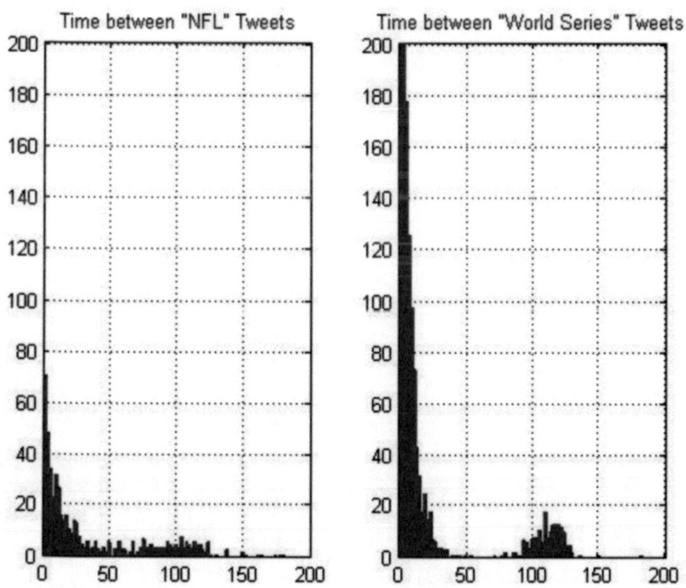

Figure 16. Histogram plot for NFL versus World Series time between tweets, Saturday 8 PM to 11 PM.

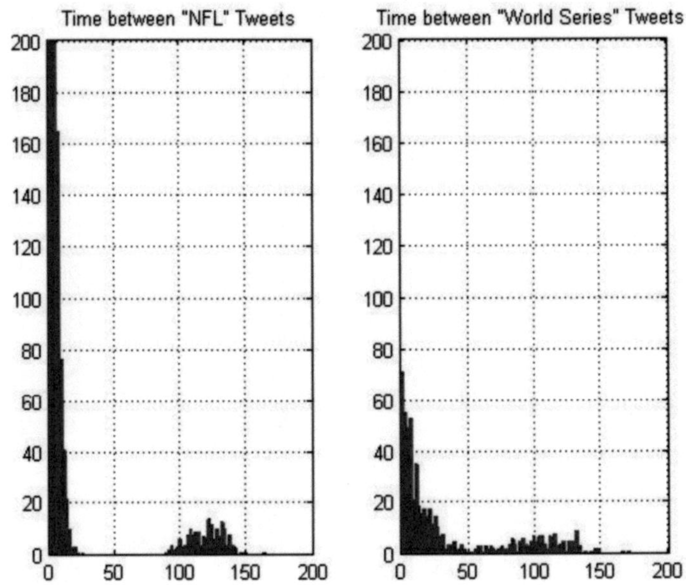

Figure 17. Histogram plot for NFL versus World Series time between tweets, Sunday 1 PM to 4 PM.

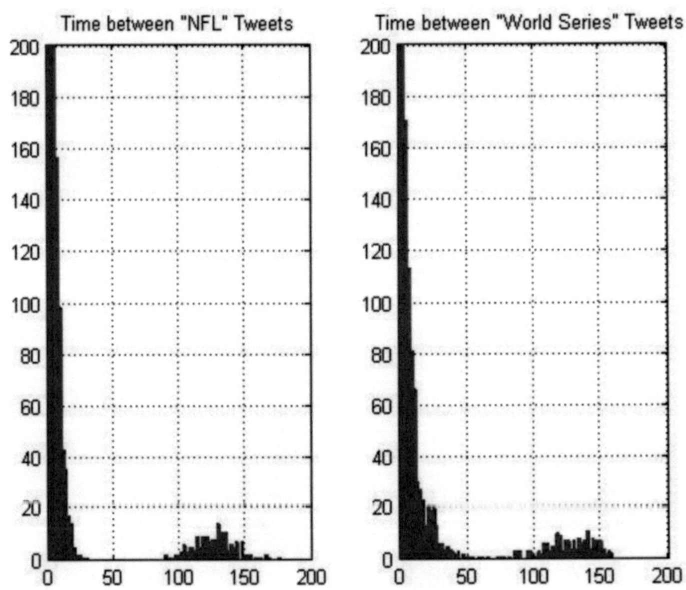

Figure 18. Histogram plot for NFL versus World Series time between tweets, Sunday 5 PM to 8 PM.

http://dx.doi.org/10.5772/58895

5.4. Scatter plots

Twitter queries provide additional data beyond the time and text of the tweet. For example, the number of friends, number of followers, user screen name, date of account creation, and time zone of user are also available and easily extract from the queries. This information can be used to determine if any significant differences or similarities exist among users of Twitter.

Within MATLAB, scatter plots can be used to visually identify clusters of data. Figures 19–22 illustrate the use of scatter plots to compare the number of friends and number of followers for NFL (blue Xs) and World Series (red circles) tweeters during each of the four data collection periods. Although a significant amount of overlap exists in the groups, particularly for small numbers of friend and followers, outliers can be identified in all four plots. Additional variables and analysis may be needed to further isolate these groups.

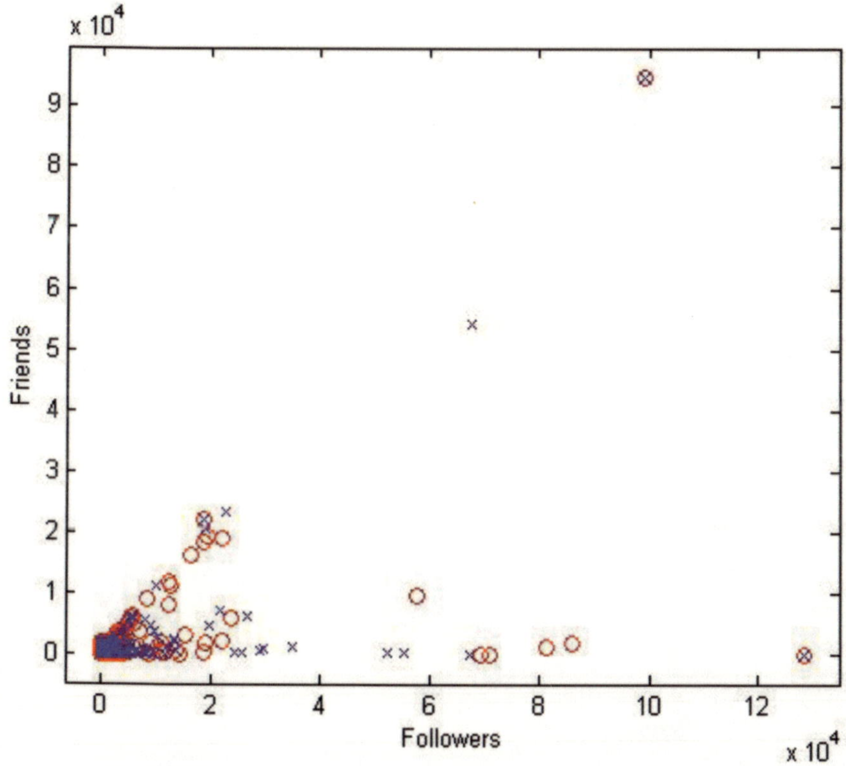

Figure 19. Scatter plot for friends versus followers, Saturday 5 PM to 8 PM.

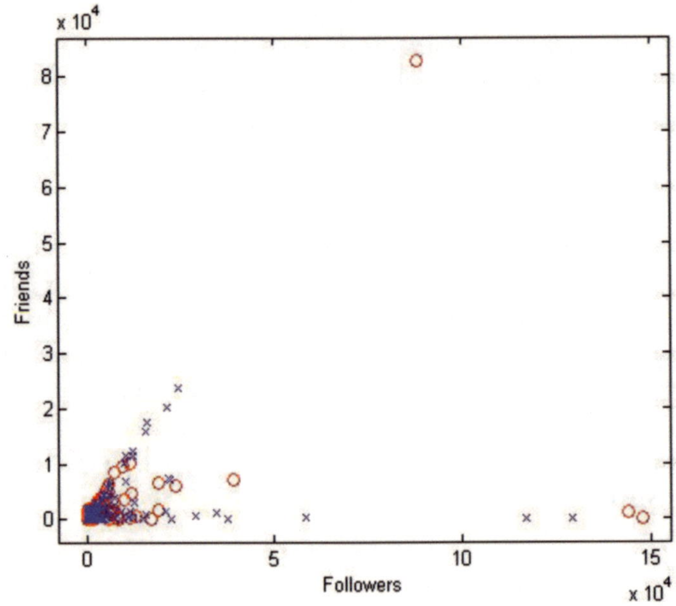

Figure 20. Scatter plot for friends versus followers, Saturday 8 PM to 11 PM.

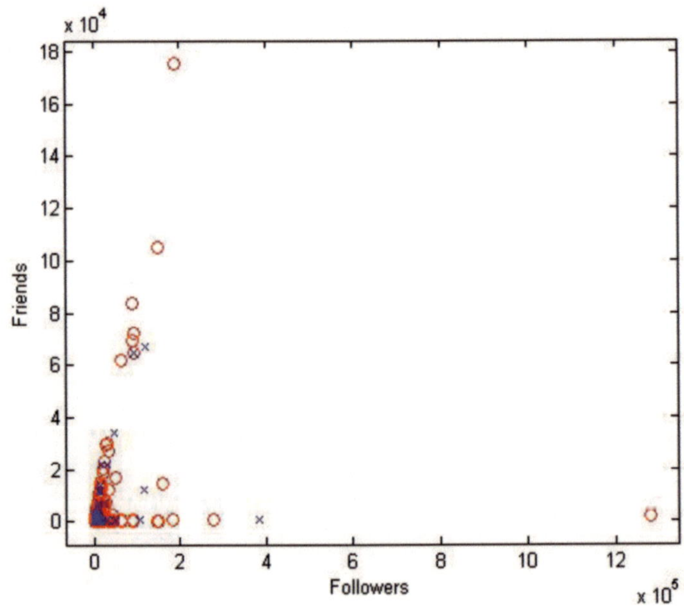

Figure 21. Scatter plot for friends versus followers, Sunday 1 PM to 4 PM.

http://dx.doi.org/10.5772/58895

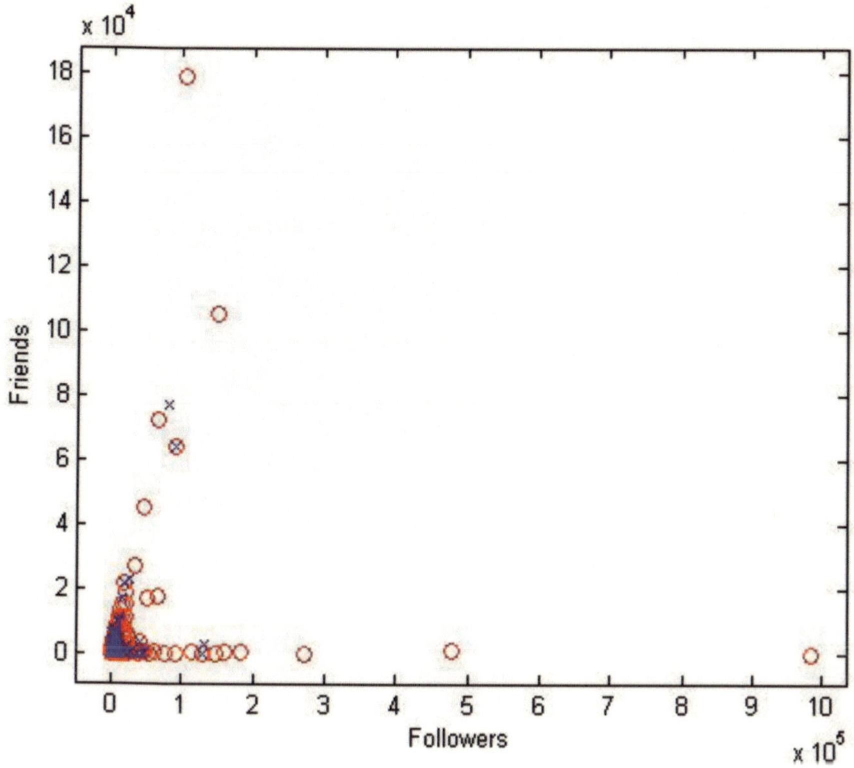

Figure 22. Scatter plot for friends versus followers, Sunday 5 PM to 8 PM.

5.5. Silhouette plots

Running the *k*-means algorithm in MATLAB for the Twitter feature sets further reveals the similarity in both NFL and World Series sets of tweets for all four time collection periods. Figures 23–26 illustrate the results of the applying the *k*-means algorithm for three clusters.

In all cases, one very large cluster with silhouette values very close to 1 is observed. However, the other two clusters are very small with both negative and lower positive silhouette values. This indicates that the separation into unique clusters is difficult for this set of data and features. Additional selection of features and analysis would be needed to better identify clusters of similar Twitter users.

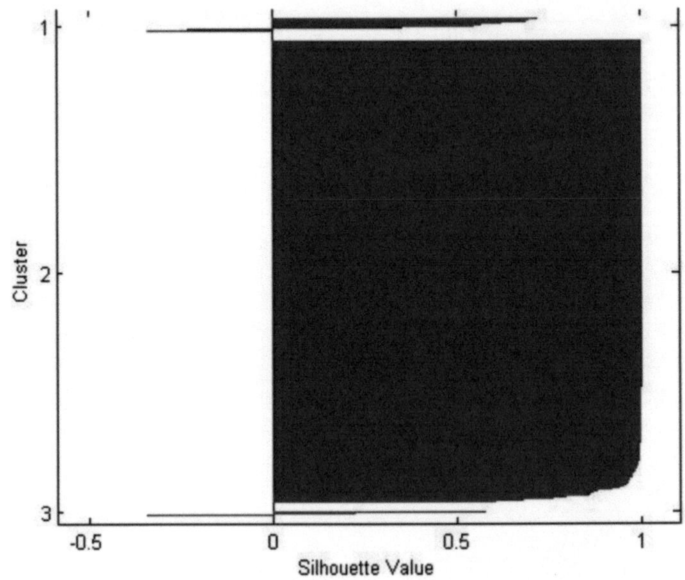

Figure 23. Silhouette plot of NFL versus World Series tweet features, Saturday 5 PM to 8PM.

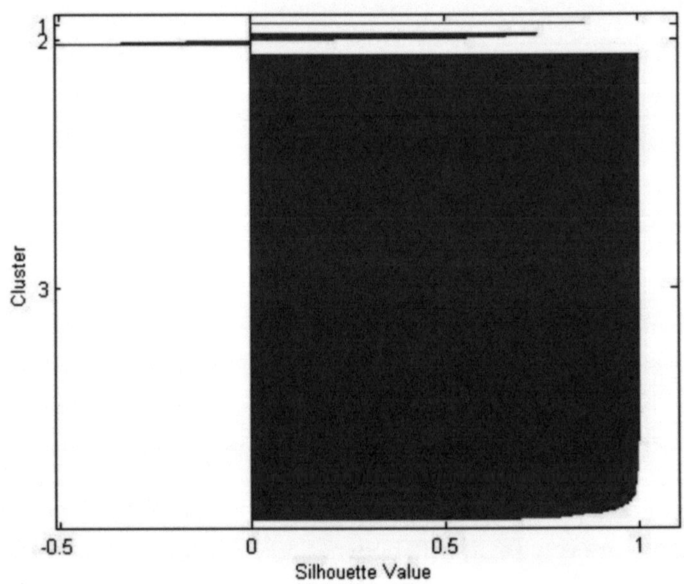

Figure 24. Silhouette plot of NFL versus World Series tweet features, Saturday 8 PM to 11 PM.

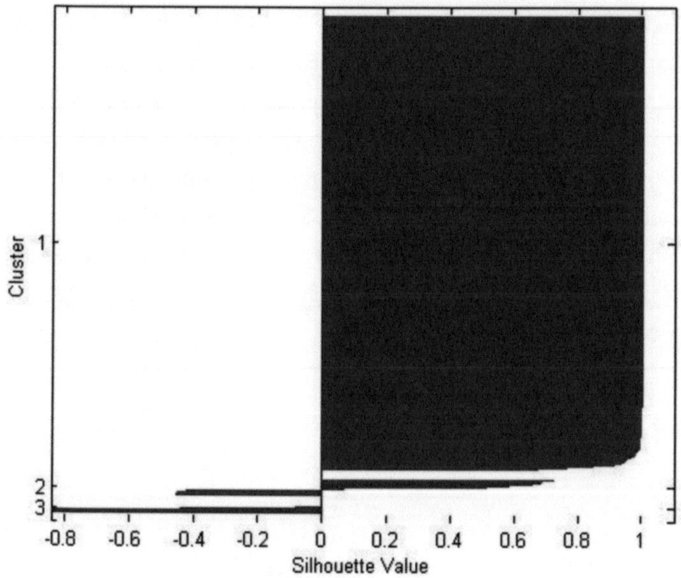

Figure 25. Silhouette plot of NFL versus World Series tweet features, Sunday 1 PM to 4 PM.

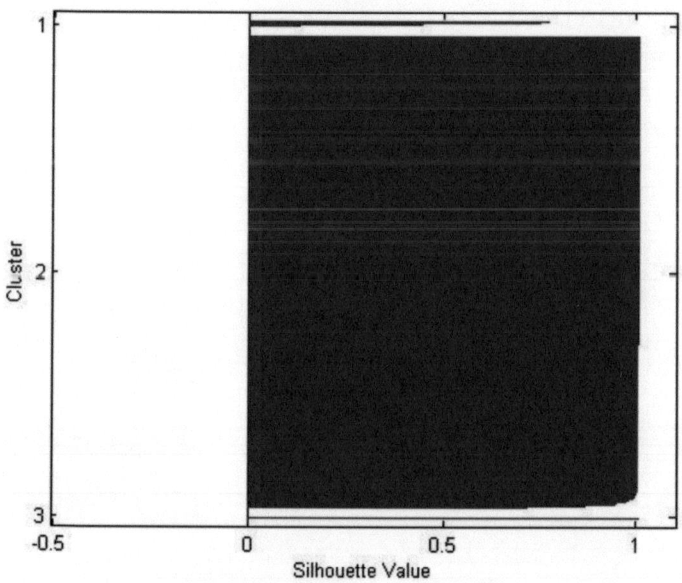

Figure 26. Silhouette plot of NFL versus World Series tweet features, Sunday 5 PM to 8 PM.

5.6. Hierarchical plots

Hierarchical clustering provides an additional visualization of possible cluster separation for the tweet data. In all cases, the number of cluster and representatives within that cluster matches the *k*-means clustering results. Specifically, one large cluster was identified along with at most one or two very small clusters as illustrated in Figures 27–30 where the left portion of the tree has many nodes whereas the right portion just has one or two. The size of the cluster grows over the collection periods with the final collection period on Sunday resulting in the largest cluster with the least amount of additional clusters. For example, on Sunday, the tree's one small branch is evident on the right side of the graph with the larger branch on the left side containing most observations.

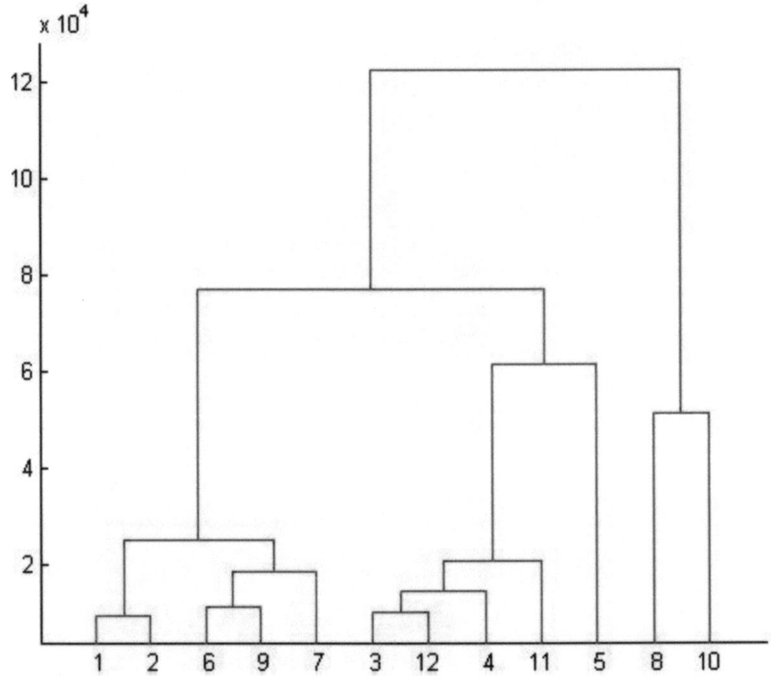

Figure 27. Hierarchical clustering of NFL versus World Series tweet features, Saturday 5 PM to 8 PM.

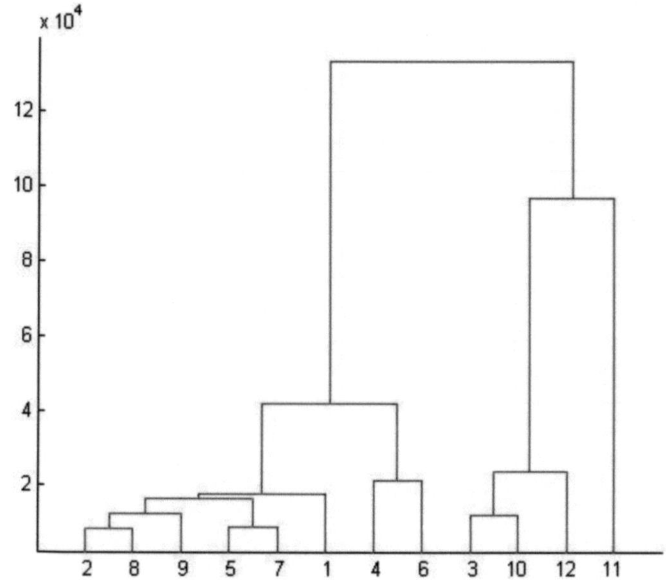

Figure 28. Hierarchical clustering of NFL versus World Series tweet features, Saturday 8 PM to 11 PM.

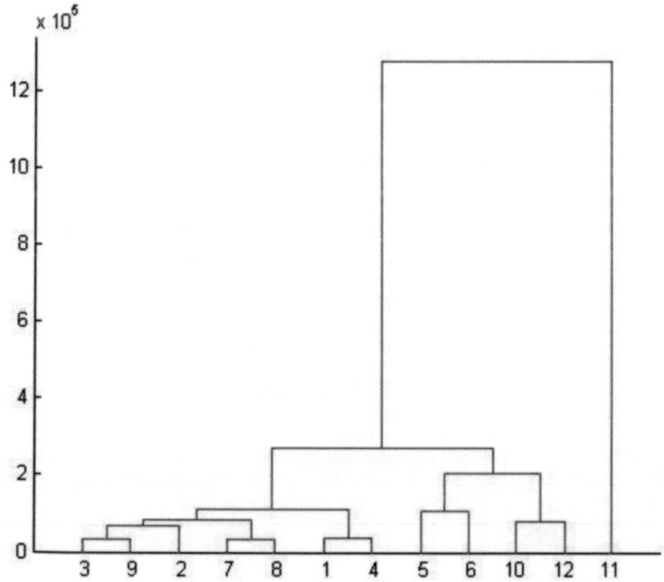

Figure 29. Hierarchical clustering of NFL versus World Series tweet features, Sunday 1 PM to 4 PM.

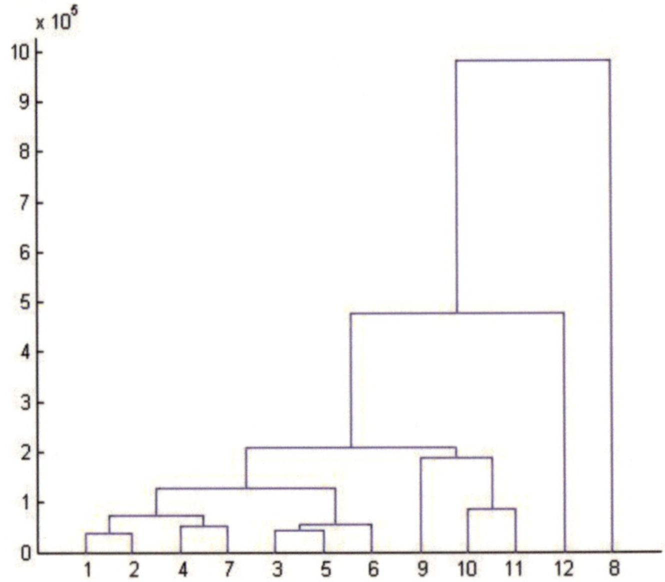

Figure 30. Hierarchical clustering of NFL versus World Series tweet features, Sunday 5 PM to 8 PM.

5.7. Self-Organizing Maps (SOM) plots

MATLAB's Neural Network Toolbox was also used to cluster the tweets through the self-organizing maps function. A hextop topology of 10 ×10 nodes was selected with 200 training epochs. After training, several visualizations are available to help determine how the input is distributed across the nodes. The locations of the data points and the weight vectors are shown by selecting the weight positions plot. With this display, only two weights can be shown at one time. Figure 31 shows that most of the data points cluster in one area and they are not very well distributed. This type of clustering was observed in both the hierarchical and *k*-means results.

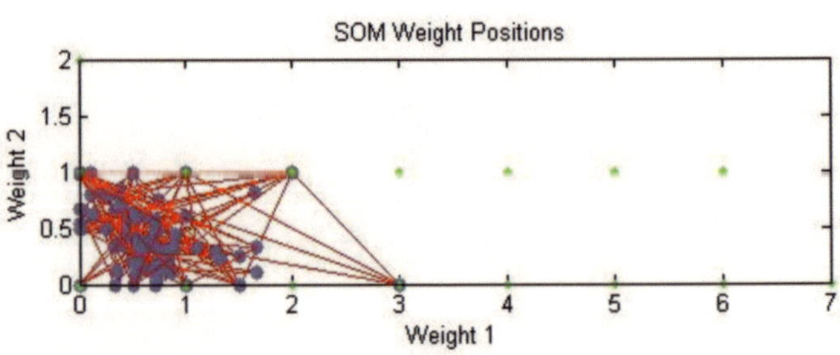

Figure 31. SOM weight positions, Saturday 5 PM to 8 PM.

http://dx.doi.org/10.5772/58895

5.7.1. SOM weight distance plots

The SOM neighbor weight distances plot, using multiple dimensions, provides more information. In Figures 32–35 SOM neighbor weight distance plots are displayed for each of the four time collections. The following diagram colors and description should be used when interpreting these plots:

1. Neurons are represented by blue hexagons
2. Red lines connect neighboring neurons
3. Dark-colored regions represent larger distances between neurons
4. Light-colored regions represent smaller distances between neurons

Figures 32–35 show one large cluster, with small distances between the member records, present in all four collection periods. One or two very small clusters are also present, with relatively large distances between the member records.

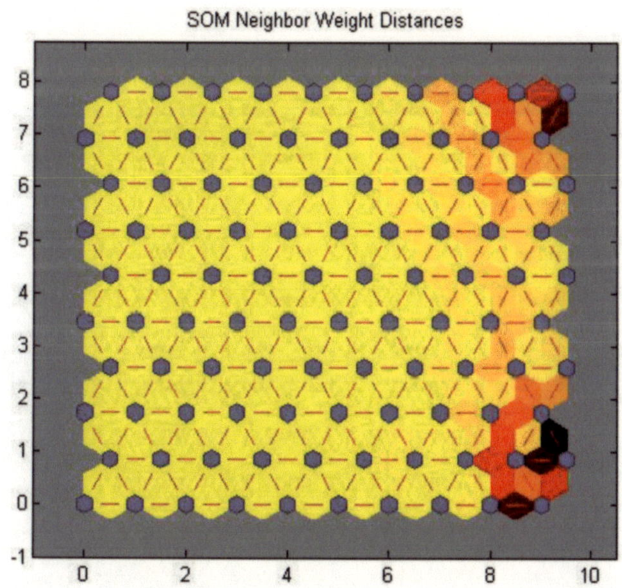

Figure 32. SOM weight distances, Saturday 5 PM to 8 PM.

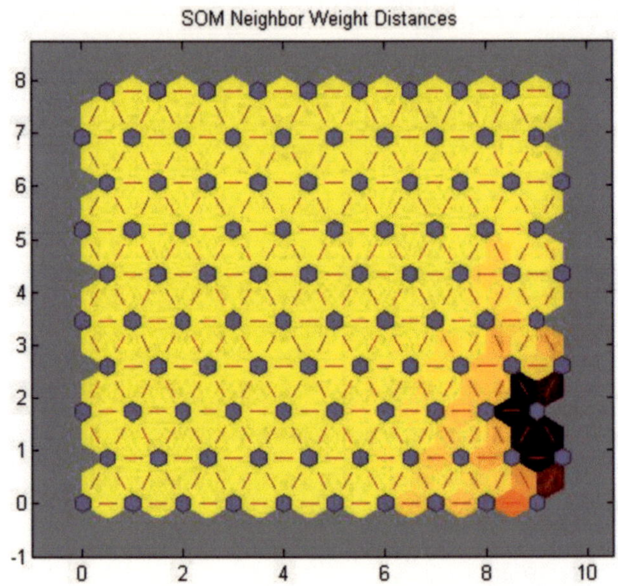

Figure 33. SOM weight distances, Saturday 8 PM to 11 PM.

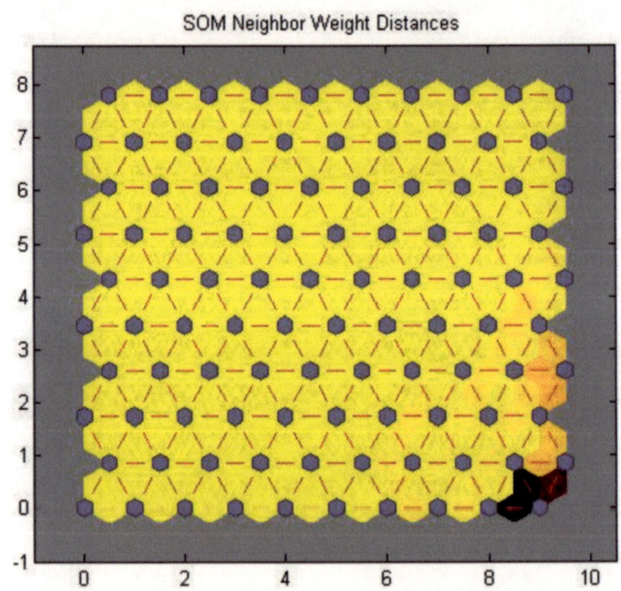

Figure 34. SOM weight distances, Sunday 1 PM to 4 PM.

http://dx.doi.org/10.5772/58895

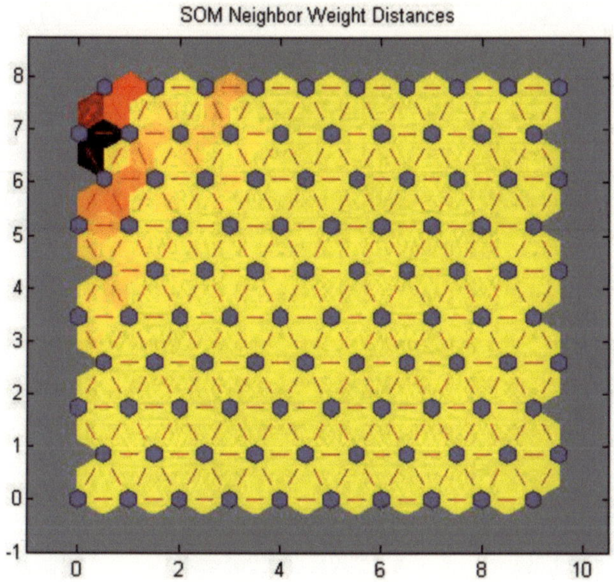

Figure 35. SOM weight distances, Sunday 5 PM to 8 PM.

5.7.2. SOM weight plane plots

The SOM weight plane plots are used to visualize the strength of weights that connect each input to each of the neurons. For our experiment, five inputs were used; therefore, five subplots were generated for each experiment. The five input features included, for each tweet, the number of user mentions, URL mentions, hashtag mentions, followers, and friends. Lighter colors in the plots represent larger weights whereas darker colors represent smaller weights. Similar connection patterns of the inputs indicate a high correlation.

Weight plane plots are shown for each of the collection times in Figures 36–39. Inputs 4 and 5 appeared to be similar in all collection times and were interpreted as highly correlated. Input from variables 1, 2, and 3 seemed to contribute the smallest amount of cluster separation in the data sets as they appear to be the least similar and less correlated. This seems reasonable because the number of friends and followers do seem to be correlated with Twitter users as a large number of friends also have a large number of followers. The information from the user-, URL-and hashtag-mentions shows some promise as the maps show these as not being highly correlated. Additional features and analysis are recommended to enhance the differences in these maps and to perform better clustering.

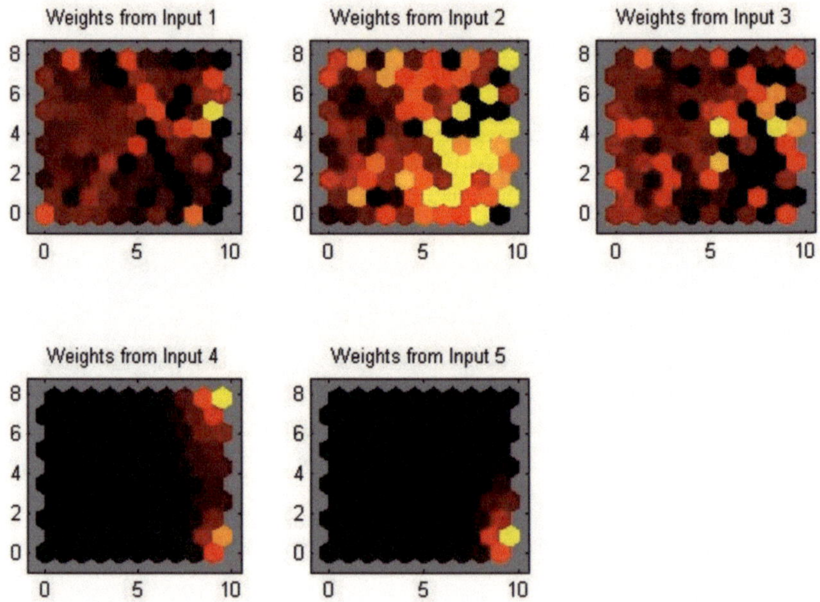

Figure 36. SOM weight planes, Saturday 5 PM to 8 PM.

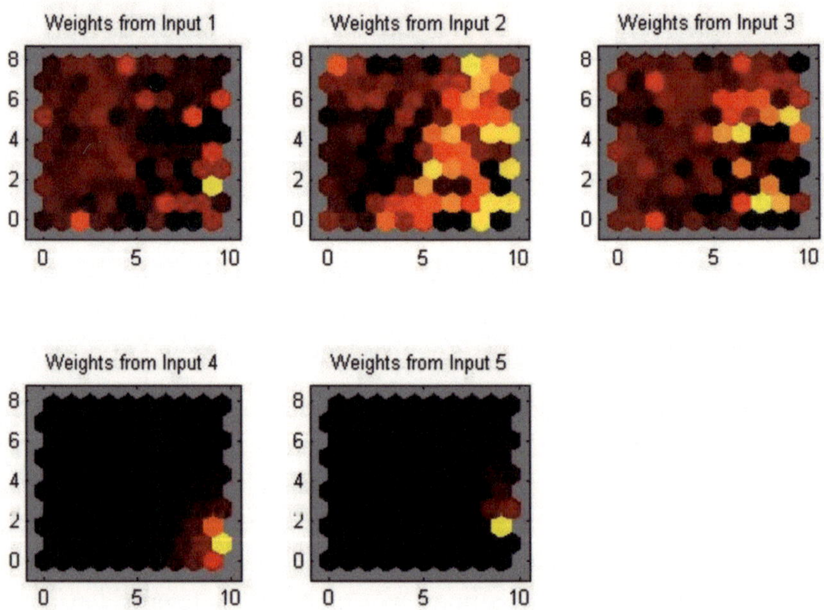

Figure 37. SOM weight planes, Saturday 8 PM to 11 PM.

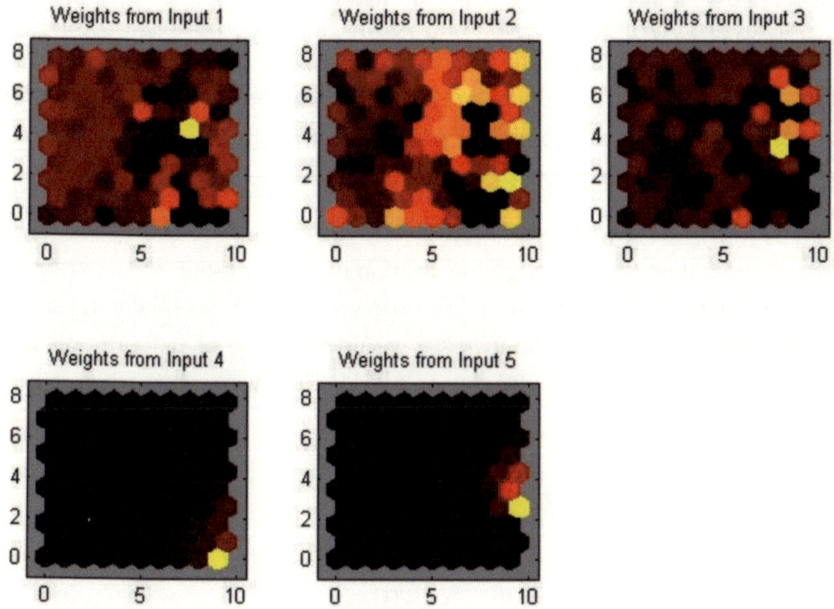

Figure 38. SOM weight planes, Sunday 1 PM to 4 PM.

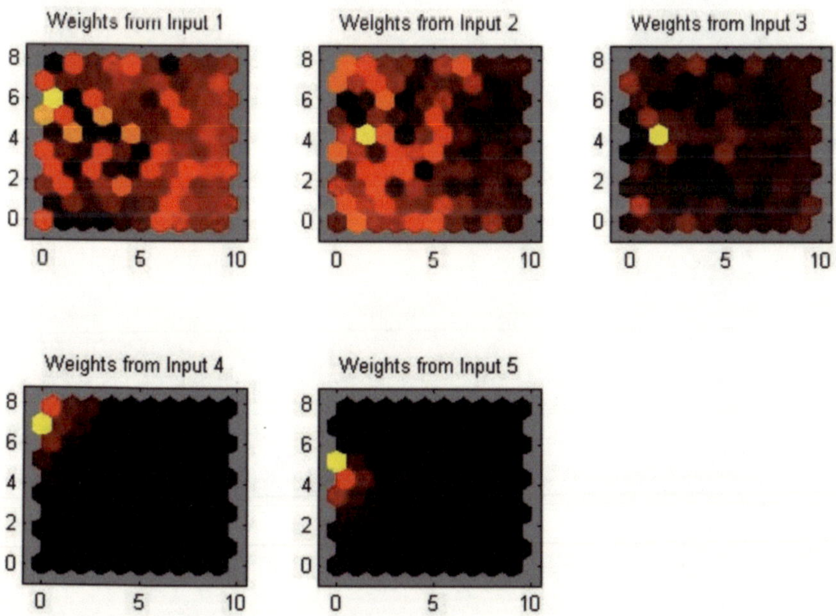

Figure 39. SOM weight planes, Sunday 5 PM to 8 PM.

5.7.3. SOM sample hits plots

One additional and useful visual plot provided by the MATLAB SOM function is the SOM sample hits plot. The sample hits plot counts the number of data records associated with each neuron. In an ideal situation, a relatively even distribution across the neurons is desired.

Figures 40–43 show the distribution across the neurons was not even in our experiment. In most cases, the distribution was clustered in one area, which indicates very similar data without much separation. Even though the location of concentration seems to shift from one area of the map to another for each time frame, the results are essentially the same for each collection time. The exception is the increase in concentration of data around the "heavy-hitting" neurons on Sunday as both NFL and World Series events were scheduled.

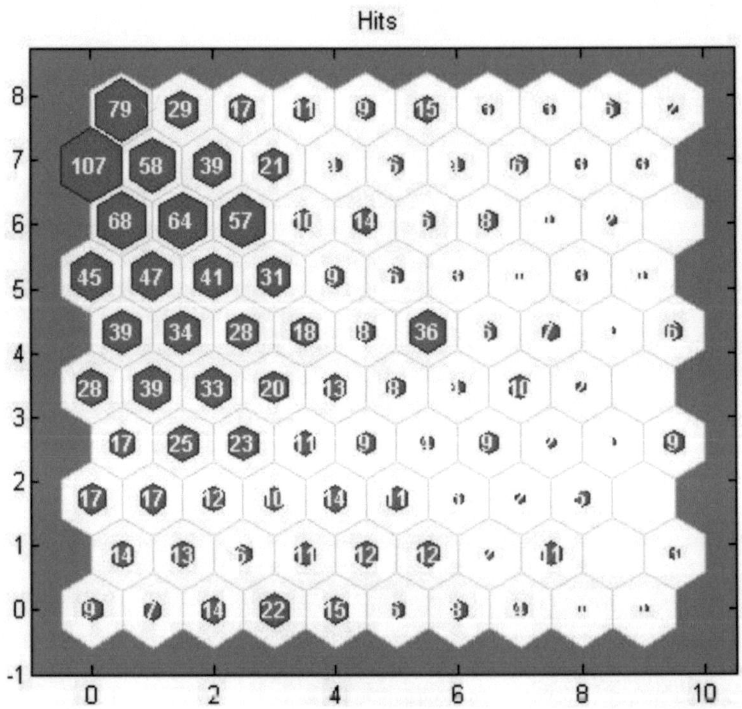

Figure 40. SOM sample hits, Saturday 5 PM to 8 PM.

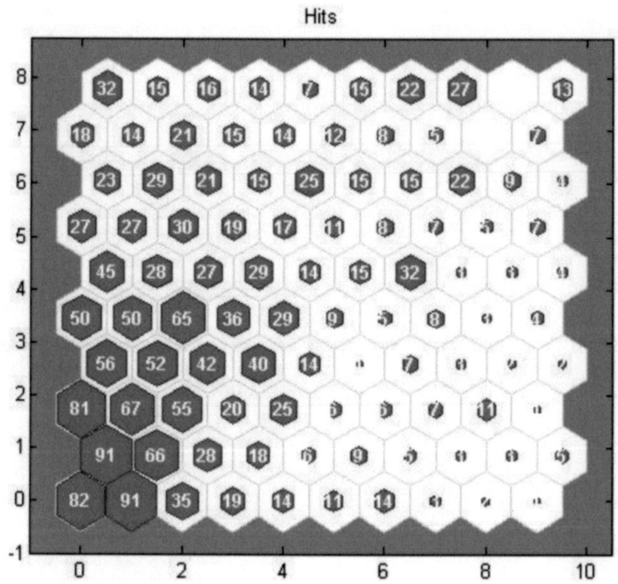

Figure 41. SOM sample hits, Saturday 8 PM to 11 PM.

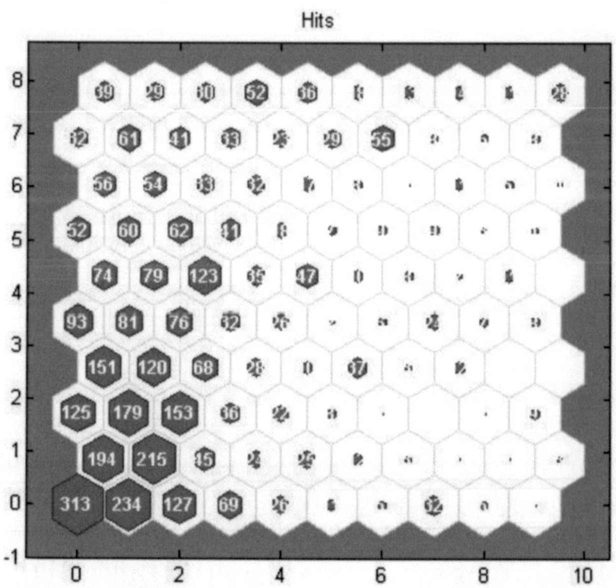

Figure 42. SOM sample hits, Sunday 1 PM to 4 PM.

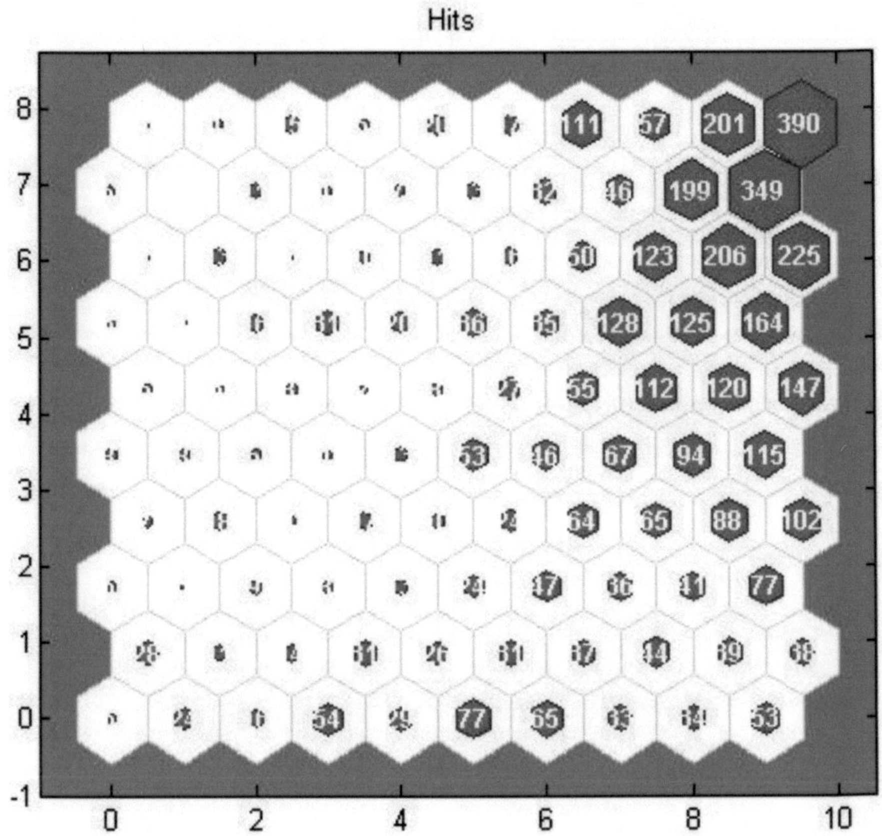

Figure 43. SOM sample hits, Sunday 5 PM to 8 PM.

6. Conclusion

This research used MATLAB tools to extract and analyze social networking data sets and leverage cloud technologies and infrastructures. AWS was used to spin up a Windows 2008 server and install MATLAB and its associated toolboxes for data mining and statistics. In addition, a community MATLAB m file interfaced with the Twitter API to search specific text queries and retrieve associated data. The setup process on AWS was straightforward and provided a cost-effective and free solution for the hardware and operating system. The MATLAB license was still needed in this implementation to be able to use the toolboxes and associated m files.

http://dx.doi.org/10.5772/58895

AWS provided cost savings, including all server-related hardware and software. Since MATLAB was used, the development costs for some very specialized analysis visualization tools were also reduced. Further cost savings are envisioned as MATLAB provides cloud options for running its software for short durations using a pay-as-you-go cost model.

At the time of publishing, access to MATLAB Distributed Computing Server on the cloud is available as part of an Early Adopter Program for MATLAB Distributed Computing Server on Elastic Compute Cloud (EC2). Future efforts could take advantage of this option to speed up implementations, run algorithms in parallel, and possibly further reduce licensing costs.

The twitty.m and parse_json.m community files were successfully used to interface with the Twitter API to search for tweets related to specific queries including "NFL" and "World Series" sporting events. In addition to the tweet texts, other information used in the experiment included user data such as number of friends, number of followers, time between tweets, number of URL mentions, number of Hashtag mentions, and number of user mentions in each text.

The MATLAB Statistics and Neural Network Toolboxes were then used to extract and display descriptive statistics and perform unsupervised clustering using *k*-means, hierarchical, and self-organized maps. Initial analysis of the visualization and data output revealed that sports events and the associated popularity and frequency of tweets increases as the time of the event gets closer. The frequency of tweets also persisted throughout the event.

Tweet users were also shown to have similar characteristics and profiles and would be difficult to separate based on just a few features. Referencing the SOM weight distance plots, smaller clusters were observed in all the plots, however, the distance among the members of the cluster were large compared to the one large cluster observed in each plot. Additional research with larger data sets and more robust features are needed to form predicative models.

7. Recommendations

This research demonstrated the use of MATLAB for social networking site analysis using AWS servers to reduce costs is feasible, cost-effective, and efficient. Further research is recommended to Investigate MATLAB's AWS Parallel computing license options and costs. It is believed even more cost-savings could be realized with a pay-as-you-go model. This is particularly attractive for smaller companies and start-ups that might have limited financial resources, yet have the personnel skills to conduct some excellent research.

This initial experiment collected data from four different, but relatively short, time periods for two sports-related tweets. Only a handful of features were used to identify clusters and perform statistical analysis. We recommend expanding the time frame, number of tweet queries, and features to be able to provide further insight and understanding from the information available from social networking sites, such as Twitter.

Appendix A: Example MATLAB Code

```
% Test Twitty call account
% Clear variables
clear;
% Set up the credentials based on Twitter account
credentials.ConsumerKey = 'YourKey';
credentials.ConsumerSecret = 'Yoursecret';
credentials.AccessToken = yourAccess;
credentials.AccessTokenSecret = 'youraccesssecret';

% Create Tweet instance based on credentials
% tw = twitty(credentials);
% Create a Tweet example
% Pick Topeka Kansas for Center of Continental U.S.
% Set the last ID to Any value to start
LastID = 123456;
LastIDQ2 = 123456;
NumIts = 180;
TweetCnt=0; % Initialize to 0 counts
TweetCntQ2=0;
PauseTime = 60;
% Start a timer
Tic;
% Loop several times gathering data
for j=1:NumIts
j
% clear old data
clear S;
clear Q2;
% Time out issues establish new tw each iteration
tw = twitty(credentials);
% Run the First Query
S     =     tw.search('NFL',     'count',20,     'include_entities','true','geoco-
de','39.051300,-95.724660,1700mi','since_id',LastID);
% Let us see how many we got
StatCnt = length(cellfun('ndims',S{1,1}.statuses));
for i=1:StatCnt
 TweetCnt = TweetCnt+1;
 MyTweets=S{1,1}.statuses{1,i}.text ;
 % Put the data in
 Tweets{TweetCnt}=MyTweets;
 % Put the dates/time in
 Dates{TweetCnt} = S{1,1}.statuses{1,i}.created_at;
 % Gather other stuff
 FollowerCount(TweetCnt) = S{1,1}.statuses{1,i}.user.followers_count;
 FriendsCount(TweetCnt) = S{1,1}.statuses{1,i}.user.friends_count;
 TZones = S{1,1}.statuses{1,i}.user.time_zone;
 TimeZones{TweetCnt} = TZones;
 % Get screen name
 SName = S{1,1}.statuses{1,i}.user.screen_name;
```

http://dx.doi.org/10.5772/58895

```
 ScreenName{TweetCnt} = SName;
 % Get the User Mentions Count
  UserMentionCnt{TweetCnt} = length(cellfun('ndims',S{1,1}.statuses{1,i}.enti-
ties.user_mentions));
  URLMentionCnt{TweetCnt} = length(cellfun('ndims',S{1,1}.statuses{1,i}.enti-
ties.urls));
 HashTagsMentionCnt{TweetCnt} = length(cellfun('ndims',S{1,1}.statuses{1,i}.en-
tities.hashtags));
 end

 % Get the lastID to eliminate Dups
 if (StatCnt > 0)
 LastID = S{1,1}.statuses{1,1}.id_str;
 end
 % Run the World Series Query
Q2 = tw.search('World Series', 'count',20, 'include_entities','true','geoco-
de','39.051300,-95.724660,1700mi','since_id',LastIDQ2);
% Let us see how many we got
StatCntQ2 = length(cellfun('ndims',Q2{1,1}.statuses));

for i=1:StatCntQ2
 TweetCntQ2 = TweetCntQ2+1;
 MyTweetsQ2=Q2{1,1}.statuses{1,i}.text ;
 % Put the data in
 TweetsQ2{TweetCntQ2}=MyTweetsQ2;
 % Put the dates/time in
 DatesQ2{TweetCntQ2} = Q2{1,1}.statuses{1,i}.created_at;
 % Gather other stuff
 FollowerCountQ2(TweetCntQ2) = Q2{1,1}.statuses{1,i}.user.followers_count;
 FriendsCountQ2(TweetCntQ2) = Q2{1,1}.statuses{1,i}.user.friends_count;
 TZonesQ2 = Q2{1,1}.statuses{1,i}.user.time_zone;
 TimeZonesQ2{TweetCntQ2} = TZonesQ2;
 % Get screen name
 SNameQ2 = Q2{1,1}.statuses{1,i}.user.screen_name;
 ScreenNameQ2{TweetCntQ2} = SNameQ2;
 % Get the User Mentions Count
    UserMentionCntQ2{TweetCntQ2}    =    length(cellfun('ndims',Q2{1,1}.sta-
tuses{1,i}.entities.user_mentions));
 URLMentionCntQ2{TweetCntQ2} = length(cellfun('ndims',Q2{1,1}.statuses{1,i}.en-
tities.urls));
   HashTagsMentionCntQ2{TweetCntQ2}   =   length(cellfun('ndims',Q2{1,1}.sta-
tuses{1,i}.entities.hashtags));
 end
 % Get the lastID to eliminate Dups
 if (StatCntQ2 > 0)
 LastIDQ2 = Q2{1,1}.statuses{1,1}.id_str;
 end
 % Pause a few seconds
 pause(PauseTime);
end
```

Appendix B: Example Data Analysis MATLAB M-File

```
% Combine the Data into a vector
measWS = [cell2mat(UserMentionCntQ2)' cell2mat(URLMentionCntQ2)' cell2mat(Hash-
TagsMentionCntQ2)' FollowerCountQ2' FriendsCountQ2'];
measNFL= [cell2mat(UserMentionCnt)' cell2mat(URLMentionCnt)' cell2mat(HashTags-
MentionCnt)' FollowerCount' FriendsCount'];
% Combine
meas = [measWS;measNFL];
% Now let's do some Stats and Clustering
[cidx2,cmeans2] = kmeans(meas,2,'dist','sqeuclidean');
figure;
[silh2,h] = silhouette(meas,cidx2,'sqeuclidean');
% Look for maximum number of clusters
[cidx3,cmeans3] = kmeans(meas,3,'display','iter');
% Now do some clustering an
figure;
[silh3,h] = silhouette(meas,cidx3,'sqeuclidean');
% Some plots Might want to plot with NFL versus World Series
% Hierarchical Clustering
eucD = pdist(meas,'euclidean');
clustTreeEuc = linkage(eucD,'average');
myCop = cophenet(clustTreeEuc,eucD)
figure;
[h,nodes] = dendrogram(clustTreeEuc,0);
set(gca,'TickDir','out','TickLength',[.002 0],'XTickLabel',[]);
% Reduce nodes
figure;
[h,nodes] = dendrogram(clustTreeEuc,12);
toc
% World Series tweet Gaps
for i=1:length(Dates)-1
time1 = [str2num(Dates{i}(26:30)) 10 str2num(Dates{i}(9:10)) str2num(Dates{i}
(12:13)) str2num(Dates{i}(15:16)) str2num(Dates{i}(18:19))];
time2 = [str2num(Dates{i+1}(26:30)) 10 str2num(Dates{i+1}(9:10))
str2num(Dates{i+1}(12:13)) str2num(Dates{i+1}(15:16)) str2num(Dates{i+1}
(18:19))];
deltaWorldSeries(i) = abs(etime(time1,time2));
end
% NFLtweet gaps
for i=1:length(DatesQ2)-1
time1 = [str2num(DatesQ2{i}(26:30)) 10 str2num(DatesQ2{i}(9:10)) str2num(Da-
tesQ2{i}(12:13)) str2num(DatesQ2{i}(15:16)) str2num(DatesQ2{i}(18:19))];
time2 = [str2num(DatesQ2{i+1}(26:30)) 10 str2num(DatesQ2{i+1}(9:10))
str2num(DatesQ2{i+1}(12:13)) str2num(DatesQ2{i+1}(15:16)) str2num(DatesQ2{i+1}
(18:19))];
deltaNFL(i) = abs(etime(time1,time2));
end
figure (1)
subplot(2,1,1)
plot (deltaNFL,'r');
```

http://dx.doi.org/10.5772/58895

```
ylabel('Time between Tweets')
xlabel ('Tweet Number')
title('"NFL" Time between Tweets');
grid;
subplot(2,1,2)
plot(deltaWorldSeries, 'b');
ylabel('Time between Tweets')
xlabel ('Tweet Number')
title('"World Series" Time between Tweets');
grid;
% Stats
% Quick histograms for the 2 delta times
xvalues = -1:2:800;
figure (2)
subplot (1,2,1)
hist(deltaNFL,xvalues);
grid;
title ('Time between "NFL" Tweets')
axis ([-1 200 0 200]);
subplot (1,2,2)
hist(deltaWorldSeries,xvalues);
grid;
title ('Time between "World Series" Tweets')
axis ([-1 200 0 200]);
% Box plots for Descriptive visualization
figure(3)
subplot(1,2,1)
boxplot(deltaNFL)
title ('Time between "NFL" Tweets')
grid;
subplot(1,2,2)
boxplot(deltaWorldSeries)
title ('Time between "World Series" Tweets')
grid;
% Group Scatter
% Put everything together
MyGroup1 = zeros(1,length(HashTagsMentionCnt));
MyGroup2 = ones(1,length(HashTagsMentionCntQ2));
MyGroups = [MyGroup1 MyGroup2];
A1 = cell2mat(HashTagsMentionCnt);
B1 = FollowerCount;
C1 = FriendsCount;
D1 = cell2mat(UserMentionCnt);
E1 = cell2mat(URLMentionCnt);
A2 = cell2mat(HashTagsMentionCntQ2);
B2 = FollowerCountQ2;
C2 = FriendsCountQ2;
D2 = cell2mat(UserMentionCntQ2);
E2 = cell2mat(URLMentionCntQ2);
MyVars = [A1' B1' C1' D1' E1'; A2' B2' C2' D2' E2'];
varNames = {'HashTagMention' 'FollowerCount' 'FriendCount' 'URLMention' 'Hash-
TagMention'};
```

```
figure(4)
gplotmatrix(MyVars(:,2),     MyVars(:,3),MyGroups,['r'     'b'],['O'     'X'],
[],'off','hist',['Followers'],['Friends']);
grid;
```

Author details

Kelly Bennett[1] and James Robertson[2]

1 U.S. Army Research Laboratory, Sensors and Electron Devices Directorate, Adelphi, MD, USA

2 Clearhaven Technologies LLC, Severna Park, MD, USA

References

[1] Rahman, M. Mining social data to extract intellectual knowledge. doi:10.5815/ijisa.2012.10.02

[2] Das TK., Kumar P. BIG Data Analytics: A Framework for Unstructured Data Analysis. International Journal of Engineering Science and Technology 2013;5(2) 153-156.

[3] Daehoon K., Daeyong K., Seungmin R., Eenjun H. Detecting Trend and Bursty Keywords Using Characteristics of Twitter Stream Data. International Journal of Smart Home 2013;7(1) 209-220.

[4] Karandikar A. Clustering short status messages: A topic model based approach. Master's thesis. University of Maryland; 2010. http://ebiquity.umbc.edu/_file_directory_/papers/518.pdf (accessed 29 October 2013).

[5] Perera R. Twitter Analytics: Architecture, Tools and Analysis, Proc. The 2010 Military Communications Conference, MILCOM2010, Oct. 31, 2010-Nov. 3, 2010, San Jose Convention Center, CA; 2010.

[6] Turner and Malleson (2011). Applying geographical clustering methods to analyze geo-located open micro-blog posts: A case study of Tweets around Leeds since June 2011, https://docs.google.com/document/d/1yaRBUwJy8Cb3JWlN-fJOZZRN1JnXvpdWzhRDctqwcoI/edit?pli=1#heading=h.rx5m14o2e6yw (accessed 30 September 2013).

[7] MathWorks. MATLAB Products and Services. Overview. http://www.mathworks.com/products/matlab/ (accessed 8 October 2013).

[8] MathWorks. MATLAB Central. File Exchange. twitty by Vladimir Bondarenko. 30 January 2012 (Updated 12 July 2013). Interface-class to access the Twitter REST API

http://dx.doi.org/10.5772/58895

v1.1. http://www.mathworks.com/matlabcentral/fileexchange/34837-twitty/content/twitty.m. (accessed 21 September 2013).

[9] Twitter API. https://dev.twitter.com/docs/api/1.1 (accessed 12 July 2013).

[10] MathWorks. MATLAB Central. File Exchange. JSON Parser. JSON Parser by Joel Feenstra. 3 July 2008 (Updated 18 June 2009). http://www.mathworks.com/matlabcentral/fileexchange/20565-json-parser. (accessed 23 September 2013).

[11] MathWorks. Statistics Toolbox. Overview. http://www.mathworks.com/products/statistics/ (accessed 1 October 2013).

[12] MathWorks. Neural Network Toolbox Overview. http://www.mathworks.com/products/neural-network/ (accessed 18 September 2013).

[13] Kohonen T. Self-Organizing Maps. 3rd ed. Springer Series in Information Sciences. Springer-Verlag Heidelberg: New York; 2001.

[14] Bennett K, Robertson J. Signal and image processing algorithm performance in a virtual and elastic computing environment, Proc. SPIE Vol. 8734, Active and Passive Signatures IV, 87340B (2013).

Section 2

Control, System, and Design Applications

Chapter 2

A MATLAB-based Microscope

Milton P. Macedo

Additional information is available at the end of the chapter

http://dx.doi.org/10.5772/58532

1. Introduction

When someone intends to build a laboratorial prototype of a microscope there are two major tasks. One is in the optical side which is the selection of adequate optical and mechanical components of the optical setup taking into account budget restrictions. However the major challenge is to find the adequate overall environment that enables a easy and effective integration of the different parts of the microscope in order to arrange an efficient instrument.

This is a consequence of the great evolution in microscopy field in the last decades that naturally follows the progress in science and particularly in electronics and computer science. Currently the microscopes have little similarity with the general concept of an ancient microscope. In fact those former stand-alone microscopes that were used in biology laboratories at school have moved on to a complete instrumentation system. Different areas such as optics, mechanics, electronics and software have now to be integrated in order to get a digital image of an object. Ultimately a modern microscope is a user computer-controlled instrument.

Surely this configures an instrumentation field where it is very attractive to use MATLAB. In this chapter it is presented a practical example of MATLAB application as the fundamental tool in a three-dimensional (3D) microscopy platform. The first stage of this research project consisted on the selection of a one-dimensional (1D) array CCD/CMOS sensor and the subsequent development of the sensor readout module. Afterwards the laboratory platform has been built. Besides the sensor readout module the main components of this bench-microscope are the optical layout and computer software.

The choice of an efficient computer software is fundamental as the configuration of acquisition parameters, control of data acquisition, visualization of microscope images and data processing are to be performed by the user in a computer. The versatility of this platform is probably the most important feature in order to accommodate such different tasks as:

INTECH
open science | open minds

© 2014 The Author(s). Licensee InTech. This chapter is distributed under the terms of the Creative Commons Attribution License (http://creativecommons.org/licenses/by/3.0), which permits unrestricted use, distribution, and reproduction in any medium, provided the original work is properly cited.

- Acquisition of data from stand-alone sensor readout module-implementation of a data communication channel from sensor readout module to the computer;
- Positioning control of the object stage – implementation of the interface of stage actuators to computer;
- Visualization of data in real-time in a computer display;
- Development of 3D reconstruction algorithms;
- Development of Graphical User Interfaces (GUI) for the different applications.

A brief reference has to be made to the use of the Borland C compiler as computer software development tool at an initial stage of this work. Namely when testing a different acquisition hardware using a different sensor and to test this sensor readout module. But next the integration of those different tasks enumerated above had to be accomplished. At this point MATLAB had been naturally considered owing to its versatility given by the functionalities from its core and toolboxes.

In this chapter the focus is the description of MATLAB applications. However for a deeper comprehension of MATLAB functionalities implemented in these applications some details of the bench-microscope prototype have to be stated. Then firstly some hardware features as the sensor readout module and object stage positioning are reported. The particularities in image build and visualization owing to the use of a linear image sensor in this bench-microscope are also covered.

On the other hand the best mode of evaluating the effectiveness of the MATLAB applications is showing the results obtained with this bench-microscope. Four applications have been developed for the implementation of image acquisition and visualization as well as for the assessment of image quality and image processing in some practical applications of this platform in materials science field.

Lastly a summary of the overall functionalities of these different MATLAB applications and a discussion of the advantages of a platform that use such a diversity of integrated tools is presented.

2. Microscope implementation

The challenge of assembling a microscope with the diversity of areas of knowledge that it demands had led to the development of open-source microscopy software. In this manner different research groups in universities as well as in industry work together in order to build software platforms that make easier the implementation of the different tasks in order to accomplish the acquisition of an image on a microscope.

Obviously the use of an open source microscopy software should be considered whenever a new microscope setup is assembled. Amongst these open source microscopy software, *Micro-Manager* and *OME* (*Open Microscopy Environment*) are probably the better established.

Micro-Manager is a complete microscopy software that include control of microscope itself and associated hardware. A long list of microscope models as well as cameras, stages and other peripherals can be controlled. It runs as a plugin to *ImageJ* and provides an easy to use software to control microscope experiments.

OME aims at the storage and manipulation of biological data. It comprises a client-server software (*OMERO*) for visualization, management and analysis of images and a *Java* library (*Bio-Formats*) for reading and writing biological image files. This library can be used as an *ImageJ* plugin, MATLAB toolbox or in our own software. *ImageJ* is a public domain *Java* image processing program. It is a very complete image tool that can be used with many image formats as well as raw-images.

As this is a research project a fast and easy access to hardware in order to test other acquisition and control configurations would be important. Surely if a software platform is developed from the zero it is more versatile and flexible. On the other hand the graphical user interface (GUI) was adapted from the one used in the preliminary tests which had been developed in C/C++language. These two issues together with other particularities listed in table 1 were decisive to the choice of developing in MATLAB an entirely original and dedicated software for this project.

Micro-Manager	OME	Original MATLAB applications
Disadvantages		Advantages
Sensor and stage actuators devices not supported	Do not perform microscope control	Versatility and flexibility in hardware configuration
Time consuming and energy investment in Micro-Manager	Optimized to work with biological data	GUI layout previously developed in C/C++ language
No previous experience in using ImageJ	No previous experience in using ImageJ	Experience in programming languages / MATLAB

Table 1. Advantages and disadvantages of using an open source microscopy software or develop original Matlab applications for this project.

3. Description of bench-microscope

The purpose of this work was to build a platform to develop and test algorithms able to obtain 3D images. The own microscope optics is based on a linear-array image sensor. At an initial stage an hardware previously developed in our research team, named PAF (*Photodiode Array Fluorometer*), had been used. After the implementation of a few and plain adjustments in the PAF software the first tests were performed. A scheme of this system is shown in figure 1.

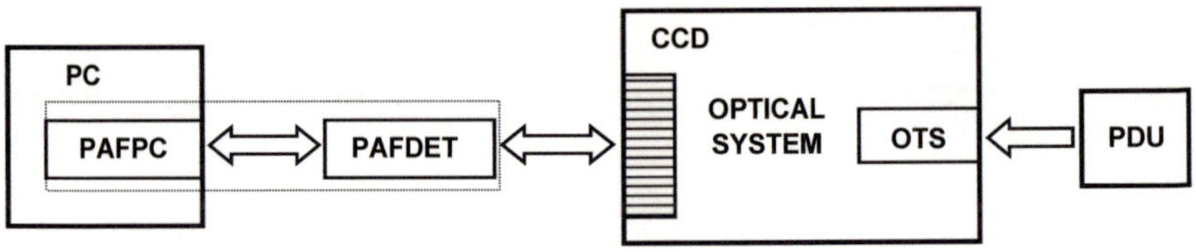

Figure 1. Test system using PAF. PAFPC e PAFDET are PAF hardware modules in computer bus and with detector, respectively; OTS – Object Translation Stage; PDU – Piezoelectric Drive Unit.

Owing to the excessive pixel width in the linear-array CCD used in PAF other sensor must be searched. A new sensor in the market (*LIS-1024 from Photon-Vision Systems*) with 1024 pixels of 7,8 μm width had been selected. Afterwards the development of a sensor readout had also enabled to assemble the sensor in the optical bench. The block diagram showing microscope architecture is presented in figure 2 as well as a photo of the optical layout showing the sensor-readout module and stage actuators both controlled from MATLAB. The optical layout is beyond the scope of this chapter but for clarity a brief description of sensor-readout module and positioning of the object platform is essential.

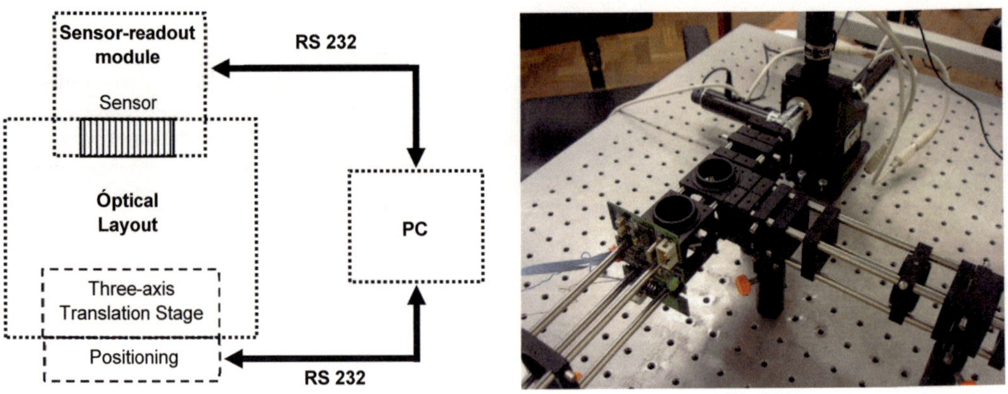

Figure 2. Block diagram and a photo of the bench-microscope.

3.1. Sensor-readout module

This stand-alone module is based on a microcontroller of PIC family *(PIC16F876)* from Microchip. It had been selected amongst a set of similar devices as it completely meets the predefined specifications, namely: a 10-bit ADC, three timers and an high versatility owing to an interrupt structure with thirteen interrupt sources.

Its weakness lies in communication options. It only has a USART for RS232 communication. So sensor data is transferred to the computer through its serial port (RS232). However the optimization of the system regarding acquisition speed is not a goal of this project. Otherwise other PIC microcontroller, *PIC16C745*, with an USB serial port would be the right choice. But

http://dx.doi.org/10.5772/58532

the overall specifications of *PIC16F876* are more adequate to the system needs namely because of its 10-bit ADC in comparison to the 8-bit ADC in *PIC16C745*.

Figure 3 shows the block diagram of the module. Besides the sensor and microcontroller it contains a RS-232 *driver* (*MAX242 from Maxim*) that receive/transmit signals from/to PIC serial port. This driver also put data in electric format of RS-232 standard and manage control signals for data communication with the computer. As serial ports have been gradually disappearing of computers in recent years there is the possibility of using an USB to RS232 adapter and connect this module to a more modern and powerful computer.

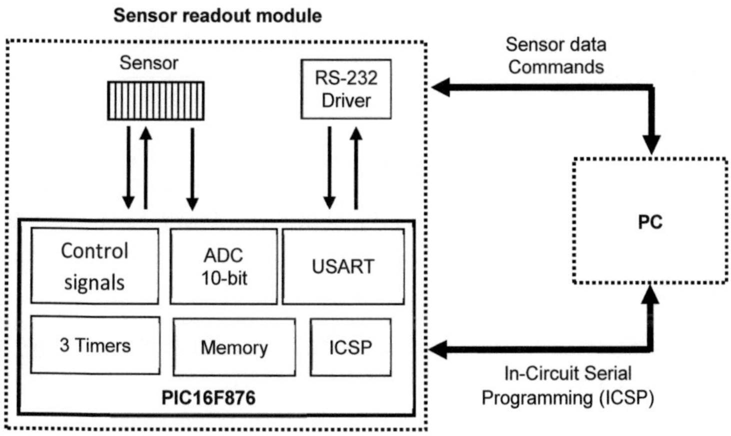

Figure 3. Block diagram of the sensor readout module.

Another important functionality of this PIC microcontroller, shown in this block diagram, is called ICSP (*In-Circuit Serial Programming*). This enables an easy mode for programming the PIC, changing its configurations, namely the sensor readout mode, without the need of take the hardware module out of optical layout.

3.1.1. Sensor readout

The ICSP functionality also enables a fast and easy configuration of the sensor operation mode taking advantage of its flexibility that comes out from CMOS technology. It is very useful as the more adequate sensor operation mode depends on the type of application in which the bench-microscope is used.

The sensor readout mode normally used was the destructive Dynamic Pixel Reset (DPR). The reset of each pixel is executed as the respective readout is concluded. This assures an equal integration time for every pixel. To ensure the correct timing of the readout start of the next set of 1024 pixels, the PIC waits by a specific control signal from the sensor.

The verification of timing specifications for sensor readout is ensured by the three *timers* of the PIC. Therefore the internal clock of the sensor with a duty-cycle of 50%, the readout of each pixel data in the second half of the respective readout time window and the acquisition time in accordance with precision specifications of the ADC are easily implemented.

The acquisition cycle is based on the appropriate interrupt structure of the PIC. Figure 4 presents the timing diagram of the acquisition cycle. It is also shown the timing of data transfer to computer through RS-232 serial port.

No external memory exists in this stand-alone module. As there is no way to store the data in the module memory, each pixel value of 10 bits, the result of the ADC conversion of the analog value read from each sensor pixel, has to be sent to computer till the end of the timeslot. In this case the timeslot is the time lapse from one ADC conversion to the next one.

These 10 bits value from each pixel is packed in a frame with three words of 8 bits (bytes) as it is shown in figure 5. Thus each timeslot must be long enough for the USART complete the transfer of this frame.

Using the *Instrument Control Toolbox* the configuration of the computer serial port was performed. Preliminary tests had shown that using the maximum baud rate of 59200 bps the communication errors were very scarce. In spite of this it had been considered that a baud rate of 19200 bps was the best compromise between speed and reliability. The option had been to completely avoid these error relaxing the speed goals.

This lower baud rate imposes a rate of pixel sensor readout slightly above 1 kHz. This is achieved from a timeslot width (T_{cycle}) of nearly 900 μs. Therefore the acquisition of all 1024 sensor pixels takes around one second.

In many applications of this bench microscope it is unnecessary to perform the acquisition of the 1024 pixels. Owing to the easiness of programming the PIC that arises from the ICSP functionality described above it is plain to change the sensor readout configuration namely the timing issues in order to adequate it to the specific needs of each situation.

In these cases instead of wasting time for the acquisition of data without relevant information it is clearly useful the definition of a region of interest (ROI). The dimension of this ROI in image plane depends on the magnification of the objective used. One of the objective lenses in this bench microscope is 40x / 0.65 NA (numerical aperture is a number related to the width of the cone of light gathered by the lens). So the image with 1024 pixels corresponds to $200\ \mu m$ in the sample (in object plane). If in one specific application this is excessive a ROI should be defined and consequently the acquisition rate is increased. For a ROI with 256 or 128 pixels the acquisition rate is increased by a factor of 4 or 8, respectively.

3.2. Positioning actuators

This bench microscope is intended to be used in reflection mode. Its optical layout is an epi-illumination configuration, typical of confocal microscopes. In this case light travelling from the light source to the sample has a fraction of its path in common to light reflected by the sample. Due to budget constraints it has been made the option by a stage-scanning instead of the beam-scanning configuration.

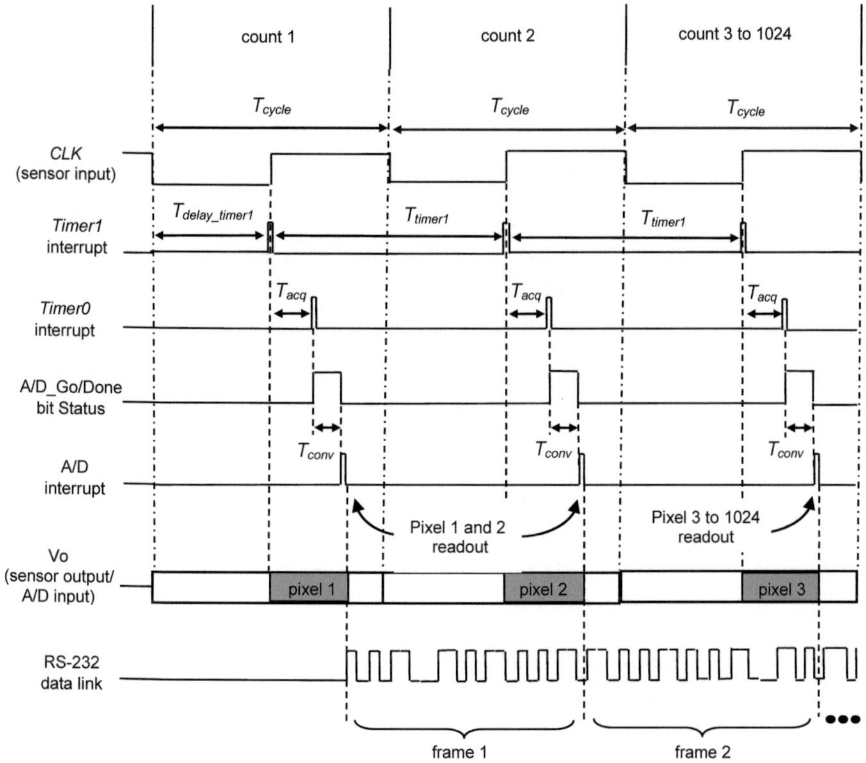

Figure 4. Timing diagram of the acquisition cycle of sensor data (time intervals not in scale). Pixel acquisition time (T_{cycle}) of 888 µs, A/D acquisition time (T_{acq}) of 30 µs and conversion time (T_{conv}) of 20 µs.

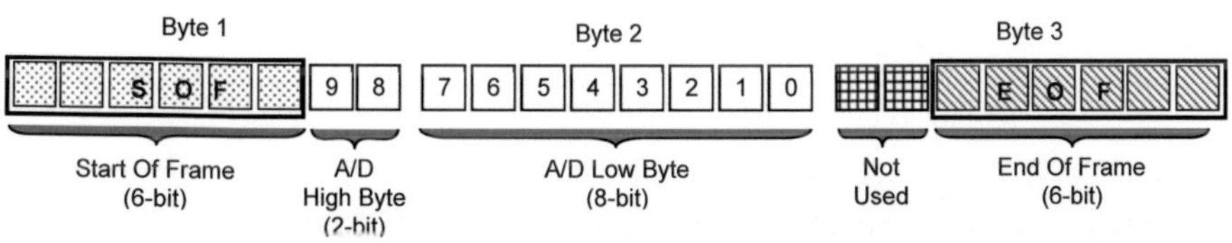

Figure 5. Format of the *frame* used in RS-232 communication.

There are a wide range of positioning devices that use, e.g., stepper motors, acousto-optic deflectors (AOD), galvanometric mirrors or piezoelectric drivers. The selection of the actuators to control the positioning of the object translation stage had been based on the following issues:

- Easiness to accommodate in the three-axis translation stage (*Melles Griot 17 AMB 003*);
- Computer-controlled;
- Cost effective (nice compromise between cost and performance).

T-series positioning products from Zaber™ and in particular linear actuators are ready to mount in the translation stage. These computer controlled positioning products use stepper motors to achieve open loop position control. These devices turn by a constant angle called a step for every electrical impulse sent to them. This allows a system to be built without feedback, reducing total system cost.

However, being incremental (as opposed to absolute) in nature, the stepper motor must initially be zeroed by going to a home sensor. As there is no encoder, the actual position of the device will become different from the position shown in the computer display. Also these positioning products use a direct drive system for a simplified mechanical design with no coupling, gear, belt or other expensive components.

Likewise the specifications of this linear actuators in terms of resolution and repeatability comply with the purposes of the bench-microscope thence the option by the linear actuator T-LA 28, with a 28 mm range.

The resolution (or addressability) is the distance equivalent to the smallest incremental move the device can be instructed to make. In other words, it is the linear or rotational displacement corresponding to a single microstep of movement. The resolution for T-LA products is 0.09921875 mm (or approximately 0.1 mm).

The repeatability is the maximum deviation in the position of the device when attempting to return to a position after moving to a different position. The typical repeatability for T-LA actuators is about 0.3 mm. Also the typical backlash, which is the deviation of the final position that results from reversing the direction of approach, is 2.2 mm. T-LA devices have built in anti-backlash routines that do not affect motion in the positive direction (increasing absolute position, plunger extending). For negative motion, however, the device will overshoot the desired position by roughly 600 microsteps and return, approaching the requested position from below.

3.2.1. Positioning control

Image acquisition with this bench-microscope requires to control the positioning of the object stage. Automatic scanning in the three-axis (XYZ) is performed. One T-LA 28 actuator controlled through the RS232 port of a computer is used to implement the scanning in each axis. However the three units are connected in a daisy-chained mode thus sharing the same serial port in the computer. The configuration of the computer serial port and the control of RS232 communication was implemented in a MATLAB application.

Communications settings must be: 9600 baud, no hand shaking, no parity, one stop bit. After power-up, the units in the chain will each initialize itself as unit #1 and thus each will execute the same instructions. To assign each unit a unique identifier, a renumber instruction must be issued after all the units in the chain are powered up and every time a unit is added or removed from the chain. Instructions must not be transmitted while the chain is renumbering or the renumbering routine may be corrupted. Renumbering takes less than a second, after which instructions may start to be issued over the RS232 connection.

All instructions consist of a group of 6 bytes. They must be transmitted with less than 10 ms between each byte. If the unit has received less than 6 bytes and then a period of more than 10 ms passes, it ignores the bytes already received. The table 2 below shows the instruction format:

Byte 1	Byte 2	Byte 3	Byte 4	Byte 5	Byte 6
Unit #;	Command #	Data (least significant byte)	Data	Data	Data (most significant byte)

Table 2. Instruction format.

The first byte is the unit number in the chain. Unit number 1 is the unit closest to the computer, unit number 2 is next and so forth. If the number 0 is used, all the units in the chain will execute the accompanying command simultaneously.

The second byte is the command number. Bytes 3, 4, 5 and 6 are data in long integer, 2's complement format with the least significant byte transmitted first. How the data bytes are interpreted depends on the command.

Most instructions cause the unit to reply with a return code. It is also a group of 6 bytes. The first byte is the device #. Byte 2 is the instruction just completed or 255 if an error occurs. Bytes 3, 4, 5 and 6 are data bytes in the same format as the instruction data byte. For some instructions in this reply it is sent the actual effective position.

Therefore the communication between the computer and T-LA 28 is executed in both directions. From the graphical user interface (GUI) of the MATLAB application the user gives an order to perform a command, e.g., reset, home, renumber, move absolute, move relative, using the instruction format presented in table 1.

The slow data communication between these linear actuators and the computer, 9600 *baud,* is one of the most important weaknesses of these actuators. Image acquisition rate is consequently low but it is assumed that in this work the concern is not to optimize this rate. The aim of this project is to obtain microscope images from which a three-dimensional reconstruction is made. Therefore with this goal in mind the easiness in the integration of this actuators in the optical layout combined with programming versatility largely compensate the imposed low acquisition rate.

4. Image visualization

Raw-data provided in one sensor readout consists of 1024 analogue values that the A/D in microcontroller converts in 10-bit digital values. And these values compose a linear image of a region-of-interest (ROI) in the object with a length that depends on the objective magnification. It corresponds to 200 μm and 400 μm for 40X and 20X objectives, respectively,

Usually the object plane is considered as the XY plane. Hence the optical axis which is perpendicular to this plane is the z-axis. When using a linear sensor normally the x-axis represents the direction of the sensor pixels. Thus the acquisition of a two-dimensional (2D) image implies the scanning of the object on the translation-stage in the other lateral direction perpendicular to sensor (y-axis).

4.1. 2D image view

Two-dimensional image build is schematically shown in figure 6. This diagram illustrates its dependence on spatial sampling rate in both lateral axes.

Sampling rate in x-axis is imposed by pixel width which is 7,8 μm. It is possible to join contiguous pixels and consequently the correspondent photoelectrons are added. This process is denominated by binning. The advantages are a faster image acquisition rate, reduced exposition time or an improved signal-to-noise ratio (SNR). However it is achieved at expense of a degradation in image resolution [1]. Spatial sampling rate in object space also depends on objective magnification. For the objectives 40x and 20x these values are 195 nm and 390 nm, respectively, without binning. Consequently putting together e.g., four contiguous pixels, the sampling rate is decreased by the same factor.

Spatial sampling in y-axis is imposed by the minimum length in XYZ stage movements in that direction. Based on the specifications of the positioning devices the option was to use the minimum scanning step of 1 μm. On the other hand in microscope applications that demand a larger field-of-view (FOV), wider scanning steps, till the maximum of 20 μm, were used at expense of image lateral resolution.

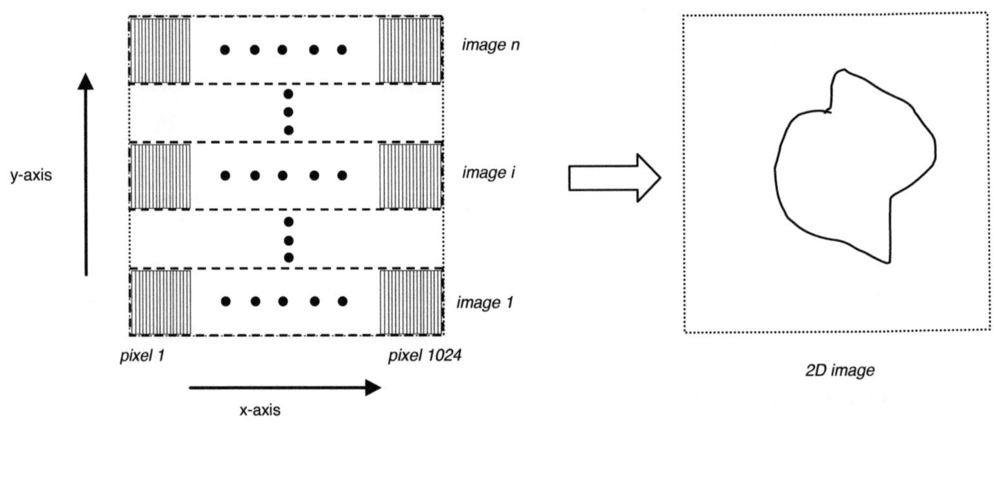

Figure 6. Schematic of 2D image build. Pixel width is 7,8 μm at image space. Sampling rate in y-axis at object space range from one to twenty microns.

To build a 2D image that is a faithful representation of the relative dimensions of the object in the two lateral directions it is necessary to have an equal scale in both axes. As spatial

http://dx.doi.org/10.5772/58532

sampling rate in the two axes generally is different, the MATLAB function *imresize* is used. One of its parameters is exactly the ratio of sampling rate values in both axes. This parameter acts as a multiplicative factor to be used for the values in the axis with lower sampling rate. If the 20x objective is used together with the minimum scanning step in y-axis a multiplicative factor of 2,56 should be used in *imresize* function. Other parameter is the interpolation method that may be chosen from the following three: nearest-neighbor, bilinear or bicubic.

This process for 2D image build is illustrated in the scheme of figure 7. It is presented as example one image of the USAF resolution target used in this work for image quality assessment.

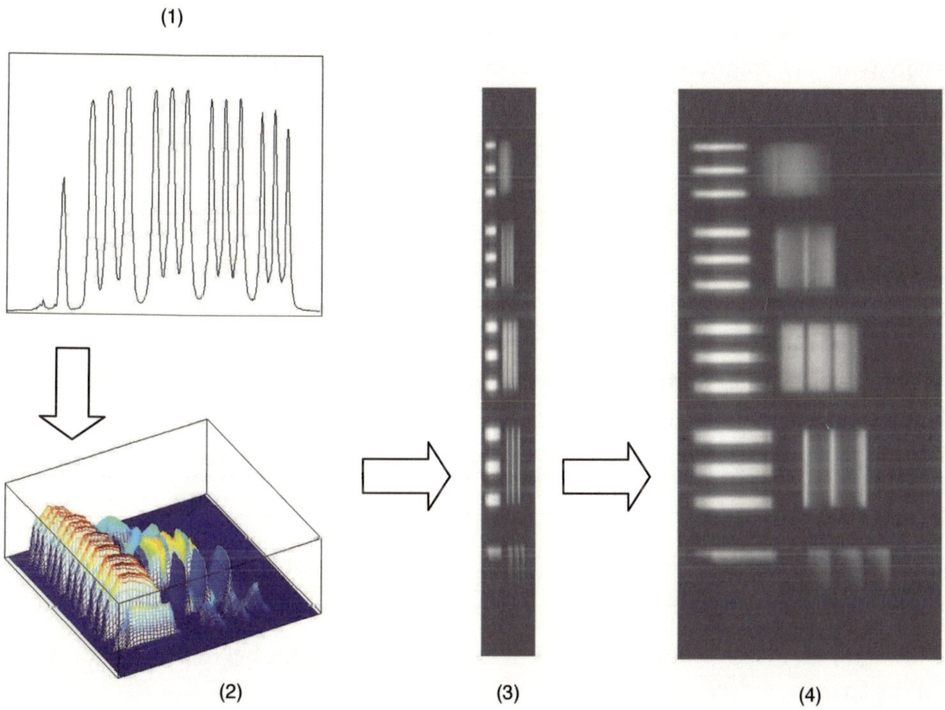

Figure 7. Diagram depicting the 2D image build in the case of the USAF resolution target. (1) Linear image (data from one sensor readout); (2) 3D representation of the intensity values in the XY plane (after the scanning along y-axis); (3) 2D image using data from sensor readout (no data processing); (4) 2D image with equal scales in both lateral axes (output of *imresize* function). In (3) and (4): horizontal direction – y-axis; vertical direction – x-axis.

In some microscope applications the field-of-view from each sensor readout is insufficient. However this microscope is able to increase the field-of-view through the scanning also along sensor direction (x-axis). The overall width of the 1024 sensor pixels gives a total field-of-view of approximately 400 μm and 200 μm, for 40x and 20x objective lenses, respectively. In order to build the 2D image with a larger field-of-view it is necessary to use an adequate method to mount contiguous images in x-axis. The MATLAB function *montage* performs this action assuring a correct position alignment. In the overall image these transitions are undistinguishable.

4.2. Extraction and visualization of 3D information

Linear images from each sensor readout of its 1024 pixels as well as 2D images obtained in result of the scanning in y-axis are blurred by light collected from reflection on points of the object at different depths. Then this blur in an ideally focused image is a result of light coming from reflection on points in planes in front or behind the focal plane.

Scanning optical microscopes (SOM) and particularly the confocal microscope, which is the most widely used, are suitable to get three-dimensional (3D) information. To achieve an image with 3D information the acquisition of different optical sections must be performed. It consists on images of object planes at different depths. Its acquisition is performed through the scanning along the direction of the optical axis, usually known as the axial direction.

Thus as this bench-microscope is intended for the acquisition of images with 3D information, scanning of the XYZ object translation stage is also performed along optical axis (z-axis). Spatial sampling rate in this axis is similar to the used in y-axis. Sampling intervals range from the minimum of 1 μm till 20 μm. The axial resolution depends on the numerical aperture (NA) of the objective. So the selection of the spatial sampling rate must have in consideration which objective is used, namely the 0.4 NA or 0.65 NA.

Amongst the different modes of visualization of 3D information the following two are the more usual:

- Auto-focus images – images with three-dimensional information as points in image are focused at different depths.
- Topographic maps – a three-dimensional representation of the height, $h(x_i, y_i)$, of each point in XY plane.

A more detailed description of the methods implemented in this microscope will be presented together with the presentation of several microscope applications. However to illustrate how 3D information can be visualized and simultaneously to evidence the ability of this bench-microscope to achieve this goal see figure 8. It is the result of the application of a particular non-automatic method. In this case the user select for each lateral position the best focus on the bonding wire amongst the overall axial positions. It is clearly distinguishable the wire inclination that departs from the pad on the integrated circuit and increases its height from the left to the right.

http://dx.doi.org/10.5772/58532

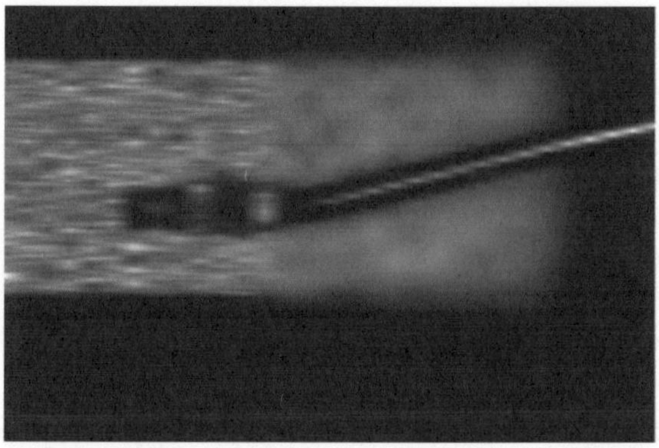

Figure 8. *Best-focus* image (bonding wire). FOV: 620 μm x 400 μm (horizontal direction – y-axis; vertical direction – x-axis).

5. Results

5.1. Image acquisition

The image acquisition as well as its visualization is configured by the computer user. Even in the early stage of this bench-microscope in which preliminary tests were performed with PAF hardware and software it was accomplished. Using PAF system as well as in the initial tests using this sensor readout module the software development tool had been Borland C. This occurred mainly because the software already developed with this tool for PAF was in an easy and fast mode applied to this new hardware module.

However a point had been reached in which the need of improving the quality of the graphical user interface and of creating a more user-friendly interface had demanded the change to other software environment. Borland C had been a great tool to develop code for someone that has learned C language in the first step of programming learning. Nevertheless it was not directed for the development of graphical user interfaces (GUI). Consequently it was a time consuming task and the graphical interface had not reached the desired quality.

As already mentioned the option had been to use MATLAB. In fact it is a very complete tool as through the use of its objects it is easy and much faster to create a graphical user interface, to add or remove any functionality at any time. But in this bench-microscope there is also the necessity of implement the acquisition of sensor data as well as the control of the positioning of the object stage. Yet MATLAB covers this scope through its toolboxes namely *Instrument Control* or *Data Acquisition*. The mode how this functionalities had been easily implemented in MATLAB had been probably the major proof that it was the best choice.

CompleteGUI had been the first MATLAB application developed for this bench-microscope. It is the more general in the sense it is used anytime the user intends to get a microscope image. Besides the initialization of the sensor and positioners the user has to define the acquisition parameters in terms of the scanning axes, range and steps.

As the sensor readout is performed with an acquisition rate of about one frame of 1024 pixels per second and it is a linear image sensor it is necessary to complete the acquisition of a set of frames to build a two-dimensional (2D) image. It usually takes a few tens of seconds. This image is then built from a set of one-dimensional (1D) images which are also displayed in real-time. One functionality of this application is to build this 2D image giving the possibility of image visualization immediately after its acquisition is completed. This GUI is shown in figure 9 with an example of real-time visualization of raw-data from sensor which is the 1D image.

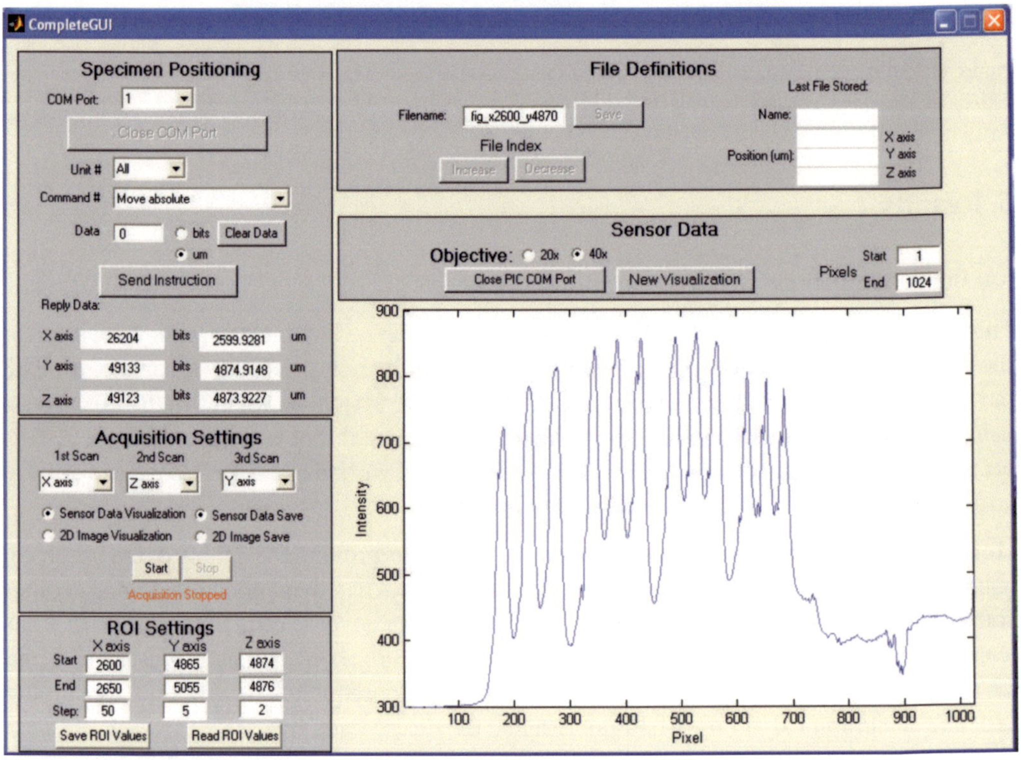

Figure 9. Graphical User Interface – *CompleteGUI* – developed for configuration settings and acquisition control and visualization.

The functionalities of *CompleteGUI* application are summarized below:

- Object-stage positioning
  - User definition of the order of scanning in the three axes (through the GUI);
  - User definition of the region-of-interest limits in the three axes (through the GUI);
  - Send commands to positioners through a computer serial port.

http://dx.doi.org/10.5772/58532

- Sensor data readout
  - Send a command to the sensor readout module to signal acquisition start (through a computer serial port).
  - Receive the sensor data, 10-bit values of the 1024 pixels (through a computer serial port).
- Image visualization
  - Real-time visualization (preview) of each sensor readout, i.e., a 1D image that shows sensor raw-data;
  - Visualization of each 2D image as soon as the acquisition of the set of sensor data is completed
- Data-files creation
  - Open Excel data-files
  - Store data files in the computer hard disk.

5.2. Image quality assessment

One of the most important tasks to be performed had been image quality assessment. After the implementation of overall system architecture that includes the optical layout it was necessary to know whether the images obtained with this bench-microscope are in good agreement with theoretical expressions. In fact the performance of a microscope is determined by the quality of its output image. There are two different approaches for this assessment:

- Quantitative assessment through the determination of the modulation transfer function (MTF) and point spread function (PSF) which are a measure of contrast and resolution, respectively.
- Qualitative assessment using images of specific objects with known dimensions [2]

Usually only one of these two different methods is selected. It depends on the specificity of the system. Owing to practical reasons a method for quantitative assessment was used. Namely because this is a bright-field microscope in reflection mode and a new method for the determination of PSF would be implemented.

5.2.1. Contrast measurement (determination of MTF)

Firstly it was measured the MTF which is an usual representation of the performance of imaging systems. It is used as a measure of image contrast. The general definition of MTF is given by the ratio of modulation depth in the output and input of an optical system in function of the spatial frequency when a sinusoidal target is used as input [3]. Modulation depth (*M*), normally called contrast, has the following definition:

$$M = \frac{I_{\max} - I_{\min}}{I_{\max} + I_{\min}}, \tag{1}$$

where I_{max} and I_{min} are the maximum and minimum intensity values, respectively. It is relative either to irradiance emitted by the object or collected in the image, which are system output and input, respectively. Thus MTF definition is:

$$MTF(\xi) = \frac{M_{output}(\xi)}{M_{\underset{input}{\sin usoidal}}(\xi)}, \tag{2}$$

whereξ is the spatial frequency (rigorously it is its component along sinusoidal grid direction)

From the different methods for MTF determination [4], the choice had been the scanning method. It consists on the measurement of the dependence of the contrast on spatial frequency using a sinusoidal grid as object. Although the MTF concept is applied to sinusoidal grids, for practical reasons, it is much easier to use square grids.

A widely used square grid is the USAF (*United-States Air Force*) resolution target. Then MTF determination was accomplished through contrast measurement for each group / element in images of the USAF target. This target consists on groups of three lines with different densities. The separation of the lines ranges from a minimum of approximately 2 μm (that corresponds to a maximum spatial frequency of 228 lp/mm) to tens of microns (one line pair/mm).

In this manner this method consists on the measurement of the system response to an input which is a square and not a sinusoidal grid. This is the definition similar to MTF but designated by contrast transfer function (CTF), in accordance to:

$$CTF(\xi_f) = \frac{M_{output}(\xi_f)}{M_{\underset{input}{square}}(\xi_f)}, \tag{3}$$

whereξ_f is the fundamental spatial frequency.

To materialize this implementation the MATLAB application *USAF_image* had been developed. Its graphical user interface is presented in figure 10.

The functionalities of *USAF_image* application are summarized below:

- Region-of-interest (ROI)
  - User definition of ROI limits in the two axes (through the GUI);
  - ROI visualization;

- Image files
  - Store image files in JPEG format in the computer hard disk;
  - Parameter acquisition
- Selection of a ROI containing one line;
  - Determination of maximum and minimum value in that ROI;
  - Determination of line width given in number of pixels using a predetermined threshold value (usually average of maximum and minimum values).

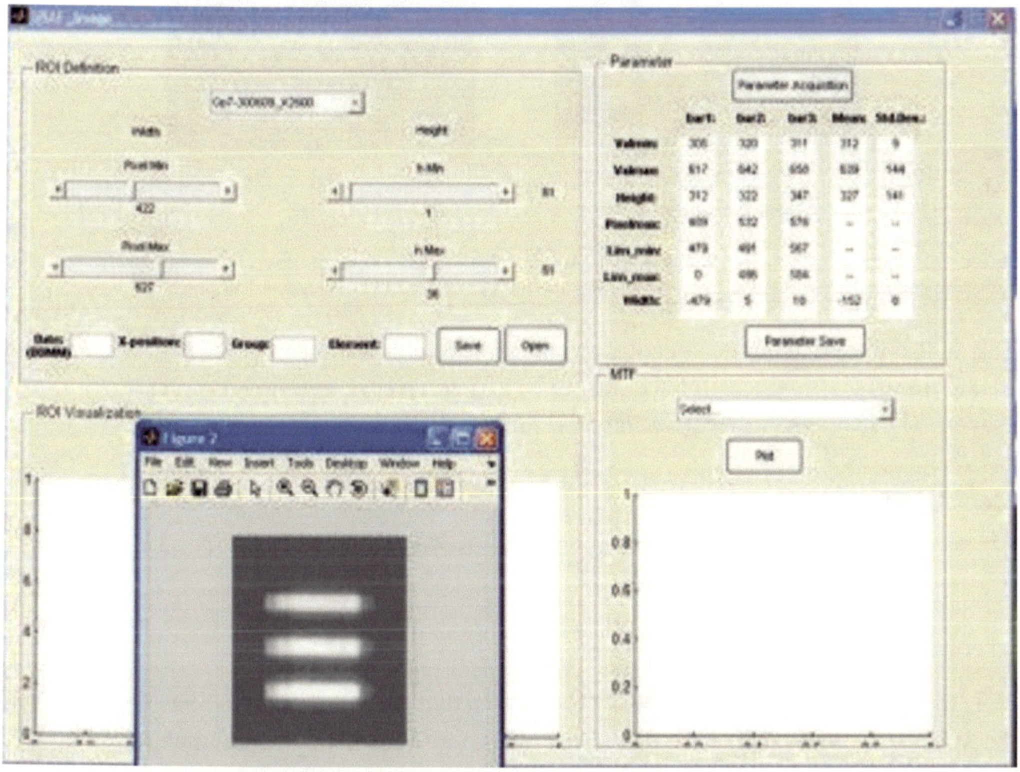

Figure 10. Graphical User Interface – *USAF_image* – developed for image quality assessment namely contrast measurements.

CTF values were then calculated for each spatial frequency, using the groups of three lines in USAF target images as shown in figure 11. Different optical configurations had been used in the acquisition of these two images. Images on the left and right correspond to wide-field and line-illumination, respectively. Despite the importance of the illumination mode for the success of this bench-microscope, it is out of the scope of this chapter. Just for completeness the comparison of image contrast on these two illumination modes will be presented.

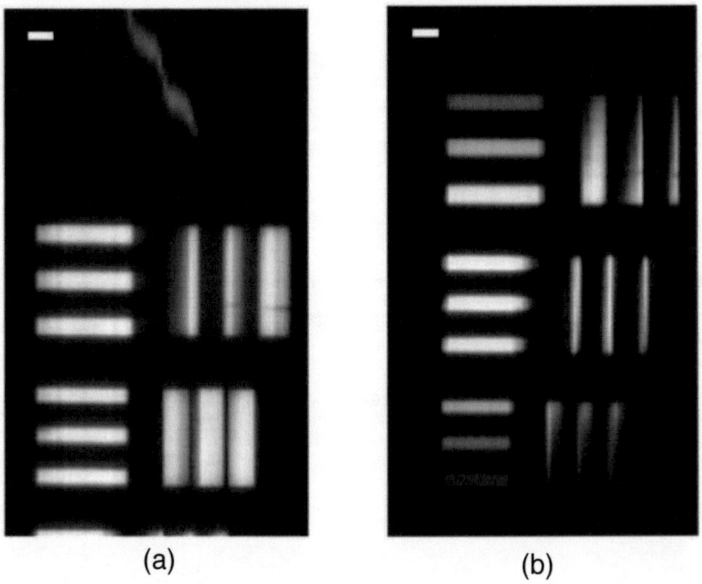

Figure 11. Images of USAF target showing some elements (sets of three lines) of group 7 (higher density). (a) wide-field illumination; (b) line-illumination. Scale bar is 5 μm (horizontal direction – y-axis; vertical direction – x-axis).

This is also the reason why a detailed explanation of how the measured CTF (response to a square input) is converted to MTF (response to a sinusoidal input) is not presented in this chapter. The mathematical expression used for this conversion is:

$$MTF(\xi_f) = \frac{\pi}{4}\sum_{n=0}^{N} B_{2n+1}\frac{CTF\left[2n+1(\xi_f)\right]}{2n+1} \quad para \; \frac{\xi_f}{2N+3} < \xi \leq \frac{\xi_f}{2N+1} \tag{4}$$

where B_{2n+1} is equal to-*1*, *0* or *1*.

Thus the selection of the line is made in an interactive mode using *USAF_image* GUI. When the ROI is exactly as desired the user gives the order to calculate the parameters namely I_{max} and I_{min}, already described and previously shown in equation 1. The range of spatial frequencies used for the determination of MTF is much lower than the range of frequencies the system is able to pass. However this is considered adequate in several applications [4,5,6].

Results are presented in figure 12. In wide-field and line-illumination experimental data range from 32 lp/mm to 228 lp/mm and 128 lp/mm to 228 lp/mm, respectively. Experimental cutoff frequencies (maximum spatial frequency the system is able to pass) are 719 *lp/mm* and 975 lp/mm for wide-field and line-illumination, respectively. It had been used a 40X 0.65 NA objective lens which diffraction-limited (ideal system with no aberrations) cutoff frequency is *1136 lp/mm*.

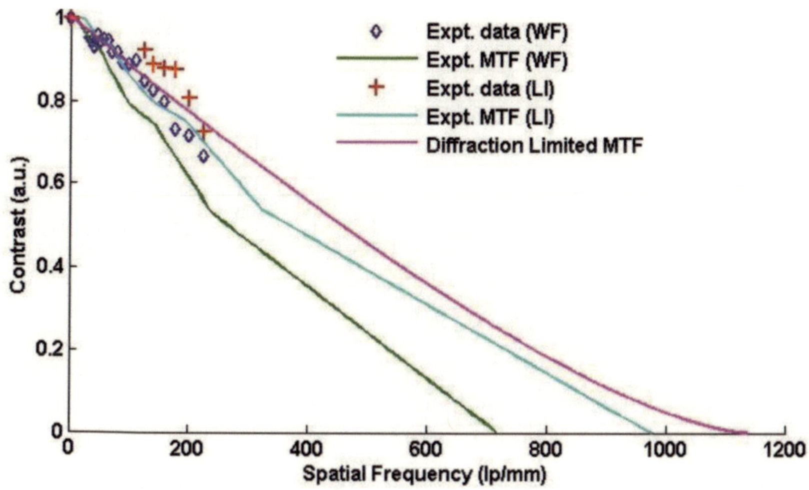

Figure 12. Comparison of wide-field (WF) to line-illumination (LI) for experimental data and calculated diffraction-limited MTF.

5.2.2. Lateral resolution measurement (new method for the determination of PSF)

Images of this bench-microscope have contributions of light coming from planes in front and behind the focal plane. A mathematical model describing the image formation process is used frequently in these cases to remove this blur. From a compromise between data processing demands and required accuracy it had been used one simplified model as follows:

$$\mathrm{I} = H\,O + b \tag{5}$$

where I is the image collected in sensor, H is the sampled PSF (matrix representing blur) sometimes space variant, O is a discrete object and b is background light.

To use this model it is necessary to calculate the PSF. In this method that is performed using as object one line of USAF target. It obeys the fundamental condition that object spatial parameters are well-known. So it was applied using lines of higher spatial frequencies in the range from 64 to 228 lp/mm, as those shown previously in figure 11.

For the implementation of this method some code was developed in MATLAB and included in *USAF_image*. It consists on the steps presented in table 3. Owing to anisotropy imposed by the use of a linear image sensor, the PSF in x-axis and y-axis, respectively, parallel and perpendicular to sensor, are different. Thus the method was applied separately for lines in both directions.

This algorithm was applied to obtain PSF_{xx} using a line along x-axis in the group 6 of USAF target. This one-dimensional function was used as image (I). The object (O), built in MATLAB, was a step function. Its width is 8 μm according to target specifications.

Step #	Description	Function
1.	Selection of one line from the USAF target	$I(Image)$
2.	Subtraction of background	$I-b$, $b(background)$
3.	Calculation of its FFT (*Fast Fourier Transform*)	$fft(I-b)$
4.	Definition of correspondent theoretical line as object	$O(Object)$
5.	Calculation of FFT of the object	$fft(O)$ fft(O)
6.	Determination of FFT of the PSF (application of model)	$fft(H)=fft(I-b)/fft(O)$
7.	Calculation of its inverse FFT (corresponds to PSF)	$H=ifft(fft(H))$

Table 3. Description of the algorithm executed for the determination of the PSF.

The PSF_{yy} was calculated in a similar mode. In this case an image of a line along y-axis in the group 7 was used with a step function of 3.1 μm width.

For the 40X 0.65NA objective the Nyquist limit is 258 nm. Therefore the minimum sampling interval of 1 μm used in y-axis, which corresponds to the used unit space in the scanning of object stage, is above Nyquist limit. This impairs the result concerning PSF_{xx}.

Apart from sampling issues results agree with theory in the sense that PSF_{yy} is narrower than PSF_{xx}. Ratio of lateral resolution in both axes is near the 1.4 factor which is the typical improvement of confocal microscopy. The full width of half maximum of PSF_{yy} is close to 300 nm.

To illustrate and close this subject, in figure 13 it is represented the two-dimensional point spread function in the XY plane. It had been built putting together the one-dimensional PSF curves in each axis.

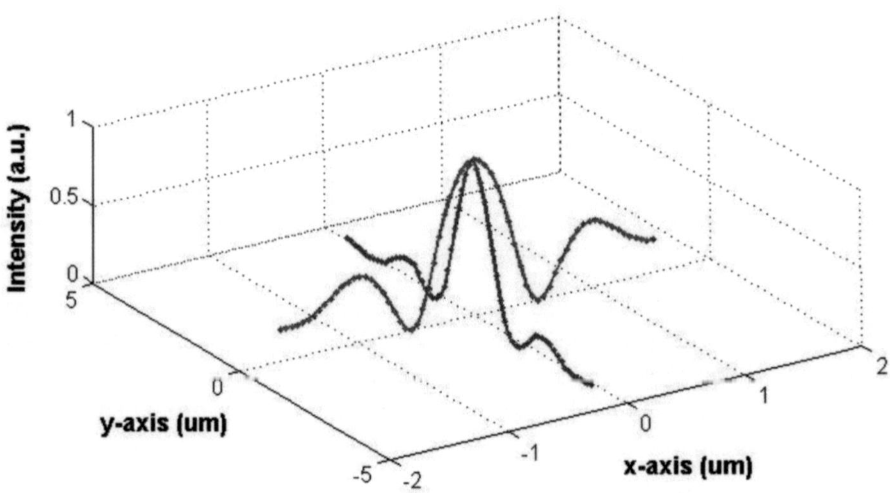

Figure 13. Representation of two-dimensional point spread function (PSF) built from one-dimensional PSF in both x- and y-axis (different scales in the two axes)

http://dx.doi.org/10.5772/58532

5.3. Integrated circuit and printed circuit board inspection

One inspection task in the manufacturing of integrated circuits occurs after the bonding process in which a metallic wire (copper, gold or aluminum) is used to connect a silicon die to package terminals. The diameter of this bonding wire depends on the required specifications of each integrated circuit (IC). Typically it is of the order of magnitude of a few tens of microns.

Another inspection procedure is relative to quality assurance of a printed circuit board (PCB) in order to comply with customer specifications. It consists on the measurement of track dimensions namely its width and thickness.

These inspection processes were performed with this bench-microscope. The graphical user interface of the developed MATLAB application, *IC_image*, is presented in figure 14.

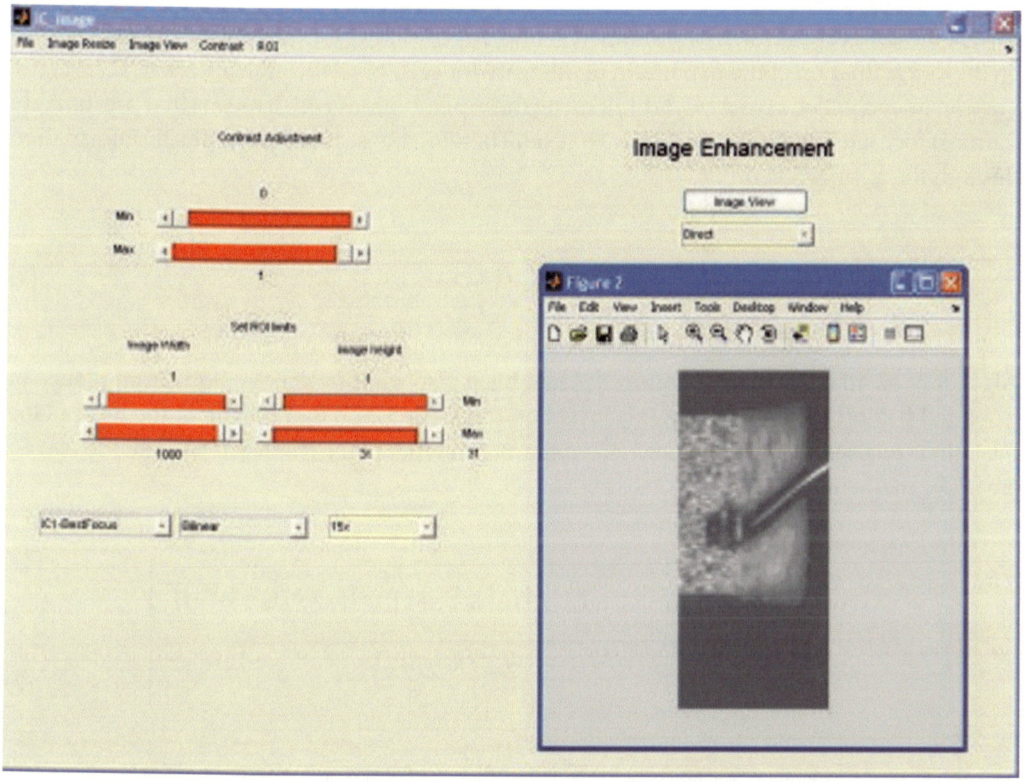

Figure 14. Graphical User Interface – IC_image-developed for the inspection of bonding wire in integrated circuits.

The functionalities of *IC_image* application are summarized below:

- Image settings
  - User definition of ROI limits in the two axes (through the GUI);
  - User definition of contrast adjustment (through the GUI)

- Image visualization
  - User selection of the set of sensor images previously acquired (through the GUI);
  - User definition of the *imresize* method and parameter (through the GUI);
  - User selection of the visualization mode (through the GUI);
  - Visualization of 2D or 3D images

5.3.1. Determination of bonding wire diameter

As it will be shown later, for the determination of wire diameter as well as PCB track dimensions it was necessary to implement algorithms for the reconstruction of 3D images. Then besides the operations for image visualization it had been necessary to include these algorithms in the *IC_image* application.

Two of these algorithms will be presented below. Algorithm #1 is more simplified and consists on the determination of the maximum of intensity for each pixel through a stack of 2D images. Then an image, called *auto-focus*, is built using these pixel values which means that presumably the most focused XY plane is find for each pixel. Therefore these images contain 3D information through the application of:

$$I(x_i, y_i) = \underset{k=1}{\overset{N}{MAX}}\, I(x_i, y_i, z_k) \tag{6}$$

Algorithm #2 adapted from literature [7] had been also used to remove light from planes in front and behind the focal plane. It is based on the assumption that ideally at the focal plane the light is focused on one point and as it departs from that plane it spreads over an increasing area. The mathematical expressions are:

$$\begin{gathered} I_{ext}(x_i, y_i) = \underset{k=1}{\overset{S}{MAX}} \left[\frac{\sum\limits_{a=-(N-1)/2}^{(N-1)/2} \sum\limits_{b=-(M-1)/2}^{(M-1)/2} \left(I_m(x_i, y_i, z_k) - I(x_i + a, y_i + b, z_k) \right)^2}{I_m^{\,2}(x_i, y_i, z_k)} \right] \\ I_m(x_i, y_i, z_k) = \frac{1}{(N \cdot M)} \sum\limits_{a=-(N-1)/2}^{(N-1)/2} \sum\limits_{b=-(M-1)/2}^{(M-1)/2} I(x_i + a, y_i + b, z_k) \end{gathered} \tag{7}$$

where:

- N and M are spatially parameters used for the definition of a ROI to be considered around each pixel. These values had been established from specific geometrical and sampling parameters of this bench-microscope. N and M represent the number of pixels and linear images, respectively.

http://dx.doi.org/10.5772/58532

- *Inda* and *indb* are adjustable and obey the requirement of $-0.5 \leq inda, indb \leq 0$. After some tests, in this inspection task middle values had been used ($inda = indb = -0.25$). *S* is the amount of 2D images to be used.

The output of this algorithm #2 provide data that may be presented through three visualization modes. So the user may select in *IC_image* GUI one of the following modes:

1. Processed image $I_{ext}(x_i, y_i)$ (matrix values obtained directly with the mathematical expression in equation 7)

2. Raw-data image $I(x_i, y_i, z_k)$ where z_k is the position along z-axis in which the pixel values are maxima in each pixel of the processed image, $I_{ext}(x_i, y_i)$.

3. Processed topographic map $h(x_i, y_i)$ representing the z_k values already described in the previous mode.

Image in visualization mode (2) is also an *auto-focus* image as the image obtained by equation 6. These two images are shown in figure 15 for one example where six two-dimensional images (parameter S in equation 6 and equation 7) and a ROI (defined by *N* x *M* in equation 7) equal to 17 x 1 had been used.

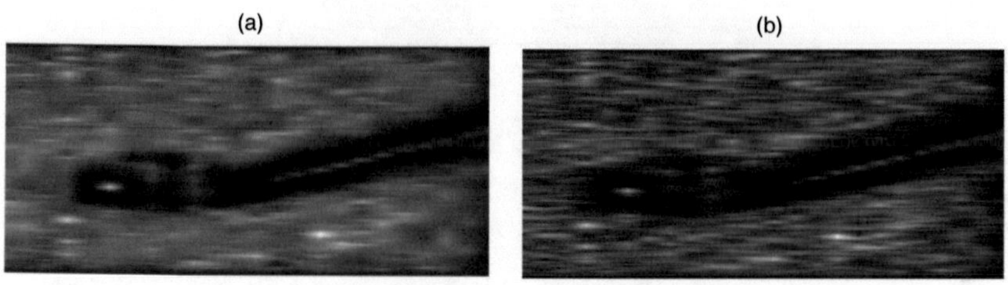

Figure 15. Auto-focus images: (a) algorithm #1 (from Equation 6); (b) algorithm #2 (from Equation 7) using visualization mode (2). FOV: 460 µm x 210 µm (horizontal – y-axis; vertical – x-axis)

In a very similar mode in figure 16 are presented the respective 3D maps. It means that the data shown in part (a) had been obtained from algorithm #1 and the visualization is similar to mode (3).

For the determination of the gold wire diameter the following three images had been used, for comparison purposes:

1. Raw-data auto-focus image $I(x_i, y_i, z_k)$ where z_k is the position along z-axis in which the pixel values are maxima in each pixel of the raw-data image $I(x_i, y_i)$.

2. Processed auto-focus image $I(x_i, y_i, z_k)$ where z_k is the position along z-axis in which the pixel values are maxima in each pixel of the processed image $I_{ext}(x_i, y_i)$.

3. Processed height image such as $I(x_i, y_i, z_k) = h(x_i, y_i)$ where $h(x_i, y_i)$ represents the z_k values already described for the previous image.

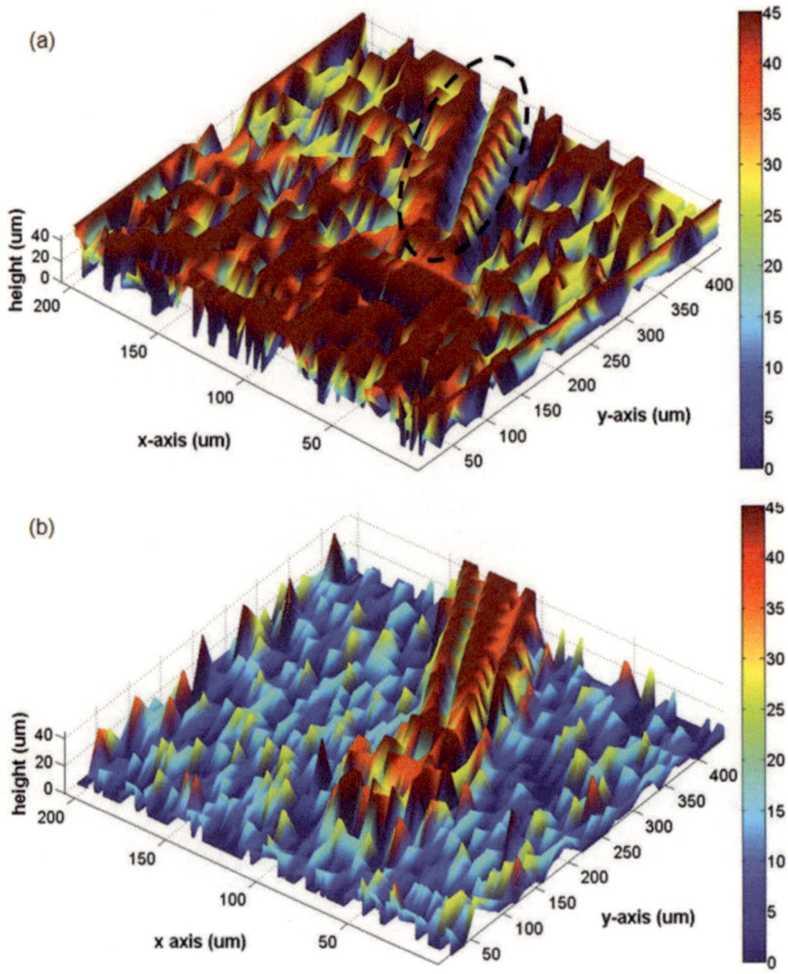

Figure 16. 3D maps achieved using visualization mode (3): (a) algorithm #1; (b) algorithm #2. Dashed oval in part (a) surrounds a linear structure with the same orientation of the structure that is extremely clear in part (b).

In this image (3) shown in figure 17. (a) as well as in images (1) and (2) both shown in figure 15 a ROI with 300 pixels (117 μm) and twelve linear images (220 μm) had been defined. This ROI should contain a part of the wire which is away from the package terminal. In this manner the diameter measurement is not affected by the stress imposed in the wire to make the connection.

However this implies that the MATLAB application must use a 3D reconstruction algorithm to obtain a focused image of this part of the wire because its height is not constant. This ROI in the three images (1) to (3) is shown in figure 17 (b) to (d).

The aim is to develop a method that for each linear image in the ROI is able to find the amount of pixels that belong to wire. So this algorithm is adjustable depending on the image. For images

(1) and (2) it calculates the number of pixels with intensity lower, and in image (3) higher, than a pre-defined threshold.

Using a threshold value of 50% it corresponds to the calculation of FWHm (Full Width at Half minimum) and FWHM, respectively. A geometric correction factor should be used as the wire is not horizontal in image because it is not perpendicular to sensor.

The results of the application of this algorithm on the three images are presented in table 4. Besides average values of wire diameter its standard deviation was also calculated. The diameter from image (2) is considerably larger than from the other two images. The definition of a threshold different than 50% would mitigate this difference induced by lower image contrast in this particular image.

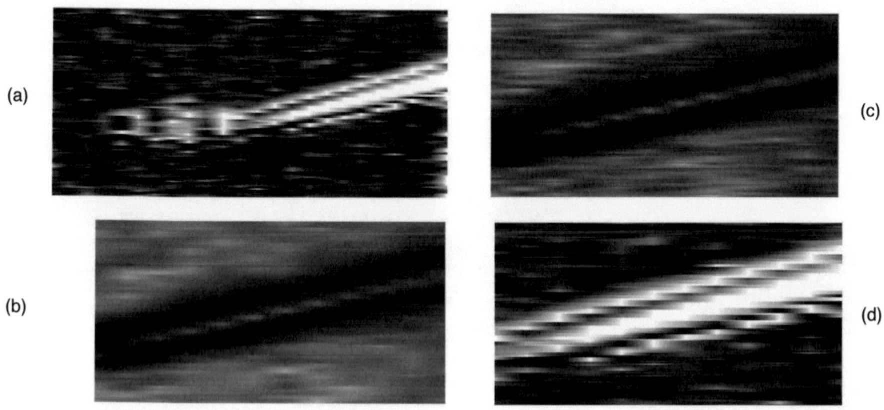

Figure 17. (a) Complete image (3). FOV: 460 µm x 210 µm. (b) to (d) images of the ROI extracted from images (1) to (3), respectively. FOV: 220 µm x 117 µm (horizontal – y-axis; vertical – x-axis). Image in part (a) uses a different scale.

Image	Wire diameter (µm)	
	Average	Std. deviation
(1)	43,06	4,51
(2)	61,78	6,83
(3)	36,24	7,97

Table 4. Wire diameter average and standard deviation values calculated from images (1) to (3) using the ROIs shown in figure 17. (a) to (c), respectively.

5.3.2. Determination of width and thickness of PCB tracks

Both track orientations, parallel and perpendicular to sensor, had been used. However it was accomplished using a very similar method. For illustration it is presented the parallel one in which twelve two-dimensional images had been acquired.

Using the equation 6 it was calculated the *auto-focus* image, designated previously by image (1). This image is shown in figure 18. Also the topographic (3D) map $h(x_i, y_i)$ representing the z_k values that correspond to the position along z-axis in which the pixel values are maxima in each pixel of the raw-data image $I(x_i, y_i)$. To represent a two-dimensional (2D) profile it was selected the pixel n of the sensor and $h(x_n, y_i)$ is the height of that pixel n for each sensor line.

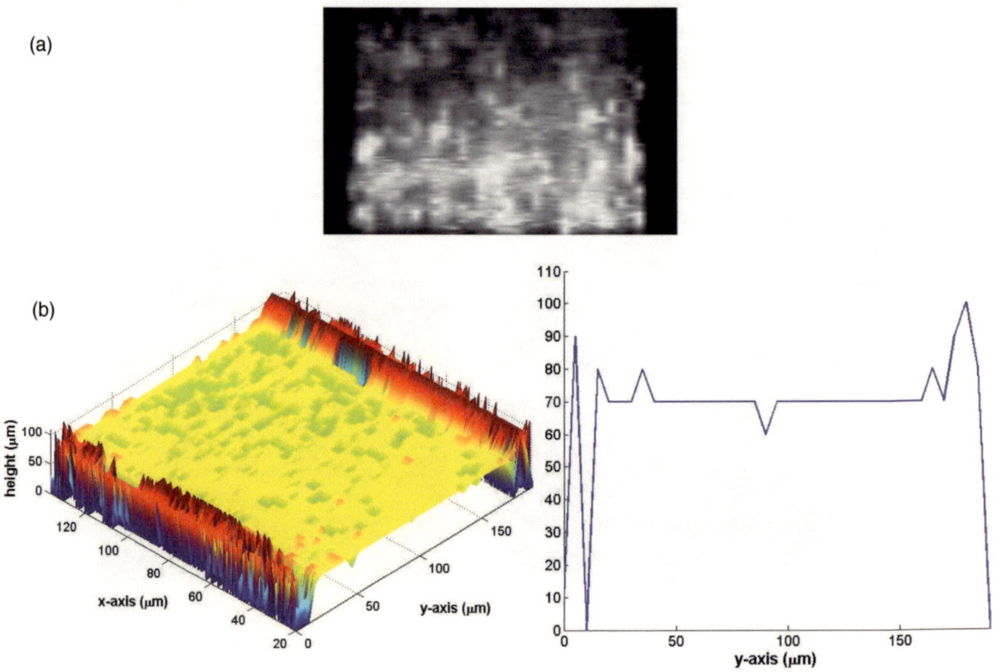

Figure 18. PCB track parallel to the sensor. (a) raw-data *auto-focus* image. FOV: 190 μm x 115 μm (horizontal – y-axis; vertical – x-axis). Same scale in both axes. (b) raw-data topographic (3D) map and a 2D profile drawn for pixel *n*.

In spite of the ringing effects present at track borders, that hamper the measurement of its width and reduce precision and accuracy, an algorithm had been developed for its calculation. This algorithm implemented in *IC_image* application consists on the following steps:

1. Definition of a ROI completely inside the track;
2. Determination of height $h(x_i, y_i)=z_k$ where z_k is the position along z-axis in which the pixel values are maxima for each pixel of the raw-data image $I(x_i, y_i)$.
3. Determination of height mean (h_{mean}) and standard deviation (h_{std}).
4. Definition of the lower (h_{min}) and upper (h_{max}) height limits inside the track. The considered limits had been: $h_{\substack{\max \\ \min}} = h_{mean} \pm h_{std}$.

5. Definition of other ROI including the complete field of view along y-axis (perpendicular to the track);

6. Calculation of the number of lines (position in y-axis) in which the height lays in the range $h_{min} \leq h \leq h_{max}$ (over all the pixels inside the ROI);

7. Determination of track width mean and standard deviation expressed in number of lines;

8. Conversion to microns and mils.

The height value $h(x_i, y_i)$ represents the axial position of the track. Therefore the track height is easily calculated through the determination of the height of the exterior side plane and its subsequent subtraction. This calculation had been made for a track perpendicular to sensor but this example is not covered in this chapter. Table 5 shows the results of the implementation of this algorithm.

Track parameter	Mean	Std. deviation
Height	4,2890*	0,5963*
Width	120,40 µm (4,74 mils)	9,74 µm (0,38 mils)

Table 5. Mean and standard deviation values of the track height and width obtained using a ROI inside the track and over the complete y-axis, respectively. (*) rigorously it indicates only the axial plane and not the height.

5.3.3. *Application in profilometry*

Owing to its depth discrimination ability, optical techniques as confocal microscopy have been used in profilometry. It consists on build three-dimensional profiles in order to measure different surface or geometrical dimensions such as roughness, height / depth or width.

Another MATLAB application, *Profilometry_SiFrame*, which GUI is presented in figure 19 had been developed.

This MATLAB application has the following functionalities:

- Profile settings
    - User definition of ROI limits in the two axes (through the GUI);
- Profile visualization
    - User selection of the set of sensor images previously acquired (through the GUI);
    - User selection of the visualization mode (2D or 3D) (through the GUI);
    - User definition of the scanning sequence to be used in 2D visualization (through the GUI);
    - User selection of the 3D reconstruction algorithm (through the GUI);
    - Interactive visualization of a sequence of 2D profiles (stop by an user order).

◦ Visualization of 3D profiles

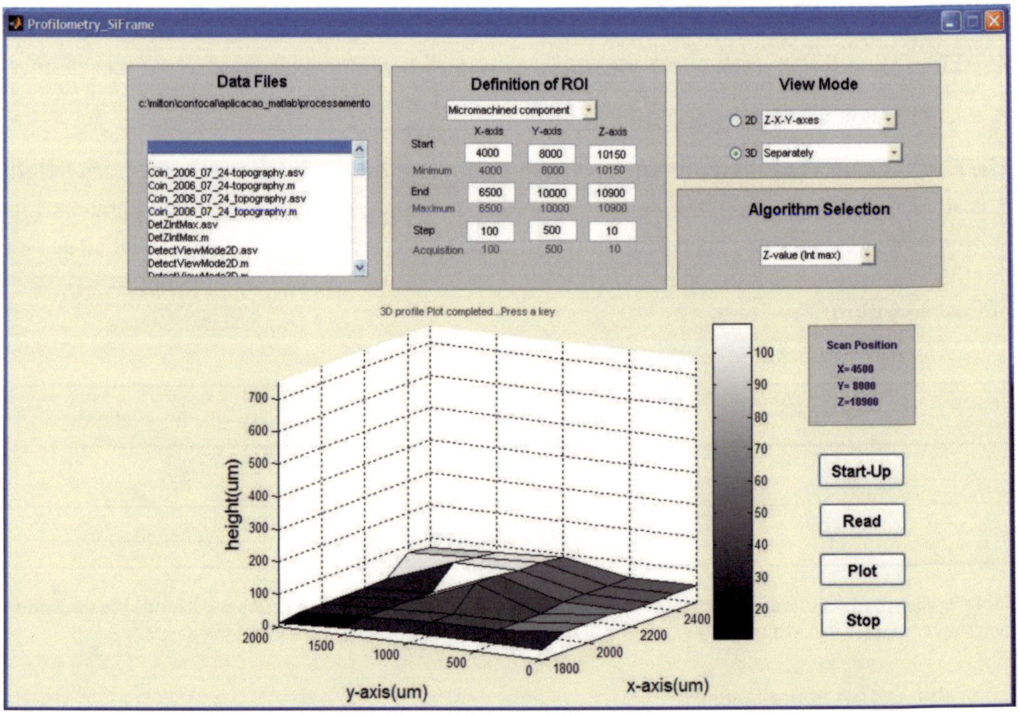

Figure 19. Graphical User Interface – *Profilometry_SiFrame* – developed for building and visualization of micromachined component profiles.

A micromachined component that contains a three-dimensional silicon frame had been the test object. For the assessment of the quality of the results, a scheme with frame specification is also presented in figure 20.

Experimental profiles shown in figure 20 are a raw-data topographic (3D) map and a 2D profile where height is represented versus x-axis (sensor orientation). This profile had been drawn from topographic map in (b) representing one of the lines across the frame. Experimental values of width, height or slope of silicon frame are superimposed in the 2D profile.

The lateral side of the silicon frame had been aligned with y-axis. Thus lateral walls of the frame are perpendicular to sensor. On the other hand three different ROI were defined over x-axis. In ROI separation the slope of the frame wall is higher than its maximum value considering the particular objective used. Owing to this slope the light reflected in frame surface is not gathered by the objective and consequently it is not collected in the sensor.

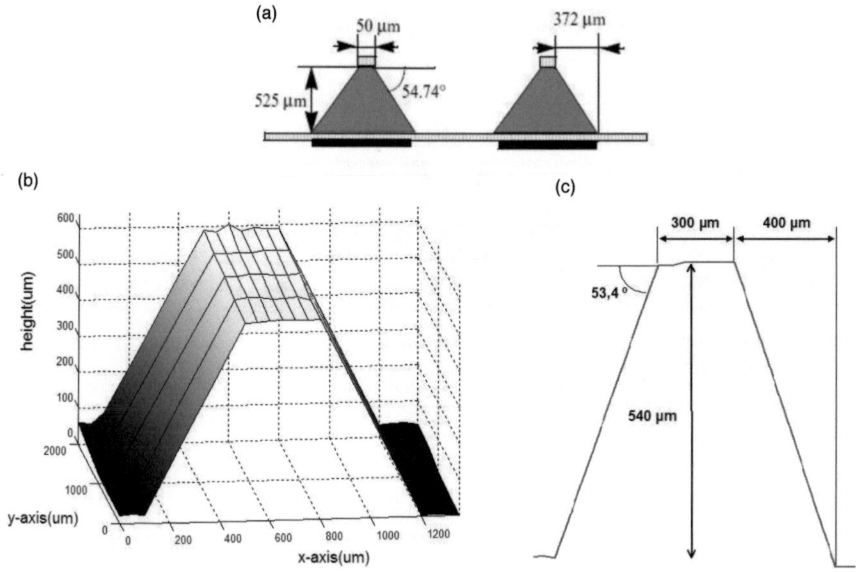

Figure 20. (a) Scheme of the silicon frame illustrating its dimensions (reproduced from [8]). (b) experimental 3D profile of the frame (x-and y-axis represent parallel and perpendicular directions relative to sensor, respectively). (c) 2D profile showing the results for frame dimensions (not to scale).

6. Conclusion

The challenge of building a laboratorial prototype of a microscope using a linear image sensor had been successfully attained. It had been shown its ability to perform the acquisition and visualization of images containing three-dimensional information as well as its potential application in materials science field.

MATLAB has played a fundamental role for this outcome. Apart from the optical layout every task since sensor readout through communication of sensor data to the computer for image visualization to image reconstruction algorithms had been implemented in MATLAB applications. In this manner the result is a bench-microscope completely controlled by a computer user. Figure 21 summarizes overall functions implemented in the four MATLAB applications in order to achieve this computer-controlled platform.

The essential graphical user interface had been developed in a much faster and easier mode using functions of MATLAB core than previously with Borland C. Besides it is important to emphasize the versatility provided by its toolboxes. Particularly *Instrument Control toolbox* that made the implementation of all acquisition and control tasks, commanded from the computer through its serial port, look like a trivial task. Also *Image Processing toolbox* had shown how the implementation of reconstruction algorithms and of any image related operation may be performed in an easy way despite the complexity that people might assume because of matrix approach. In summary, with every sense, it is a MATLAB-based microscope.

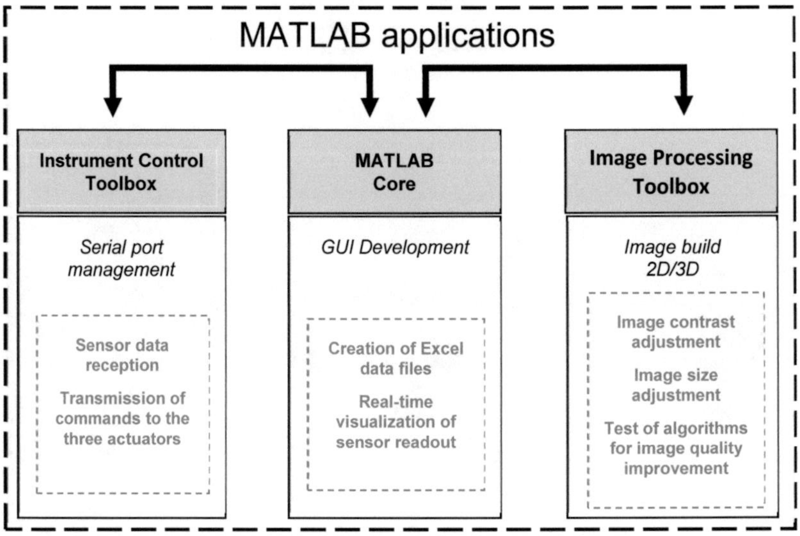

Figure 21. Diagram of the functionalities of the MATLAB applications.

Author details

Milton P. Macedo[1,2]

1 Instituto Politécnico de Coimbra, ISEC, DFM, Coimbra, Portugal

2 Centro de Instrumentação, Department of Physics, University of Coimbra, Coimbra, Portugal

References

[1] Murphy DB. Fundamentals of light microscopy and electronic imaging. USA: Wiley-Liss; 2001.

[2] Lee J, Rogers JD, Descour MR. Imaging quality assessment of multi-modal miniature microscope. Optics Express 2003; 11(12) 1436-1451.

[3] Boreman GD, Yang S. Modulation transfer function measurement using three-and four bar target, Applied Optics supplement 1995; 8050-8052.

http://dx.doi.org/10.5772/58532

[4] Williams TL. The Optical Transfer Function of Imaging Systems. USA: IoP; 1999.

[5] Williams CS, Becklund OA. Introduction to the Optical Transfer Function. USA: SPIE Press; 2002

[6] Sabharwal S et al. Slit-scanning confocal microendoscope for high-resolution in vivo imaging. Applied Optics 1999; 38 (34) 7133-7144.

[7] Tympel V. Three dimensional animation with a conventional light microscopy. In: Cogswell CJ, Conchello JA, Wilson T. (eds) BiOS1997: proceedings of three-dimensional microscopy: image acquisition and processing IV, 12-13 February 1997, San Jose, USA. Washington: SPIE Press; 1997. p190-198.

[8] Correia JH, Bartek M, Wolffenbuttel RF. Load-deflection of a low-stress SiN-membrane/Si-frame composite diaphragm. In: First International Conference on Modeling and Simulation of Microsystems, Semiconductors, Sensors and Actuators: conference proceedings, 6-8 April 1998, Santa Clara Marriott, CA, USA. Boston: Computational Publications; 1998. p563-568.

Chapter 3

Obstacle Avoidance Task for a Wheeled Mobile Robot – A Matlab-Simulink-Based Didactic Application

R. Silva-Ortigoza, C. Márquez-Sánchez,
F. Carrizosa-Corral, V. M. Hernández-Guzmán,
J. R. García-Sánchez, H. Taud,
M. Marciano-Melchor and J. A. Álvarez-Cedillo

Additional information is available at the end of the chapter

http://dx.doi.org/10.5772/58392

1. Introduction

In recent years, the development of wheeled mobile robots (WMR) has allowed for significant progress in various fields of science due to the wide scope of applications in which such robots can be employed [1]. These fields include medical assistance, space and marine exploration, leisure, entertainment, technology research and development, metal-mechanics and chemical industries, military research, cleaning in diverse surroundings, agriculture, inspection, security, and transportation, among others. The discussion regarding mobile robotics has been undergoing a slowly-evolving transition and continues even now to be a topic of great interest at the international level.

Mobile robots can be classified according to their locomotion method into three types [1]: wheeled, legged, and caterpillar track. Although both legged and caterpillar track locomotion have been widely researched, most mobile robots that have been built, evaluated, and reported use wheels to move. This reflects their increasing use in applications such as planetary exploration, mining, inspection, security, rescue operations, hazardous waste clean-up, and medical assistance. A review associated with WMR can be found in [1]; although much of the research that has been carried out thus far has provided a significant contribution to the topic, the development and conception of a mobile robot that has total autonomy of operation remains a distant prospect.

In order to improve the autonomy of mobile robots, experiments examining control have generally focused on solving the following problems: (1) mobile robot positioning,

INTECH
open science | open minds

© 2014 The Author(s). Licensee InTech. This chapter is distributed under the terms of the Creative Commons Attribution License (http://creativecommons.org/licenses/by/3.0), which permits unrestricted use, distribution, and reproduction in any medium, provided the original work is properly cited.

(2) stabilization, (3) trajectory tracking control, (4) trajectory planning, and (5) obstacle avoidance. In this respect, significant progress (albeit not total) has been achieved. The present work focuses on the obstacle avoidance problem, whose objective is providing a mobile robot with collision-free navigation through a workspace in which obstacles have been predeterminately distributed. In particular, we develop, step-by-step, a Matlab-Simulink application that describes the experimental implementation of a WMR controller which allows collision-free navigation.

According to the robotics literature, a variety of different methods are available with which to perform the obstacle avoidance task, the most relevant being: edge detection [2], cell decomposition [3], map building [4], and artificial potential fields [5]; a description of all of these methods can be found in [1], with the artificial potential field method notably the most cited. In the present work the artificial potential field technique is employed to carry out an obstacle avoiding task with a WMR. Developed by Khatib [5], in this method the mobile robot can be considered as a particle, the obstacles presented within the workspace as particles that exert a repulsive force on the mobile robot, and the goal as a particle that exerts an attractive force on the mobile robot. Thus, a resultant potential field is achieved that leads the trajectory that the mobile robot must follow in order to evade the obstacles –which might be considered previously in the method, or else detected via a sensor– and reach the goal. It is worth mentioning that applying the artificial potential field method does not require a great deal of computational complexity because it is based on the implementation of mathematical functions representing the attractive and repulsive forces exerted on the mobile robot. Finally, since the initial establishment of the artificial potential field method, a number of different modifications and implementations have been developed in conjunction with other techniques. Hence, some variations of the method have been reported in [6–13].

Whereas the works cited above introduce research examining the obstacle avoidance task using the artificial potential field method with WMRs, the present document describes the step-by-step experimental implementation of a hierarchical control which is performed along with the artificial potential field method in carrying out the obstacle avoidance task with the differentially-driven WMR built and reported in [14]. This work is aimed at helping students integrate theoretical and practical knowledge through the use of a relevant and modern open-architecture testbed that allows rapid prototyping [15]. On the one hand, simulations are carried out using Matlab-Simulink. On the other hand, Matlab-Simulink, ControlDesk, and the DS1104 electronic board (dSPACE) are employed for the real-time experiments since the graphical environment provided by Simulink facilitates the analysis, design, and construction of dynamic systems.

The present work is structured as follows. Section 2 describes the basis of the artificial potential field method for the obstacle avoidance task. The hierarchical control applied to the WMR in performing the obstacle avoidance task is detailed in Section 3. In Section 4, a description of the block diagrams programmed in Matlab-Simulink, along with the simulation results associated with the closed-loop system, are presented. The subsystems of the prototype employed are then described in Section 5, with Section 6 containing a description of the blocks developed in Matlab-Simulink for the experimental implementation of the hierarchical control via Matlab-Simulink, ControlDesk, and the DS1104 in the prototype. Finally, conclusions drawn from the study are presented in Section 7.

http://dx.doi.org/10.5772/58392

2. Artificial potential field

This section describes the artificial potential field method, which in conjunction with a controller allows the accomplishment of the obstacle avoidance task. Although the method has been modified by various authors in order to solve some of its inherent problems, these modifications account for individual problems separately and not necessarily in an optimal manner. Therefore, the classic method is employed herein. The artificial potential field method consists of the creation of artificial potential fields, with the goal being the development of an attractive pole and obstacles acting as repulsive surfaces for the mobile robot. Whereas the attractive force produced by the artificial potential field associated with the goal generates a continuous trajectory towards it, the repulsive force produced by the fields associated with the obstacles move the mobile robot away from them. When combining both forces a third force is produced which enables an effective control. It is worth noting that when the attractive and repulsive forces are equal in magnitude and opposite in orientation, as generated by a specific goal and obstacle distribution, the mobile robot cannot accomplish the obstacle avoidance task. When this occurs, the mobile robot is said to be trapped within a local minimum.

The present study addresses a problem involving a WMR, an obstacle, and the goal which is directly extendable to the general case, namely, the n obstacles problem. Consider a bidimensional workspace and a fixed coordinate system X-Y in which the coordinates of a point associated with the WMR are determined by $q = (x_1, y_1)$ (see Figure 4), the obstacle by $q_{obs} = (x_o, y_o)$, and the goal by $q_m = (x_m, y_m)$. Moreover, suppose that the obstacle and the goal separately exert a force on the WMR, generating a resultant force, F_{total}, given by

$$F_{total} = F_{at}(q) + F_{rep}(q), \tag{1}$$

where $F_{at}(q)$ is the attractive force produced by the goal and $F_{rep}(q)$ is the repulsive force generated by the obstacle.

The resultant force is considered to be exerted by an artificial potential field determined by

$$U(q) = U_{at}(q) + U_{rep}(q), \tag{2}$$

with $U_{at}(q)$ and $U_{rep}(q)$ being the artificial potential fields associated with the goal and the obstacle, respectively, where

$$F_{at}(q) = -\nabla U_{at}(q), \tag{3}$$
$$F_{rep}(q) = -\nabla U_{rep}(q), \tag{4}$$

and the operator ∇ is defined as $\left(\frac{\partial}{\partial x}, \frac{\partial}{\partial y}\right)$. The attractive and repulsive forces are represented by the negative gradient of the potential fields, as expressed in (3) and (4). Hence, depending on the positions of the obstacle and the goal, the resultant force will lead the mobile robot's point q, collision-free, towards the goal.

2.1. Attractive potential

One of the most commonly-used attractive potential fields was presented in [16], and is determined by

$$U_{at}(q) = \frac{1}{2}\xi\rho^{k}(q, q_m), \tag{5}$$

where ξ is a positive scale factor, q is the mobile robot's reference point, q_m is the goal's coordinate, $\rho(q, q_m) = \|q - q_m\|$ is the distance between q and q_m, and $k = 1, 2$.

- For $k = 1$, the attractive potential field presents a conic shape, as shown in Figure 1. The attractive force generated by U_{at} has constant amplitude except at the goal, where U_{at} is non-differentiable, as given by

$$F_{at}(q) = -\nabla U_{at}(q) = -\frac{1}{2}\xi\frac{(q - q_m)}{\|q - q_m\|}. \tag{6}$$

- For $k = 2$, the attractive potential field presents a parabolic shape, as shown in Figure 2. The corresponding attractive force is determined by the negative gradient of the attractive potential, i.e.,

$$F_{at}(q) = -\nabla U_{at}(q) = -\xi(q - q_m), \tag{7}$$

which converges linearly to zero as the mobile robot approaches the goal.

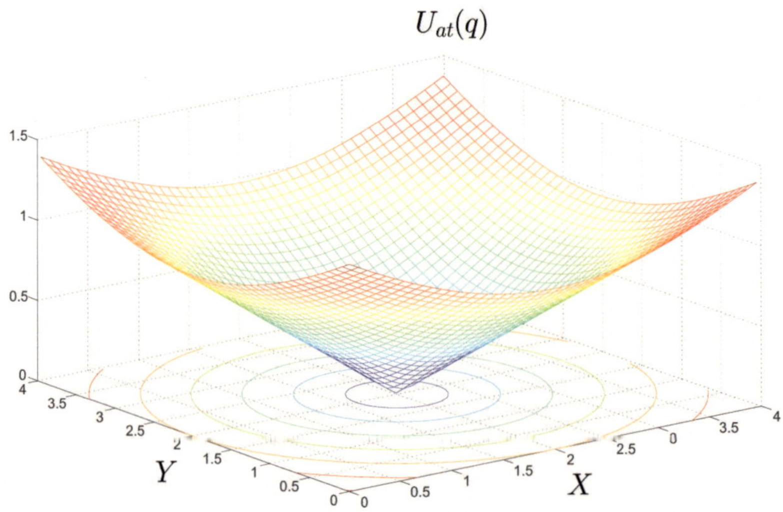

Figure 1. Attractive potential field for $k = 1$.

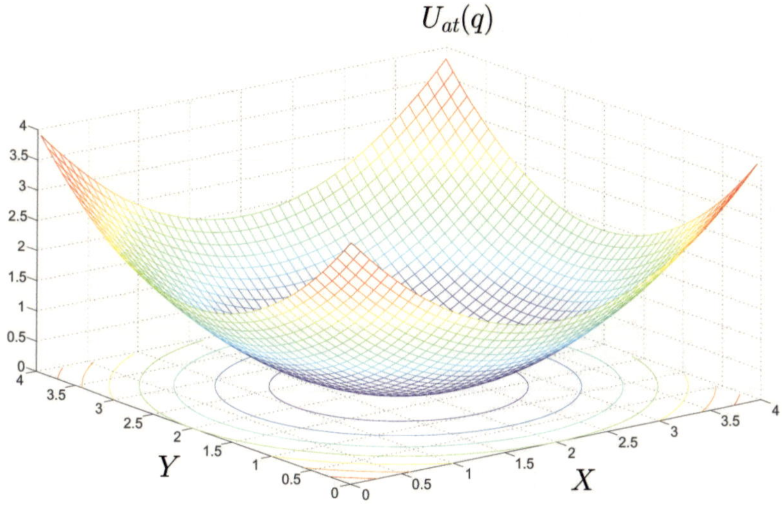

Figure 2. Attractive potential field for $k = 2$.

2.2. Repulsive potential

One commonly-used repulsive potential function takes the following form [16]:

$$U_{rep}(q) = \begin{cases} \frac{1}{2}\eta\left[\frac{1}{\rho(q,q_{obs})} - \frac{1}{\rho_0}\right]^2, & \text{for } \rho(q,q_{obs}) \leq \rho_0, \\ 0, & \text{for } \rho(q,q_{obs}) > \rho_0, \end{cases} \tag{8}$$

where η is a positive scale factor, $\rho(q,q_{obs}) = \|q - q_{obs}\|$ is the shortest distance between the mobile robot and the obstacle, and ρ_0 is a positive constant that represents the distance of the obstacle's influence. The graphical representation associated with the obstacle defined by (8) is shown in Figure 3. Hence, the repulsive force, $F_{rep}(q)$, associated with (8), is determined by

$$F_{rep}(q) = -\nabla U_{rep}(q) = \begin{cases} \eta\left[\frac{1}{\rho(q,q_{obs})} - \frac{1}{\rho_0}\right]\frac{q - q_o}{\rho^3(q,q_{obs})}, & \text{for } \rho(q,q_{obs}) \leq \rho_0, \\ 0, & \text{for } \rho(q,q_{obs}) > \rho_0. \end{cases} \tag{9}$$

Finally, it is worth mentioning that the described artificial potential field method depends upon the relative position of the mobile robot to the obstacle, unlike other methods such as that of Krogh [17] in which the potential field is sensitive to the impact time. Furthermore, implementing the presented method requires knowledge of the coordinates of the mobile robot, the obstacle, and the goal, i.e., $q = (x_1, y_1)$, $q_{obs} = (x_o, y_o)$, and $q_m = (x_m, y_m)$, respectively. In the present work, it is assumed that these coordinates are already known; nevertheless, the employed method can also be extended to sensors that allow the acquisition of these coordinates in real-time.

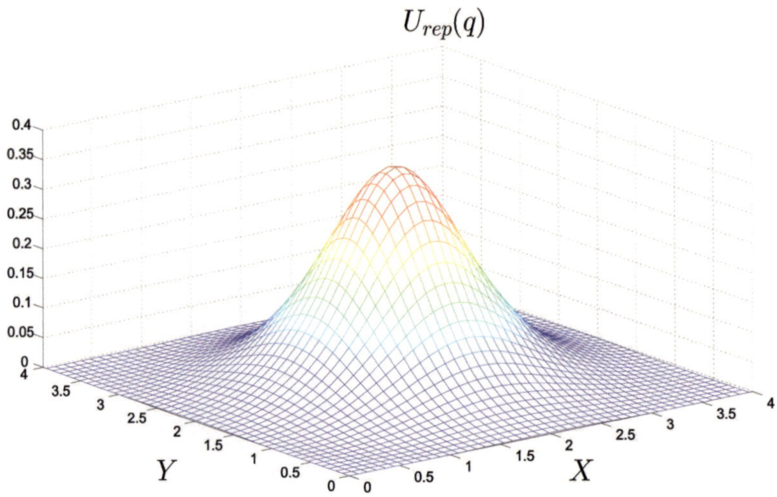

Figure 3. Repulsive potential field.

3. Control for obstacle avoidance of WMR

This section presents the hierarchical control developed in [18], and analyzed in [26] for a trailer-like vehicle. Using the kinematic model associated with the differentially-driven WMR, an input-output linearization control is proposed that, in conjunction with the artificial potential field method, enables the accomplishment of the obstacle avoidance task. A PI control is then proposed for each DC motor, allowing the WMR to move. Finally, with the ultimate aim of experimentally accomplishing the obstacle avoidance task with a WMR prototype, a hierarchical control is proposed which merges the said controls, similar to the structure presented in [14, 19–23].

3.1. Control of the kinematic model

The mobile robot under study is a vehicle comprising two traction wheels, left and right. These two wheels are identical, parallel to each other, non-deformable, and joined by a shaft. The robot also comprises two omnidirectional wheels, front and rear, that ensure the robot platform remains on a plane. Supposing movement is restricted on an XY plane and that there is no wheel slip, existing literature (see [24]) describe the WMR kinematics as given by

$$\begin{aligned} \dot{x} &= \frac{(\omega_r + \omega_l)\, r}{2} \cos\varphi, \\ \dot{y} &= \frac{(\omega_r + \omega_l)\, r}{2} \sin\varphi, \\ \dot{\varphi} &= \frac{(\omega_r - \omega_l)\, r}{2l}, \end{aligned} \tag{10}$$

where (x, y) denotes the position of the mid-point of the shaft that joins the wheels, φ is the angle formed by the WMR symmetry axis and the positive X-axis, ω_r and ω_l are the

http://dx.doi.org/10.5772/58392

angular velocities of the right and left wheels, respectively, r is the wheel ratio, and $2l$ is the separation between the wheels. Parameters and variables associated with the WMR are shown in Figure 4. This WMR configuration is known as differential traction.

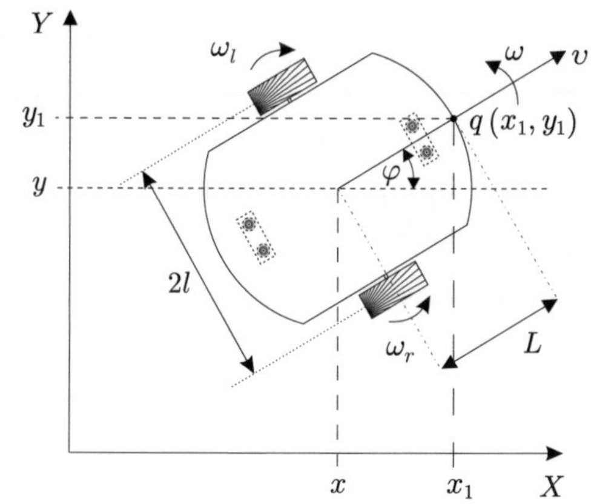

Figure 4. WMR diagram.

Whereas the derivative with respect to time t, associated with the state variables, is denoted by a dot in equations (10) and (12), in the rest of the chapter it is represented explicitly, i.e., $\frac{d}{dt}$.

Since the mathematical model described by (10) presents a noninvertible relationship between the controls, (ω_r, ω_l), and the outputs, (x, y), it is not possible to propose a control via input-output linearization. For simplicity, another reference point associated with the WMR that can therefore be considered is the front part which has the coordinates $q = (x_1, y_1)$ (see Figure 4). The coordinates of q expressed in terms of x, y, and φ are determined by

$$\begin{aligned} x_1 &= x + L\cos\varphi, \\ y_1 &= y + L\sin\varphi, \end{aligned} \tag{11}$$

where L is the distance from the mid-point of the wheel shaft, (x, y), to the point q in the direction perpendicular to the shaft. Deriving system (11) with respect to time obtains the WMR kinematic model associated with point $q = (x_1, y_1)$, which is given by

$$\begin{pmatrix} \dot{x}_1 \\ \dot{y}_1 \end{pmatrix} = A(\varphi) \begin{pmatrix} \omega_r \\ \omega_l \end{pmatrix}, \tag{12}$$

with

$$A(\varphi) = \begin{pmatrix} \cos\varphi & -L\sin\varphi \\ \sin\varphi & L\cos\varphi \end{pmatrix} \begin{pmatrix} \frac{r}{2} & \frac{r}{2} \\ \frac{r}{2l} & -\frac{r}{2l} \end{pmatrix}.$$

Since $\det A(\varphi) = -\frac{Lr^2}{2l} \neq 0$, it is clear that an input-output linearization scheme can be proposed for $(\omega_r, \omega_l) - (x_1, y_1)$. According to [18], an input-output linearization control that allows the WMR to accomplish the obstacle avoidance task and reach the goal can be written as follows:

$$\begin{pmatrix} \omega_r \\ \omega_l \end{pmatrix} = \frac{v_d}{\sqrt{f_x^2 + f_y^2 + \varepsilon}} \frac{1}{Lr} \begin{pmatrix} L\cos\varphi - l\sin\varphi & l\cos\varphi + L\sin\varphi \\ L\cos\varphi + l\sin\varphi & -(l\cos\varphi - L\sin\varphi) \end{pmatrix} \begin{pmatrix} f_x \\ f_y \end{pmatrix}, \tag{13}$$

where v_d is a desired constant velocity, ε is a constant value close to zero, and f_x and f_y are the components of F_{total} in directions X and Y, respectively.

When there are n obstacles located within the workspace, f_x and f_y are determined by

$$\begin{pmatrix} f_x \\ f_y \end{pmatrix} = \begin{pmatrix} f_{x\,at} + f_{x\,1rep} + f_{x\,2rep} + \ldots + f_{x\,nrep} \\ f_{y\,at} + f_{y\,1rep} + f_{y\,2rep} + \ldots + f_{y\,nrep} \end{pmatrix}, \tag{14}$$

with $f_{x\,at}$ the attractive force component associated with the goal in direction X, and $f_{x\,1rep}, f_{x\,2rep}, \ldots, f_{x\,nrep}$ the repulsive force components in direction X associated with obstacles $1, 2, \ldots, n$, respectively. The description of the terms associated with f_y is highly similar to that for the terms associated with f_x.

Here we present the equations explicitly associated with (14) when it is supposed that, within the workspace, there are one and two obstacles, respectively.

- One obstacle:
  In this situation, in accordance with (5) and (7), the attractive potential fields associated with the goal and its force components in directions X and Y, respectively, are given by

$$U_{at}(q) = \frac{1}{2}\xi\left[(x_1 - x_m)^2 + (y_1 - y_m)^2\right], \tag{15}$$

$$f_{x\,at} = -\xi(x_1 - x_m), \tag{16}$$

$$f_{y\,at} = -\xi(y_1 - y_m). \tag{17}$$

  Whereas, in accordance with (8) and (9), the repulsive potential fields associated with the obstacle and its force components in directions X and Y, respectively, are determined by

$$U_{1rep}(q) = \begin{cases} \frac{1}{2}\eta\left[\frac{1}{\rho(q,q_{obs1})} - \frac{1}{\rho_{01}}\right]^2, & \text{for } \rho(q,q_{obs1}) \le \rho_{01}, \\ 0, & \text{for } \rho(q,q_{obs1}) > \rho_{01}. \end{cases} \tag{18}$$

$$f_{x\,1rep} = \begin{cases} \eta\left[\frac{1}{\rho(q,q_{obs1})} - \frac{1}{\rho_{01}}\right]\left[\frac{1}{\rho^3(q,q_{obs1})}\right](x_1 - x_{o1}), & \text{for } \rho(q,q_{obs1}) \le \rho_{01}, \\ 0, & \text{for } \rho(q,q_{obs1}) > \rho_{01}. \end{cases} \tag{19}$$

$$f_{y\,1rep} = \begin{cases} \eta\left[\frac{1}{\rho(q,q_{obs1})} - \frac{1}{\rho_{01}}\right]\left[\frac{1}{\rho^3(q,q_{obs1})}\right](y_1 - y_{o1}), & \text{for } \rho(q,q_{obs1}) \le \rho_{01}, \\ 0, & \text{for } \rho(q,q_{obs1}) > \rho_{01}. \end{cases} \tag{20}$$

Therefore, for a scenario involving one obstacle, (14) is given by

$$\begin{pmatrix} f_x \\ f_y \end{pmatrix} = \begin{pmatrix} f_{x\,at} + f_{x\,1rep} \\ f_{y\,at} + f_{y\,1rep} \end{pmatrix}. \tag{21}$$

- Two obstacles:

  The attractive force components associated with the goal, $f_{x\,at}$ and $f_{y\,at}$, are determined by (16) and (17), respectively. Whereas the repulsive force components associated with one of the obstacles, $f_{x\,1rep}$ and $f_{y\,1rep}$, are determined by (20) and (20), respectively, the second obstacle, which is associated with the repulsive potential field $U_{2rep}(q)$, has the following force components:

$$U_{2rep}(q) = \begin{cases} \frac{1}{2}\eta \left[\frac{1}{\rho(q,q_{obs2})} - \frac{1}{\rho_{02}}\right]^2, & \text{for } \rho(q,q_{obs2}) \le \rho_{02}, \\ 0, & \text{for } \rho(q,q_{obs2}) > \rho_{02}. \end{cases} \tag{22}$$

$$f_{x\,2rep} = \begin{cases} \eta \left[\frac{1}{\rho(q,q_{obs2})} - \frac{1}{\rho_{02}}\right] \left[\frac{1}{\rho^3(q,q_{obs2})}\right] (x_1 - x_{o2}), & \text{for } \rho(q,q_{obs2}) \le \rho_{02}, \\ 0, & \text{for } \rho(q,q_{obs2}) > \rho_{02}. \end{cases} \tag{23}$$

$$f_{y\,2rep} = \begin{cases} \eta \left[\frac{1}{\rho(q,q_{obs2})} - \frac{1}{\rho_{02}}\right] \left[\frac{1}{\rho^3(q,q_{obs2})}\right] (y_1 - y_{o2}), & \text{for } \rho(q,q_{obs2}) \le \rho_{02}, \\ 0, & \text{for } \rho(q,q_{obs2}) > \rho_{02}. \end{cases} \tag{24}$$

Thus, in a scenario two obstacles, (14) adopts the following expression:

$$\begin{pmatrix} f_x \\ f_y \end{pmatrix} = \begin{pmatrix} f_{x\,at} + f_{x\,1rep} + f_{x\,2rep} \\ f_{y\,at} + f_{y\,1rep} + f_{y\,2rep} \end{pmatrix}. \tag{25}$$

Finally, it is worth mentioning that for each obstacle present within the workspace there will exist a repulsive potential field; as a consequence, the terms associated with f_x and f_y will be increased depending on the number of obstacles.

3.2. DC motor control

In order to execute the obstacle avoidance task experimentally, the angular velocity profiles ω_r and ω_l, determined by the upper hierarchy (13), must be reproduced by the DC motors associated with the WMR prototype employed in the present work (see [14]). Thus for the right and left angular velocities of the DC motors to approach ω_r and ω_l, respectively, a PI controller is implemented for each motor.

A DC motor mathematical model expressed in terms of the motor shaft speed ϖ is given by

$$\begin{aligned} L_a \frac{di_a}{dt} &= u - R_a i_a - k_e \varpi, \\ J \frac{d\varpi}{dt} &= -b\varpi + k_m i_a, \end{aligned} \tag{26}$$

where u is the motor armature voltage, i_a is the armature current, k_e is the back-electromotive force constant, k_m is the motor torque constant, L_a is the armature inductance, R_a is the armature resistance, J is the rotor and load inertia, and b is the viscous friction constant due to both motor and load.

Since motor manufacturers do not generally provide all of the parameter values associated with (26), these values can be simply obtained via the reduction of (26) to a first order system that relates ϖ to u. This is accomplished by assuming that $L_a \approx 0$ in (26). Hence, the simplified model is determined by

$$\frac{d\varpi}{dt} = -\alpha\varpi + \beta u. \tag{27}$$

Characterization of α and β associated with the prototype's DC motors –two Engel GNM3150s (24 V, 55 W) with G2.6 gearboxes– was previously carried out in [14]. In this latter study it was found that the simplified model (27) of the right and left motors can be respectively expressed by

$$\begin{aligned} \frac{d\varpi_r}{dt} &= -10.20\varpi_r + 5.51u_r, \\ \frac{d\varpi_l}{dt} &= -10.20\varpi_l + 5.99u_l, \end{aligned} \tag{28}$$

where ϖ_r and ϖ_l are the right and left angular velocity of the motors, and u_r and u_l represent the armature voltages of the right and left motors, respectively. Hence, a PI control for (27) that achieves $\varpi \to \varpi^*$ is determined by

$$u = K_p e + K_i \int_0^t e d\tau, \tag{29}$$

with

$$e = \varpi^* - \varpi, \tag{30}$$

where e is the tracking error, ϖ^* is the desired angular velocity trajectory, K_p is the proportional gain, and K_i is the integral gain. Next, (29) is applied to the DC motors of the WMR.

3.3. Hierarchical control

This subsection presents the connection of the control laws developed via a hierarchical control, a block diagram of which is shown in Figure 5. At the upper level, an input-output linearization control was used for the WMR model, generating the desired velocity profiles, ω_r and ω_l, for the robot wheels to track. These velocity profiles ensure that the WMR moves from the starting point to the goal point while avoiding the obstacles placed in between.

At the lower level, two PI controllers for the DC motors were considered, ensuring that the actual wheel velocities followed the desired velocity profiles generated at the upper level.

In accordance with (28), the mathematical models associated with the right and left motors are expressed as follows:

$$\begin{aligned} \frac{d\varpi_r}{dt} &= -10.20\varpi_r + 5.51u_r, \\ y_r &= \varpi_r, \end{aligned} \tag{31}$$

and

$$\begin{aligned} \frac{d\varpi_l}{dt} &= -10.20\varpi_l + 5.99u_l, \\ y_l &= \varpi_l. \end{aligned} \tag{32}$$

Thus, two controls, u_r and u_l, are required; in accordance with (29), these are given by

$$u_r = K_{pr}e_r + K_{ir}\int_0^t e_r d\tau, \tag{33}$$

$$u_l = K_{pl}e_l + K_{il}\int_0^t e_l d\tau, \tag{34}$$

where u_r and u_l are the control voltages for the right and left motors, respectively, and K_{pr}, K_{ir}, K_{pl}, and K_{il} are the constant gains (proportional and integral) associated with each motor. Finally, e_r and e_l represent the angular velocity tracking errors defined by

$$\begin{aligned} e_r &= \varpi_r^* - \varpi_r, \\ e_l &= \varpi_l^* - \varpi_l, \end{aligned} \tag{35}$$

with

$$(\varpi_r^*, \varpi_l^*) = (\omega_r, \omega_l). \tag{36}$$

This means that the desired angular velocity trajectories (ϖ_r^*, ϖ_l^*) are determined by (ω_r, ω_l), which are obtained from (13).

4. Simulations

Using Matlab-Simulink, which allows the programming of mathematical models by means of blocks that facilitate the establishment of equations in a transparent and simple manner, this section presents the numerical simulations associated with the obstacle avoidance task developed previously, with the general results then applied to a scenario involving three obstacles within the WMR workspace. As mentioned earlier, the positions of the obstacles

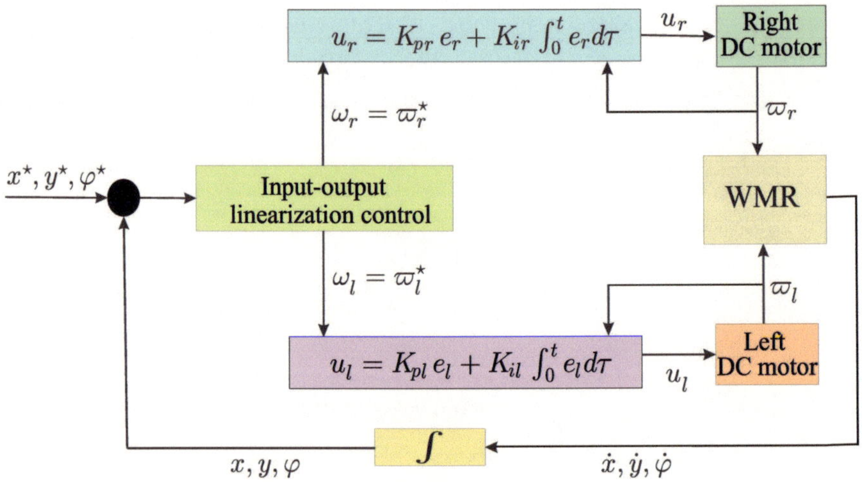

Figure 5. Block diagram of the WMR hierarchical control.

within the workspace is assumed to be already known. The following subsections outline the stages of the simulation process, namely: the definition of the parameters of the system and of the hierarchical control, the implementation of the control via Matlab-Simulink, and finally the obtained results.

4.1. Definition of parameters

When implementing simulations associated with the closed-loop system, both WMR and control parameters must first be considered in order to use them later to program (via Matlab-Simulink) the block associated with the hierarchical control. In this case, the parameters associated with the WMR are l, r, and L, and those associated with the hierarchical control being v_d, ε, η, ξ, and ρ_0 due to the use of the artificial potential field method. The values of these parameters are shown in Table 1. It is worth mentioning that the values associated with the WMR, i.e., l, r, and L, correspond to the prototype reported in [14]. Finally, the coordinates associated with the goal, q_m, and the obstacles, q_{obs}, (for a three obstacle scenario) are presented in Table 2, where $\rho_0 = \rho_{01} = \rho_{02} = \rho_{03}$. The declarations elaborated in Matlab-Simulink for all the above-mentioned parameters are shown in the upper part of Figure 6.

Constant	Definition	Value
l	Distance from (x, y) to the wheels	0.220 m
r	Wheel ratio	0.075 m
L	Distance from (x, y) to q	0.250 m
v_d	Desired constant velocity	0.5 m/s
ε	Constant value close to zero	0.1
η	Positive scale factor (repulsive)	2
ξ	Positive scale factor (attractive)	1
ρ_0	Distance of the obstacle's influence	0.5 m

Table 1. Parameters employed in the development of the simulations.

http://dx.doi.org/10.5772/58392

$q(x_1,y_1)$	$q_m(x_m,y_m)$	$q_{obs\,1}(x_{o1},y_{o1})$	$q_{obs\,2}(x_{o2},y_{o2})$	$q_{obs\,3}(x_{o3},y_{o3})$
$x_1 = 0$ m	$x_m = 2.2$ m	$x_{o1} = 0.2$ m	$x_{o2} = 1.2$ m	$x_{o3} = 1.5$ m
$y_1 = 0$ m	$y_m = 1.7$ m	$y_{o1} = 0.4$ m	$y_{o2} = 0.4$ m	$y_{o3} = 1.6$ m
		$\rho_{01} = 0.5$ m	$\rho_{02} = 0.5$ m	$\rho_{03} = 0.5$ m

Table 2. Coordinates associated with the goal and the obstacles.

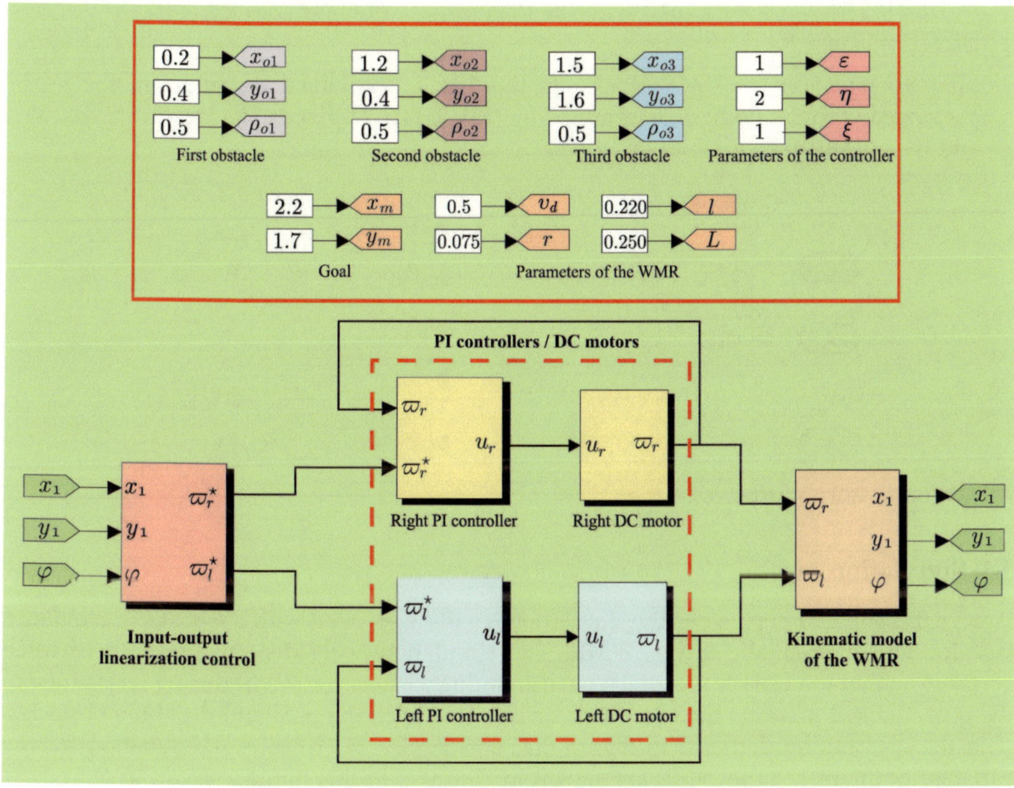

Figure 6. Implementation of the hierarchical control in Matlab-Simulink for the WMR.

Once the values of the parameters associated with the WMR and the control have been defined, the hierarchical control can be programmed in Matlab-Simulink to simulate the closed-loop system.

4.2. Implementing the control via Matlab-Simulink

Figure 6 (bottom part) shows the three blocks associated with the hierarchical control programmed using Matlab-Simulink: *Input-output linearization control*, *PI controllers/DC motors*, and *Kinematic model of the WMR*.

1.- *Input-output linearization control* block. In this block, the control determined by (13), which accomplishes the obstacle avoidance task, is programmed. The inputs are the variables (x_1, y_1, φ), and the outputs the desired velocity profiles $(\omega_r, \omega_l) = (\varpi_r^*, \varpi_l^*)$, the latter being tracked by the angular velocities of the right and left DC motors, respectively. Figure 7 presents the block's constituent sub-blocks.

2.- *PI controllers/DC motors* block. In this block, the PI controls, associated with the right and left motors, respectively determined by (33) and (34), are implemented. The inputs are determined by (ϖ_r^*, ϖ_l^*) and the angular velocities produced by the motors (ϖ_r, ϖ_l), respectively, with the outputs being the controls u_r and u_l in such a way that $(\varpi_r, \varpi_l) \to (\varpi_r^*, \varpi_l^*)$. The gains associated with the PI controls were here selected as $K_{pr} = 2$, $K_{ir} = 50$, $K_{pl} = 2$, and $K_{il} = 50$.

3.- *Kinematic model of the WMR* block. In this block, the kinematic model of the WMR associated with the point q, determined by (12), is programmed. The inputs are (ϖ_r, ϖ_l), and the outputs the variables (x_1, y_1, φ).

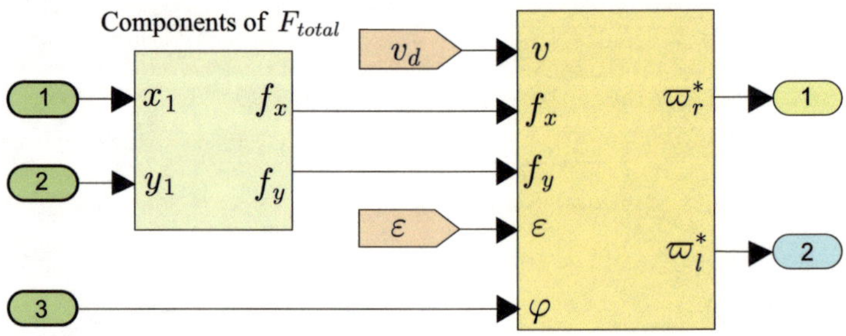

Figure 7. Input-output linearization control block.

4.3. Simulation results

Finally, this subsection presents the simulation results associated with the obstacle avoidance task for the differentially-driven WMR. The simulations consider the presence of three obstacles within the workspace which have an influence over the WMR during its journey to the goal. Table 2 presents the coordinates associated with the goal and the three obstacles, with the distribution depicted in Figure 8(a) and Figure 14. The results obtained for the variables of interest to the WMR are shown in Figure 8; in this figure one can observe how the WMR successfully evades the obstacles and reaches the goal.

5. Description of the employed prototype

This section provides a general description of the WMR prototype reported in [14], which was built to carry out various control tasks associated with WMRs. Figure 9 displays a block diagram describing the existent connections between the different stages of the employed WMR, namely: *Subsystems*, *Power system*, and *Data acquisition and control system*.

Here we present a summarized description of the blocks composing the WMR prototype, including its connection with the DS1104 board, as shown in Figure 9.

- Stage 1: *Subsystems*. This stage (see Figure 10) comprises the mechanical subsystems **a** and **b**, which include the actuators, sensors, and the mechanical structure of the WMR. Subsystem **a**, *actuators and sensors*, generates the movement of the WMR wheels in a specified workspace, and discrete position sensing, respectively. Subsystem **b**, *mechanical*

http://dx.doi.org/10.5772/58392

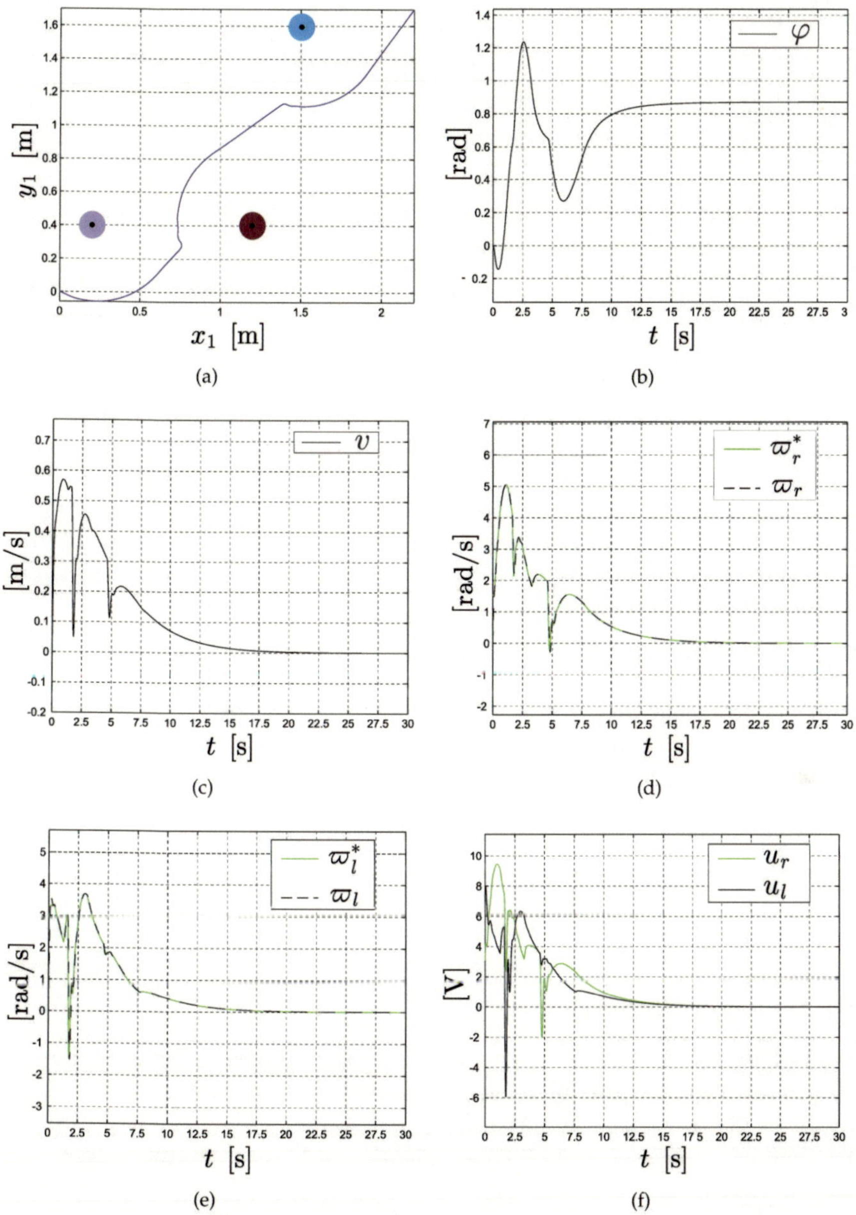

Figure 8. Simulation results in the three obstacles scenario.

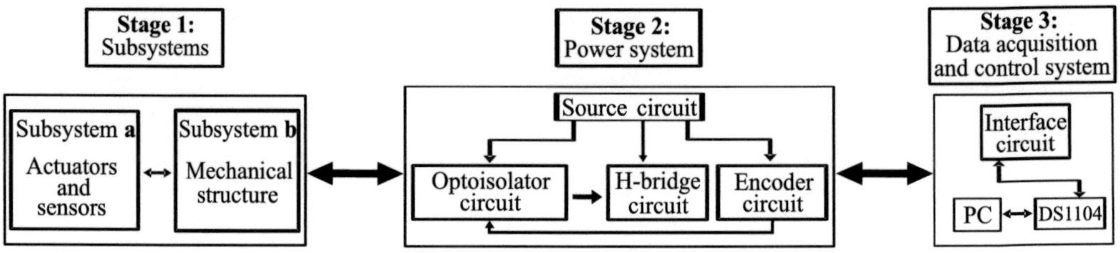

Figure 9. General block diagram of the WMR prototype.

structure, corresponds to the mechanical topology associated with the differentially driven WMR.

- Stage 2: *Power system*. This stage enables interaction between the electronic control interface (stage 3) and the mechanical subsystems (stage 1). A block diagram of stage 2 is shown in Figure 11. This block comprises the following four substages, numbered from 1 to 4: *source circuit*, *optoisolator circuit*, *H-bridge circuit*, and *encoder circuit*. In substage 1, the power supply, via the source circuit, distributes the different voltages to the general electronic system. Substage 2 enables electrical signal isolation between the DS1104 electronic board and substage 3. Substage 3 enables the direction of rotation of the DC motors to be controlled via the use of a positive or a negative voltage, which is determined by the control exerted by the DS1104 board. Finally, substage 4 involves the acquisition of the encoders' signals, which can then be used to estimate the position of the WMR within the workspace.
- Stage 3: *Data acquisition and control system*. The main device involved in this stage is the DS1104 board, which performs the acquisition of the variables of interest to the experimental implementation of the WMR hierarchical control. This board was selected due to the potential for integration between Matlab-Simulink and the board's firmware. Moreover, the high programming level available in Simulink makes it a practical selection for the programming of complex control strategies in a graphical environment. Stage 3 also includes an *interface circuit* (see Figure 9) which establishes communication between the DS1104 board and the WMR.

Figure 12 shows pictures of the real WMR, including the employed instrumentation.

6. Real-time experiments

In order to validate the data obtained via numeric simulation presented in Section 4, here we present the experimental results obtained using the WMR in real-time. These experiments were performed using Matlab-Simulink, ControlDesk, and a DS1104 board (dSPACE), with the distribution of the obstacles and the goal identical to that in the simulations.

6.1. Real-time control of the WMR via Matlab-Simulink

Whereas the mathematical models associated with the WMR and the DC motors were used to obtain the simulation results, these models were replaced by the WMR prototype in obtaining the experimental results. However, it is worth mentioning that the robot kinematic model

Figure 10. Bottom view of the mechanical structure.

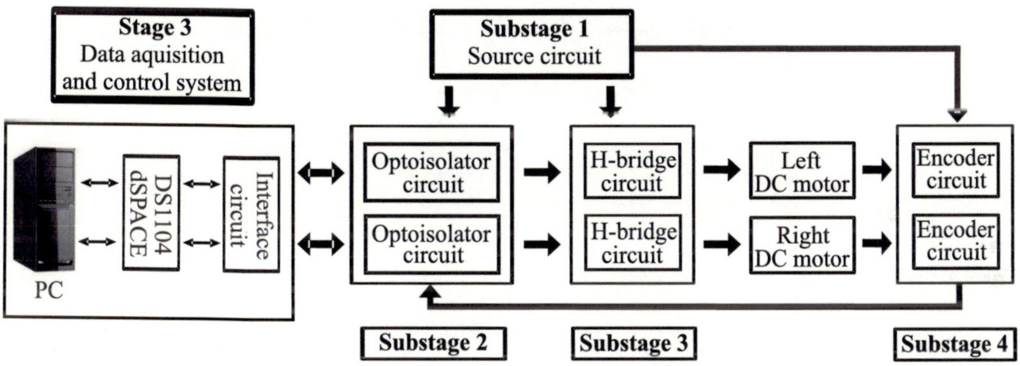

Figure 11. Block diagram of the power system.

was employed here to provide an estimation of the WMR position, since no localization sensor was used for the WMR in the present study.

The Matlab-Simulink program associated with the hierarchical control used to obtain the experimental results for the closed-loop system is shown in Figure 13, which consists of the following blocks: *System parameters*, *Input-output linearization control*, *PI controllers/DC motors*, and *Kinematic model of the WMR*. Figure 13 also depicts the connections between the WMR and the hierarchical control. A comparison of Figures 6 and 13 reveals that the two are highly similar, with the only block experiencing any significant changes being the one associated with the *PI controllers/DC motors*. Hence, we can focus our attention solely on this block.

- *PI controllers/DC motors* block. This block describes the implementation of the PI controls, u_r and u_l, associated with the right and left motors, respectively, which allow $(\varpi_r, \varpi_l) \rightarrow$

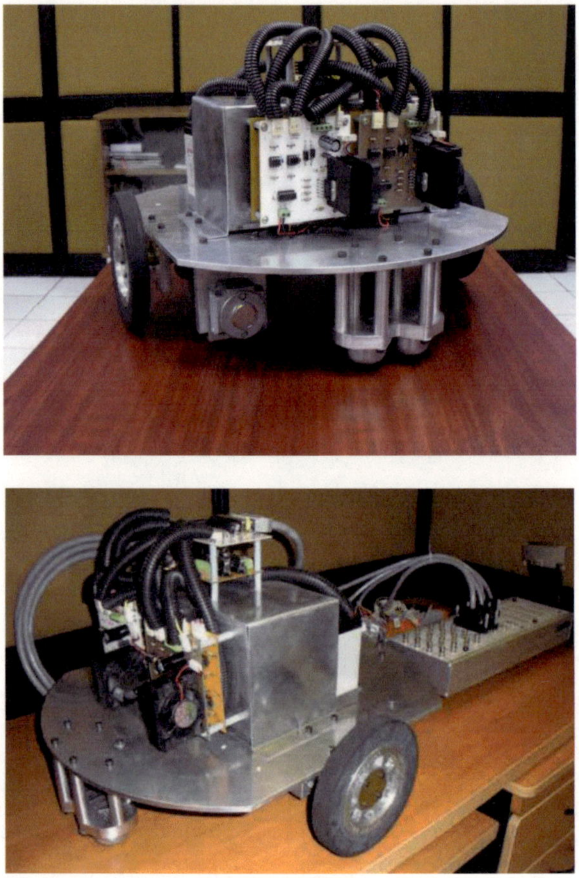

Figure 12. WMR prototype.

(ω_r^*, ω_l^*). In order to start the DC motors, the u_r and u_l voltages must be conditioned through PWM blocks, which are implemented via the DS1104 board. The PWM signals then go through the *power system* stage illustrated in Figure 9. For the acquisition of the angular velocities ω_r and ω_l, two E50S8 incremental encoders (Autonics) were employed in combination with Matlab-Simulink blocks.

6.2. Experimental results

This subsection presents the experimental results associated with the distribution of the obstacles and the goal mentioned in Table 2. Likewise, the locations of the WMR, obstacles, and goal within the workspace are illustrated in Figure 14. The corresponding experimental results for such a scenario, in which the parameters of the WMR and the gains of the controls were the same as those employed in the simulations, are shown in Figure 15. Additionally, supplementary material associated with these results can be seen through Video S1 (see [25]). Also, experimental results for the scenarios involving two and zero obstacles within

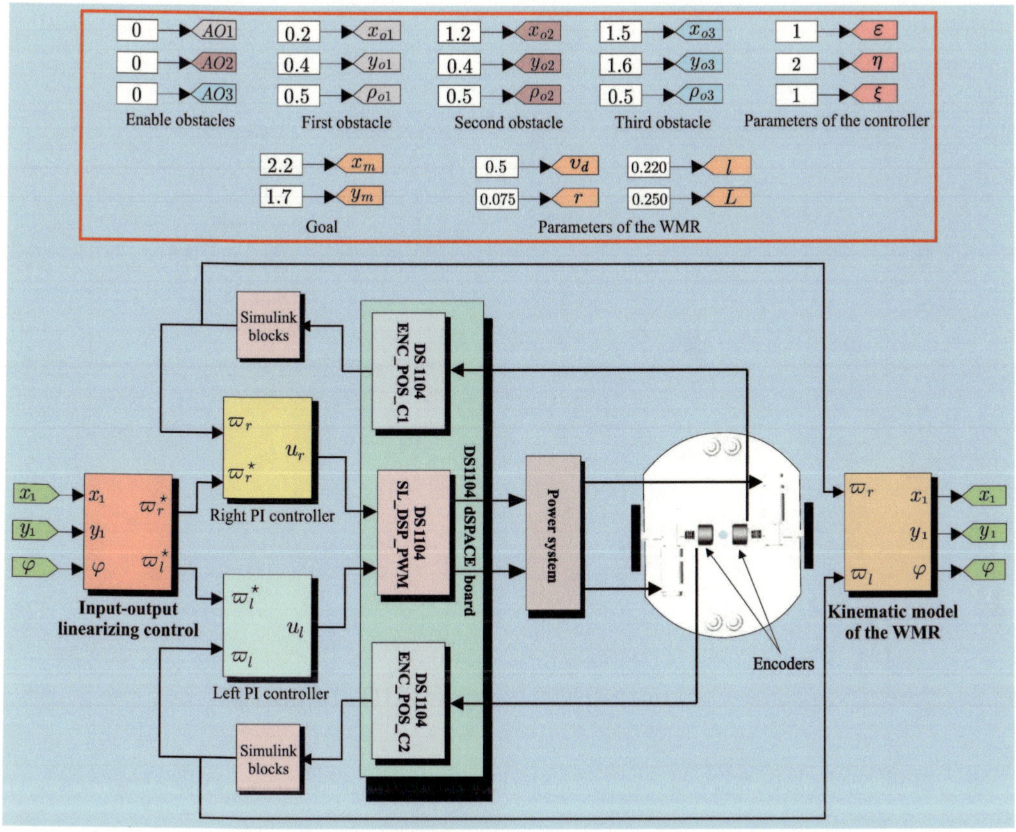

Figure 13. Experimental implementation of the controller via Matlab-Simulink and its connection with the WMR.

the workspace are presented in Videos S2 and S3, respectively, (see [25]). The aforementioned videos are available online at: www.controlautomatico.com.mx/trabajos.html

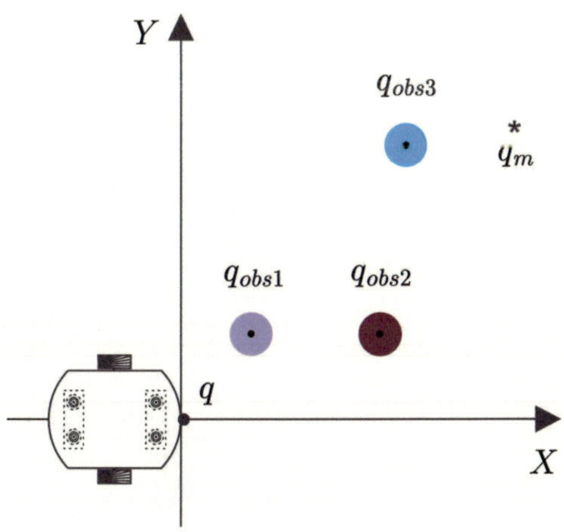

Figure 14. Position and orientation of the starting point of the WMR.

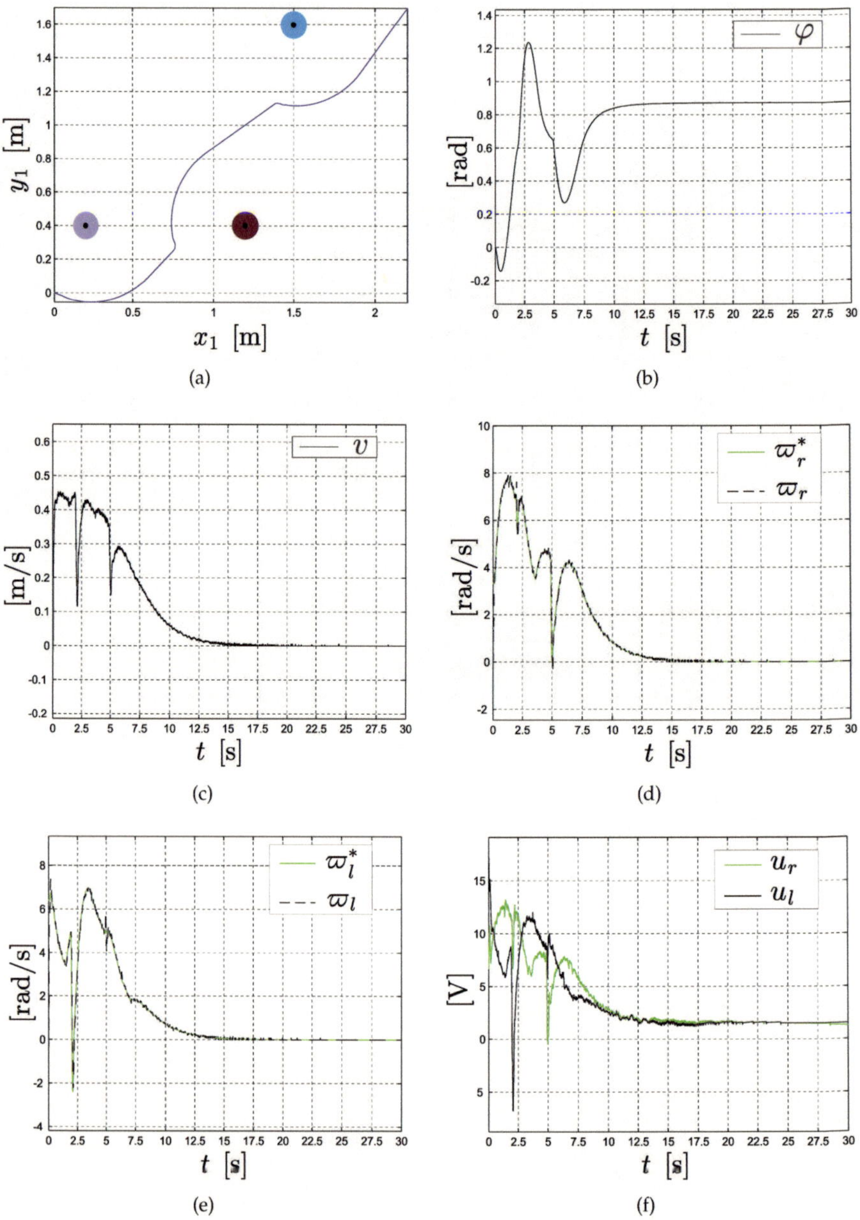

Figure 15. Experimental results for the three obstacles scenario.

http://dx.doi.org/10.5772/58392

6.3. Discussion of the results

Similar results were obtained in the simulation and experimental tests; in both cases the angular velocities of the DC motors, ω_r and ω_l, tracked the desired velocity profiles imposed by the WMR kinematic model, ω_r^* and ω_l^*, respectively. Hence, the obstacle avoidance task was successfully carried out by the WMR, as verified experimentally in Figure 15(a). However, it is worth mentioning that an error arose that could only be appreciated visually and which thus does not appear in Figure 15(a): a gap of approximately 10 cm was observed between point q and point q_m. This discrepancy likely occurred due to the fact that the position of q within the workspace was calculated indirectly via the WMR kinematic model. It was also observed that the voltages u_r and u_l, associated with the DC motors, did not surpass the $(-24$ V, $+24$ V) voltage interval: this was convenient since the nominal voltage of the employed DC motors is in the range of ± 24 V. As a result it can be confirmed that the developed hierarchical control performed successfully.

7. Conclusions

Based on the artificial potential field approach, the present work has provided a solution to the obstacle avoidance task for a differentially-driven WMR via the design of a hierarchical control, for which a step-by-step guide has been presented that details the theory, simulation, and experimental implementation. Simulation results were obtained by developing a Matlab-Simulink program, since Simulink provides a graphical environment that facilitates the analysis, design, and construction of dynamic systems. In order to obtain experimental results, a Matlab-Simulink program was again employed, this time alongside ControlDesk and the DS1104 board. A comparison of the simulation and experimental results associated with the obstacle avoidance task revealed the good performance of the developed hierarchical control. However, as mentioned earlier, an error between the WMR and the goal arises that can only be observed visually, likely due to the fact that the position of the robot is calculated via the kinematic model of the WMR. Future work will aim to locate the WMR via a sensor in order to reduce or eliminate said error.

Acknowledgments

R. Silva-Ortigoza, H. Taud, M. Marciano-Melchor, and J. A. Álvarez-Cedillo acknowledge financial support from the Secretaría de Investigación y Posgrado del Instituto Politécnico Nacional (SIP-IPN), SNI-México, and the IPN programs EDI and COFAA. The work of C. Márquez-Sánchez was supported by CONACYT and BEIFI scholarships. V. M. Hernández-Guzmán acknowledges financial support from SNI-México. Finally, Rhomina and Joserhamón deserve a special mention from R. Silva-Ortigoza for their moral support and for being the inspiration for his introduction to the thrilling world of robotics.

Author details

R. Silva-Ortigoza[1], C. Márquez-Sánchez[1], F. Carrizosa-Corral[2], V. M. Hernández-Guzmán[3], J. R. García-Sánchez[1], H. Taud[1], M. Marciano-Melchor[1], and J. A. Álvarez-Cedillo[1]

1 Instituto Politécnico Nacional, CIDETEC, Área de Mecatrónica, Unidad Profesional Adolfo López Mateos, México, DF, Mexico

2 Instituto Tecnológico de Culiacán, Departamento de Metal-Mecánica, Culiacán, Sin, Mexico

3 Universidad Autónoma de Querétaro, Facultad de Ingeniería, Querétaro, Qro, Mexico

References

[1] R. Silva-Ortigoza, M. Marcelino-Aranda, G. Silva-Ortigoza, V. M. Hernández-Guzmán, M. A. Molina-Vilchis, G. Saldaña-González, J. C. Herrera-Lozada, and M. Olguín-Carbajal, "Wheeled mobile robots: A review," *IEEE Latin America Transactions*, vol. 10, no. 6, pp. 2209–2217, 2012. Available at http://www.ewh.ieee.org/reg/9/etrans/eng/

[2] J. L. Crowley, "World modeling and position estimation for a mobile robot using ultrasonic rangin," *in Proceedings of the IEEE International Conference on Robotics and Automation*, pp. 674–680, May 1989.

[3] J. T. Schwartz and M. Sharir, "On the piano movers problem. II. General techniques for computing topological properties of real algebraic manifolds," *Advances in Applied Mathematics*, vol. 4, no. 3, pp. 298–351, 1983.

[4] N. J. Nilsson, "A mobile automaton: An application of artificial intelligence techniques," *in Proceedings of the International Joint Conference on Artificial Intelligence*, pp. 509–520, May 1969.

[5] O. Khatib, "Real-Time obstacle avoidance for manipulators and mobile robots, " *The international Journal of Robotics Research*, vol. 5, no. 2, pp. 90–98, 1986.

[6] J. Borenstein and Y. Koren, "Obstacle avoidance with ultrasonic sensors," *IEEE Journal of Robotics and Automation*, vol 4, no. 2, pp. 213–218, 1988.

[7] J. Borenstein and Y. Koren, "Real-Time obstacle avoidance for fast mobile robots, " *IEEE Transactions on Systems, Man and Cybernetics*, vol. 19, no. 5, pp. 1179–1187, 1989.

[8] R. Tilove, "Local obstacle avoidance for mobile robots based on the method of artificial potentials," *in Proceedings of the IEEE International Conference on Robotics and Automation*, pp. 566–571, May 1990.

[9] J. Borenstein and Y. Koren, "Potential field methods and their inherent limitations for mobile robot navigation," *in Proceedings of the IEEE International Conference on Robotics and Automation*, pp. 1398–1404, April 1991.

[10] J. Guldner and V. I. Utkin, "Sliding mode control for gradient tracking and robot navigation usig artificial potential fields," *IEEE Transactions on Robotics and Automation*, vol. 11, no. 2, pp. 247–254, 1995.

[11] K. Valanavis, T. Hebert, R. Kolluru, and N. Tsourveloudis, "Mobile robot navigation in 2-D dynamic enviroments using an electrostatic potential field," *IEEE Transactions on Systems, Man and Cybernetics, Part A: Systems and Humans*, vol. 30, no. 2, pp. 187–196, 2000.

[12] F. Xu, H. Van Brussel, M. Nuttin, and R. Moreas, "Concepts for dynamic obstacle avoidance and their extended application in underground navigation," *Robotics and Autonomous Systems*, vol. 42, no. 1, pp. 1–15, 2003.

[13] W. Huang, B. Fajen, J. Fink, and W. Warren, "Visual navigation and obstacle avoidance using a steering potential function," *Robotics and Autonomous Systems*, vol. 54, no. 4, pp. 288–299, 2006.

[14] R. Silva-Ortigoza, C. Márquez-Sánchez, M. Marcelino-Aranda, M. Marciano-Melchor, G. Silva-Ortigoza, R. Bautista-Quintero, E. R. Ramos-Silvestre, J. C. Rivera-Díaz, and D. Muñoz-Carrillo, "Construction of a WMR for trajectory tracking control: Experimental results," *The Scientific World Journal*, vol. 2013, Article ID 723645, pp. 1–17, 2013. Available at http://dx.doi.org/10.1155/2013/723645

[15] V. M. Hernández-Guzmán, R. Silva-Ortigoza y R. V. Carrillo-Serrano, *Control Automático: Teoría de Diseño, Construcción de Prototipos, Modelado, Identificación y Pruebas Experimentales*, Colección CIDETEC–IPN, Mexico, DF, Mexico, 2013. Available at http://www.controlautomatico.com.mx

[16] S. S. Ge and Y. J. Cui, "New potential functions for mobile robot path planning," *IEEE Transactions on Robotics and Automation*, vol. 16, no. 5, pp. 615–620, 2000.

[17] B. H. Krogh, "A generalized potential field approach to obstacle avoidance control," *International Robotics Research Conference*, Bethlehem, PA, August 1984.

[18] J. R. García Sánchez, *Diseño y construcción de un robot móvil, aplicando el método de campos potenciales en la evasión de obstáculos*. Tesis de Maestría. CIDETEC del Instituto Politécnico Nacional, Mexico City, Mexico, 2008.

[19] A. W. Divelbiss and J. T. Wen, "Trajectory tracking control of a car-trailer system," *IEEE Transactions on Control Systems Technology*, vol. 5, no. 3, pp. 269–278, 1997.

[20] R. Silva-Ortigoza, G. Silva-Ortigoza, V. M. Hernández-Guzmán, V. R. Barrientos-Sotelo, J. M. Albarrán-Jiménez, and V. M. Silva-García, "Trajectory tracking in a mobile robot without using velocity measurements for control of wheels," *IEEE Latin America Transactions*, vol. 6, no. 7, pp. 598–607, 2008. Available at http://www.ewh.ieee.org/reg/9/etrans/eng/

[21] R. Silva-Ortigoza, J. R. García-Sánchez, J. M. Alba-Martínez, V. M. Hernández-Guzmán, M. Marcelino-Aranda, H. Taud, and R. Bautista-Quintero, "Two-stage control design of a Buck converter/DC motor system without velocity measurements via a $\Sigma-\Delta$-modulator," *Mathematical Problems in Engineering*, vol. 2013, Article ID 929316, pp. 1–11, 2013. Available at http://dx.doi.org/10.1155/2013/929316

[22] R. Silva-Ortigoza, C. Márquez-Sánchez, F. Carrizosa-Corral, M. Antonio-Cruz, J. M. Alba-Martínez, and G. Saldaña-González, "Hierarchical velocity control based on differential flatness for a DC/DC Buck converter-DC motor System," *Mathematical Problems in Engineering*, vol. 2014, Article ID 912815, pp. 1–12, 2014. Available at http://dx.doi.org/10.1155/2014/912815

[23] R. Silva-Ortigoza, V. M. Hernández-Guzmán, M. Antonio-Cruz, and D. Muñoz-Carrillo, "DC/DC Buck power converter as a smooth starter for a DC motor based on a hierarchical control," *IEEE Transactions on Power Electronics*, Article in Press, Available with DOI: 10.1109/TPEL.2014.2311821

[24] H. Sira-Ramirez and S. K. Agrawal, *Differentially Flat Systems*, Marcel Dekker, New York, 2004.

[25] Supplementary Material. Available at http://www.controlautomatico.com.mx/trabajos.html

[26] T. A. Vidal Calleja, *Generalización del método de campos potenciales artificiales para un vehículo articulado*. Tesis de Maestría. Sección de Mecatrónica del Departamento de Ingeniería Eléctrica del CINVESTAV-IPN, Mexico City, Mexico, 2002.

Chapter 4

Dual Heuristic Neural Programming Controller for Synchronous Generator

Mato Miskovic, Ivan Miskovic and Marija Mirosevic

Additional information is available at the end of the chapter

http://dx.doi.org/10.5772/58377

1. Introduction

This chapter describes the development of voltage control system of a synchronous generator based on neural networks. Recurrent (dynamic) neural networks (RNN) are used, as a type that has great capabilities in approximation of dynamic systems [1]. Two algorithms are used for training – Dual Heuristic Programming (DHP) and Globalized Dual Heuristic Programming (GDHP). The algorithms have been developed for the optimal control of nonlinear systems using dynamic programming principles.

Neural voltage controller is developed in MATLAB and Simulink environment. For training purposes a mathematical model of synchronous generator is designed and applied in Simulink. DHP and GDHP algorithms are designed in Simulink, with matrix calculations in S-functions. Algorithms are used for offline training of neural networks (NN). In the second part, the same functions are redesigned as real time controllers, based on the Real Time Windows Target Toolbox.

DHP or GDHP algorithms provide a significant improvement over conventional PI controller with, in some cases, power system stabilizer (PSS). Conventional linear controller can only provide optimal control in single operating point. Algorithms described in the chapter provide significantly better control over the whole operating range by minimization of the user defined cost function during the training of the neural network.

Digital voltage controller is implemented on real system in two basic steps. First step is neural network design and training in Matlab environment on desktop computer. Second step consists of transfer of controller with computed coefficients to the digital control system hardware.

INTECH
open science | open minds

© 2014 The Author(s). Licensee InTech. This chapter is distributed under the terms of the Creative Commons Attribution License (http://creativecommons.org/licenses/by/3.0), which permits unrestricted use, distribution, and reproduction in any medium, provided the original work is properly cited.

For the controller to have optimal performance in all real operating conditions, neural networks must be trained for the whole working range of the plant. Procedure described in the chapter can be applied on standard voltage control systems by replacing the PI controller with the offline-trained neural network. Most modern digital control systems have sufficient hardware and software support for neural network implementation.

2. Recurrent neural networks

Neural networks are computational models capable of machine learning and pattern recognition. They can also be used as universal approximators of continuous real functions. Typical dynamic neural network is shown in Figure 1.

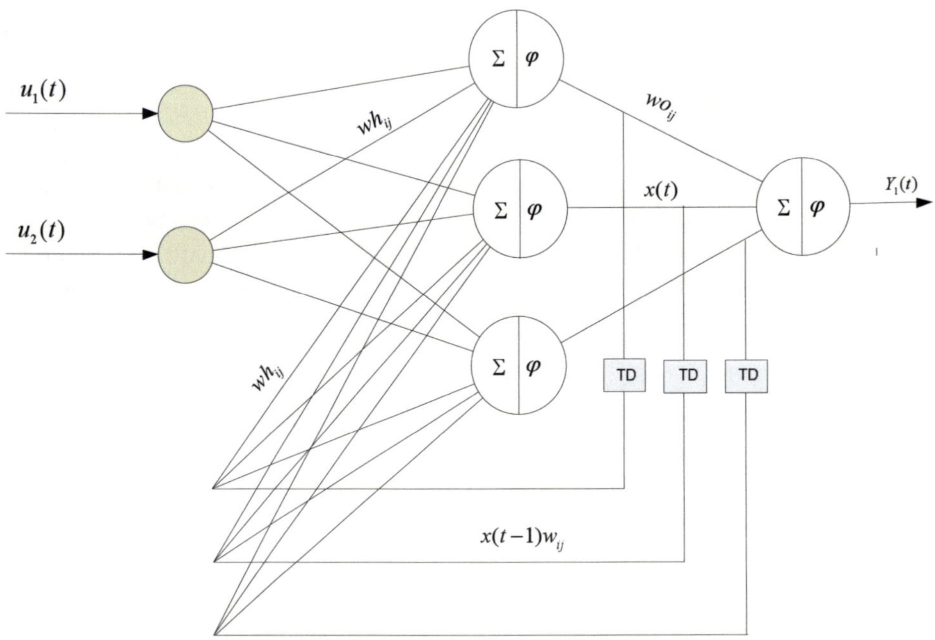

Figure 1. Recurrent neural network structure

Neural network is formed from interconnected layers of neurons. Output of each neuron is calculated from:

$$y_k = \varphi\left(\sum_{j=0}^{m}\left(w_{kj} \cdot x_{kj}\right) + b\right) \tag{1}$$

http://dx.doi.org/10.5772/58377

where

φ is activation function,

w_{kj} and x_{kj} are weights and outputs from previous layer and b is bias.

Typical activation function maps input values $u(t) \in [-\infty, \infty]$ to output $y(t) \in [0, 1]$ or $y(t) \in [-1, 1]$. Activation function must be derivable over the whole range. Among typically used nonlinear activation functions are *logsig*, *tansig* and Gaussian.

Dynamic behavior is added by introducing a memory element (step delay) that stores neuron output and reintroduces it as input to all neurons in the same layer in next time step.

This type of network is named recurrent or dynamic neural network. An example of tansig (*Hyperbolic Tangent Sigmoid Transfer Function*) activation function, $\phi(u) = \frac{2}{1+e^{-2u}} - 1$, and its derivative $\phi(u)' = 1 - \phi(u)^2$ is shown in Figure 2.

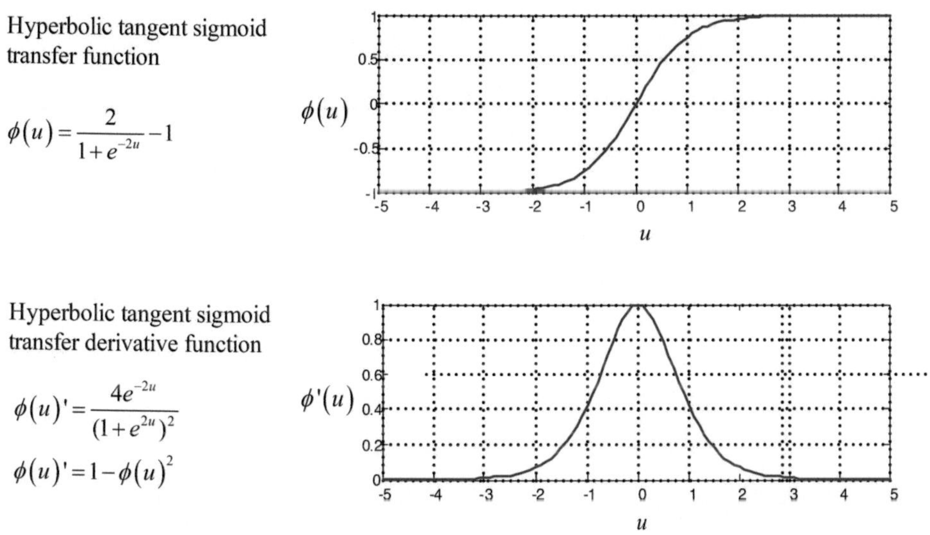

Figure 2. Tansig activation function and its derivative

Input values are in range of $u \in [-\infty, \infty]$, with output values in range $\varphi(u) \in [-1, 1]$.

Use of function with simple derivative significantly improves calculation times of numerical procedures.

Dynamic (recurrent) neural networks provide good approximation of time-dependent functions. However, training of recurrent neural networks is more complex than training static networks.

2.1. Recurrent neural networks training

There are many methods for training neural networks, and most of them rely on some form of backpropagation – calculation of partial derivative of system output over network weight coefficients $\left(\frac{\partial y}{\partial w}\right)$. Partial derivatives are determined using chain rule, by finding derivatives of weight coefficients in output layer, using intermediate results to calculate next layer, with respect to network structure. Calculation is repeated until all layers are processed.

Described procedure is valid for static neural networks, but is of no use in recurrent networks, as each neuron has inputs from previous time step from the same layer. Two procedures are often used in calculation of partial derivatives: *Backpropagation Through Time* (*BPTT*) and *Real Time Recurrent Learning* (*RTRL*).

In BPTT recurrent neuron inputs are replaced with the same neural network delayed by one time step. Process is iterated N times. Thus, recurrent network is approximated by N feedforward networks with delayed outputs. Network weight coefficients, recurrent inputs and outputs must be preserved for past N time steps. Obtained derivative $\left(\frac{\partial y(t)}{\partial w(t)}\right)$ is used to determine new weight coefficients. One advantage of BPTT is that all methods used for training feedforward networks can be utilized in training recurrent networks.

This chapter will describe use of RTRL procedure in training dynamic networks. Output of recurrent network with one hidden and one output layer has the following form:

$$\begin{aligned} x(t) &= \tanh\left(W_1 \cdot p_1\right) \\ y(t) &= W_2 \cdot x(t) \end{aligned} \tag{2}$$

where

p_1– hidden layer input, p_1=[$u(t)$; $x(t-1)$; 1],

$x(t)$– hidden layer output,

y(t) – network output,

W_1– hidden layer weight coefficients,

W_2– output layer weight coefficients, p_2=[$x(t)$; 1]

Equation (2) can easily be expanded for multi layer recurrent networks. Partial derivative of network output over output layer weight coefficients is

$$\frac{\partial y(t)}{\partial w_{ij}^{o}(t)} = p_2(t) \tag{3}$$

For hidden layer, partial derivatives are

$$\frac{\partial y(t)}{\partial w_h(t)} = \frac{\partial y(t)}{\partial w_2(t)} \frac{\partial x(t)}{\partial w_2(t)} \tag{4}$$

Partial derivative of hidden layer output over weight coefficients is

$$\frac{\partial x_l(t)}{\partial w_{i,j}(t)} = f[x(t)]'_i \left(p_j(t)\delta_{li} + \sum_{k=1}^{N_{W1}} w(t)_{l,N_{in}+k} \frac{\partial x_k(t-1)}{\partial w_{i,j}(t-1)} \right) \tag{5}$$

where

N_{W1}– number of neurons in hidden layer,

N_{in}– number of neurons in input layer.

Value of $\frac{\partial x_l(t)}{\partial w_{i,j}}$ is calculated using four nested loops (Appendix A).

Matrix of output derivatives over weight coefficients is of the form $[N_{W1}, N_{W1} \cdot (N_{in} + N_{W1} + 1)]$.

2.2. Neural network training algorithms

2.2.1. Gradient descent

Gradient descent is the most commonly used method in neural networks training. Difference between real and desired network output can be expressed as

$$e(t) = y(t) - \hat{y}(t) \tag{6}$$

Differentiation of (5) provides update values of weight coefficients:

$$w_{ij}(t) = w_{ij}(t-1) - \beta \frac{\partial \hat{y}(t)}{\partial w_{ij}(t)} \tag{7}$$

Parameter β defines learning rate and must be in range $0<\beta<1$.

2.2.2. *Kalman filter based training*

Kalman filter [5] was developed as a recursive procedure of optimal filtering of linear dynamic state-space systems. For RNN training extended Kalman filter (EKF) is used. It is also applicable to nonlinear systems using linearization around operating point. The algorithm is used as a predictive-corrective procedure.

Kalman filter based recurrent network training is described in [6] and [7].

Training is performed in two steps. The first step is calculation of prediction values of weight coefficients. Second step is correction of predicted variables based on measured state space.

Algorithm is defined by the following relations:

$$K(t) = P(t)H(t)\left(\eta(t)I + H^T(t)P(t)H(t)\right) \tag{8}$$

$$W(t) = W(t-1) + K(t)\varepsilon(t) \tag{9}$$

$$P(t+1) = P(t) - K(t)H^T(t)P(t) + Q(t) \tag{10}$$

where

$K(t)$– Kalman gain matrix, determined form network output derivatives over weight coefficients $H(t) = \frac{\partial y(t)}{\partial w}$. System linearization is accomplished by calculating $H(t)$.

$P(t)$– Error covariance matrix, calculated in every iteration

To escape local minima during training, a diagonal matrix $Q(t)$ is added to covariance matrix $P(t)$ in each time step.

Updates to weight coefficients are determined from (9), as a product of Kalman gain and $\varepsilon(t)$ in current step.

Training based on Kalman filter is fast, has good rate of convergence and is often the only practical solution for recurrent networks training. However, the procedure is demanding in terms of computational power and memory requirements.

3. System identification

Nonlinear dynamic systems are identified as input-output system model, or as a state space system. For the selected process, identification is performed by minimization of the cost function

$$E(t) = \frac{1}{2} \cdot \left[y(t) - \hat{y}(t) \right]^T \cdot \left[y(t) - \hat{y}(t) \right] \tag{11}$$

where $[y(t) - \hat{y}(t)]$ is the difference of the measured system outputs and output values of the model.

Selected cost function represents squared error of the identified model.

Dynamic system identification can be performed according to [9], using either series-parallel or parallel structure.

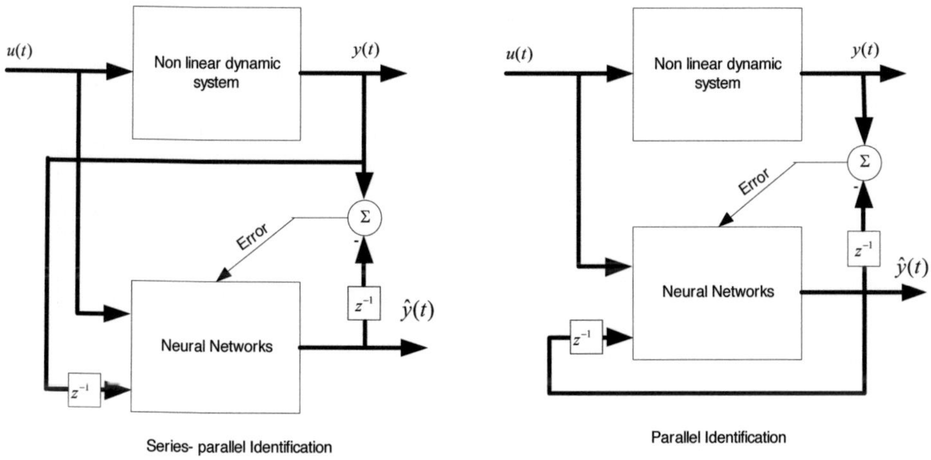

Figure 3. Nonlinear dynamic system identification

In series-parallel structure Figure 3, model neural network input vector is expanded with system outputs from previous steps. In parallel structure Figure 3, network output from previous states is added to input vector. Series-parallel identification provides estimated system output for next time step only, while parallel identification can predict multiple future iterations. However, parallel structure is harder to train and is susceptible to state drifting.

To verify the validity of the RTRL algorithm, neural networks were trained on several discrete mathematical functions. Supervised training has been used, with control value expressed as difference between desired and actual network output.

A parallel identification structure was used on dynamic SISO system $y(t+1) = \frac{y(t)}{1 + y(t)^2} + u(t)^3$. Training has been performed on Recurrent Neural Network with four neurons in hidden layer, and one neuron in linear output layer. Identification results are shown in Figure 4.

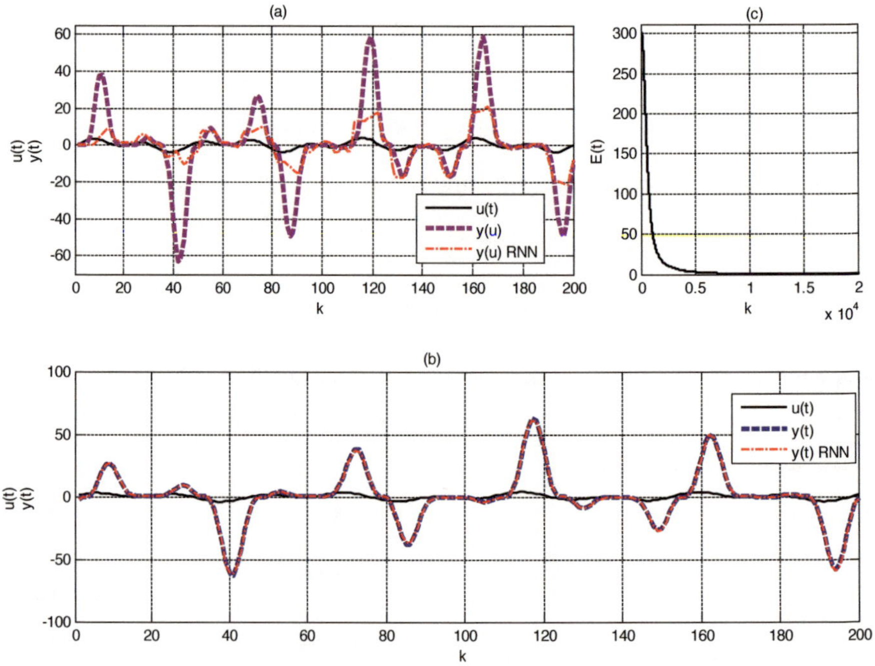

Figure 4. Identification of dynamic function 1

Figure 4a compares initial response of model output $y(t)$ and network output $\hat{y}(t)$. Figure 4b represents the same values with trained network. There is a perfect match between function output values and output of the trained NN. Figure 4c displays training rate as error square $(y(t)-\hat{y}(t))^2$. Training was completed in 20000 steps.

Input signal used for training and verification is $u(t)=\sin(\frac{2\pi}{50})+\sin(\frac{2\pi}{12})$, with sample time $(T_D=1s)$.

In second test, a system with one input, two state variables and one output has been identified:

$$x_1(t+1)=0.5x_2\cdot(t)+0.2\cdot x_1(t)\cdot x_2(t)$$
$$x_2(t+1)=-0.3\cdot x_1(t)+0.8\cdot x_2(t)+u(t)$$
$$y(t+1)=(x_1(t)+x_2(t))^2$$

System was identified using series-parallel structure with RNN with 5 neurons in hidden layer, and one linear neuron in output layer. Identification results are shown in Figure 5.

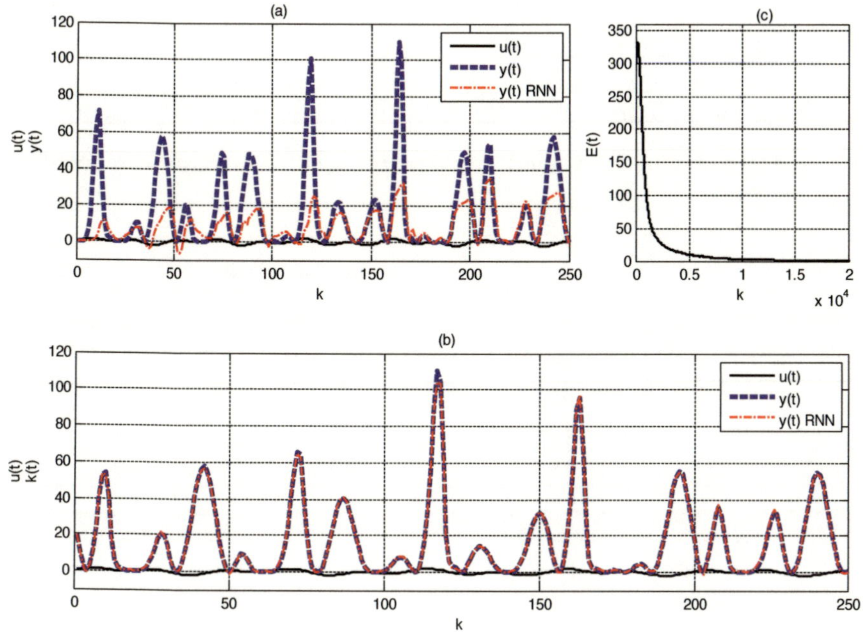

Figure 5. Identification of dynamic function 2

Input signal used for training and verification is the same as in previous example:

$$u(t)=\sin(\frac{2\pi}{50}kT_D)+\sin(\frac{2\pi}{22}kT_D), \text{ where } (T_D=1s).$$

Both examples were designed in Matlab and Simulink. Neural network was trained using c-language S-function (Appendix B). Although the training took 10000 steps, all important system dynamics were visible on trained network after 2000 steps.

3.1. Determination of partial derivatives of functions using neural networks

One of the most important features of neural network modeling is the possibility to determine system output derivatives over inputs $\left(\frac{\partial y_i(t)}{\partial u_j(t)}\right)$. After finding output derivatives, various optimization algorithms can be used.

Partial derivative is calculated from (2)

$$\frac{\partial y_i(t)}{\partial u_j(t)}=\sum_{j=1}^{N_{W1}}\left(W_{i,j}\cdot\sum_{k=1}^{N_p}\left(f_k'(x)\cdot W_{k,j}\right)\right) \tag{12}$$

where $N_p = N_{W1} + N_{in} + 1$ is number of hidden layer inputs. Partial derivative $\left(\frac{\partial y_i(t)}{\partial u_j(t)}\right)$ is obtained from network backpropagation.

For nonlinear function $y(t) = u(t-1)^2 + 6 \cdot u(t-1)^3$, partial derivative $\frac{\partial y(t)}{\partial u(t)}$ was first calculated analytically, and then obtained from model network using (12). Results are compared in Figure 6a and 6b.

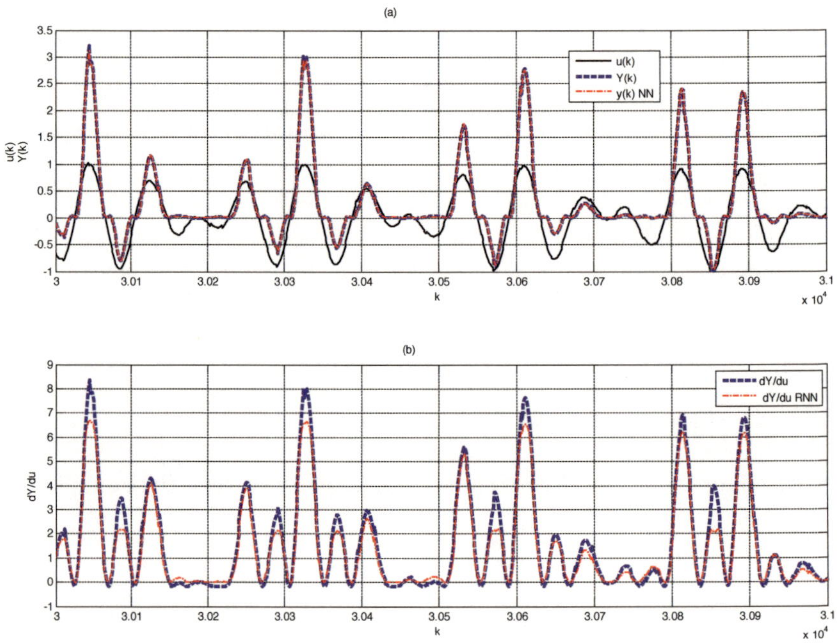

Figure 6. Identification of nonlinear function and calculation of partial derivatives using neural networks

Results from Figure 6b show good match between calculated function derivatives and values obtained from neural network of identified model.

In S-function for training RNN (Appendix B) a procedure is shown for online calculation of partial derivatives of $\left(\frac{\partial y_i(t)}{\partial u_j(t)}\right)$, using (12).

4. Adaptive critic design

Adaptive critic design (ACD) is a set of optimal control procedures of nonlinear systems. It is based on dynamic programming and neural networks. Optimal control is achieved by training neural networks and using them in the structure according to the selected ACD algorithm. ACD algorithms are implemented using a heuristic approach – system state space variables, control values and cost function are selected based on process characteristics. This text focuses on the Heuristic Dynamic Programming (HDP), Dual Heuristic Programming (DHP) and General Dual Heuristic Programming (GDHP) [1,2].

4.1. Heuristic dynamic programming

Heuristic dynamic programming (*HDP*) is the simplest (by structure) ACD algorithm. The basis of all HDP algorithms is minimization of Bellman dynamic programming function $J(t)$:

$$J(t) = \sum_{k=0}^{\infty} \gamma^k U(t+k) \tag{13}$$

where

γ represents discount factor with value in range $0<\gamma<1$, ensuring the convergence of Bellman sum $J(t)$ and cancellation of old values,

$U(t+1)$ is user defined utility function based on system state space variables.

Control signal that minimizes Bellman sum is generated using one of the Adaptive Critic algorithms. In practical control systems, HDP optimization is realized with three neural networks with a structure as shown in Figure 7.

Model neural network in *7a* is used for model identification. Network inputs are control signal $u(t)$ and output state in the previous time step $y(t-1)$. Network output represents estimated model output in the current time step $\hat{y}(t)$. Only systems outputs used in utility function need to be estimated. Model NN is structured according to the selected process model, where the control value is input to the NN, and NN output represents predicted system output. The same NN output values are used to calculate the cost function.

Model neural network is trained to minimize the quadratic criterion:

$$\|E_M\| = \sum_t E_M^T(t) \cdot E_M(t) \tag{14}$$

where:

$$E_M = y(t) - \hat{y}(t) \tag{15}$$

For adaptive control systems, model NN is trained continuously, allowing for adaptation to change of system parameters, and optimal control. Model neural network is trained simultaneously with other networks over time.

Critic neural network in *7b* is used for identification of Bellman sum $J(t)$.

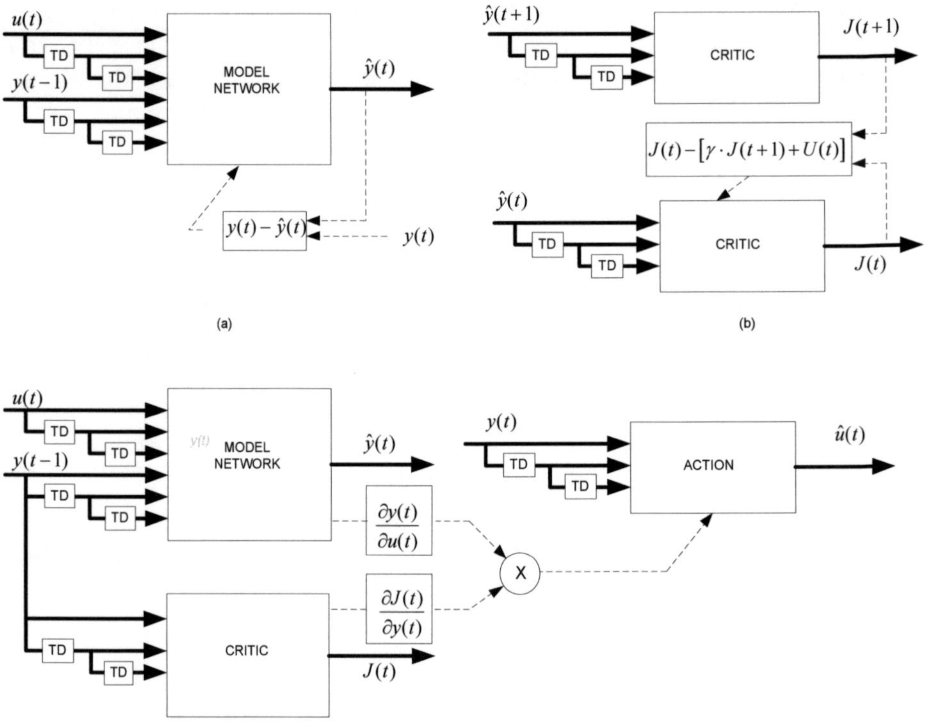

Figure 7. HDP Control structure

Training is used to minimize

$$\|E_C\| = \sum_t E_C^T(t) \cdot E_C(t) \tag{16}$$

where:

$$E_C(t) = J(t) - [\gamma \cdot J(t+1) + U(t)] \tag{17}$$

Critic neural network training is performed with a copy of the same network which is fed with predicted future system outputs $\hat{y}(t+1)$, thus approximating $J(t+1)$.

Action neural network training is based on model and critic network outputs, by minimizing criterion:

$$\|E_A\| = \sum_t E_A^T(t) \cdot E_A(t) \tag{18}$$

where:

$$E_A(t) = \frac{\partial y(t)}{\partial u(t)} \cdot \frac{\partial J(t)}{\partial y(t)} \tag{19}$$

Partial derivatives $\frac{\partial y(t)}{\partial u(t)}$ and $\frac{\partial J(t)}{\partial y(t)}$ are determined from model network using backpropagation in the manner described in section 2.5.

Minimization of scalar product $\| E_A \|$ in (18) by training of action network results in minimization of Bellman sum in $J(t)$ in (13). Minimum of $J(t)$ is achieved when $\frac{\partial J(t)}{\partial y(t)} \approx 0$, as action network training criterion approaches zero, thus ensuring end of training process.

Action neural network is trained from the output network (unsupervised algorithms). Training of neural networks is carried out using (19) with the training concept shown in Figure 7c.

4.2. Dual heuristic programming

Dual Heuristic Programming optimal control algorithm is developed with a goal of increasing procedure efficiency by increasing training speed.

Model network training is the same as in HDP procedure. The improvement is in the direct calculation of the Bellman sum partial derivative over state space variables $\frac{\partial J(t+1)}{\partial y(t)}$ as output of critic network.

Structure of DHP control system is shown in Figure 8.

Training of critic neural network minimizes scalar product:

$$\|E_C\| = \sum_t E_C^T(t) \cdot E_C(t) \tag{20}$$

with

$$E_C(t) = \frac{\partial J[\hat{y}(t)]}{\partial \hat{y}(t)} - \gamma \frac{\partial J[\hat{y}(t+1)]}{\partial y(t)} - \frac{\partial U[y(t)]}{\partial y(t)} \tag{21}$$

where $\frac{\partial J[\hat{y}(t)]}{\partial \hat{y}(t)}$ represents partial derivative of Bellman sum over state space variables, and is estimated from critic network. The second part of (21) is determined by deriving

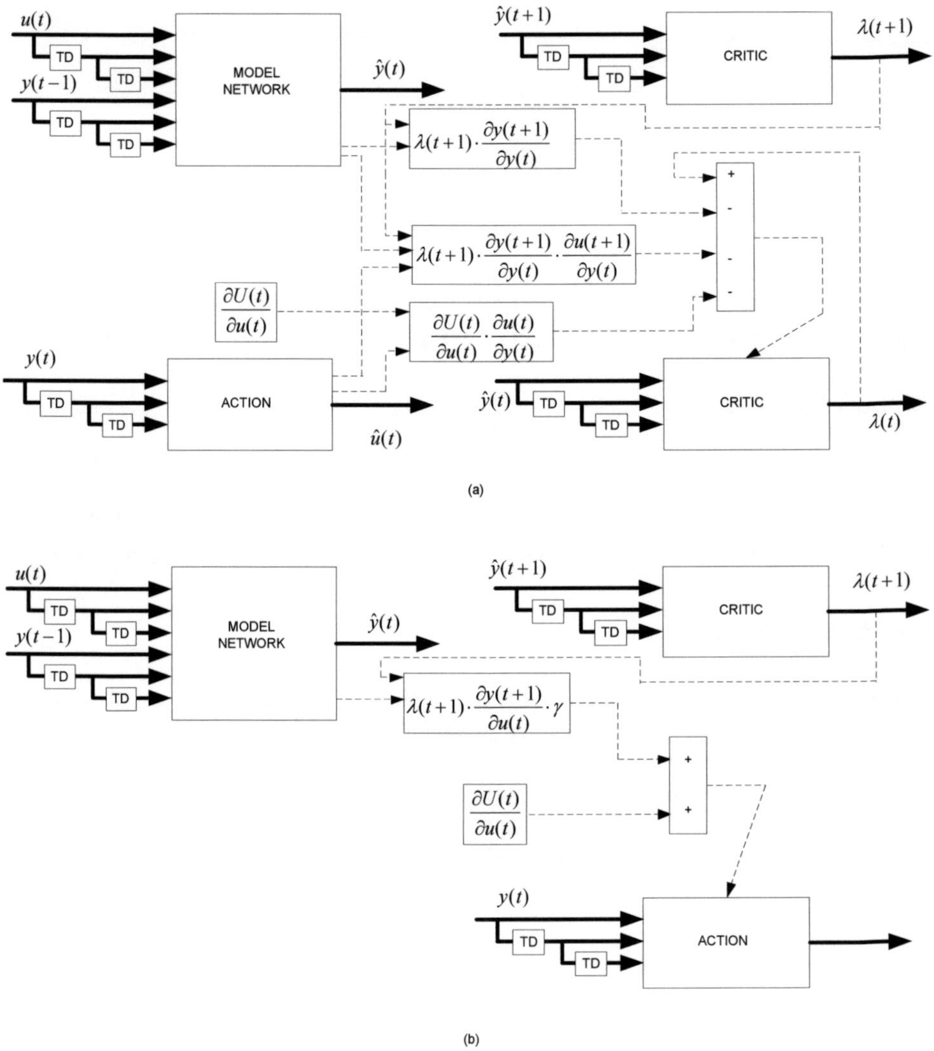

Figure 8. DHP structure, (a) Critic NN training, (b) action NN training

$$\frac{\partial J(t+1)}{\partial \hat{y}_j(t)} = \sum_{i=1}^{n} \lambda_i(t+1) \frac{\partial \hat{y}_i(t+1)}{\partial \hat{y}_j(t)} + \sum_{k=1}^{m} \sum_{i=1}^{n} \lambda_i(t+1) \frac{\partial \hat{y}_i(t+1)}{\partial \hat{u}_k(t)} \frac{\partial \hat{u}_k(t+1)}{\partial \hat{y}_j(t)} \tag{22}$$

where

$\hat{\lambda}(t+1) = \frac{\partial J[\hat{y}(t+1)]}{\partial \hat{y}(t+1)}$,

n is size of model network output vector $\hat{y}(t)$,

m is size of control vector $\hat{u}(t)$.

http://dx.doi.org/10.5772/58377

Third part of equation (22) is determined from deriving

$$\frac{\partial U(t)}{\partial Y(t)} = \sum_{k=1}^{m} \frac{\partial U(t)}{\partial u_k(t)} \frac{\partial u_k(t+1)}{\partial y_j(t)} \tag{23}$$

Somewhat simplified structure of DHP is shown in Figure 8a. Partial derivatives $\frac{\partial \hat{y}_i(t+1)}{\partial \hat{y}_j(t)}$, $\frac{\partial \hat{y}_i(t+1)}{\partial \hat{u}_k(t)}$, $\frac{\partial U(t)}{\partial u_k(t)}$ are determined from model network, and partial derivatives $\frac{\partial \hat{u}_k(t+1)}{\partial \hat{y}_j(t)}$ from action network. Prediction of states $\hat{y}(t+1)$ and $\lambda(t+1)$ is determined from model network.

Action neural network is trained to minimize Bellman sum, $\min[J(t)]$, from the criterion $\frac{\partial J[\hat{y}(t)]}{\partial \hat{y}(t)} \approx 0$.

Thus, equation (22) can be transformed to

$$\gamma \frac{\partial J[\hat{y}(t+1)]}{\partial y(t)} + \frac{\partial U[y(t)]}{\partial y(t)} = 0 \tag{24}$$

Training of Action Network minimizes scalar product:

$$\|E_A\| = \sum_t E_A^T(t) \cdot E_A(t) \tag{25}$$

with

$$E_A(t) = \gamma \frac{\partial J[\hat{y}(t+1)]}{\partial y(t)} + \frac{\partial U[y(t)]}{\partial y(t)} \tag{26}$$

Simplified training procedure of action NN is shown in Figure 8a.

Cross training of critic and action networks results in slower approximation. In order to reduce training time, it is recommended to begin the procedure with action network pre-trained as linear controller.

4.3. Global dual heuristic programming

Globalized Dual heuristic optimal control algorithm uses both algorithms described.

Critic neural network provides approximation of Bellman sum $J(t)$ and derivative $\frac{\partial J(t+1)}{\partial y(t)}$

Action network is trained using the same procedure as described for HDP and DHP.

5. Neural networks based control of excitation voltage

Main elements of electric power system are generators, transmission and distribution network and consumers. Transmission and distribution network form a power grid, which is usually very large in geographic terms. Grid control is implemented on both local and global level, mostly on the power generation side of the grid. Specific to power grid control is large number of closed control loops governing the power and voltage of synchronous generators. Transmission network is governed by setting voltage on transformers in order to minimize transmission losses. Governing of generator power and voltage achieves balance of power as well as reactive power flow on the transmission system. Voltage control also has a large impact on the dynamic system behavior.

Generator power output is governed on the generator unit. For water and steam turbine generators, it defines local power transmission to the grid, while also influencing system frequency. Considering the inertness of the generator systems, power output is not difficult to govern. Voltage control manages the balance between generator and grid voltage, and determines reactive power flow. A change in generator voltage setpoint has impact on system state variables and parameters. Disregarding system transients, a change of generator voltage causes a change on generator busbars, generator current and reactive power.

If we also consider system dynamics, generator voltage change also changes system parameters influencing system damping. Synchronous generator connected to the power grid is dominantly nonlinear in characteristics. Generator output power is proportional to generator and grid voltage, while the relation to angle between generator and grid voltage is a sinus function. Maximum theoretical output power is realized with a load angle being $\delta = \frac{\pi}{2}$. Exceeding of maximum value of load angle causes large disturbances and disconnection from power grid.

Operating point of generator connected to the grid is determined by steady state excitation current. Excitation voltage and current values dictate generator voltage, reactive power and load angle.

Frequent small disturbances expected and part of normal operating conditions, resulting in oscillations of generator electromechanical variables. Especially pronounced is the swinging of generator power, reaching several percents of nominal value, with a frequency around 1Hz. It is caused by low system damping and outer disturbances on the grid. Also present on the grid are oscillations caused by the system characteristic frequencies, usually around 0.1Hz.

Power grid can be represented as a single machine connected to an infinite bus system. For each operating point a characteristic frequency and damping can be determined.

In case of small disturbances with a synchronous generator working around predefined operating point, system can be considered linear, but only if it returns to the same operating

http://dx.doi.org/10.5772/58377

point after each disturbance. For those conditions, power system stabilizer (*PSS*) is added to AVR. Based on change of output power and load angle, it modifies voltage regulator setpoint and increases system damping. PSS is configured using linear control theory, and is presently a standard part of automatic voltage regulator systems [10].

Large disturbances occur after short circuits on the power grid, transmission and generator outages, and connection and disconnection of large loads.

Electromechanical oscillations occurring as a consequence of disturbances cause damped oscillations of all electrical and mechanical values (generator voltages and currents, active and reactive power, speed and load angle). Oscillations are also propagated by AVR to excitation system values.

Large system disturbances can cause significant changes to local parameters relevant for generator stability. Due to the linear nature of the voltage regulator system, a change in grid voltage or configuration leads to generator working in non optimal state. Even if the system returns to the same operating conditions, passing through nonlinear states during disturbance causes non optimal control, diminishing the stabilizing effects of the voltage regulator on the system. This can in turn cause another disturbance or, in case of larger units, disruption of the whole power grid. Limitations of the use of linear control systems call for an improved system which can provide optimal control of generator excitation system [13]- [15].

There is a lot of research effort directed toward design of excitation control system based on neural networks. However, very few of the demonstrated solutions have been implemented on real plants.

The goal of the chapter is to develop a practical-to-use system. This is mainly achieved by separating the design on preparation and implementation phase. Almost all algorithm steps are executed in off-line mode, up to the final step of digital voltage regulator implementation.

To implement the voltage regulator described in the chapter following equipment is needed:

- data acquisition hardware and software
- personal computer with Matlab and Simulink environment
- automatic voltage regulator with neural network support (no training support is needed)

Described controller is not adaptive. Adaptive critic design (ACD) algorithm is used for optimal control.

Classic voltage regulators (AVR) equipped with PSS can be very effective in voltage control and power system stabilization if it is used in well configured transmission grid. In such conditions the generator stays in the linear operating range and the controller maintains optimal configuration on change of active and reactive power. Voltage regulator accuracy, balance of reactive power, stabilizing effect during large disturbances and active stabilization in normal operating conditions are achieved.

If the generator is connected to relatively weak transmission grid, with possible configuration changes during operation, use of neural network based control of excitation voltage leads to better results.

5.1. HDP algorithm implementation

In order to achieve optimal control of synchronous generator connected to the power grid, it is necessary to select a minimum of two system variables – generator voltage and either output power or angular velocity. Selected variables must reflect system oscillations during disturbances. It is also necessary to choose cost function that is minimized during training. System optimization is achieved by minimization of squared generator voltage governing error $\Delta U(t)=U_{G_{REF}}-U_G$ and minimization of output power change ΔP obtained from:

$$\begin{aligned} U(t) &= \left(K_{u1}\cdot\Delta U_G(t)+K_{u2}\cdot\Delta U_G(t-1)+K_{u3}\cdot\Delta U_G(t-2)\right)^2 + \\ &\left(K_{P1}\cdot\Delta P(t)+K_{P1}\cdot\Delta P(t-1)+K_{P1}\cdot\Delta P(t-2)\right)^2 \end{aligned} \tag{27}$$

It is important to notice that the two demands are in conflict. Increase in gain in main control loop reduces static control error, but also reduces system damping and increases power output deviation ΔP. Use of cost function (27) ensures training process that increases system damping without sacrificing controller responsiveness.

System identification is carried by training model neural network. Figure 8 shows training process of model neural network. Identification of nonlinear system is made by series-parallel structure.

For ACD algorithm optimal control two output state space variables are chosen – generator voltage and output power, $y=[\Delta U_G;\Delta P]$. Vector y is used to form the cost function. Input vector is

$$u(t)=\left[\, y_r(t)\ y_r(t-1)\ y_r(t-2)\ y(t-1)\ y(t-2)\ y(t-3)\right]^T \tag{28}$$

where

$y_r=U_{GREF}$ represents generator voltage setpoint,

u_f – exciter control signal,

$y=[\Delta U_G\ \Delta P\,]^T$ is system output.

Model NN has 9 inputs and 2 outputs.

Figure 9 shows simulation block diagram of identification procedure, implemented in Matlab and Simulink environment.

http://dx.doi.org/10.5772/58377

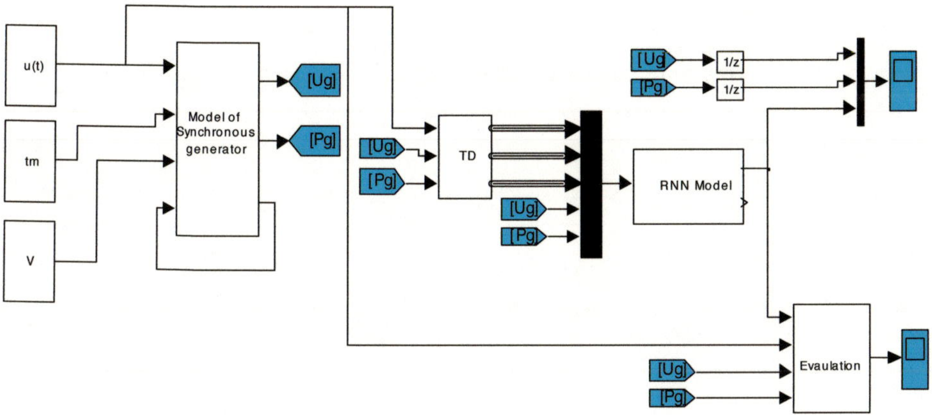

Figure 9. Model identification block diagram

A third order nonlinear mathematical model was used as a synchronous generator [20]. Synchronous generator is modeled as a single machine connected to an infinite bus. Although the model ignores initial magnetic flows, it proves to be a good approximation of an actual generator. A predictor-corrector method is used to solve differential equations.

Selected mathematical model, used with well conditioned state space variables and described methods, achieves good numerical stability during simulation, allowing for relatively large sample time (T_D=0.02s). Described model of synchronous generator is implemented in C-language S-function and used for further simulations.

For model identification, recurrent neural network is used, with five neurons in hidden layer and two neurons in output layer. Hidden layer is implemented with full recursion and *tansig* activation function. Output layer uses linear activation function.

Initial learning rate value η (21) is set to $\eta = 10^5$. It was reduced during training to $\eta = 10^2$. Training was completed in ~10000 steps. Results are shown in Figure 10. Signals U_G NN(0) and U_G NN(1) represent generator voltage at the start and at the end of RNN training. Figure 10a compares responses of control error of generator model and neural network. Voltage setpoint is generated as a pulse signal with a magnitude of ± 10%. In figure 10b, response to the change of generator power is shown. Figure 10c shows squared sum of RNN error during training.

In the same experiment efficiency of the algorithm was verified. Training was stopped after 100000 steps. For the rest of the simulation, network output is calculated without the change of weight coefficient, thus eliminating the recency effect.

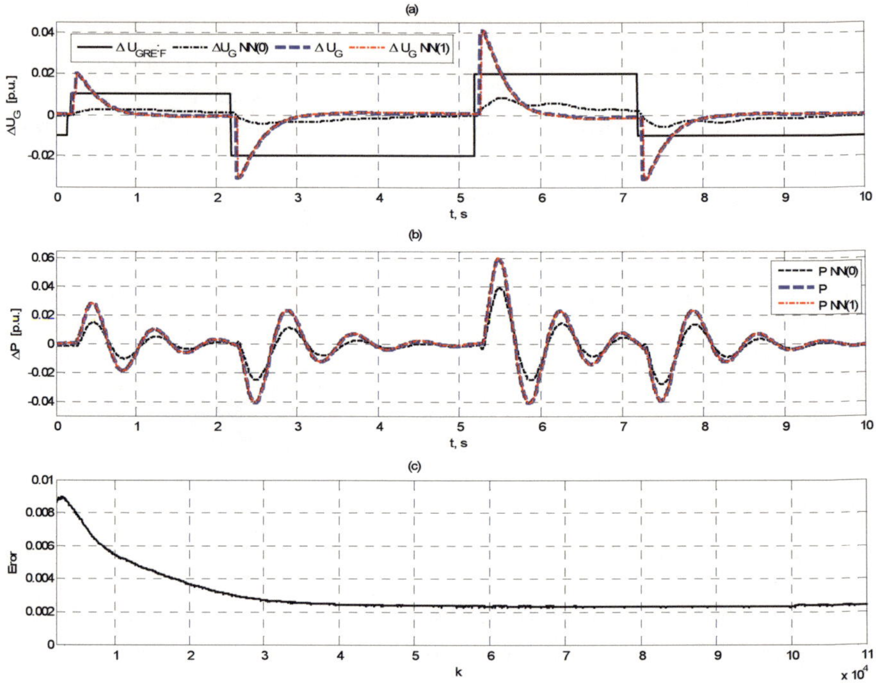

Figure 10. Training results of model neural network

Once the model neural network is trained, it is possible to create simulation for training critic and action neural networks. Simulink model of the simulation is shown in Figure 11.

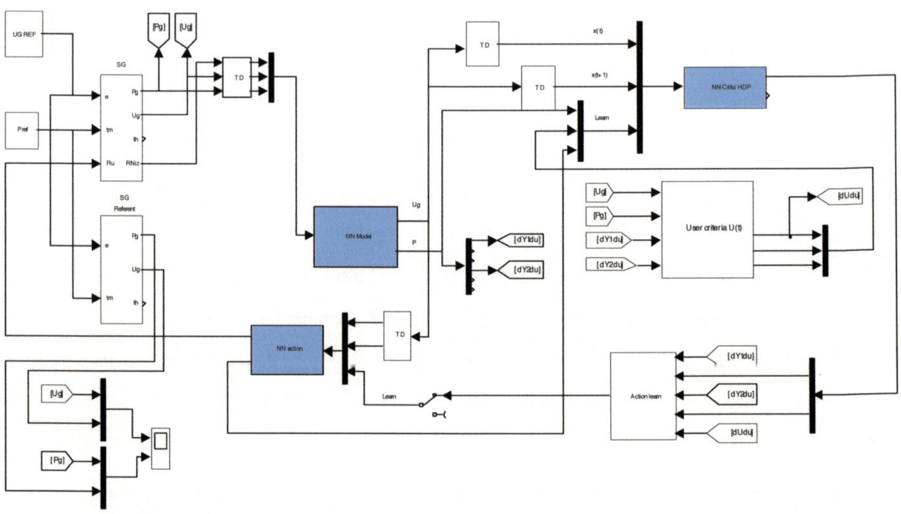

Figure 11. Simulink model for training action and critic networks

Simulation uses expressions (21), (22) and (23).

Neural network training is implemented in Matlab S-functions, written in C programming language.

Input of the S function is formed of system signals and desired value. S-function returns RNN output signals and partial derivatives of outputs $\left(\frac{\partial y_i(t)}{\partial u_j(t)}\right)$. Critic and action networks are trained in parallel.

Training results are shown in Figure 12. Figure 12a compares generator voltage response using conventional automatic voltage regulator (AVR) to neural network based controller trained using HDP algorithm. It can be seen that voltage rate of change was not degraded as a result of system damping. It is important to emphasize that generator voltage rate of change is key to system stability during large disturbances.

Figure 12b compares active power output oscillation of conventional and HDP controller. Figure 12c shows load angle, which is indicative of system stability $\left(\delta < \frac{\pi}{2}\right)$. System damping is significantly increased by use of neural network controller.

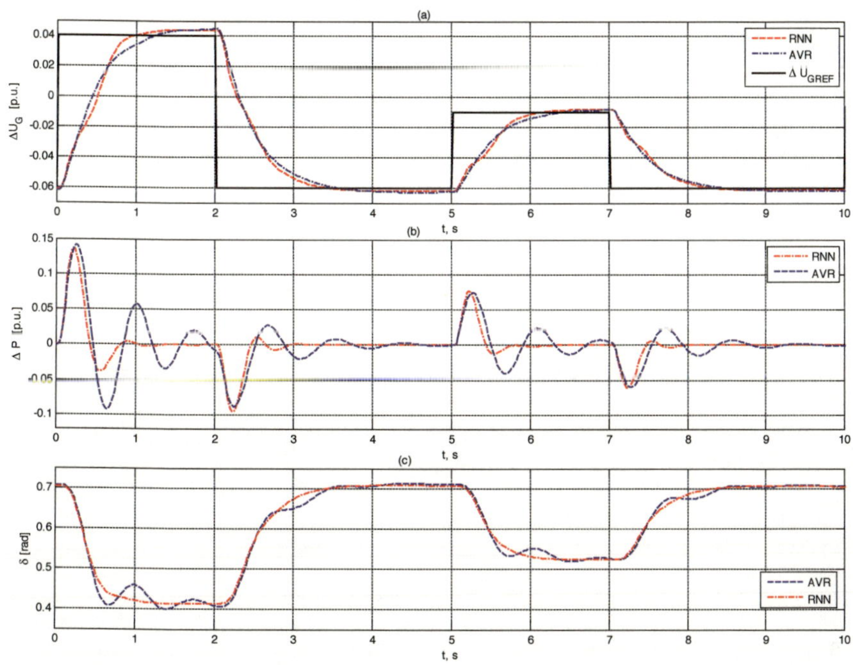

Figure 12. Response comparison of conventional AVR and HDP controller. a) generator voltage; b) generator active power; c) load angle

HDP algorithm is also verified on voltage control of synchronous generator from Simulink SimPower System block library (Synchronous Machine).

Model network is designed with one hidden recursion layer with 5 neurons. Critic and action networks use the same structure, but with four neurons in hidden layer.

HDP algorithm shown in Figure 11 is applied. Training of neural networks is performed in two steps– in first step action NN is trained to mimic classic voltage regulator, and in second step DHP algorithm is used to train both action and critic NN. It is important to get initial values of action NN in first step, as DHP needs network partial derivatives in training critic NN. Figure 13 shows training results.

Figure 13a shows comparison of classic and NN controller responses. Generator voltage rate of change is almost the same for both controllers.

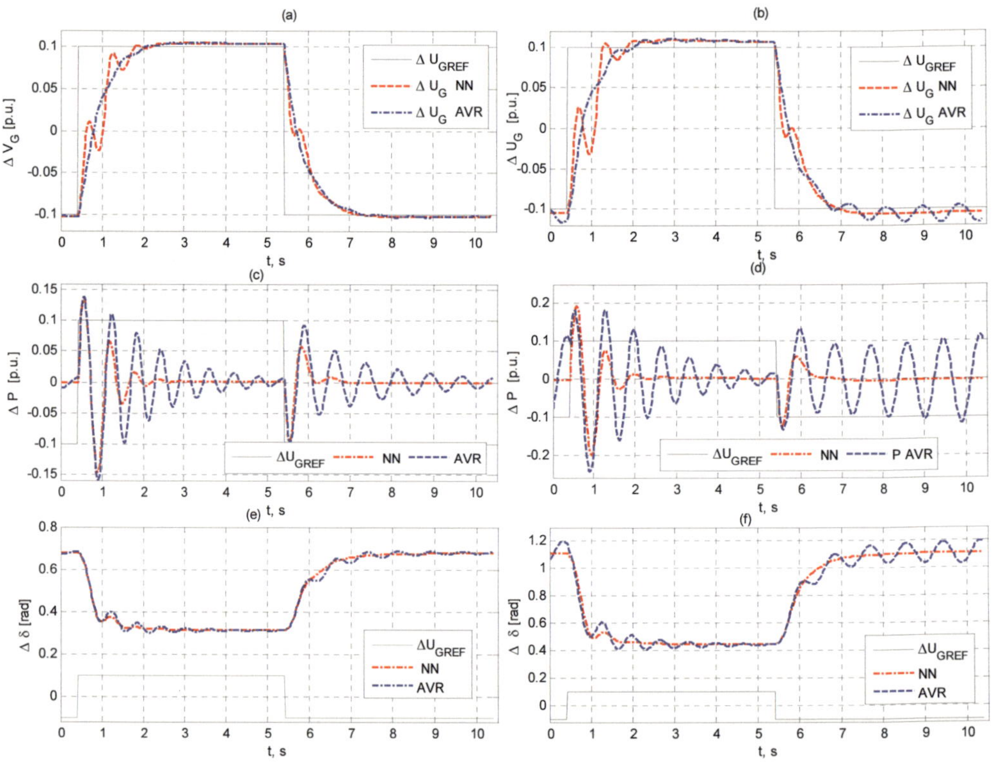

Figure 13. Response comparison of conventional AVR and HDP controller a), b) generator voltage; c), d) generator active power; e), f) load angle

Figure 13c and 13e show comparison of output power and load angle change. It is obvious that the HDP neural network controller shows significant improvement over classic regulator.

Figure 13b shows comparison of voltage transient in the condition generator voltage reduced to 90% of nominal value. Rate of change of generator voltage is maintained even during such extreme operating conditions.

Figure 13d shows conventional automatic voltage regulator (AVR) operating on the edge of stability, while the DHP controller is completely stable. Comparison of load angle values demonstrates significantly better behavior of DHP controller. On large load angles DHP controller maintains stability while conventional AVR provides low system damping, leading to instability and possible outages.

Neural network HDP voltage controllers were developed using DHP algorithm. Experimental results showed that DHP algorithm is more efficient than ADC algorithm. Implementation of GDHP does not bring significant improvements over DHP.

Application of developed S-functions enables simple use of described algorithms, as well as experimenting with different function parameters.

6. Real time windows target implementation

DHP optimal control algorithm has also been implemented using Matlab Real Time Windows Target Toolbox (RTWT), based on [18] and [19]. Simulation hardware consists of desktop PC equipped with National Instruments data acquisition card NI DAQ 6024.

Use of RTWT platform enables direct implementation of developed controllers on the real system.

In Figure 14, a system consisting of synchronous generator and RTWT controller is shown. Signal acquisition is achieved using DAQ 6062E Input, with AD conversion of the input values. Line voltage and phase current signals are processed in "Clark" S-function, using Clarke transformation. Transformed values of generator voltage U_G and generator power P are used as control feedbacks. Digital to analog conversion is performed by output module DAQ 6062 Output. All simulation blocks are part of a standard Simulink library except Clark transformation and RNN S-functions.

ACD algorithm is implemented in two steps. Classic voltage controller is used in the first step (Figure 14). In the second step it is replaced with NN controller.

During testing, generator active power and voltage were changed for a wide range of values. A pulse signal was superimposed to the generator voltage set-point value, resulting in large disturbances on the generator. To obtain measurement records RTWT Signal Visualization was used, with measured data saved in Workspace Simulink block yP. Recorded data was used to train neural network in offline mode.

A RNN was used with one hidden layer containing 5 tansig neurons. Model NN had 9 inputs and 2 outputs. Results of NN training are displayed in Figure 15.

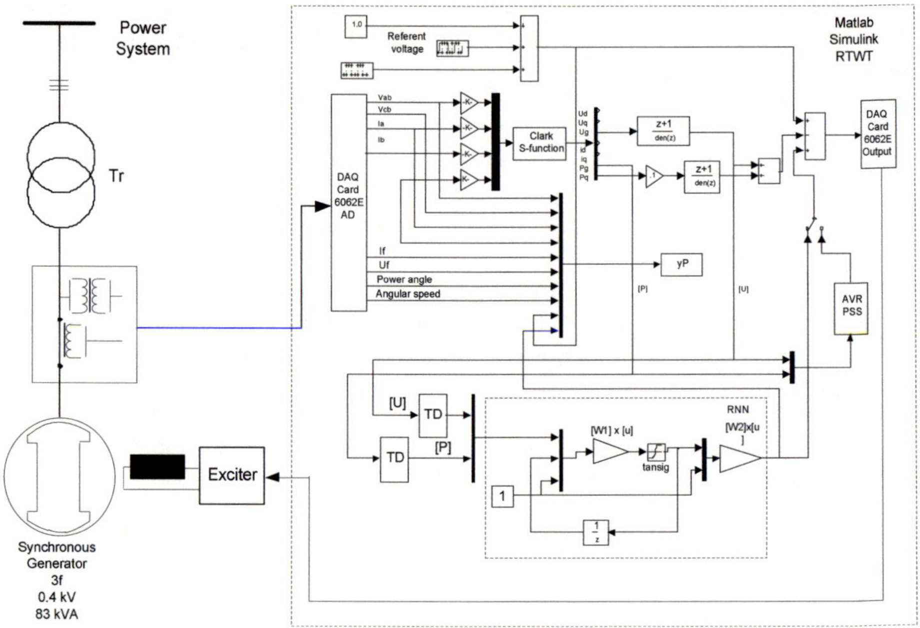

Figure 14. Automatic voltage control of synchronous generator using RTWT platform

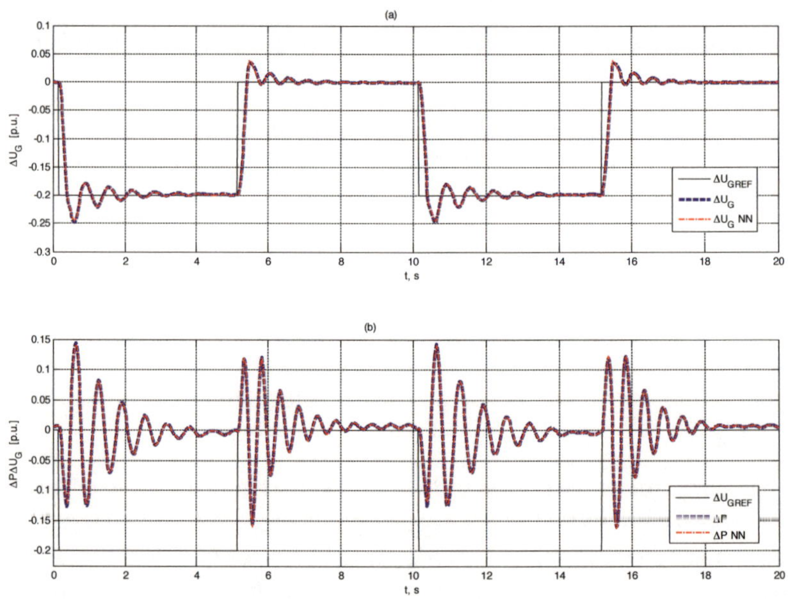

Figure 15. Results of Model NN training a) generator voltage; b) generator active power

Obtained model NN was used to train critic and action RNN using procedure described in 3. The trained action NN was transferred to Simulink block (Figure 14) and prepared for use in real time. Using RTWT module system was run in real-time mode, with trained action RNN as a voltage controller.

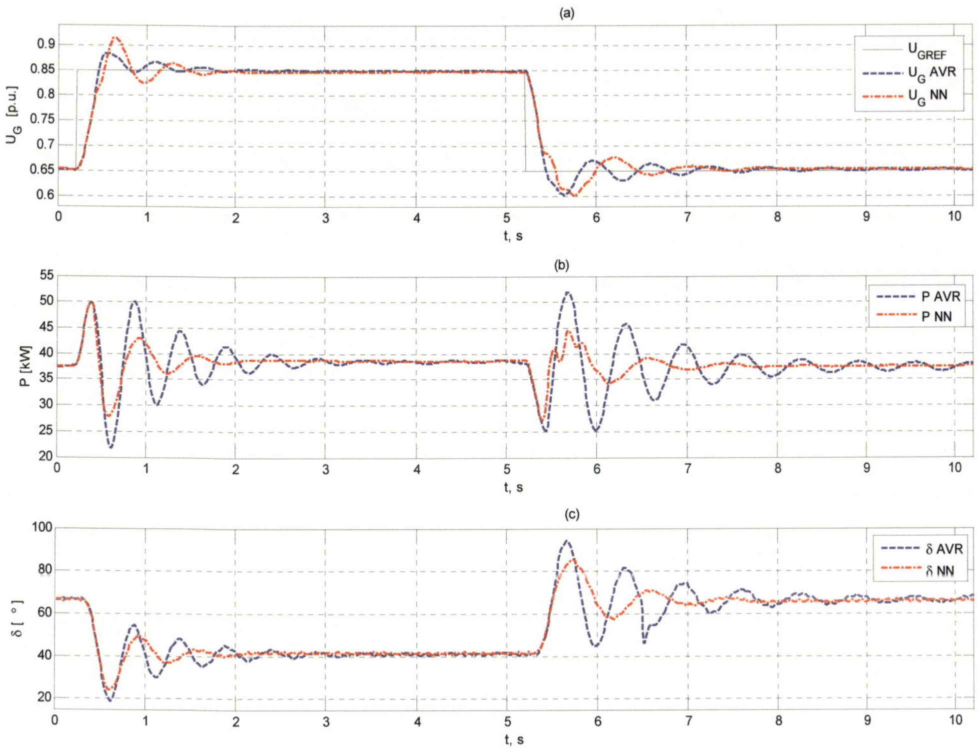

Figure 16. Classic controller and HDP NN controller – system responses: a) generator voltage; b) generator active power; c) load angle

Simulation results are shown in Figure 16, comparing classic and DHP voltage controllers. Figure 16a represents comparison between generator voltage responses and shows satisfactory rate of generator voltage change and high control accuracy. In Figure 16b, generator active power outputs are compared. Considerable damping was achieved using DHP controller. Improved system stability during large disturbances is visible in Figure 16c, where the maximum load angle deviation is significantly lower for DHP controller.

RTWT controller was implemented in sample-time mode with sample time set to $T_s = 2.5 \cdot 10^{-4} s$. Control loop sample time is $T_D = 0.02 s$.

Matlab Simulink RTWT Toolbox simplifies the transfer of developed procedures to the hardware platform.

7. Conclusion

In the chapter, a complete process of development and implementation of neural network based controller is described. Optimal control is achieved by training neural network using data obtained from real system. Developed algorithms were tested on voltage control of synchronous generator connected to the power grid.

Optimal control algorithm is implemented in Matlab and Simulink environment. Neural network training is implemented in C programming language Matlab S-function. S-function execution time was sufficiently low to achieve real time performance.

Developed algorithm is tested using Matlab Real Time Windows Target Toolbox, using the same models with minimal modifications.

Experiments performed on laboratory system show possibility of building optimal controller based on special network training procedure with no need for adaptive features.

Obtained simulation results show advantages of neural networks based controller over classic controllers. Developed procedure can relatively easily be adapted for use on real systems.

Appendices

Appendix A

Matlab function for calculating hidden layer derivatives of outputs over weight coefficients of hidden layer.

```
function[dadWR,a]=dadWR(WW1,WW2,p,a_1,dadWR_1,NW1,NW2);
%function determines the partial derivative  output recursive hidden%layers to weight coefficients matrix WW1% WW1 matrix of hidden layer% WW2 matrix of output layer% NW1 number of neurons in the hidden layer% NW2 length of the output vector neural networks% Ni  length of the input vector neural networks% J  target output value of the neural network% a output value of hidden layer neurons % p  input vector of the hidden layer of recurrent neural network

Ni=length(p)-NW1;
a_temp=WW1*[p; 1];
a=tansig(a_temp);
Ia=ones(NW1,1)-(a.*a);  %value of derivative tansig activation function of neurons -
%y=WW2*a;
%J=J-y;
for l=1:NW1
    for i=1:NW1
        for j=1:Ni+NW1
            dadar_temp=0;
            for k=1:NW1;
                dadar_temp=dadar_temp+WW1(l,Ni+k)*dadWR_1(k,(i-1)*Ni+j);
```

```
            end
            dadWR(l,(i-1)*(Ni+NW1)+j)=Ia(i)*((l==i)*p(j)+dadar_temp);

        end,
    end,
end,

%end  function dadWR
```

Appendix B

S-function for RNN training with one hidden layer.

The first part defines sample time, number of inputs, outputs and neurons. Input is formed of values used for training. Output 1 is RNN output. Output 2 is partial derivative of output over input. Training is performed using Kalman filter.

```
/*  File    : model.c *  Abstract: *  For more details about S-functions, see
simulink/src/sfuntmpl_doc.c. *  Copyright 1990-2002 The MathWorks, Inc. *  $Re-
vision: 1.12 $ */
                        /* ================model===================== * This s-
function is used for learning recurrent neural network (RNN) in programming en-
vironment Matlab Simulink * Learning RNN is implemented using the Kalman
filter * This program supports RNN with one hidden layer * In the first part
defines the time discretization, number of inputs, number of outputs and * the
number of neurons in a single hidden layer * Simultaneously with learning RNN
this function account the partial derivative of output per inputs * Port num-
ber of the s-function is equal to the number of inputs in RNN + number of out-
puts * Mato Miskovic Imotica */#define S_FUNCTION_NAME model
#define S_FUNCTION_LEVEL 2
#include "simstruc.h"
#include <math.h>
#include <string.h>

#define TS 1    //sample time
#define N_ULD 3 //number of inputs
#define N_TD 1  //number of steps backwards (t-1), (t-3),(t-3), (t-N_TD)
#define NUL     (N_ULD*N_TD)
#define NIZ 1   //number outputs
#define W1 5    // number of neurons in the hidden layer
#define W1_j    (NUL+W1+1)    //
#define W2_j    (W1+1)
#define W1_ij   (NUL+W1+1)*W1
#define W2_ij   NIZ*W2_j
#define N_W1    0
#define N_W2    N_W1+W1_ij
#define SIZE_P   (W1_ij+W2_ij)
#define N_P     N_W2+W2_ij
#define NH_1    N_P+ SIZE_P*SIZE_P
#define N_dadWR NH_1+W1
#define N_OUT   N_dadWR+W1*W1_ij
#define N_dnet  N_OUT+NIZ
```

```
#define N_ON     N_dnet+NIZ*N_ULD
#define NX       N_ON+10 //
#define ETTAMI 10.0   //final value of the   learning rate
#define ETTAQ .051    // Q
#define ITER_UCI 20000  //number of steps to stop learning RNN
#define NDISCSTATES NX

static
                    void ttsig(real_T x, real_T *y)  //tansig
{
    *y=2.0/(1.0+exp(-2.0*x))-1.0;
}
//AxB=C multiplying matrices in line form
static
                      void aputab_c(real_T *aa, real_T *bb, real_T *cc, int_T
a_r, int_T a_c, int_T b_c){
    int_T i, j, k;
    real_T priv;
    for(i=0; i<a_r  ;i++){
        for(j=0;j<b_c;j++){
            priv=0;
            for(k=0;k<a_c;k++)  {
                priv=priv+aa[k+i*a_c]*bb[j+b_c*k];
            }
            cc[i*b_c+j]=priv;
        }
    }
}
//XxB=C multiplying matrices in line form,  x from SimStruc
static
                      void xputab_c_pok(SimStruct *S, real_T *bb, real_T *cc,
int_T a_r, int_T a_c, int_T b_c, int_T x_p){
    int_T i, j, k;
    real_T priv;
    real_T *x       = ssGetRealDiscStates(S);
    for(i=0; i<a_r  ;i++){
        for(j=0;j<b_c;j++){
            priv=0;
            for(k=0;k<a_c;k++)  {
                priv=priv+x[x_p+k+i*a_c]*bb[j+b_c*k];
            }
            cc[i*b_c+j]=priv;
        }
    }
}
//AxX=C multiplying matrices in line form,  x from SimStruc
static
                      void aputax_c_pok(SimStruct *S, real_T *aa, real_T *cc,
int_T a_r, int_T a_c, int_T b_c, int_T x_p){
    int_T i, j, k;
    real_T priv;
    real_T *x       = ssGetRealDiscStates(S);
```

```
    for(i=0; i<a_r  ;i++){
        for(j=0;j<b_c;j++){
            priv=0;
            for(k=0;k<a_c;k++)  {
                priv=priv+aa[k+i*a_c]*x[x_p+j+b_c*k];  }
            cc[i*b_c+j]=priv;
        }
    }
}
//AxB=X multiplying matrices in line form,  x to SimStruc
static
                    void aputab_x_pok(SimStruct *S, real_T *aa, real_T *bb,
int_T a_r, int_T a_c, int_T b_c, int_T x_p){
    int_T i, j, k;
    real_T priv;
    real_T *x       = ssGetRealDiscStates(S);
    for(i=0; i<a_r  ;i++){
        for(j=0;j<b_c;j++){
            priv=0;
            for(k=0;k<a_c;k++)  {
                priv=priv+aa[k+i*a_c]*bb[j+b_c*k];
            }
            x[x_p+i*b_c+j]=priv;
        }
    }
}
static
                    void transp(real_T *aa, real_T *bb, int_T a_r, int_T a_c)
{ //transposed matrix
    int_T i, j;
    for(i=0; i<a_c  ;i++){
        for(j=0; j<a_r  ;j++){
            bb[i*a_r+j]=aa[i+j*(a_c)];  }}
}
static
                    void invmatrix(real_T *aa, int_T n){ // inverse matrixin
inline form
    int_T l, m, p;
    int_T pos, p_old;
    int_T p_old2;
    for(l=0;l<n;l++){
        p_old2=l*n+l;
        aa[p_old2]=1/(aa[p_old2]);
        for(m=0;m<n;m++)
            if(m!=l){
            p_old=m*n+l;
            aa[p_old]=aa[p_old]*aa[p_old2];
            }
        for(m=0;m<n;m++){
            for(p=0;p<n;p++){
                if(m!=l){
                    if(p!=l){
```

```
                        pos=m*n+p;
                        p_old=m*n+l;
                        p_old2=l*n+p;
                        aa[pos]=aa[pos]-(aa[p_old]*aa[p_old2]);
                    }
                }
            }
        }

        p_old=l*n+l;
        for(p=0;p<n;p++)
            if(p!=l){
            pos=l*n+p;
            aa[pos]=-aa[p_old]*aa[pos];
            }
    }
    pos=n*n;
}
/*=====================*
 * S-function methods *
 *=====================*/
static
                    void mdlInitializeSizes(SimStruct *S) {
    ssSetNumSFcnParams(S, 0);  /* Number of expected parameters */
    if (ssGetNumSFcnParams(S) != ssGetSFcnParamsCount(S)) {
        return; /* Parameter mismatch will be reported by Simulink */
    }
    ssSetNumContStates(S, 0);
    ssSetNumDiscStates(S, NDISCSTATES);
    if (!ssSetNumInputPorts(S, 1)) return;
    ssSetInputPortWidth(S, 0, NUL+NIZ);
    if (!ssSetNumOutputPorts(S, 2)) return;
    ssSetOutputPortWidth(S, 0, NIZ);
    ssSetOutputPortWidth(S, 1, NIZ*N_ULD);
    ssSetNumSampleTimes(S, 1);
    ssSetNumRWork(S, 0);
    ssSetNumIWork(S, 0);
    ssSetNumPWork(S, 0);
    ssSetNumModes(S, 0);
    ssSetNumNonsampledZCs(S, 0);
    ssSetOptions(S, SS_OPTION_EXCEPTION_FREE_CODE);
}
static
                    void mdlInitializeSampleTimes(SimStruct *S) {
    ssSetSampleTime(S, 0, TS);
    ssSetOffsetTime(S, 0, 0.0);
}
#define MDL_INITIALIZE_CONDITIONS
// Function: mdlInitializeConditions ========================================
static
                    void mdlInitializeConditions(SimStruct *S) {
    real_T *x0 = ssGetRealDiscStates(S);
```

```
    int_T  i, j;
    real_T  tempRAND[22]={0.66, 0.01, 0.42, -0.14, -0.39, -0.62, -0.61, 0.36,
-0.39, 0.08, -0.69, 0.39, -0.24, 0.72, 0.7, 0.18, -0.01, 0.79, 0.64, 0.28,
0.6359, 0.32};
    for (i=0; i<W1_ij+W2_ij; i++){
        x0[i]=.1*tempRAND[i-(i/20)*20];}
    for (i=0; i<SIZE_P; i++){
        for (j=0; j<SIZE_P; j++){
            if (i==j){
                x0[N_P + i*SIZE_P+j]=1000;
            }
        }
    }
}
// Function: mdlOutputs ==========================================================


static
                    void mdlOutputs(SimStruct *S, int_T tid) {
    real_T              *Y     = ssGetOutputPortRealSignal(S, 0);
    real_T              *DY    = ssGetOutputPortRealSignal(S, 1);
    real_T              *x     = ssGetRealDiscStates(S);
    int_T i;

    //InputRealPtrsType uPtrs = ssGetInputPortRealSignalPtrs(S,0);
    UNUSED_ARG(tid); /* not used in single tasking mode */

    for (i=0;i<NIZ;i++)
        Y[i]=x[N_OUT+i];
    for (i=0; i<NIZ*N_ULD; i++)
        DY[i]= x[N_dnet+i];
}
#define MDL_UPDATE
//Function: mdlUpdate =========================================================
static
                    void mdlUpdate(SimStruct *S, int_T tid) {
    int_T  i, j, k, priv_i;
    real_T priv;
    real_T   WW1[W1][W1_j];
    real_T   WW2[NIZ][W2_j];
    real_T   a_pr[W1]={0};
    real_T   a[W1+1]={0};
    real_T   JJ[NIZ]={0};
    real_T   W1R[W1*W1]={0};
    real_T   oout[NIZ];
    real_T   WW2pr[NIZ*W1]={0};
    real_T   dadWR[W1*W1_ij];
    real_T   I_a[W1];
    real_T   PP[W1*W1_ij];
    real_T   dYdW[NIZ*SIZE_P]={0};
    real_T   dYdW_T[NIZ*(SIZE_P)];
    real_T   h_WxP [NIZ*SIZE_P];
```

```
    real_T   K[SIZE_P*NIZ];
    real_T   Ppr[SIZE_P*SIZE_P];
    real_T   Kxh_W[SIZE_P*SIZE_P];
    real_T   pu[W1_j];
    real_T   Apr[NIZ*NIZ]={0};
    real_T   Pxh_W[SIZE_P*NIZ] ;
    real_T   NNx[SIZE_P] ;
    real_T   dnet[NIZ*N_ULD]={0};
    real_T   ettami=0;
    int_T    SIZE_PxSIZE_P=SIZE_P*SIZE_P;
    int_T    W1xW1_ij=W1*W1_ij;
    real_T              *x        = ssGetRealDiscStates(S);
    InputRealPtrsType uPtrs       = ssGetInputPortRealSignalPtrs(S, 0);
    x[N_ON]=x[N_ON]+TS;
    pu[NUL+W1]=1.0;
    for (i=0; i<NUL; i++){
        pu[i]=*uPtrs[i];
    }
    for (i=0; i<W1; i++){
        pu[NUL+i]=x[NH_1+i];
    }
    pu[NUL+W1]=1.0;
    for (i=0; i<NIZ; i++){
        JJ[i]=*uPtrs[NUL+i];
    }
    for (i=0; i<W1; i++) {
        for (j=0; j<W1_j; j++) {
            WW1[i][j]=x[N_W1+i*W1_j+j];
        }
    }
    for (i=0; i<NIZ; i++) {
        for (j=0; j<W2_j; j++) {
            WW2[i][j]=x[N_W2+i*W2_j+j];
        }
    }
    for (i=0; i<W1; i++) {
        for (j=0; j<W1; j++) {
            W1R[i*W1+j]=WW1[i][NUL+j];
        }
    }
     xputab_c_pok(S, pu, a_pr, W1, W1_j, 1, 0);//xputab_c_pok(S,bb, cc, a_r,
a_c,  b_c, x_p)
    for (i=0; i<W1; i++)  {               //a
        ttsig(a_pr[i], &a[i]);       // ttsig(real_T x,real_T *y)
        x[NH_1+i]=a[i];
    }
    a[W1]=1.0;
    for (i=0; i<W1; i++)
        I_a[i]=1.0-a[i]*a[i];
    xputab_c_pok(S, a, oout, NIZ, W2_j, 1, N_W2);           //Y=WW2*[a;1];
    for (i=0; i<NIZ; i++){
        x[N_OUT+i]=oout[i];
```

```
        JJ[i]=JJ[i]-oout[i];
    }
    for (i=0; i<W1*W1_ij; i++)
        PP[i]=0;
    for (i=0; i<W1_j; i++)
        PP[i]=pu[i];
    for (i=1; i<W1; i++){
        for (j=0; j<W1_j; j++){
            PP[i*(W1_ij+W1_j)+j]=pu[j];
        }
    }
    //dnet
    for (i=0; i<NIZ; i++){
        for (j=0; j<N_ULD; j++){
            priv=0.0;
            dnet[i*N_ULD+j]=0.0;
            for (k=0; k<W1; k++){
                priv=priv+WW2[i][k]*(1.0-(a[k]*a[k]))*WW1[k][j*N_TD];}
            x[N_dnet+i*N_ULD+j]=priv;
        }
    }
    aputax_c_pok(S, W1R, dadWR, W1, W1, W1_ij, N_dadWR);
    for (i=0; i<W1xW1_ij; i++)
        PP[i]=PP[i]+0.9*dadWR[i];
    for(i=0;i<W1;i++){
        for(j=0;j<W1_ij;j++){
            x[N_dadWR+i*W1_ij+j]=I_a[i]*PP[i*W1_ij+j];
        }
    }
    for(i=0;i<NIZ;i++){
        for(j=0;j<W1_ij;j++){
            priv=0.0;
            for(k=0;k<W1;k++){
                priv=priv+x[N_W2+i*W2_j+k]*x[N_dadWR+k*W1_ij+j];
            }
            dYdW[i*SIZE_P+j]=priv;
        }
    }

    for(i=0; i<NIZ; i++) {                                   // dydW2
        for(j=0; j<W2_j; j++){
            dYdW[W1_ij+i*(W1_ij+W2_ij+W2_j)+j]=a[j];
        }
    }
    //Kalman
    transp(dYdW, dYdW_T, NIZ, SIZE_P); //dYdW_T=dYdW'
    aputax_c_pok(S, dYdW, h_WxP, NIZ, SIZE_P, SIZE_P, N_P);
    aputab_c(h_WxP, dYdW_T, Apr, NIZ, SIZE_P, NIZ);
    if ( x[N_ON] > ITER_UCI )
        etttami=1e90*ETTAMI;
    else etttami=ETTAMI+1000*ETTAMI/(x[N_ON]+1.0);
    for (i=0; i<NIZ*NIZ; i=i+NIZ+1){
```

```
        Apr[i]=Apr[i]+etttami;
    }
    invmatrix(Apr, NIZ);
    xputab_c_pok(S, dYdW_T, Pxh_W, SIZE_P, SIZE_P, NIZ, N_P);
    aputab_c(Pxh_W, Apr, K, SIZE_P, NIZ, NIZ);     //K=PM*h_WM*A;
    aputab_c(K, JJ, NNx, SIZE_P, NIZ, 1);
    for(i=0; i<SIZE_P; i++){
        x[i]=x[i] +NNx[i];
    }
    aputab_c(K, dYdW, Kxh_W, SIZE_P, NIZ, SIZE_P); //K*h_WM
    aputax_c_pok(S, Kxh_W, Ppr, SIZE_P, SIZE_P, SIZE_P, N_P);
     for (i=0; i<SIZE_P; i++){     Ppr[i*(SIZE_P+1)]=Ppr[i*(SIZE_P+1)] - ETTAQ/
(x[N_ON]+1.0);
    }
    for (i=0; i<SIZE_PxSIZE_P; i++)
        x[N_P+i]=x[N_P+i]-1*Ppr[i];
    UNUSED_ARG(tid);
}
// mdlTerminate
static
                    void mdlTerminate(SimStruct *S) {
    int_T i, j;
    real_T          *x       = ssGetRealDiscStates(S);
    printf("\n");
    for(i=0; i<W1*W1_j+NIZ*W2_j; i++){
        printf("%f\t", x[i]);
    }
    UNUSED_ARG(S);
}

#ifdef  MATLAB_MEX_FILE    /* Is this file being compiled as a MEX-file? */
#include "simulink.c"      /* MEX-file interface mechanism */
#else
#include "cg_sfun.h"       /* Code generation registration function */
#endif
```

Author details

Mato Miskovic[1], Ivan Miskovic[2] and Marija Mirosevic[3]

1 HEP Hydro-power Dubrovnik, Dubrovnik, Croatia

2 Brodarski Institute, Zagreb, Croatia

3 University of Dubrovnik, Dubrovnik, Croatia

References

[1] P.Werbos "Aproximate dynamic programming for real-time control and neural modeling" in Handbook of Intelligent Control, White and Sofge Eds. New York: Van Nostrand Reinhold, pp493-525.

[2] D. Prokhorov: "Adaptive critic design", IEEE Trans. Neural Networks, vol. 8, pp. 997-1007, Sept 1997.

[3] Wiliams, R. J. and Zisper D: "A learning agorithm for continually running fully recurrent neural networks", Neural Copmutation, 1:270-280.

[4] Pedro DeLima: "Application of Adaptive Critic Designs for Fault Tolerant Control", IEEE Computational intelligence Society Walter J Karplus Summer Research Grant 2004.

[5] R.E. Kalman, "A new approach to linear filtering and prediction problems,"Transactions of the ASME, Ser. D, Journal of Basic Engineering, 82, 35–45 (1960).

[6] G.V. Puskorius and L. A. Feldkamp: "Neurocontrol of Nonlinear Dynamic Systems with Kalman Filter Trained Recurrent Networks", IEEE Trans. on Neural Networks, 5(14), 279-297.

[7] Simon S. Haykin: "Kalman Filtering and Neural Networks", 2001

[8] M. Cernasky, L. Benuskova:" Simple recurrent network trained by RTRL and extended Kalman filter algorithms" Neural Network World 13(3) (2003) 223–234

[9] Narendra K.S., Parthasarathy K. "Identification and Control of Dynamical Systems Using Neural Networks", IEEE transaction on Neural Networks, 1:4-27, March 1990.

[10] IEEE recommended practice for excitation system models for power system stability studies, : IEEE St. 421.5-2002 (Section 9).

[11] W. Mielczarski and A. M. Zajaczkowski "Nonlinear Field Voltage Control of a Synchronous Generator using Feedback Linearization", Automatica Vol 30, pp1625-1630, 1994.

[12] P. Shamsollahi, O. P. Malik, "Real time Implementation and Experimental Studies of a Neural Adaptive Power System Stabilizer", IEEE Trans. on Energy Conversion, Vol. 14. No. 3, September 1999.

[13] G. K. Venayagamoorthy, Ronald G. Harley, and Donald Wuncsh "Implementation off an adaptive neural network for efective control of turbogenerators" *IEEE Budapest Power Tech. Conf. 1999. paper BPT99 pp 431 – 23.*

[14] T. Kobayashi and A. Yokoyama, "An Adaptive Neuro-Control System of Synchronous Generator for Power system stabilization", IEEE Trasaction on Energy Conversion, Vol. 11, No. 3, September 1996.

[15] D.Flynn, S. McLonne, G. W. Irwin, M. D. Brown, E. Swidenbank, and B. W. Hogg, "Neural control turbogeneraroe systems", Automatica, vol 33, no,11, pp. 1961 – 1973, 1997.

[16] Q.H. Wu, B.W. Hogg, G.W. Irwin " A neural network regulator for turbogenerators," IEEE Trans. on Neural Network, vol. 3, no. 1, pp. 95-100, Jan 1992.

[17] G. K. Venayagamoorthy, Ronald G. Harley, and Donald Wuncsh "Implementation off an adaptive neural network for efective control of turbogenerators" IEEE Budapest Power Tech. Conf. 1999. paper BPT99 pp 431 – 23.

[18] MATLAB the Language of Technical Computing, http://www.mathworks.com/help/rtwin/index.html

[19] MATLAB the Language of Technical Computing, http://www.mathworks.com/products/matlab

[20] M.Miskovic " Extended Synchronous Generator Operation Region Using Neural Network Based Adaptive Control ", PhD thesis, FER Zagreb 2007.

[21] M. Miskovic, M.Mirosevic, G.Erceg *"Load angle estimation of a synchronous generator using dynamical neural networks"*//Energija 02 (2009.) ; 174-191.

[22] Miskovic, Mato; Mirosevic, Marija; Miskovic, Ivan. On-line Identification of Synchronous Generator Mathematical Model // ICRERA 2012 Proceedings / Kurokawa, Fujio (ur.). Nagasaki, Japan : University of Nagasaki, 2012. 1-3

[23] Matuško, Jadranko; Petrović, Ivan; Perić, Nedjeljko. Neural network based tire/road friction force estimation. Engineering Applications of Artificial Intelligence. (2007), 15 pages

[24] Sumina, Damir; Bulic, Neven; Miskovic, Mato. Parameter tuning of power system stabilizer using eigenvalue sensitivity. // Electric power systems research. 81 (2011), 12; 2171-2177

Chapter 5

Design of Fractionation Columns

Hassan Al-Haj Ibrahim

Additional information is available at the end of the chapter

http://dx.doi.org/10.5772/57249

1. Introduction

Distillation is a physical process used to separate a fluid mixture of two (binary) or more (multi-component) substances into its component parts. In most cases, the components to be separated are miscible liquids with different volatilities and boiling points. This separation process is a thermal unit operation that utilizes the differences of vapour pressure to produce the separation. In this process, the vapour or liquid mixture is heated whereby the more volatile components are evaporated, condensed and allowed to drip or drip apart, i.e. distil or destillare, as it was originally called in Latin. It is from this fact of 'Dripping' that the name of the distillation process was derived.

Distillation may be carried out in an intermittent or batch process or it may be carried out in a continuous steady-state process with a continuous feed stream. Distillation systems may also operate at different pressures, with higher pressures used for the separation of the more volatile materials and reduced pressures, in vacuum distillation systems, for heavier higher boiling-point materials, lowering thereby their boiling points.

Simple distillation of alcoholic beverages and petroleum has been practiced for a very long time. In the Middle Ages, Damascus played a part as a distilling centre, where distillation came into its own as the best and quickest way of obtaining pure chemical substances [1]. In the writings of the thirteenth century Syrian Scholar, Al-Dimashki, we find the earliest reference to the industrial distillation of crude oil or petroleum. Al-Dimashki says: "Many types of petroleum are water white by nature and so volatile that they can not be stored in open vessels. Others are obtained from a kind of pitch or bitumen in a turbid and dark condition, but by further treatment they can be made clear and white by distilling them like rose-water" [1].

An earlier account of crude oil distillation was given by Rhases (865-925) in his book Sirr alasrar (Secretum secretorum or Secret of secrets), and in 1512 Hieronymus Brunschwig wrote a book

INTECH
open science | open minds

© 2014 The Author(s). Licensee InTech. This chapter is distributed under the terms of the Creative Commons Attribution License (http://creativecommons.org/licenses/by/3.0), which permits unrestricted use, distribution, and reproduction in any medium, provided the original work is properly cited.

on the true art of distillation (Das Buch der wahren Kunst zu destillieren). The theory of distillation, however, was first studied by Sorel in 1893 in his book on the distillation (Rectification) of alcohol, in which, interestingly, he says that the aim of distillation is the production (Fabrication) of alcohol and alcoholic liquors [2]. Mathematical analysis of the distillation (of binary mixtures) was first carried out in 1902 by Lord Rayleigh [3].

2. Fractional distillation

In common industrial jargon, distillation is used sometimes to mean fractional, and not merely simple, distillation. Fractional distillation, or fractionation, however, is in fact a special type of distillation, and as a separation technique, is much more effective than simple distillation and more efficient. In effect, fractionation is equivalent to a series of distillations, where the separation is achieved by successive distillations or repeated vaporization-condensation cycles[1]. Each vaporization-condensation cycle makes for an equilibrium stage, commonly known as a theoretical stage. A number of such theoretical stages may be required for the efficient fractionation and separation of the vapour or liquid mixture. The McCabe-Thiele method is a graphical method that may often be used to calculate the required number of theoretical stages. These theoretical stages will then have to be converted to actual plates or an equivalent packed height depending upon separation efficiency for a particular service.

In fractional distillation the components are separated through continuous heat and mass transfer between counter-current streams of a rising vapour and a descending liquid. As in all thermal separation processes, the motive force for the separation is the drive towards thermodynamic equilibrium between the different phases (VLE or vapour liquid equilibrium). This equilibrium is continuously disturbed by the mixing of the colder descending liquid and the hotter rising vapour, where the more volatile components of the descending liquid are vaporized and the less volatile components of the rising vapour are condensed and the driving force for the separation process is thereby maintained. The concentration of the lighter components will be greater in the vapour phase and conversely the concentration of the heavier components will be greater in the liquid phase, and only in the case of pure components or azeotropic mixtures will the equilibrium composition be the same in both phases.

Fractional distillation is much more recent than simple classical distillation. Its invention is often attributed to an illiterate French workman from Rouen, Edouard Adam by name, who succeeded in obtaining concentrated alcohol in a single distillation (Seule distillation). Although he patented his rectification still in 1801, he was not successful in commercializing his invention and several distillers built similar stills and he died poor in 1807 [4].

In recent years, fractional distillation has become one of the most important unit operations in chemical engineering industries. It is by far the most common specialized separation technology. It has been variously estimated that the capital investment in separation

1 In fact, the term used in Arabic for fractional distillation (Takreer) is derived from this repeated vaporization-condensation cycles.

equipment is 40-50% of the total for a conventional fluid processing unit. In the USA, fractionators are used in 90 to 95% of the separations [5]. In 1992, Darton estimated the world-wide throughput of distillation columns at 5 billion tonnes of crude oil and 130 million tonnes of petrochemicals per year.

In petroleum refineries in particular, atmospheric fractionation of crude oil, variously known as topping, is the first and the most important process of the series of oil refinery operations [6]. The crude oil feedstock, which is a very complex multi-component mixture, is separated into a number of products or fractions, with each product or fraction being composed of groups of compounds within a relatively small range of boiling points. These straight-run products or fractions are the origin of the term fractional distillation or fractionation. Fractionation, however, is not used in the petroleum refining industry only, but is also used in other chemical, petrochemical, beverage and pharmaceutical industries and in natural gas processing plants.

Fractionation, though widely used, is one of the most energy intensive operations. In fact, distillation may be the largest consumer of energy in petroleum and petrochemical processing. Of the total energy consumption of an average unit, the separation steps accounts for about 70% and distillation alone can consume more than 50% of a plant's operating energy cost [7]. Fractional distillation accounts for about 95% of the total distillation consumption [8]. Back in 1988, speaking of distillation, Dr. Frits Zuiderweg wrote:

"Distillation is the most important and most visible separation technology. The skyline of many refineries and chemical plants is dominated by tall distillation towers, and it cannot be denied that their spatial arrangements often amount to architectural beauty. Less spectacular, but also visible are the smoke stacks of these industrial complexes; they represent the energy used in processing, the major part of which is consumed by distillation processes" [9].

Replacing fractionation by other separation techniques in such industries as petroleum and petrochemical industries is, however, highly unlikely despite its energy intensiveness. The pre-eminence of distillation for the separation of fluid mixtures is fundamental for both kinetic and thermodynamic reasons [9]. It may also be the most economical process for the separation and production of high-purity products. In general, distillation is favoured over other separation techniques when large rates are desired of products that are thermally stable with relative volatility greater than 1.2 and where no extreme corrosion, precipitation, sedimentation or explosion issues are present [10].

The lunar environment would offer some unique advantages for distillation processes, as has been pointed out in an interesting paper on fractional distillation in a lunar environment [11]. Due to the cryogenic temperatures available on the moon, vacuum distillation would be possible with lower heat loads and cleaner separations [11].

3. Fractionation columns

In normal practice, fractionation is carried out in isolated, vertical, cylindrical fractionation columns or towers using different types of contacting devices, with condensers at the top for cooling and partially condensing the top products and reboilers at the bottom for heating and partial evaporation of the bottom products. Fractionation towers may also have several outlets at intervals up the column allowing for the withdrawal of different products having different boiling points or boiling ranges. When the liquid mixtures to be separated are similar in boiling points, spinning band distillation may sometimes be used in which a spinning helical band made of an inert material is used to push the rising vapours and descending liquids to the sides of the column, bringing them into close contact with each other and providing for a greater number of vaporization-condensation cycles and thereby speeding equilibration. Spinning band distillation was first used by Harold Clayton Urey for the separation of different compositions of isotopic water, but was later used in normal, non-isotopic, distillations, where it proved to be much superior to other distillation techniques.

In industrial fractionation towers, reflux is normally used to improve the efficiency of separation of the fractionation products. Reflux refers to the portion of the condensed overhead product that is returned to the tower. The reflux flowing downwards provides the cooling required for condensing the vapours flowing upwards. The reflux ratio, which is the ratio of the (internal) reflux to the overhead product, is conversely related to the theoretical number of stages required for efficient separation of the distillation products, with the two extreme theoretical and impractical possibilities being the use of a minimum reflux ratio with an infinite number of stages or else the use of total reflux with a minimum number of stages. From the standpoint of design, total reflux can be thought of as a column of infinite diameter operating at infinitely large vapour and liquid rates [12]. In practice, the optimum choice of the reflux ratio and the number of theoretical stages is based on economical considerations. Increasing the reflux ratio reduces the number of theoretical stages and thus reduces the construction cost of the column. On the other hand, increasing the reflux ratio leads at the same time to an increase in both the construction and operating costs of the fractionation columns, as increasing the reflux ratio leads to an increase of the column diameter and a corresponding increase of the size of coolers and condensers required for cooling and condensing the reflux (Fig. 1). Most columns are designed to operate between 1.2 to 1.5 times the minimum reflux ratio because this is approximately the region of minimum operating costs [13]. For an existing distillation tower with a fixed number of stages, the reflux ratio can be used to influence the steady-state operation of the unit and maximize the operating profit [8].

Fractionation columns are generally composed of two sections: an upper rectifying section and a lower stripping section. Rectification in general is used to mean purification or purification by distillation in particular, and in other languages, such as French (Rectification) or German (Rektifikation), it is used to refer to fractionation. In the strict technical sense, however, rectification in English refers only to that part of the fractionation process in which the concentration of the more volatile components is increased in the upper section of the fractionation column. Stripping, on the other hand, refers to the part of the fractionation process in which the more volatile components are stripped from the liquid in the lower section of the fractionation column or, sometimes, in a separate stripping column or stripper. In most stripping sections or columns, steam is normally used to strip the volatile components from the descending liquid.

http://dx.doi.org/10.5772/57249

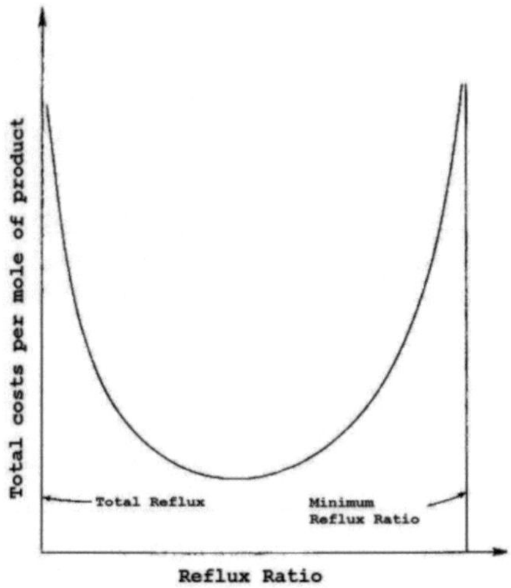

Figure 1. Total costs for a specified separation [12]

The two major types of contacting devices used in fractionation columns or towers are packing and trays. Packed columns, also called continuous-contact columns, use packing that may be grid, random dumped or structured (sheet metal) packing, while tray columns, also called staged-contact columns, use trays or plates. Trays used in tray columns can be of many different types and designs including not only conventional trays such as bubble-cup, perforated and valve trays but also baffle, tunnel, high capacity, dual-flow and multiple downcomer trays. The first vertical columnar continuous distillation still was developed by Collier-Blumenthal in France in 1813, but tray columns, along with feed preheating and the use of internal reflux, first appeared on the scene in the 1820s. The first generation of random packings was developed as early as 1907, but structured packing was only developed in the 1940s.

Packing is usually preferred for loads that are temperature sensitive or corrosive, as the range in packing materials is wider than that commonly available for trays. Packing is further preferred for foaming systems where the low gas and liquid velocities in packing suppress foam formation. Packing pressure drop is also much lower than trays. Kister et al. states that packing pressure drop is typically three to five times lower than that of trays [14]. For this reason, packing columns are favoured in vacuum services and wherever pressure drop is important or where it is economical to minimize it. In addition, packing columns are normally used for lower loads because of the mass transfer characteristics of packing. The mass transfer in packing applications takes place on a thin film of liquid that is spread over the surface area of the packing. If the liquid rate is high this boundary layer will increase, reducing the mass transfer. Packing columns are also used for smaller towers, with diameters less than 3 ft, as it is difficult to access such towers from the inside in order to install and maintain the trays. Although an oversized diameter may be used to overcome this difficulty, packing is normally a cheaper and more desirable alternative [9, 10, 15].

Tray columns, on the other hand, are used for larger columns with high liquid loads. With lower liquid loads trays can have high residence times leading to undesired effects such as fouling and sedimentation. In addition trays will have difficulty maintaining a good weir loading and distribution across the tray, resulting in lower than expected tray efficiencies. For such reasons, it is often more economical to handle high liquid loads in tray columns. Whereas packings are prone to severe maldistribution problems in large-diameter columns, these problems are far less severe in tray columns. Tray columns are also to be preferred where fouling or solid accumulation and deposition is anticipated because of the long history of success trays have had in fouling service applications. Trays can handle solids a lot easier than packed columns, as solids tend to accumulate in packing voids, but the higher gas and liquid velocities on trays provide a sweeping action that keeps tray openings clear. In addition, cleaning trays is easier than cleaning random packing, while cleaning structured packing is practically impossible. In many situations, tray columns are favoured because of performance prediction which is generally much better with tray columns. A major difficulty often encountered in packed-tower design is the inability to predict performance. This difficulty was, for many years, circumvented by grossly oversizing packed towers. Finally, tray columns weigh less than packed columns, which mean lower costs for foundations, support and column shell, the cost of the column being usually estimated on the basis of weight [9, 10, 15]. Tower casing cost, for example, can be estimated from this equation, in USA dollars [16]:

$$\text{Tower casing cost} = 8750\left(\frac{wt,\quad lb}{6000}\right)^{0.75}$$

In most oil refinery operations, tray columns are mainly used for the separation of petroleum fractions at different stages of oil refining [6]. Apart from the general advantages, already referred to, of using trays for larger columns and higher liquid loads, other factors as well argue for the use of tray columns in the oil industry. These include better performance prediction, feed composition variation and the need to incorporate side drawoffs, reboilers, condensers and other complexities. Feed composition variation is generally allowed for by installing alternate feed points, but in packed towers, every alternate feed point requires expensive distribution equipment. Complexities are also more easily incorporated in tray than in packed columns where every complexity requires additional distribution and/or liquid collection equipment [9, 15].

4. Design of fractionation columns

Fractionation columns are designed to achieve the required separation of fluid mixtures or miscible liquids efficiently. The energy intensiveness of distillation added to the continued increase in energy costs has made it of paramount importance to develop rapid calculation procedures for the design of distillation columns.

In general, the design methods for fractionation columns are similar to the design methods used for other separation processes such as absorption and extraction. With reference to the different types of fractionation columns, design procedures for tray columns are better established than for packed columns. This is particularly so with respect to separation efficiency since tray efficiency can be estimated more accurately than packed height equivalent to a theoretical plate (HETP) [17].

The design of fractionation columns is normally made in two steps; a process design, followed by a mechanical design. The purpose of the process design is to calculate the number of required theoretical stages and stream flows including the reflux ratio, heat reflux and other heat duties. The purpose of the mechanical design, on the other hand, is to select the tower internals and calculate column diameter and height. For the efficient selection of tower internals and the accurate calculation of column height and diameter, many factors must be taken into account. Some of the factors involved in design calculations include feed load size and properties and the type of distillation column utilized. This phase of column design has a major impact on column costs, for the choice of internals influences all costs of the distillation system including the column, attendant structures, connecting piping and auxiliaries such as reboiler, condenser, feed heater, and control instruments [15].

Over the years, a considerable amount of work has been done to develop efficient and reliable computer-aided procedures for the mechanical design of fractional distillation columns. Reliable design methods for fractionation columns and other equipment have been developed by commercial organisations such as Fractionation Research Inc. (FRI), but their work is of a proprietary nature and is not freely available in technical literature. Besides being costly to license, using the available rigorous commercial simulation programmes of fractional distillation columns often requires some time to learn. Short-cut design calculation methods have also been presented but mainly for specific and limited applications such as for binary or pseudo-binary systems [18, 19]. In most cases, however, the correct design of multi-component fractionation columns with multiple feeds and side-streams is not straightforward and is not always a simple task, particularly in the oil industry where the fractions to be separated are not simple mixtures composed of two or three components but are complex mixtures of varying composition and properties and which are composed of tens or hundreds of different compounds.

In the oil refining industry, the design and operation of fractionation towers is still largely accomplished on an empirical basis. The calculations involved in the design of petroleum fractionation columns require in the usual practice the use of numerable charts, tables and complex empirical equations. Such charts, tables, equations and other design aids have long been available in the literature, but their use is often lengthy and tedious, and the results are not always dependable [6]. Using Matlab computer programming in the design of fractionation columns can, therefore, be of great help and assistance in facilitating the design calculations and improving their accuracy and dependability. The use of charts, tables and empirical equations can then be dispensed with and the different available calculation methods can be directly compared and evaluated in order to achieve better design results. Using Matlab computer programming is, furthermore, time saving which is often an important consideration from a designer's perspective. In the remaining part of this chapter, the clear advantages of using Matlab programming in the design calculations of fractionation columns will be illustrated by the calculation of column diameters.

5. Calculation of column diameter

In industrial applications, diameters of fractionation columns vary greatly and may range from about 65 cm in smaller towers to about 6 m and more in larger columns, even up to 15 m or 50 feet in some applications [12]. In general, column diameter is relatively insensitive to changes in operating temperature or pressure. Nonetheless, the proper sizing of the column diameter is essential for the efficient performance and operation of fractionation columns. If the column diameter is not sized properly, operational problems may occur and the desired separation will not be achieved. Proper sizing of the column diameter is also crucial for other economic considerations as the costs of fractionation equipment are markedly influenced by the column diameter. The investment cost of a distillation column is a function of its diameter, and so is the cost factor for capacity for the estimation of the cost of trays [20]. For sieve trays, for example, the cost, in USA dollars, has been estimated as equal to 151 $\left(\frac{D}{3}\right)^{1.63}$ where D is the tower diameter in feet [16].

The accurate calculation of column diameter will depend on many factors of column design and, conversely, many factors of column design and construction will depend on the column diameter. Furthermore, in the choice of the contacting devices to be used in fractionation columns, the column diameter is the main factor to consider. As was indicated above, packing is preferred for smaller towers while trays are mainly used in lager columns, with diameters greater than 3 ft. The use of tray columns with diameters in the l-ft, 6-in. to 2-ft range is not usually economical and a packed tower in such cases will prove the best economically. On the other hand, packed towers are not limited to small units and the use of larger-diameter packing columns may still provide the less expensive choice for some specific applications [21].

In packed columns, some of the ultimate performance depends on the column diameter. When random packings are used, there are many reports of an increase in HETP with column diameter [15]. Tower diameter is related also to the packing size, and Robbins recommends that the tower diameter should be at least 8 times the packing size, and if not, the diameter calculations should be repeated with different packing. The ratio of maximum random packing size to tower diameter depends, however, on the type of packing used. Although the 1:8 ratio is in more common use for most packings, some types of packing require a larger ratio of about 1:15, and recent data indicates that Raschig rings require a ratio approaching 1:20 [7, 21].

In tray column design, the calculation of the column diameter is of special significance. Factors of column design that depend on the column diameter include such factors as the choice of plate type and liquid flow arrangement. The choice of plate type is often related to column diameter. Using dual-flow trays, for example, has numerous advantages over other types of trays, particularly in heavy fouling services, but their use in larger diameter towers may lead at the same time to maldistribution. The choice of both liquid flow, reverse or direct flow, and number of passes, single or multiple pass, depend on the column diameter. The common design practice is to minimize the number of passes, and trays smaller than 1.5-m diameter seldom use more than a single pass; those with 1.5- to 3-m diameters seldom use more than two passes. Four-pass trays are only used in towers larger than 5-m diameter [15]. In general, increasing column diameter leads to liquid flow rate increase as the square of the diameter. As the area available for liquid flow also increases in proportion to the diameter, the liquid load per unit length of outlet weir will increase in proportion to the column diameter. In larger column diameters, liquid level difference across the tray increases leading to inefficient mixing of liquid and vapour and trays may have to be fitted with multiple downcomers to reduce the liquid load across each active area section. This reduces the weir load and liquid head on the tray deck resulting in higher vapour capacity, lower pressure drop and improved operating turndown range. Tray efficiency, which typically varies in well-designed trays between 40 and 120%, may be affected by the column diameter. Because of a cross-flow effect, higher efficiency values may be achieved in large-diameter towers [17]. Finally, trays for columns larger than about 900 mm in diameter are normally manufactured in sections sized to fit through the column manways and are assembled inside the column.

Calculation of the column diameter, on the other hand, will in turn depend on many factors of column design such as plate spacing, the type of tray used in the column, surface tension and other physical properties of the vapour and liquid at the tray conditions and other factors. The interrelationship of these different factors is not clearly understood, and diameters are, therefore, determined by relations correlated by empirical factors [21].

Greater plate spacing raises capacity, leading to a smaller tower diameter, but at the same time it raises tower height. In this case, an economic tradeoff is to be considered between tower height and diameter. With accessibility in mind, plate spacing should be from 450 to 600 mm. In towers with larger than 1.5-m diameter, tray spacing is typically 600 mm to allow easy access for maintenance, but in very large towers (>6-m diameter), tray spacings of 750 mm are often used. For a tower diameter below 1.5 m, on the other hand, a tray spacing of 450 mm is adequate as the column wall can be reached from the manway [7, 15].

The factors influencing the different tray types are somewhat different. Column diameter is a function of both tray efficiency and its capacity characteristics as represented by velocity effects including entrainment, and the pressure of the operation. Low-pressure operations require generally larger diameter Columns [21].

The reflux ratio is another factor that affects the calculation of tower diameter. Increasing the reflux ratio means more vapour being boiled up and the required column diameter will be greater.

The principal factor that determines the column diameter, however, is the vapour flow rate. The minimum vapour flow rate required is determined by weeping, but the flooding condition fixes the upper limit of vapour velocity. A high vapour velocity will be needed for high plate efficiencies, but the vapour velocity must at the same time be below that which would cause excessive liquid entrainment or a high pressure drop. In general, vapour velocity will normally be between 70 to 90 per cent of that which would cause flooding. For design purposes, a value of 80 to 85 per cent of the flooding velocity should be used [22].

Calculation of the column diameter is often based on a trial and error approach. The preliminary diameter calculated may have to be refined by checking against the performance correlations of the column. In any case the calculated diameter should also be rounded appropriately for fabrication standardisation. A number of general rules of thump may be used as a general guide before carrying out the actual calculations, but these rules often have exceptions and may not apply in all cases. Such rules as related to column diameter include the following four rules [10]:

1. The length to diameter ratio should be less than 30, preferably below 20, and tower height is to be limited to 60 meters because of wind load and foundation concerns. If the tower is higher than 60 m, then a design with smaller tray spacing should be considered [7, 23].

2. The ratio of tower diameter to random packing size is greater than 10.

3. The tower diameter should be maintained at 1.2 meters at the top for vapour disengagement.

4. The tower diameter should be maintained at 2 meters at the bottom for liquid level and reboiler return.

In normal practice, however, only one diameter is calculated for the whole column. Different column diameters would only be used where there is a considerable change in flow-rate. Changes in liquid rate can be allowed for by adjusting the liquid downcomer areas [22]. If two or more diameters are calculated, say for the top and bottom sections of the column, then roughly speaking, when the difference in the calculated diameters exceeds 20%, different diameters for the top and bottom sections are likely to be economical and sections having different diameters should be at least 600 cm (20 ft) in length. Otherwise the diameter should be uniform. The preliminary column diameter would then be the larger of the two calculated diameters [9].

6. Calculation procedures for column diameter

The equation most often used for the calculation of column diameter is based on the well-known empirically-correlated Souders and Brown equation. Equation 1, or the chart of Fig. 2, may then be used to estimate the maximum allowable superficial vapour velocity, and hence the column area and diameter.

$$U_V = \frac{K}{3600}\left(\frac{\rho_L - \rho_V}{\rho_V}\right)^{0.5} \tag{1}$$

Where:

U_V = Maximum allowable superficial vapour velocity (ft/sec or m/sec)

ρ_L = Liquid density (kg/m^3 or lb/ft^3)

ρ_V = Vapour density (kg/m^3 or lb/ft^3)

K in the above equation is an entrainment-related factor that depends on several variables which differ from one correlation to another. From a consideration of the balance of forces acting on the liquid droplets, the acceleration due to gravity must be included in the K factor, although it does not appear as a separate parameter in the above equation. This is to be explained by the fact that the Souders and Brown equation is based on empirical correlation of experimental data and has no theoretical derivation. The other main variables that affect the K factor include plate spacing, type of tray, physical properties, liquid load, hole diameter and fractional hole area.

Of such variables, plate spacing is the most important. In general, the K factor rises with plate spacing, where it is proportional to plate spacing to the power of 0.5 to 0.6. At low plate spacing (<38 cm) the power maybe somewhat higher due to the proximity of the froth envelop and/or excessive splashing from dispersion at the plate [9]. For the calculation of the K factor in terms of plate spacing, the following equation may be used:

$$K = 3600\left(-0.171\,T^2 + 0.27\,T - 0.047\right) \tag{2}$$

Where:

T = plate spacing (m).

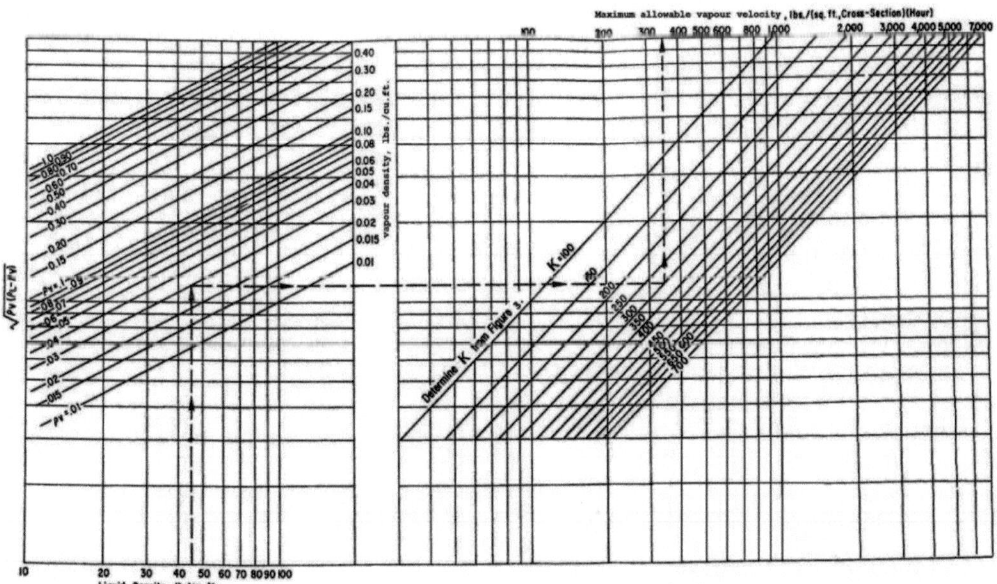

Figure 2. Allowable vapour velocity for fractionation, absorption, and stripping columns.

This K factor may also be estimated from charts available in the literature such as shown in Figure 3 (curve 3, for normal performance of bubble plates through normal range of liquid

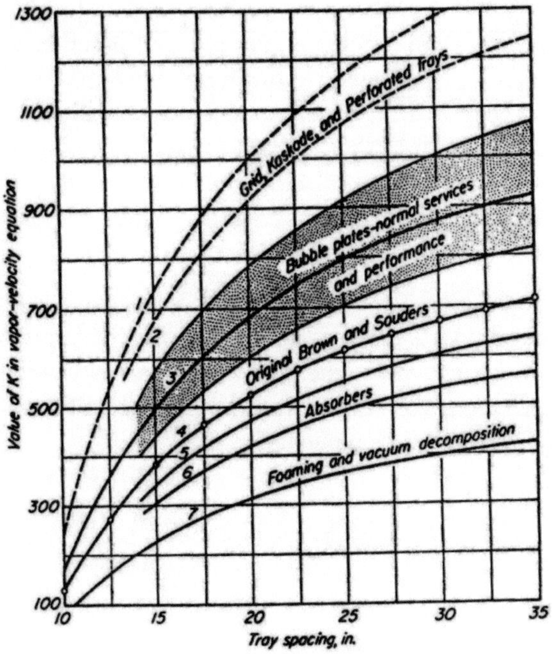

Figure 3. Effect of tray spacing and type of service allowable vapour load in fractionators [24]

loads at atmospheric and higher pressures, or curve 2 for other tray types). Using the value of the K factor from this chart often gives a lower estimate of the column diameter as compared to the other charts and procedures. This will be clearly seen when the K factor from this chart is used in the calculation of the two fractionators given later on in this chapter.

Although it has been suggested by certain workers that the K factor is at most a weak function of physical properties, there are several correlations that tend to contradict this suggestion [9]. Surface tension, in particular, may have a significant effect on the value of the K factor, as evidenced by such charts as are shown in figures 4 and 5. Equation 2 may also be modified to include the effect of surface tension for bubble cap trays as follows:

$$K = (36.71 + 5.456\,T - 0.08486\,T^{2})\ln\sigma - 312.9 + 37.62\,T - 0.5269\,T^{2}$$

Correlation ranges are:

K = 0 to 700

σ = Surface tension (dynes/cm) 0.1 to 100.

T = plate spacing (in) = 18 to 36.

The K factor increases with fractional hole area increase and hole diameter decrease. Roughly speaking, it increases with the reciprocal of hole diameter to a power of 0.1 to 0.2 [9].

Finally, liquid load can have a significant effect on the value of the K factor. As liquid load increases, the K factor first rises then declines [9].

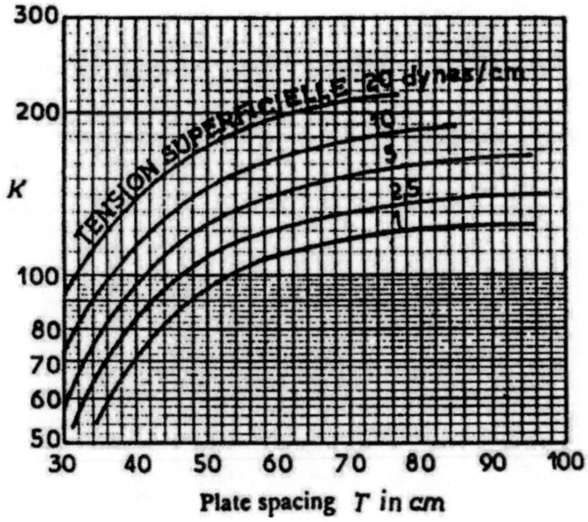

Figure 4. Coefficient of entrainment as a function of plate spacing and surface tension [25]

Taking all the above effects into consideration, the K factor may be calculated (for valve and sieve trays) using the Kister and Haas Correlation [9]:

$$K = 0.144\left(\frac{d_H^2\,\sigma}{\rho_L}\right)^{0.125}\left(\frac{\rho_V}{\rho_L}\right)^{0.1}\left(\frac{T}{h_c}\right)^{0.5}$$

Where:

d_H = Hole diameter (in)

ϱ_L = Liquid density (kg/m^3 or lb/ft^3)

ϱ_V = Vapour density (kg/m^3 or lb/ft^3)

h_c = Clear liquid height (in).

In Fair's correlation, the value of the K factor is a function of the flow parameter F_{lv}, plate spacing, surface tension and fractional hole area (Fig. 6), where:

$$F_{lv} = \frac{L}{V}\sqrt{\frac{\rho_v}{\rho_L}} \tag{3}$$

L = Liquid flow rate (lb/h)

V = Vapour flow rate (lb/h)

Fair's correlation was recommended by most designers, but, according to some workers, it may be on the conservative side.

The K factor is normally determined at the top and bottom (or intermediate) positions of the column in order to evaluate the point of maximum required diameter.

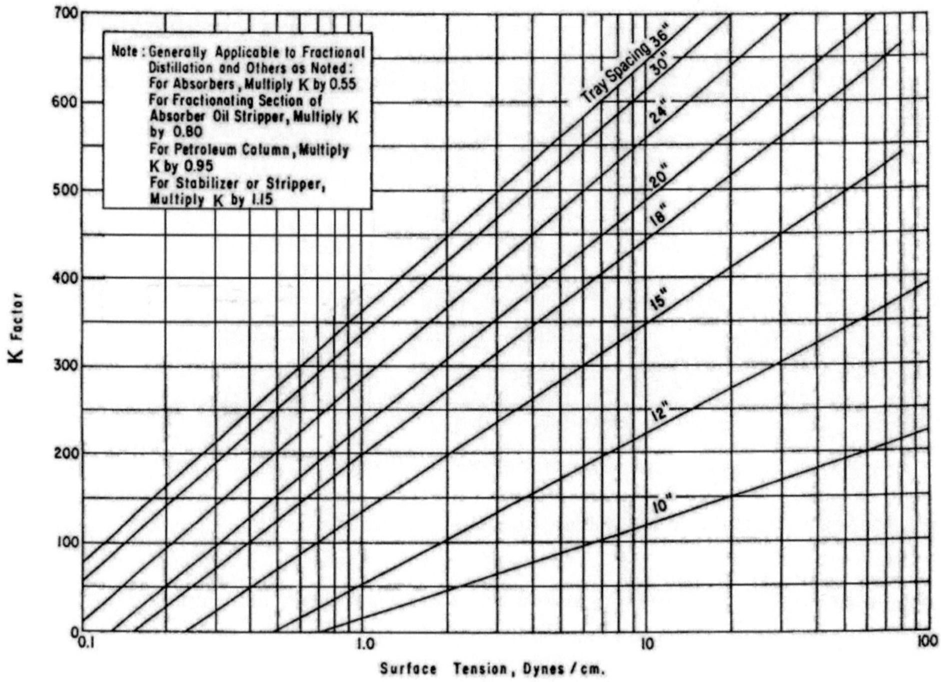

Figure 5. K factors for column diameter using bubble cap trays

It has been suggested that, for perforated trays in particular, the Souders-Brown method is rather conservative and that a better first approximation and often a more economical tower diameter is determined using the following equation for the calculation of vapour velocity [21]:

$$e_w = 0.22\left(\frac{73}{\sigma}\right)\left(\frac{u_V}{T'}\right) \tag{4}$$

where:

e_w = Weight of liquid entrained/unit weight of vapour flowing in perforated tray column. Entrainment values of 0.05 lbs liquid/lb vapour are usually acceptable, with 0.001 and 0.5 lb/lb being the extremes.

T'= Effective tray spacing, distance between top of foam and next plate above

$= T \quad 2.5\, h_c$

h_c = Height of clear liquid in bubbling zone. This is based on an aerated mixture density of 0.4 that of the clear liquid on the tray, and has been found to be a reasonable average for several mixtures.

Equation 4 was derived primarily for perforated trays with downcomers, but, because of the very close similarity between a perforated plate without downcomers and one with downcomers, it can also be used for trays without downcomers, although the liquid level and foam-froth height will generally be higher on trays without downcomers. The value of h_{cl}, clear liquid on the tray, may therefore range from 1 in. to 6 in. depending on the service [21].

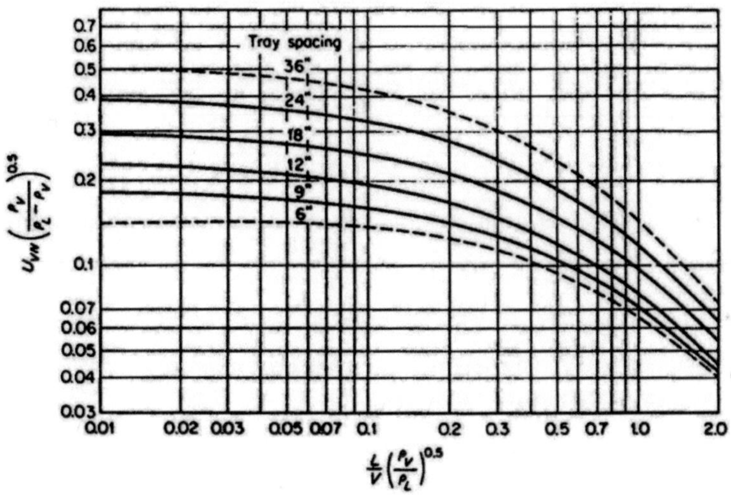

Figure 6. Flooding limits for bubble-cap and perforated plates [26]

From the calculated vapour velocity U_V, the column diameter can then be calculated using the following equation:

$$D = \left[\frac{4V}{3600 \pi \rho_V U_V} \right]^{0.5} \tag{5}$$

Where:

D = Column diameter (m or ft)

V = Maximum allowable vapour flow rate (kg/h or lb/h)

The diameter obtained in this solution, corresponding to the maximum allowable flow rate, is the minimum acceptable diameter for operation with essentially no entrainment carryover from plate to plate. If irregularities in capacity, system pressure or other significant variables are anticipated, the maximum allowable flow rate can then be divided by a safety, or ignorance, factor of 1.10 to 1.25. Alternatively, the maximum flow rate may be multiplied by 1.05 to 1.15 for satisfactory operation at conditions tolerating some entrainment with no noticeable loss in fractionation efficiency or capacity.

In another procedure based on Fair's correlation that may also be used for the estimation of column diameter, the chart of Figure 6 may be used to determine the maximum vapour velocity relative to the net area for vapour flow (U_{VN}) for a given value of flow parameter and plate spacing, the net area being defined as the tower cross-sectional area minus the downflow area. This may be used for both bubble-cap plates and perforated plates with the following restrictions:

1. The distilling system is non-foaming or low-foaming type. Foaming makes liquid disengagement from vapour flow difficult, and when foaming becomes severe it can lead to a reduction in capacity and loss of efficiency. To counter this effect distillation equipments that operate in foaming systems are run at lower vapour, and liquid, rates to reduce the amount of froth generated.

2. The weir height is less than 15% of the tray spacing.

3. In perforated trays, the perforation diameters are equal to or less than 0.25 in. Entrainment may be greater with larger hole sizes.

4. The plate spacings of 6 and 9 in. do not apply to bubble-cap plates.

5. The ratio of slot area, or hole area, to active plate area must be equal to or greater than 0.1, and the system surface tension 20 dynes/cm.

For hole-to-active area ratios of less than 0.1, it is recommended by Fair that the vapour velocity from the chart be modified by the following factors:

A_s/A_A	Multiply U_{VN} by
0.10	1.00
0.08	0.90
0.06	0.80

The base surface tension assumed in the chart of Figure 6 is 20 dynes/cm. The decrease in surface tension as equilibrium temperature rises promotes foaming in distillation systems, and, as mentioned earlier, distillation equipment may have to be run in foaming systems at lower vapour rates. For surface tensions different from 20 dynes/cm, the velocity from the chart is therefore modified by:

$$\text{Corrected } U_{VN} = U_{VN} \left(\frac{\sigma}{20}\right)^{0.2}$$

Alternatively, the maximum vapour velocity (U_{VN}) from the chart of Fig. 6 may be used for estimating the flooding vapour velocity (U_f). Taking the above considerations into account and assuming operation at 80% flooding, the following equation may then be used for calculating the flooding velocity.

$$U_f = 0.80\, U_{VN}.\, C_s.\, C_F.\, C_A$$

Where:

http://dx.doi.org/10.5772/57249

C_s = Surface tension correction factor = $\left(\frac{\sigma}{20}\right)^{0.2}$

C_F = Foaming correction factor (1, for non-foaming systems; 0.50-0.75 for foaming systems)

C_A = Hole-to-active area ratio correction factor (1, for $A_s/A_A \geq 0.1$; $5(A_s/A_A)+0.5$, for $0.06 \leq (A_s/A_A) < 0.1$). For valve trays $C_A = 1$.

The flooding vapour velocity is usually about 50-60% of the maximum vapour velocity value, and can be as high as 85% or even 95% if sufficient information is available about the system foaming characteristics.

The net area for vapour flow (A_N) can then be calculated, and hence, using the flooding vapour velocity, the column diameter can be calculated.

Assuming that the downflow area (A_d) is 10% of the total cross-sectional area of the column (A),

$$A_N = 0.90\ A = 0.90 \times 0.785\ D^2 = \frac{Q_V}{3600\ U_F}$$

$$D^2 = \frac{1.4}{3600}\ \frac{Q_V}{U_F}$$

Where:

Q_V = Vapour volume flow rate (m^3/h or ft^3/h).

A correlation similar to Fair's correlation, applicable to columns having bubble caps, sieve or valve trays, was later proposed by Smith et al [27]. In this correlation, settling height, defined as tray spacing minus clear liquid height in bubbling zone, was used as parameter instead of tray spacing, where:

Clear liquid height = $h_c = h_w + h_{ow}$

h_w = Height of outlet weir.

h_{ow} = Height of liquid over weir.

In a similar correlation by Gerster, this clear liquid height (h_c) was used as a parameter [28]. The deviation in the flooding velocity data from manufacturers of valve trays, as reported by Smith et al., was six percent on average [27].

For checking designs one can roughly relate tower diameter (ft) to reboiler duty as follows [29]:

Situation	Reboiler Duty, MM/BTU/hr
Pressure distillation	$0.5\ D^2$
Atmospheric pressure distillation	$0.3\ D^2$
Vacuum distillation	$0.15\ D^2$

In a lunar environment with its reduced gravity, fractionation column area and diameter would be larger, as both are inversely related to the acceleration due to gravity. In his paper on distillation in a lunar environment, Pettit concluded that the ratio of the column diameters on earth and moon will be proportional to the square root of the accelerations due to gravity [11].

$$\frac{A_m}{A} \propto \sqrt{\frac{g}{g_m}}$$

Where:

A = Cross-sectional area of the column on earth

A_m = Cross-sectional area of the column on the moon

g = Gravity constant on earth

g_m = Gravity constant on the moon.

Considering that the lunar gravity is about one sixth of the earth gravity, an earthly fractionation column of one-meter diameter would correspond to a lunar column of 1.6 m diameter.

7. MATLAB programming for column diameter calculation

For the calculation of the fractionation column diameter using the various charts and calculation methods available in the literature, a computer programme is written in Matlab (See appendix). Using this programme simplifies the procedure of the calculation of column diameter and dispenses with the tedious use of the different charts and eliminates the errors that may result from reading such charts. There is a minimal data requirement for the calculation using this programme, with the possibility of calculating the surface tension and other required data being built in the programme. Furthermore, using the programme makes comparison of the different calculation methods an easy and straightforward matter. The order of the calculated diameters using the programme is as follows:

D_1 based on Fig. 3;

D_2 based on Fig. 4;

D_3 based on Fig. 5;

D_4 based on Fig. 6;

D_5 based on Eq. 2.

The use of this programme will be illustrated by two examples in which the diameters of two fractionation columns used at the Homs oil refinery, in Syria, are calculated.

Example 1

Fractionation column data

T = Plate spacing = 22 in. = 56 cm

Q_V = Vapour volume flow rate = 29 × 10^2 m^3/h = 10 × 10^4 ft^3/h

L = Liquid flow rate = 65.3 × 10^2 kg/h = 14.4 × 10^3 lb/h

V = Maximum allowable vapour flow rate = 83.3 × 10^2 kg/h = 18.3 × 10^3 lb/h

ρ_L = Liquid density = 684 kg/m^3 = 42.7 lb/ft^3

ρ_V = Vapour density = 2.9 kg/m^3 = 0.18 lb/ft^3

t = Temperature = 141°C

M = Average molecular weight = 110

The calculated tower diameter varied between 1.0 and 1.2 m depending on the method or chart used for calculation. The results are as follows:

D_1 = 1.0 m

D_2 = 1.2 m

D_3 = 1.2 m

D_4 = 1.2 m

D_5 = 1.1 m

The diameter of the actual tower is 1.2 m which happens to be also the diameter calculated using the charts of Figures 4, 5 and 6. As was earlier indicated, the surface tension of the system is not taken into account in the estimation of the K factor using Fig. 3 or Eq. 2, and using the values of the K factor from Eq. 2 or from the chart of Fig. 3 often gives lower estimates of the column diameter, with Eq. 2 giving a better estimate of the tower diameter (1.1 m) than Fig. 3 (1.0 m). Neglecting the diameter calculated using the K value of Fig. 3 gives an average calculated diameter of 1.2±0.09 m with a maximum difference between the calculated values of less than 9% of the average, which is quite acceptable and falls well within the accuracy limits of the methods of calculation.

Example 2

Fractionation column data

T = plate spacing = 18 in. = 46 cm

Q_V = Vapour volume flow rate = 96 × 10^2 m^3/h = 33.1 × 10^4 ft^3/h

L = Liquid flow rate = 25.6 × 10^3 kg/h = 56.5 × 10^3 lb/h

V = Maximum allowable vapour flow rate = 11.5 × 10^3 kg/h = 25.4 × 10^3 lb/h

ρ_L = Liquid density = 7.2 × 10^2 kg/m^3 = 45 lb/ft^3

ρ_V = Vapour density = 1.2 kg/m^3 = 0.075 lb/ft^3

t = Temperature = 149°C

M = Average molecular weight = 98

The calculated diameter varied between 1.6 and 2.0 m, and the results are as follows:

D_1 = 1.6 m

D_2 = 2.0 m

D_3 = 2.0 m

D_4 = 2.0 m

D_5 = 1.8 m

The actual column diameter in this case is 2.0 m, which is also the diameter calculated using the charts of Figures 4, 5 and 6. As mentioned before, using Eq. 2 or the chart of Fig. 3 gives lower estimates of the tower diameter (1.8 and 1.6 m respectively). Neglecting the diameter calculated using the K value of Fig. 3 gives an average diameter of 2.0±0.18 m with a maximum difference of 10%.

8. Conclusion

The use of the Matlab programme for the calculation of fractionation column diameters greatly simplified the calculation procedure and made it possible to compare calculated diameters based on different calculation procedures and/or assumptions.

The results obtained on applying the programme on the two fractionation columns at the Homs Oil Refinery indicate clearly the significance of surface tension in the calculation of tower diameters. In all three procedures in which the surface tension is taken into account, accurate and equal estimates of the tower diameter were obtained. When using, however, Eq. 2 or the chart of Fig. 3, where the surface tension is not considered, lower estimates were generally obtained, although in both instances Eq. 2 gave a much better estimate than the chart of Fig. 3. The calculation results obtained were found to be comparable in general and mostly fall well within the accuracy limits of the methods of calculation.

As indicated above, the calculated column diameter will have to be further refined, by checking against the performance correlations of the column. Following this refinement, the eventual choice of the column diameter will be made.

http://dx.doi.org/10.5772/57249

Nomenclature

A = Cross-sectional area of the column (m^2 or ft^2)

A_A = Active area (m^2 or ft^2)

A_m = Cross-sectional area of the column on the moon

A_N = Net area for vapour flow (m^2 or ft^2)

A_s = Slot area (or hole area) (m^2 or ft^2)

C_A = Hole-to-active area ratio correction factor (1, for $A_s/A_A \geq 0.1$; $5(A_s/A_A)+0.5$, for $0.06 \leq (A_s/A_A) < 0.1$)

C_F = Foaming correction factor (0.85-0.95, for non-foaming systems; 0.50-0.60 for foaming systems)

C_s = Surface tension correction factor $= \left(\frac{\sigma}{20}\right)^{0.2}$

D = Column diameter (m or ft)

d_H = Hole diameter (in).

e_w = Weight of liquid entrained/unit weight of vapour.

g = Gravity constant on earth

g_m = Gravity constant on the moon.

h_c = Height of clear liquid in bubbling zone (in).

h_{ow} = Height of liquid over weir.

h_w = Height of outlet weir.

K = A factor that depends on plate spacing.

L = Liquid flow rate (kg/h or lb/h)

M = Average molecular weight

Q_V = Vapour volume flow rate (m^3/h or ft^3/h).

T = plate spacing (in., cm or m)

T'= Effective tray spacing (in.)

t = Temperature (°C)

U_F = Flooding vapour velocity (m/sec or ft/sec).

U_V = Maximum allowable superficial vapour velocity (m/sec or ft/sec).

U_{VN} = Vapour velocity relative to the net area for vapour flow (m/sec or ft/sec).

V = Maximum allowable vapour flow rate (kg/h or lb/h)

ρ_L = Liquid density (kg/m^3 or lb/ft^3)

ρ_V = Vapour density (kg/m^3 or lb/ft^3)

σ = Surface tension (dynes/cm)

Appendix

```
disp('Matlab programme for the calculation of fractionation column diameter')
N = input('N = ')
switch N
Case 1
disp('Fig –3')
t = input('T = ')
x = t;
y = ((0.0254 * x ^ 3 - 2.793 * x ^ 2 + 110.6 * x - 616.6) + 0.5);
k = y
disp(['K=' int2str(k)])
EL = input ('EL');
EV = input ('EV');
V = input ('V');
Uv = k / 3600 * ((EL - EV) / EV) ^ 0.5;
W = 3600 * EV * Uv;
D = (4 * V / (3.14 * W)) ^ 0.5;
disp(['D=' num2str(D * 0.3048)])
Case 2
disp(' Fig - 4')
t = input ('t= ');
M = input ('M = ');
if t == -20 Then
x = M;
y = 0.000006446 * x ^ 3 - 0.0033908 * x ^ 2 + 0.61513 * x - 9.3259;
s = y;
Else if t == 40
x = M;
y = -0.000000018 * x ^ 4 + 0.000014 * x ^ 3 - 0.0044 * x ^ 2 + 0.675 * x – 17;
s = y;
Else if t > -20 & t < 40
x = M;
y = 0.000006446 * x ^ 3 - 0.0033908 * x ^ 2 + 0.61513 * x - 9.3259;
S1 = y;
x – M;
y = -0.000000018 * x ^ 4 + 0.000014 * x ^ 3 - 0.0044 * x ^ 2 + 0.675 * x – 17;
S2 = y;
s = S1 - (S1 - S2) / (-20 - 40) * (-20 - t);
Else if t == 90
x = M;
y = -0.00000001 * x ^ 4 + 0.00001 * x ^ 3 - 0.0036 * x ^ 2 + 0.601 * x – 20;
```

http://dx.doi.org/10.5772/57249

```
s = y;
Else if (t > 40) & (t < 90)
x = M;
y = -0.000000018 * x ^ 4 + 0.000014 * x ^ 3 - 0.0044 * x ^ 2 + 0.675 * x – 17;
S1 = y;
x = M;
y = -0.00000001 * x ^ 4 + 0.00001 * x ^ 3 - 0.0036 * x ^ 2 + 0.601 * x – 20;
S2 = y;
s = S1 - (S1 - S2) / (90 - 40) * (90 - t);
Else if t == 150
x = M;
y = 0.00000235 * x ^ 3 - 0.00154 * x ^ 2 + 0.387 * x - 17.71;
s = y;
Else if (t > 90) & (t < 150)
x = M;
y = -0.00000001 * x ^ 4 + 0.00001 * x ^ 3 - 0.0036 * x ^ 2 + 0.601 * x – 20;
S1 = y;
x = M;
y = 0.00000235 * x ^ 3 - 0.00154 * x ^ 2 + 0.387 * x - 17.71;
S2 = y;
s = S1 - (S1 - S2) / (150 - 90) * (150 - t);
end
disp(['s=' num2str( s)])
t = input ('T = ');
if s == 20
x = t;
y = -0.049 * x ^ 2 + 7.941 * x - 97.82;
k = y;
Else if s == 10
x = t;
y = -0.045 * x ^ 2 + 7.359 * x - 107.2;
k = y;
Else if s > 10 & s < 20
x = t;
y = -0.049 * x ^ 2 + 7.941 * x - 97.82;
k1 = y;
x = t;
y = -0.045 * x ^ 2 + 7.359 * x - 107.2;
K2 = y;
k = k1 - (k1 - K2) / (20 - 10) * (20 - s);
Else if s == 5
x = t;
y = -0.034 * x ^ 2 + 5.834 * x - 81.98;
```

```
k = y;
Else if (s > 5) & (s < 10)
x = t;
y = -0.045 * x ^ 2 + 7.359 * x - 107.2;
k1 = y;
x = t;
y = -0.034 * x ^ 2 + 5.834 * x - 81.98;
K2 = y;
k = k1 - (k1 - K2) / (10 - 5) * (10 - s);
Else if s == 2.5
x = t;
y = -0.032 * x ^ 2 + 5.4 * x - 83.02;
k = y;
Else if (s > 2.5) & (s < 5)
x = t;
y = -0.034 * x ^ 2 + 5.834 * x - 81.98;
k1 = y;
x = t;
y = -0.032 * x ^ 2 + 5.4 * x - 83.02;
K2 = y;
k = k1 - (k1 - K2) / (5 - 2.5) * (5 - s);
Else if t == 1
x = t;
y = -0.029 * x ^ 2 + 4.918 * x - 77.79;
k = y;
Else if s > 1 & s < 2.5
x = t;
y = -0.032 * x ^ 2 + 5.4 * x - 83.02;
k1 = y;
x = t;
y = -0.029 * x ^ 2 + 4.918 * x - 77.79;
K2 = y;
k = k1 - (k1 - K2) / (2.5 - 1) * (2.5 - s);
end
disp( ['K=' int2str(k)] )
EL = input ('EL');
EV = input ('EV');
V = input ('V');
Uv = k / 3600 * ((EL - EV) / EV) ^ 0.5;
W = 3600 * EV * Uv;
D = (4 * V / (3.14 * W)) ^ 0.5;
disp( ['D=' num2str(D)])
```

Case 3

http://dx.doi.org/10.5772/57249

```
disp( ' Fig - 5')
t = input ('t= ');
M = input ('M = ');
if t == -20
x = M;
y = 0.000006446 * x ^ 3 - 0.0033908 * x ^ 2 + 0.61513 * x - 9.3259;
s = y;
Else if t == 40
x = M;
y = -0.000000018 * x ^ 4 + 0.000014 * x ^ 3 - 0.0044 * x ^ 2 + 0.675 * x – 17;
s = y;
Else if t > -20 & t < 40
x = M;
y = 0.000006446 * x ^ 3 - 0.0033908 * x ^ 2 + 0.61513 * x - 9.3259;
S1 = y;
x = M;
y = -0.000000018 * x ^ 4 + 0.000014 * x ^ 3 - 0.0044 * x ^ 2 + 0.675 * x – 17;
S2 = y;
s = S1 - (S1 - S2) / (-20 - 40) * (-20 - t);
Else if t == 90
x = M;
y = -0.00000001 * x ^ 4 + 0.00001 * x ^ 3 - 0.0036 * x ^ 2 + 0.601 * x – 20;
s = y;
Else if (t > 40) & (t < 90)
x = M;
y = -0.000000018 * x ^ 4 + 0.000014 * x ^ 3 - 0.0044 * x ^ 2 + 0.675 * x – 17;
S1 = y;
x = M;
y = -0.00000001 * x ^ 4 + 0.00001 * x ^ 3 - 0.0036 * x ^ 2 + 0.601 * x – 20;
S2 = y;
s = S1 - (S1 - S2) / (90 - 40) * (90 - t);
Else if t == 150
x = M;
y = 0.00000235 * x ^ 3 - 0.00154 * x ^ 2 + 0.387 * x - 17.71;
s = y;
Else if (t > 90) & (t < 150)
x = M;
y = -0.00000001 * x ^ 4 + 0.00001 * x ^ 3 - 0.0036 * x ^ 2 + 0.601 * x – 20;
S1 = y;
x = M;
y = 0.00000235 * x ^ 3 - 0.00154 * x ^ 2 + 0.387 * x - 17.71;
S2 = y;
s = S1 - (S1 - S2) / (150 - 90) * (150 - t);
```

```
end
disp([ 's=', num2str(s)])
t = input ('T = ')
if t == 36
x = s;
y = 123.2 * Log(x) + 363.9;
k = y;
Else if t == 30
x = s;
y = 120.7 * Log(x) + 337.3;
k = y;
Else if t < 36 And t > 30
x = s;
y = 123.2 * Log(x) + 363.9;
k1 = y;
x = s;
y = 120.7 * Log(x) + 337.3;
K2 = y;
k = k1 - (k1 - K2) / (36 - 30) * (36 - t);
Else if t == 24
x = s;
y = 118.6 * Log(x) + 287.4;
k = y;
Else if t < 30 And t > 24
x = s;
y = 120.7 * Log(x) + 337.3;
k1 = y;
x = s;
y = 118.6 * Log(x) + 287.4;
K2 = y;
k = k1 - (k1 - K2) / (30 - 24) * (30 - t);
Else if t == 20
x = s;
y = 113.2 * Log(x) + 231.1;
k = y;
Else if t < 24 And t > 20
x = s;
y = 118.6 * Log(x) + 287.4;
k1 = y;
x = s;
y = 113.2 * Log(x) + 231.1;
K2 = y;
k = k1 - (k1 - K2) / (24 - 20) * (24 - t);
```

http://dx.doi.org/10.5772/57249

```
Else if t == 18
x = s;
y = 107 * Log(x) + 197.9;
k = y;
Else if t < 20 And t > 18
x = s;
y = 113.2 * Log(x) + 231.1;
k1 = y;
x = s;
y = 107 * Log(x) + 197.9;
K2 = y;
k = k1 - (k1 - K2) / (20 - 18) * (20 - t);
Else if t == 15
x = s;
y = 92.91 * Log(x) + 136.55;
k = y;
Else if t < 18 And t > 15
x = s;
y = 107 * Log(x) + 197.9;
k1 = y;
x = s;
y = 92.91 * Log(x) + 136.55;
K2 = y;
k = k1 - (k1 - K2) / (18 - 15) * (18 - t);
Else if t == 12
x = s;
y = 74.62 * Log(x) + 53.18;
k = y;
Else if t < 15 And t > 12
x = s;
y = 92.91 * Log(x) + 136.55;
k1 = y;
x = s;
y = 74.62 * Log(x) + 53.18;
K2 = y;
k = k1 - (k1 - K2) / (15 - 12) * (15 - t)
Else if t == 10
x = s;
y = 46.68 * Log(x) + 15.74;
k = y;
Else if t < 12 And t > 10
x = s;
y = 74.62 * Log(x) + 53.18;
```

```
k1 = y;
x = s;
y = 46.68 * Log(x) + 15.74;
K2 = y;
k = k1 - (k1 - K2) / (12 - 10) * (12 - t);
end
disp( ['k=' int2str(k)])
EL = input ('EL');
EV = input ('EV');
V = input ('V');
Uv = k / 3600 * ((EL - EV) / EV) ^ 0.5;
W = 3600 * EV * Uv;
D = (4 * V / (3.14 * W)) ^ 0.5;
disp([ ('D=' num2str (D * 0.3048)])
```

```
Case 4
disp( 'Fig - 6')
t = input ('t= ');
M = input ('M = ');
if t == -20 Then
x = M;
y = 0.000006446 * x ^ 3 - 0.0033908 * x ^ 2 + 0.61513 * x - 9.3259;
s = y;
Else if t == 40
x = M;
y = -0.000000018 * x ^ 4 + 0.000014 * x ^ 3 - 0.0044 * x ^ 2 + 0.675 * x – 17;
s = y;
Else if t > -20 & t < 40
x = M;
y = 0.000006446 * x ^ 3 - 0.0033908 * x ^ 2 + 0.61513 * x - 9.3259;
S1 = y;
x = M;
y = -0.000000018 * x ^ 4 + 0.000014 * x ^ 3 - 0.0044 * x ^ 2 + 0.675 * x – 17;
S2 = y;
s = S1 - (S1 - S2) / (-20 - 40) * (-20 - t);
Else if t == 90
x = M;
y = -0.00000001 * x ^ 4 + 0.00001 * x ^ 3 - 0.0036 * x ^ 2 + 0.601 * x – 20;
s = y;
Else if (t > 40) & (t < 90)
x = M;
y = -0.000000018 * x ^ 4 + 0.000014 * x ^ 3 - 0.0044 * x ^ 2 + 0.675 * x – 17;
S1 = y;
x = M;
```

http://dx.doi.org/10.5772/57249

```
y = -0.00000001 * x ^ 4 + 0.00001 * x ^ 3 - 0.0036 * x ^ 2 + 0.601 * x – 20;
S2 = y;
s = S1 - (S1 - S2) / (90 - 40) * (90 - t);
Else if t == 150
x = M;
y = 0.00000235 * x ^ 3 - 0.00154 * x ^ 2 + 0.387 * x - 17.71;
s = y;
Else if (t > 90) & (t < 150)
x = M;
y = -0.00000001 * x ^ 4 + 0.00001 * x ^ 3 - 0.0036 * x ^ 2 + 0.601 * x – 20;
S1 = y;
x = M;
y = 0.00000235 * x ^ 3 - 0.00154 * x ^ 2 + 0.387 * x - 17.71;
S2 = y;
s = S1 - (S1 - S2) / (150 - 90) * (150 - t);
end
disp(['s=' num2str( s)])
L = input ('L = ');
V = input ('V = ');
EV = input ('EV = ');
DL = input ('DL = ');
t = input ('T = ');
Qv = input ('Qv = ');
pF = (L / V) * (EV / dL) ^ 0.5;
if t == 36
x = pF;
y = 0.104 * x ^ 4 - 0.52 * x ^ 3 + 0.974 * x ^ 2 - 0.916 * x + 0.508;
pc = y;
Else if t == 24
x = pF;
y = 0.111 * x ^ 4 - 0.524 * x ^ 3 + 0.903 * x ^ 2 - 0.765 * x + 0.399;
pc = y;
Else if t > 24 And t < 36
x = pF;
y = 0.104 * x ^ 4 - 0.52 * x ^ 3 + 0.974 * x ^ 2 - 0.916 * x + 0.508;
PC1 = y;
x = pF;
y = 0.111 * x ^ 4 - 0.524 * x ^ 3 + 0.903 * x ^ 2 - 0.765 * x + 0.399;
PC2 = y;
pc = PC1 - (PC1 - PC2) / (36 - 24) * (36 - t);
Else if t == 18
x = pF;
y = 0.058 * x ^ 4 - 0.295 * x ^ 3 + 0.555 * x ^ 2 - 0.518 * x + 0.298;
```

```
pc = y;
Else if (t > 18) And (t < 24)
x = pF;
y = 0.111 * x ^ 4 - 0.524 * x ^ 3 + 0.903 * x ^ 2 - 0.765 * x + 0.399;
PC1 = y;
x = pF;
y = 0.058 * x ^ 4 - 0.295 * x ^ 3 + 0.555 * x ^ 2 - 0.518 * x + 0.298;
PC2 = y;
pc = PC1 - (PC1 - PC2) / (24 - 18) * (24 - t);
Else if t == 12
x = pF;
y = -0.053 * x ^ 5 + 0.292 * x ^ 4 - 0.618 * x ^ 3 + 0.663 * x ^ 2 - 0.438 * x + 0.234;
pc = y;
Else if (t > 12) And (t < 18)
x = pF;
y = 0.058 * x ^ 4 - 0.295 * x ^ 3 + 0.555 * x ^ 2 - 0.518 * x + 0.298;
PC1 = y;
x = pF;
y = -0.053 * x ^ 5 + 0.292 * x ^ 4 - 0.618 * x ^ 3 + 0.663 * x ^ 2 - 0.438 * x + 0.234;
PC2 = y;
pc = PC1 - (PC1 - PC2) / (18 - 12) * (18 - t);
Else if t == 9
x = pF;
y = 0.034 * x ^ 4 - 0.161 * x ^ 3 + 0.284 * x ^ 2 - 0.269 * x + 0.186;
pc = y;
Else if t > 9 And t < 12
x = pF;
y = -0.053 * x ^ 5 + 0.292 * x ^ 4 - 0.618 * x ^ 3 + 0.663 * x ^ 2 - 0.438 * x + 0.234;
PC1 = y;
x = pF;
y = 0.034 * x ^ 4 - 0.161 * x ^ 3 + 0.284 * x ^ 2 - 0.269 * x + 0.186;
PC2 = y;
pc = PC1 - (PC1 - PC2) / (12 - 9) * (12 - t);
Else if t == 6
x = pF;
y = -0.013 * x ^ 4 + 0.042 * x ^ 3 - 0.002 * x ^ 2 - 0.11 * x + 0.147;
pc = y;
Else if t > 6 And t < 9
x = pF;
y = 0.034 * x ^ 4 - 0.161 * x ^ 3 + 0.284 * x ^ 2 - 0.269 * x + 0.186;
PC1 = y;
x = pF;
y = -0.013 * x ^ 4 + 0.042 * x ^ 3 - 0.002 * x ^ 2 - 0.11 * x + 0.147;
```

http://dx.doi.org/10.5772/57249

```
PC2 = y;
pc = PC1 - (PC1 - PC2) / (9 - 6) * (9 - t);
end
disp( pc)
disp('pF=')
disp (pF)
disp( 'pc=')
disp (pc) )
corpc = pc * (s / 20) ^ 0.2;
Uvn = corpc / (EV / (DL - EV )) ^ 0.5;
D = Sqrt((4 * Qv / (0.54 * 3.14 * Uvn))/60;
disp([ 'D=' num2str(D * 0.3048)])
Case 5
disp( 'Eq')
T = input ('T');
EL = input ('EL');
EV = input ('EV');
V = input ('V');
k = 3600 * (-0.171 * T ^ 2 + 0.27 * T - 0.047);
Uv = k / 3600 * ((EL - EV) / EV) ^ 0.5;
W = 3600 * EV * Uv;
D = ((4 * V) / (3.14 * W))^.5;
disp( ['k=' num2str (k)])
disp( [('D=' num2str(D)])
End
```

Author details

Hassan Al-Haj Ibrahim*

Address all correspondence to: sanjim84@yahoo.com

Dept of Chemical Engineering, Al-Baath University, Homs, Syria

References

[1] Forbes RJ. A short history of the art of distillation. Leiden: E. J. Brill; 1970.

[2] Sorel E. La rectification de l'alcool. Paris: Gauthier-Villars et fils; 1893.

[3] (Lord) Rayleigh. On the distillation of binary mixtures. Philosophical Magazine1902; 4:521-537.

[4] Urbain G and Boll M. La science, ses progrès, ses applications. Vol. 2, Les applications et les théories actuelles, Paris: Librairie Larousse; p. 304, 1934.

[5] Humphrey JL. and Keller, G. E., Separation Process Technology, New York: McGraw-Hill; 1997.

[6] Al-Haj Ibrahim H and Daghistani N. Petroleum refinery engineering (In Arabic). vol. 3, Homs, Syria: Al-Baath University; 2008.

[7] Distillation Column Selection and Sizing. KLM Technology group, 2011, available at: www.klmtechgroup.com.

[8] Chen H and Lin Y. Case Studies on Optimum Reflux Ratio of Distillation Towers in Petroleum Refining Processes. Tamkang Journal of Science and Engineering 2001; 4(2):105-110.

[9] Kister HZ. Distillation design. New York: McGraw-Hill Book Co.; 1992.

[10] Kolmetz K et al. Optimize Distillation Column Design for Improved Reliability in Operation and Maintenance. 2nd Best Practices in Process Plant Management, Kuala Lumpur, Malaysia, March 14-15, 2005.

[11] Pettit DR. Fractional distillation in a lunar environment. Los Alamos National Laboratory, MS P952, Los Alamos, NM87545.

[12] Holland CD. Fundamentals of multi-component distillation. New York: McGraw-Hill; 1997.

[13] Tham MT. Distillation, an introduction. available at: http://lorien.ncl.ac.uk/ming/distil/distil0.htm.

[14] Kister HZ et al. How Do Trays and Packing Stack Up? Chemical Engineering Progress, February 1994.

[15] Kister HZ et al. Equipment for Distillation. Gas Absorption, Phase Dispersion and Phase Separation, Section 14, Perry's Chemical Engineers Handbook, 8th Edition, New York: McGraw-Hill; 2008.

[16] Razia SS. Equipment Design and Costs for Separating Homogeneous Mixtures. Bangladesh University of Engineering and Technology, Dhaka.

[17] Seader JD, Siirola JJ, Barnicki SD. Distillation. Ch. 13 of Perry's Chemical Engineers Handbook, 7th Edition, New York: McGraw-Hill; 1997.

[18] Youssef S et al. Calcul d'une colonne de rectification à multiples alimentations et soutirages latéraux. The Chemical Engineering Journal 1989, 42(3):153–165.

[19] Jevric J, and Fayed ME. Shortcut Distillation Calculations via Spreadsheets. Dec. 2002, available at: www.cepmagazine.org.

[20] Guthrie KM. Data and techniques for preliminary capital cost estimating. Chem. Eng. 142, Mar. 24, 1969.

[21] Ludwig EE. Applied process design for chemical and petrochemical plants. vol. 2, Gulf Professional Publishing; 1997.

[22] Sinnott RK. Coulson & Richardson's Chemical Engineering. Elsevier, vol. 6, 2006.

[23] Douglas J. Conceptual Design of Chemical Processes. McGraw-Hill, Section A.3, 1988.

[24] Nelson WL. Petroleum refinery engineering. McGraw-Hill Book Co., New York, 1958.

[25] Wuithier P. editor. Le pétrole: Raffinage et génie chimique. Paris: L'institut français du pétrole; Vol. 2, 1972.

[26] Van Winkle M. Distillation. New York: McGraw-Hill Book Co.; 1967.

[27] Smith RB et al. Tower capacity rating ignores trays. Hydrocarbon process. and pet. Refiner 1963; 40(5):183.

[28] Gerster JA. Recent advances in distillation. Davis-Swindin memorial lecture, University of Loughborough, 1964.

[29] Branan CR. The Process Engineer's Pocket Handbook. Vol. 1, Gulf Publishing Co., 1976.

Section 3

Modeling, Simulation, and Analysis

Chapter 6

Remotely Train Control with the Aid of PIC32 Microcontroller

Mostefa Ghassoul

Additional information is available at the end of the chapter

http://dx.doi.org/10.5772/57365

1. Introduction

Automatic train control is very difficult due to two main reasons. One is the metrological conditions such as wind, rain, snow, heat, tear and wear which affects its behavior and secondly the changing load whether that load is passengers or goods, where the number of passengers may change from station to station, or change in goods as well. This renders the system to be highly non linear. So a non linear scheme is required. One feasible technique is by combining a PI with a fuzzy controller. To make the controller efficient, a 32 bits microchip PIC32 microcontroller is used. Programming PIC32 using fuzzy is very tedious, so it would be far better to use the MATLAB SIMULINK fuzzy block set. To program the controller using SIMULINK, special block sets are used called MICROCHIP block sets. Those have been developed by somebody called Kerhuel (1) and are offered for demo purpose with limited inputs. The chapter is divided into five sections. After this introduction, Section2 addresses the speed capture using a PIC18F452 mounted on the train, as well as the data transmission and data reception by the PIC32 level. Section3 discusses the train modeling. Section4 discusses the PI fuzzy logic controller and its implementation in SIMULINK. Section5 addresses the testing of the system, first by simulating the train, then two station test and three station test. Section6 presents the conclusion of the work presented here. The chapter is concluded by looking at possible alternatives to SIMULINK such as NI LABVIEW and Inform Fuzzy TECH. Last but not the least, a list of references is presented at the end of the chapter. A block diagram of the scheme is shown in figure (1).

INTECH
open science | open minds

© 2014 The Author(s). Licensee InTech. This chapter is distributed under the terms of the Creative Commons Attribution License (http://creativecommons.org/licenses/by/3.0), which permits unrestricted use, distribution, and reproduction in any medium, provided the original work is properly cited.

2. Train speed capture

Before any control takes place, the train speed has to be captured. This is done by using a light source (LED), which emits narrow rays towards a reflector mounted on one of the train wheels. The reflected light is picked up by a phototransistor. The output of the phototransistor is in the range of 1.62-2.07 V on no light, and 2.31- 2.89V on reflected light presence. This voltage is fed to a buffer (LM358N) for matching purpose. The buffer output is compared with a 2.25V voltage through another LM358N operational amplifier, to produce a pulse train, with zero volt for low voltage (<2.25V) and 5 V for high voltage (>2.25V). The duration of the pulse is proportional to the train speed. The speed capture circuit is shown in figure (2).

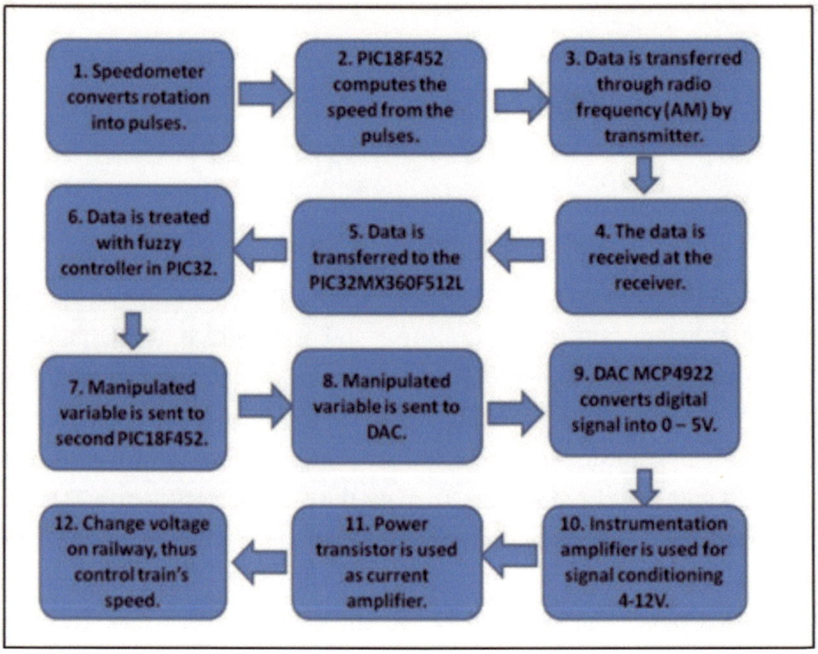

Figure 1. Block diagram of the system

The pulses are captured through the data capture port of the microchip PIC18F452 microcontroller, where each two successive leading edges are detected. The PIC18F452 has four 16 bit timers. In this project only Timer0 is used and programmed as a free running timer. On each leading edge, the timer value is read in a buffer. Then its value is read on the following leading edge into a second buffer. The difference between the two values gives the duration of the pulse. The shorter is the pulse, the faster is the train. So the speed is inversely proportional to the pulse duration.

V = K/T where V is the speed, T is the pulse period and K is the proportionality constant. It was found that the value of k is equal to 0.14192 V.S.

http://dx.doi.org/10.5772/57365

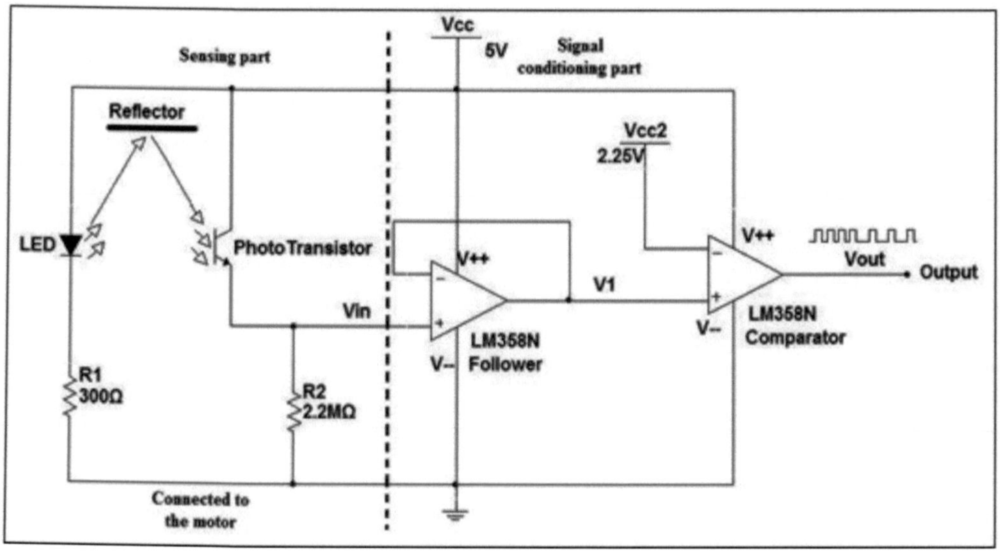

Figure 2. Train speed capture circuit

2.1. Speed transmission

The speed capture circuit is mounted on the train. So once the speed is computed, The signal is sent from the microcontroller using the Universal Synchronous Asynchronous Receiver Transmitter serial port (USART). it is then modulated using amplitude shift keying (ASK) in order to be radio transmitted. The modulator is of type SHY-J6122TR transmitter/receiver. It is capable of transmitting radio frequencies in the band 300-450MHz. In the control room, is the main controller which is nothing less than the powerful 32 bit PIC32 microcontroller. The choice of this device is for several reasons. 1- It has a 512 Kbytes of flash memory; so it could accommodate any program of this type of application. 2- It has a large stack, so it could accommodate all the if statements, produced by SIMULINK fuzzy controller algorithm, no matter how many rules are implemented without jumping the stack. 3- No truncation is needed because of the size of mantissa which is 32 bits. 4- The availability of the SIMILINK block sets, which makes the programming of the controller very easy. 5- up to 32 kbytes of RAM, for storing variables and tables when required. The speed signal is read into the controller through the USART, after being received and demodulated using a second SHY-J6122TR transmitter/ receiver. The transmitting microcontroller was programmed using PCC C language, and the subroutine is shown below:

Result1 and result2 are the current and previous timer readings, corresponding to edge capture of the current and previous edge. Line 18 defines the configuration of the serial port (USART). Line 26 configures the data capture1, where data is captured on every rising edge. Line 29 configures TIMER 1 as a 16 bit timer, with 1:1 prescaler, and timer source is capture1 (CCP), and the configuration circuit is shown in figure (3).

```
#include <p18f452.h>
#include <capture.h>
#include <timers.h>
#include <stdlib.h>
#include <usart.h>

#pragma config WDT = OFF

unsigned int result1;
unsigned int result2;
unsigned int delta;
unsigned int speed;

void main (void)
{

	//configure USART
	OpenUSART ( USART_TX_INT_OFF & USART_RX_INT_OFF &
	USART_ASYNCH_MODE & USART_EIGHT_BIT & USART_CONT_RX &
	USART_BRGH_HIGH, 207 );

	//configure PORTC, bit3 must be input RC2, bit6 must be output RC6
	TRISC = 0x04;

	// Configure Capture1
	OpenCapture1 ( C1_EVERY_RISE_EDGE & CAPTURE_INT_OFF );

	// Configure Timer1, internal clock is used which means Fosc/4
	OpenTimer1 ( TIMER_INT_OFF & T1_16BIT_RW & T1_SOURCE_INT &
		T1_PS_1_1 & T1_OSC1EN_OFF & T1_SOURCE_CCP );

	while (1)
	{

		while (!PIR1bits.CCP1IF); // Wait for event
		result1 = ReadCapture1(); // read result
		PIR1bits.CCP1IF = 0;//clear

		while (!PIR1bits.CCP1IF);
		result2 = ReadCapture1();
		PIR1bits.CCP1IF = 0;

		delta = result2 - result1;

		speed = 141952/delta;

		WriteUSART ( speed );
	}
}
```

http://dx.doi.org/10.5772/57365

2.2. Speed reception by the main controller

Once the speed is air transmitted, it is received into the main controller which is no more than the microchip PIC32MX360F512L microcontroller. The choice of this controller is because of the availability of the SIMILINK block sets to drive it. At start, the microcontroller has to be configured.

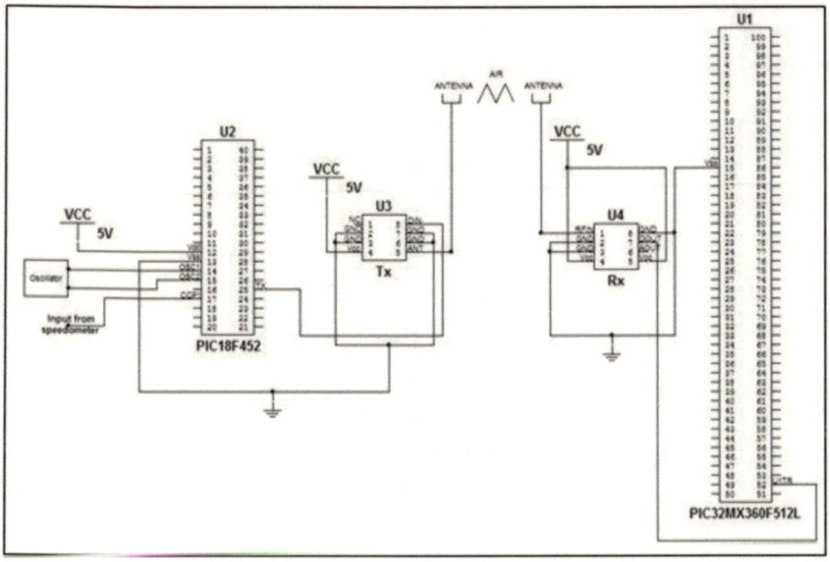

Figure 3. Circuit showing the transmitter and the receiver of the speed

This is done using three SIMULINK block sets. The first one is called "master". By clicking its icon, a windows opens where one configures the PIC, by selecting the type of controller, the port used, the clock which UART is used. Then UART1 icon (two UARTs are available on the chip) is clicked so that UART1 configuration pops up so it could be configured by setting the baud rate etc. Figure (4) shows the block set configuration.

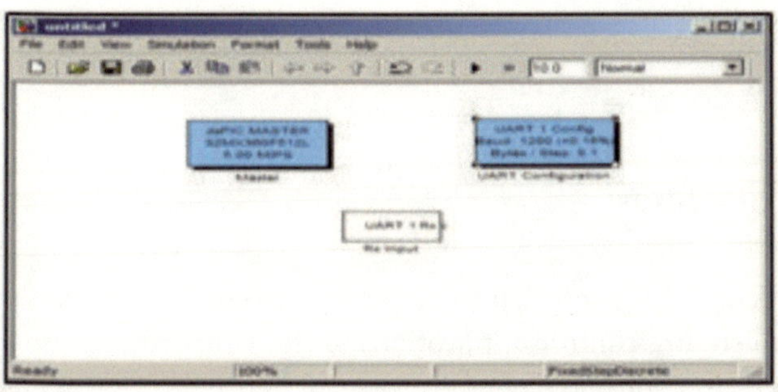

Figure 4. PIC32 port configuration using SIMULINK

3.Train model

Before any control to be applied, the train was first modeled using MATLAB system identification tool (SIT). This is done by entering a series of input voltages together with corresponding speeds. Table (1) shows the input voltage and the corresponding train speed. After opening SIT, "Time Domain Data" was selected to write workspace variables (voltage and speed) as shown in figure (5). After importing the data and estimating the model to be second order system with a time delay which represents the model for a DC motor, process model parameters were found. This is shown in figure (6).

	>> voltage=v
speed =	voltage =
1.7100	3.9900
3.4700	5.0000
5.1900	6.0400
6.3700	6.9900
7.8700	7.9900
9.5900	9.0000
11.2900	10.0100
13.2100	11.0000
14.8900	11.9900

Table 1. Speed (cm/s) as a function of input voltage (V)

4. Fuzzy logic controller

In any standard book on fuzzy control, fuzzy logic control is defined to be a practical alternative for a variety of challenging control applications since it provides a convenient method for constructing non-linear controllers via the use of heuristic information. Since heuristic information may come from an operator who has acted as "a human in the loop" controller for a process. In the fuzzy control design methodology, a set of rules on how to control the

http://dx.doi.org/10.5772/57365

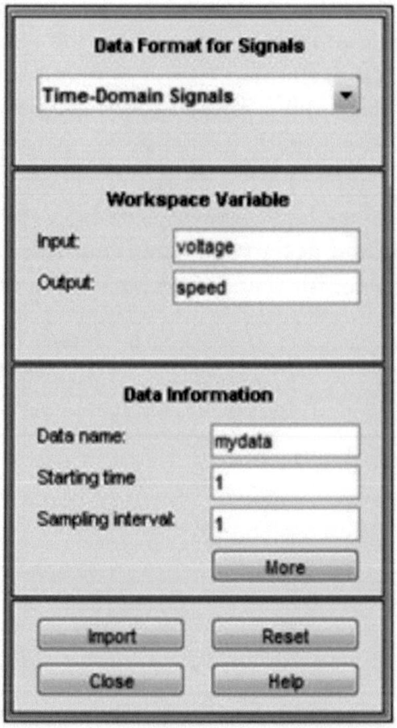

Figure 5. Importing data from workspace

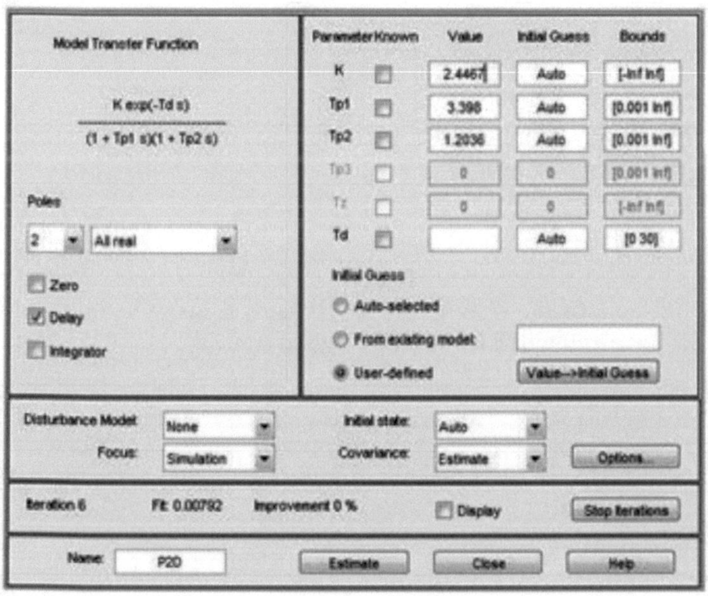

Figure 6. The modeling parameter of the train

process is written down and then it is incorporated into a fuzzy controller that emulates the decision making process of the human. In other cases, the heuristic information may come from a control engineer who has performed extensive mathematical modelling, analysis and development of control algorithms for a particular process. The ultimate objective of using fuzzy control is to provide a user-friendly formalism for representing and implementing the ideas we have about how to achieve high performance control. Apart from being a heavily used technology these days, fuzzy logic control is simple, effective and efficient(2). In this section, the structure, working and design of a fuzzy controller is discussed in detail through an in-depth analysis of the development and functioning of a fuzzy logic speed controller.

The general block diagram of a fuzzy controller is shown in figure (7). The controller is composed of four elements:

- A Rule Base
- An Inference Mechanism
- A Fuzzification Interface
- A Defuzzification Interface

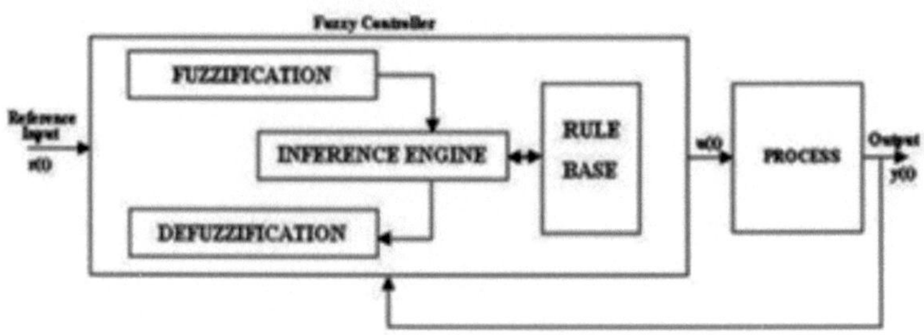

Figure 7. Fuzzy controler model

4.1. Rule base

This is a set of "If ……..then….." rules which contains a fuzzy logic quantification of the expert's linguistic description of how to achieve good control.

4.2. Inference mechanism

This emulates the expert's decision making in interpreting and applying knowledge about how best to control the plant.

4.3. Fuzzification interface

This converts controller inputs into information that the inference mechanism can easily use to activate and apply rules.

4.4. Defuzzification interface

It converts controller inputs into information that the inference mechanism into actual inputs for the process.

4.5. Selection of inputs and outputs

It should be made sure that the controller will have the proper information available to be able to make good decisions and have proper control inputs to be able to steer the system in the directions needed to be able to achieve high-performance operation.

The fuzzy controller is to be designed to automate how a human expert who is successful at this task would control the system. Such a fuzzy controller can be successfully developed using high-level languages like C, Fortran, etc. Packages like MATLAB® also support Fuzzy Logic.

4.6. Fuzzy sets and membership function

Given a linguistic variable Ui with a linguistic value Aij and membership function μ Aij(Ui) that maps Ui to [0, 1], a 'fuzzy set is defined as

Aij= {(Ui, μ Aij (Ui)); Ui ε υi}

The above written concept can be clearly understood by going through the following example. Suppose we assign Ui="VOLTAGE" and linguistic value A11="base", then A11 is a fuzzy set whose membership function describes the degree of certainty that the numeric value of the temperature, Ui ε υi, possesses the property characterized by A11. This is made even clearer by the fig (8).

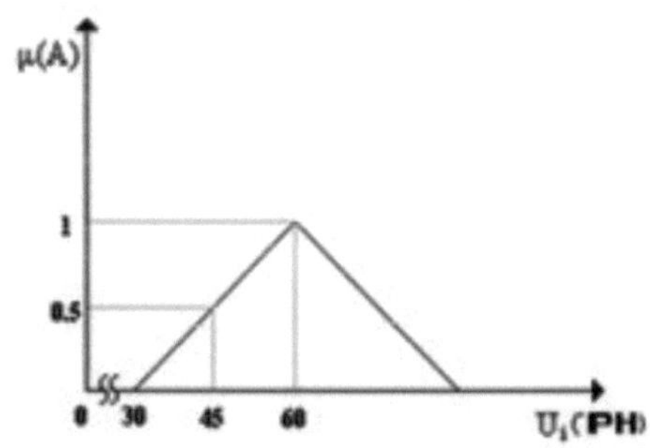

Figure 8. Triangular membership function

In the above example, the membership function chosen is triangular. There are some other membership functions lime Gaussian, Trapezoidal, Sharp peak, Skewed triangle, etc. Depending on the application and choice of the designer, the required one can be chosen (figure(9)).

It is well known that the train load is highly nonlinear due to the fact that the number of passengers keeps changing, as well as the goods, adding to that the unpredictable climatic conditions.. This makes the application of linear control techniques very difficult to implement.

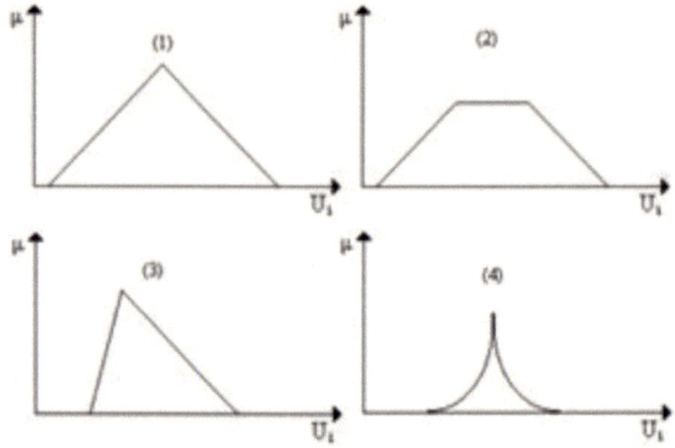

Figure 9. Triangular, 2) Trapezoid, 3) Skewed triangular, 4) Sharp peak

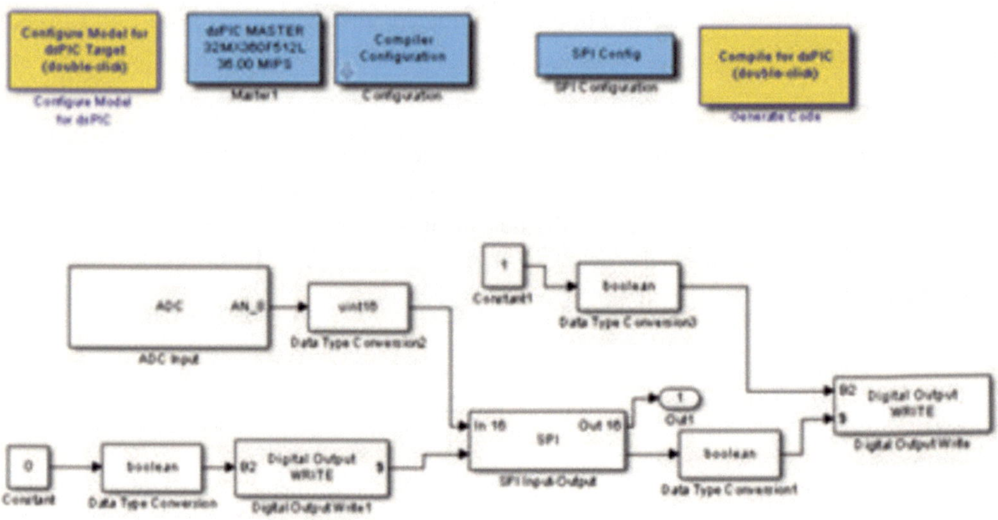

Figure 10. Different PIC32 block sets inserted into a SIMULINK model

So a feasible solution to make call to nonlinear techniques. A very suitable one for this type of application One is the fuzzy logic controller. On top of being simple to use because no transfer function is required, it could solve the nonlinearity problem if designed and tuned properly. To implement a fuzzy controller, using microcontroller, is a very tedious, time consuming and certainly not optimized whether it is developed using C language or assembly language. A better way is to make use of the optimized SIMULINK fuzzy controller block sets. But to do this, the PIC32 microcontroller resources have to be interfaced to SIMULINK. Luckily, this has been developed by a French researcher (1) and made available as a demo version with limited inputs/outputs. Those block sets are click and drag type, where they could be easily placed in a SIMULINK pane and configured. Figure (10) shows the different PIC32 block sets inserted into a SIMULINK model to control the train.. Once the model is compiled, they are two ways on how to download it into the microcontroller. After compiling the model using MATLAB real time workshop (RTW), if successful, it will produce two files, one with extension exe and one with extension mcp. The executable (exe) file could be downloaded directly into the microcontroller using a boot loader and executed. But unfortunately there is no way it could be debugged. A better solution is to use the mcp file, by downloading into MPLAB by clicking on outside the MATLAB (refer to figure (11). This will open the project within MPLAB, with all the required files and headers. It is then rebuilt and downloaded it into the controller and executed. The advantage of doing so is that the project could be debugged on line using MPLAB facilities and if necessary, it could be modified. Figure (12) shows MPLAB project window, with all the required files.

Figure 11. Exporting file from MATLAB to MPLAB

Figure 12. Train project with all the required files and headers produced by SIMULINK

4.7. Fuzzy control implementation

In the case in hand (train control), the constructed fuzzy controller has two inputs which are the distance and the speed and one output which is the voltage which drives the train. Before using the fuzzy block set in SIMULINK, we have first to define the rules and conditions, by importing the fuzzy software into MATLAB environment. Then define the memberships, rules and conditions. Once that is done, the file has to be exported to MATLAB workspace so it will be recognized by the SIMULINK fuzzy logic block set call.

4.7.1. Fuzzy memberships and rules

The fuzzy controller is shown in figure (13). The model has two inputs, distance and speed and one output is the voltage.

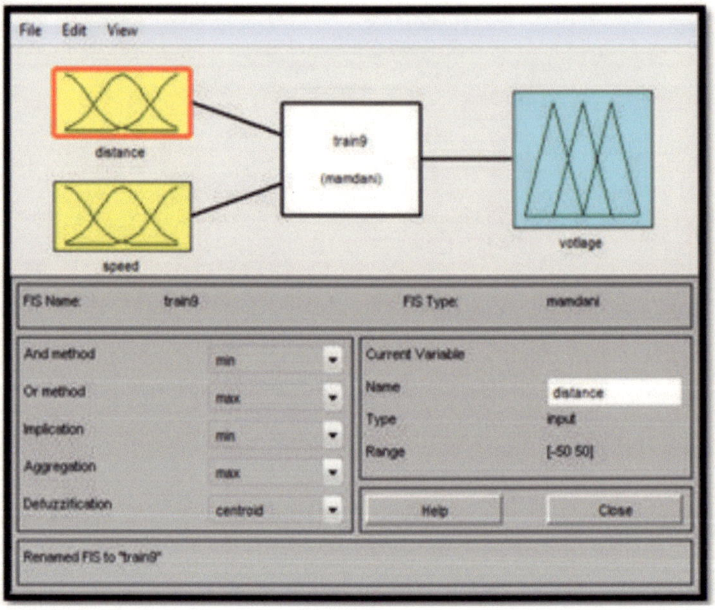

Figure 13. Train fuzzy model

The memberships were set. It is worth mentioning here that the train only accelerates at the start, then it cruises to its cruising speed and keeps the speed constant until it reaches the proximity of the breaking distance, it decelerates until it comes to a standstill. Figure (14) and figure (15) show the memberships of the inputs and output respectively. The memberships are of triangular type for accelerating and decelerating and trapezoidal shape for cruising. Using MATLAB software we design the rules and the functions we need for controlling the speed of the train. Figure (16) shows the fuzzy rules at the beginning, the train accelerates until it reaches cruising speed.

http://dx.doi.org/10.5772/57365

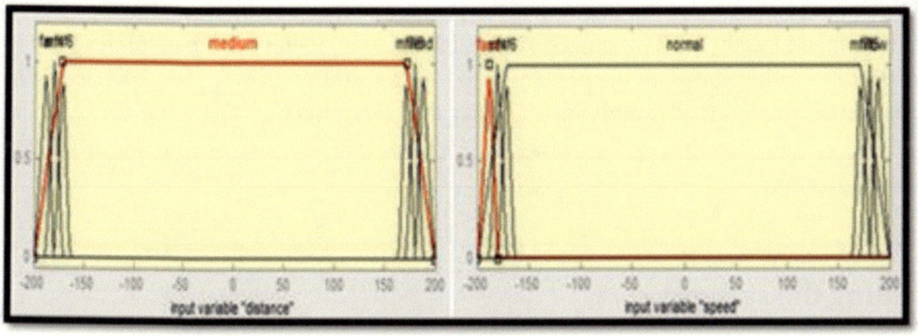

Figure 14. Membership of the inputs (distance and speed)

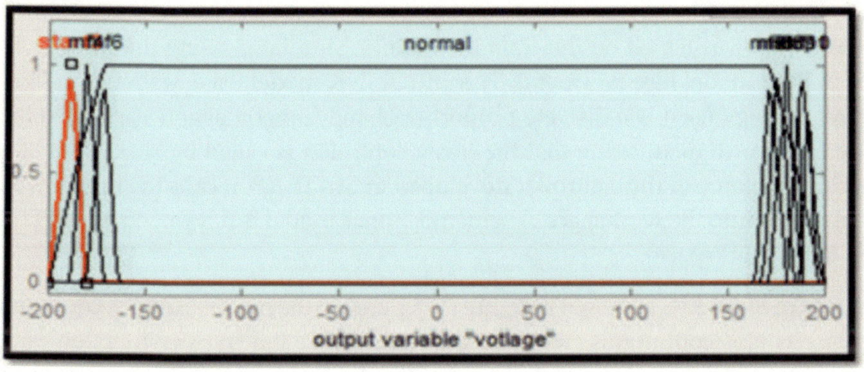

Figure 15. Membership of the output (voltage)

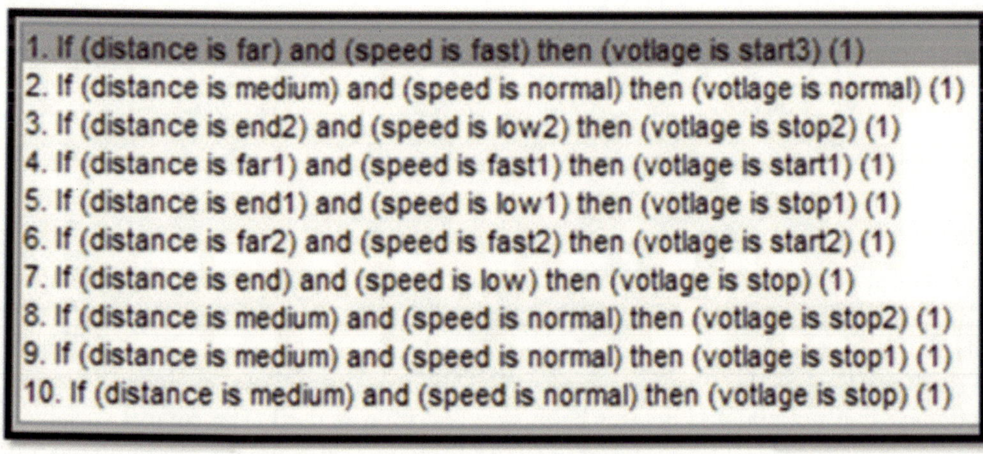
1. If (distance is far) and (speed is fast) then (votlage is start3) (1)
2. If (distance is medium) and (speed is normal) then (votlage is normal) (1)
3. If (distance is end2) and (speed is low2) then (votlage is stop2) (1)
4. If (distance is far1) and (speed is fast1) then (votlage is start1) (1)
5. If (distance is end1) and (speed is low1) then (votlage is stop1) (1)
6. If (distance is far2) and (speed is fast2) then (votlage is start2) (1)
7. If (distance is end) and (speed is low) then (votlage is stop) (1)
8. If (distance is medium) and (speed is normal) then (votlage is stop2) (1)
9. If (distance is medium) and (speed is normal) then (votlage is stop1) (1)
10. If (distance is medium) and (speed is normal) then (votlage is stop) (1)

Figure 16. Fuzzy rules for train control

For controlling the train, at the beginning the memberships are tuned so that the train cruises to normal speed (-200 _ -160 range). Once this is achieved, it stays there no mater how long is the trajectory, until it comes to the proximity of the stop station (range 160 _ 200), it decelerates until it comes to standstill following the stopping membership. Once the control action is computed, a deffuzification process takes over to generate the crisp output. Figure (17) shows the deffuzification.

5. Testing the system

Before the system was tested, the train was first modeled and simulated.

5.1. Simulating the system

Before the model was tested on the train, it was first simulated using the transfer function obtained in train model (see figure (6)), The SIMULINK model used is shown in figure (18). The control strategy used is a discrete proportional and integral action applied to the fuzzy controller. It is worth mentioning that the fuzzy controller is called by clicking on its action, and entering the name of the controller developed in MATLAB, it calls the model which was already exported into the workspace.. (Remember once model is developed in MATLAB, it is exported to the workspace).

The response of the model is shown in figure (19). Because the model used is a continuous one, the response is also continuous. This could be noticed in the transfer function and the PI controller where the S domain is used instead of the discrete sample. This is confirmed by the smoothness of the response. This will not be the case when online control of the train is implemented. It also shows the smoothness of the response whether at the start or stop phases.

5.2. Testing the controller using real data

The testing was carried out on a small train where the speed could be varied from zero to 31cm/s by varying the input voltage from zero to 12 V, first using only two stations then three stations.

5.2.1. Two station test

The model used for the test is shown in figure (20). The controller is reading the speed UART1 receiver(UART1 RX) of the PIC32, which was radio transmitted from the train. This feeds the PI controller. This time, a discrete digital integrator is used. This because the MATLAB real time workshop only complies PIC32 block sets using discrete form. It is worth mentioning that no model is present because a real train is used. The control variable is outputted using the UART1 transmitter (TX UART1) (how this signal is controlling the train will be discussed later). The train response is shown in figure (21). Figure (21) shows the smoothness by which the train accelerates, then cruise at a constant speed, then decelerates and stop exactly at the right stop.

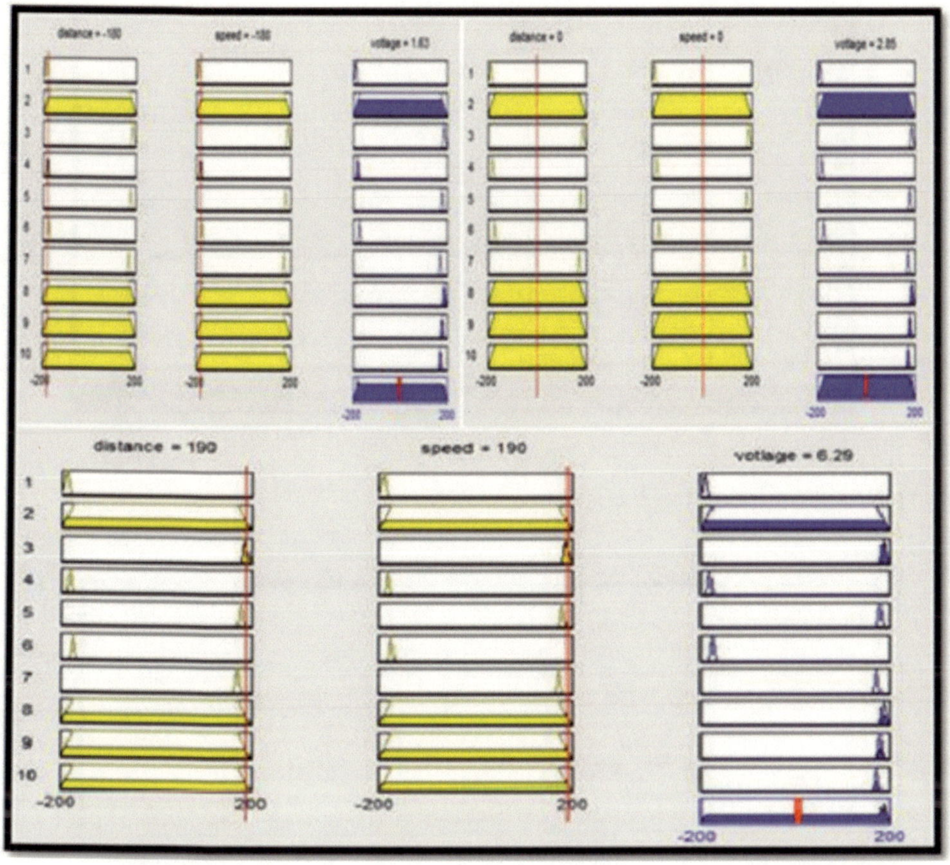

Figure 17. Deffuzification process

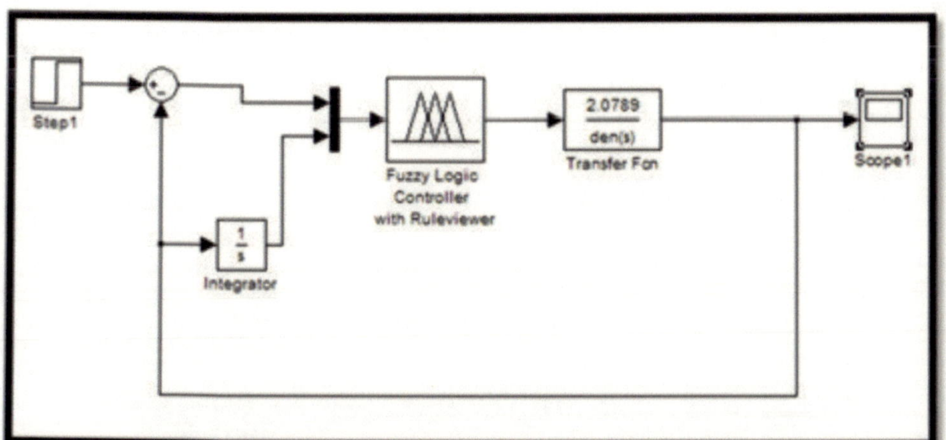

Figure 18. Simulation of the SIMULINK of the train model

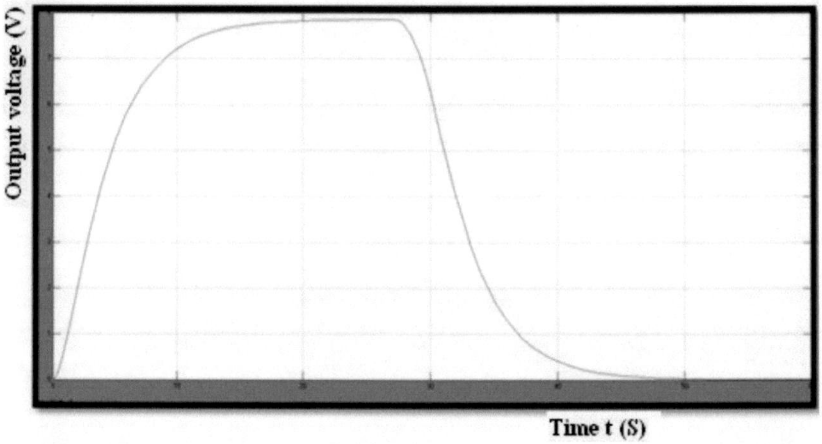

Figure 19. SIMULINK simulation of the train model

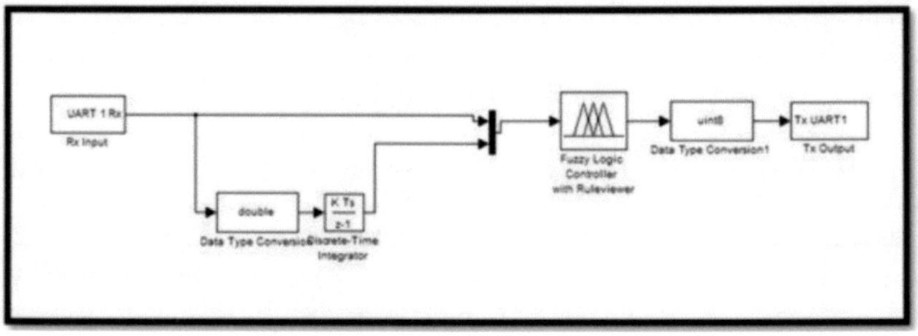

Figure 20. Train control between two stations

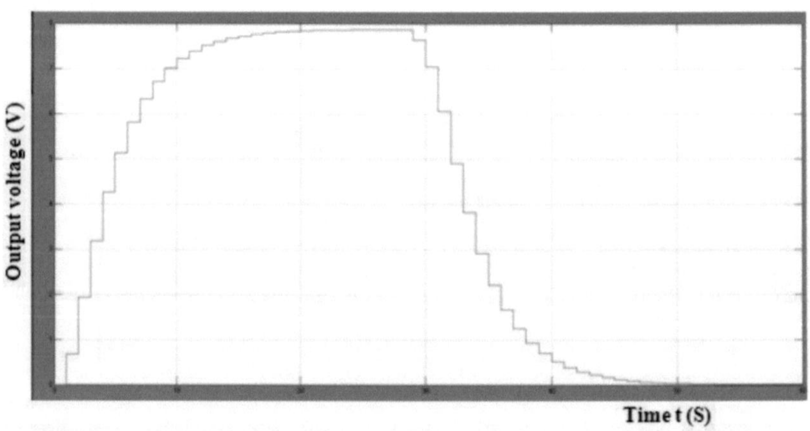

Figure 21. Train trajectory between two stations

http://dx.doi.org/10.5772/57365

5.2.2. Three station test

The train was then tested using three stations. Initially, it leaves station1 and accelerates, cruises, then decelerates at station2 and stops where it waits for ten seconds, then it accelerates again, until it reaches station3 where it decelerates and stops. The SIMULINK model is shown in figure (22).

The fuzzy memberships are shown in figure (23).

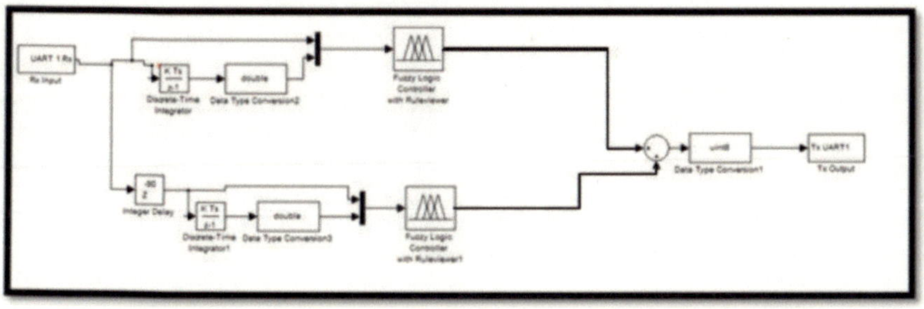

Figure 22. Three station controler

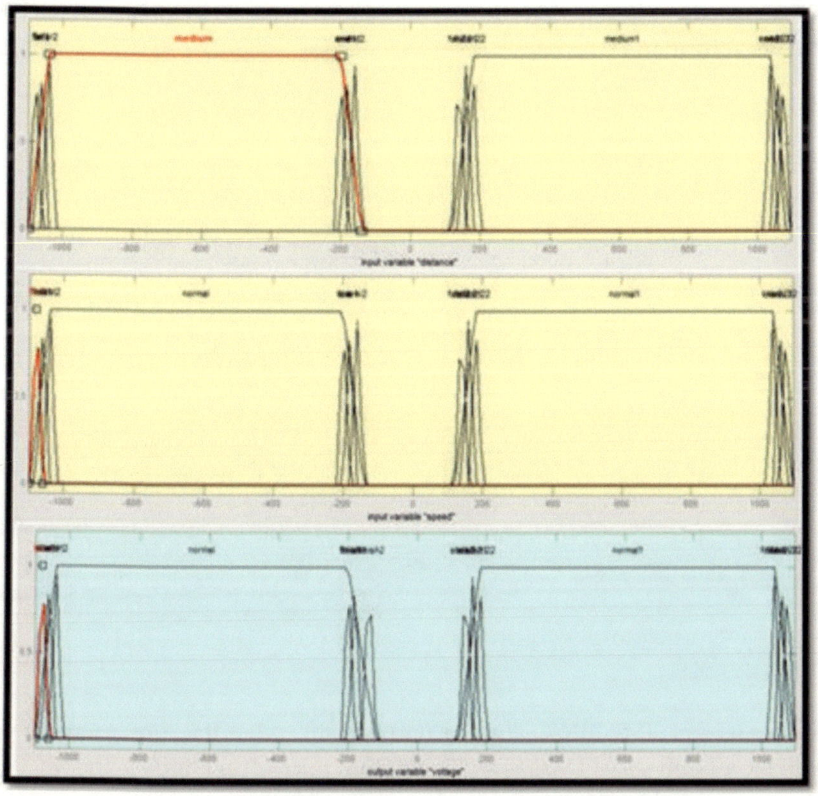

Figure 23. Input/output memberships for three stations

It could be noticed that each membership is divided into seven parts; acceleration at station1, then cruising between station1 and 2, then decelerating at station2, then waiting, then accelerating at station2, then cruising between station2 and 3 and finally stopping at station3. The trajectory rules are shown in figure (24).

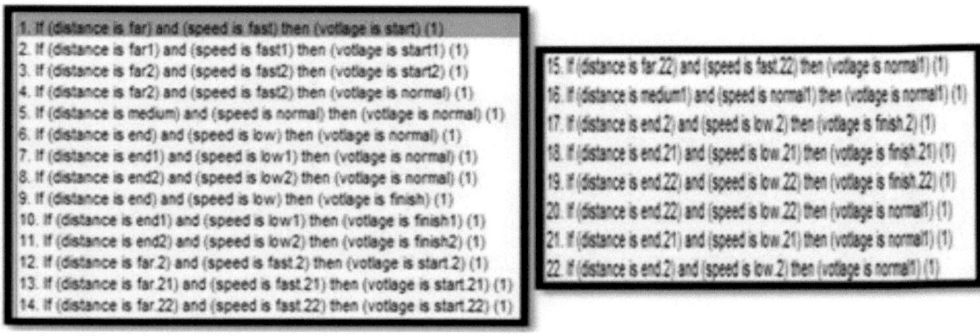

Figure 24. Fuzzy rules for three station system

The response of the system is shown in figure (25). To emulate a real system, the distances between station s to be different. Yet the response looks to be very smooth, if one ignores the steps due to discretization.

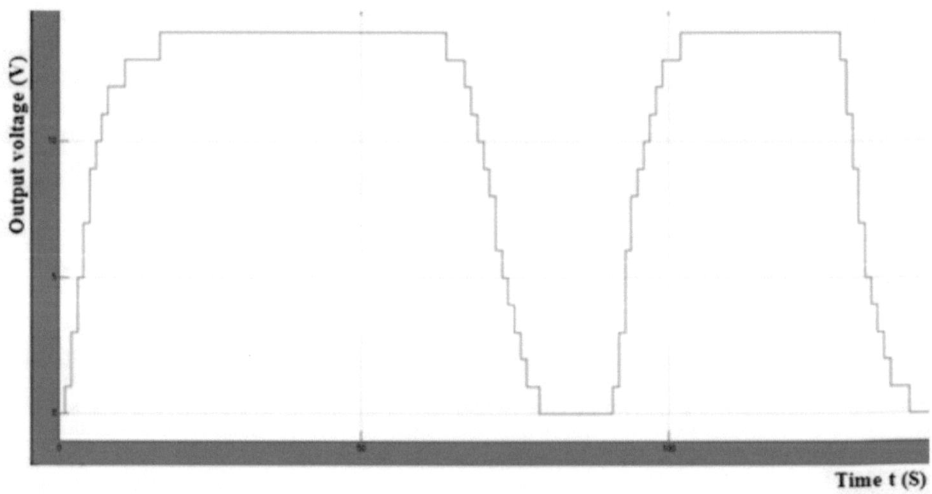

Figure 25. Three train station

The digital output from SIMULINK cannot drive the train, unless it is converted to an analogue signal. To do so, a 12 bit serial DAC is available from microchip which is the MCP4922. This converter has got a synchronous serial interface (SPI) with three connections; one is the serial data, one is the synchronizing clock and the third one is the chip select. On the output side, it

http://dx.doi.org/10.5772/57365

has two analogue channels A and B. In the application in hand, only channel A is used. The output of the converter is between 0 and 5V, so one requires to amplify this from zero to 12V. It was also noticed that the train starts moving only if the voltage reaches 4V. To do this we use the instrumentation amplifier INA114A together with a -5V regulator (LM7905T). The -5C is used to feed the negative rail on one side, and to obtain the exact required voltage of -4V at the inverting rail of the amplifier by using a potential divider. The output of the amplifier feeds an emitter follower to obtain enough current to drive the train electric motor. The voltage is applied to the train through the rails, so no extra arrangement is required. Figure (26) shows the output interfacing circuitry between the microcontroller and the train.

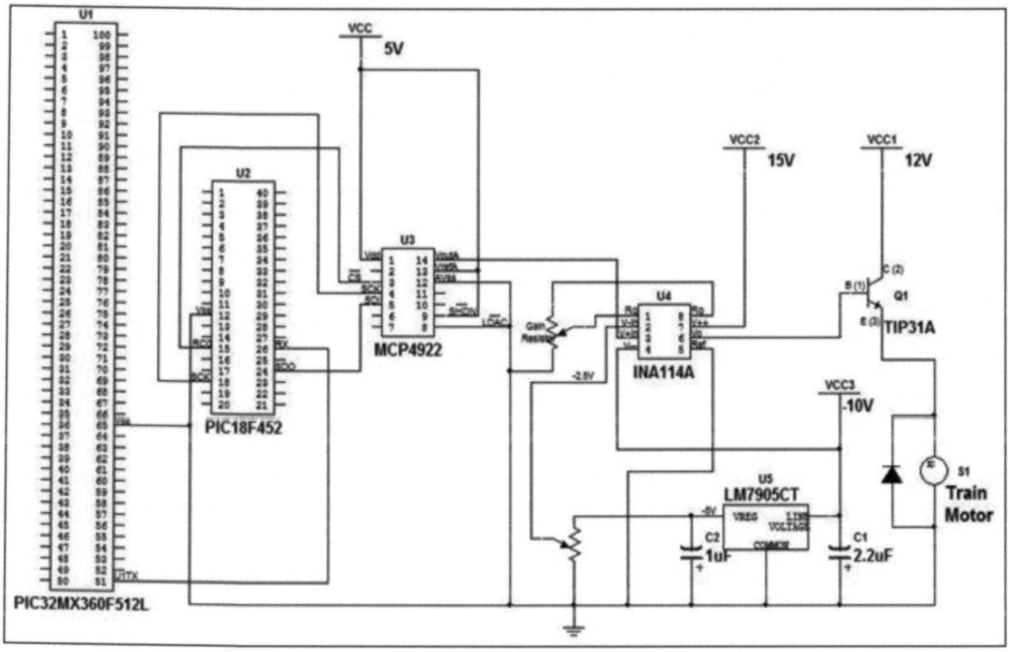

Figure 26. Output interface between the controler and the train

6. Conclusions

Though at the beginning MATLAB and SIMULINK were simulation tools to aid students and researchers to develop and simulate models. But there was a major drawback. That is it was difficult to interface those models to a real process. But in last few years things have changed where several companies have developed interfacing cards, together with their block sets (4& 5). Better still, in the last few years, block sets have been developed to program advanced microcontrollers such as dsPIC30 and dsPIC33 (6& 7) together with the powerful 32 bit PIC32 (7). This has renders the task of developing advanced control such as fuzzy logic, relatively simple and interesting as well. Instead of going into the process of developing fuzzy control algorithm from scratch with all the problems which come with it in terms of time and bugs, it would be better to use on line a well established, easy to use algorithm such as SIMULINK based block set. This had made the simulating modeling straight forward (figures (5 & 6) and table (1)). The model representation was just click and drag type. (figures(18, 20 & 22)), so are the memberships (figures(14, 15 & 23)). One important factor, unlike other algorithms, the SIMULINK one could accommodate a big number of rules. (figures(16 & 24)).. In fact it could accommodate more than 100 rules.

On the design side, a remotely controlled train system was designed and tested. Though, the prototype is too small to be loaded to see its effect on the algorithm, nevertheless it has shown to be very effective. The beauty of the algorithm that we only bother at the transition periods (acceleration and decelerations) where special care has to be taken to fine tune the memberships and the rules no matter how many stations are used. Once the train enter the cruise trajectory, only a single trapezoidal membership is required This is demonstrated in simulation mode (figure (19)) though this looks to be very smooth, That is due to using continuous simulation. For real test, discrete integration was used. That is shown on the on line response (figures (21 & 25)) either for two stations or three stations respectively. This did not affect the response of the motor. Last but not the least, the compatibility of the electronics (figures (3 & 26)) such as the type of the microcontroller and its large stack and memory to accommodate all the if statements required by the fuzzy algorithm, plus the different ports such as the UART and SPI, to the serial converter and the signal conditioning circuitry to drive the train.

Though this chapter has shown the greatness of SIMULINK in rendering programming a very powerful and wonderful microcontroller such as the PIC32 relatively easy, it still faces a main challenge. That is how to monitor the speed online. Luckily, a call to the PIC serial port (USART) came to the rescue, where the port is interfaced to the computer serial port RS232, through a MAXIM max232 transceiver (7). Then a MATLAB input m-input function block is called. This block displays the speed response online as it shown in figures (21,25)

7. Alternative tools to SIMULINK

Practically there are alternative solutions other than SIMULINK such as LABVIEW and Fuzzy TECH. A company known as 3D micro Tools (3DμT) has developed a tool (10), compatible with NI LABVIEW, which generates PIC C code in similar manner as SIMULINK which could be fired into the PIC. The generated code could be fired into the PIC using the microchip MPLAB platform. However it is quite difficult at this stage to make a fair comparison between SMULINK based and NI LABVIEW based platforms, for the simple reason I have not tried yet. However, there is a will to do that in the near future. For the Fuzzy TECH, it looks though it is only implemented on certain old PIC microcontrollers such as PIC16C5x, PIC16Cxx and PIC17Cxx (11). As mentioned earlier, it looks though it is very difficult to implement a relatively accurate fuzzy algorithm on such controllers for the simple reason, that the stack memory is very limited. This in turn, makes the number of rules hence number of calls in fuzzy rules very limited as well. This may not produce accurate results.

http://dx.doi.org/10.5772/57365

Author details

Mostefa Ghassoul*

Address all correspondence to: mghassoul@uob.edu.bh

Chemical Engineering Department, College of Engineering, University of Bahrain, Bahrain

References

[1] http://www.kerhuel.eu/wiki/Download (This is the site where a demo SIMULINK block sets could be downloaded from).

[2] http://www.microchip.com/search/searchapp/searchhome.aspx?id=2&q=matlab (PIC32 is not included)

[3] Ghassoul, M. "pH control using MATLAB" Chapter in book MATLAB: A fundamental tool for scientist and engineering applications Volume 1 Edited by V.N.Katsikis, Intech PP243 – 268

[4] Ghassoul " Design of a Fuzzy System to Control a Small Electric Train Using Microchip PIC32 With the Aid of MATLAB Blocksets" IEEE Computer Science and Automation Engineering (CSAE) 2011 International Conference, Shanghai, Vol 03, PP 242-246

[5] Noor,S.B.M, Khor, W.C and Ya'acob,M.E. " Fuzzy logic control of a nonlinear pH neutralisation in waste water treatment" International Journal of Engineering and Technology,VOL. 1, No 2, 2004, pp 197-205

[6] Sang-Hoon Lee, Yan_Fan Li and Vikram Kapila " Development of a MATLAB-based graphical user interface environment for PIC microcontroller projects" Proceedings of the 2004 American Society for Engineering Education Annual Conference and Exposition Session 2220

[7] HUMUSOFT MF 624 Multifunction I/O card

[8] National Instruments PCI 6221 data acquisition card

[9] 3Dmicro Tools "Design, develop and download code on PIC microcontroller with NI LabView" This product was developed in collaboration with Prof. David Scaradozzi and supported by LabMACS, Laboratory of Modeling, Analysis and Control of Dynamical Systems, Department of Information Engineering, Universita' Politecnica delle Marche, Ancona (IT). January 2013

[10] Fuzzy TECH is a trademark of Inform GmbH and Inform Software Corporation

Chapter 7

Integration of MATLAB and ANSYS for Advanced Analysis of Vehicle Structures

A. Gauchía, B.L. Boada, M.J.L. Boada and V. Díaz

Additional information is available at the end of the chapter

http://dx.doi.org/10.5772/57390

1. Introduction

During vehicle structure design several parameters have to be considered, not only to pass vehicle approval tests but also to manufacture an efficient vehicle. Therefore, initial gross designs have to be optimized in order to reach the best compromise between two main antagonistic parameters: vehicle stiffness and weight. Optimization has proved to be a powerful tool in order to achieve the best possible design.

In the engineering field several programs, focused in vehicle structure analysis and based on the finite element method (FEM), are available (i.e. ANSYS, Abaqus, etc). Some of these programs allow the user to perform optimization algorithms of the vehicle structure. Even though finite element analysis of structures can also be done with MatLab it is not a FEM-focused software. However, MatLab is a powerful program that provides not only different optimization algorithms already implemented but the possibility to run a defined user optimization algorithm. Therefore, it seems that the best solution is to couple the FEM software (such as ANSYS) with MatLab in order to get the best from both while allowing total control by the user. In addition, due to the fact that the user can modify the optimization parameters as well as the vehicle geometry, the overall proposed loop has proven to be a successful tool in advanced mechanical engineering analysis. The main difference with respect to other researches that combine ANSYS and MatLab is that the proposed methodology is done completely automatically and that the developed optimization script does not require user intervention until the solution is found or stopping criteria is achieved.

The present chapter details how to carry out this coupling and how to manage the files between them. To clarify, a complex bus structure, shown in Figure 1, optimization loop is described as an example. The aim is to explain how to generate the needed files in order to establish an automatic loop that does not need user intervention. In addition, some

INTECH
open science | open minds

© 2014 The Author(s). Licensee InTech. This chapter is distributed under the terms of the Creative Commons Attribution License (http://creativecommons.org/licenses/by/3.0), which permits unrestricted use, distribution, and reproduction in any medium, provided the original work is properly cited.

specific hints on ANSYS and MatLab programming are provided in order to achieve success in the final implementation.

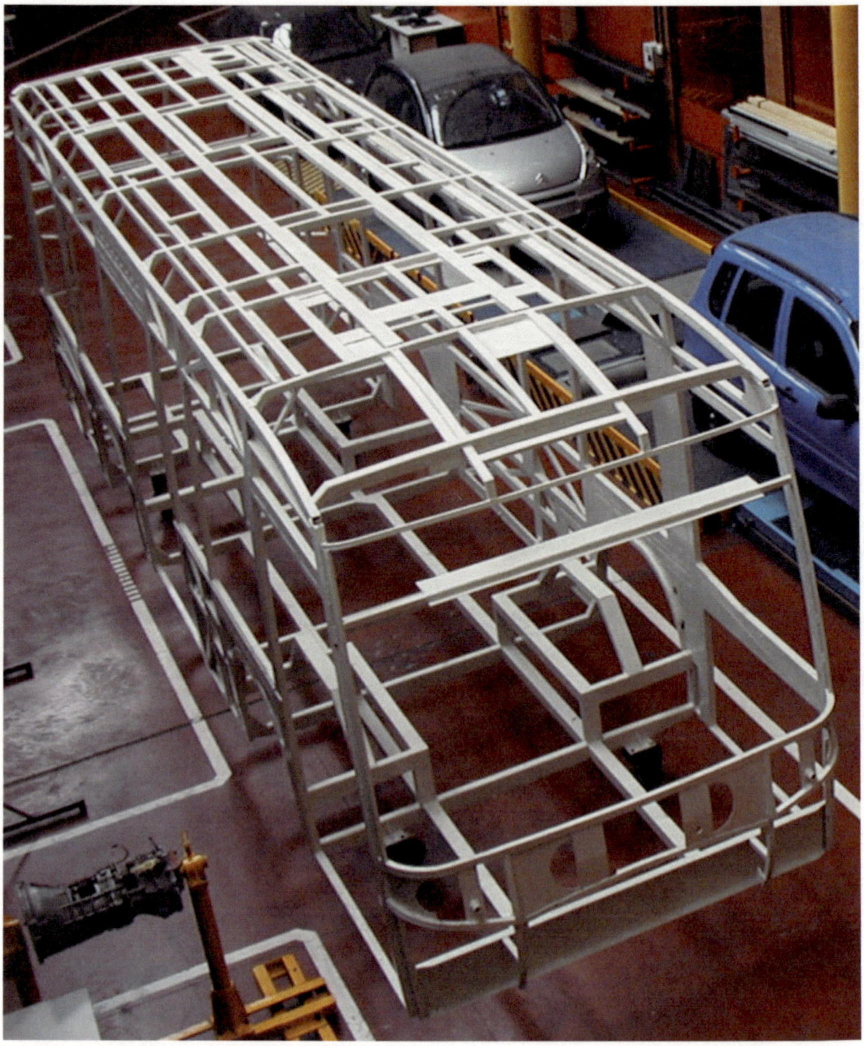

Figure 1. Real bus structure

The layout of the chapter is as follows. In section 2 the overall flow diagram is described. The aim of section 2 is to show the overall file flow which has been applied to optimize in torsion stiffness and vehicle weight a real urban bus structure. In section 3 a brief description of the bus structure model is provided as well as how to generate the output files. The genetic algorithm optimization is described in section 4. This section not only shows how the genetic algorithm is done but how to define the fitness function. In addition, this section describes and reveals how to call ANSYS from MatLab so that ANSYS is run under the operating system

http://dx.doi.org/10.5772/57390

(batch mode) automatically until the optimized value is achieved. Section 5 shows some of the obtained results to prove the effectiveness of the proposed advanced analysis. Finally, section 6 provides conclusions of the described methodology.

2. The overall flow diagram

The aim is to optimize a complex bus structure in weight and stiffness. The bus structure has to have a certain amount of bending and torsional stiffness, being torsion the most demanding effort [1]. Torsion loads appear during vehicle cornering, unequal bumps or potholes. A bus torsion stiff structure is desirable in terms of handling and lateral rollover dynamics [2, 3]. However, increasing vehicle torsion stiffness usually requires of adding beams to the structure, thus increasing vehicle weight. An increased vehicle sprung weight penalizes the vehicle lateral dynamics as more weight is transferred between the wheels of the same axle, thus reducing tire lateral grip. In addition, for the analyzed vehicle structure, the vehicle centre of gravity height has a massive influence in rollover. For the same torsion stiffness it is desirable that the heavier beams are placed as low as possible while being able to protect passenger from a possible rollover [4]. Therefore, for a given structure configuration and layout of beams, the optimization tool should provide the optimal structure that allows achieving a certain value of torsion stiffness by changing the thickness of the appropriate vehicle beams while keeping the vehicle weight to a minimum [5].

From the different optimization algorithms available in MatLab [6], genetic algorithms have been selected to optimize the bus structure. Genetic algorithms are being applied in many areas of the mechanical engineering field, having proved to be a suitable tool to optimize vehicle structure. In fact, genetic algorithms are particularly suitable for optimization in which a multidimensional global search with multiple local minimum is required. In addition, genetic algorithm is especially well-suited when the search space is not well known, being able to combine the best solutions yielding an even better one.

The bus structure analysis will be carried out with ANSYS [7], which is a finite element software. It is worth highlighting that any other finite element software (either licensed or opened source) may be used to be coupled with MatLab. The requirement to be fulfilled is that the software must allow programming the finite element model by means of a text file in order to be able to automate the proposed optimization methodology shown in Figure 2. The coupling between MatLab and the finite element software is done by means of line code which will be later detailed. For the particular case analyzed in this paper ANSYS has been used. The complete creation and solving of a structure may be done either by picking on the different menus or by programming in Ansys Parametric Design Language (APDL). The main advantage of creating and solving a model by means of APDL is that the model can be defined in terms of variables, thus creating a parametric model. In general, the variable that is employed to create a parametric model is beam thickness as it greatly influences vehicle stiffness and weight. Other variables such as the length of the beam could be considered, but modify the overall vehicle geometry. In terms of the optimization loop it is very convenient to create a parametric model as an automatic loop can be created without user intervention. The values of the different variables will be changing according to the optimization loop until a minimum is reached. APDL allows, among other features, creation of files in text format to store the results of the analyzed model. These files will be used by the optimization tool in order to re-define better values for the variables of the vehicle structure.

Figure 2 resumes the optimization loop. In the depicted figure the output of each of the steps is also shown. It can be seen that the information between ANSYS and MatLab is based on text files which are overwritten in each loop. All of the created files must be placed on the same folder.

The optimization loop will flow through the following steps:

- The file "OptiBus.m" creates the file "parameters.inp" which stores the value of the thickness of the beams. This file is the one that runs the genetic algorithm, which needs to evaluate the fitness function.
- Once the file "parameters.inp" stores the assigned values of the thickness of the beams the finite element model can be run. The finite element model is programmed, by means of APDL, in a text file ("BusModel.txt"). This text file retrieves the values of the beam thickness from file "parameters.inp". Once the model is solved, the results ("Displacement.txt", "ReactionForce.txt", "Stress.txt" and "Weight.txt") are stored in different files. These results will be used to evaluate the fitness function, which represents the objective function that has to be minimized.
- Next, the genetic algorithm mutates the value of the thickness so as to achieve a minimum in the fitness function. The new values for the beam thickness are stored and overwritten in "parameters.inp".
- The loop will continue until a stopping criteria or minimum is achieved.

Although an optimization loop has been presented in this chapter as an example of how to couple MatLab and ANSYS, any other loop vehicle calculation could be performed.

It is worth highlighting that prior to any optimization, a sensitivity analysis of the vehicle structure must be performed [8]. The aim of the sensitivity analysis is to find the beams of the vehicle structure so that a change of beam thickness is highly sensitive to weight and torsion stiffness. Therefore, the optimization process will be focused on the beams whose change in beam thickness generates great changes on weight and torsion stiffness. Thus, the optimization loop will only be applied to certain beams of the bus structure. For the particular case analyzed in the current chapter, the main optimized beams belong to the bus chassis, as shown in Figure 3. The sensitivity analysis is performed by measuring the change of weight and torsion stiffness when 1 mm increase is applied to the beams of the vehicle structure. By computing the ratio variation of weight to variation of thickness (sensitivity to weight) and comparing this result for the different beams the most sensitive beams to weight can be selected. In addition, by computing the ratio of the variation of torsion stiffness to the variation of thickness (sensitivity to torsion stiffness) the most sensitive beams to torsion stiffness can be found. Due to the fact that the aim is to select the beams that are most sensitive to both parameters at the same time,

http://dx.doi.org/10.5772/57390

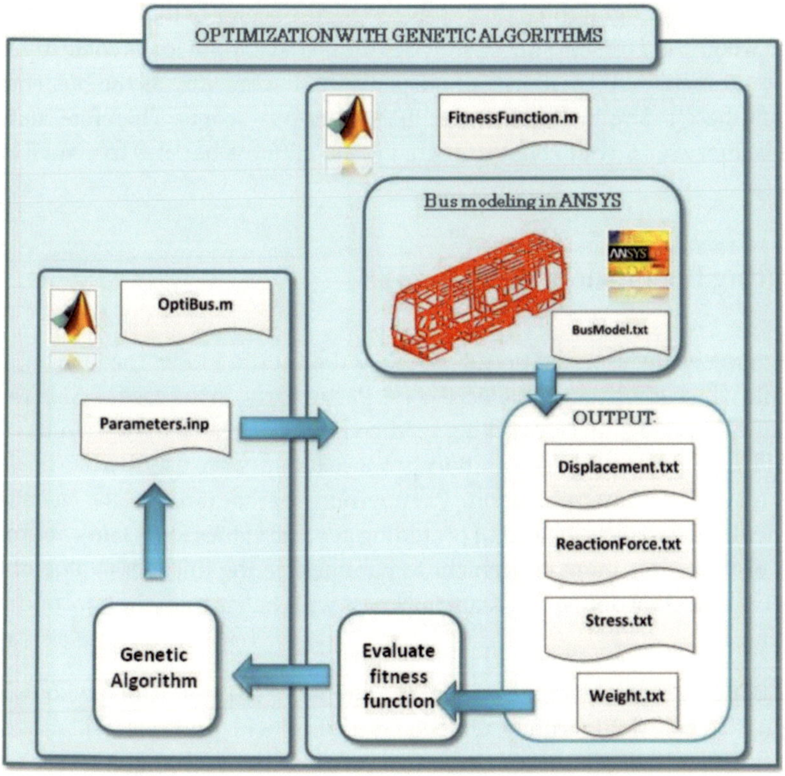

Figure 2. Optimization flow diagram

a ratio between the sensitivity to weight and the sensitivity to torsion stiffness may be defined. In addition, it is worth checking if the results of the sensitivity analysis are coherent with the expected. For the analyzed bus structure, it is expected that the beams placed at the chassis (lower part of the superstructure represented in Figure 1) are very sensitive to torsion stiffness. The reason is that these beams are the connection link between both bus axles and also to the superstructure.

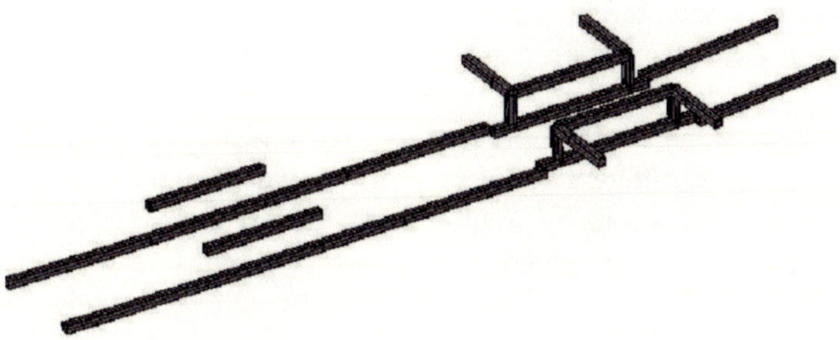

Figure 3. Beams of the bus chassis most sensitive to weight and torsion stiffness

From Figure 3 it can be highlighted that, as expected, the beams of the bus chassis have a great influence on weight and torsion stiffness. Due to the fact that input loads come from the wheels and these are transmitted, by means of suspension attachments, to the bus structure, it is expected that these beams will be heavier than other bus beams. Therefore, not only these beams will be more sensitive to bus structure torsion stiffness but also to overall bus weight.

3. Generating the bus model in ANSYS

Most of the finite element model programs allow the user to model the vehicle structure by means of a file which is written in a special code. Particularly, in the case of ANSYS the vehicle structure can be created either by picking on the various available options in the menu or by means of APDL programming. The authors propose for advance users to use the latter as it is the most suitable for parametrization. Parametric programming of the vehicle structure consists of defining variables instead of providing specific values to certain variables. Thus, in the present example it is more convenient to parametrize the thickness value of the vehicle beams. The variables that define this beam thickness will change until the final optimized value is achieved.

It is worth noting that the aim of the present chapter is not to provide detail knowledge of the optimization with genetic algorithms nor become skillful with finite element modeling, but to learn how to create the complete calculation progress by coupling ANSYS and MatLab. Therefore, in depth concepts of APDL programming are not explained in this chapter.

Modeling of a vehicle structure, and in general, of any engineering process by means of the finite element method, must follow three steps: Pre-processor, Solution and Post-processor. During the Pre-processor the geometry of the bus structure and material properties are defined. Once the geometry of the structure is generated the user must specify in the Solution step the loading condition and constraints. Finally, during the Post-processor results can be visualized.

3.1. Pre-processor

Regarding the Pre-processor, the bus structure is defined by means of beam elements. Prior to generate the beam elements the structure geometry is built with lines and keypoints. In addition, the user must define the cross section of all of the beams of the bus structure, which are 2445 beams. During the meshing process each beam is defined with it's corresponding cross section. More than 50 different beam cross sections were defined. Due to the fact that the entire described bus model is done by programming, instead of providing a specific value for the thickness a variable ("T") was given. In fact, each of the thicknesses of the each beam is defined as Ti (view Figure 4).

The bus beam cross sections are made of hollow rectangular steel beams. The material of the bus structure is steel with the material properties shown in Table 1.

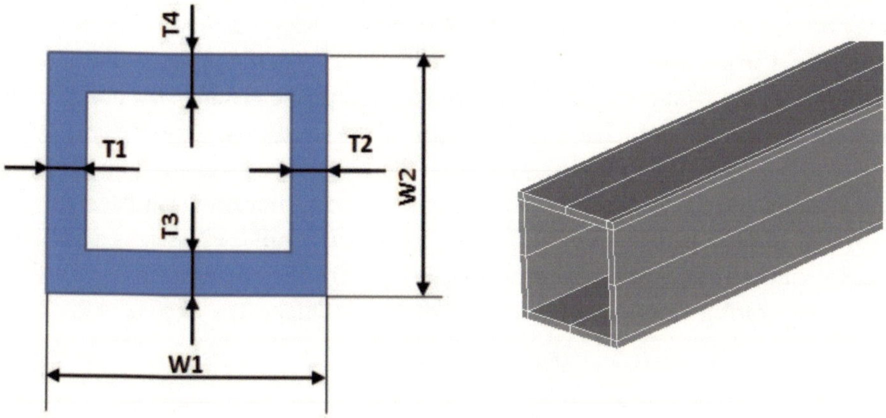

Figure 4. A parametric beam cross section (left) and the corresponding beam of the bus structure (right).

Material	Modeled as	Elasticity modulus (GPa)	Poisson ratio	Density (kg/m^3)
Steel	Linear elastic	200	0.3	7850

Table 1. Bus structure material properties

The bus structure is modeled as linear elastic. All of the applied loads are intended to be computed in the linear range of the material. The reader must recall that the loading conditions must provide the bus structure torsion stiffness and the weight, thus, none of these loads requires information regarding its plastic behavior. Figure 5 depicts the geometry of the complete bus structure.

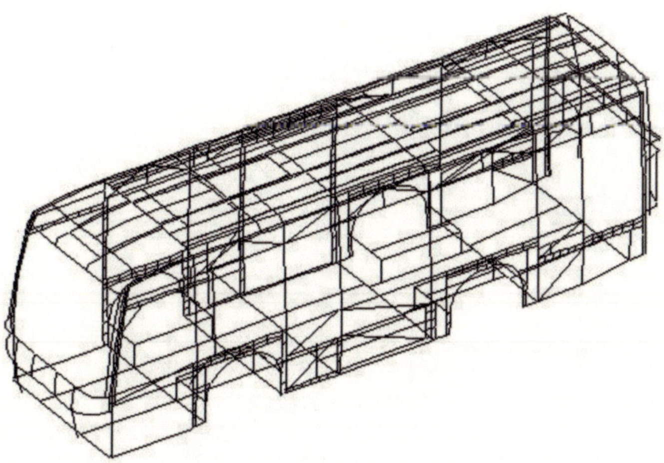

Figure 5. Finite element of the bus structure.

The complete bus structure does not include side panels nor windows, seats, etc. However, they may be included in the designer needs them to be considered. Figure 6 shows an example of how the bus structure geometry by means of APDL programming, is defined. It can be observed that a file "parameters.inp" is needed as an input to generate the bus structure as it contains the values of the thickness of the beams. Afterwards, the type of element is created (Beam 44) and the material properties are provided. Next, the geometry of each of the cross sections is generated. It can be observed that cross section 1 thickness has been parametrized with T1, T2, T3 and T4 (see Figure 4). The "parameters.inp" just assigns values for each thickness variable by stating for example that T1=1.5. The file "parameters.inp" is the output of the genetic algorithm implemented in MatLab, which will be described later on the chapter.

```
/inp,parameters,inp

/PREP7

/TITLE,BUS-4: BUS STRUCTURE OPTIMIZATION



ET,3,BEAM44
ET,4,MPC184
KEYOPT,4,1,1
MP,EX,1,210000
MP,NUXY,1,0.3
MP,DENS,1,7.85e-9



SECTYPE,    1, BEAM, HREC, 6P303015, 0
SECOFFSET, USER, 15, 15
SECDATA,30,30,T1,T2,T3,T4,0,0,0,0

SECTYPE,    2, BEAM, HREC, 252515, 0
SECOFFSET, CENT
SECDATA,25,25,1.5,1.5,1.5,1.5,0,0,0,0
```

Figure 6. APDL programming to generate the bus structure ("Busmodel.txt")

In Figure 7 an example of the "parameters.inp" is shown.

http://dx.doi.org/10.5772/57390

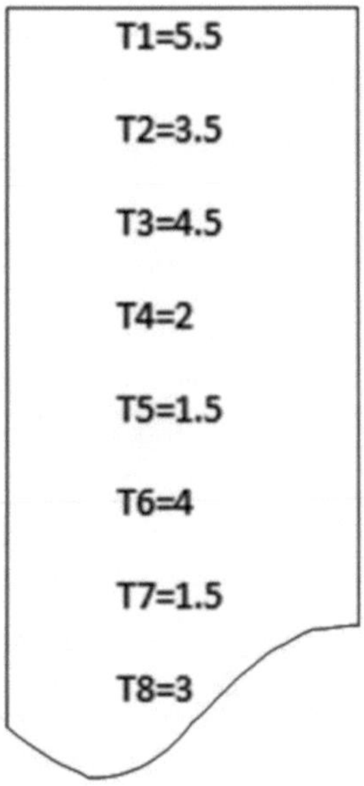

Figure 7. Example of value of thickness parameters ("parameters.inp")

3.2. Solution

During the solution step the loading condition and constraints must be applied. In this particular case, the aim is to optimize the vehicle structure in torsion stiffness and weight. Therefore, two loading conditions must be defined:

- Load condition to compute bus structure weight: Gravity (g=9810 N/mm^2) must be applied to the body structure and the four suspension supports must be constrained. It must be highlighted that while at the front axle there is one suspension support per wheel, at the rear axle there are two suspension attachments per wheel, thus, the whole bus structure sprung mass is supported by six suspension supports. During the post-processor step, the sum of the reactions at these supports will provide the bus structure weight.
- Load condition to compute torsion stiffness: A specific vertical displacement (Δz) is applied at one of the suspension supports while the others supports are constrained. Torsion stiffness is computed by means of the following equation:

$$K_T = \frac{M_T}{\Delta\phi} = \frac{F_z \cdot B}{\tan^{-1}\left(\frac{\Delta z}{B}\right)} \quad [\mathrm{N{\cdot}m/deg}] \tag{1}$$

where F_z is the vertical force measured at the suspension support at which the vertical displacement Δz is applied and B is the wheeltrack. In addition to the loads, constraints must be applied to the model. In Figure 8 the loads and constraints applied to the bus structure for the torsion loading condition are depicted.

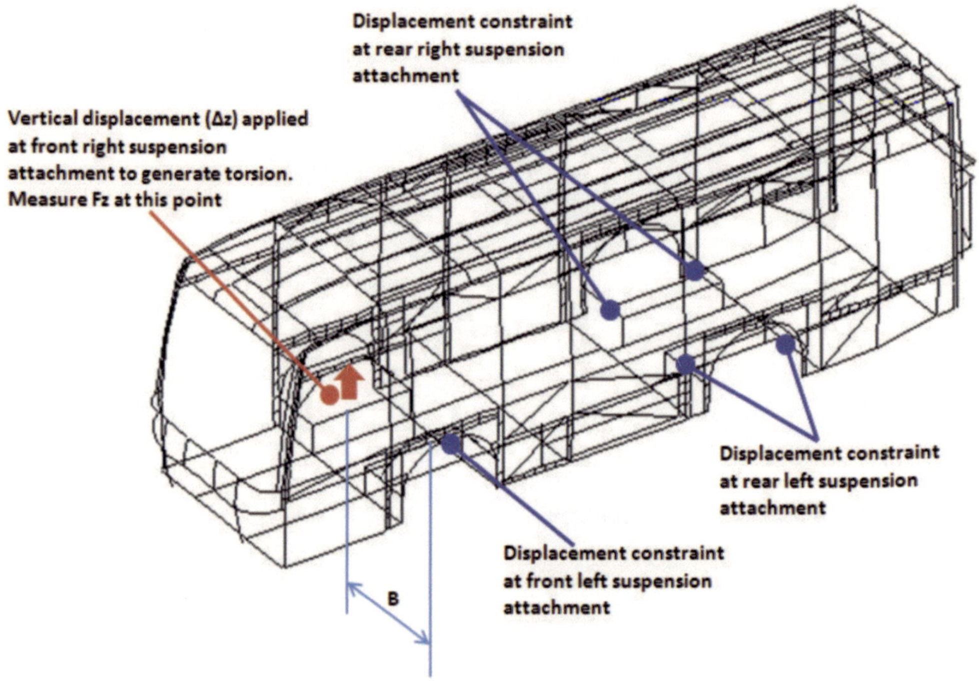

Figure 8. Constraints and loads for the torsion load case

The rotation angle generated in the structure (φ) due to the applied vertical displacement is measured by means of the vertical displacement (Δz) of the lifted suspension strut and the wheeltrack (B). It is worth highlighting that if a massive vertical displacement is applied to the bus structure it would reach permanent deformation, shown in Figure 9, which is a scenario not desired to be achieved. The reason is that the bus structure can be considered to behave as a torsion spring under torsion loads. Therefore, the value of the measured torsion stiffness should be measured during the elastic linear range of the bus structure material; otherwise, it would not represent the elastic bus structure performance correctly. As shown in Figure 9, for the applied vertical displacement in one of the suspension struts the maximum stress at the bus structure must be below the yield stress of the bus structure material, which in the particular example shown in this chapter must be below 250 MPa. Therefore, during the post-processor the maximum stress measured in the bus structure must be below the yield stress during the torsion load condition.

http://dx.doi.org/10.5772/57390

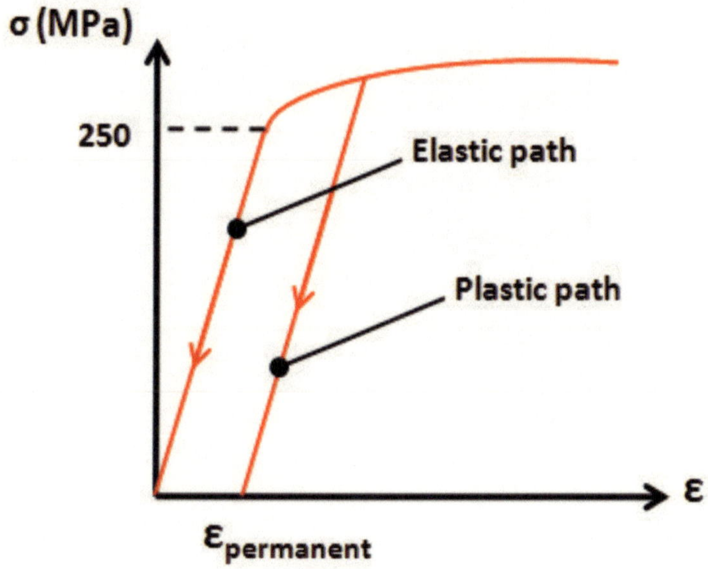

Figure 9. Bus material behaviour

Due to the fact that the value of the torsion stiffness is computed in the elastic range its value is independent of the applied vertical displacement. A bigger applied vertical displacement will provide the same value for the bus structure stiffness, as the value of the measured vertical force (F_z) will change to provide the same amount of stiffness. More complex models that account for a damping factor for the bus structure can be considered, but the frequency of the applied torsion loads is usually small, thus the torsion spring is the main activated component. Most of the vertical displacement is absorbed by the bus pneumatic suspension travel. Bigger torsion loads take place during very fast cornering or large potholes, being for the former mass longitudinal distribution an important parameter.

3.3. Post-processor

Finally, results can be viewed and stored in files for further usage. The value of the weight of the bus structure is done in the APDL file. The outputs are four files: "Displacement.txt", "ReactionForce.txt", "Stress.txt" and "Weight.txt". These files will be used to evaluate the fitness function. As an example, the programming in APDL in order to write the file "Weight.txt" is shown in Figure 10.

Similarly, by means of programming in APDL a file with the value of stress will be stored in a specific file ("Stress.txt"), as shown in Figure 11.

The Postprocessor allows viewing results by means of plots, as depicted in Figure 12, where von Misses stress is represented.

```
/POST1

*GET,P1,NODE,2512,RF,FZ
*GET,P2,NODE,2527,RF,FZ
*GET,P3,NODE,621,RF,FZ
*GET,P4,NODE,2612,RF,FZ
*GET,P5,NODE,2623,RF,FZ
*GET,P6,NODE,1052,RF,FZ

P=P1+P2+P3+P4+P5+P6

/OUT,Weight,txt
*VWRITE,P
(F15.5,'                    ')
```

Figure 10. Example of how to save variables and store them in a file ("Weight.txt")

```
/POST1

ETABLE,SMAXI,NMISC, 1
ETABLE,SMINI,NMISC, 2
ETABLE,SMAXJ,NMISC, 3
ETABLE,SMINJ,NMISC, 4

SMAX,SMAXVAI,SMAXI,SMAXJ,1,1
SMAX,SMAXVAJ,SMAXI,SMAXJ,1,1
SMAX,SMAXVAEL,SMAXVAI,SMAXVAJ,1,1

ESORT,SMAXVAEL
*GET,STRS,SORT,,MAX
PARSAV,ALL

/OUT,Stress,txt
*VWRITE,STRS
(F10.5,'                    ')
PARSAV,ALL
```

Figure 11. Example of how to save variables and store them in a file to create file "Stress.txt"

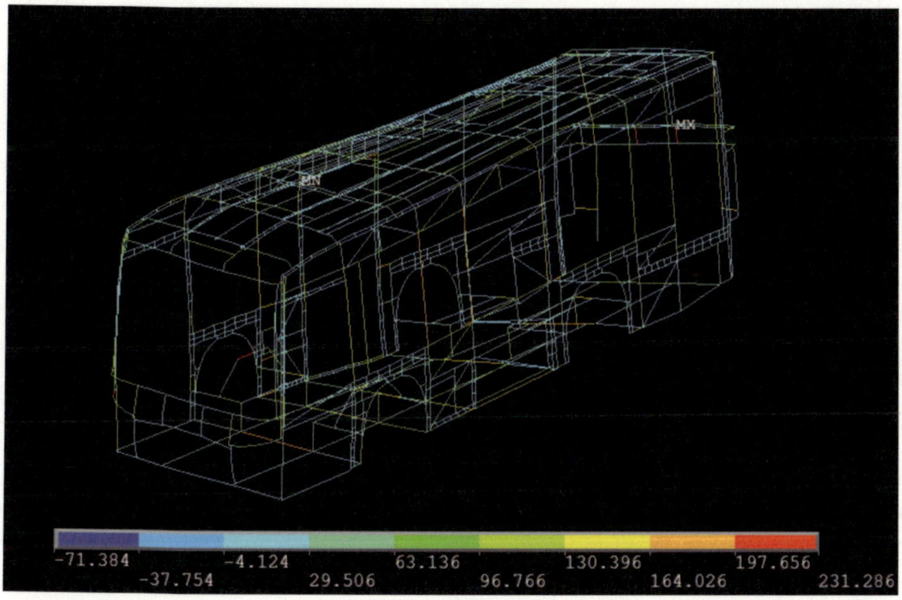

Figure 12. Postprocessing of the bus structure during a torsion rear right load

4. Optimization with genetic algorithms

Genetic algorithms (GA) have been used in this particular case because they are especially suited for multidimensional global search problems where the search space potentially contains the multiple local minimum. In addition, GA do not require having an extensive knowledge of the search space, thus, computing time can be reduced. Last but not least, GA finds better solutions by combining good solutions.

GA has proved to be a suitable tool to solve many optimization problems in the mechanical engineering field, for example, to find the optimum diameter of a rotor shaft as in [9]. In the field of structures it has also been successfully used to optimize truss structures [10, 11]. GA have also been applied for crack detection in shafts [12] as well as to estimate the overall elastic stiffness [13]. In the field of mechanism it has been used for the synthesis of complaint mechanisms [14, 15].

Genetic algorithms consist of three main steps: selection, genetic operation and replacement [16, 17]. The cycle is repeated until a termination criterion is achieved. The criterion can be defined in terms of the maximum number of cycles, the amount of variation of individuals between different generations or of a predefined value of fitness. The best value of the parameters achieved during search will be the final result of the genetic algorithm loop. The function that quantifies the evolutionary mechanism is the fitness function. The fitness function is the function that the user desires to minimize. Therefore, it represents the main link between the real system (for this particular case, the bus structure) and the genetic algorithm. The two main parameters of a genetic algorithm are the fitness function and the search space.

The search space is the area in which the genetic algorithm will search the solution that best minimizes the fitness function. The genetic algorithm is able to search in the whole search space but this would increase computational effort and time. Thus, a specific search space in which the best solution can be found is provided to the genetic algorithm. For the particular analyzed case, the criteria to specify the genetic algorithm the search space can be based, for example, on minimum allowable thickness to weld two beams or in the minimum standard available beam thickness, etc. For the bus structure, the search space is restricted to values of thickness ranging from 0,25 mm to 9 mm. These values have been selected because they represent standard common beam cross section used in busses.

The fitness function is a function that must be defined by the user. The aim is to minimize this function. Therefore, for the particular case analyzed in this chapter, this function must be proportional to the bus structure weight. In addition, it must be inversely proportional to bus structure torsion stiffness. From equation 1 it can be found that torsion stiffness is proportional to the measured vertical force (F_z). In order to reduce computation time and taking into account that the fitness function is minimized; it must be inversely proportional to the measured vertical force (F_z) at the node at which the vertical displacement is applied in order to maximize torsion stiffness.

A simple genetic algorithm is shown in Figure 13. This genetic algorithm has been implemented in MatLab by means of an integrated toolbox.

One of the most important steps is to define the fitness function. The fitness function will consider the weight, the stress level and the reaction force measured during the torsion stiffness computation for a given applied vertical displacement. This reaction force is an indirect measurement of how stiff a chassis is, as explained above. For the particular example the fitness function defined by the authors is the following one:

$$\begin{gathered} if\left\{\left(\frac{\sigma_{\max}}{S_{steel}}<1\right)\&\left(\frac{W}{W_o}<1\right)\&\left(\frac{F_{zo}}{F_z}<1\right)\right\} \\ ff3=\left(\frac{\sigma_{\max}}{S_{steel}}\right)+\left(\frac{W}{W_o}\right)^4+\left(\frac{F_{zo}}{F_z}\right)^2 \\ \text{else ff3} = \text{infinity} \end{gathered} \tag{2}$$

where S_{steel} is the steel yield stress (250 MPa), σ_{max} is the maximum stress measured during the virtual torsion test, W is the weight of the bus structure for each loop, W is the initial value of the weight of the bus (W_o=1580 kg), F_z is the reaction force at the location at which the vertical displacement is applied in order to generate torsion in the bus structure for each loop and F_{zo} is a fixed value of 5500 N.

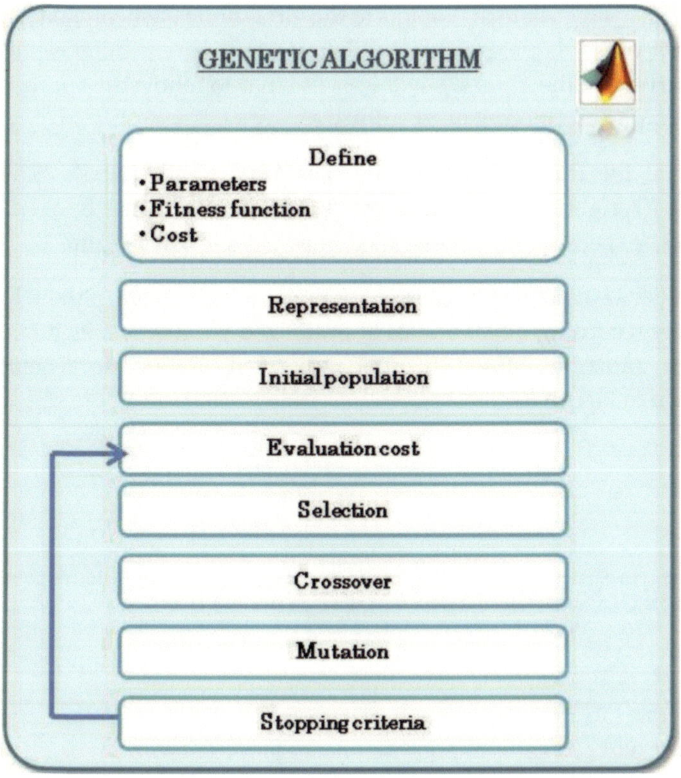

Figure 13. Genetic algorithm done in MatLab

The fitness function is defined in a MatLab file which is the one that will call ANSYS so that it runs in batch mode, that is, so that it runs under the operating system without intervention of the user. The file "fitnessfunction.m" stores the optimized parameters in the file "parameters.inp", executes ANSYS in batch mode and evaluates the fitness function.

The first part of "fitnessfunction.m" is depicted in Figure 14.

Programming of the fitness function, defined by equation (2), is shown in Figure 15.

During the first part the developed program stores the provided values of beam thickness from the GA ("OptiBus.m") to individual variables. Next, these individual variables are stored in the file "parameters.inp" which will be used to create the bus geometry. Afterwards, ANSYS is executed from "fitnessfunction.m" by means of the command specified in Figure 16.

If another type of finite element software is employed "C:\Program Files (x86)\Ansys Inc\..... \ANSYS.exe" must be substituted by the appropriate executable route file. In addition, it must be checked on the help tool how to run the finite element software in batch mode. Batch mode allows the software to be run under system without specifically opening it by providing an input text file in which the finite element model is programmed. For ANSYS, batch mode is run with the specific commands described in Figure 16. The third part of the code provided in the figure specifies the file route that points to the input finite element model text file in which the finite element model is programmed. When using different finite element software the programming written in the input file will vary as it has to follow the appropriate commands for the specific employed finite element software.

Next, to evaluate the fitness function, the files "ReactionForce.txt", "Displacement.txt", "Stress.txt" and "Weight.txt" generated by "BusModel.txt" must be read. Thus, reading commands must be specified in "fitnessfunction.m", as shown in Figure 17.

In addition, another MatLab file will call the GA tool to which several parameters will be given. Other parameters regarding initial values of optimized parameters, its minimum and maximum values, etc. must be defined in order to correctly define the genetic algorithm. An example is shown in Figure 18.

```
function salud=fitnessfunction(T)

T1=abs(T(1));
T2=abs(T(2));
T3=abs(T(3));
T4=abs(T(4));
T5=abs(T(5));
T6=abs(T(6));
T7=abs(T(7));
T8=abs(T(8));

fid=fopen('parameters.inp','w+');
fprintf(fid,'T1=%f\n',T1);
fprintf(fid,'T2=%f\n',T2);
fprintf(fid,'T3=%f\n',T3);
fprintf(fid,'T4=%f\n',T4);
fprintf(fid,'T5=%f\n',T5);
fprintf(fid,'T6=%f\n',T6);
fprintf(fid,'T7=%f\n',T7);
fprintf(fid,'T8=%f\n',T8);
fclose(fid);
```

Figure 14. First part of file "fitnessfunction.m"

http://dx.doi.org/10.5772/57390

```
fid=fopen('ReactionForce.txt','r');
FR=fscanf(fid,'%f',[1,1]);
fclose(fid);

fid=fopen('Weight.txt','r');
P=fscanf(fid,'%f',[1,1]);
fclose(fid);

fid=fopen('Stress.txt','r');
STRS=fscanf(fid,'%f',[1,1]);
fclose(fid);

%Torsion stiffnesss in Nm/deg
%atan(5,1592)=0.179948 degrees
R=(FR*1.592)/0.179948;


if ((STRS/250)<1) && ((P/15508.826)<1) &&  ((5500/FR)<1)
   salud=((STRS/250)+((P/15508.826)^4)+((5500/FR)^2));
else
    salud=1000000000;
end
```

Figure 15. Programming of the fitness function in "fitnessfunction.m"

```
!"C:\Program Files (x86)\Ansys Inc\..... \ANSYS.exe" -b -p
ANSYSUL -i "C:\Documents and Settings\.....\ BusModel.txt"
```

Figure 16. Command to run ANSYS in batch mode from "fitnessfunction.m"

Additional values for options must be defined, such as the population size, etc. Please refer to MatLab help for further information. In Figure 18 it can be seen that there are 8 variables of thickness (T) and a minimum value for all of them has been set to 1 mm. The maximum value of each thickness is set to 8 mm. It is worth highlighting that all of the files generated either by the MatLab scripts and by ANSYS (by means of programming in APDL) must be placed on the same folder so as to be recognized.

In Figure 19 depicts an example of the options that the user must specify in order to set the genetic algorithm options.

```
fid=fopen('Reactionforce.txt','r');
FR=fscanf(fid,'%f',[1,1]);
fclose(fid);

fid=fopen('Displacement.txt','r');
DP=fscanf(fid,'%f',[1,1]);
fclose(fid);

fid=fopen('Weight.txt','r');
P=fscanf(fid,'%f',[1,1]);
fclose(fid);

fid=fopen('Stress.txt','r');
STRS=fscanf(fid,'%f',[1,1]);
fclose(fid);
```

Figure 17. Commands written in "fitnessfunction.m" to read the values of the files generated by the FEM "BusModel.txt"

```
function OptiBus


options = gaoptimset('PopInitRange',[1 1 1 1 1 1 1 1;8 8 8 8 8 8 8 8],'Generatior
[T,fval,output,population] = ga(@fitnessfunction, 8,options)
```

Figure 18. Defining the genetic algorithm parameters for optimization ("OptiBus.m")

```
options = gaoptimset('PopInitRange',[1 1 1 5 1 1 1 1;2 2 2 10 8 8 8 8],
'Generations';100;'PopulationSize';100;'EliteCount';2;'MigrationFraction';0.2;
'MigrationInterval';50;'PopulationType';'doubleVector';'StallGenLimit';Inf,
'SelectionFcn'; @selectionroulette;'PlotFcns';(@gaplotbestf))
[T,fval,output,population] = ga(@fitnessfunction, 8,options);
```

Figure 19. Defining the options of the genetic algorithm ("OptiBus.m")

http://dx.doi.org/10.5772/57390

5. Results

In order to show the effectiveness of the proposed methodology this section shows some of the obtained results. Figure 20 shows the evolution of the fitness function until a minimum value of the fitness function was achieved. In the figure it can be seen that the initial values of the fitness function are very big. The reason is that the initial thickness of the bus beam cross sections are not optimized in weight, as expected. The genetic algorithm searches the search space and for the different feasible thickness values inside the defined search space the fitness function is evaluated. For the thickness values that provide lower values of the fitness function are combined between them in order to obtain an even better solution. Finally, an optimum is found, for the defined fitness function. It is worth noting that the user must define different fitness functions in order to see which one better suits the optimization which is being performed. A better minimum might be reached with a different defined fitness function. In addition, it must also be checked that the genetic algorithm has stopped due to a minimum solution and not due to have reached a maximum number of iterations. If the genetic algorithm has stopped for having reached the maximum number of iterations, either the defined maximum number of iterations is too small or the defined fitness function is not the most appropriate to find the minimum.

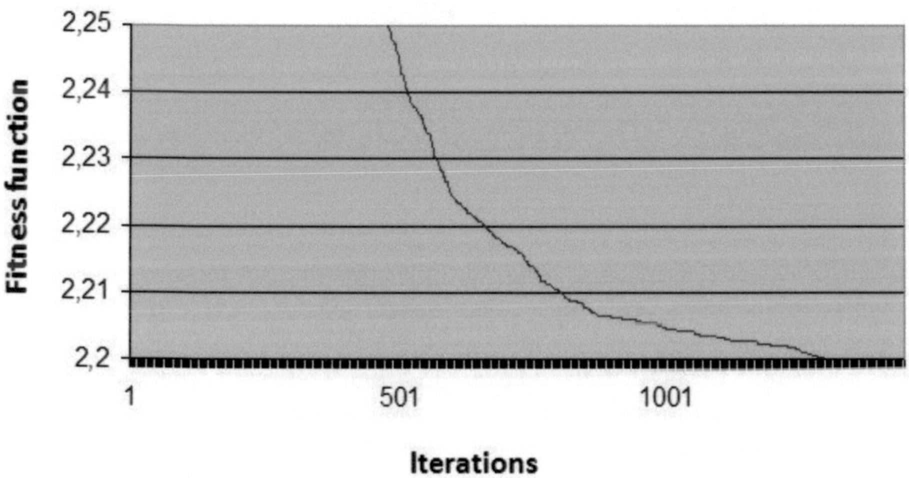

Figure 20. Evolution of the fitness function value

In addition, as an example of some of the obtained results, Figure 21 shows the evolution of the thickness value of one of the beam cross sections.

From Figure 21 it can be observed that although very big values of the beam thickness were obtained, once smaller values minimize the fitness function the genetic algorithm converges to a solution.

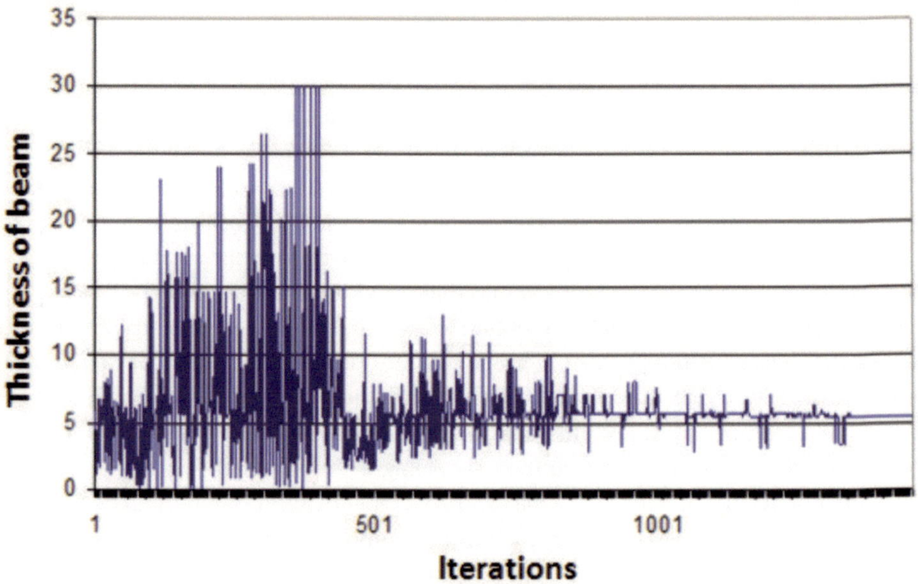

Figure 21. Example of the evolution of the value of beam thickness

The optimized vehicle structure achieved the optimized reductions shown in Table 2.

Weight	Torsion stiffness
Reduction of 4%	Increased 0,23%

Table 2. Optimization results

A reduction of 4% of the weight was achieved while improving the torsion stiffness in 0,23%. Prior to this optimization a sensitivity analysis was carried out in order to apply the optimization loop on certain beams more sensitive to variations in weight and torsion stiffness. It is worth highlighting that the optimization that has been performed keeps the original bus structure geometry. Thus, further weight reduction and torsion stiffness improved results may arise by changing the beam placement in the bus structure.

6. Conclusions

In the current chapter the authors have shown, by means of an optimization of a real bus structure, how to perform an advance analysis in the automotive field based on the usage of MatLab and ANSYS. The methodology to couple both programs has been presented, as well as all of the files necessary to optimize the beam thickness of a real bus structure in weight and torsion stiffness. On one hand, MatLab provides an advanced software environment in which the user may, either program complex scripts or use available toolboxes. For the optimization loop analyzed in this chapter the genetic algorithm toolbox has been employed, having shown to be a very useful tool. On the other hand, due to the fact that the optimization problem to be solved required of vehicle structure calculations, finite element software (ANSYS) was employed. In addition, for each iteration of the optimization loop, both programs require of calculations, thus, having to be coupled together and perform such computations without user intervention. The present chapter has shown how to couple both programs as well as how to manage the different files created during the simulations. In addition, in order to perform the bus structure calculations and due to the fact that the thickness value changes during each loop, the bus finite element model must be defined in terms of parametric variables. It has been shown how to use the ANSYS Parametric Design Language (APDL) in order to parametrize the bus structure finite element model. The methodology presented has shown to be a very successful tool for advance analysis in the automotive field.

Author details

A. Gauchía*, B.L. Boada, M.J.L. Boada and V. Díaz

*Address all correspondence to: agauchia@ing.uc3m.es

Mechanical Engineering Department, Research Institute of Vehicle Safety (ISVA), Carlos III University, Madrid, Spain

References

[1] Gauchía, A., Boada, M.J.L., Boada, B.L., Díaz, V. Simplified dynamic torsional model of an urban bus. Int. J. Heavy Vehicle Systems 2009; 16(3) 341-353.

[2] Gauchía, A., Díaz, V., Boada, M.J.L., Olatunbosun, O.A., Boada, B.L. Bus structure behaviour under driving manoeuvring and evaluation of the effect of an active roll system. Int. J. Vehicle Structures & Systems 2010; 2(1) 14-19.

[3] Gauchía, A., Olmeda, E., Aparicio, F., Díaz, V. Bus mathematical model of acceleration threshold limit estimation in lateral rollover test. Vehicle System Dynamics 2011; 49(10) 1695-1707.

[4] Cazzola, G.J., Alcalá, E., Aparicio Izquierdo, F. Study of the bending response of metal foam-filled beams applied to enhace the rollover behavior of coach structure. International Journal of Chrashworthiness 2013. DOI: 10.1080/13588265.2013.831516.

[5] Lan, F., Chen, J., Lin, J. Comparative analysis for bus side structures and lightweight optimization. Proc. IMechE Part D: J. Automobile Engineering 2004; 218 1067-1075.

[6] MATLAB 2011, The MathWorks Inc. 2011.

[7] ANSYS. Structural Analysis Guide. Ansys Inc 2001.

[8] Gauchía, A., Díaz, V., Boada, M.J.L., Boada, B.L. Torsional stiffness and weight optimization of a real bus structure. International Journal of Automotive Technology 2010; 11(1) 41-47.

[9] Choi, B., Tang, B. Optimum shape design of rotor shafts using genetic algorithm. Journal of Vibration and Control 2000; 6 207-222.

[10] Gil, L., Andreu, A.. Shape and cross section optimisation of a truss structure. Computers and Structures 2001; 79 681-689.

[11] Adeli, H., Cheng, N.-T. Concurrent genetic algorithm for optimization of large structures. Journal of Aerospace Engineering 1994; 7(3) 276-296.

[12] Xiang, J., Zhong, Y., Chen, X., He, Z.. Crack detection in a shaft by combination of wavelet-based elements and genetic algorithm. International Journal of Solids and Structures 2008; 45 (17) 4782-4795.

[13] Li, S., 2000. The micromechanics theory of classical plates: a congruous estimate of overall elastic stiffness. International Journal of Solids and Structures 37 (40), 5599-628.

[14] Joo, J., Kota, S., Noboru, K. Nonlinear synthesis of compliant mechanisms: Topology design. In: DETC2000/MECH-14141 (Ed.), Proceedings of 2000 ASME Biannual Mechanism Design Conference.

[15] Saxena, A. Topology optimization of large displacement compliant mechanisms with multiple materials and multiple ports. Structural and Multidisciplinary Optimization 2005; 30(6) 477-490.

[16] Mitchell, M. An Introduction to Genetic Algorithms. The MIT Press. Cambridge. Massachusetts. London. England 1996.

[17] Goldberg, D. E. Genetic Algoritmhs in Search, Optimization and Machine Learning.Addinson-Wesley Publishing Company, Inc 1989.

Chapter 8

Modelling and Analysis of Higher Phase Order (*HPO*) Squirrel Cage Induction Machine

A.A. Jimoh, E.K. Appiah and A.S.O. Ogunjuyigbe

Additional information is available at the end of the chapter

http://dx.doi.org/10.5772/57468

1. Introduction

The need for more power per volume, or mass and reliability has promoted the advancement of higher phase order (*HPO*) electric machines. The *HPO* machines are electric machines with the number of phases higher than the conventional arrangement of three (3). These machines are considered to have several advantages and useful applications. So far *HPO* machines have found applications in electric ship propulsion, hybrid electric vehicles and many other industrial applications (Yong Le A, et al, 1997), (Lipo T.A., 1980). Also, they can operate with an asymmetrical winding structure in the case of loss of one or more machine phases thus making them fault tolerant (Apsley J., et al, 2006).

In this chapter, an approach of modelling and analysis of the higher phase order machine will be explored where the stator has a symmetrical winding layout. The machine stator winding is connected to a balanced phase supply and the machine performance characteristics observed during normal operation and under fault conditions, both in loaded and unloaded conditions. The performance under fault is considered to demonstrate the fault tolerance of the machine. Though rating may fall during the loss of 1 or more phases due to fault, unlike the conventional 3-phase ones, does not stop the machine from running as long as the condition for the production of rotating magnetic field in the air-gap is met.

Furthermore, a six phase squirrel cage induction machine was investigated using the classical field analysis method, the generalised theory method and the finite element method (*FEM*). The six phase squirrel cage induction machine is modelled and simulated in Matlab\Simulink environment. Steady-state and the dynamic results characterising the performance of the six phase squirrel cage induction machine were generated. Laboratory tests were conducted on a constructed 1.5 kW experimental machine to validate the performance characteristics results obtained from the theoretical simulations. The results of the three methods used were

INTECH
open science | open minds

© 2014 The Author(s). Licensee InTech. This chapter is distributed under the terms of the Creative Commons Attribution License (http://creativecommons.org/licenses/by/3.0), which permits unrestricted use, distribution, and reproduction in any medium, provided the original work is properly cited.

compared among themselves, and also with the experimental to appraise the suitability of each method for modelling and analysis of *HPO* machines. Even though six-phase machine is considered it is believed that the methods as applied in this work are generally applicable to *HPO* squirrel cage induction machine of any number of phases.

2. Mathematical modelling of the six phase squirrel cage induction machine

The arbitrary reference frame theory is used in the dynamic analysis of electrical machines. The highly coupled nature of the machine, especially the inductances within the winding makes it rather challenging to perform the dynamic simulations and analysis on this machine (Ogunjuyigbe A.S.O., 2009), (Krause P.C., Wasynczuk O., et al, 2002). By using this method as applied to the three phase case, a six-phase machine is also transformed to a four-phase machine with their magnetic axis in quadrature. This method is also commonly referred to as the *dqxy0102* transformation. Figure 1 shows the symmetrical layout of the machine in the natural reference frame, where the stator is represented by the six phase symmetrical winding and the rotor by the three phase winding.

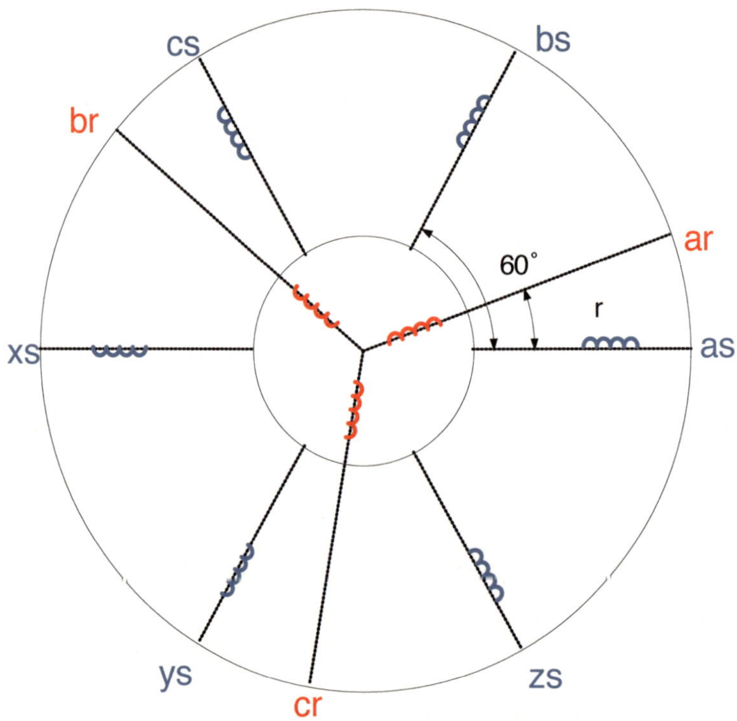

Figure 1. The Machine Diagram in natural reference frame

The matrix transformation of the *dqxy*0102 and *abcxyz* for the stator phases is given in Equation (1) and Equation (2) as (Levi E., 2006):

$$\begin{bmatrix} f_{ds} \\ f_{qs} \\ f_{dxs} \\ f_{qys} \\ f_{os1} \\ f_{os2} \end{bmatrix} = \frac{2}{6}\begin{bmatrix} \cos(\theta) & \cos\left(\theta-\frac{\pi}{3}\right) & \cos\left(\theta-\frac{2\pi}{3}\right) & \cos(\theta-\pi) & \cos\left(\theta-\frac{4\pi}{3}\right) & \cos\left(\theta-\frac{5\pi}{3}\right) \\ \sin(\theta) & \sin\left(\theta+\frac{\pi}{3}\right) & \sin\left(\theta+\frac{2\pi}{3}\right) & \sin(\theta+\pi) & \sin\left(\theta+\frac{4\pi}{3}\right) & \sin\left(\theta+\frac{5\pi}{3}\right) \\ \cos(2\theta) & \cos\left(2\theta-\frac{2\pi}{3}\right) & \cos\left(2\theta-\frac{4\pi}{3}\right) & \cos(2\theta-2\pi) & \cos\left(2\theta-\frac{8\pi}{3}\right) & \cos\left(2\theta-\frac{10\pi}{3}\right) \\ \sin(2\theta) & \sin\left(2\theta+\frac{2\pi}{3}\right) & \sin\left(2\theta+\frac{4\pi}{3}\right) & \sin(2\theta+2\pi) & \sin\left(2\theta+\frac{8\pi}{3}\right) & \sin\left(2\theta+\frac{10\pi}{3}\right) \\ \frac{1}{2} & \frac{1}{2} & \frac{1}{2} & \frac{1}{2} & \frac{1}{2} & \frac{1}{2} \\ \frac{1}{2} & -\frac{1}{2} & \frac{1}{2} & -\frac{1}{2} & \frac{1}{2} & -\frac{1}{2} \end{bmatrix}\begin{bmatrix} f_{as} \\ f_{bs} \\ f_{cs} \\ f_{xs} \\ f_{ys} \\ f_{zs} \end{bmatrix} \tag{1}$$

$$\begin{bmatrix} f_{as} \\ f_{bs} \\ f_{cs} \\ f_{xs} \\ f_{ys} \\ f_{zs} \end{bmatrix} = \begin{bmatrix} \cos(\theta) & \sin(\theta) & \cos(2\theta) & \sin(2\theta) & 1 & 1 \\ \cos\left(\theta-\frac{\pi}{3}\right) & \sin\left(\theta+\frac{\pi}{3}\right) & \cos\left(2\theta-\frac{2\pi}{3}\right) & \sin\left(2\theta+\frac{2\pi}{3}\right) & 1 & -1 \\ \cos\left(\theta-\frac{2\pi}{3}\right) & \sin\left(\theta+\frac{2\pi}{3}\right) & \cos\left(2\theta-\frac{4\pi}{3}\right) & \sin\left(2\theta+\frac{4\pi}{3}\right) & 1 & 1 \\ \cos(\theta-\pi) & \sin(\theta+\pi) & \cos(2\theta-2\pi) & \sin(2\theta+2\pi) & 1 & -1 \\ \cos\left(\theta-\frac{4\pi}{3}\right) & \sin\left(\theta+\frac{4\pi}{3}\right) & \cos\left(2\theta-\frac{8\pi}{3}\right) & \sin\left(2\theta+\frac{8\pi}{3}\right) & 1 & 1 \\ \cos\left(\theta-\frac{5\pi}{3}\right) & \sin\left(\theta+\frac{5\pi}{3}\right) & \cos\left(2\theta-\frac{10\pi}{3}\right) & \sin\left(2\theta+\frac{10\pi}{3}\right) & 1 & -1 \end{bmatrix}\begin{bmatrix} f_{ds} \\ f_{qs} \\ f_{dxs} \\ f_{qys} \\ f_{os1} \\ f_{os2} \end{bmatrix} \tag{2}$$

Likewise, the rotor matrix transformation between ABC and *dq0* is also given in Equation (3) and Equation (4) as (Jimoh A.A., Jac-Venter P, Appiah E.K., 2012):

$$\begin{bmatrix} f_{dr} \\ f_{qr} \\ f_{or} \end{bmatrix} = \begin{bmatrix} \cos\beta & \cos\left(\beta-\frac{2\pi}{3}\right) & \cos\left(\beta-\frac{4\pi}{3}\right) \\ \sin\beta & \sin\left(\beta+\frac{2\pi}{3}\right) & \sin\left(\beta+\frac{4\pi}{3}\right) \\ \frac{1}{2} & \frac{1}{2} & \frac{1}{2} \end{bmatrix}\begin{bmatrix} f_{ar} \\ f_{br} \\ f_{cr} \end{bmatrix} \tag{3}$$

$$\begin{bmatrix} f_{ar} \\ f_{br} \\ f_{cr} \end{bmatrix} = \begin{bmatrix} \cos\beta & \sin\beta & 1 \\ \cos\left(\beta - \frac{2\pi}{3}\right) & \sin\left(\beta - \frac{2\pi}{3}\right) & 1 \\ \cos\left(\beta - \frac{4\pi}{3}\right) & \sin\left(\beta + \frac{4\pi}{3}\right) & 1 \end{bmatrix} \begin{bmatrix} f_{dr} \\ f_{qr} \\ f_{or} \end{bmatrix} \tag{4}$$

Where *f* can be expressed as the voltage, current or the flux linkage and the subscript *ABC-XYZ* represents the phases of the machine winding.

In developing the equations which describe the behaviour of the six phase induction machine the following assumptions were made:

1. The air-gap is uniform.

2. Eddy currents, friction and windage losses and saturation are neglected.

3. The windings are distributed sinusoidally around the air gap.

4. The windings are identical.

2.1. Voltage and flux linkage equations

The voltage equation of the six phases (*abcxyz* to *dqxy0102*) is derived using the similar concept as applied to the three phase case (Jimoh A.A., Jac-Venter P, Appiah E.K., 2012). The symmetrical *dqxy0102* voltage equation with flux linkage as state variables is expressed as (Appiah E.K., et al, 2013):

$$V_{ds} = r_s\left(\frac{\lambda_{ds} - \lambda_{md}}{l_{ls}}\right) + \frac{d}{dt}\lambda_{ds} - \omega\lambda_{qs} \tag{5}$$

$$V_{qs} = r_s\left(\frac{\lambda_{qs} - \lambda_{mq}}{l_{ls}}\right) + \frac{d}{dt}\lambda_{qs} + \omega\lambda_{ds} \tag{6}$$

$$V_{dr} = r_r\left(\frac{\lambda_{dr} \quad \lambda_{md}}{l_{lr}}\right) + \frac{d}{dt}\lambda_{dr} - (\omega - \omega_r)\lambda_{qr} \tag{7}$$

$$V_{qr} = r_r\left(\frac{\lambda_{qr} - \lambda_{mq}}{l_{lr}}\right) + \frac{d}{dt}\lambda_{qr} + (\omega - \omega_r)\lambda_{dr} \tag{8}$$

$$V_{dxs} = r_r\left(\frac{\lambda_{dxs}}{l_{ls}}\right) + \frac{d}{dt}\lambda_{dxs} \tag{9}$$

$$V_{qys} = r_s\left(\frac{\lambda_{qys}}{l_{ls}}\right) + \frac{d}{dt}\lambda_{qys} \tag{10}$$

$$V_{os1} = r_s\left(\frac{\lambda_{os1}}{l_{ls}}\right) + \frac{d}{dt}\lambda_{os1} \tag{11}$$

$$V_{os2} = r_s\left(\frac{\lambda_{os2}}{l_{ls}}\right) + \frac{d}{dt}\lambda_{os2} \tag{12}$$

The flux linkage equations are expressed as current dependent variables (Levi E., 2006):

$$i_{ds} = \frac{\lambda_{ds} - \lambda_{md}}{l_{ls}} \tag{13}$$

$$i_{qs} = \frac{\lambda_{qs} - \lambda_{mq}}{l_{ls}} \tag{14}$$

$$i_{dr} = \frac{\lambda_{dr} - \lambda_{md}}{l_{lr}} \tag{15}$$

$$i_{qr} = \left(\frac{\lambda_{qr} - \lambda_{mq}}{l_{lr}}\right) \tag{16}$$

$$i_{dxs} = \left(\frac{\lambda_{dxs}}{l_{ls}}\right) \tag{17}$$

$$i_{dys} = \left(\frac{\lambda_{dys}}{l_{ls}}\right) \tag{18}$$

$$i_{os1} = \left(\frac{\lambda_{os1}}{l_{ls}} \right) \tag{19}$$

$$i_{os2} = \left(\frac{\lambda_{os2}}{l_{ls}} \right) \tag{20}$$

The mutual inductances between the stator and the rotor are given as:

$$\lambda_{md} = L_m \left(i_{ds1} + i_{dr} \right) \tag{21}$$

$$\lambda_{mq} = L_m \left(i_{qs1} + i_{qr} \right) \tag{22}$$

Where λ is the flux linkage, L_m the magnetizing inductance and Ll_s and Ll_r *are the* stator and rotor inductances respectively.

2.2. Mechanical equations voltage and flux linkage equations

The mechanical equations for the six phase squirrel cage induction machine comprises of the electromagnetic torque and the speed as expressed in Equations (23) and (24). These equations are derived using the same concept of the three phase case (Ogunjuyigbe A.S.O., 2009), (Krause P.C., Wasynczuk O., et al, 2002).

$$T_{em} = \left(\frac{6}{2} \frac{P}{2} \right) \left(\lambda_{ds1} i_{qs1} - \lambda_{qs1} i_{ds1} \right) \tag{23}$$

$$J \left(\frac{2}{P} \right) \frac{d\omega_r}{dt} + T_L = T_{em} \tag{24}$$

Where P is number of poles, J is moment of inertia, T_{em} is the electromagnetic torque, T_L is torque connected to the shaft, and ω_r is the angular rotational speed of the rotor.

2.3. Equivalent circuit

The equivalent circuit diagram of figure 2 summarises the voltage and flux linkage equations of the six phase squirrel cage machine in *dqxy0102* transformation. The figure 2 (a) and figure 2 (b) illustrates the equations with its corresponding stator and rotor mutual coupling of the machine as expressed in equations (5)-(8) and (13)-(16). From the equivalent circuit presentation, only these equations take part in the electromechanical energy conversion process.

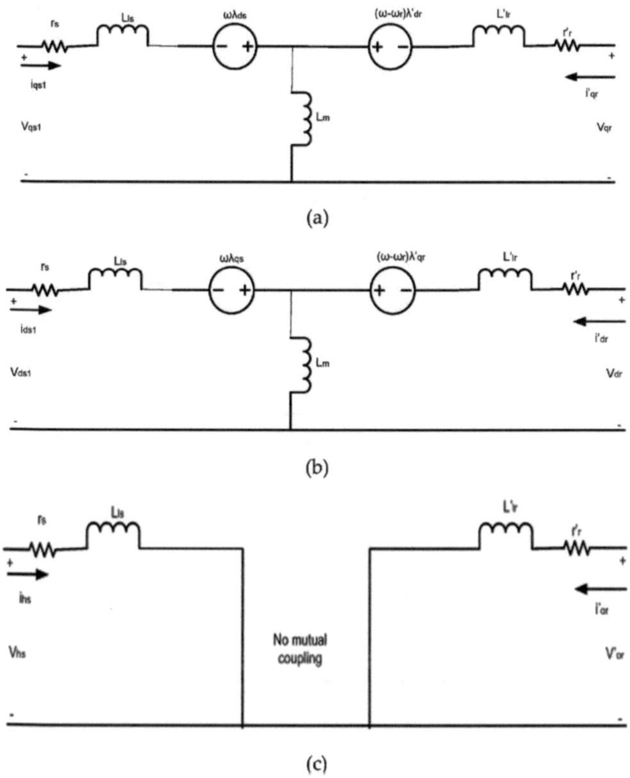

Figure 2. The *dqxy0102* equivalent circuit of the six phase squirrel cage induction machine (a) The *q* equivalent circuit (b) The *d* equivalent circuit, (c) The *h* non-coupling equivalent circuit

There is no mutual coupling in the equations (9)-(12) and (17)-(20) as presented in figure 2(c) where h denotes $xy0102$ voltage equations. These equations do not take part in the energy conversion process and therefore contribute to losses in the system. (Aroquiadassou G., Mpanda-Mabwe A., 2009).

3. Modelling of six-phase squirrel cage induction machine under fault conditions

The operation of the machine under fault is considered here to demonstrate its fault tolerance ability. This machine consists of a symmetrical six phase supply with a fault at the stator terminal, assuming the phase *a* winding. To investigate the performance of the machine under faulty conditions, the open and short circuit faults were simulated for both no-load and loaded states of operation. The winding arrangement for an open circuit in phase *a* is as shown in figure 3. The short circuit faults winding arrangement between the phases *a* and *b* is shown in figure 4.

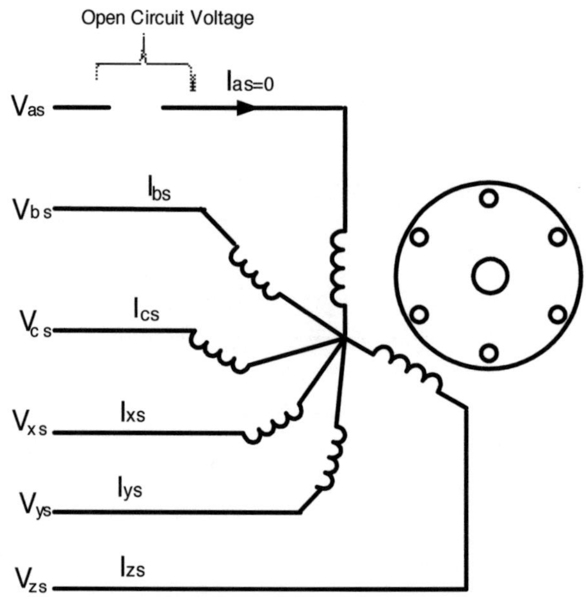

Figure 3. Arrangement of the machine under fault for open circuit in phase *a* stator winding

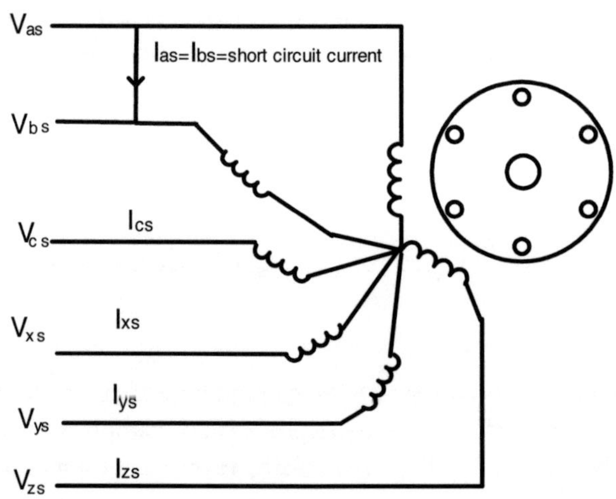

Figure 4. Arrangement of the machine under short circuit in phases *a* and *b* stator winding.

3.1. Open circuit fault

With phase *a* opened the machine is modelled for ease of referral in the stationary reference frame where $\omega=0$ is substituted in equation (5). The open circuit fault is simulated by simply assuming that the current ceases to flow in phase *a* after a normal steady state current, and an open circuit voltage is assumed across the open circuit terminals (Singh G.K., Pant V., 2000), (Krause P.C., Thomas C.H., 1965). The machine is assumed to be operating as a motor, hence a balanced six phase supply is applied to the stator. The six phase squirrel cage induction machine has no neutral connections and therefore, all the zero sequence currents are zero before the fault. However, at the loss of a phase the machine operates in asymmetry, and zero sequence current flow in the rest of the winding.

For a balanced six phase, the total phase currents may be expressed as:

$$I_{as} + I_{bs} + I_{cs} + I_{xs} + I_{ys} + I_{zs} = 0 \tag{25}$$

From equation (2), assuming $\theta=0$, the stator current of phase *a* is expressed as:

$$I_{as} = I_{ds1} + I_{dxs} \tag{26}$$

From equation (26), as $I_{as}=0$,

$$I_{ds1} = -I_{dxs} \tag{27}$$

The open circuit voltage is also expressed as:

$$V_{as} = V_{ds1} + V_{dxs} \tag{28}$$

Putting I_{ds1}=0 into equation (13) and (21) and back substituting into equation (5) gives the new *d*-axis voltage equation as:

$$V_{ds} = \frac{d}{dt}\left(\frac{L_m}{L_m + L_r^{'}}\right)\lambda_{dr} \tag{29}$$

There is no mutual coupling between the stator and the rotor winding of the *x*-axis voltage. As such, putting I_{dxs}=0 into equation (9) gives the new *x*-axis voltage as:

$$V_{dxs} = 0 \tag{30}$$

Back substituting equations (29) and (30) into (28) gives the open circuit voltage as:

$$V_{as} = \frac{d}{dt}\left(\frac{L_m}{L_m + L_r^{'}}\right)\lambda_{dr} \tag{31}$$

Where $L_s = L_{ls} + L_{lr}$ and $L_r^{'} = L_{lr} + L_m$.

The open circuit voltage in equation (31) is placed across the open circuit terminal in the simulation.

3.2. Short circuit fault simulations

In this section we consider a short circuit between two phases during a normal operation of the machine. For this instance, the balanced six phase total phase voltages may be expressed as:

$$V_{as} + V_{bs} + V_{cs} + V_{xs} + V_{ys} + V_{zs} = 0 \tag{32}$$

With phase *a* and phase *b* short circuited, the line to line voltage between these two phases become zero. The short circuit fault is simulated by putting this line voltage to zero, implying the connection of phase *a* to phase *b* at a certain point at a time t when the fault occurs.

3.3. Classical field analysis

In this section, the classical field analysis is used to determine the magnetic field distribution in the air-gap of the machine. With this magnetic field distribution, the performance behaviour of the machine at steady state was determined using the equivalent circuit in figure 2. The corresponding smooth air-gap flux density distribution of the stator and the rotor is given in more details by (Appiah E.K. *et al*, 2013):

$$\begin{aligned} B_{gs}(\theta,t) &= \frac{\mu_0 MMF(\theta,t)}{l_g} \\ B_{gr}(\theta,t) &= \frac{\mu_0 MMF_r(\theta,t)}{l_g} \end{aligned} \tag{33}$$

The permeance factor Λ is expressed as (Jimoh A. A., 1986):

$$\Lambda = \frac{1-y}{\left[(a-y)(b-y)\right]^{\frac{1}{2}}} \tag{34}$$

$$\theta = \frac{g}{\pi}\left[-In\left|\frac{1+p}{1-p}\right| + In\left|\frac{b+p}{b-p}\right| + 2\frac{b_{os}}{l_g} + a\tan\frac{p}{\sqrt{b}} \right] - 0.5\frac{b_{os}}{l_g} \tag{35}$$

Where B_g represents the flux density distribution of the stator and the rotor, *MMF* represents the magnetomotive force, l_g represents the air-gap length, μ_o represents the permeability of air, θ represents space, and t represents time.

The six phase air-gap power can be expressed as:

$$P_{ag} = 6\left|I_r^{'}\right|^2 \frac{R_r^{'}}{s} \tag{36}$$

Where:

$$s = \frac{\omega_s - \omega_r}{\omega_s}, R_2 = R_r^{'} \tag{37}$$

The electromechanical power and torque of the machine is expressed as:

$$P_{em} = P_{ag}\left(1-s\right) \tag{38}$$

$$T_{em} = \frac{P_{ag}}{\omega_s} \tag{39}$$

Similarly, the input power, output power and the power factor are also expressed as:

$$P_{in} = P_{ag} 6\left|I_r^{'}\right|^2 R_s \tag{40}$$

$$P_{out} = P_{ag} - P_{loss} \tag{41}$$

$$PF = \frac{P_{in}}{6V_s I_s} \tag{42}$$

Also s denotes the slip, ω_s is the synchronous speed, ω_r is the rotor speed, P_{in} is the input power, V_s is the supply voltage, I_s is the stator supply current, PF is the power factor, P_{ag} is the air-gap power, P_{em} is the electromagnetic power, P_{out} is the output power, P_{loss} is the losses-which includes stator and rotor winding losses, core loss, windage and friction and other stray losses- and the subscripts s and r denotes the stator and the rotor respectively.

As the permeance factor of equation (34) is superimposed on the flux density distribution expressed in equation (33), the effects of slot opening on the flux density distribution is accounted.

3.4. Finite element analysis

In this section, the finite element analysis using a two dimensional Quickfield software package is used to evaluate the performance behaviour of the machine. The magnetic vector potential is employed in the numerical solution to give the magnetic flux density distribution. The magnetic vector potential is expressed as (Pyrhonen T. P., Valeria H., 2008), (Appiah E.K., Jimoh A. A., et al, 2013):

$$\vec{B} = \nabla \times \vec{A} \tag{43}$$

$$B_x = \frac{\partial A_x}{\partial y} \tag{44}$$

$$B_y = \frac{\partial A_y}{\partial x} \tag{45}$$

For a two dimensional problem of the vector potential, the Poisson equation is expressed as:

$$\begin{aligned} \nabla^2 A_x &= \frac{\partial^2 A_x}{\partial x^2} + \frac{\partial^2 A_x}{\partial y^2} = -\mu.\vec{J}_x \\ \nabla^2 A_y &= \frac{\partial^2 A_y}{\partial x^2} + \frac{\partial^2 A_y}{\partial y^2} = -\mu.\vec{J}_y \end{aligned} \tag{46}$$

The performance behaviour of the machine at steady state was evaluated by loading the machine in AC magnetics in Quickfield software. The governing equation for the slip and torque is given by (Appiah E.K. *et al*, 2013):

$$\omega_r = -s\omega_s + \omega_s \tag{47}$$

The torque derivation of the *FEA* is given as:

$$T = \frac{1}{2}\int_s ((rxH)(n.B) + (rxB)(n.H) - (rxn)(H.B)ds \tag{48}$$

where r is a radius vector of the point of integration and n denotes the unit vector normal to the surface.

The geometry of the whole machine was developed using the software package. Two boundary conditions were used for this analysis within the entire structure: the Dirichlet's boundary condition for the outer layer of the machine structure and the homogeneous Neumann boundary condition for the change over from one geometry or medium to another such as from the core to the air-gap and vice versa. The automatic meshing of the machine geometry which is generated by the software and spread over the whole cross section is shown in figure 6(a (i)). The field solution is now obtained by running the mesh geometry in the software solver by solving the Maxwell's equation. The machine winding has been excited with balanced stator currents for no-load and full load conditions.

4. Simulation results

In this section, the simulation results for the three methods; the generalised theory of machine, the classical field, and the finite element analysis are presented. The dynamic performance behaviour of the machine was determined using the derived mathematical modelling in *dqxy0102* (generalised theory), and implemented in Matlab/Simulink environment. This simulation results are generated in the Matlab/Simulink environment for the machine performance characteristics, during normal operation and under fault conditions in loaded and unloaded conditions. The performance behaviour of the machine at steady state was determined using the equivalent circuit, and the models implemented in Matlab for classical field analysis and Quickfield environment for *FEA*. The effect of slot opening on the magnetic flux density distribution of the air-gap for the field and other results obtained from finite element analysis are shown in the remaining part of the section.

4.1. Magnetic flux density distribution of the classical field

To obtain the air-gap flux density distribution the permeance factor distribution, which reflects the effects of the slot openings, is superimposed on the flux density distribution. If saturation is to be accounted for, the *B-H* characteristics of the magnetic core would have been incorporated in the flux density distribution (Jimoh A. A., 1986). Figure 5 shows the permeance flux density distribution and the air-gap flux density distribution, for the no load and the full load conditions.

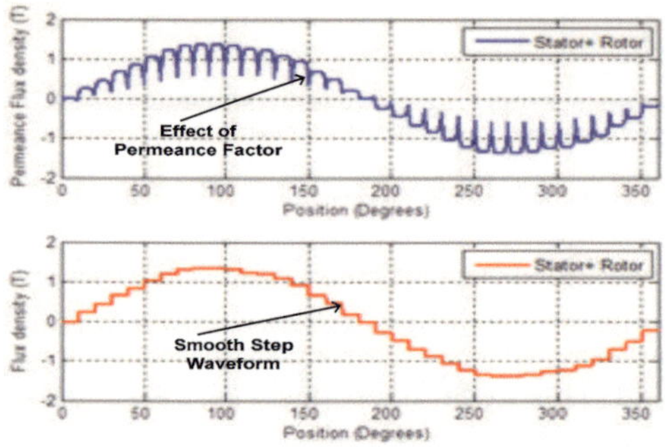

(i)

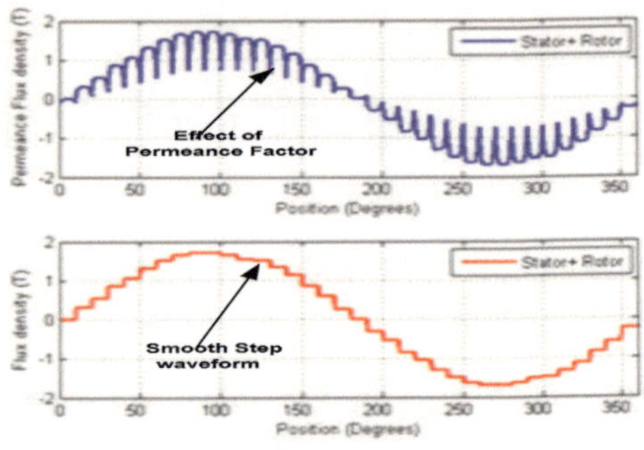

(ii)

Figure 5. The plot of air-gap flux density (i) no-load, (ii) full load conditions

4.2. Magnetic flux density distribution of the *FEA*

In this section, the automatic meshing of the machine and the magnetic flux lines are shown in figure 6 (a).The colour map of the magnetic flux line shows that most of the portion of the yoke is under high flux density. The effect of slot opening on the magnetic flux density distribution of the air-gap is shown in figure 6 (b), for no-load and rated load condition. This is achieved by clicking the mid-air-gap of the whole geometry in Quickfield. The magnetic saturation of the materials is taken care of by the magnetization curve.

4.3. Steady state analysis

This section presents the results of the analysis of the machine in steady state for the three methods; the generalised theory of machine, the classical field and the finite element analysis. For test performance under load condition the machine has been loaded to approximately 125% of rated torque. The values obtained for torque, efficiency, input power, output power, power factor and reactive power were respectively plotted against the loading as shown in figures 7-9. Experimental measurements were also plotted on the same curve for validation of the theoretical work. The machine performance characteristics increase with increasing load. The range of loading of the machine from 0 to 0.2 per unit shows that the three scenarios under study have the same effects until they begin to deviate from each other. However, the case of the reactive power is different in such that it deviates from each other from 0 to 125% of the rated load. It is further observed during the load study that the reactive power at start is high but decreases with loading and vice versa for the active power. The difference in deviation could be so because of the rotor losses when the machine is being loaded. The effect of the reactive power at start gives a very poor power factor to the machine but the performance improves with loading. The experimental results validate the theoretical model and are plotted alongside those of the three methods.

http://dx.doi.org/10.5772/57468

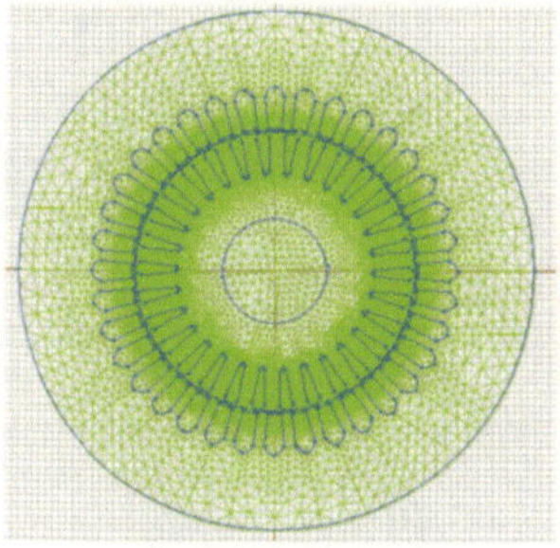

(i)

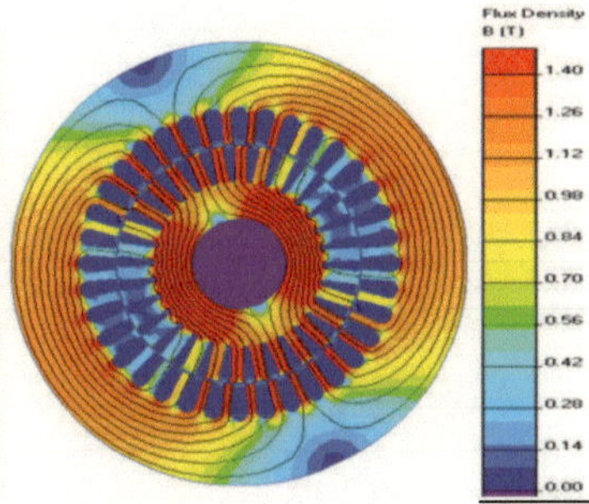

(ii)

(a)

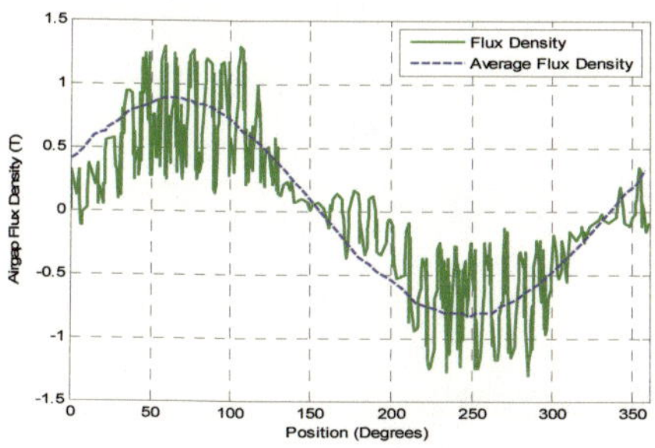

(i)

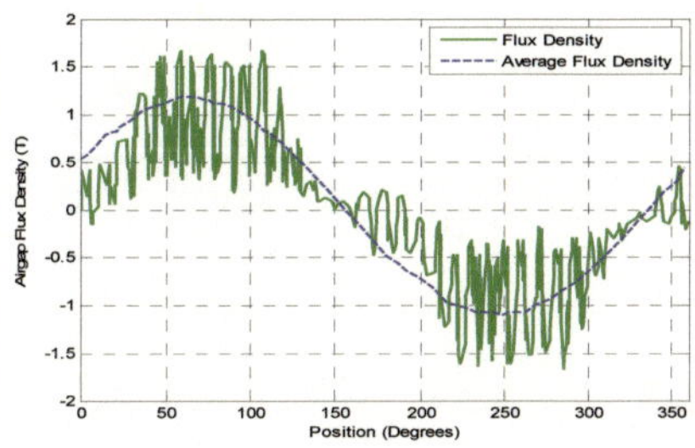

(ii)

(b)

Figure 6. (a) (i) mesh of the full geometry, (ii) magnetic flux lines, (b) (i) air-gap magnetic flux density distribution at no-load, (ii) air-gap magnetic flux density distribution at full load

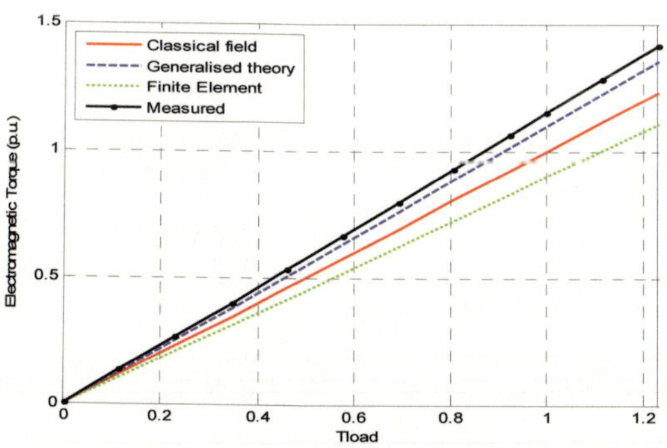

(i)

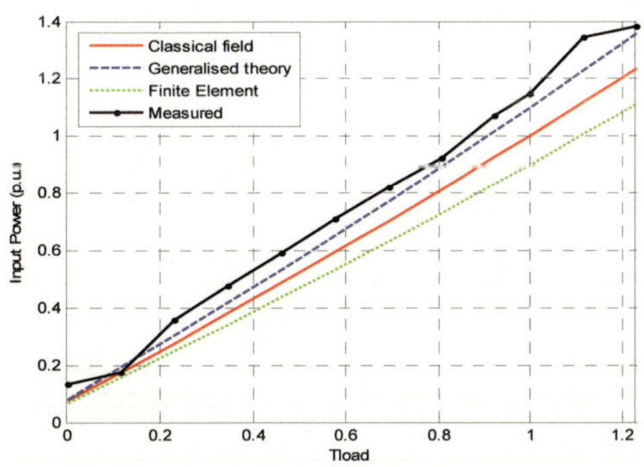

(ii)

Figure 7. The steady state (i) electromagnetic torque, (ii) input power versus load

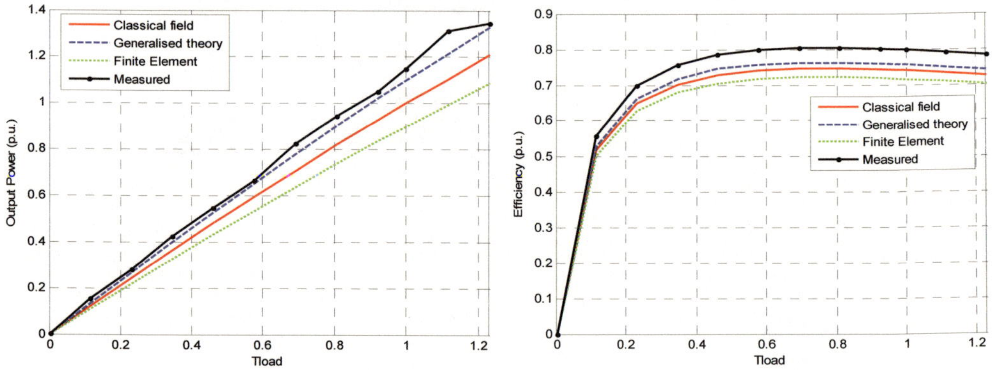

(i) (ii)

Figure 8. The steady state (i) output power, (ii) efficiency versus load

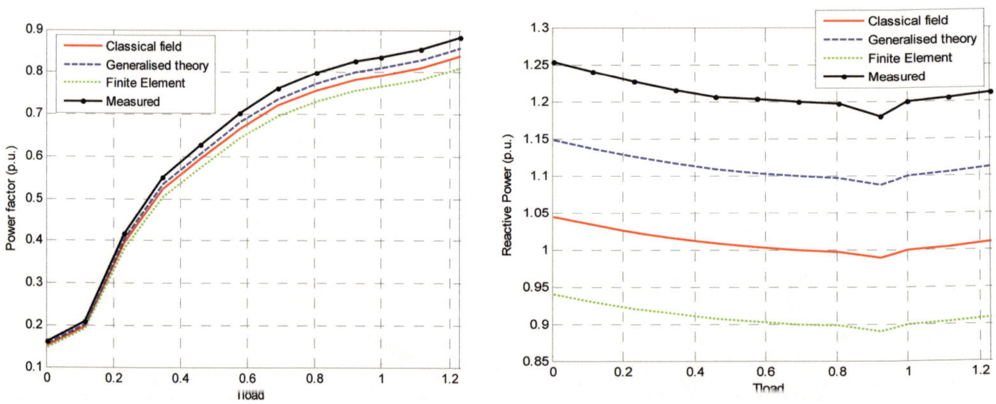

(i) (ii)

Figure 9. The steady state (i) power factor, (ii) reactive power versus load

4.4. Dynamic analysis

Steady-state analysis is not always sufficient in determining the behaviour of an electrical machine. The behaviour of the machine under changing conditions is also necessary. The dynamic model will show the exact behaviour of the machine during transient and or dynamic periods. The derived voltage, flux linkage and mechanical equations for the squirrel cage six phase induction machine is implemented in Matlab/ Simulink as follows:

1. All partial differential variables are converted to integral variables. This concept is similarly applicable to the three phase case (Chee Mun Ong, 1998).

2. The flux linkage equations are resolved into state variables and current as dependent variables. (Ogunjuyigbe A.S.O., 2009), (Krause P.C., Wasynczuk O., et al, 2002).

3. The entire equations are then modelled, implemented and simulated within the Matlab/ Simulink environment.

4.4.1. Simulation of healthy machine

The dynamic and transient simulation of the six phase squirrel cage induction machine is done in the arbitrary reference frame. The Simulink model built using equations (5-24) is shown in figure 10. Figure 10a shows the complete model of the six-phase machine system, while the power block is represented in Figure 10b. The power supply block converts the machine variables from the balanced *abcxyzs* supply voltage to the *dqxy0102* using the Park transformation matrix. This is used as an input to supply the squirrel cage induction machine which is modelled in the *dqxy0102* reference frame. The simulation of these models is carried out with all the phases connected. Two scenarios: (1) at no load and (2) at rated load were investigated. The free acceleration characteristics under no-load and rated load are shown in figure 11.

The results in figure 11 show that the speed settles a little below synchronous speed at 314.1 rad/sec for the 50 Hz supply system. It is to be noted that the friction and the windage losses have been neglected in this model and as such the speed is almost equal to the synchronous speed. This effect is shown in the torque versus speed curve, and the speed versus time. From the theoretical simulations, it is observed that the starting current is about 10.8 A as compared to the rated current of 1.8 A. At the steady state settling of the current at no-load, the current is not zero but is at 0.8 A. This accounts for the magnetizing current present in the machine at no-load. The speed versus time, torque versus speed curve characteristics and the waveforms of the two stator currents, phases *a* and *x*, are as shown in figure 11a. The machine settles into a steady state at about 1.8 seconds.

Furthermore, the results of figure 11b show that the speed of the machine settles at rated load to 293.194 rad/sec, corresponding to a slip of 0.07. The simulation was done by applying the rated load of 1 pu at the time of 2.5 seconds, after the settling of the free oscillation at no-load. It is observed that the current immediately increased to show the presence of load. The speed versus time, torque versus speed curve characteristics and the waveforms of the two stator currents, phases *a* and *x* for sudden increase in load are as shown in figure 11b.

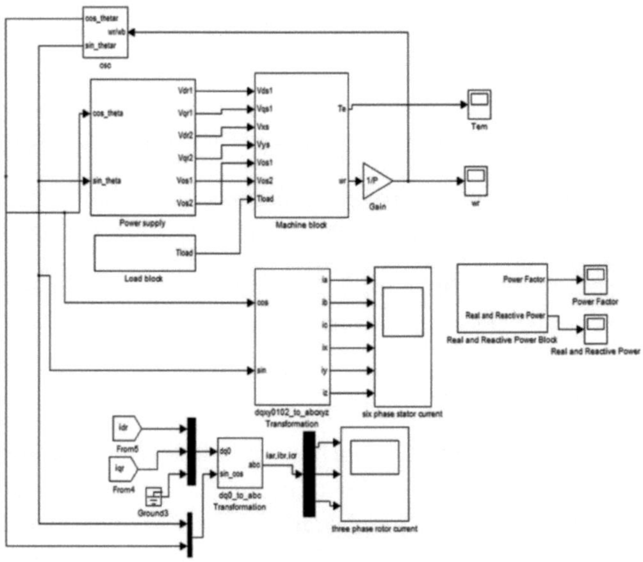

(a)

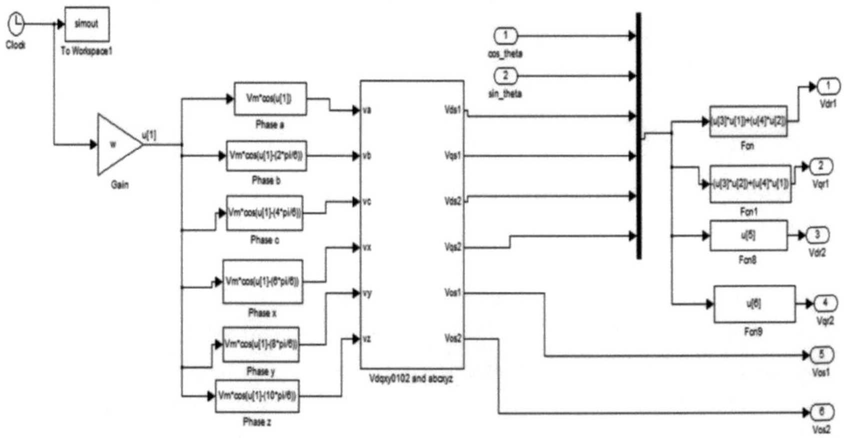

(b)

Figure 10. The Simulink representation for the healthy six phase squirrel cage induction machine model (a) The main block, (b) The conversion from *abcxyzs* supply voltage to *dqxy0102* block

http://dx.doi.org/10.5772/57468

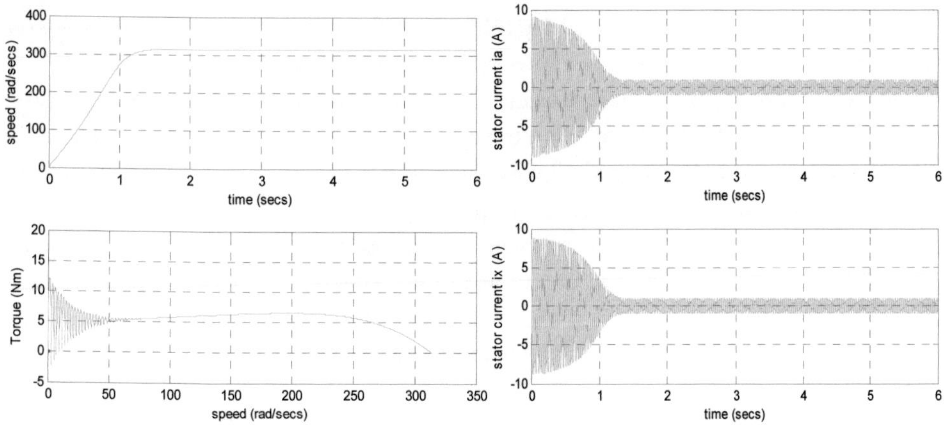

(i) (a) (ii)

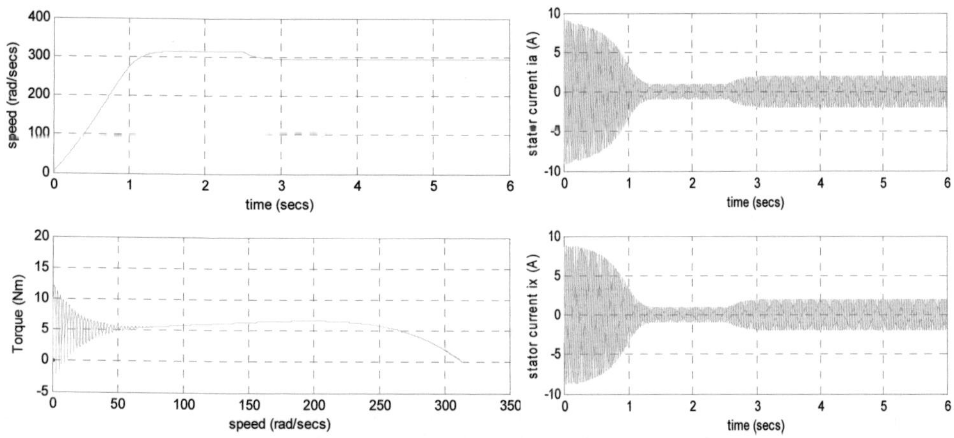

(i) (b) (ii)

Figure 11. The healthy machine (a) no-load simulation results of (i) speed-time, torque-speed, (ii) starting transient characteristics of phase *a* and phase *x* currents, (b) rated-load simulation results of (i) speed-time, torque-speed, (ii) starting transient characteristics of phase *a* and phase *x* currents in loaded conditions

4.4.2. Simulation results of faulty machine under open circuit condition

Equation (31) is used to obtain the performance characteristic of the machine under no-load and loaded conditions during fault. The Simulink representation of the open circuit voltage (*Vop*) model block is represented in figure 12. This is replaced with the supply voltage (*a*-phase)

using a signal builder as a timer, via a multiport switch for the simulation. The fault was created at a time 4 seconds, and the simulated results are shown in figure 13.

From the occurrence of fault at 4 seconds, the current in the faulty phase *a* is zero as expected. The amplitude of the oscillations in phase *x* rose to reach a constant value. Although there is no much significant change in speed during this period, the torque lead to oscillations as shown in the torque versus speed curve of figures 13a and 13b. This is true especially in loaded conditions when the amplitude of torque oscillations is nearly twice that observed in no load conditions. During the full load condition the speed dropped from 314 to about 280 rad\secs which is demonstrated in the step liked waveform in figure 13b. This created the oscillations in the performance characteristics. Although the machine was able to run at the rated torque under fault, severe precautions must be taken into account in other not to damage the entire winding of the machine. The speed versus time, torque versus speed, torque versus time curves and the waveforms of the two stator currents, phases *a* and *x* are as shown in figures 13 a and 13 b for no-load and rated load conditions respectively.

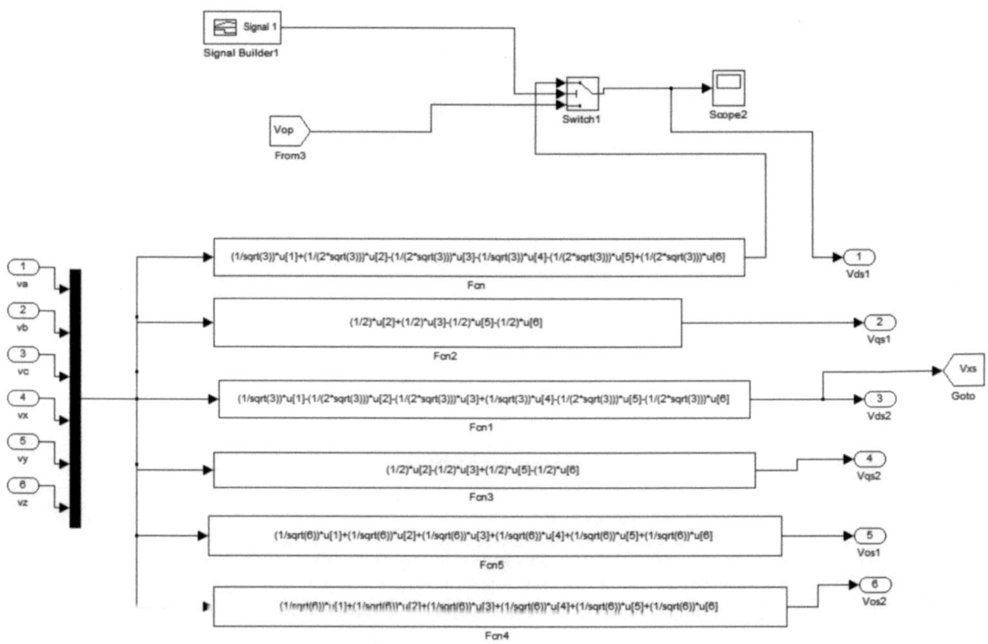

Figure 12. The Simulink representation for the unhealthy (open circuit) six phase squirrel cage induction machine model

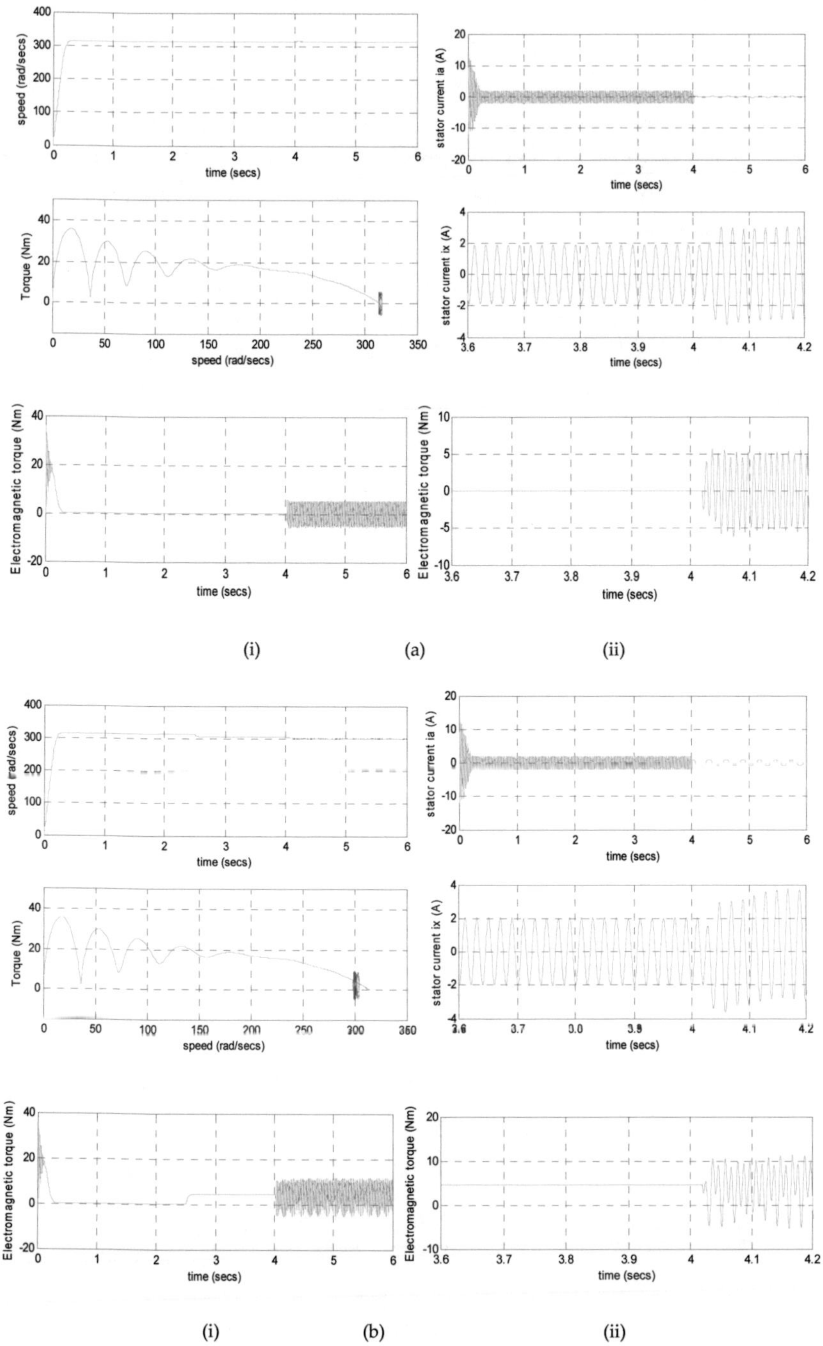

Figure 13. The open circuit (a) no-load simulation results of (i) speed-time, torque-speed, torque-time (ii) starting transient characteristics of phase *a* and phase *x* currents, (b) rated-load simulation results of (i) speed-time, torque-speed,torque-time (ii) starting transient characteristics of phase *a* and phase *x* currents in loaded conditions

4.4.3. Simulation results of faulty machine under short circuit condition

The short circuit voltage is achieved by making the supply voltages equal to zero by short circuiting two phases using the signal builder. The Simulink representation of the short circuit voltage model blocks is represented in figure 14. For the theoretical analysis of short circuit, a fault was created at 4 seconds for phases *a* and *b* after the machine started from standstill at no-load. The simulation of the rated load was done by applying the load at 2.5 seconds after the free oscillation settling of the no-load.

In this instance currents in both phase *a* and phase *x* are subject to oscillations having the same impact on the torque as in the open circuit fault but simply the amplitude of the oscillations appearing is slightly greater. Conversely, the speed drops and oscillates around a certain average value. From the effects of the short circuit simulated below on the torque and speed, it is apparent that this is a case of the most severe fault. However, the performance of the machine is not critically affected. The results, shown in figure 15 are the speed versus time, torque versus speed, torque versus time curves and the waveforms of the two stator currents, phases *a* and *x* for no-load and rated load conditions.

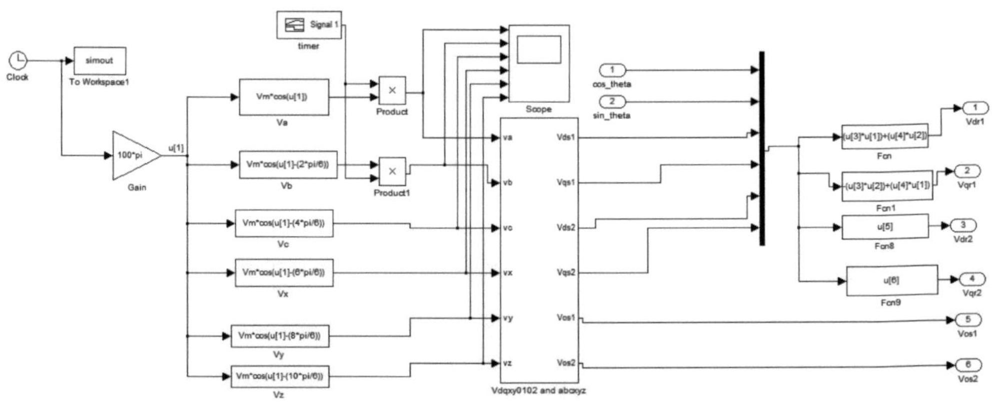

Figure 14. The Simulink representation for the unhealthy (short circuit) six phase squirrel cage induction machine model

http://dx.doi.org/10.5772/57468

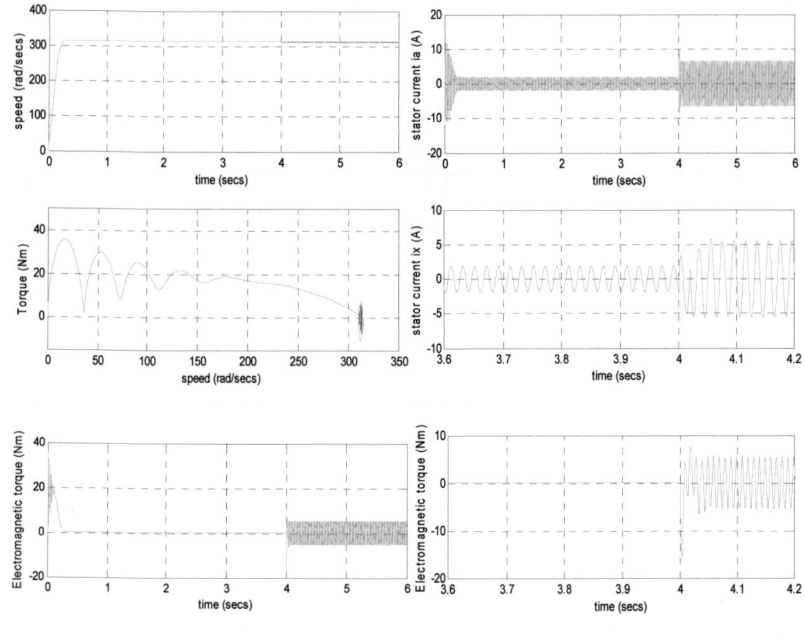

(i) (a) (ii)

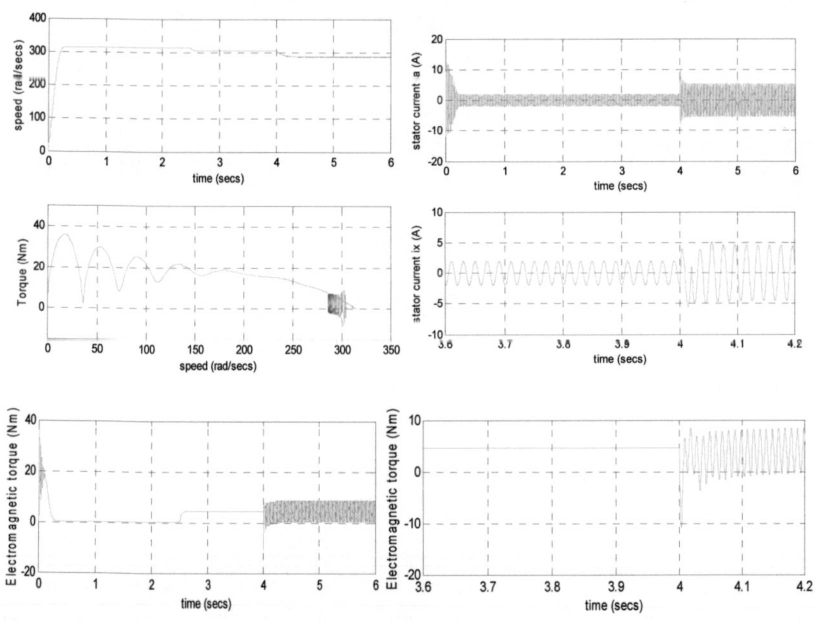

(i) (b) (ii)

Figure 15. The shot circuit (a) no-load simulation results of (i) speed-time, torque-speed, (ii) starting transient characteristics of phase *a* and phase *x* currents, (b) rated-load simulation results of (i) speed-time, torque-speed, (ii) starting transient characteristics of phase *a* and phase *x* currents in loaded conditions

5. Experimental validation

In order to validate the theoretical results with the experimental results, the experimental set up shown in figure 16 is utilised. The experimental results are used to validate the theoretical model. The set up consists of an induction motor which was reconstructed to a six phase machine, data acquisition equipment, torque transducer and computer system for waveform acquisition and a six phase supply. The machine performance at steady state has been plotted alongside the theoretic figures 7-9.

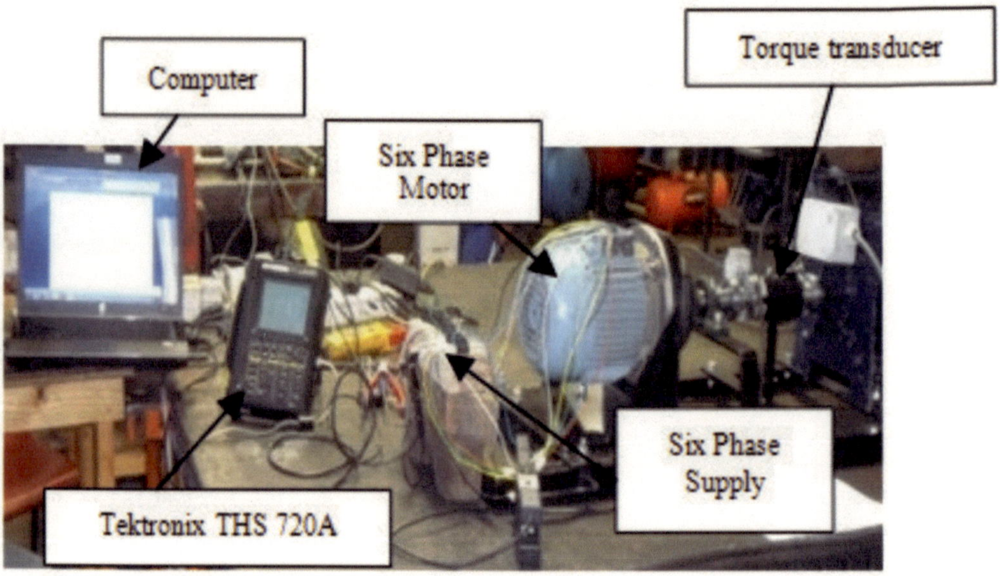

Figure 16. The six-phase experimental machine system

The dynamic simulations of the stator currents have been observed for the machine performance characteristics during normal operation and under fault conditions, both in loaded and unloaded conditions. These are shown in the figures 17 and 18. Given a fault condition, the current drawn at full load under fault condition is higher than that of the no load. This means that operating the machine for a long period of time under full load fault without de-rating can damaged the machine winding. The good agreement, shown by the curves, between theoretical and experimental results tends to validate the model.

http://dx.doi.org/10.5772/57468

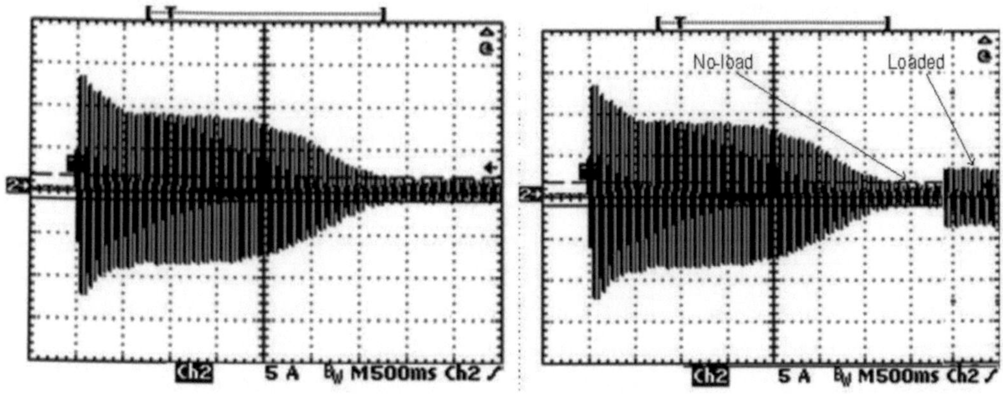

(i) (ii)

Figure 17. The experimental results, (i) no-load, (ii) loaded condition

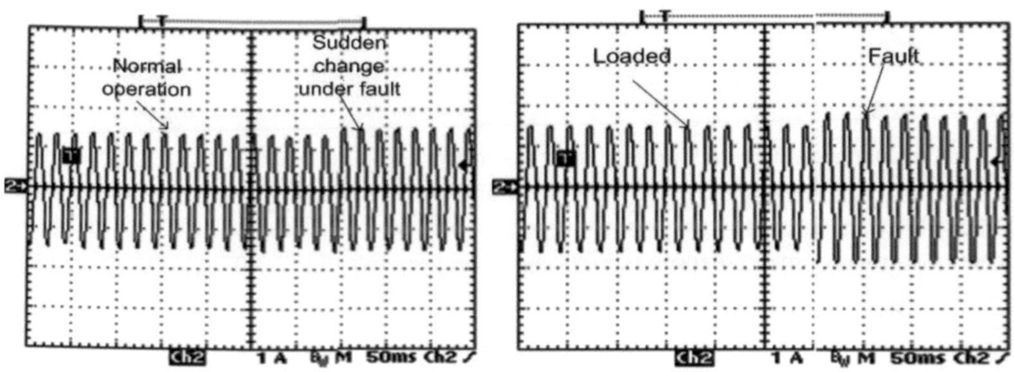

(i) (ii)

Figure 18. The experiment results, (i) no-load, (ii) loaded condition

6. Application possibility in electric vehicles (EV) and hybrid electric vehicles (HEV)

In view of the need to reduce the continued dependency on petroleum as a source of energy for powering cars and the drive to reduce CO_2 emissions, EV/HEV has received huge research interest. The applications of HEV range from small cars to buses, and even trucks. Researchers are generally working towards developing more efficient drive systems for EV/HEV vehicles. With different vehicle applications and requirements, it is clear that no single electric motor design fits all. As such motors designed for electric vehicle applications have to meet rigorous demands, with space limitations and the driving environment key factors. Reports of achievements has demonstrated that the specific performance characteristic of HPO machines matches the technical demands of HEV and also has the potential to further improve its quality. HPO machines finds application in areas where high power, high torque as well as high reliability is demanded. This is because it has a reduced amplitude and increased frequency of torque oscillation, reducing the rotor harmonic current per phase without increasing the voltage per phase, lowers the dc-link current harmonics, high fault tolerance (in the case of loss of one or more phases), reduction of required power rating per inverter leg and increase torque per ampere for the same volume of machine. HPO has been utilised also for integrated stator/alternator in HEV and ordinary vehicles with combustion engines Miller et al (2001) and Miller and Stefanovic (2002). The integrated idea replaced two electrical machines with a single machine and matches the goal of reducing the number of assemblies to have lighter vehicles.

The major types of electric motors adopted for EV/HEV includes DC motor, Induction motor, permanent magnet motor and Switched reluctance motor. A general review of the state of the art in EV/HEV shows that cage induction motors and the permannet magnet motors are highly dominant, whereas, study on the use of DC motors are going down.

6.1. Comparative study

6.1.1. Dc motor

DC motors have established presence in electric propulsion because their torque-speed characteristics suit traction requirement well and their speed controls are simple, Wildi (2004). However, dc motor drives have large assemblage, low efficiency, low reliability and continuous need of maintenance, mainly due to the presence of the mechanical commutator (brush).

Contrary to this, the continuous development of rugged solid-state power semiconductors has made it increasingly practicable to introduce AC induction and synchronous motor drives that are mature to replace dc motor drive in EV/HEV /traction applications.

The motors without commutator are attractive, as high reliability and maintenance-free operation are prime considerations for electric propulsion. Nevertheless, with regard to the cost of the inverter, ac drives are used generally just for higher power. At low power ratings, the dc motor is still more than an alternative (Zeraoulia, 2006).

6.1.2. Induction motor

Cage induction motors has wide acceptance as a potential candidate for the electric propulsion of EV/HEVs based on their reliability, ruggedness, low maintenance, low cost, and the ability to operate in a hostile environment. They are particularly well suited for the rigors of industrial and traction drive environments. Today, induction motor drive, Chris (2007) is the most mature technology among various commutatorless motor drives.

The introduction of, as well as the level of development in the HPO machines has further strengthened the position of Induction machine for electric propulsion in EV/HEV, particularly

http://dx.doi.org/10.5772/57468

Propulsion **Characteristics**	 DC	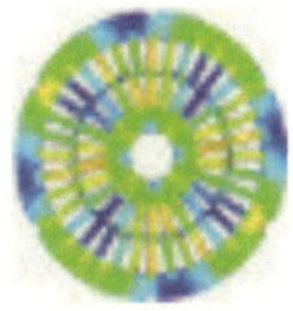 IM	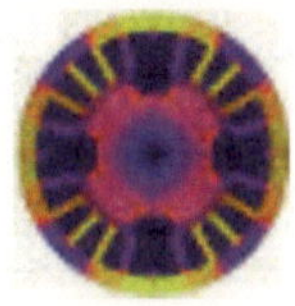 PM	 SRM
	DC	IM	PM	SRM
Power Density	2.5	3.5	5	3.5
Efficiency	2.5	3.5	5	3.5
Controllability	5	5	5	3
Reliability	3	5	4	5
Technology Maturity	5	5	4	4
Cost	4	5	3	4
			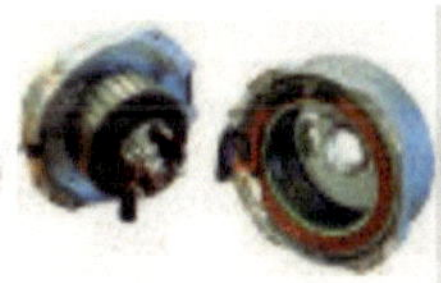	
ΣTotal	22	27	25	23

Table 1. Evaluation of Electric Propulsion Systems (Zeraoulia, 2006)

because of the possibility of high power, high torque and high torque per ampere for same volume of machine.

Zeraoulia (2006) carried out an evaluation of electric propulsion systems based on the main characteristics EV/HEV's propulsion, table 6.1. It was consensually established that induction motor is the most adapted for the propulsion of urban HEV's. This report is pre-the recent developments in the design and control of HPO machines.

7. Conclusions

A study of *HPO* machine using six-phase squirrel cage induction machine as a case study has been presented in this chapter. An experimental 1.5 KW six phase induction machine with 220V, 50Hz supply has been used for the study. Three different methods have been applied for modelling and analysis of the study and the performance behaviours of the machine have been considered under no-load and loaded conditions for a healthy machine and a machine with faults.

The results obtained showed that in both healthy and unhealthy cases the machine is able to produce the starting torque. However, it has been observed that the torque produced by the healthy machine is greater in magnitude and produces fewer oscillations than the machine with faults at the stator phases. The significant observation is that the machine settles down to a new steady state with the fault, thus confirming fault tolerance, albeit the performance of the signal variables is compromised.

The steady state performance of real power, reactive power, power factor, electromagnetic torque, the stator currents and efficiency have been shown. In the steady state results, the performance characteristics obtained from the simulations were compared with the experimental results, while the dynamic ones were similarly compared. While good agreements were generally observed the generalized theory gave closer result to the experiment than the classical field and the finite element methods.

Author details

A.A. Jimoh[1], E.K. Appiah[1] and A.S.O. Ogunjuyigbe[2]

1 Tshwane University of Technology, Pretoria, South Africa

2 University of Ibadan, Ibadan, Nigeria

References

[1] Appiah E.K., Mboungui G., Jimoh A.A., Munda J.L. & Ogunjuyigbe A.S.O. 2013. Symmetrical Analysis of a Six-Phase Induction Machine under Fault Conditions. Paper presented at the *World Acadeny of Science Engineering and Technology*, Brazil.

[2] Appiah E.K., Jimoh A.A., Mboungui G.&Munda J.L. "Effects of slot opening on the performance of a six phase squirrel cage induction machine using Finite Element and Field Analysis", Paper Accepted and presented at the *IEEE* Africon Conference in Mauritius, September 2013.

[3] Apsley J. & Williamson S. 2006. Analysis of Multiphase Induction Machines with Winding Faults. *IEEE Transactions On Industry Applications*, 4?(?)

[4] Aroquiadassou G., Mpanda-Mbawe A., Betin F. & Capolino G. A. 2009. Six Phase Induction Machine Drive Model for Fault-Tolerant Operation. Paper presented at the *IEEE Transactions*. Retrieved

[5] Bianchi N. 2005. *Electrical Machine Analysis using Finite Elements*. CRC Press, Taylor and Francis Group.

[6] Boldea I. & Tutelea L. 2010. *Steady State, Transients, and Design with Matlab*. CRC Press, Taylor & Francis Group.

[7] Ghuru B. S. & Hiziroglu H. R. 2005. *Electromagnetic Field Theory Fundamentals*. Cambridge University Press.

[8] Jimoh A. A. 1986. Stray load losses in Induction Machine. Doctor of Philosophy, McMaster University, McMaster University.

[9] Jimoh A. A., Jac-Venter P. & Appiah E.K. (2012). *Modelling and Analysis of Squirrel Cage Induction Motor with leading Power factor Injection*. Chapter in a book "Induction Motors - Modelling and Control", Edited by Prof. Rui Esteves Araújo, ISBN 978-953-51-0843-6, Published by Intech: November 14, 2012 under CC BY 3.0 license, in subject Energy Engineering, Chapter 4, pp. 99-126.

[10] Krause P. C. & Thomas C.H. 1965. Simulation of Symmetrical Induction Machinery. Paper presented at the *IEEE Transactions on Power Apparatus and Systems*.

[11] Krause P. C., Wasynczuk O. & Sudhoff S.D. 2002. Analysis of Electrical Machinery and Drive Systems. In: University, P. (Ed.). *Analysis of Electrical Machinery and Drive Systems*. IEEE Power Engineering Society

[12] Levi E. 2006. Recent Developments in High Performance Variable-Speed Multiphase Induction Motor Drives. Belgrade, SASA, Serbia: Sixth International Symposium Nikola Tesla.

[13] Lipo T. A. 47907. A d q model for Six Phase Induction Machines [Electronic Version].

[14] Ogunjuyigbe A.S.O. 2009. Improved Synchronous Reluctance Machine With Dual Stator Windings And Capacitance Injection. Doctor of Technology, A thesis submitted to the Department of Electrical Engineering, Tshwane University of Technology.

[15] Pyrhonen T. P. & Val'Eria H. 2008. *Design Of Rotating Machines*. First Ed. United Kingdom: John Willey and Sons Limited.

[16] Singh G.K. & Pant V. 2000. Analysis of a Multiphase Induction Machine Under Fault Condition in a Phase-Redundant A.C. Drive System [Electronic Version]. 577-590.

[17] Yong-Le A., Kamper M. J. & Le Roux A. D. 2007. Novel Direct Flux and Direct Torque Control of Six-Phase Induction Machine With Special Phase Current Waveforms. Paper presented at the *IIEEE Transactions on Industry Applications*.

[18] Chris;, M. 2007. Field-Oriented Control of Induction Motor Drives with Direct Rotor Current Estimation for Application in Electric and Hybrid Vehicles *Journal of ASIA electric vehicles*, 5(2):4.

[19] Wildi T. 2004. *Electrical Machines, Drives, and Power Systems*. Sixth Edition ed.: Pearson Prentice Hall.

[20] Miller, J.M., Stefanovic, V., Ostovic, V. and Kelly, J., (2001), Design considerations for an automotive integrated starter-generator with pole-phase modulation, *Proc. IEEE Ind. Appl. Soc. Annual Meeting IAS,* Chicago, Illinois, CD-ROM Paper 56_06.

[21] Miller, J.M. and Stefanovic, V., (2002), Prognosis for integrated starter alternator systems in automotive applications, *Proc. Power Electronics and Motion Control Conf. PEMC,* Cavtat, Croatia, CD-ROM Paper T5-001.

[22] M. Zeraoulia, IEEE, M.E.H. Benbouzid and D. Diallo (2006) Electric Motor Drive Selection Issues for HEV Propulsion Systems: A Comparative Study, 1756 IEEE Transactions On Vehicular Technology, Vol. 55, No. 6, November 2006.

Chapter 9

Atmospheric Propagation Model for Satellite Communications

Ali Mohammed Al-Saegh, A. Sali, J. S. Mandeep, Alyani Ismail, Abdulmajeed H.J. Al-Jumaily and Chandima Gomes

Additional information is available at the end of the chapter

http://dx.doi.org/10.5772/58238

1. Introduction

As the radio frequency signal radiates through an Earth-sky communication link, its quality degrades as it propagates through the link because of the absorption and scattering by the particles in space [1]. This degradation significantly affects the received information, particularly with the recent advances in satellite technologies and services, which require a high information rate. Furthermore, the extent of degradation depends on the link, atmospheric, transmitted signal, and receiver antenna parameters.

Two types of signal fluctuations caused by atmospheric phenomena, fast and slow fluctuations [2], as shown in Figure 1. The former is called scintillation, which is typically caused by rapid variations of signal performance attributed to the turbulent refractive index inhomogeneity in the medium. Meanwhile, slow fluctuations are usually caused by the absorption and scattering of the signal energy by the particles, particularly water droplets, in the link between the satellite and the earth station.

With respect to the atmospheric layers, the satellite signal may be subjected to different types of scintillations. Ionospheric scintillation occurs because of the irregularities in electron density in the ionosphere [3] (approximately from 85 km to 600 km above sea level) and, thus, irregularities in the refractive index. Whereas, tropospheric scintillation is caused by irregularities in radio refractivity as the wave travels along different medium densities in the troposphere (approximately 0 km to 10 km above sea level) [2].

The variation of the transmitted signal parameters (frequency f and elevation angle θ, in particular) has the major impact on the amount of the atmospheric impairments. For the transmitted signal frequencies below 3 GHz, the ionospheric scintillation has a significant

INTECH
open science | open minds

© 2014 The Author(s). Licensee InTech. This chapter is distributed under the terms of the Creative Commons Attribution License (http://creativecommons.org/licenses/by/3.0), which permits unrestricted use, distribution, and reproduction in any medium, provided the original work is properly cited.

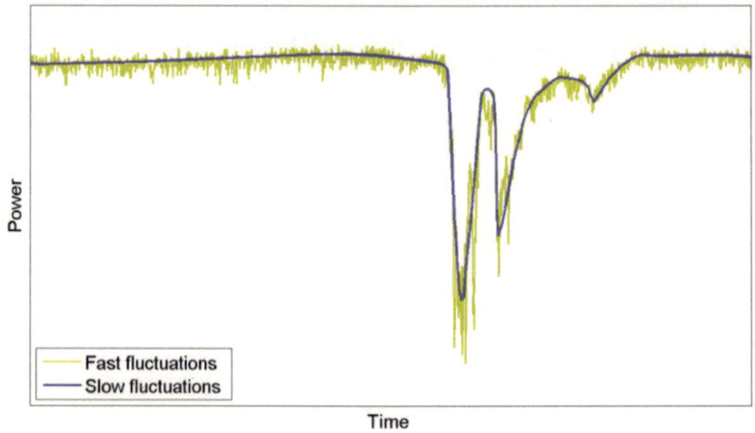

Figure 1. Fast and slow fluctuations

effect. However, this phenomenon becomes negligible as the frequency increases [4]. Consequently, for frequencies above 10 GHz, other phenomena, such as rain and clouds, impose a serious impact on the signal attenuation [5]. The oxygen and water vapor particles in space have a significant effect at higher signal frequencies [3].

Transmission at a low-elevation angle during the rain, condensed clouds, water vapor and Oxygen will increase the effective rain, clouds, water vapor, and Oxygen path of the signal on the medium, respectively, which in turn causes degradation in the received signal level. Therefore, the engineers in earth stations try to access the nearest possible satellite in order to increase the elevation angle, and hence, decrease the effect of atmospheric parameters.

The atmospheric impairments effects on the earth sky communication quality increase the need for developing prediction models in order to index the atmospheric fade level as well as select the proper fade mitigation technique (FMT).

This chapter proposes a complete model of atmospheric propagation to improve the estimation and the analysis of atmospheric effects on the signal quality in satellite communications using actual measured parameters. The model is composed of correlated modules that include channel modules and quality assessment extended modules.

2. Channel model

The general satellite system model contains three main components: Earth station(s), satellite(s), and the link(s) between them (channel/s). The channel and receiver models have been built using MATLAB as explained in the following subsections.

The satellite link may suffer from poor signal quality owing to atmospheric impairments. Raindrops cause significant effect at higher transmission frequencies, particularly above 10

http://dx.doi.org/10.5772/58238

GHz [5]. Other atmospheric phenomena, such as clouds, water vapor, and oxygen, significantly affect signal attenuation, especially at higher transmission frequencies. The models were implemented in Matlab based on the radiowave sector recommendations from the International Telecommunication Union (ITU) which proved to be suitable for satellite communications.

2.1. Rain attenuation

Rain droplets absorb and scatter the signal energy and cause its power level to attenuate to a value depending on the size, amount, and shape of the droplets that the signal passes through as well as the rain rate [6]. Rain usually occurs at different heights above sea level depending on a region on the earth.

Several rain attenuation prediction models have been developed which gained world agreements, such as Crane [7], group of researchers from International Telecommunication Union-Radiowave sector (ITU-R) [8, 9], DAH [10], and SAM [11]. These models were developed through many years of monitoring and observations. However, less than 5% of annual time usually contains rainy events. ITU-R [8] used this percentage as a starting point for their rain attenuation prediction model. To recognize the characteristics of rainy conditions in any area in the world, a percentage of less than 1% of the time of the year, which includes the rainfall that causes a significant amount of attenuation as the signal propagated through, is required to be taken into consideration.

The rain attenuation model shown in Figure 2 has been built and implemented based on modified ITU-R prediction model. In Particular, the actual measured rain rate in [6], rather than the predicted values by the ITU-R model, has been applied to construct a more accurate rain estimation model. The model has been implemented using Matlab. The initialization contains values for earth station position parameters (latitude, and height above sea level), rain parameters (rain rate, rain height, and percentage of exceedance time p), and transmitter parameters (frequency f, elevation angle θ, and polarization angle τ).

The developed program performs two procedures simultaneously. The first procedure starts with obtaining the frequency-dependent rain attenuation empirical values [12] before calculating the rain specific coefficients k and α through Eq. (1) and (2).

$$k = \frac{\mathrm{k_H} + \mathrm{k_V} + (\mathrm{k_H} - \mathrm{k_V})\cos^2\theta\cos(2\tau)}{2} \tag{1}$$

$$\alpha = \frac{\mathrm{k_H}\alpha_H + \mathrm{k_V}\alpha_v + (\mathrm{k_H}\alpha_H - \mathrm{k_V}\alpha_v)\cos^2\theta\cos(2\tau)}{2k} \tag{2}$$

The rain specific attenuation (the rain attenuation per 1 km) is then calculated using Eq. (3) depending on the actual measured rainfall rate (at p=0.01%) listed in [6] rather than the ITU predicted values in [9].

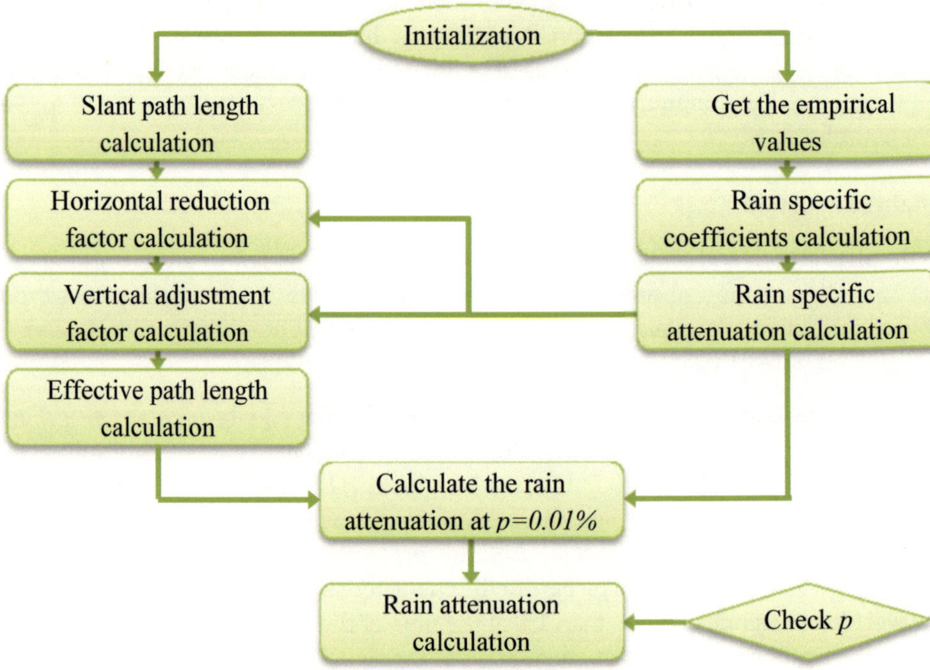

Figure 2. Rain attenuation model

$$\gamma_{Rain} = \alpha(R_{0.01})^k \tag{3}$$

This value will be used in the second procedure to identify the effective path length as well as to predict the overall rain attenuation. The horizontal reduction factor (r_H) for 0.01% of the time can be calculated using Eq. (4).

$$r_H = \frac{1}{1 + 0.78\sqrt{\frac{P_H \gamma_R}{f} - 0.38\left(1 - e^{-2P_H}\right)}} \tag{4}$$

where P_H is the horizontal projection which depends on the slant path length and the elevation angle, as imposed by Eq. (5)

$$P_H = L_S \cos\theta \tag{5}$$

The slant path length depends on the vertical height from the earth station to the rain height as well as on θ, as shown in Eq. (6).

$$L_S = \begin{cases} \dfrac{H_R - H_S}{\sin\theta} & \text{for } \theta \geq 5^\circ \\ \dfrac{2(H_R - H_S)}{\sqrt{\sin^2\theta + \dfrac{2(H_R - H_S)}{E_R}} + \sin\theta} & \text{for } \theta < 5^\circ \end{cases} \tag{6}$$

where H_R and H_S are the rain and earth station heights above sea level, respectively; and E_R is the earth radius (8500 km). The vertical adjustment factor (V_F) can be calculated at 0.01% of the time using Eqs. (7) to (9).

$$\xi = \tan^{-1}\left(\frac{H_R - H_S}{P_H r_H}\right) \tag{7}$$

$$L_R = \begin{cases} \dfrac{P_H r_H}{\cos\theta} & \text{for } \xi > \theta \\ \dfrac{H_R - H_S}{\sin\theta} & \text{for } \xi \leq \theta \end{cases} \tag{8}$$

$$V_F = \frac{1}{1 + \sqrt{\sin\theta}\left[31\left(1 - e^{-\frac{\theta}{1-x}}\right)\frac{\sqrt{L_R \gamma_R}}{f^2} - 0.45\right]} \tag{9}$$

where x depends on the latitude (φ) of the earth station. The calculation of the horizontal reduction and vertical adjustment factors in the ITU-R model is based on 0.01% of the time exceedance because these factors actually indicate the temporal variability of rain drop dimension and rain height, respectively [13]. The effective path length can be obtained using Eq. (10), whereas the total rain attenuation at 0.01% of time ($A_{0.01}$) can be calculated using Eq. (11).

$$L_E = L_R V_F \tag{10}$$

$$A_{0.01} = L_E \gamma_R \tag{11}$$

Consequently, the predicted rain attenuation at any percentage of time (p) can be calculated using Eqs. (12) and (13).

$$\beta = \begin{cases} 0 & \textit{If } p \geq 1\% \textit{ or } |\varphi| \geq 36^\circ \\ -0.005(|\varphi| - 36) & \textit{If } p < 1\% \textit{ and } |\varphi| < 36^\circ \textit{ and } \theta \geq 25^\circ \\ -0.005(|\varphi| - 36) + 1.8 - 4.25\sin\theta & \textit{Otherwise} \end{cases} \tag{12}$$

$$A_{rain} = A_{0.01}\left(\frac{p}{0.01}\right)^{-\left[0.655+0.033\ln(p)-0.045\ln(A_{0.01})-\beta(1-p)\sin\theta\right]} \tag{13}$$

The signal performance during rain events at different transmission parameters is analyzed along with received signal strength and error rates assessments.

2.2. Cloud attenuation

The cloud content of liquid water also causes absorption and scattering of electromagnetic energy especially for frequencies above 10 GHz, but with less intensity than that of rain [6]. Cloud attenuation, in addition to the transmission parameters such as the signal frequency and the elevation angle θ, depends on the cloud parameters such as average height and thickness, as well as the total columnar content of liquid water in Kg/m^2 (liquid water contents *LWC*) and temperature.

Several models have been developed to estimate cloud attenuation, such as Salonen & Uppala [14], ITU-R [15], DAH [16], and Altshuler & Marr [17]. Salonen & Uppala and ITU-R are identical in terms of the procedure used to predict the cloud attenuation, as shown in Figure 3. The only difference between these two models is in the prediction of the *LWC*.

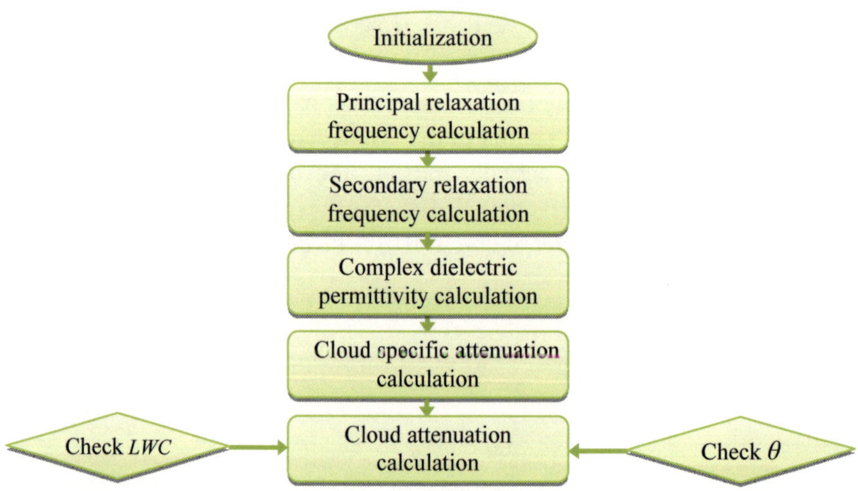

Figure 3. Cloud attenuation model

The cloud attenuation estimation model has been implemented based on the Salonen & Uppala and ITU-R models. The implemented model started with the initialization of the aforementioned parameters.

The principal and secondary relaxation frequencies are calculated using Eqs. (14) and (15), respectively.

$$fr_{pri} = 20.09 - 142(\Lambda - 1) + 294(\Lambda - 1)^2 \tag{14}$$

$$fr_{\sec} = 590 - 1500(\Lambda - 1) \tag{15}$$

where $\Lambda = 300/T$, and T is the temperature in Kelvin. The complex dielectric permittivity of water contents in the cloud is given by:

$$\varepsilon' = \frac{\varepsilon_0 - \varepsilon_1}{1 + \left(\frac{f}{fr_{pri}}\right)^2} + \frac{\varepsilon_1 - \varepsilon_2}{1 + \left(\frac{f}{fr_{\sec}}\right)^2} + \varepsilon_2 \tag{16}$$

$$\varepsilon'' = \frac{f(\varepsilon_0 - \varepsilon_1)}{fr_{prp}\left[1 + \left(\frac{f}{fr_{pri}}\right)^2\right]} + \frac{f(\varepsilon_1 - \varepsilon_2)}{fr_{\sec}\left[1 + \left(\frac{f}{fr_{\sec}}\right)^2\right]} \tag{17}$$

where ε_0=77.6+103.3(Λ– 1), whereas ε_1 and ε_2 are equal to 5.48 and 3.51, respectively. However, the cloud specific attenuation coefficient can be calculated using Eq. (18).

$$\gamma_{clouds} - \frac{0.819 f}{\varepsilon''\left[1 - \left(\frac{2 + \varepsilon'}{\varepsilon''}\right)^2\right]} \tag{18}$$

The cloud attenuation at any probability depends on the *LWC* that can be obtained from radiosonde or radiometric measurements for the region of interest.

$$A_{clouds} = \gamma_{clouds}\left(\frac{LWC}{\sin\theta}\right) \tag{19}$$

However, the *LWC* can be predicted using either Salonen & Uppala [14] or ITU-R study group 3 [15] prediction values. The former implies that *LWC* is obtained from a proposed map depending on the temperature and height from the cloud base. The latter implies the use of the annual values of *LWC* exceeded at some specific locations for several percentages of annual time from digital maps they proposed containing *LWC* values. The values for other desired locations on Earth can be derived by interpolation.

2.3. Water vapor and oxygen attenuations

The signal propagating through the atmosphere undergoes a degradation in signal level owing to the water vapor and dry air components in the transmission medium [18]. Water particles absorb and scatter the wave energy more than oxygen.

Water vapor attenuation depends on the weather parameters such as temperature, water vapor content, and altitude above sea level. The attenuation increases proportionally once the temperature and relative humidity (RH) increase. However, oxygen has the paramount effect among all other gases because the dry atmosphere contains 20.946% oxygen, thus resulting in a significant effect on satellite wave frequencies above 50 GHz [3, 19]. The oxygen attenuation analysis differs from other atmospheric impairments, because its effect on all the regions on the earth remains constant and independent.

Numerous experiments have been conducted [19, 20] using radiosonde for the purpose of observing and predicting the water content and oxygen attenuation. However, the ITU-R propagation sector came up with a prediction model [21] that has gained global agreement.

Figures. 4(a) and (b) shows the water vapor and oxygen attenuation models, respectively. The models, which have been implemented based on the ITU-R approximate estimation model, were initialized with related parameters such as the transmitted frequency, relative humidity, mean temperature, and pressure.

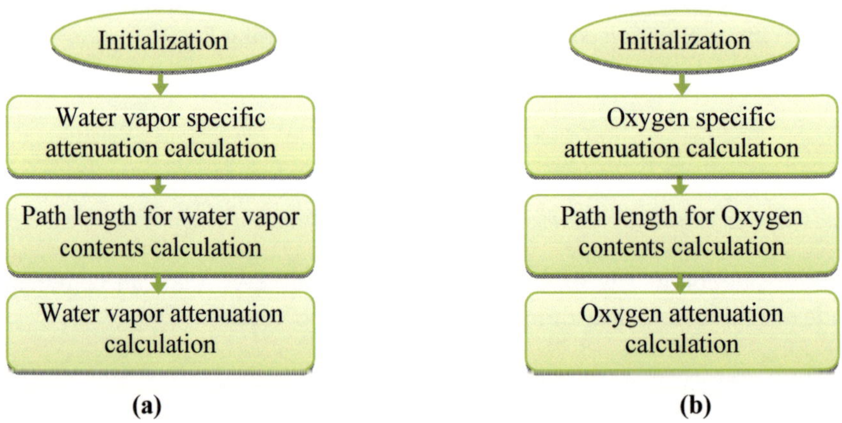

Figure 4. Water vapor and oxygen attenuation models (a) water vapor, and (b) oxygen

Oxygen specific attenuation can be determined for frequencies up to 350 GHz from the equations listed in Table 1.

Frequency (GHz)	Equation
$f \leq 54$	$\gamma_O = f^2 r_p{}^2 \left[\dfrac{7.2 r_T{}^{2.8}}{f^2 + 0.34 r_p r_T{}^{1.6}} + \dfrac{0.62 \xi_3}{(54-f)^{1.16\xi_2}} \right] \times 10^{-3}$
$54 < f \leq 60$	$\gamma_O = \exp\left[\dfrac{\ln \vartheta_{54}}{24}(f-58)(f-60) - \dfrac{\ln \vartheta_{58}}{8}(f-54)(f-60) + \dfrac{\ln \vartheta_{60}}{12}(f-54)(f-58) \right]$
$60 < f \leq 62$	$\gamma_O = \vartheta_{60} + \dfrac{f-60}{2}(\vartheta_{62} - \vartheta_{60})$
$62 < f \leq 66$	$\gamma_O = \exp\left[\dfrac{\ln \vartheta_{62}}{8}(f-64)(f-66) - \dfrac{\ln \vartheta_{64}}{4}(f-62)(f-66) + \dfrac{\ln \vartheta_{66}}{8}(f-62)(f-64) \right]$
$66 < f \leq 120$	$\gamma_O = f^2 r_p{}^2 \left[3.02 \times 10^{-4} r_T{}^{3.5} \dfrac{0.283\ r_T{}^{3.8}}{(f-118.75)^2 + 2.91\ r_p{}^2 r_T{}^{1.6}} + \dfrac{0.502\ \xi_6 (1 - 0.0163\ f\ \xi_7 - 1.0758\ \xi_7)}{(f-66)^{1.4346\ \xi_4} + 1.15\ \xi_5} \right] \times 10^{-3}$
$120 < f \leq 350$	$\gamma_O = f^2 r_p{}^2 r_T{}^{3.5} \left[\dfrac{3.02 \times 10^{-4}}{1 + 1.9 \times 10^{-5} f^{1.5}} + \dfrac{0.283\ r_T{}^{0.3}}{(f-118.75)^2 + 2.91\ r_p{}^2 r_T{}^{1.6}} \right] \times 10^{-3} + \delta$

Table 1. Oxygen specific attenuation calculation [21]

Where r_p and r_T are coefficients related to pressure (r_p=*Pressure*/1013) and temperature (r_T=288/ *T*) respectively. ξ_n, ϑ_n, and δ can be obtained from [21]. The path length for oxygen content can be determined using Eq. (20).

$$L_O = \frac{6.1(1 + z_1 + z_2 + z_3)}{1 + 0.17\ r_p{}^{-1.1}} \tag{20}$$

where

$$z_1 = \frac{4.64}{1 + 0.066\ r_p{}^{-2.3}} \exp\left[-\left(\frac{f - 59.7}{2.87 + 12.4\exp(-7.9\ r_p)} \right)^2 \right] \quad \text{(a)}$$

$$z_2 = \frac{0.14\exp(2.12\ r_p)}{(f-118.75)^2 + 0.031\exp(2.2\ r_p)} \quad \text{(b)} \tag{21}$$

$$z_3 = \frac{0.0114 f}{1 + 0.14\ r_p{}^{-2.6}} \left(\frac{-0.0247 + 0.0001 f + 1.61 \times 10^{-6} f^2}{1 - 0.0169 f + 4.1 \times 10^{-5} f^2 + 3.2 \times 10^{-7} f^3} \right) \quad \text{(c)}$$

Meanwhile, Eq. (22) is used to calculate the water vapor specific attenuation in (dB/km).

$$\gamma_W = f^2 r_T^{2.5} \rho \left[s_1 + s_2 + s_3 + s_4 + s_5 + s_6 + s_7 + s_8 + s_9 \right] \times 10^{-4} \tag{22}$$

Where ϱ is the water vapor density in (g/m³). $S_{1..9}$ can be obtained from Table 2.

Par	Equation	*Par*	Equation
S_1	$\frac{3.98\eta_1 \exp\left[2.23(1-r_T)\right]}{(f-22.235)^2 + 9.42\eta_1^2}\left[1+\left(\frac{f-22}{f+22}\right)^2\right]$	S_6	$\frac{17.4\eta_1 \exp\left[1.46(1-r_T)\right]}{(f-448)^2}$
S_2	$\frac{11.96\eta_1 \exp\left[0.7(1-r_T)\right]}{(f-183.31)^2 + 11.14\eta_1^2}$	S_7	$\frac{844.6\eta_1 \exp\left[0.17(1-r_T)\right]}{(f-557)^2}\left[1+\left(\frac{f-557}{f+557}\right)^2\right]$
S_3	$\frac{0.08\eta_1 \exp\left[6.44(1-r_T)\right]}{(f-321.226)^2 + 6.29\eta_1^2}$	S_8	$\frac{290\eta_1 \exp\left[0.41(1-r_T)\right]}{(f-752)^2}\left[1+\left(\frac{f-752}{f+752}\right)^2\right]$
S_4	$\frac{3.66\eta_1 \exp\left[1.6(1-r_T)\right]}{(f-325.153)^2 + 9.22\eta_1^2}$	S_9	$\frac{8.3328\times 10^4 \eta_2 \exp\left[0.99(1-r_T)\right]}{(f-1780)^2} \cdot \left[1+\left(\frac{f-1780}{f+1780}\right)^2\right]$
S_5	$\frac{25.37\eta_1 \exp\left[1.09(1-r_T)\right]}{(f-380)^2}$	η_1	$0.955 r_p r_T^{0.68} + 0.006\rho$
		η_2	$0.735 r_p r_T^{0.5} + 0.0353 r_T^4 \rho$

Table 2. Water vapor density calculation [21]

The effective path length may vary with respect to season, latitude, and/or climate change. However, the ITU-R estimated the effective water vapor path length in the troposphere for $f \leq 350$ GHz using Eq. (23).

$$L_W = 1.66\left(1 + \frac{1.39\sigma_W}{(f-22.235)^2 + 2.56\sigma_W} + \frac{3.37\sigma_W}{(f-183.31)^2 + 4.69\sigma_W} + \frac{1.58\sigma_W}{(f-325.1)^2 + 2.89\sigma_W}\right) \tag{23}$$

where

$$\sigma_W = \frac{1.013}{1 + \exp\left(4.902\text{-}8.6 r_p\right)} \tag{24}$$

The effective water vapor path length is based on the assumption of an exponential atmosphere to describe the relation between water vapor density and altitude. At this point, the total gases attenuation A_{Gases} (oxygen and water vapor attenuations) can be predicted using Eq. (25).

$$A_{Gases} = \frac{A_O + A_W}{\sin\theta} = \frac{\gamma_O L_O + \gamma_W L_W}{\sin\theta} \tag{25}$$

3. Extended model

The extended model has been added to improve the signal quality assessment in satellite communication networks for several modulation schemes to propose the optimal *FMT*. According to the Friis transmission equation [18, 22], the received power in dB is the summation of the power transmitted P_T, the antenna gains of the transmitter G_T, and the receiver G_R, and the subtraction of the losses. The link losses are composed of two types, namely, the free space loss (*FSL*), and the atmospheric losses. The *FSL*, which depends on the link distance (*d*) and transmitted frequency f=$(3\times 10^8)/\lambda$, can be calculated using Eq. (26).

$$FSL = 20\log\left(\frac{4\pi d}{\lambda}\right) \tag{26}$$

The atmospheric losses discussed in Section 2 are the second type of link losses. The received carrier power-to-noise ratio is estimated to identify the total degradation of the power in dB. The total noise depends on the bandwidth, in addition to the system and antenna noise temperatures. Based on the Friis transmission equation and to analyze the communication signal quality, the bit energy-to-noise ratio E_b/N_o can be calculated using Eq. (27).

$$E_b/N_{o\,dB} = EIRP + G_r - FSL - L_A - L_S - N_o - 10\log(R_b) \tag{27}$$

where *EIRP* is the Effective Isotropic Radiated Power; and L_A, L_s, N_o and R_b are the atmospheric losses, system losses, noise spectral density, and bit rate, respectively. The atmospheric impairments negatively affect the data after being demodulated in the receiver. The effects appear as a decrease in E_b/N_o and bit error rate (*BER*). These two metrics are used in selecting the optimal *FMT* at the time instants. The *BER* caused by atmospheric impairments can be approximated based on a Gray-code using Eq.28 [23].

$$BER \approx \frac{SER}{\log_2(M)} \tag{28}$$

where the symbol error rate (*SER*) is calculated using the equations listed in [6] for three modulation schemes: QPSK, 8-PSK and 16-PSK. The extended model has been added in order to improve the signal quality assessment in satellite communication networks for several modulation schemes to propose the optimal FMT. The extension includes several steps in the receiver side of the system, and comprises the calculation of the received signal power with the extraction of the atmospheric effects, E_b/N_o that indicates the signal quality, and *BER*.

4. Indexing and FMT

Recent satellite communications technologies make massive use of resource management procedures such as channel state reporting and *FMT*. The procedure for channel state reporting (indexing) is a fundamental feature of satellite networks utilizing *FMT* since it enlists the estimated channel quality level at the receiver, and then send this report to the transmitter to apply specific technique in the next period of time. Each index is calculated as a quantized and scaled measure of the experienced E_b/N_o, E_s/N_o, *BER or SER*. The reported values can be used to make decisions concerning the resource allocation to users experiencing specific channel conditions or application of a certain *FMT*. In TDM/TDMA transmitters, the decision is applied for a time period called transmission time interval (*TTI*). For every *TTI*, the allocation decision or *FMT* is performed with a validation until the next *TTI*.

FMT is usually classified into two types [6]. The first type mainly deals with a variation in signal characteristics (such as Adaptive coding and modulation ACM, time diversity, or frequency diversity). The second type does not concern the signal modifications (such as power control, or site diversity).

The reporting procedure is related to the FMT module, which selects the proper modulation and coding scheme in a case where a satellite network use the ACM technique for the process of maximizing the supported throughput with a given target error rate. Therefore, a user experiencing higher E_b/N_o will be served with higher bitrates, whereas a user experiencing poor channel conditions, will be served with lower bitrates to maintain active connections with lower error bits. It is worth to mention that the number of modulation and coding schemes is limited. Therefore, the throughput is upper-bounded over a specific threshold and the increase in the E_b/N_o does not result in any gain in throughput. This is the main reason of applying ACM technique accompanied with the power control technique.

The power control technique (uplink or downlink power control) is a dynamic procedure that adjusts transmission power to compensate for instantaneous channel condition variations [24]. These adjustments reduce power while maintaining a constant bitrate, or boost power to decrease losses when a higher modulation and coding scheme are selected, thus, increasing the bitrate. Henceforth, the aim is to keep the expected error rate below a target threshold.

However, some satellite networks consist of two or more ground stations spatially separated by at least 20 km [25] to provide separate propagation paths to the signal. This technique is called site diversity. The idea is to provide two different satellite channels that will not be significantly affected by rain attenuation simultaneously. This process enables the use of the best channel condition with a higher received signal level.

The transmitted signal can also be repeated at different time frames. Therefore, the receiver will receive more than one copy of the data transmitted. This technique is called time diversity. The time separation between successive repetitions should be greater than the channel coherence time to prevent the correlation of the received signals. Finally, frequency diversity involves transmitting the same message simultaneously at sufficiently separated (more than the coherence bandwidth) transmitted frequencies.

5. Complete proposed propagation model

The complete proposed propagation model for the satellite network is shown in Figure 5. The model consists of three parts: the transmitter, channel, and receiver. The modules in the channel and the receiver are the main concern of this chapter.

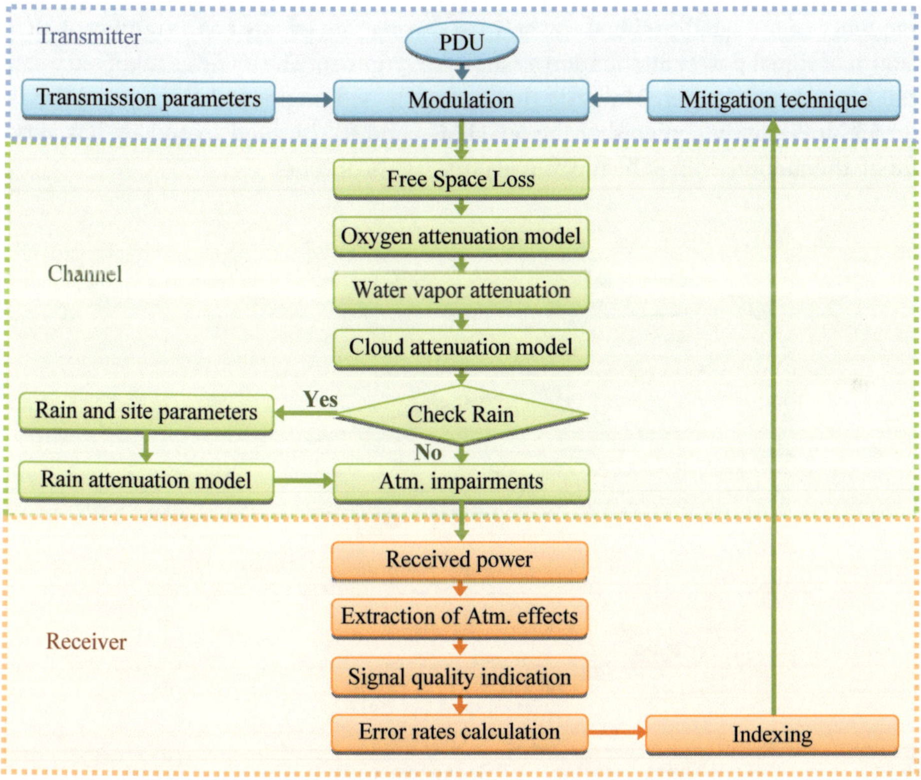

Figure 5. Complete propagation model

The packet data units are transmitted using specific transmission parameters and mitigation technique selected through the reported satellite channel. The effect of FSL, dry air (oxygen), and water vapor attenuation are added before the cloud attenuation module. The availability of rain attenuation is then checked. The rain and position parameters are also identified for the purpose of determining the effect of rain to the signal power. The total atmospheric impairments are then calculated to evaluate the received signal power as mentioned in section 3.

The atmospheric impairments and their effects on the received signal signified by E_b/N_o are then evaluated at different elevation angles. E_b/N_o is used for the signal quality indication and BER evaluation at different modulation schemes. The obtained values are then indexed in the process of estimating the instantaneous satellite channel quality. These values are then reported to the transmitter for the selection of the appropriate FMT to the next TTI. The model has been applied and the results were obtained at specific modules with signal evaluation and assessment under different atmospheric and transmission parameters.

6. Results and discussion

The frequency of the satellite signal transmitted during rain events has a significant effect on the amount of signal power attenuation as shown in Figure 6. The analysis involved a satellite terminal located in Selangor, Malaysia (Latitude 3.01 N, Longitude 101.6 E), and the θ was fixed to 45º. It is clearly shown that the 6 GHz C-band transmitted frequency has very low amount of attenuation even at heavy rain events (0.01% of time).

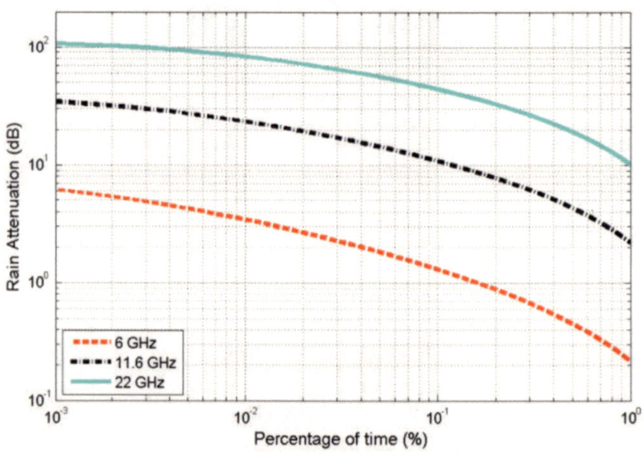

Figure 6. Rain attenuation at different percentages of time and frequencies

At 11.6 GHz Ku-band frequency, the rain attenuation at 0.01% of time ($A_{0.01}$) is approximately 23.4 dB and reached approximately 34.5 dB at 0.001% of the time, whereas $A_{0.01}$ reached approximately 83 dB if the signal was transmitted at 22 GHz Ka-band carrier frequency. The elevation angle is a highly effective parameter for the signal quality degradation. Figure 7 shows the amount of rain attenuation at different frequencies and elevation angles.

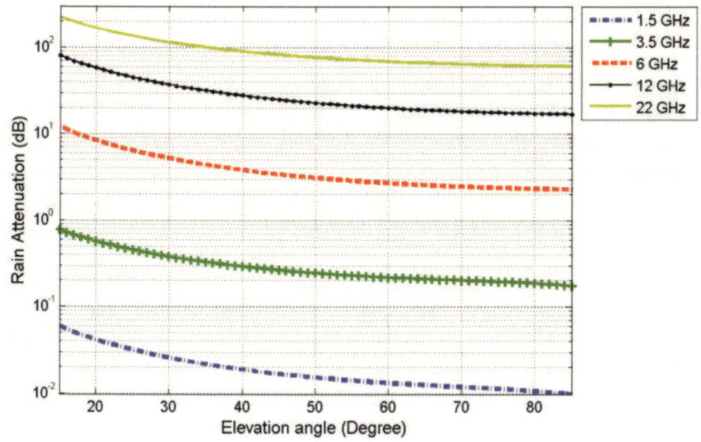

Figure 7. Rain attenuation at different θ and f

During rain events, the transmission link elevation angle is inversely proportional to the effective rain path of the signal and hence the amount of rain attenuation, whereas the transmitted frequency is directly proportional to the rain attenuation value. Consequently, the satellite position in space and the earth station terminal identifies the θ of the communication link. With the aid of the results in Figure7, the rain attenuation at three different satellites connected to earth station in Selangor has been analyzed as shown in results listed in table 3 for several frequencies.

Satellite	Elevation angle (θ)	Rain attenuation (dB) 1.5GHz L-Band	3.5 GHz S-Band	6 GHz C-Band	12 GHz Ku-Band	22 GHz Ka-Band
MEASAT 3/3A (91.5° E)	77.5°	0.01	0.2	2.36	17.6	62.5
SUPERBIRD C2 (144° E)	41.1°	0.02	0.29	3.73	27.3	88.7
INTLESAT 19 (166° E)	17.4°	0.05	0.67	9.93	67.8	191

Table 3. Rain attenuation at different satellites and transmission frequencies

It's obvious that there is a difference in the amount of rain attenuation at the same frequency but with different satellite (different θ). Consequently, there is a significant change in rain attenuation as the frequency band changed for the same satellite (fixed θ).

For cloud attenuation, the transmitted frequency and amount of liquid water in the cloud have a major effect on signal power attenuation. Figure 8 displays these effects on the amount of cloud attenuation.

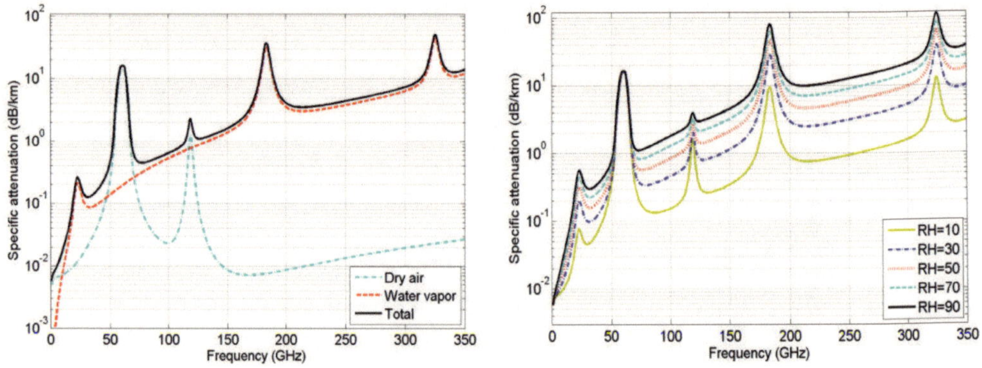

(a) (b)

Figure 9. Gases attenuation.

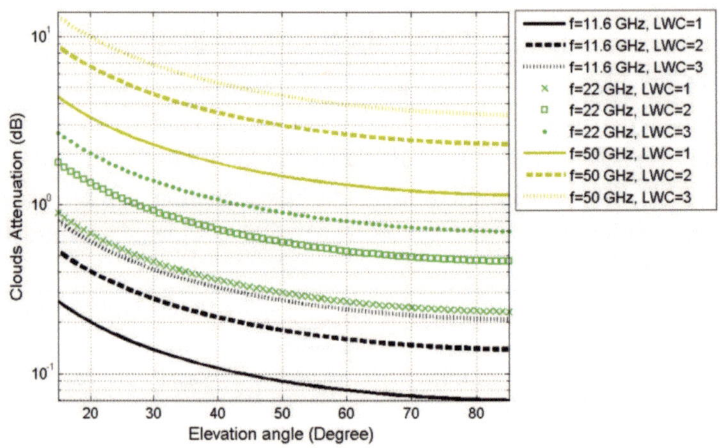

Figure 8. Cloud attenuation at different *f*, *θ*, and *LWC*

Figure 8 shows that the effect of clouds at Ku band frequencies is almost negligible for all θ and LWC, whereas the cloud attenuation at 22 GHz Ka frequency band are below 1 dB for a different *LWC* at $\theta > 45^{\circ}$, and below 3 dB for lower θ at 2 and 3 Kg/m^2 *LWC*. At 50 GHz V frequency band, a significant amount of cloud attenuation exceeding 10 dB for *LWC*=3 Kg/m^2 and θ below 20º was observed. Whereas it reached 1.8 dB, 3.6 dB, and 5.3 dB for θ=41.1º and *LWC* was 1, 2, and 3 Kg/m^2, respectively. Consequently, cloud attenuation reached approximately 1.17 dB, 2.3 dB, and 3.5 dB if the if θ=77.5º and *LWC* was 1, 2, and 3 Kg/m^2, respectively.

The significant amount of dry air and water vapor specific attenuation appears at specific regions across the frequency spectrum, and hence the total correlated gases attenuation, as shown in Figure 9(a)

The significant specific attenuation started at frequencies above 55 GHz mainly due to the effect of oxygen, and then the attenuation level went down. The effect appeared again at frequencies above 170 GHz, but this time mainly due to water vapor attenuation. The gases attenuation at fixed 40% *RH* reached higher level at approximately 325 GHz. The relative humidity (*RH*) is directly proportional to the amount of signal power attenuation due to the water vapor particles in space, and hence the total gases attenuation as shown in Figure 9b. However, the regions near the sea and the equator usually suffer from higher *RH* which indicates increased gases attenuation.

The channel quality level can be identified by the value of E_b/N_o. This leads to the selection of the proper *FMT* for the next *TTI*. The channel quality during atmospheric impairments is varied according to several parameters. θ is one of the major parameters that specify the channel quality during atmospheric dynamics. Figure 10 shows the E_b/N_o with various rainfall events at different θ for 11.6 GHz transmitted frequency.

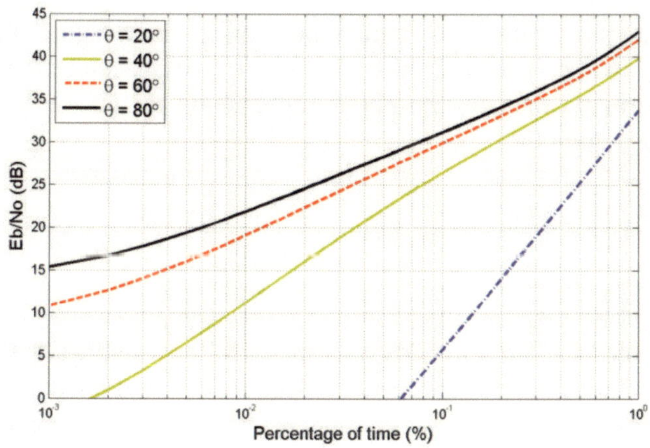

Figure 10. Bit energy to noise ratio for different θ

The higher the elevation angle, the lower the attenuation and therefore the higher the value of E_b/N_o. During very heavy rain (around 0.001% of annual time), bad channel quality imposes serious problems to the users of the satellite networks. This leads to communication link outage at lower θ. The BER calculations depends on the E_b/N_o along with the transmission bit rate and bandwidth. Figure 11 shows the BER approximated for three modulation schemes: QPSK, 8-PSK, and 16-PSK.

As the number of bits per second increased with the M-ary[1] modulation scheme, the number of error bits increased simultaneously during the signal propagation through the atmosphere. For rainy weather events, the higher the M-ary modulation scheme, the higher the *BER* due to

1 M-ary is a term derived from the word binary. M represents a digit that corresponds to the modulation order. M=4, 8, and 16 for the QPSK, 8-PSK, and 16-PSK modulation schemes, respectively. more details in [26].

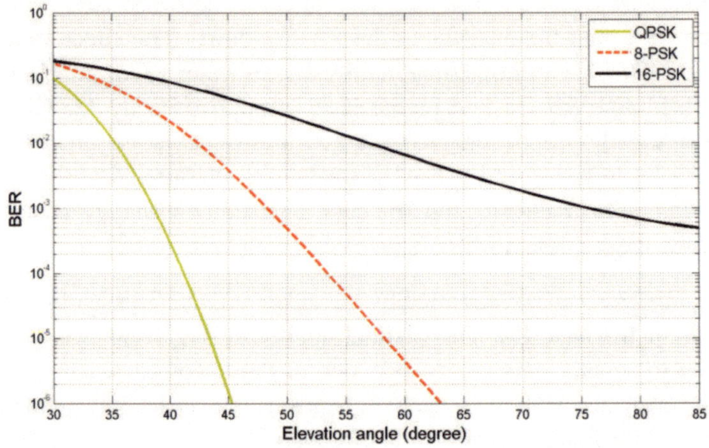

Figure 11. Bit error rate

the higher number of transmitted bits in unit time. Consequently, Figure 10 also clarifies that the θ is inversely proportion to *BER*. QPSK modulation can be considered the most appropriate modulation scheme in case of high atmospheric impairments, but at the cost of a lower number of transmitted bits per unit time.

7. Conclusion

This chapter presented the atmospheric impairments to the satellite signal quality in terms of performance evaluation and assessments concerning various effective atmospheric and transmission parameters during dynamic weather conditions. The impairments presented were caused by rain, clouds, dry air (oxygen), and water vapor attenuation. An overview of ionospheric and tropospheric scintillations, channel status reporting (indexing), and FMT was provided. The atmospheric propagation model was introduced. The model included a transmitter, channel, and receiver modules built using Matlab which was revealed to be appropriate for building mathematical and analytical models. Channel conditions were evaluated along with quality and error rate estimation extensions. The atmospheric impairments results were obtained based on actual measured real-world parameters. The performance analysis of the proposed extended and propagation modules for the satellite system included atmospheric attenuation, signal-to-noise ratios, bit energy-to-noise ratios, as well as BER. The results showed that the rain attenuation effect started at frequencies above 10 GHz and exhibited the largest effects among other atmospheric phenomena, followed by cloud attenuation, and gases attenuation that have the least effects. Moreover, the results revealed that the transmitted frequency, rainfall rates, *LWC*, and relative humidity are directly proportional to the signal quality degradation, whereas θ is inversely proportional. The reported channel quality, which indicated by E_b/N_o, under poor

http://dx.doi.org/10.5772/58238

conditions may suffer from link outage at heavy rain events for low θ. This condition corresponds to low BER, particularly at a higher M-ary modulation scheme. The chapter would be useful for satellite system designer to accurately predict the atmospheric impairments that may affect the channel, and identifying signal quality performance with error rates during weather dynamics.

Appendix: Matlab code

```
%-----------------------------------------------------------------------------------------
% Initialization
%-----------------------------------------------------------------------------------------
 % Input parameters:
% The values of these parameters can be adjusted according to the scenario or region of interest.

% Transmission parameters
disp('Transmission parameters:');
command = 'Input the elevation angle (Degree): ';
Elev = input(command);
if Elev<5 || Elev>90
   error('please input value from 5 to 90 ')
end
command = 'Input the transmission frequency (GHz): ';
f=input(command);
if f<0.1 || f>350
   error('please input value from 0.1 to 350 ')
end
command = 'Input the polarization? (1 for Horizontal, 2 for Vertical, and 3 for Circular): ';
pol= input(command);
if pol==1
tau=0;
elseif pol==2
tau=90;
elseif pol==3
tau=45;
else
   error('please input integers from 1 to 3 ')
end
disp('=======================');

% Atmospheric parameters
disp('Atmospheric parameters:');
command = 'Input percentage of exceedance time (from 0.001% to 5%): ';
P = input(command);
command = 'Input Rain Rate for 0.01% of time (mm/h): ';
Rrate = input(command);
% Some actual measured rain rate values can be obtained from [6].
command = 'Input Rain height above sea level (km): ';
hR = input(command);
command = 'Input liquid water contents LWC (Kg/m^2): ';
LWC = input(command);
command = 'Input Temperature (K): ';
T = input(command);
command = 'Input the relative humidity (%): ';
RH = input(command);
```

```
if RH<0 || RH>100
   error('please input value from 0 to 100 ')
end
command = 'Input pressure (hPa): ';
p = input(command);
disp('========================');

% Satellite and earth station parameters
disp(Satellite and earth station parameters:');
command = 'Input the Effective Isotropic radiated power (dBW): ';
EIRP = input(command);
command = 'Input earth station Latitude : ';
Lat = input(command);
command = 'Input Station height above sea level (km): ';
hs = input(command);
command = 'Input receiver gain (dBi): ';
gr = input(command);
disp('========================');

%--------------------------------------------------------------------------------------
% Rain attenuation
%--------------------------------------------------------------------------------------

% Frequency-dependent rain attenuation empirical values (K and alpha)
% In order not to take much space, the empirical values are defined here for
% frequency range from 11 to 14 GHz
% other frequency values can be obtained from ITU-R P.838 recommendation.
% Source: http://www.itu.int/dms_pubrec/itu-r/rec/p/R-REC-P.838-3-200503-I!!PDF-E.pdf
if f==11
   kH=0.01772;
   kV=0.01731;
   alphaH=1.2140;
   alphaV=1.1617;
elseif f<12 && f>11
   kH=(((f-11)/(12-11))*(0.02386-0.01772))+0.01772;
   kV=(((f-11)/(12-11))*(0.02455-0.01731))+0.01731;
   alphaH=(((f-11)/(12-11))*(1.1825-1.2140))+1.2140;
   alphaV=(((f-11)/(12-11))*(1.1216-1.1617))+1.1617;
elseif f==12
   kH=0.02386;
   kV=0.02455;
   alphaH=1.1825;
   alphaV=1.1216;
elseif f<13 && f>12
   kH=(((f-12)/(13-12))*(0.03041-0.02386))+0.02386;
   kV=(((f-12)/(13-12))*(0.03266-0.02455))+0.02455;
   alphaH=(((f-12)/(13-12))*(1.1586-1.1825))+1.1825;
   alphaV=(((f-12)/(13-12))*(1.0901-1.1216))+1.1216;
elseif f==13
```

```
    kH=0.03041;
    kV=0.03266;
    alphaH=1.1586;
    alphaV=1.0901;
  elseif f<14 && f>13
    kH=(((f-13)/(14-13))*(0.03738-0.03041))+0.03041;
    kV=(((f-13)/(14-13))*(0.04126-0.03266))+0.03266;
    alphaH=(((f-13)/(14-13))*(1.1396-1.1586))+1.1586;
    alphaV=(((f-13)/(14-13))*(1.0646-1.0901))+1.0901;
elseif f==14
    kH=0.03738;
    kV=0.04126;
    alphaH=1.1396;
    alphaV=1.0646;
% Update the frequency-dependent rain attenuation empirical values here
end

k=(kH+kV+((kH-kV)*((cosd(Elev)).^2)*cosd(2*tau)))/2;
alpha=((kH*alphaH)+(kV*alphaV)+(((kH*alphaH)-
(kV*alphaV))*((cosd(Elev)).^2)*cosd(2*tau)))/(2*k);

gamaR=k*(Rrate.^alpha);           % The rain specific attenuation (dB/km)
disp(['Rain specific attenuation= ', num2str(gamaR),' dB/km']);
if Elev >=5
   Ls=(hR-hs)/(sind(Elev));          % slant-path length below the rain height (km)
end
   LG=Ls.*cosd(Elev);               % The horizontal projection of the slant path length (km).

 % Calculation of the horizontal reduction factor for 0.01% of the time
   c=0.78.*sqrt(LG.*gamaR/f);
   d=0.38.*(1-exp(-2.*LG));
   ro_o1=1/(1+c-d);

 % Calculation of the vertical adjustment factor for 0.01% of the time
   eta=atand((hR-hs)/LG.*ro_o1);
    if eta >Elev
       LR=(LG.*ro_o1)/cosd(Elev);
    else
       LR=(hR-hs)/sind(Elev);
    end;
     abslat=abs(Lat);
     if abslat<36
        kye=36-abslat;
     else
        kye=0;
     end;
   e=31.*(1-exp(-Elev/(1+kye)));
   fff=sqrt(LR.*gamaR)/f.^2;
   vo_o1=1/(1+sqrt(sind(Elev)).*(e.*fff-0.45));
```

```
% Effective path length (km)
LE=LR*vo_o1;

% Rain attenuation at P=0.01% of time (dB)
RAtt01=LE*gamaR;

% Calculation of rain attenuation at different percentages of time
  if P >=(1)||(abs(Lat)>=36)
   beta=0;
  elseif P <(1)&& (abs(Lat)<36)&&(Elev>=25)
   beta=-0.005.*(abs(Lat)-36);
  else
   beta=-0.005.*(abs(Lat)-36)+1.8-4.25.*sind(Elev);
  end
if P >=(0.001) && (P <=5)
 pu=(-1).*(0.655+(0.033.*log(P))-(0.045.*log(RAtt01))-(beta.*(1-P).*sind(Elev)));
 RainAttP=RAtt01.*(P/0.01).^(pu);
else  error('Percentage of exceedance time should be from 0.001% to 5% for...
 predicting the rain attenuation' )
end
disp(['Rain attenuation= ', num2str(RainAttP),' dB']);

%-----------------------------------------------------------------------------------------
% Cloud attenuation
%-----------------------------------------------------------------------------------------

% Calculation of the principal & secondary relaxation frequencies:
theta=300/T;
eo=77.6+103.3.*(theta-1);
e1=5.48;
e2=3.51;
fp=20.09-142.*(theta-1)+294.*(theta-1)^2;  %GHz
fs=590-1500.*(theta-1);                    %GHz

% Calculation of the complex dielectric permittivity of water:
eta2=(f/fp).*((eo-e1)/(1+(f/fp)^ 2))+(f/fs).*((e1-e2)/(1+(f/fs)^2));
eta1=((eo-e1)/(1+(f/fp)^2))+((e1-e2)/(1+(f/fs)^2))+e2;
n=(2+eta1)/eta2;

% cloud specific attenuation coefficient ((dB/km)/(g/m^3))
Kl=0.819.*f/(eta2.*(1+n^2));

CAtten=LWC.*Kl/sind(Elev);
disp(['Cloud attenuation= ', num2str(CAtten),' dB']);
```

http://dx.doi.org/10.5772/58238

```
%----------------------------------------------------------------------------------------
% Gases attenuation
%----------------------------------------------------------------------------------------

% (1) Water vapor

% calculation of the water vapor specific attenuation
th=300/T;
pw=(RH/5.752)*th*(10.^(10-(9.834*th))); % Water vapor density (g/m^3)
rt=288/T;
rp=p/1013;
n1=0.955*rp*(rt.^0.68)+(0.006*pw);
n2=0.735*rp*(rt.^0.5)+(0.0353*(rt.^4)*pw);
Yw=(((3.98*n1*exp(2.23*(1-rt)))/(((f-22.235).^2)+9.42*(n1.^2)))*(1+((f-22)/(f+22)).^2)+...
   ((11.96*n1*exp(0.7*(1-rt)))./(((f-183.31).^2)+11.14*(n1.^2)))+((0.081*n1*exp(6.44*(1-rt)))/...
   (((f-321.226).^2)+(6.29*(n1.^2))))+((3.66*n1*exp(1.6*(1-rt)))/(((f-325.153).^2)+9.22*(n1.^2)))+...
   ((25.37*n1*exp(1.09*(1-rt)))/((f-380).^2))+((17.4*n1*exp(1.46*(1-rt)))/((f-448).^2))+...
   ((844.6*n1*exp(0.17*(1-rt)))/((f-557).^2))*(1+((f-557)/(f+557)).^2)+((290*n1*exp(0.41*(1-t)))/...
   ((f-752).^2))* (1+((f-752)/(f+752)).^2)+ ((83328*n2*exp(0.99*(1-rt)))/...
   ((f-1780).^2))* (1+((f-1780)/(f+1780)).^2))*((f.^2)*(rt.^2.5)*(pw*10.^(1-5)));
disp(['water vapor specific attenuation= ', num2str(Yw),' dB/km']);

% calculation of the path length for water vapor contents (km)
conw=1.013/(1+exp((0-8.1)*(rp-0.57)));
hw=1.66*(1+((1.39*conw)/(((f-22.235).^2)+(2.56*conw)))+((3.37*conw)/(((f-183.31).^2)+...
   (4.69*conw)))+((1.5*conw)/(((f-325.1).^2)+(2.89*conw))));

Aw=Yw*hw; %water vapor attenuation in zenith angle path (dB)

% (2) Dry air

% Definitions:
ee1=(rp.^0.0717)*(rt.^(0-1.8132))*exp(0.0156*(1-rp)-1.6515*(1-rt));
ee2=(rp.^0.5146)*(rt.^(0-4.6368))*exp((0-0.1921)*(1-rp)-5.7416*(1-rt));
ee3=(rp.^0.3414)*(rt.^(0-6.5851))*exp(0.2130*(1-rp)-8.5854*(1-rt));
ee4=(rp.^(0-0.0112))*(rt.^(0.0092))*exp((0-0.1033)*(1-rp)-0.0009*(1-rt));
ee5=(rp.^0.2705)*(rt.^(0-2.7192))*exp((0-0.3016)*(1-rp)-4.1033*(1-rt));
ee6=(rp.^0.2445)*(rt.^(0-5.9191))*exp(0.0422*(1-rp)-8.0719*(1-rt));
ee7=(rp.^(0-0.1833))*(rt.^(6.5589))*exp((0-0.2402)*(1-rp)+6.131*(1-rt));
Y54=2.192*(rp.^1.8286)*(rt.^(0-1.9487))*exp(0.4051*(1-rp)-2.8509*(1-rt));
Y58=12.59*(rp.^1.0045)*(rt.^(3.5610))*exp(0.1588*(1-rp)+1.2834*(1-rt));
Y60=15*(rp.^0.9003)*(rt.^(4.1335))*exp(0.0427*(1-rp)+1.6088*(1-rt));
Y62=14.28*(rp.^0.9886)*(rt.^(3.4176))*exp(0.1827*(1-rp)+1.3429*(1-rt));
Y64=6.819*(rp.^1.4320)*(rt.^(0.6258))*exp(0.3177*(1-rp)-0.5914*(1-rt));
Y66=1.908*(rp.^2.0717)*(rt.^(0-4.1404))*exp(0.4910*(1-rp)-4.8718*(1-rt));
ss=(0-0.00306)*(rp.^3.211)*(rt.^(0-14.94))*exp(1.583*(1-rp)-16.37*(1-rt));
```

```
% Calculation of the dry air specific attenuation
if f<=54
Yo=(((7.2*(rt.^2.8))/((f.^2)+(0.34*(rp.^2)*(rt.^1.6))))+((0.62*ee3)/(((54-...
        f).^(1.16*ee1))+(0.83*ee2))))*((f.^2)*(rp.^2)*(10.^(0-3)));
elseif f>54 && f<=60
    Yo=exp(((log(Y54)./24)*(f-58)*(f-60))-((log(Y58)./8)*...
        (f-54)*(f-60))+((log(Y60)./12)*(f-54)*(f-58)));
elseif f>60 && f<=62
    Yo=Y60+((Y62-Y60)*((f-60)/2));
elseif f>62 && f<=66
    Yo=exp(((log(Y62)./8)*(f-64)*(f-66))-((log(Y64)./4)*(f-62)*...
        (f-66))+((log(Y66)./8)*(f-62)*(f-64)));
elseif f>66 && f<=120
    Yo=((3.02*(10.^(0-4))*(rt.^3.5))+((0.283*(rt.^3.8))/(((f-...
        118.75).^2)+(2.91*(rp.^2)*(rt.^1.6))))+...
        ((0.502*ee6*(1-(0.0163*ee7*(f-66))))/(((f-66).^(1.4346*ee4))+...
        (1.15*ee5))))*((f.^2)*(rp.^2)*(10.^(1-4)));
elseif f>120 && f<=350
    Yo=(((3.02*(10.^(0-4)))/(1+(1.9*(10.^(0-5))*(f.^1.5))))+...
        ((0.283*(rt.^0.3))/(((f-118.75).^(2))+(2.91*(rp.^2)*...
        (rt.^1.6)))))*((f.^2)*(rp.^2)*(rt.^3.5)*(10.^(0-3)))+ss;
end
disp(['Dry air specific attenuation= ', num2str(Yo),' dB/km']);

% Calculation of the equivalent height
t1=(4.64/(1+(0.066*(rp.^(0-2.3)))))*exp(0-((f-59.7)/(2.87+(12.4*exp((0-7.9)*rp)))).^2);
t2=(0.14*exp(2.12*rp))/(((f-118.75).^2)+0.031*exp(2.2*rp));
t3=(0.0114/(1+(0.14*(rp.^(0-2.6)))))*f*((0-0.0247+(0.0001*f)+...
        (1.61*(10.^(0-6))*f.^2))/(1-(0.0169*f)+(4.1*(10.^(0-5))*f.^2)+ (3.2*(10.^(0-7))*f.^3)));
ho=(6.1/(1+(0.17*(rp.^(0-1.1)))))*(1+t1+t2+t3);

Ao=Yo*ho;    % Dry air attenuation in zenith angle path (dB)

% Total gases attenuation

Ytot=(Yo+Yw)./sin(Elev);
disp(['Total gases specific attenuation= ', num2str(Ytot),' dB/km']);
Atot=(Ao+Aw)./sin(Elev);
disp('=========================');

%------------------------------------------------------------------------------------------
% Extended model
%------------------------------------------------------------------------------------------

disp('Extended model');
disp('=============');
disp('Other Input parameters:');
command = 'Input the bit rate (kb/s): ';
brate = input(command)*1000;
```

```
command = 'Input the noise spectral density: ';
No = input(command);
command = 'Input total system losses (dB) : ';
Ls = input(command);

% Calculating the free space loss (FSL)
lambda=(3*1e8)/(f*10^9);
fsl= 20*log10((4*pi*3.6*1e7)./lambda);
disp(['Free space Loss = ', num2str(fsl),' dB']);

command = 'Input the atmospheric loss (dB) : ';
La = input(command);
% Here you can define the atmospheric loss (La) according to the specifiedscenario,
% or you can use the outputs from the aforementioned models.
% Error rate mathematical model can be added as mentioned in section 3.

% Quality indication: Calculating the bit energy to noise ratio
Rpower=EIRP+gr-fsl-La-Ls;          % received power (dBW)
ebnor=Rpower-No-10*log10(brate);
disp(['Eb/No = ', num2str(ebnor),' dB']);

%-----------------------------------------------------------------------------------------
```

Acknowledgements

Ministry of Higher Education (MoHE) in Malaysia is thankfully acknowledged for the grant with code ERGS/1-2012/5527096.

Author details

Ali Mohammed Al-Saegh[1], A. Sali[1], J. S. Mandeep[2], Alyani Ismail[1], Abdulmajeed H.J. Al-Jumaily[1] and Chandima Gomes[3]

1 Department of Computer and Communication Systems Engineering, Universiti Putra Malaysia, Serdang, Selangor, Malaysia

2 Department of Electrical, Electronic and Systems Engineering, Universiti Kebangsaan Malaysia, Bangi, Selangor, Malaysia

3 Department of Electrical and Electronic Engineering, Universiti Putra Malaysia, Serdang, Selangor, Malaysia

References

[1] J. Mandeep and Y. Ng, "Satellite Beacon Experiment for Studying Atmospheric Dynamics," *Journal of Infrared, Millimeter and Terahertz Waves,* vol. 31, pp. 988-994, 2010.

[2] A. Adhikari, A. Bhattacharya, and A. Maitra, "Rain-Induced Scintillations and Attenuation of Ku-Band Satellite Signals at a Tropical Location," *Geoscience and Remote Sensing Letters, IEEE,* vol. 9, pp. 700-704, 2012.

[3] M. Zubair, Z. Haider, S. A. Khan, and J. Nasir, "Atmospheric influences on satellite communications," *Przeglad Elektrotechniczny,* vol. 87, pp. 261-264, 2011.

[4] A. D. Panagopoulos, P. D. M. Arapoglou, and P. G. Cottis, "Satellite communications at KU, KA, and V bands: Propagation impairments and mitigation techniques," *Communications Surveys & Tutorials, IEEE,* vol. 6, pp. 2-14, 2004.

[5] T. V. Omotosho and C. O. Oluwafemi, "Impairment of radio wave signal by rainfall on fixed satellite service on earth–space path at 37 stations in Nigeria," *Journal of Atmospheric and Solar-Terrestrial Physics,* vol. 71, pp. 830-840, 2009.

[6] A. M. Al-Saegh, A. Sali, J. S. Mandeep, and A. Ismail, "Extracted atmospheric impairments on earth-sky signal quality in tropical regions at Ku-band," *Journal of Atmospheric and Solar-Terrestrial Physics,* vol. 104, pp. 96-105, 2013.

[7] R. K. Crane, "Prediction of Attenuation by Rain,"*Communications, IEEE Transactions on,* vol.28, pp.1717-1733, Sep 1980.

[8] I. T. U. ITU, "Propagation data and prediction methods required for the design of Earth-space telecommunication systems.," ed: International Telecommunication Union-Recommendation P.618-11, 2013.

[9] ITU, "Characteristics of precipitation for propagation modelling.," ed: International Telecommunication Union-Recommendation P.837-6, 2012.

[10] A. Dissanayake, J. Allnutt, and F. Haidara, "A prediction model that combines rain attenuation and other propagation impairments along Earth-satellite paths," *Antennas and Propagation, IEEE Transactions on,* vol. 45, pp. 1546-1558, 1997.

[11] W. L. Stutzman and W. K. Dishman, "A simple model for the estimation of rain-induced attenuation along earth-space paths at millimeter wavelengths," *Radio Sci.,* vol. 17, pp. 1465-1476, 1982.

[12] ITU, "Specific attenuation model for rain for use in prediction methods ", ed: International Telecommunication Union-Recommendation P.838-3, 2005.

[13] S. D. A. Adhikari, A. Bhattacharya, and A. Maitra, "Improving rain attenuation estimation: modelling of effective path length using ku-band measurements at a tropical location," *Progress In Electromagnetics Research B,* vol. 34, pp. 173-186, 2011.

[14] E. Salonen and S. Uppala, "New prediction method of cloud attenuation," *Electronics Letters,* vol. 27, pp. 1106-1108, 1991.

[15] I. T. U. ITU, "Attenuation due to clouds and fog.," ed: International Telecommunication Union-Recommendation P.840, 2012.

[16] A. Dissanayake, J. Allnutt, and F. Haidara, "Cloud attenuation modelling for SHF and EHF applications," *International Journal of Satellite Communications,* vol. 19, pp. 335-345, 2001.

[17] E. E. Altshuler and R. A. Marr, "Cloud attenuation at millimeter wavelengths," *Antennas and Propagation, IEEE Transactions on,* vol. 37, pp. 1473-1479, 1989.

[18] L. J. Ippolito, *Satellite communications systems engineering: atmospheric effects, satellite link design and system performance*: Wiley, 2008.

[19] R. Bhattacharya, R. Das, R. Guha, S. D. Barman, and A. B. Bhattacharya, "Variability of millimetrewave rain attenuation and rain rate prediction: A survey," *Indian Journal of Radio & Space Physics (IJRSP),* vol. 36, pp. 325-344, Aug-2007 2007.

[20] A. Maitra and S. Chakraborty, "Cloud Liquid Water Content and Cloud Attenuation Studies with Radiosonde Data at a Tropical Location," *Journal of Infrared, Millimeter and Terahertz Waves,* vol. 30, pp. 367-373, 2009.

[21] I. T. U. ITU, "Attenuation by atmospheric gases.," ed: International Telecommunication Union-Recommendation P.676-10, 2013.

[22] V. K. Sakarellos, D. Skraparlis, A. D. Panagopoulos, and J. D. Kanellopoulos, "Outage Performance Analysis of a Dual-Hop Radio Relay System Operating at Frequencies above 10GHz," *Communications, IEEE Transactions on,* vol. 58, pp. 3104-3109, 2010.

[23] K. K. Teav, Z. Zhendong, and B. Vucetic, "On the Asymptotic Bit Error Probability of M-QAM for MIMO Y Channels," *Communications Letters, IEEE,* vol. 16, pp. 577-580, 2012.

[24] L. Castanet, M. Bousquet, and D. Mertens, "Simulation of the performance of a Ka-band VSAT videoconferencing system with uplink power control and data rate reduction to mitigate atmospheric propagation effects," *International Journal of Satellite Communications,* vol. 20, pp. 231-249, 2002.

[25] J. S. Mandeep, S. I. S. Hassan, and K. Tanaka, "Rainfall measurements at Ku-band satellite link in Penang, Malaysia," *Microwaves, Antennas & Propagation, IET,* vol. 2, pp. 147-151, 2008.

[26] M. K. Simon and M.-S. Alouini, *Digital communication over fading channels*, Second ed. vol. 95. New Jersey: John Wiley & Sons, Inc., 2005.

Chapter 10

Stateflow® Aided Modelling and Simulation of Friction in a Planar Piezoelectric Actuator

G. M'boungui, A.A. Jimoh, B. Semail and F. Giraud

Additional information is available at the end of the chapter

http://dx.doi.org/10.5772/57569

1. Introduction

Research works have focused on friction over more than 500 years. It is indeed a complex phenomenon arising at the contact of the surfaces that is encountered in a wide variety of engineering disciplines including contact mechanics, system dynamics and controls, aeromechanics, geomechanics, fracture and fatigue, structural dynamics, and many others [1]. Recently, the action of friction generated by a surface under the finger has been exploited in continuous structure tactile (sensorial touch) interfaces.

Indeed, in daily life, various tasks may be more speedily and efficiently completed if kinaesthetic feedback is exploited [2]. However, human beings are only using visual and audio feedback when interacting with numerous interfaces such as computers, mobile phones, etc. In such a context, the utilization of haptic devices to get back forces corresponding to feelings from virtual objects manipulation enhances the realism of the global experience. This is even true in the instance of forces and pressure applied on fingers and hand in tele-robotics applications. As a matter of fact, as soon as one has to grasp, touch, and feel objects it becomes necessary to involve haptic devices. Thus, for many researchers, such interfaces represent a new human-machine communication medium, which is a growing topic of interest and prime importance to the research community. Developments in the field have been observed over the last years. Besides tele-operation, haptic feedback can have so many over applications either in engineering, CAD, electronic games, education, learning, etc. Force feedback devices are commercialised. Phantom from Sensable® or Virtuose from Haption®, are examples of haptic feedback pen [3]. Some other solutions have been proposed including « exoskeleton » devices that directly apply forces on the hand or the finger. Typically, these haptic peripherals have an essential place in design, simulation and virtual assembly for instance in car production in the automobile industry. So many additional illustrations in terms of utilisation are

INTECH
open science | open minds

© 2014 The Author(s). Licensee InTech. This chapter is distributed under the terms of the Creative Commons Attribution License (http://creativecommons.org/licenses/by/3.0), which permits unrestricted use, distribution, and reproduction in any medium, provided the original work is properly cited.

available and helping a user in identifying limits and virtual shape changes may be achieved by such interfaces.

Nevertheless, it is remarkable that force feedback devices are mostly based on electromagnetic technologies. Consequently, numerous mechanical links are often involved in movement transformation. This results in systems integration and dynamic problems, etc. For this reason piezoelectric actuators present a reliable alternative especially since high forces, rapid response and compactness are seen to be added advantages. It is indeed shown that piezoelectric actuators make variable friction phenomena available [4] and exploitable for the purpose of haptic feedback.

The actuator to be discussed follows this trend: it is based on electro mechanical conversion principle specific to piezoelectric systems.

Indeed, exciting a plate in certain conditions of vibratory amplitude and frequency the texture represented in Figure 1 e.g. can be simulated [5][6]. For that it suffices to correlate the vibratory amplitude with the level of friction reduction between an exploring finger and the textured plate. To complete the process, the control of the finger position over the plate enables textures feeling. In fact, during the touching of the excited surface, that is vibrating, the finger perceives smoothness. If the vibrations source is switched off a roughness is perceived. To reform a given texture, we can thus measure the finger displacement and control the vibratory amplitude as a function of the explored feeling (smoothness or roughness) and the finger position. This example is chosen to illustrate that controlled friction is an interesting alternative in terms of tactile feelings generation. The challenge is however in modelling the friction and to deduce appropriate control laws.

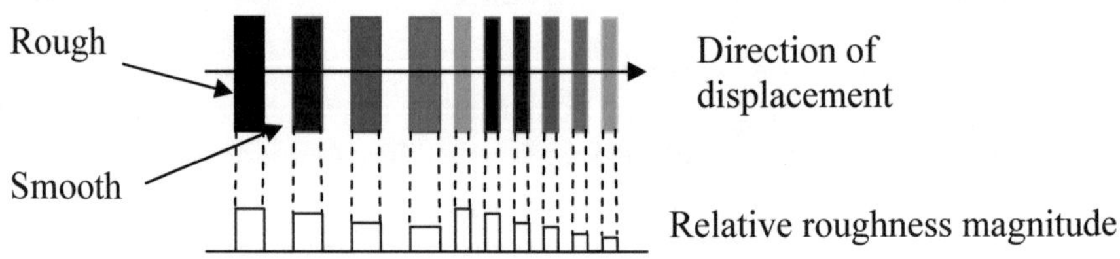

Figure 1. Image of the texture

A feature of stick-slip vibration is a saw tooth displacement time evolution with stick and slip phases clearly defined in which the two surfaces in contact stick respectively slip over each other [7]. From the later definition a relative similarity may be perceived between the modelling of stick-slip vibration and the texture in figure 1. In the chapter is presented the approach we propose using Matlab-Simulink-Stateflow® to deal with our structure as a finite state structure.

Thus an overview of piezoelectric materials and the impact they may have on resulting piezoelectric systems, in particular on transducers technology is given. This is followed by a brief discussion on tactile feedback designs using actuation other than piezoelectric and the drawbacks and advantages of piezoelectric actuators versus other types. From now on

http://dx.doi.org/10.5772/57569

we present the design, modelling and implementation of our proposal which is a passive 2Dof (two Degree of freedom) device able to provide different resistant feelings when a user moves it.

2. Piezoelectric materials contribution to transducers technology

In this section, piezoelectric materials such as lead zirconium titanate (PZT) utilised elsewhere in our design are briefly discussed. We focus on the benefits that transducers technology in general can draw from those materials.

Piezoelectric materials produce an electric charge when subjected to mechanical loads (direct effect) and/or vibrations. Those materials deform when subjected to a magnetic field (inverse effect) [8]. The piezoelectric effect is expressed in materials such as single crystals, ceramics, polymers, composites, thin films and relaxor-type ferroelectric materials.

Of the existing piezoelectric materials polymers and ceramics have been widely explored as transducers materials [8]. Ceramic piezoelectric materials comprise barium titanate (BaTiO3), lead zirconate – lead titanate of general formula $Pb(Zr\text{-}Ti)O_3$-PZT and lead titanate ($PbTiO_3$, PCT). Those materials have been extensively studied because most of them have in common a perovskite (ABO_3) structure [9][8], a material in which the application of an intense electric field aimed at aligning polarization of elementary ferroelectric microcrystal (polarization operation) enables introduction of necessary anisotropy to piezoelectric existence. The dielectric and piezoelectric constants of barium titanate vary with temperature, stoichiometry, microstructure and doping [10] whereas the piezoelectric constants for PZT are not strongly dependant upon temperature but rather on material composition. However, piezoelectric constants for certain stoichiometry compositions of PZT are far more sensitive to temperature dependencies than others [11]. In [12] it can be seen that the characteristics of BaTiO3 single crystal favoured their usage in certain applications such as electromechanical transducers for operation at high frequencies. However, nowadays, PZT have been the material of reference in the field of piezoelectric motors. Regarding, lead titanate material, Samarium-modified PCT was investigated for application in infrared sensors, electro-optic devices and ferroelectric memory devices [13].

Polymer piezoelectric material such as polyvinylidene difluoride (PVDF) or PVF2 demonstrate the piezoelectric effect when they are stretched or formed during fabrication [10]. However, it is among composite piezoelectric materials made of a piezoelectric and a polymer that composites comprised of PZT rods embedded within a polymer matrix are predicted to be one of the most promising structures for transducers and acoustic applications [10].

Relaxor-type ferroelectric materials differ from traditional ferroelectric material because they have a broad phase transition from paraelectric to ferroelectric state, dielectric relaxation and weak remnant polarization. Indeed those materials have the ability to become polarized when subjected to applied electric field. Unlike in traditional ferroelectric materials, this can happen even if there is no permanent electric dipole that exists in the material. The result of removing the field is polarisation in the material returning to zero [14]. Single crystals of $Pb(Mg_{1/3}Nb_{2/3})O_3$ (PMN), $Pb(Zn_{1/3}Nb_{2/3})O_3$ (PZN), PMN-PT and PZN-PT are currently under investigation for transducer technology because of their large coupling coefficients, large piezoelectric constants and high strain levels so far higher than other piezoelectric materials [15].

3. Tactile feedback interfaces overview

As we have indicated in the introduction, piezoelectric technology is promising in haptics, restricted in this chapter to tactile feedback, but other alternatives have been exploited. Therefore several methods used for tactile or coetaneous feedback and several forms of technological proposals will be described. We chose to sort those proposals by highlighting related function and technology.

Until now, two methods of tactile feedback have mainly been proposed: shape tactile display and vibrotactile stimuli application. Shape tactile display appears to designers of tactile stimulators to reforming a material state of surface [16]. Conversely, tactile stimulation, as it is perceived actually deals with direct stimulation through vibrators or skin mechanoreceptors stimulation. Each stimulator has its own domain of validity and tactile devices are divided according to discrimination and space covered by stimulation area [17][18]. From a technological point of view, tactile stimulation can be realised from different ways. Therefore, various actuation principles are discussed. So, in shape tactile displays (quasi static) actuators are of: electromagnetic, Shape Memory Alloy, pneumatic technology, etc. In a second group, vibrotactile matrices systems use piezoelectric and electromagnetic actuators. Finally, the third subset is made of vibrating systems with continuous structure and friction reduction generally actuated using piezoelectric technology.

3.1. Shape tactile displays (Quasi-static)

3.1.1. Electromagnetic actuators

Electromagnetic (EM) actuators used in shape stimuli display are generally DC rotary actuators or electromagnets. They are generally bulky because of mechanisms involved and their miniaturisation is challenging. Consequently very few electromagnetic micro actuators are available in the market. Two examples are given with a graphic illustration.

The FEELEX from University of Tsukuba is an interface actuated by rotary motors controlled in position and deforming a plane surface of 3 mm thick thanks to a rods matrix. Each rod is actuated by a DC motor which the movement is transformed.

The FEELEX2 [19] allows a maximum rods displacement and force of respectively 18 mm and 1.1 kgf; such displacements and high forces are the main advantages of EM actuation.

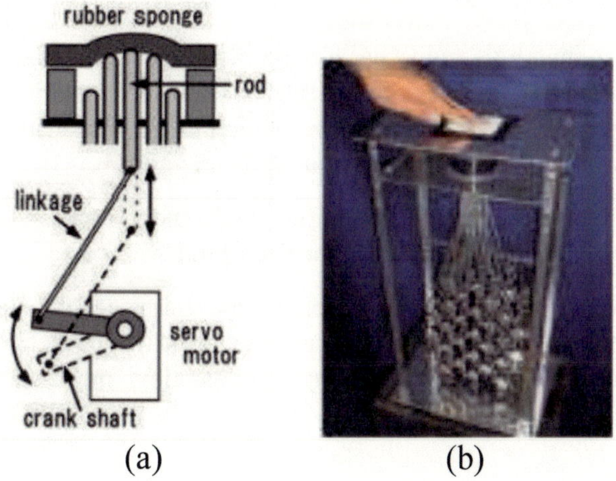

Figure 2. Feelex2 a) principle of movement transformation b) interface [19]

A device similar to the one in this study was proposed by Schneider et al [20] who developed a common computer mouse to move on a steel mat, to which force feedback function is added by including in an electromagnet. In function of cursor position on the computer screen and effort needed a reference voltage is applied inducing therefore a magnetic field and then a continuous friction force depending upon the voltage value. The modified mouse is a Hewlett-Packard 5187-1556 (Figure 3). The maximum friction force obtained is 2.0 N which is still relatively high. However, a notable problem came from the localized magnetic force at the back of the mouse, causing a rotation around the magnet; a rotation which needed to be counterbalanced.

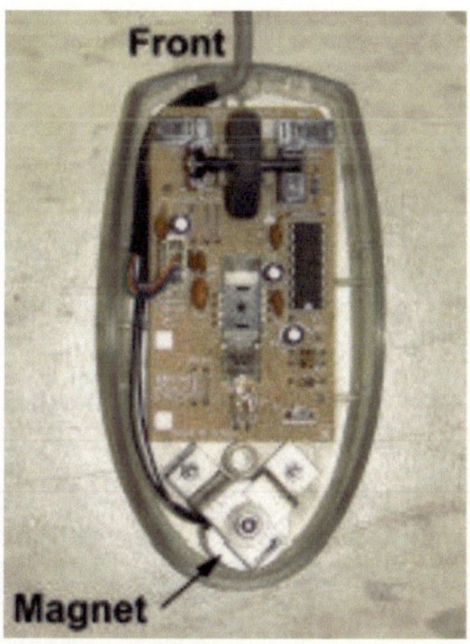

Figure 3. Hewlett-Packard 5187-1556 modified mouse [20]

3.1.2. Shape Memory Alloys (SMA)

SMA are alloys of tremendous properties among metal materials wherein the capability to "keep in memory" an initial shape and to get back even after a deformation. Usually SMA follows a plastic deformation at relatively low temperatures (Martensite) and gets back their original shape (Austenite) if they are heated at high temperature.

For teleoperation and virtual reality applications, researchers from Harvard University have developed a tactile prototype [21] made of one line of rods.

Reduced space between rods, significant force and roughness developed, and displacements amplitude make up SMA technologically adapted to tactile feedback. However, SMA are not so often used because of their relatively long response time and their integration remains challenging.

3.1.3. Pneumatic technology

Apart from air bladders inserted in the gloves of TeleTact Glove and filled up by a compressor, other devices exist. That is the case for pistons actuated by motors [22] allowing the feeling of a variable roughness membrane, the case as well of devices using a pump to expel [23] or aspire some air by means of binary electromagnet micro valves [24]. Although those devices from pneumatic technology can generate high forces, they are not always comfortable and are relatively heavy.

3.1.4. Electro-Rheologic Fluids (ERF)

A matrix of bladders full of ERF can allow space distribution of normal forces on the finger pulp that pre constrains the device then. Indeed, a local change of fluid viscosity by electric field application yields a variable roughness under the finger pulp. It turns out that some progress in terms of precision is necessary [25].

3.1.5. Other technologies

In this field of application, research groups have investigated other solutions such as MEMS (Micro-Electro Mechanical Systems) [26] and active polymers but developments are still marginal.

3.2. Vibro tactile matrices systems

The chosen approach in this sub section differs from the latter one because this time it is the vibro tactile stimuli application that generates the prospected feeling. Previously the prospected effect was obtained by means of normal indentation of the skin according to shape reconstitution usually related to discrete representation of the state of surface or 3D explored asperity. High amplitude and low frequency of rods displacement feature those structures whereas in vibro tactile stimulators rods have a high frequency (around 200 Hz) and very low amplitude (around 10 μm) displacements. "Reproducing" surface asperities is no longer the aim but conversely, producing a sort of appropriate excitation on different skin mechanoreceptor populations. Conceptually, electromagnetic and piezoelectric technologies are resorted to.

In this category the Vital [17] is an example of electromagnetic system.

The devices belonging to the family to be discussed in next section are based on electro mechanical conversion principle specific to piezoelectric systems. That principle will be used in the rest of this work.

3.3. Continuous structure based vibro tactile systems

In order to create shape displays or vibro tactile feelings, the technologies described above generally have the particularity to communicate the explored feeling to the user finger through a rods matrix. The advantage of that rods matrix structure is to allow refinement in control (each rod being independently controllable) but the structure is limited in integration. Conversely, some other devices present a continuous structure producing a pulse or a controllable friction under the finger.

Using this principle, the impulse display proposed by Poupyrev et al [27] was able to be incorporated on the sensitive screen of a PDA (Personal Digital Assistant).

3.4. Variable friction devices

3.4.1. Variable friction creation principle

The action of friction generated by a surface under the finger is a second alternative exploited in continuous structure tactile interfaces. Watanabee [28] pioneered friction coefficient adjustment. Let's describe Watanabee experience briefly for the slot it opened in the design of number of structures in this category. Watanabee used a steel beam which one end was attached to a Langevin transducer [29]. The Langevin transducer excited at 77 kHz communicates its maximum 2 μm vibrations to the beam. As a result, the feeling procured to a finger that explored the surface of the non excited beam was different from the feeling obtained with the vibrating beam: in the latter case the surface is very slippery and smooth. Watanabee also observed that as long as the vibratory frequency is grater than 20 kHz it has no influence on the perceived feeling.

In the follow up T. Nara [30] proposed a tapered plate and as in the introduction the idea inspired among others the designs presented in [2] and [3].

From the description of the later devices it can be seen that controlled friction is an interesting alternative in terms of tactile feelings production. Controlled friction is generated by continuous surfaces, limited in size and hence fully inerrable. In addition the control of these devices is rather global since it is the entire structure that is excited not a matrix rods. The accurate knowledge of the finger position is necessary and texture to be explored have to be processed in terms of friction coefficient in order to provide reference inputs to the effecter.

4. The system

4.1. Description

Figure 4 shows the proposed structure; a resonant physical device that in this specific case is a piezoelectric transducer converting electrical energy into mechanical energy. Driven in a simple bending mode of vibration, the structure consists of a set of PZT polarised piezo-ceramics of 12x12x1mm glued on the upside of a cupper-beryllium substrate whose size is 64x38x3 mm. On the opposite side (Figure 1), four built-in feet support the plate. Considering this polarisation, piezo-ceramic electrodes are conveniently supplied by a sinusoidal voltage of some ten Volts to create a standing wave using the piezoelectricity inverse effect with 40.7 kHz driving frequency (resonant frequency). Earlier some studies have been carried out using a system closed to this structure [31][32]. The main difference is that this plate will only move normally. Indeed, as we will see later, this particular structure is not supposed to move by itself along the tangential direction.

In Figure 4 b), alongside the four feet appears also a measurement ceramic glued on the plate. That flat round ceramic is acting as a vibratory sensor without altering the structure voltage supply that is kept unbroken.

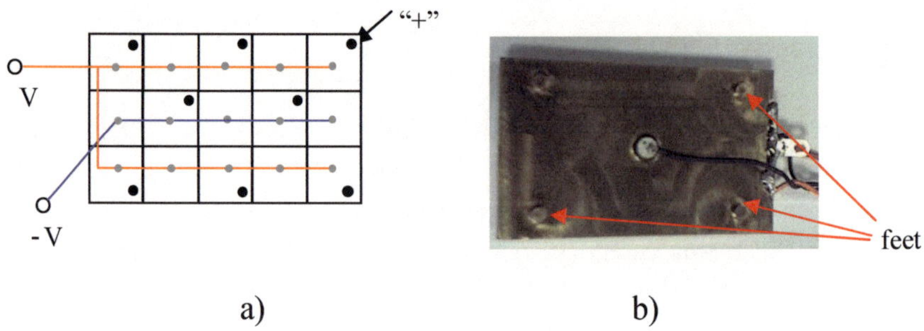

Figure 4. Up and down view of the actuator: a) electrical connection b) four feet and measurement ceramic location

4.2. Working principle

The feet are positioned exactly at the antinodes (Figure 5) of the vibrating plate and they are in contact with a plane steel substrate for example. Therefore, when no voltage is applied to the ceramics, if users move the actuator, they can feel the classical Coulomb friction force (R_t in Figure 7 a) acting at the interface feet-substrate.

When voltage is applied to the ceramic electrodes, a standing wave is generated and the friction between feet and substrate is decreased: this happens according to amplitude vibration. As a matter of fact, from a given wave amplitude, an intermittent contact may occur at the interface. Consequently, at the feet base, transitions between stick or slip conditions are created.

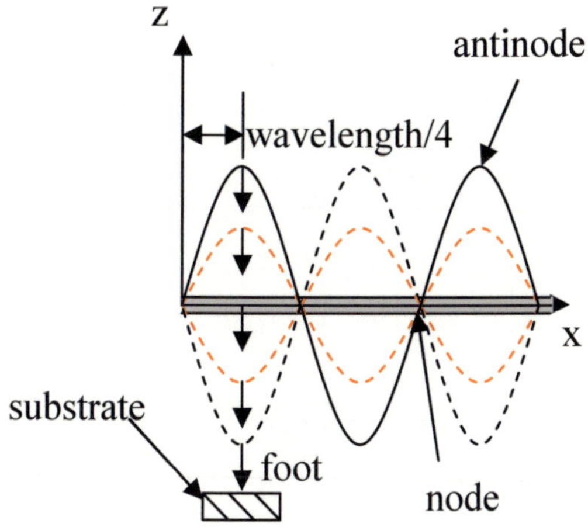

Figure 5. Standing wave and foot trajectory

4.3. Modelling

Many researchers studied stick-slip vibrations with switch models which Leine et al. [7] claim the solution they proposed is an improved version. The model proposed by Leine treats the system as three different sets of ordinary differential equations (ODE): one for the slip phase, a second for the stick phase and a third for the transition from stick to slip. Restricted to its normal movement component, our system can be seen as the "stick-slip" defined above with the "same" (contact, separation and transition from contact to separation) three states. The problem is solved using Simulink-Stateflow®, a convenient tool for finite state machine simulation and control: here is all the interest that is to see how it provides with a "switch block" to deal with the transition phase source of some difficulties including dealing with equation for stick to slip transition in the pseudo code used by Leine et al., sensitivity analysis, etc, as developed in [7].

4.3.1. Feet-plan Contact model

The structure in study involves contact and separation sequences between the feet of a body and the floor or substrate: contact and separation are induced by the foot elasticity. The movement so defined on the component normal to the plane of contact is broken down into compression – relaxation – separation sequences. This approach identifies the feet in contact with the floor to a mass-spring system.

The particular surface topology required by the device, that is a substrate highly rigid and a minimal surface roughness ($R_a \leq 0.6 \mu m$), the low clearances of the effecter tip in the range of a few micrometers make the approximation a priori acceptable.

The model will enable characterizing the contact intermittence.

4.3.1.1. *Foot mass – spring model*

From the plate which the kinetic is briefly reminded here, a refined analysis of the bond up effecter can be carried out. For sake of convenience, figure 6 shows the plate kinetic diagram in an *Oxyz* coordinates system. For a plate constrained in pure bending mode as in figure 6, more precisely a plate in vibratory mode (0,6) as in figure 5 with feet located at $\lambda/4$, it can be shown [33] [34][35] that:

$$w_A(u,v,t) = w(t) = W(t)\sin(\omega t) \tag{1}$$

A is the foot end located at intersection of the foot and the plate.

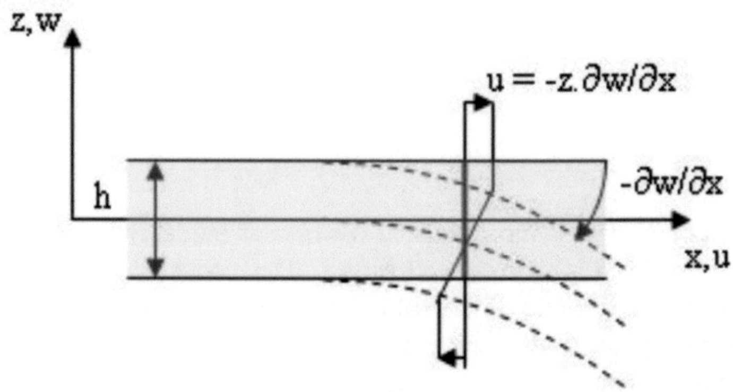

Figure 6. Kinematic of plate deformation

W(t) is the dynamic vibration amplitude at the actuator centre and ω the vibratory mode pulsation.

It is recalled in the preceding that only the displacement w is considered. Also, the feet location which the tip is at antinode ($\lambda/4$) is assumed constant because of the pure bending mode assumption. In addition, from the similar feet positioning with respect to the wave, the mechanical study may be restricted to that of one foot subjected to a pre stress F_n equally distributed upon n feet. Moreover, external loads are reported to the plate partial centre of gravity G. Conversely, the plate has four feet, making the problem hyperstatic because of many number of unknown contact variables. Elsewhere, planarity of the contact surface may contribute to invalidate the load equal distribution upon the feet. Nevertheless, considering the global contact approach, the load equal repartition is retained.

That yields the equivalent mechanical diagram used to define the system dynamic relations.

Each foot can now on be described as a mass-spring system and we represented it in Figure 7 a. In Figure 7 a, M_{ext} depicts the load applied on the top of the device to assume pre-stress. This load lies on an elastic element whose stiffness k_m is low enough to assume that the force

http://dx.doi.org/10.5772/57569

F_n due to M_{ext} (F_n=9.81M_{ext}) is constant. The mass of the vibrating plate is denoted m and the number of feet, n. The foot mass m_f is too low to be considered and its normal stiffness is k_n. Finally the displacement $w_A(t)$ is imposed by the plate vibrations whereas R_n denotes the normal reaction force at the foot tip.

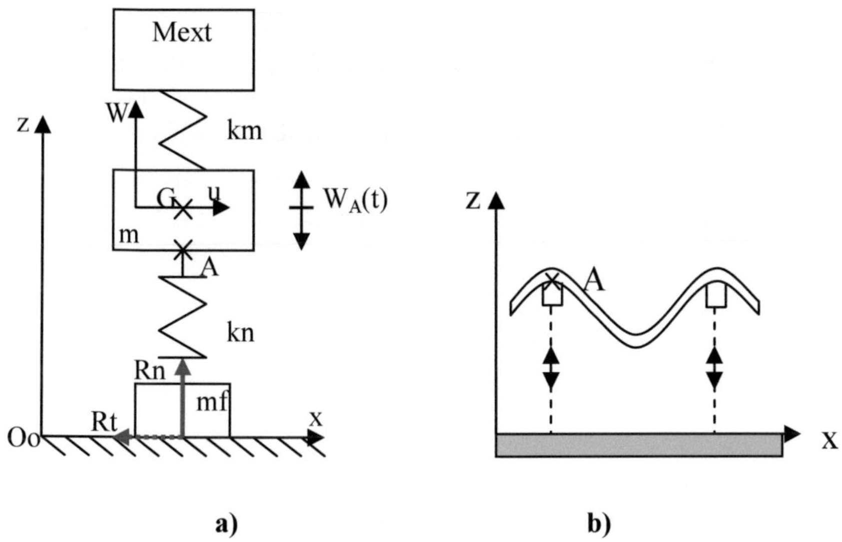

Figure 7. a) equivalent mechanical scheme and forces acting on the foot b) system

4.3.1.2. Actuator behaviour along the normal axis

Describing the behaviour of actuator along the normal axis *Oz* amounts to writing the foot tip equation of movement characterizing the induced separation and contact periods along that *Oz* axis. The separation phase is also called flight. Equation obtained by applying the general dynamic laws to the system assuming the substrate is ideally rigid and therefore only the foot is storage element of potential energy, which yields:

$$\frac{m}{n}\ddot{z}_A = \frac{m}{n}\ddot{w}_A - \frac{F_n}{n} - \frac{m}{n}g + R_n(t) \quad (2)$$

with

$$\frac{m}{n}\ddot{z}_A = \frac{m}{n}\ddot{w}_A - \frac{F_n}{n} - \frac{m}{n}g + R_n(t), \qquad \text{during the contact phase} \quad (3)$$

$$R_n(t) = 0, \qquad \text{during the separation phase} \quad (4)$$

Where k_n is the elasticity of the foot, h the height of the foot when no pressure is exerted on it and d_n a damping coefficient on the main compression of the foot induced by variation of z_G.

Prior to solving equation (2) let us examine the detail of transition conditions from contact to separation phase. At rest, under external mass M_{ext}, the plate plane is located from the ground at a distance z_G lesser than h, the height of relaxed/released foot: the foot is compressed. Vibrating, the plate imposes a sinusoidal normal displacement of the foot end z_A. In the instance of a displacement large enough for the ordinate z_A to be greater than the height h, there is separation. It is underlined that for k_n a priori high, eventual longitudinal vibrations of the foot are neglected during the separation. The following transition condition results:

$$z_A > h, \qquad \text{foot in separation} \tag{5}$$

$$z_A \leq h, \qquad \text{foot in contact} \tag{6}$$

Taking

$$z_A = z_G - w_A, \tag{7}$$

yields

$$(z_G + w_A) \leq h: \quad \text{contact} \tag{8}$$

$$(z_G + w_A) > h: \quad \text{separation} \tag{9}$$

Taking into account equation (7), equation (2) may be rewritten:

$$\frac{m}{n}\ddot{z}_G = -\frac{F_n}{n} - \frac{m}{n}g + R_n(t) \tag{10}$$

or after rewriting equation (2):

$$\frac{m}{n}\ddot{z}_G + d_n \dot{z}_G + k_n z_A = -\frac{F_n}{n} - \frac{m}{n}g + k_n h \quad \text{If there is contact} \tag{11}$$

$$\frac{m}{n}\ddot{z}_G = -\frac{F_n}{n} - \frac{m}{n}G. \quad \text{If there is separation} \tag{12}$$

The set of these two equations may mathematically describe the system. The solutions of the piecewise ODE are of course function of the initial conditions and the focus is only on the steady state in presence of an intermittent contact; without the intermittence we are in the instance of a spring which one end is fixed while to the other end is attached a mass in sinusoidal motion. It is assumed that the first phase is a contact phase governed by equation (11) and the final conditions of the contact phase $(z_A > h)$ are the initial conditions of the separation phase $(z_A \leq h)$ governed by equation (12) and so on.

The structure requires taking into account vibratory phenomena alternating transient-steady-transient states. For an arbitrary value of vibratory amplitude high enough to induce intermittent contact, that behaviour is graphically illustrated in Figure 8 where t_{ci} denotes the start up of the ith phase arising after a transient state of the periodic phenomenon described by Equation 11 of period T. $t_{c(i+1)}$ represents the beginning of the $(i+1)^{th}$ contact phase.

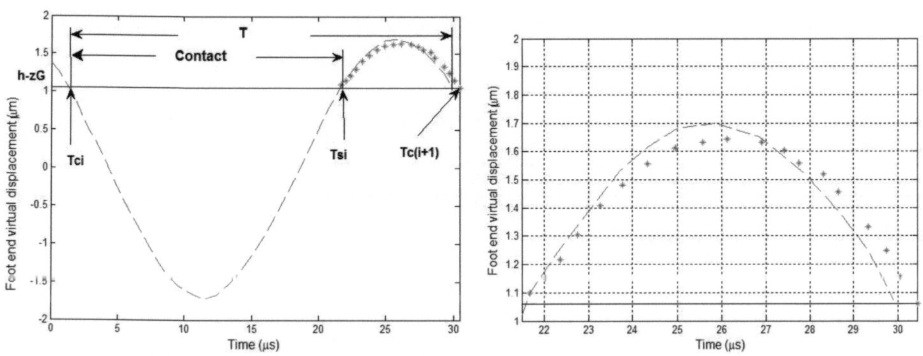

Figure 8. Contact-separation-contact sequence and post t_{si} detail

Bearing in mind that the aim is to compute the normal reaction R_n, it is worth the while to look at the set of ODE implementation. Figure 9 shows the Simulink implementation of equation (10). The subsystem that is a self defined Simulink system uses the Constant, Sum, Integrator, Outport and Gain templates taken from the linear block library of Simulink. The first summation generates the quantity in the right hand side of equation (10). The later sum is divided by the gain "1/n" and then integrated twice to obtain z_m from which z_G is derived. The reason for integrators chain (two integrators) is because we are dealing with a second order equation.

Therefore we integrate $\ddot{z}$ twice to get z.

Of course, the integrators must be initialized to correspond to initial values; thus in this specific case, the initial value of first integrator is set to 0 according to the system initial conditions (null foot speed). The initial value of the second integrator is set to h according to the initial conditions.

A second sum is used to get z_A as in equation (7).

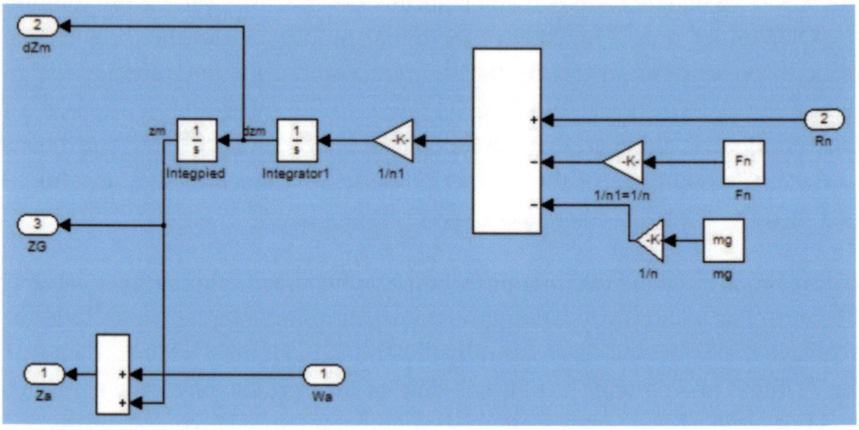

Figure 9. Implementation of equation (10)

To proceed further, we use the Simulink system shown in Figure 10. The distinctive feature of this system is that it contains an algebraic loop and a Stateflow® chart.

As can be seen in Figure 10, R_n is delivered to the input of FPDnorm broke down above.

On the other hand, this input depends directly on the output function given variables as expressed in equation (10). But, R_n is conditional, which suggests resorting to Stateflow® through "motion state" chart.

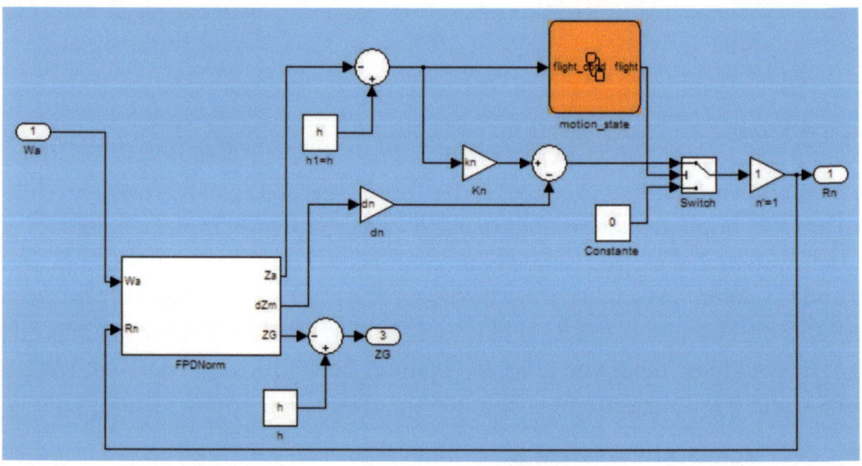

Figure 10. Normal reactive force R_n computation

Stateflow® is a Simulink toolbox convenient for modelling and simulating finite state machines. A finite state machine being a representation of an event-driven system that is a system making a transition from one state (mode) to another prescribed state, provided that the condition defining the change is true.

In Stateflow® representations states and transitions form the basic building blocks of the system.

Stateflow® block is used within the Simulink model here to dynamically simulate the system state changes. The chart block where the system is modelled is open in Figure 11. The device has two states: contact and separation that are represented by a rectangular block and named accordingly. Transition lines indicate the next state that the system in the current state can transit to. According to our algorithm these lines are from contact to fly and vice versa. Also, a default transition is assigned to a default or very first state, the state machine has to be in when it starts, chosen to be the "contact" state. In this case, the first state will be "contact" when the execution begins.

Actions to be taken when entering each state are defined. In this case, this is fly ($flight=1$) or its logic complement, not fly ($flight=0$) for contact and flight state respectively. For the Simulink model it is the machine output (0 or 1) that is present at the Stateflow® chart output port. Entry command will be executed when entering the state.

Conversely, let us notice the chart block input port set to control the Stateflow® chart that "sees" $(h - z_A)$ component from Simulink model. This is the "flight_cond" standing for flight condition associated to transition lines.

Next, at its input 2, from Stateflow® chart, a switch block compares the machine output (0 or 1) to a threshold chosen to have the arbitrary value 0.5 as criterion for the switch to pass either through switch input 1 where $k_n(h - z_A(t)) - d_n\dot{z}_G$ is present or through switch input 3 holding the 0 value. One or the other later amount will ultimately output the switch yielding the $R_n(t)$ (see equation (11) and (12)) of the subsystem output. In every iteration step, Simulink will try to bring the algebraic loop mentioned earlier which involves R_n "into balance".

This block enables watching state changes when simulating.

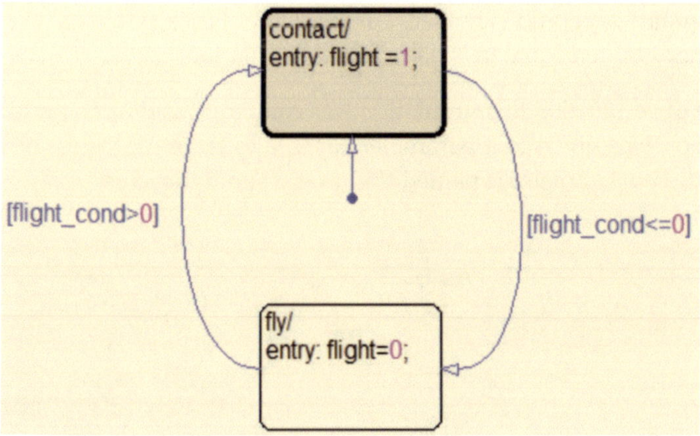

Figure 11. Open chart block named "motion state" in figure 10

Regarding the diagrams in Figure 9 and 10 the interested reader may connect outport carrying R_n to corresponding inport, the same for inports Wa, replaces outports dz_m, z_G and z_A with scopes e.g., set up a sinewave for Wa and use the given values to run the simulation. The solution may be calculated using the ode23 (Bogacki-Shampine) procedure with step size control activated (parameters: Initial Step Size=Auto, Max Step Size=1e-7, Min Step Size=Auto, relative and absolute tolerance=Auto), over the time interval [0, 0.5]. Here is an example of numerical values set: k_n=*9.7* MN/m, F_n=*10* N, *m=0.0723* kg, d_n=*200* N/ms^{-1}, *h=0.004* m. A MATLAB *function*, similar to the one in Appendix may be used to calculate the quantities of the example above, to be supplied to Simulink interfaces.

In Figure 12 are shown the time evolution of normal reaction R_n: for low vibratory amplitude, the normal reaction does not get null but is modulated at the excitation frequency and according to the vibratory amplitude. For higher vibratory amplitudes

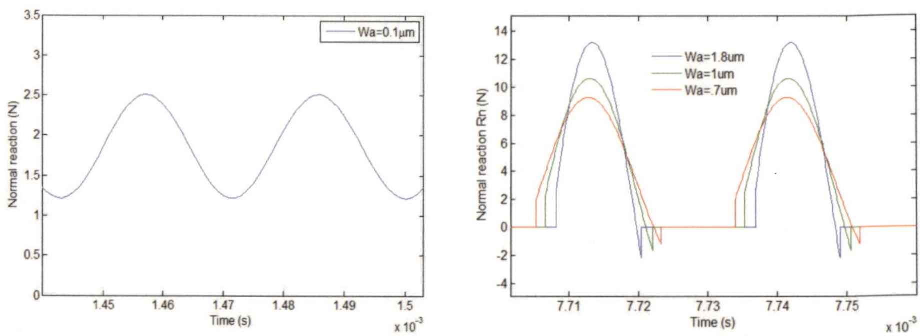

a) b)

Figure 12. Continuous-time variation of normal reaction Rn a) low b) high vibratory amplitude

Figure 12 shows an annulment of R_n and thus an intermittent contact. The impact of the switch in transitions contact-separation-contact is remarkable. For a purpose, in steady state the exciting frequency is taken equal to 35 kHz in this simulation.

For the purpose of verification this simulation was compared to the one performed in [36]. To that end, attention was given to a parameter capable to learn on the flight duration over a vibratory period. The parameter is named flight ratio and defined as:

$$\beta = \frac{t_s - t_c}{T} \times 100 \quad (13)$$

with

t_s: instant of separation debut

and

t_c: instant of contact debut.

Figure 13 shows results for β that are compared to those obtained by [37] for feet located at λ/ 8. Since our simulation is somehow validated by this result, we show in Figure 9 b) the flight rate variations as a function of vibratory amplitude for our actuator.

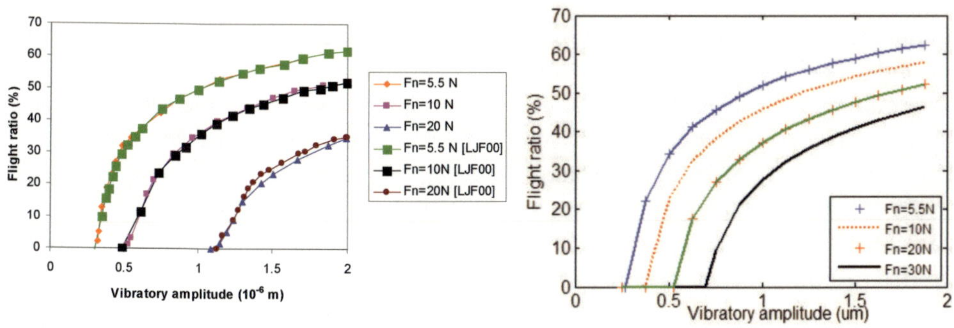

a) b)

Figure 13. Flight ratio as a function of vibratory amplitude a) for kn equals 10 MN/m ; comparison with [LJF00]; feet at λ/8 b) feet at λ/4.

In steady state, for different preload values, for a stiffness of 10 MN/m and feet located at λ/8, results in Figure 13 a) show the expected flight ratio variations that increase with the vibratory amplitude and decrease with the preload.

Experimental tests performed by [36] to measure the flight ratio allowed the verification of the model relevance observing foot contact intermittence with the floor. Also, the phenomenon remains periodic and of same period with the vibratory wave in steady state.

Regarding the simulation results in conditions of feet located at the wave crest, they show the same trend with a general curves shift toward the left that is a flight ratio greater for given vibratory amplitude.

The "similarity" introduced earlier on when the system was restricted to its normal movement component and the "stick-slip" vibrations as defined by Leine et al. [7] has been used up to this point.

4.3.1.3. Actuator behaviour along the tangential axis

To calculate the tangential force variation, a classical approach would have consisted of applying at the contact surface Coulomb friction modelling. It turns out that if the device is manipulated by a user, non-zero relative tangential speed always exists between the foot and the substrate. Coulomb law suggests therefore that $R_t = \mu R_n$ during contact phase and $R_t = 0$ otherwise. Since in flight event $R_n = 0$, it is possible to generalize that $R_t = \mu R_n$.

Calculating R_t average value over a vibratory period, if a constant friction coefficient μ is considered, $<R_t>=\mu<R_n>$ (<f> denotes average value of f). But, Equation 10 shows that in steady state $<R_n>=\frac{F_n}{n}+\frac{m}{n}g$. It follows hence that regardless the flight ratio, $<R_t>$ is constant for constant μ. That is not what was experimentally observed, justifying thus the consideration of a time variable friction coefficient.

The approach consists of considering in a more refined way the sliding triggering phenomena occurring over every vibratory period. Indeed it has been seen that feet – substrate contact can be intermittent. In such an instance, at every resuming contact, while the actuator is tangentially moving due to the user action, the feet are first in adhesion on the substrate, then speedily in partial slip and finally in total slip before flying again: the consideration of partial slip phase is source of tangential force average variation. That phase may be characterized by an elastic behaviour of the foot, characterized by its tangential stiffness k_t. This corresponds to the definition of a time varying friction coefficient μ obeying Coulomb – Orowan law [38].

Figure 14 depicts friction coefficient as a function of δ and the plot is divided approximately in two parts. The first part, relative to tangential stiffness of the contact, is linear and describes the partial slip. Then, from a critical displacement (δ_{crit}) corresponding to total slip, μ is constant.

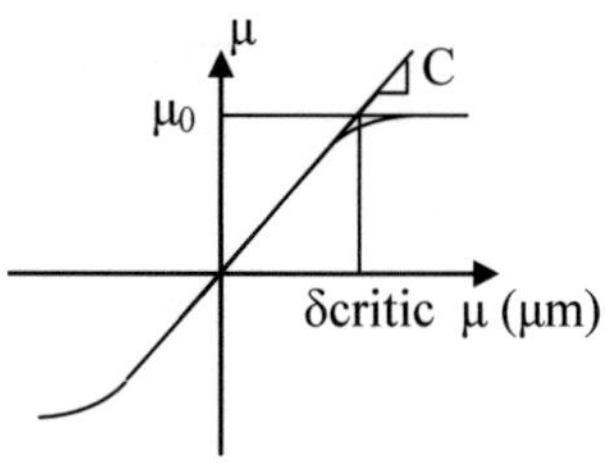

Figure 14. Coulomb-Orowan model

As explained above, the feet are positioned exactly at the antinodes (Figure 5) of the vibrating plate and they are in contact with a plane steel substrate for example. Therefore, when no voltage is applied to the ceramics, if users move the actuator, they can feel the classical Coulomb friction force acting at the interface feet/substrate.

δ_{crit} is defined from the following relationship after prior identification of tangential stiffness k_t:

$$\delta_{crit} = \mu_0 C R_n = \frac{\mu_0 R_n}{k_t} \tag{14}$$

where C (m/N) is the compliance and μ_0, the maximum friction coefficient at the interface (static friction).

As a consequence, we are able to obtain μ(t) during the foot/substrate contact time, limited by t_c and t_s which are respectively the contact and separation instants during one period of our vibrating device. We can then write:

$$\text{if } t \in \left]t_c, t_s\right[\text{ and } \delta < \delta_c \text{ then } \mu(t) = \frac{\mu_0}{\delta_{crit}}\delta(t) \tag{15}$$

$$\text{if } t \in \left]t_c, t_s\right[\text{ and } \delta > \delta_c \text{ then } \mu = \mu_0 \tag{16}$$

The displacement δ(t) is computed from the tangential speed integration.

$$\delta(t) = \int_0^t V_t(t)dt \tag{17}$$

where V_t is the relative sliding speed between the two surfaces in contact.

The determination of $\langle R_t \rangle$ is a key point for this study since it is the reactive force sensed by the device user and, equations (11) and (12) show that it is a function of the pre-load, displacement speed and wave amplitude. To this end, we will have to control the wave amplitude, the two other variables being not suitable for control: the tangential speed will be imposed externally by the user, and the normal pre-load is set at a fixed value.

5. Control of the vibration amplitude

The control of the vibratory amplitude may be achieved following different approaches. In [39], the wave amplitude control is done thanks to the phase control of the standing wave according to the voltage signal supply. The advantage of this method is its high robustness against resonance frequency variations. One drawback is a lower dynamic behaviour due to the response time imposed by a phase locked loop (PLL).

Another way to control the wave amplitude is to tune the supply frequency around the resonance value. This approach comes from the characteristic frequency – vibratory amplitude which shows that beyond the resonant frequency, the wave amplitude W decreases quasi – linearly, making possible its control [40]. The method presents the advantage of being easy to implement and the loop dynamic is fast. Conversely, it has the disadvantage that changes in temperature displace the resonant frequency and lead to discrepancies in the control. Rigorously, to avoid that inconvenience, an algorithm to track the resonant frequency should be implemented to anticipate the preload influence on the resonant frequency. Nevertheless we have chosen this approach, also easier to implement.

6. Features of friction forces

From equations introduced in section 5, it was possible to compute the behaviour of the actuator for a given wave amplitude, a given tangential speed and a given normal load. The obtained results are as shown in Figure 15.

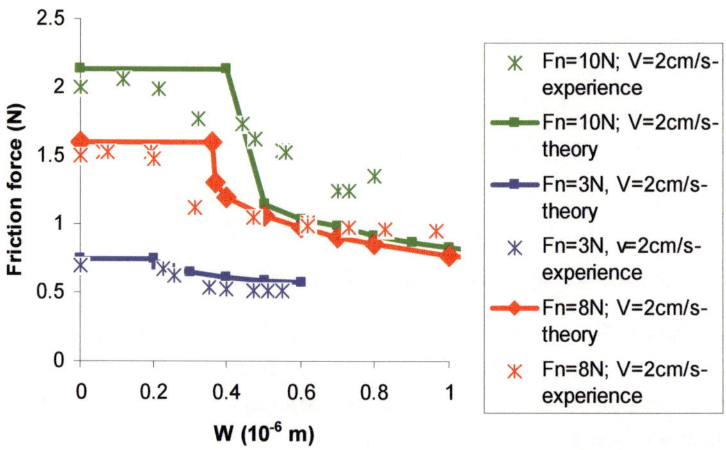

a)

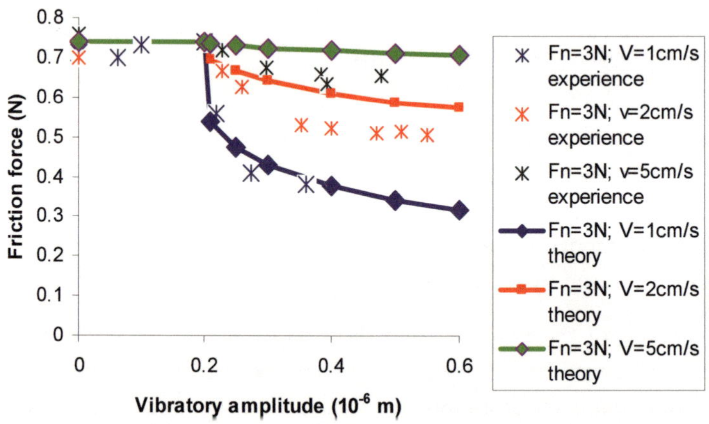

b)

Figure 15. Friction force for a) a fixed preload as a function of vibratory amplitude and tangential displacement speed, b) a given tangential speed as a function of the wave amplitude and the normal pre-load.

To characterize the friction forces we use, for different vibratory amplitudes, a DC motor Maxon® controlled in speed to which the plate is attached by means of an inextensible cable and a 10 mm diameter pulley. The measured motor current is therefore an image of torque and thus force developed by the motor. That force is in absolute value equal to the explored friction force.

An optical encoder is used to measure the motor rotational speed and the so constituted setup is controlled by a dSPACE DS1104 application. Several simulations based on the contact conditions described all along were performed and the results as compared to the experimental are shown in Figure 15.

The experimental results presented in Figure 15 were obtained in such a way that a load M_{ext} was applied on the top of the device to assume pre-load. This load lied on an elastic element whose stiffness was low enough to consider constant the force F_n due to M_{ext} (F_n=9.81M_{ext}). Also, a steel substrate (μ=0.2) was used for these trials. Finally the time variable displacement w is imposed by the plate vibrations.

These results illustrate the overall behaviour of the structure and show the existence of a critical wave amplitude beyond which friction reduction is noticed.

7. Evaluation of the device for touch feedback application

The aim of the evaluation of the device for tactile feedback is to determine whether the device qualifies or not for the dedicated application. In his study, U. Spälter [41] indicates that there is no standard evaluation procedure for haptic devices. In this specific case, the profile in Figure 16 that shows an alternation of "notches" was considered. One aspect of the evaluation was to know if the alternation of apparent friction coefficient (μ_1, μ_2) induced by vibratory amplitude enabled generation of "notches". In Figure 16, μ_1 and μ_2 correspond respectively to friction coefficient before and beyond the critical wave amplitude identified in Figure 12.

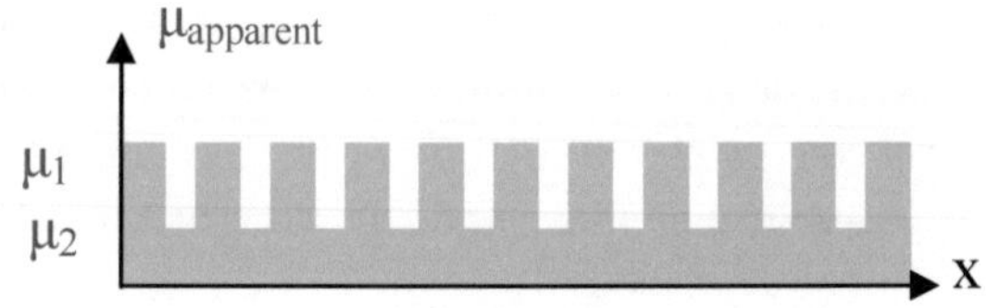

Figure 16. Profile of alteration of notches

The other aspect of the evaluation was to determine if it was possible to discriminate the two profiles in Figure 17.

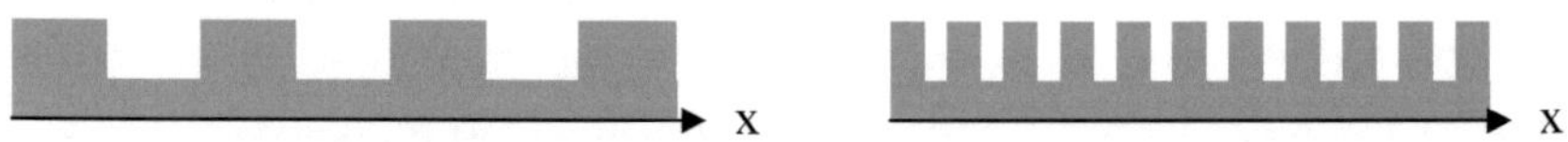

Figure 17. Simulated notches (different spatial periods)

A preliminary psychophysical evaluation discussed in [42] showed how to assess the validity of the structure to low force feedback application.

8. Summary

The concept of friction coefficient reduction has been presented to design a 2Dof passive low force feedback device in this chapter. For a design utilizing piezoelectric technology, piezoelectric materials and their effect in transducers technology mainly, together with several existing solutions using technologies other than piezoelectric actuation in the field of touch feedback were briefly discussed. Modelling of the device with an emphasis on the normal reaction force, leading to the expression of the tangential force felt by a user moving the actuator the way he moves a common computer mouse was also presented. In particular, some details were given on a way to use Stateflow® to deal with modelling and simulation aspects of the normal reaction force in the system, regarded as finite state machine when restricted to its normal movement component. We also showed how results from experimental and theoretical investigations agree on the fact that it is possible to control the resulting friction force even if this force highly depends on normal pre-load and tangential speed.

Finally, the proposed device may be a solution to cope with the lack of compactness and simplicity often encountered in haptics interfaces. Complementary experiments are needed to assess its response to touch feedback. Also required is a study of the device behaviour over the time to consider feet wear, or at least variation of contact conditions so that the initial vibratory amplitude control can anticipate such changes. Consequently a direct comparison between the solution proposed in this study and the demonstrated high-performance and practical electromagnetic mouse described in section 3.1.1 e.g. may not be easily sustainable. However, apart from simplicity and compactness characteristics common to both of them, it is an additional advantage in terms of behaviour that this design anticipated issues like the observed rotation of the electromagnetic mouse which resulted from the localized magnetic force.

http://dx.doi.org/10.5772/57569

Appendix

```
function [m,kn,dn,Fn,h,n] = planeactuatpm(Li,l,h_s,h_p,rho_s,rho_p)
%
% Function activebrakepm
%
% Call: [m,kn,dn,Fn,h,n]=planeactuatpm(Li,l,h_s,rho_s,rho_p)
%
% MATLAB function for parametrizing the Simulink system
% could be called activebrake.mdl
%
% Input data: Li      plate width [m]
%             l       plate length [m]
%             h_s     thickness of the metal layer of the plate [m]
%             h_p     thickness of the ceramic layer of the plate [m]
%             rho_s   metal layer density [kg/m^3]
%             rho_p   ceramic layer density[kg/m^3]
%
% with the parameters of the Simulink simulation window not set here
%
% Output data: the parameters of Equation (11) and (12)
%

%******************************%
% declaration of the pre-load  %
%******************************%
% The pre-load is constant

Fn=10;    % [N/m]

%*****************************************************%
% declaration of the foot length and number of feet   %
%*****************************************************%
% The length of the foot and the number of the feet are constant

h=0.0040;                  % length of the foot [m]

n=3;                       % chosen number of the feet

%
% Calculation of the mass of the plate

m=rho_s*(h_s*l*Li)+rho_p*(h_p*l*Li);

% gravity is constant
g=9.81;                % [N/kg]

% Calculation of the weight 'mg'

mg=g*m;

%*************************************%
%   Damping and stiffness coefficient  %
%*************************************%

% normal damping coefficient is constant

dn=200; %[kg/m]

%
% The stiffness coefficient function of the pre-load
% is taken constant

kn=9.7e6; % [N/m]
```

A call for the parameters of our actuator then yields:

```
[m,kn,dn,Fn,h,n]=planeactuatpm(0.038,0.064,0.003,0.00065,8250,7650)

m=

0.0723

kn=

9700000

dn=

200

Fn=

10

h=

0.0040

n=

3
```

Author details

G. M'boungui[1*], A.A. Jimoh[1], B. Semail[2] and F. Giraud[2]

*Address all correspondence to: mboungui@yahoo.fr

1 Department of Electrical Engineering, Tshwane University of Technology, Pretoria, RSA

2 Laboratoire d'Electrotechnique et d'Electronique de Puissance de Lille, université Lille IRCICA, Villeneuve d'Ascq, France

References

[1] E. J. Berger, Friction Modelling for Dynamic System Simulation, Appl. Mech. Rev vol. 55, no 6, pp. 535-536, Nov. 2002.

[2] G. Casiez, P. Plenacoste, C. Chaillou, B. Semail, Elastic Force Feedback With a New Multi-finger Haptic Device : The DigiHaptic, Eurohaptics 2003

[3] http://www.fcs-cs.com HapticMaster

[4] L. Garbuio, F. Pigache, J.F. Rouchon, B. Semail, Ultrasonic Friction Drive for Passive Force Feedback Devices, Electromotion, Vol.14, 2007, n°2, April-June 2007

[5] L. Winfield, J. Glassmire, J. E. Colgate, M. Peshkin, T-PaD: Tactile Pattern Display through Variable Friction Reduction, Second Joint Eurohaptics Conference and Symposium on Haptic Interfaces for Virtual Environment and Teleoperator Systems (WHC'07), 2007.

[6] M. Biet, F. Giraud, B. Semail. Squeeze film effect for the design of an ultrasonic tactile plate, in: IEEE Transactions on Ultrasonic, Ferroelectric and Frequency Control, December 2007.

[7] R I Leine, D. H. Van Campen, and A. De Kraker, Stick-slip Vibrations Induced by Alternate Friction Models, Nonlinear Dynamics 16: 41-54, 1998.

[8] A. Arnau, 2004; Piezoeletric Transducers and Applications (New York: Springer)

[9] B. Nogarède, Moteurs piézoélectriques. Les techniques de l'ingénieur, DFB(D3765), juin 1996.

[10] K A Cook-Chennault, N Thambi and A M Sastry, Powering MEMS portable devices — a review of non-regenerative and regenerative power supply systems with special emphasis on piezoelectric energy harvesting systems, Smart Mater. Struct. 17 (2008) 04300.

[11] R. A. Wolf and S. Troiler-McKinstry, Temperature dependence of the Piezoelectric response in lead zirconate titanate films, J. Appl. Phys. 95, 1397.

[12] A. H. Meitzler, and H. L. Stadler, (1958), Piezoelectric and Dielectric Characteristics of Single-Crystal Barium Titanate Plates. Bell System Technical Journal, 37: 719–738. doi: 10.1002/j.1538-7305.1958.tb03884.x

[13] S Singh, O P Thakur, C Prakash and K K Raina, 2005, Dilatometric and dielectric behaviour of Sm modified PCT ceramics Physica B 355 280–5

[14] http://answers.yahoo.com/question/index?qid=20090731111309AANblRO

[15] S E Park and T R Shrout 1997 Ultrahigh strain and piezoelectric behavior in relaxor based ferroelectric single crystals J. Appl. Phys. 82 1804–11

[16] F. Martinot, Characterisation of Touch Role in the Touch Dynamic in Textures Perception, PhD Thesis (2006), USTL

[17] M. B. Khoudja, M. Hafez, J. M. Alexandre, A. Kheddar, "Electromagnetically Driven High-Density Tactile Interface Based on a Multi-Layer Approach", Best Paper in International Symposium on Micromechatronics and Human Science, pp.147_152, Nagoya, Japan, 2003

[18] http://www.cim.mcgill.ca/~jay/index_files/research_files/actuators.htm

[19] H. Iwata, H. Yano, F. Nakaizumi, and R. Kawamura, Project feelex: Adding haptic surface to graphics, In proceedings of SIGGRAPH 2001, pp 469-476, 2001

[20] C. Schneider, T. Mustufa, and A. M. Akamura, A magnetically-actuated friction feedback mouse. In Proceedings of EuroHaptics 2004, Munich, Germany, pages 330 – 337, 2004

[21] P. Wellman, W. Peine, G. Favalora, R. Howe, " Mechanical Design and Control of a High-Bandwidth shape Memory Alloy Tactile Display", International Symposium on Experimental Robotics, Barcelona, Spain. June 1997

[22] K. Fujita and H. Ohmori, A new Softness Display Interface by Dynamic Fingertip Contact Area Control, in proc. 5th World Multiconference on Systemics, Cybernetics and Informatics, pp.78-82, 2001

[23] G. Moy, C. Wagner, R.S. Fearing. Compliant Tactile Display for Teleaction, ICRA, 2000

[24] Y. Makino, H. Shinoda, "Selective Simulation to Superficial Mechanoreceptors by Temporal Control of Suction Pressure", First Joint Eurohaptics Conference and Symposium on Haptics Interfaces for Virtual Environment and Teleoperator Systems, pp. 229-234, 2005

[25] P. M. Taylor, D. M. Pollet, A. Hosseini-Sianaki, C. J. Varley, "Advances in An Electro rheological Fluid-based Tactile Array", Elsevier Displays 18(1998) 135-141

[26] M. Siegel,"Tactile display development: The driving-force for tactile sensor development". Int. Workshop Haptic Virtual Environments and Their Applications, pp. 115-118, IEEE, 2002

[27] J. Pasquero, V. Hayward, "STReSS: A practical Tactile Display System with One Millimetre Spatial Resolution and 700Hz Refresh Rate". Proc. Of Eurohaptics 2003, Dublin, Ireland, July 2003. pp. pp.94-110

[28] T. Watanabe, S. Fukui: a method for controlling tactile sensation of surface roughness using ultrasonic vibration, 1995 IEEE Int. Conf. on Robotics and Automation, (1995), pp 1134-1139

[29] M. Budinger, J.F. Rouchon and B. Nogarede, "Analytical modelling for the design of a piezoelectric rotating-mode motor", IEEE/ASME Transactions on Mechatronics, vol. 9, n° 1, pp.1-9, 2004

[30] T. Nara, T. Maeda, Y. Yanagida, S. Tachi. A Tactile Display Using Elastic Waves in a Tapered Plate, Proceedings of the 8th Int. Conf. Artif. Real Telexistence, Page. 109-116(1998)

[31] F. Pigache, F. Giraud and B. Lemaire-Semail, "Modelling and identification of a planar standing wave ultrasonic motor. Identification of a planar actuator", Eur. Phys. J. Appl. Phys. 34, 55-65 (2006).

[32] P. Le Moal, E. Joseph, J.C. Ferniot, "Mechanical energy transductions in standing wave ultrasonic motors: analytical modelling and experimental investigations". European Journal of Mechanics A/Solids, vol. 19, pp. 849-871, 2000.

[33] F. Pigache. Modélisation causale en vue de la commande d'un translateur piézoélectrique plan pour une application haptique. Thèse de Doctorat (2005), USTL

[34] J. Courbon. Plaques minces élastiques. Editions Eyrolles, Paris, 1980

[35] M. Géradin and D. Rixen. Théorie des vibrations. Masson, Paris, 1993

[36] P. L. Moal, E. Joseph, J.C. Ferniot. Mechanical energy transductions in standing wave ultrasonic motors: Analytical modelling and experimental investigations. Eur. J. Mech. A/Solids 19 (2000) 849-871

[37] J.C. Ferniot, Translateur piézo-électrique à ondes stationnaires : modélisation théorique et caractérisation expérimentale. Thèse de Doctorat (2002), UFR des Sciences et techniques de l'Université de Franche-Comté.

[38] L. Garbuio, Etude du phénomène de Lubrification électroactive à l'aide d'actionneurs piézoélectriques, Application à la réduction des forces de frottement sec dans un moteur à combustion interne, Thèse de Doctorat, 2006, INPT, ENSEEIHT

[39] F. Pigache, B. Lemaire-Semail, F. Giraud, A. Bouscayrol, « control of a piezo-electric actuator for adjustable brake in haptic devices », EPE 05, DRESDE, 11-14 September 2005, CD-ROM ISBN 90-75815-08-05

[40] E. Piecourt, M. Lajoie Mazenc, Electromechanical characterization and power supply of piezoelectric motors, PhD thesis, Institut national polytechnique de Toulouse, Toulouse, France, N°: 95 INPT 0102, 1995.

[41] U. Spälter, Haptic interface design and control with application surgery simulation, EPF Lausanne, Thèse n° 3529, 2006

[42] G. M'Boungui, B. Lemaire-Semail, F. Giraud, Piezo-electric actuator for force feedback application, Third Joint Eurohaptics Conference and Symposium on Haptic Interfaces for Virtual Environments and Teleoperator Systems, Salt Lake City, Utah, USA, March 18-20, 2009

Chapter 11

Modelling and Simulation Based Matlab/Simulink of a Strap-Down Inertial Navigation System' Errors due to the Inertial Sensors

Teodor Lucian Grigorie and
Ruxandra Mihaela Botez

Additional information is available at the end of the chapter

http://dx.doi.org/10.5772/57583

1. Introduction

Inertial navigation is a dead reckoning positioning method based on the measurement and mathematical processing of the vehicle absolute acceleration and angular speed in order to estimate its attitude, speed and position related to different reference. Due to the specific operation principle, the positioning errors for this method result from the imperfection of the initial conditions knowledge, from the errors due to the numerical calculation in the inertial system, and from the accelerometers and gyros errors. Therefore, the inertial sensors performances play a main role in the establishment of the navigation system precision, and should be considered in its design phase frames (Bekir, 2007; Farrell, 2008; Grewal et al., 2013; Grigorie, 2007; Salychev, 1998; Titterton and Weston, 2004).

Amazing evolution of physics and manufacturing technologies to improve the optical an electronic fields have made possible the development of opto-electronic rotation and translation sensors in parallel with the mechanical sensors. The Ring Laser Gyros (RLG) have entered the market only in 1980's even if in 1963 was first demonstrated in a square configuration. Mechanical gyroscopes dominated the market and the RLG were required in military applications, because these are ideal systems for high dynamics strap-down inertial navigation, used in extreme environments. The RLG has excellent scale-factor stability and linearity, negligible sensitivity to acceleration, digital output, fast turn-on, excellent stability and repeatability across the range, and no moving parts. Present day RLG's (Ring Laser Gyros) is considered a matured technology and its development efforts are to reduce costs more than

INTECH
open science | open minds

© 2014 The Author(s). Licensee InTech. This chapter is distributed under the terms of the Creative Commons Attribution License (http://creativecommons.org/licenses/by/3.0), which permits unrestricted use, distribution, and reproduction in any medium, provided the original work is properly cited.

to increase its performance (Barbour & Schmidt, 2001; Barbour et al., 2010; Barbour, 2010; Edu et al., 2011; Hopkins, 2010; Kraft, 2000; Lawrence, 1998).

Fiber optic gyros (FOG) are also a mature technology and were originally designed as a low-cost alternative to the RLG. Surprisingly, today they compete RLG's both in terms of manufacturing costs, as well as that of performance, gaining prominence in a series of military and commercial applications. The studies provide that the developments in solid-state optics and fiber technology could lead to 0.001-deg/h performance in miniature design. Research in the field of fiber optic gyros, similarly to those of RLG, aimed at decreasing the size and manufacturing costs at an approximately constant level of performance, if not better. Development of miniaturized FOGs was based on the technology achievements brought by the telecommunications industry. An important innovation was the discovery of photonic crystal fibers (PCF Fibers crystal photon) that have been a very important step towards the next generation of IFOG instruments, the PC-IFOG. The introduction of PCFs in IFOG applications brings significant advantages to this field, such as the significant reduction of bend losses and fiber size compared to the conventional optical fiber, minimizing the fiber optic coil diameter, the possibility of incorporating a dispersion compensation in the existing PCF, with the effect of reducing the spectral distortion, guiding light through this type of fiber allows the use of a mid-infrared optical wavelength (Barbour & Schmidt, 2001; Divakaruni & Sanders, 2006; Edu et al., 2011; KVH Industries Inc., 2007; Pavlath, 2006; Tawney et al., 2006).

In the 1980s, the Hemispherical Resonant Gyro was developed, a vibratory high performance gyro; the inertial sensing element is a fused-silica hemispherical shell coated with a thin film of metal. HRG advantages are related to the fact that it is very light, compact, operates in vacuum and has no moving parts. Its life cycle is limited only by the electronic components, which are redundant (Barbour & Schmidt, 2001; Barbour, 2010; Edu et al., 2011).

Besides the above mentioned technologies, another technology, very promising in terms of inertial detection, based on atomic interferometry (cold atom inertial sensors) is developing very fast. Atomic interferometry is a sensor-based inertial sensing that uses the atom interferometry, using cold atoms, atoms that are a millionth of a degree above absolute zero, created and then trapped using laser technology. With the researches in optical precision spectroscopy (Nobel Prize 2005) today it is possible to have precise control on the internal and external of freedom of atomic matter. Those huge progresses led to application of ultra-cold matter in fields such as precision measurements, matter wave interferometry and applications in quantum information processing. The atom interferometers are very similar in their basic principle with the optical interferometers. The difference is that the optical wave is replaced with the matter-wave represented by the atoms. The current state-of-art of atom interferometry: the atom interferometers obtained and proof-of-concept. Although, gyros and accelerometers are yet too voluminous, the miniaturization seems feasible in the near future and is developing (Dumke & Mueller, 2010; Edu et al., 2011; Hopkins, 2010; Schmidt, 2010).

The aerospace industry tendencies to realize unmanned aircraft (UAV), micro and nano-satellites, easy to launch in space and with the performances analogous with the actual satellites, imposed a nimble rhythm to the expansion of the NEMS (Nano-Electro-Mechanical-Systems) and MEMS (Micro-Electro-Mechanical-Systems) technologies in the domain of the acceleration and rotation sensors, used especially in the inertial navigation systems. The use of such miniaturized sensors creates the premises to have redundant strap-down inertial navigation systems through the miscellaneous dedicated architectures and at the low-costs comparatively with the case of non-miniaturized and very precise inertial sensors use. On the other way, the use of these miniaturization technologies for the inertial sensors allows the implementation of the entire inertial navigation system in a single chip, including here the sensors and all circuits for the signals conditioning (Bose, 2008; Grewal et al., 2013; Grigorie, 2006; Grigorie et al., 2012 a; Titterton and Weston, 2004).

From the other point of view, these miniaturized sensors have some disadvantages due to the performances decrease with the miniaturization degree increase. They are quite noises, because at the great majority of the acceleration sensors the noise density is between 100 $\mu g/Hz^{1/2}$ and a few hundreds of $\mu g/Hz^{1/2}$, for the bandwidths between 100Hz and 2500Hz, and at the gyro sensors it is between 0.001 $(^o/s)/Hz^{1/2}$ and 0.1 $(^o/s)/Hz^{1/2}$, for the pass bandwidths between 50Hz and 100Hz. Also, for the same type of sensors the noise density can vary from one sensor to the other with 20% of the catalogue value. The filtering of the noise it is not recommended because it is possible to be altered the useful signal and, so, the sensor output doesn't reflect exactly the signal applied at the input of the sensor. Beside the noise increase, through miniaturization appear negative influences on the stability and value of bias, on the scale factor calibration, on the cross-axis sensitivity for the accelerometers and on the sensitivity at the accelerations applied along any given axis for the gyros. For all of these the data sheets of the MEMS and NEMS products stipulate maximal values relatively high, without be able to specify exactly their value to be corrected (Grigorie et al., 2010 a; Grigorie et al., 2010 b).

To test the influences of the sensors errors on the solution of navigation of strap-down inertial navigators we realized Matlab/Simulink models for the acceleration and rotation sensors based on the sensors data sheets and on the IEEE equivalent models for the inertial sensors (Grigorie et al., 2010 a; Grigorie et al., 2010 b). For example, for the accelerometers was obtained the model in Figure 1. He has as inputs the acceleration a_i, applied along of the sensitive axis, and the cross-axis acceleration a_c, and as output the perturbed acceleration a (Grigorie et al., 2010 a). The analytic form of the model is:

$$a = (a_i + Na_i + B + k_c a_c + \nu)(1 + \Delta K / K); \tag{1}$$

N is sensitivity axis misalignment (in radians), B-bias (expressed in percent of span), k_c-cross-axis sensitivity (expressed in percent of a_c), ν-sensor noise (given by its density ν_d expressed in $\mu g/Hz^{1/2}$, K-scale factor (expressed in mV/g), and ΔK-scale factor error (percents of K), and a, a_i, a_c expressed in m/s^2. The model was built for few miniaturized acceleration sensors and covers theirs main errors: bias, scale factor error, sensitivity axis misalignment, cross axis sensitivity and noise.

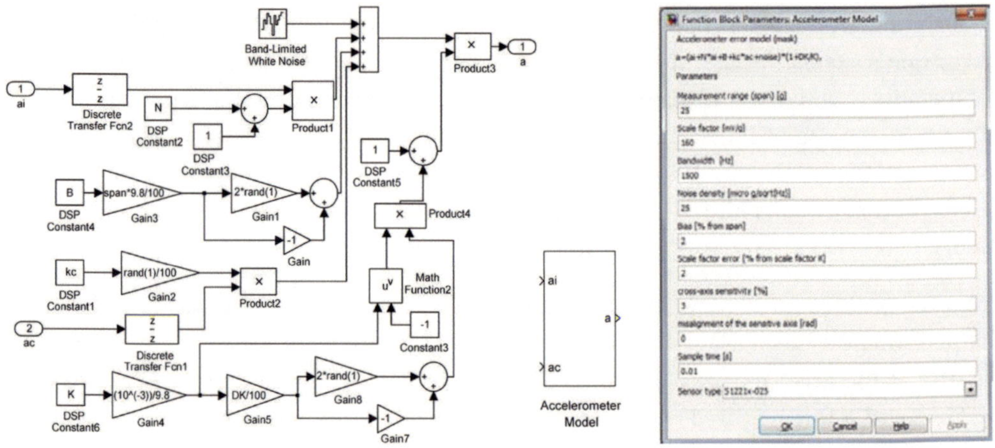

Figure 1. Accelerometers Matlab/Simulink model and its interface.

The model related to the gyro sensors was implemented in Matlab/Simulink (Figure 2) starting from the equation (Grigorie et al., 2010 b):

$$\omega = (\omega_i + S \cdot a_r + B + \nu)(1 + \Delta K / K); \qquad (2)$$

ω-sensors output angular speed (disturbed signal) expressed in °/s, ω_i-applied angular speed (°/s), S-sensitivity to the acceleration a_r applied on an arbitrary direction ((°/s)/g), B-bias (expressed in percents of span), ν-sensor noise (given by its density ν_d expressed in (°/s)/Hz$^{1/2}$), K-scale factor (expressed in mV/(°/s)), ΔK-scale factor error (percents of K).

For both models, the change of the sensor type that will be used in simulations is made using the associated interfaces. In addition, the interfaces allow the setting of the models, by the user, in custom variants. The models have the advantages to work independent with each of the sensor errors and to study in this way their influence on the inertial navigator positioning solution. Although sensors data sheets specifications are not related to the components of noise, for a more detailed study of the navigators' errors, the sensors' models can be completed with some noise terms starting from theirs Allan variance definitions. Allan's variance results are related to the seven noise terms. Five noise terms are basic terms: angle random walk, rate random walk, bias instability, quantization noise and drift rate ramp, while the other two are the sinusoidal noise and exponentially correlated (Markov) noise (Grigorie et al., 2010 c; Grigorie et al., 2012 b).

This chapter deals with solving of a navigation problem relative to terrestrial non-inertial reference frames by using attitude matrices to calculate the vehicle attitude. Once it is highlighted the general equation of inertial navigation, a numerical algorithm is developed for determining the position and speed of the vehicle based on this equation. The algorithm provides position and vehicle speed in horizontal local reference frame (ENU) and its global coordinates (latitude, longitude and altitude). For the presented algorithm is developed an error model that highlights the dependencies of the vehicle positioning, velocity and attitude errors by the strap-down inertial sensor errors used to detect acceleration and angular speed. In the development of the error model the small perturbation technique is used. Following is conducted a study of the dependence of the inertial navigator outputs errors by the errors of the used inertial sensors based on the Matlab/Simulink models built for acceleration and gyro sensors.

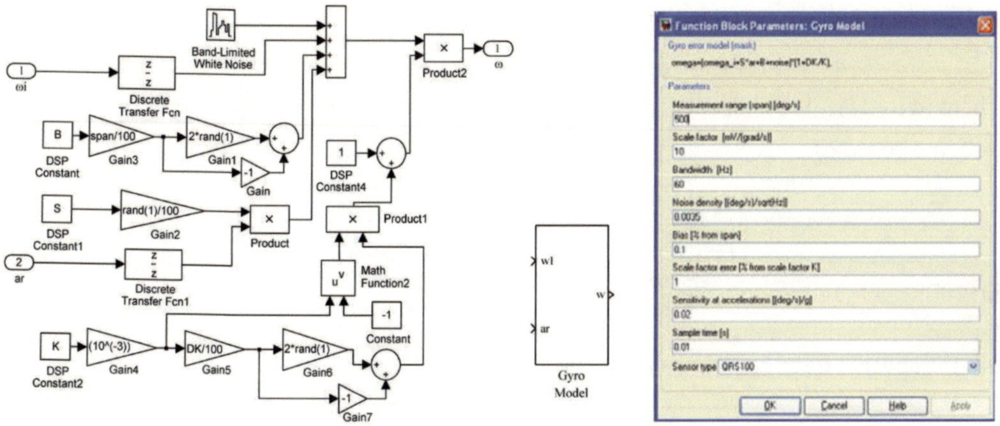

Figure 2. Gyros Matlab/Simulink model and its interface.

2. Navigation algorithm

The output $\vec{f}$ of an accelerometer is influenced by the gravitational field, it being a combination between the vehicle kinematic acceleration $\vec{a}$ and the gravitational acceleration$\vec{g}$, i.e. $\vec{f}=\vec{a}-\vec{g}$. In literature, f is very well known as specific force (Farrell, 2008; Titterton and Weston, 2004).

On the other way, according to the Coriolis formula we have:

$$\left.\frac{\mathrm{d}\vec{r}}{\mathrm{d}t}\right|_I=\left.\frac{\mathrm{d}\vec{r}}{\mathrm{d}t}\right|_P+\vec{\Omega}\times\vec{r}=\vec{v}+\vec{\Omega}\times\vec{r}, \tag{3}$$

from where it results:

$$\vec{a}=\frac{\mathrm{d}}{\mathrm{d}t}\left[\left.\frac{\mathrm{d}\vec{r}}{\mathrm{d}t}\right|_I\right]_I=\frac{\mathrm{d}}{\mathrm{d}t}\left[\vec{v}+\vec{\Omega}\times\vec{r}\right]_I=\left.\frac{\mathrm{d}\vec{v}}{\mathrm{d}t}\right|_I+\vec{\Omega}\times\left.\frac{\mathrm{d}\vec{r}}{\mathrm{d}t}\right|_I=\left.\frac{\mathrm{d}\vec{v}}{\mathrm{d}t}\right|_I+\vec{\Omega}\times\vec{v}+\vec{\Omega}\times\left(\vec{\Omega}\times\vec{r}\right); \tag{4}$$

$\vec{r}$ is the position vector of the monitored vehicle in inertial frame I, $\vec{v}$-the vehicle speed relative to the ECEF (Earth Centered Earth Fixed) reference frame (denoted with P), and $\vec{\Omega}$-Earth rotation speed around its axis.

Denoting with $\vec{\omega}_N$ the absolute angular speed of the navigation reference frame N, then the Coriolis formula applied to the $(\mathrm{d}\vec{v}/\mathrm{d}t)|_I$ term implies:

$$\left.\frac{\mathrm{d}\vec{v}}{\mathrm{d}t}\right|_I = \left.\frac{\mathrm{d}\vec{v}}{\mathrm{d}t}\right|_N + \vec{\omega}_N \times \vec{v}, \tag{5}$$

where $(\mathrm{d}\vec{v}/\mathrm{d}t)_N$ is the derivative of $\vec{v}$ relative to the navigation frame. Therefore, the acceleration $\vec{a}$ becomes:

$$\vec{a} = \left.\frac{\mathrm{d}\vec{v}}{\mathrm{d}t}\right|_N + \vec{\omega}_N \times \vec{v} + \vec{\Omega} \times \vec{v} + \vec{\Omega} \times \left(\vec{\Omega} \times \vec{r}\right), \tag{6}$$

and the specific force can be rewritten as:

$$\vec{f} = \left.\frac{\mathrm{d}\vec{v}}{\mathrm{d}t}\right|_N + \vec{\omega}_N \times \vec{v} + \vec{\Omega} \times \vec{v} + \vec{\Omega} \times \left(\vec{\Omega} \times \vec{r}\right) - \vec{g}. \tag{7}$$

Considering the expression $\vec{g}_a = \vec{g} - \vec{\Omega} \times (\vec{\Omega} \times \vec{r})$ for the apparent gravitational acceleration, eq. (7) implies:

$$\vec{f} = \left.\frac{\mathrm{d}\vec{v}}{\mathrm{d}t}\right|_N + \vec{\omega}_N \times \vec{v} + \vec{\Omega} \times \vec{v} - \vec{g}_a, \tag{8}$$

which is known as general equation of the inertial navigation.

The position and the speed of a vehicle may be obtained by the numerical integration of the eq. (8) relative to the navigation frame (Farrell, 2008; Salychev, 1998; Titterton and Weston, 2004). In the inertial navigation systems with stable platform, the axes of the acceleration sensors are kept parallel with the navigation frame axes, and, as a consequence, the components of the specific force are obtained directly in this frame. If a strap-down architecture is used for the inertial measurement unit (IMU), then the components of the specific force in the navigation frame should be calculated starting from the specific force components in the vehicle frame (SV); the acceleration sensors in IMU are fixed directly on the vehicle rigid structure. In this situation the coordinate change between the vehicle frame and navigation frame is made by using the rotation matrix describing the vehicle attitude relative to the navigation frame.

By choosing as navigation frame the local horizontal frame ENU (East-North-Up) it results $\vec{\omega}_N = \vec{\omega}_l$ (index l denotes the ENU frame). The scalar components of the eq. (8) in this frame are:

$$
\begin{aligned}
f_{xl} &= \frac{dv_{xl}}{dt} + \omega_{yl}v_{zl} - \omega_{zl}v_{yl} + \Omega_{yl}v_{zl} - \Omega_{zl}v_{yl} - g_{axl}, \\
f_{yl} &= \frac{dv_{yl}}{dt} - \omega_{xl}v_{zl} + \omega_{zl}v_{xl} - \Omega_{xl}v_{zl} + \Omega_{zl}v_{xl} - g_{ayl}, \\
f_{zl} &= \frac{dv_{zl}}{dt} + \omega_{xl}v_{yl} - \omega_{yl}v_{xl} + \Omega_{xl}v_{yl} - \Omega_{yl}v_{xl} - g_{azl},
\end{aligned} \tag{9}
$$

where f_{xl}, f_{yl}, f_{zl} are the components of the specific force in ENU frame; v_{xl}, v_{yl}, v_{zl}-components of the vehicle speed relative to ECEF frame in ENU frame; $\omega_{xl}, \omega_{yl}, \omega_{zl}$-components of the ENU frame absolute angular speed $\vec{\omega}_l$ on its own axes; $\Omega_{xl}, \Omega_{yl}, \Omega_{zl}$-components of $\vec{\Omega}$ in ENU frame; $g_{axl}, g_{ayl}, g_{azl}$-components of the apparent gravitational acceleration in ENU frame (Farrell, 2008; Grigorie, 2007; Radix, 1993):

$$
g_{xl} \cong 0,\ g_{yl} \cong 0,\ g_{zl} \cong 9{,}7803 + 0{,}0519 \cdot \sin^2\phi - 3{,}08 \cdot 10^{-6} \cdot h. \tag{10}
$$

With these considerations we have (Farrell, 2008; Grigorie, 2007; Radix, 1993):

$$
\left[\vec{\Omega}\right]_l = \left[\Omega_{xl} \quad \Omega_{yl} \quad \Omega_{zl}\right]^T = \left[0 \quad \Omega\cos\phi \quad \Omega\sin\phi\right]^T, \tag{11}
$$

$$
\left[\vec{\omega}_l\right]_l = [\omega_{xl}, \omega_{yl}, \omega_{zl}]^T = \left[-\frac{v_{yl}}{R_\phi + h}, \frac{v_{xl}}{R_\lambda + h} + \Omega\cos\phi, \frac{v_{xl}}{R_\lambda + h}\mathrm{tg}\phi + \Omega\sin\phi\right]^T, \tag{12}
$$

h is the altitude relative to the reference ellipsoid, R_ϕ şi R_λ-principal radii of curvature of the reference ellipsoid (Farrell, 2008; Grigorie, 2007; Radix, 1993):

$$
R_\phi = a\frac{1-e^2}{(1-e^2\sin^2\phi)^{3/2}},\ R_\lambda = \frac{a}{(1-e^2\sin^2\phi)^{1/2}}, \tag{13}
$$

λ and ϕ are the longitude and the latitude. The angular speed $\vec{\omega}_r$, relative to the ECEF reference frame, has in ENU frame the next components:

$$\left[\vec{\omega}_r\right]_l = [\omega_{rxl}, \omega_{ryl}, \omega_{rzl}]^T = \left[-\frac{v_{yl}}{R_\phi + h}, \frac{v_{xl}}{R_\lambda + h}, \frac{v_{xl}}{R_\lambda + h}\mathrm{tg}\phi\right]^T. \tag{14}$$

Therefore, equations (9) become:

$$\begin{aligned}
\frac{\mathrm{d}v_{xl}}{\mathrm{d}t} &= f_{xl} + \frac{v_{xl}v_{yl}}{R_\lambda + h}\mathrm{tg}\phi + 2\Omega\sin\phi v_{yl} - v_{zl}\left(\frac{v_{xl}}{R_\lambda + h} + 2\Omega\cos\phi\right) + g_{axl},\\
\frac{\mathrm{d}v_{yl}}{\mathrm{d}t} &= f_{yl} - \frac{v_{xl}^2}{R_\lambda + h}\mathrm{tg}\phi - 2\Omega\sin\phi v_{xl} - v_{zl}\frac{v_{yl}}{R_\phi + h} + g_{ayl},\\
\frac{\mathrm{d}v_{zl}}{\mathrm{d}t} &= f_{zl} + \frac{v_{yl}^2}{R_\phi + h} + \frac{v_{xl}^2}{R_\lambda + h} + 2\Omega v_{xl}\cos\phi + g_{azl}.
\end{aligned} \tag{15}$$

To integrate these equations we need to know the initial values of $\phi,\ \lambda,\ h,\ v_{xl},\ v_{yl},\ v_{zl}$, and, also, the components of $\vec{f}$ and $\vec{g}$ in ENU frame. Because the IMU of the strap-down inertial navigation system contains three accelerometers and three gyros, its inputs will be the components of the vehicle absolute acceleration and angular speed in the vehicle frame:

$$[\vec{f}]_v = [f_{xv}, f_{yv}, f_{zv}]^T, \tag{16}$$

$$[\vec{\omega}_v]_v = [\omega_{xv}, \omega_{yv}, \omega_{zv}]^T. \tag{17}$$

The components of the specific force in ENU can be determinate by using the relation:

$$[\vec{f}]_l = R_v^l[\vec{f}]_v, \tag{18}$$

where R_v^l is the rotation matrix performing the coordinate change between SV frame and ENU frame and can be calculated by solving the next Poisson equation (Farrell, 2008):

$$\dot{R}_v^l = R_v^l\tilde{\omega}_v - \tilde{\omega}_l R_v^l. \tag{19}$$

In eq. (19) $\tilde{\omega}_v$ and $\tilde{\omega}_l$ have the expressions:

$$\tilde{\omega}_v = \begin{bmatrix} 0 & -\omega_{zv} & \omega_{yv} \\ \omega_{zv} & 0 & -\omega_{xv} \\ -\omega_{yv} & \omega_{xv} & 0 \end{bmatrix}, \tilde{\omega}_l = \begin{bmatrix} 0 & -\omega_{zl} & \omega_{yl} \\ \omega_{zl} & 0 & -\omega_{xl} \\ -\omega_{yl} & \omega_{xl} & 0 \end{bmatrix}. \tag{20}$$

Can be easily observed that eq. (19) has the general form:

$$\dot{X} = XA - BX, \tag{21}$$

with $A = \tilde{\omega}_v$ and $B = \tilde{\omega}_l$. Considering that for a short period of time Δt, between t_n and t_{n+1} times, the angular speeds ω_{xv}, ω_{yv}, ω_{zv} and ω_{xl}, ω_{yl}, ω_{zl} are constant, we obtains:

$$\Delta\phi_{xv} = \int_{t_n}^{t_{n+1}} \omega_{xv} \mathrm{d}t = \omega_{xv}\Delta t,\ \Delta\phi_{yv} = \int_{t_n}^{t_{n+1}} \omega_{yv} \mathrm{d}t = \omega_{yv}\Delta t,\ \Delta\phi_{zv} = \int_{t_n}^{t_{n+1}} \omega_{zv} \mathrm{d}t = \omega_{zv}\Delta t \tag{22}$$

and

$$\Delta\phi_{xl} = \int_{t_n}^{t_{n+1}} \omega_{xl} \mathrm{d}t = \omega_{xl}\Delta t,\ \Delta\phi_{yl} = \int_{t_n}^{t_{n+1}} \omega_{yl} \mathrm{d}t = \omega_{yl}\Delta t,\ \Delta\phi_{zl} = \int_{t_n}^{t_{n+1}} \omega_{zl} \mathrm{d}t = \omega_{zl}\Delta t. \tag{23}$$

$\Delta\phi_{xv}$, $\Delta\phi_{yv}$, $\Delta\phi_{zv}$, respectively $\Delta\phi_{xl}$, $\Delta\phi_{yl}$, $\Delta\phi_{zl}$ are the increments of the angular rotations measured around the roll, pitch and yaw axes, respectively the increments of the angular rotations around the ENU frame axes calculated by the navigation processor. In this way, the value provided for the X matrix at the t_{n+1} time is given by:

$$X_{n+1} = X_n + \dot{X}_n\Delta t = X_n + X_n A\Delta t - B\Delta t X_n, \tag{24}$$

from where it is obtained:

$$X_{n+1} = X_n(I + A\Delta t) - B\Delta t X_n = X_n A_n - B_n X_n, \tag{25}$$

with:

$$A_n = \begin{bmatrix} 1 & -\Delta\phi_{zv} & \Delta\phi_{yv} \\ \Delta\phi_{zv} & 1 & -\Delta\phi_{xv} \\ -\Delta\phi_{yv} & \Delta\phi_{xv} & 1 \end{bmatrix}, B_n = \begin{bmatrix} 0 & -\Delta\phi_{zl} & \Delta\phi_{yl} \\ \Delta\phi_{zl} & 0 & -\Delta\phi_{xl} \\ -\Delta\phi_{yl} & \Delta\phi_{xl} & 0 \end{bmatrix}. \tag{26}$$

Therefore, the solution of the eq. (19) has the form:

$$R_v^l\Big|_{n+1} = R_v^l\Big|_n A_n - B_n R_v^l\Big|_n. \tag{27}$$

Through the numerical integration of the equations (15) are obtained the components of the relative speed $\vec{v}$ in ENU frame:$v_{xl},\ v_{yl},\ v_{zl}$. With the equations (Salychev, 1998):

$$\begin{aligned} \dot{\phi} &= \frac{v_{yl}}{R_\phi + h}, \\ \dot{\lambda} &= \frac{v_{xl}}{(R_\lambda + h)\cos\phi}, \\ \dot{h} &= v_{zl}. \end{aligned} \tag{28}$$

it result the geographic coordinated of the vehicle:

$$\begin{aligned} \phi(t) &= \phi(0) + \int_0^t \frac{v_{yl}}{R_\phi + h} \mathrm{d}t, \\ \lambda(t) &= \lambda(0) + \int_0^t \frac{v_{xl}}{(R_\lambda + h)\cos\phi} \mathrm{d}t, \\ h(t) &= h(0) + \int_0^t v_{zl} \mathrm{d}t. \end{aligned} \tag{29}$$

By using the rotation matrix between ENU and ECEF frames (Farrell, 2008; Salychev, 1998; Titterton and Weston, 2004):

$$[R_l^P]^T = R_P^l = \begin{bmatrix} -\sin\lambda & \cos\lambda & 0 \\ -\sin\phi\cos\lambda & -\sin\phi\sin\lambda & \cos\phi \\ \cos\phi\cos\lambda & \cos\phi\sin\lambda & \sin\phi \end{bmatrix} \tag{30}$$

the components of the relative speed $\vec{v}$ in ECEF frame result with equation:

$$[\vec{v}]_P = R_l^P [\vec{v}]_l. \tag{31}$$

By numerical integration of the relative speed $[\vec{v}]_P$ is obtained $[\vec{r}]_P$:

$$[\vec{r}]_P = [\vec{r}(0)]_P + \int_0^t [\vec{v}]_P \mathrm{d}t = [x_P \; y_P \; z_P]^T, \tag{32}$$

from which, with the model of the gravitational field for ECEF reference frame (Radix, 1993), it results:

$$[\vec{g}_a]_P = \begin{bmatrix} g_{aX^P} \\ g_{aY^P} \\ g_{aZ^P} \end{bmatrix} = \begin{bmatrix} A_1 \frac{x_P}{r^3}\left(1 + \frac{A_2}{r^2}\left(\frac{5z_P^2}{r^2} - 1\right)\right) + \Omega^2 \cdot x_P \\ A_1 \frac{y_P}{r^3}\left(1 + \frac{A_2}{r^2}\left(\frac{5z_P^2}{r^2} - 1\right)\right) + \Omega^2 \cdot y_P \\ A_1 \frac{z_P}{r^3}\left(1 + \frac{A_2}{r^2}\left(\frac{5z_P^2}{r^2} - 3\right)\right) \end{bmatrix}; \tag{33}$$

$A_1 = -3,\ 986005 \cdot 10^{14}\,\mathrm{m}^3/\mathrm{s}^2$, $A_2 = -6,\ 66425 \cdot 10^{10}\,\mathrm{m}^2$ (Radix, 1993). Components of $\vec{g}_a$ in ENU frame, starting from the model (33), are calculated by using the inverse transform ECEF to ENU:

$$[\vec{g}_a]_l = R_P^l [\vec{g}_a]_P. \tag{34}$$

Finally, the vehicle coordinates in ENU are obtained with the equation:

$$[\vec{r}']_l = [\vec{r}'(0)]_l + \int_0^t [\vec{v}]_l \mathrm{d}t = [x_l \; y_l \; z_l]^T, \tag{35}$$

where $\vec{r}'$ is the vehicle position vector in ENU reference frame. From the mathematical description of the algorithm, it results the block diagram in Fig. 3.

3. Error model of the navigation algorithm

The quality of the inertial navigator depends by the precision of the used sensors and by the numerical algorithms implemented in the navigation processor. For the error model developed in this subchapter are taken into account only the errors of the inertial sensors, considering that the numerical algorithm implemented in the navigation processor works free of errors. Thus, the model highlights the dependence of the position, velocity and attitude errors by the errors of the accelerometers and gyros in strap-down IMU. In the development of the error

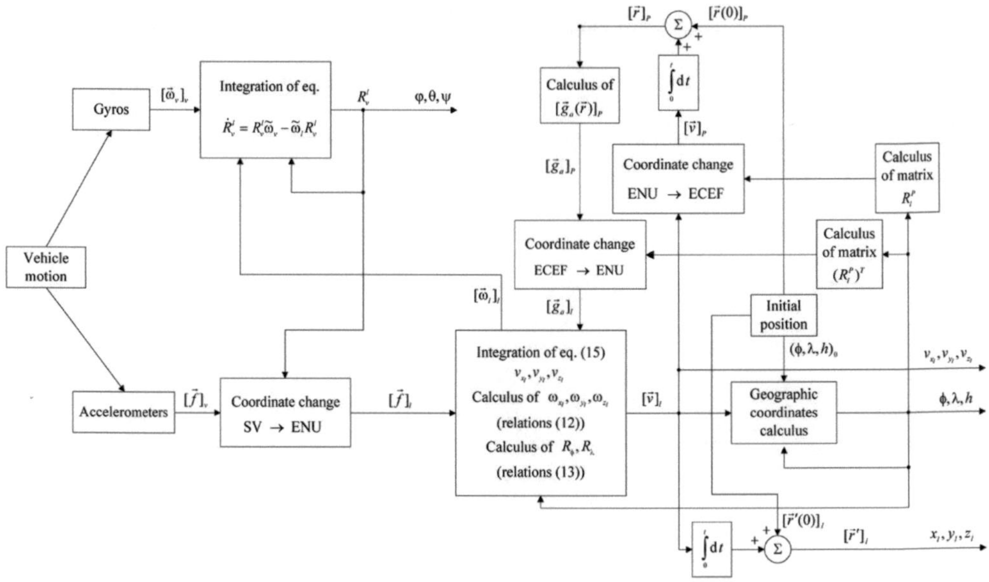

Figure 3. Block diagram of the navigation algorithm.

model are used techniques widely presented in the literature (Dahia, 2005; Farrell, 2008; Salychev, 1998; Savage, 2000).

Denoting with m the ideal value of a measurement and with $\widehat{m}$ its real value, given by the measurement system, the measurement error is calculated with the relation:

$$\delta m = m - \widehat{m}. \tag{36}$$

Starting from this expression, and having in mind that accelerometric readings are denoted with f_{xv}, f_{yv}, f_{zv}, and gyro readings are denoted with ω_{xv}, ω_{yv}, ω_{zv}, it result the errors of the accelerometric and gyro sensors under the scalar forms (the components for all three IMU axes):

$$\delta f_{xv} = f_{xv} - \widehat{f}_{xv}, \ \delta f_{yv} = f_{yv} - \widehat{f}_{yv}, \ \delta f_{zv} = f_{yv} - \widehat{f}_{yv}, \tag{37}$$

$$\delta\omega_{xv} = \omega_{xv} - \widehat{\omega}_{xv}, \ \delta\omega_{yv} = \omega_{yv} - \widehat{\omega}_{yv}, \ \delta\omega_{zv} = \omega_{zv} - \widehat{\omega}_{zv} \tag{38}$$

and, under the vector forms:

$$\delta\vec{f} = \vec{f} - \hat{\vec{f}}, \tag{39}$$

$$\delta\vec{\omega}_v = \vec{\omega}_v - \hat{\vec{\omega}}_v. \tag{40}$$

Similarly can be defined the errors of the attitude angles ($\varphi,\ \theta,\ \psi$-roll, pitch and yaw), the errors of the vehicle position over the ENU frame axes ($x_l,\ y_l,\ z_l$), and the errors of the vehicle linear speed ($v_{xl},\ v_{yl},\ v_{zl}$):

$$\delta\varphi = \varphi - \hat{\varphi},\ \delta\theta = \theta - \hat{\theta},\ \delta\psi = \psi - \hat{\psi}, \tag{41}$$

$$\begin{aligned} &\delta x_l = x_l - \hat{x}_l,\ \delta y_l = y_l - \hat{y}_l,\ \delta z_l = z_l - \hat{z}_l, \\ &\delta\vec{r}' = \vec{r}' - \hat{\vec{r}}'. \end{aligned} \tag{42}$$

$$\begin{aligned} &\delta v_{xl} = v_{xl} - \hat{v}_{xl},\ \delta v_{yl} = v_{yl} - \hat{v}_{yl},\ \delta v_{zl} = v_{zl} - \hat{v}_{zl}, \\ &\delta\vec{v} = \vec{v} - \hat{\vec{v}}. \end{aligned} \tag{43}$$

Starting from the errors of the attitude angles may be deduced the errors affecting the attitude matrices. Thus, with the equations expressing the elements of the rotation matrix R_l^v (ENU to SV) (Farrell, 2008; Salychev, 1998; Titterton and Weston, 2004) and considering as negligible the products of the attitude angles errors taken as small perturbations, ($\delta\varphi \cdot \delta\theta = \delta\varphi \cdot \delta\psi = \delta\theta \cdot \delta\psi = 0$), it results:

$$R_l^v = \hat{R}_l^v \begin{bmatrix} 1 & -\delta\psi & \delta\theta \\ \delta\psi & 1 & -\delta\varphi \\ -\delta\theta & \delta\varphi & 1 \end{bmatrix} = \hat{R}_l^v (I_3 + \tilde{R}),\ \text{with}\ \tilde{R} = \begin{bmatrix} 0 & -\delta\psi & \delta\theta \\ \delta\psi & 0 & -\delta\varphi \\ -\delta\theta & \delta\varphi & 0 \end{bmatrix}, \tag{44}$$

where R_l^v is the right matrix, and $\hat{R}_l^v$-the matrix provided by the navigation system. From eq. (44) we have:

$$R_v^l = (R_l^v)^T = (I_3 + \tilde{R})^T \cdot (\hat{R}_l^v)^T = (I_3 - \tilde{R}) \cdot \hat{R}_v^l. \tag{45}$$

In similar way, for the R_p^l matrix (ECEF to ENU) (Farrell, 2008; Salychev, 1998; Titterton and Weston, 2004), in which are considered the latitude and longitude errors:

$$\delta\lambda = \lambda - \widehat{\lambda},\ \delta\phi = \phi - \widehat{\phi}, \tag{46}$$

it results:

$$R_P^l = (I_3 - \tilde{P}) \cdot \widehat{R}_P^l, \tag{47}$$

where R_P^l is the right matrix, $\widehat{R}_P^l$-the matrix provided by the navigation system, and $\widetilde{P}$ has the form:

$$\tilde{P} = \begin{bmatrix} 0 & -\delta p_z & \delta p_y \\ \delta p_z & 0 & -\delta p_x \\ -\delta p_y & \delta p_x & 0 \end{bmatrix} \tag{48}$$

with:

$$\delta p_x = -\delta\phi,\ \delta p_y = \cos\widehat{\phi} \cdot \delta\lambda,\ \delta p_z = \sin\widehat{\phi} \cdot \delta\lambda. \tag{49}$$

One of the form of the attitude Poisson equation is (Farrell, 2008; Grigorie, 2007; Salychev, 1998; Titterton and Weston, 2004):

$$\dot{R}_l^v = R_l^v \cdot \tilde{\omega}_l - \tilde{\omega}_v \cdot R_l^v, \tag{50}$$

where $\widetilde{\omega}_l$ and $\widetilde{\omega}_v$ have the expressions given by equations (20). Due to the erroneous measurements, the inertial system integrates the next equation:

$$\dot{\widehat{R}}_l^v = \widehat{R}_l^v \cdot \widehat{\tilde{\omega}}_l - \widehat{\tilde{\omega}}_v \cdot \widehat{R}_l^v. \tag{51}$$

Thus, it results:

$$\dot{\widehat{R}}_l^v = \widehat{R}_l^v \cdot (\tilde{\omega}_l - \delta\tilde{\omega}_l) - (\tilde{\omega}_v - \delta\tilde{\omega}_v) \cdot \widehat{R}_l^v, \tag{52}$$

with

http://dx.doi.org/10.5772/57583

$$\delta\tilde{\omega}_v = \begin{bmatrix} 0 & -\delta\omega_{zv} & \delta\omega_{yv} \\ \delta\omega_{zv} & 0 & -\delta\omega_{xv} \\ -\delta\omega_{yv} & \delta\omega_{xv} & 0 \end{bmatrix},\ \delta\tilde{\omega}_l = \begin{bmatrix} 0 & -\delta\omega_{zl} & \delta\omega_{yl} \\ \delta\omega_{zl} & 0 & -\delta\omega_{xl} \\ -\delta\omega_{yl} & \delta\omega_{xl} & 0 \end{bmatrix}. \tag{53}$$

From (44) we obtain:

$$R_l^v - \widehat{R}_l^v = \widehat{R}_l^v \cdot \tilde{R}, \tag{54}$$

which, through derivation, implies:

$$\dot{R}_l^v - \dot{\widehat{R}}_l^v = \dot{\widehat{R}}_l^v \cdot \tilde{R} + \widehat{R}_l^v \cdot \dot{\tilde{R}}, \tag{55}$$

i.e.

$$\widehat{R}_l^v \cdot \dot{\tilde{R}} = \dot{R}_l^v - \dot{\widehat{R}}_l^v \cdot (I_3 + \tilde{R}). \tag{56}$$

Substituting relations (50) and (52) in (56), get to the formula:

$$\widehat{R}_l^v \cdot \dot{\tilde{R}} = \widehat{R}_l^v \cdot \tilde{R} \cdot \tilde{\omega}_l - \widehat{R}_l^v \cdot \tilde{\omega}_l \cdot \tilde{R} + (\widehat{R}_l^v \cdot \delta\tilde{\omega}_l - \delta\tilde{\omega}_v \cdot \widehat{R}_l^v)(I_3 + \tilde{R}). \tag{57}$$

Considering expressions of $\tilde{R}$, $\delta\tilde{\omega}_v$ and$\delta\tilde{\omega}_l$, in formula (57) can be neglected the products between small quantities ($\widehat{R}_l^v \cdot \delta\tilde{\omega}_l \cdot \tilde{R}and\delta\tilde{\omega}_v \cdot \widehat{R}_l^v \cdot \tilde{R}$) and we obtain:

$$\widehat{R}_l^v \cdot \dot{\tilde{R}} = \widehat{R}_l^v \cdot \tilde{R} \cdot \tilde{\omega}_l - \widehat{R}_l^v \cdot \tilde{\omega}_l \cdot \tilde{R} + \widehat{R}_l^v \cdot \delta\tilde{\omega}_l - \delta\tilde{\omega}_v \cdot \widehat{R}_l^v, \tag{58}$$

which, by multiplication on the left with$(\widehat{R}_l^v)^T$, leads to the relation:

$$\dot{\tilde{R}} = \tilde{R} \cdot \tilde{\omega}_l - \tilde{\omega}_l \cdot \tilde{R} + \delta\tilde{\omega}_l - (\widehat{R}_l^v)^T \cdot \delta\tilde{\omega}_v \cdot \widehat{R}_l^v. \tag{59}$$

With formulas (12) and (28) it results:

$$\left[\vec{\omega}_l\right]_l = [\omega_{xl},\ \omega_{yl},\ \omega_{zl}]^T = \left[-\dot{\phi},\ \dot{\lambda}\cos\phi + \Omega\cos\phi,\ \dot{\lambda}\sin\phi + \Omega\sin\phi\right]^T, \tag{60}$$

Evaluating the terms of differential equation (59), we obtain:

$$\tilde{R}\cdot\tilde{\omega}_l-\tilde{\omega}_l\cdot\tilde{R}=\begin{bmatrix}0 & -(\omega_{yl}\delta\phi-\omega_{xl}\delta\theta) & \omega_{xl}\delta\psi-\omega_{zl}\delta\phi\\ \omega_{yl}\delta\phi-\omega_{xl}\delta\theta & 0 & -(\omega_{zl}\delta\theta-\omega_{yl}\delta\psi)\\ -(\omega_{xl}\delta\psi-\omega_{zl}\delta\phi) & \omega_{zl}\delta\theta-\omega_{yl}\delta\psi & 0\end{bmatrix}, \tag{61}$$

$$[\delta\vec{\omega}_l]_l=\begin{bmatrix}\delta\omega_{xl}\\ \delta\omega_{yl}\\ \delta\omega_{zl}\end{bmatrix}=\begin{bmatrix}-\delta\dot{\phi}\\ -\sin\phi\cdot\dot{\lambda}\cdot\delta\phi+\cos\phi\cdot\delta\dot{\lambda}-\Omega\cdot\sin\phi\cdot\delta\phi\\ \cos\phi\cdot\dot{\lambda}\cdot\delta\phi+\sin\phi\cdot\delta\dot{\lambda}+\Omega\cdot\cos\phi\cdot\delta\phi\end{bmatrix}, \tag{62}$$

and for the product $(\hat{R}_l^v)^T\cdot\delta\tilde{\omega}_v\cdot\hat{R}_l^v$ the resulting matrix elements are given by the expressions:

$$\begin{aligned}
a_{11}&=a_{22}=a_{33},\\
a_{21}&=-a_{12}=-\sin\hat{\theta}\cdot\delta\omega_{xv}+\sin\hat{\phi}\cos\hat{\theta}\cdot\delta\omega_{yv}+\cos\hat{\phi}\cos\hat{\theta}\cdot\delta\omega_{zv},\\
a_{13}&=-a_{31}=\cos\hat{\theta}\sin\hat{\psi}\cdot\delta\omega_{xv}+(\sin\hat{\phi}\sin\hat{\theta}\sin\hat{\psi}+\cos\hat{\phi}\cos\hat{\psi})\cdot\delta\omega_{yv}+\\
&\qquad+(\cos\hat{\phi}\sin\hat{\theta}\sin\hat{\psi}-\sin\hat{\phi}\cos\hat{\psi})\cdot\delta\omega_{zv},\\
a_{32}&=-a_{23}=\cos\hat{\theta}\cos\hat{\psi}\cdot\delta\omega_{xv}+(\sin\hat{\phi}\sin\hat{\theta}\cos\hat{\psi}-\cos\hat{\phi}\sin\hat{\psi})\cdot\delta\omega_{yv}+\\
&\qquad+(\cos\hat{\phi}\sin\hat{\theta}\cos\hat{\psi}+\sin\hat{\phi}\sin\hat{\psi})\cdot\delta\omega_{zv}.
\end{aligned} \tag{63}$$

Therefore, the elements of the matrix $\tilde{R}$ from equation (59) are calculated by using relations of the form:

$$\begin{aligned}
r_{11}&=r_{22}=r_{33}=0,\\
r_{21}&=-r_{12}=(\omega_{yl}\delta\phi-\omega_{xl}\delta\theta)-a_{21}+\delta\omega_{zl},\\
r_{13}&=-r_{31}=(\omega_{xl}\delta\psi-\omega_{zl}\delta\phi)-a_{13}+\delta\omega_{yl},\\
r_{32}&=-r_{23}=(\omega_{zl}\delta\theta-\omega_{yl}\delta\psi)-a_{32}+\delta\omega_{xl}.
\end{aligned} \tag{64}$$

Taking into account that:

$$[\delta\vec{\omega}_v]_v=[\delta\omega_{xv},\ \delta\omega_{yv},\ \delta\omega_{zv}]^T, \tag{65}$$

can be quickly demonstrated that the elements described by formulas (63) come from a product by the form $(\hat{R}_l^v)^T\cdot[\delta\vec{\omega}_v]_v$. Thus, denoting with:

$$[\vec{\Phi}]_l = [\delta\phi,\ \delta\theta,\ \delta\psi]^T \tag{66}$$

the vector having the components equal with the errors of the attitude angles, it appears that:

$$\begin{bmatrix} \omega_{zl}\delta\theta - \omega_{yl}\delta\psi \\ \omega_{xl}\delta\psi - \omega_{zl}\delta\phi \\ \omega_{yl}\delta\phi - \omega_{xl}\delta\theta \end{bmatrix} = -[\vec{\omega}_l \times \vec{\Phi}]_l, \tag{67}$$

and the matrix equation (59) can be transfigured as:

$$[\dot{\vec{\Phi}}]_l = -[\vec{\omega}_l \times \vec{\Phi}]_l - (\widehat{R}_l^v)^T \cdot [\delta\vec{\omega}_v]_v + [\delta\vec{\omega}_l]_l, \tag{68}$$

where $(\widehat{R}_l^v)^T \cdot [\delta\vec{\omega}_v]_v$ represents the errors due to gyro measurements in ENU frame, and $[\delta\vec{\omega}_l]_l$ contains the errors of the angular velocities assessment committed by navigation processor. Equation (67) is the differential equation of the attitude error.

To derive the equation that characterizes the speed error evolution in time it starts from relation (8) in which it is considered $\vec{\omega}_N = \vec{\omega}_l$:

$$\vec{f} = \left.\frac{\mathrm{d}\vec{v}}{\mathrm{d}t}\right|_l + \vec{\omega}_l \times \vec{v} + \vec{\Omega} \times \vec{v} - \vec{g}_a. \tag{69}$$

It results:

$$[\dot{\vec{v}}]_l = [\vec{f}]_l + [\vec{g}_a]_l - [(\vec{\omega}_l + \vec{\Omega}) \times \vec{v}]_l = R_v^l \cdot [\vec{f}]_v + [\vec{g}_a]_l - [(\vec{\omega}_l + \vec{\Omega}) \times \vec{v}]_l, \tag{70}$$

that, in the hypothesis of erroneous measurement of accelerations and angular velocities, becomes:

$$[\dot{\hat{\vec{v}}}]_l = \widehat{R}_v^l \cdot [\hat{\vec{f}}]_v + [\hat{\vec{g}}_a]_l - [(\hat{\vec{\omega}}_l + \hat{\vec{\Omega}}) \times \hat{\vec{v}}]_l. \tag{71}$$

Thus, the speed error will be:

$$[\delta\dot{\vec{v}}]_l = [\dot{\vec{v}}]_l - [\dot{\hat{\vec{v}}}]_l = R_v^l \cdot [\vec{f}]_v - \widehat{R}_v^l \cdot [\hat{\vec{f}}]_v + [\vec{g}_a]_l - [\hat{\vec{g}}_a]_l - \{[(\vec{\omega}_l + \vec{\Omega}) \times \vec{v}]_l - [(\hat{\vec{\omega}}_l + \hat{\vec{\Omega}}) \times \hat{\vec{v}}]_l\}, \tag{72}$$

but, according to formula (45), $R_v^l = (I_3 - \widetilde{R}) \cdot \overset{\frown}{R}{}_v^l$, and we have:

$$\begin{aligned}[\delta\vec{v}]_l &= \widehat{R}_v^l \cdot [\delta\vec{f}]_v - \tilde{R} \cdot \widehat{R}_v^l \cdot [\vec{f}]_v + [\delta\vec{g}_a]_l - \{[(\vec{\omega}_l + \vec{\Omega}) \times \vec{v}]_l - [(\widehat{\vec{\omega}}_l + \widehat{\vec{\Omega}}) \times \widehat{\vec{v}}]_l\} = \\ &= -[\vec{\Phi}]_l \cdot [\vec{f}]_v + \widehat{R}_v^l \cdot [\delta\vec{f}]_v + [\delta\vec{g}_a]_l - [(\vec{\omega}_l + \vec{\Omega}) \times \delta\vec{v}]_l - [(\delta\vec{\omega}_l + \delta\vec{\Omega}) \times \vec{v}]_l,\end{aligned} \tag{73}$$

in which:

$$[\delta\vec{g}_a]_l = [0,\ 0,\ -3{,}08 \cdot 10^{-6} \cdot \delta h] \approx [0,\ 0,\ -2\frac{KM_P}{a^2} \cdot \frac{\delta h}{a}] = [0,\ 0,\ -2\frac{g}{a} \cdot \delta h]. \tag{74}$$

$$[\delta\vec{\Omega}]_l = [0,\ -\Omega \cdot \sin\phi \cdot \delta\phi,\ \Omega \cdot \cos\phi \cdot \delta\phi]^T. \tag{75}$$

Equations (28) give the expressions for the speed components:

$$\begin{aligned}v_{xl} &= (R_\lambda + h) \cdot \cos\phi \cdot \dot{\lambda}, \\ v_{yl} &= (R_\phi + h) \cdot \dot{\phi}, \\ v_{zl} &= \dot{h},\end{aligned} \tag{76}$$

from where are obtained the positioning errors on the axes of the ENU frame:

$$\begin{aligned}\delta x_l &= (R_\lambda + h) \cdot \cos\phi \cdot \delta\lambda, \\ \delta y_l &= (R_\phi + h) \cdot \delta\phi, \\ \delta z_l &= \delta h.\end{aligned} \tag{77}$$

By derivation with respect to time, equations (77) imply:

$$\begin{aligned}\delta\dot{x}_l &= \left[\frac{\partial R_\lambda}{\partial\phi} \cdot \dot{\phi} \cdot \cos\phi - (R_\lambda + h) \cdot \sin\phi \cdot \dot{\phi}\right]\delta\lambda + (R_\lambda + h) \cdot \cos\phi \cdot \delta\dot{\lambda} + \cos\phi \cdot \dot{h} \cdot \delta\lambda, \\ \delta\dot{y}_l &= \frac{\partial R_\phi}{\partial\phi} \cdot \dot{\phi} \cdot \delta\phi + (R_\phi + h) \cdot \delta\dot{\phi} + \dot{h} \cdot \delta\phi, \\ \delta\dot{z}_l &= \delta\dot{h},\end{aligned} \tag{78}$$

and, by differentiating the velocity components (76), we get expressions:

$$\delta v_{xl} = \left[\frac{\partial R_\lambda}{\partial \phi} \cdot \cos\phi - (R_\lambda + h) \cdot \sin\phi\right] \cdot \dot{\lambda} \cdot \delta\phi + (R_\lambda + h) \cdot \cos\phi \cdot \delta\dot{\lambda} + \cos\phi \cdot \dot{\lambda} \cdot \delta h,$$
$$\delta v_{yl} = \frac{\partial R_\phi}{\partial \phi} \cdot \dot{\phi} \cdot \delta\phi + (R_\phi + h) \cdot \delta\dot{\phi} + \dot{\phi} \cdot \delta h, \tag{79}$$
$$\delta v_{zl} = \delta\dot{h}.$$

Can be easily verified, starting from the expressions of R_λ andR_ϕ, that is valid the formula:

$$\frac{\partial R_\lambda}{\partial \phi} \cos\phi = R_\lambda \cdot \sin\phi - R_\phi \cdot \sin\phi. \tag{80}$$

Thus, relations (78) and (79) become:

$$\delta\dot{x}_l = (R_\lambda + h) \cdot \cos\phi \cdot \delta\dot{\lambda} - (R_\phi + h) \cdot \sin\phi \cdot \dot{\phi} \cdot \delta\lambda + \cos\phi \cdot \dot{h} \cdot \delta\lambda,$$
$$\delta\dot{y}_l = \frac{\partial R_\phi}{\partial \phi} \cdot \dot{\phi} \cdot \delta\phi + (R_\phi + h) \cdot \delta\dot{\phi} + \dot{h} \cdot \delta\phi, \tag{81}$$
$$\delta\dot{z}_l = \delta\dot{h}$$

and

$$\delta v_{xl} = (R_\lambda + h) \cdot \cos\phi \cdot \delta\dot{\lambda} - (R_\phi + h) \cdot \sin\phi \cdot \dot{\lambda} \cdot \delta\phi + \cos\phi \cdot \dot{\lambda} \cdot \delta h,$$
$$\delta v_{yl} = \frac{\partial R_\phi}{\partial \phi} \cdot \dot{\phi} \cdot \delta\phi + (R_\phi + h) \cdot \delta\dot{\phi} + \dot{\phi} \cdot \delta h, \tag{82}$$
$$\delta v_{zl} = \delta\dot{h},$$

from where we obtain:

$$\delta\dot{x}_l = \delta v_{xl} - (R_\phi + h) \cdot \sin\phi \cdot [\dot{\phi} \cdot \delta\lambda - \dot{\lambda} \cdot \delta\phi] + \cos\phi \cdot [\dot{h} \cdot \delta\lambda - \dot{\lambda} \cdot \delta h],$$
$$\delta\dot{y}_l = \delta v_{yl} + \dot{h} \cdot \delta\phi - \dot{\phi} \cdot \delta h, \tag{83}$$
$$\delta\dot{z}_l = \delta v_{zl}.$$

One observes that the derivative of the position error on the vertical channel is equal with the speed error.

If we denote:

$$[\vec{p}]_l = [\delta p_x,\ \delta p_y,\ \delta p_z]^T = [-\delta\phi,\ \cos\hat{\phi} \cdot \delta\lambda,\ \sin\hat{\phi} \cdot \delta\lambda]^T, \tag{84}$$

then:

$$[\vec{p}\times\vec{v}]_l=\begin{bmatrix}\cos\phi\cdot\dot{h}\cdot\delta\lambda-(R_\phi+h)\cdot\sin\phi\cdot\dot{\phi}\cdot\delta\lambda\\(R_\lambda+h)\cdot\sin\phi\cdot\cos\phi\cdot\dot{\lambda}\cdot\delta\lambda+\dot{h}\cdot\delta\phi\\-(R_\phi+h)\cdot\dot{\phi}\cdot\delta\phi-(R_\lambda+h)\cdot\cos^2\phi\cdot\dot{\lambda}\cdot\delta\lambda\end{bmatrix}. \tag{85}$$

Also, having in mind the expressions for the angular speed components relative to the ECEF frame $\vec{\omega}_r$ in ENU frame (eq. (14)), it results:

$$[\vec{\omega}_r\times\delta\vec{r}']_l=\begin{bmatrix}\cos\phi\cdot\dot{\lambda}\cdot\delta h-(R_\phi+h)\cdot\sin\phi\cdot\dot{\lambda}\cdot\delta\phi\\(R_\lambda+h)\cdot\sin\phi\cdot\cos\phi\cdot\dot{\lambda}\cdot\delta\lambda+\dot{\phi}\cdot\delta h\\-(R_\phi+h)\cdot\dot{\phi}\cdot\delta\phi-(R_\lambda+h)\cdot\cos^2\phi\cdot\dot{\lambda}\cdot\delta\lambda\end{bmatrix} \tag{86}$$

and, from there:

$$[\vec{p}\times\vec{v}]_l-[\vec{\omega}_r\times\delta\vec{r}']_l=\begin{bmatrix}\cos\phi\cdot(\dot{h}\cdot\delta\lambda-\dot{\lambda}\cdot\delta h)-(R_\phi+h)\cdot\sin\phi\cdot(\dot{\phi}\cdot\delta\lambda-\dot{\lambda}\cdot\delta\phi)\\\dot{h}\cdot\delta\phi-\dot{\phi}\cdot\delta h\\0\end{bmatrix}. \tag{87}$$

With the notation:

$$[\delta\vec{\dot{r}}']_l=[\delta\dot{x}_l,\ \delta\dot{y}_l,\ \delta\dot{z}_l], \tag{88}$$

the equation characterizing the evolution in time of the positioning error (eq. (83)) becomes:

$$[\delta\vec{\dot{r}}']_l=[\delta\vec{v}]_l+[\vec{p}\times\vec{v}]_l-[\vec{\omega}_r\times\delta\vec{r}']_l. \tag{89}$$

In conclusion, the error model of the navigation algorithm in terrestrial non-inertial reference frames by using attitude matrices is described by next equations:

$$\begin{cases}[\dot{\vec{\Phi}}]_l=-[\vec{\omega}_l\times\vec{\Phi}]_l-(\hat{R}_l^v)^T\cdot[\delta\vec{\omega}_v]_v+[\delta\vec{\omega}_l]_l,\\[\delta\dot{\vec{v}}]_l=-[\vec{\Phi}]_l\times[\vec{f}]_v+\hat{R}_v^l\cdot[\delta\vec{f}]_v+[\delta\vec{g}_a]_l-[(\vec{\omega}_l+\vec{\Omega})\times\delta\vec{v}]_l-[(\delta\vec{\omega}_l+\delta\vec{\Omega})\times\vec{v}]_l,\\[\delta\vec{\dot{r}}']_l=[\delta\vec{v}]_l+[\vec{p}\times\vec{v}]_l-[\vec{\omega}_r\times\delta\vec{r}']_l.\end{cases} \tag{90}$$

http://dx.doi.org/10.5772/57583

The resulting model consists of a system of coupled differential equations and contains nine variables: three variables are errors in the determination of the attitude angles ($\delta\phi$, $\delta\theta$, $\delta\psi$), three variables are errors in the determination of the speed (δv_{xl}, δv_{yl}, δv_{zl}), and three variables are errors in determination of the position (δx_l, δy_l, δz_l). The input variables of the model are the errors of the six inertial sensors used in the strap-down inertial navigation system. In addition to the nine variables, in the error model are involved the global positioning errors of the vehicle$\delta\lambda$, $\delta\phi$, δh, linking the nine differential equations. Numerical integration of the error model is rather difficult due to the couplings between its equations, but also due to the time evolution considered for inertial sensors errors. It can be performed, however, some numerical simulations, for different sources of error affecting the inertial sensors, in order to highlight their influence on the final errors of the navigation algorithm.

4. Numerical simulations

The validation of the navigation algorithm and of its error model is achieved by building Matlab/Simulink models for them followed by numerical simulation of these models for several navigation particular cases.

Following is conducted a study of the dependence of the inertial navigator outputs errors by the errors of the used inertial sensors. For this purpose, the Matlab/Simulink models built for acceleration and gyro sensors are used; on the inertial navigator inputs are considered three miniaturized optical integrated accelerometers (MOEMS) and three fiber optic gyros with the associated errors according to their data sheets. Due to the fact that the accelerometer and gyro software developed models allow users to work independently with each sensor error in the theoretical model, are studied the influences of the noise, bias and scale factor sensors errors on the navigation solution components. Simulations are performed for three different navigation cases, the vehicle having the same initial position in all three cases: 1) the vehicle is immobile, 2) the vehicle runs at 0.1 g acceleration on the *x*-axis, 3) The vehicle is subjected to turning with angular velocity 0.1 degree/s, while running on the track with acceleration 0.1 g along x-axis, which means the sensing of an acceleration of-0.0516 m/s^2 (-0.0053 g) along *y*-axis.

Thus, starting from the navigation algorithm block scheme in Fig. 3 the Matlab/Simulink model in Fig. 4 is obtained. Also, the software implementation of the navigator error model leads to the Matlab/Simulink model in Fig. 5.

With these two models it results the validation model in Fig. 6; "REAL" and "IDEAL" are blocks modelling the navigation algorithm (as in Fig. 4), having as inputs accelerations and angular speeds signals disturbed by the errors of strap-down inertial sensors, respectively un-disturbed by the errors of strap-down inertial sensors. "ERROR" is a block by the form in Fig. 5. The input blocks "Acc" and "Gyro" are accelerometers and gyros models as in Fig. 1 and Fig. 2, and theirs outputs are applied to the "REAL" block. The values of the input constants are considered to be ideal signals, un-disturbed by the acceleration and rotation sensors, these being applied to the "IDEAL" block.

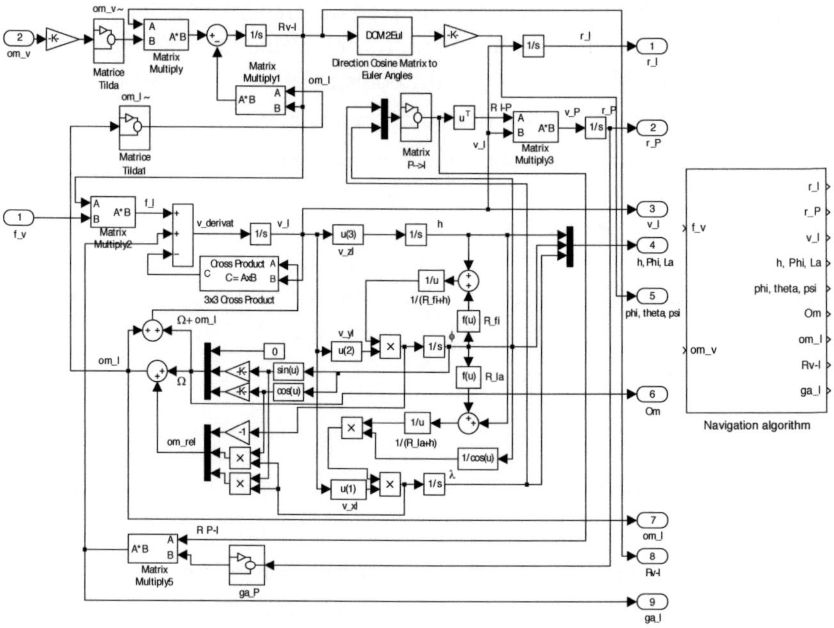

Figure 4. Matlab/Simulink model of the navigation algorithm.

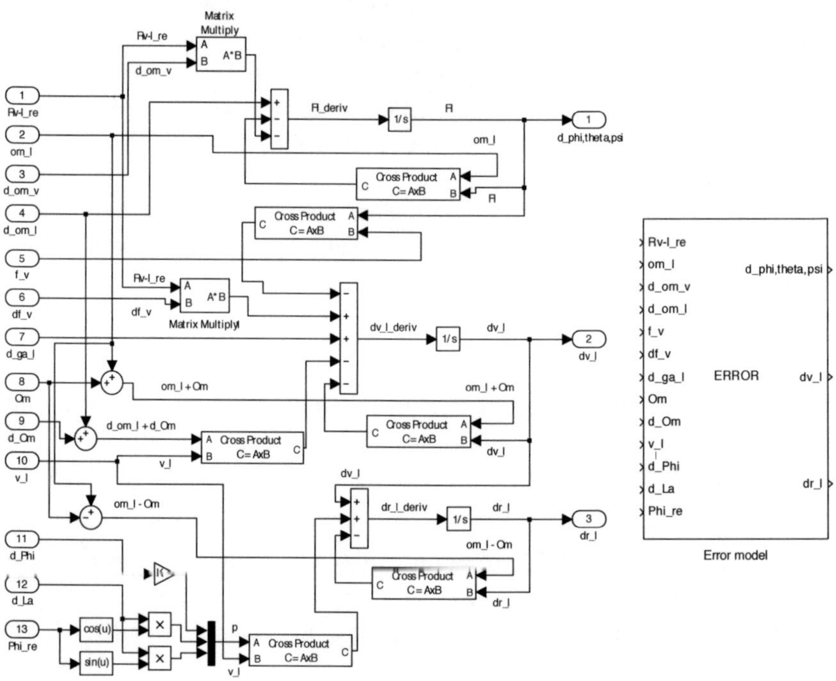

Figure 5. Matlab/Simulink implementation of the inertial navigator error model.

The error model validation is realized through the comparison of the differences between the outputs of the "IDEAL" and "REAL" blocks with the outputs of the error model. In Fig. 7 a. are depicted the attitude angles errors, the first column containing the differences between the outputs of the "IDEAL" and "REAL" blocks, and the second column-the outputs of the error model. In the same mode are built Fig. 7 b. (for the positioning errors in ENU reference frame) and Fig. 7 c. (for the speed errors in ENU reference frame).

The reading errors of the accelerometers (δf_{xv}, δf_{yv}, δf_{zv}) and of the gyros ($\delta \omega_{xv}$, $\delta \omega_{yv}$, $\delta \omega_{zv}$) applied at the error model inputs are presented in Fig. 8. For the accelerometers were neglected the effects of the cross-axis accelerations, while for the gyros were neglected the effects of the sensitivity to the accelerations; the data for three miniaturized optical integrated accelerometers (MOEMS) and three fiber optic gyros were used in sensors models.

The un-disturbed inputs were null on all rotation axes and on the x and y axes of acceleration, while for the z channel of acceleration the input was the local gravitational acceleration.

Analysing the error curves in all of the three parts of Fig. 7 can be easily concluded that the allures of the curves in the first columns are similarly with the allures of the curves in the second columns. As a consequence, the error model described by the equations (90) characterizes precisely the deviations of the attitude angles, and of the vehicle coordinates and speeds in ENU frame from their right values, free of the inertial sensors errors influence. On the other way, we can observe that the errors appearing in the altitude channel are much bigger than the errors in the two horizontal channels, and the attitude angles errors are comparable as values in all of the three channels, having an oscillatory behaviour.

For the next steps of the numerical study, just the outputs of the error model in Fig. 6 are considered. As we already mention, simulations are performed for three different navigation cases, starting from the same initial position: 1) the vehicle is immobile, 2) the vehicle runs at 0.1 g acceleration in the North (x-axis) 3) The vehicle is subjected to turning with angular velocity 0.1 degree/s, while running on the track with acceleration 0.1 g along x-axis, which means the sensing of an acceleration of-0.0516 m/s^2 (-0.0053 g) along y-axis.

For the first case, the curves in Fig. 9 are obtained and the absolute maximal values of the attitude, position and speed errors in Table 1.

According to the graphical characteristics and to the numerical results presented in Table 1, the errors of the accelerometers and gyros scale factors have an insignificant weight in the increase of the attitude angles errors, accelerometers biases cause an increase with 0.26% percent of the roll and pitch angles errors and not affect the yaw angle error, and gyros biases have important weights in all attitude angles errors, producing an increase with 76.78% in roll angle error, with 95.52% in the pitch angle error and with 149.5% in the yaw angle error. Considering simultaneously the biases and scale factor errors at accelerometers produces an increase with 0.2432% of the error in the roll channel and with 0.26% in the pitch channel, while the error in the yaw channel in approximately constant. Can be observed that the combination of the two accelerometers errors with the noise has beneficial effects in the roll channel by

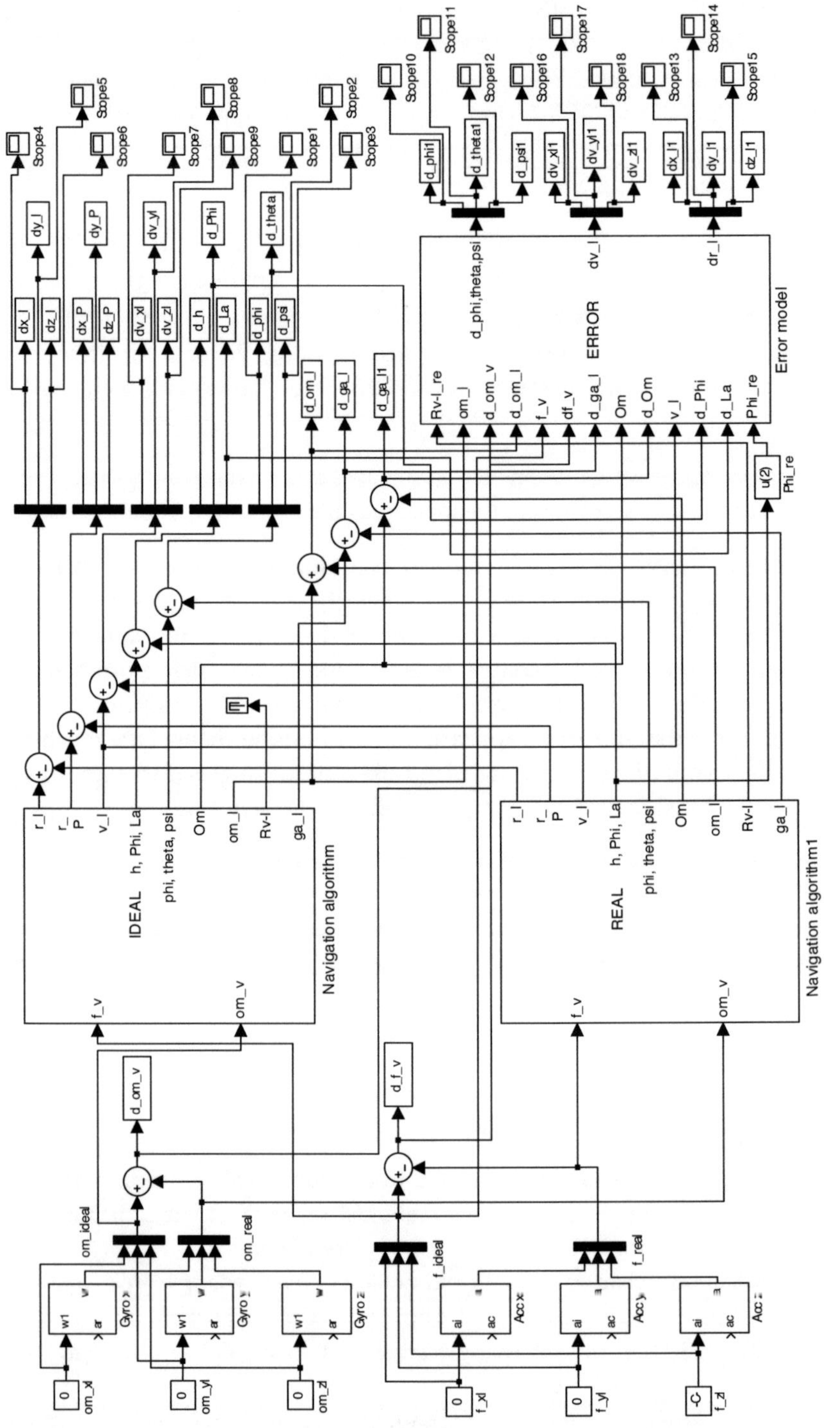

Figure 6. Matlab/Simulink validation model.

http://dx.doi.org/10.5772/57583

limiting the growth of error, compared to the situation in which is present only the bias. Proceeding similar for the gyros, the effect of the simultaneous considering of bias and scale factor errors is reflected by an increase with 76.77% of the error in the roll channel, with 95.52% in the pitch channel and with 149.5% in the yaw channel. Analysing the results obtained when all errors of the inertial sensors in IMU are taken into account, can be noticed an increase with 77.02% of the roll angle error, with 96.12% of the pitch angle error and with 149.5% of the yaw angle error. As a conclusion, the attitude angles errors are decisive influenced by the gyros biases (the strongest in the yaw channel), in a small degree by the accelerometers biases (in the roll and pitch channels) and negligible by the accelerometers and gyros scale factor errors.

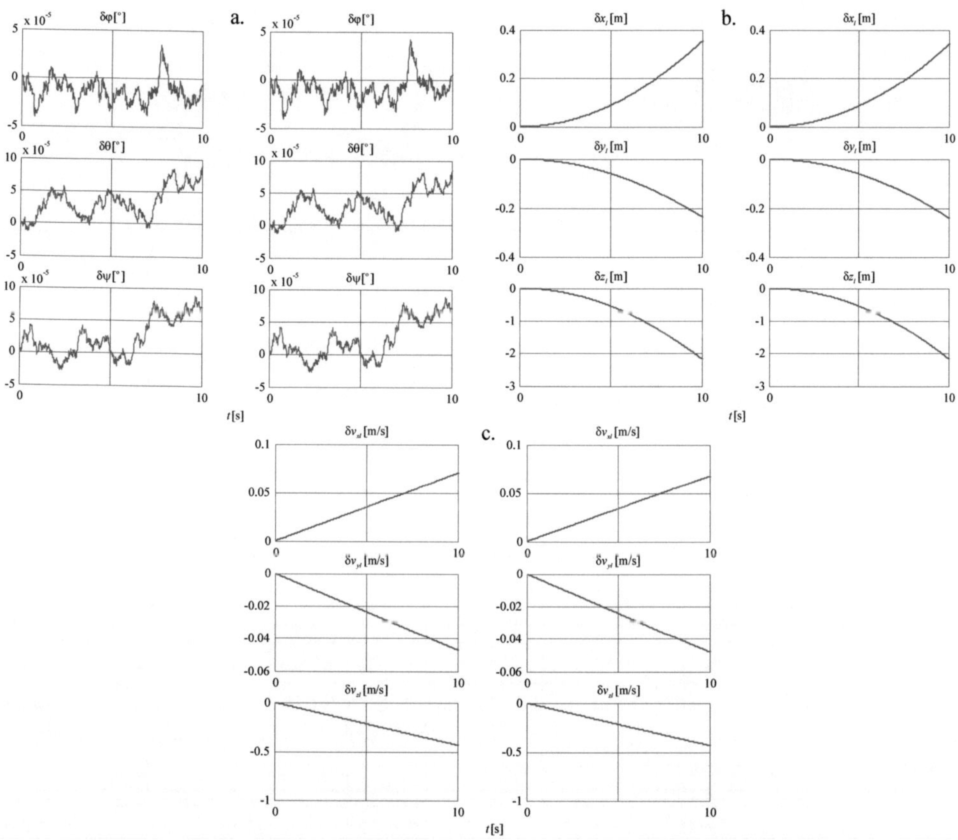

Figure 7. Errors of attitude angles, positioning and speed at validation.

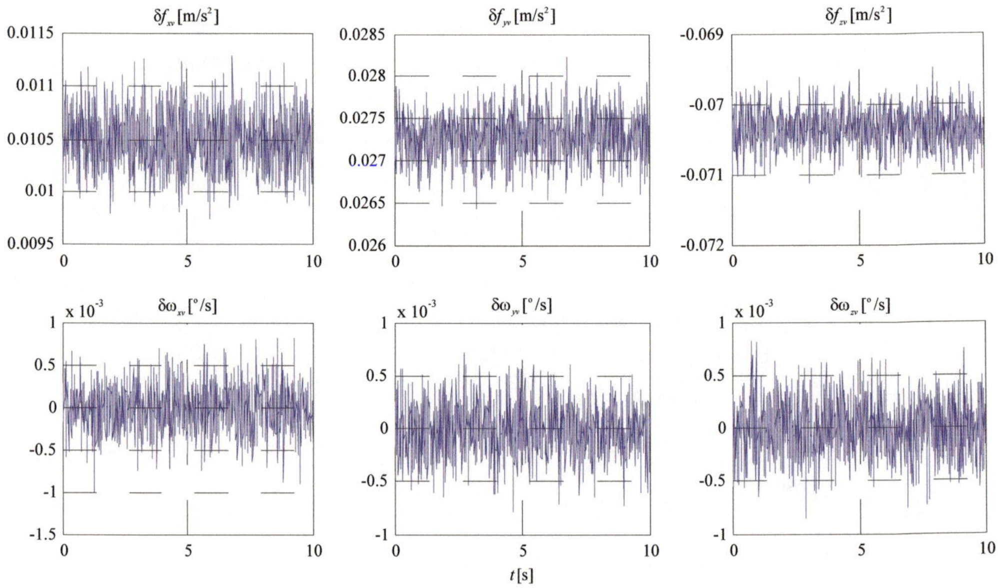

Figure 8. Reading errors of the accelerometers and of the gyros.

Sensors errors	Attitude angles errors [°]			Position errors [m]			Speed errors [m/s]		
	$\delta\varphi$	$\delta\theta$	$\delta\psi$	δx_l	δy_l	δz_l	δv_{xl}	δv_{yl}	δv_{zl}
All null (just noise)	$3.6132\cdot10^{-4}$	$1.5614\cdot10^{-4}$	$1.5281\cdot10^{-4}$	1.0329	2.0788	17.6175	0.0321	0.0984	0.5878
$B_{Acc}\neq0$	$3.6226\cdot10^{-4}$	$1.5654\cdot10^{-4}$	$1.5281\cdot10^{-4}$	11.688	6.4823	28.2643	0.3937	0.1876	0.943
$\Delta K_{Acc}\neq0$	$3.6132\cdot10^{-4}$	$1.5614\cdot10^{-4}$	$1.5281\cdot10^{-4}$	1.033	2.079	67.0058	0.0321	0.0984	2.2356
$B_{Acc}\neq0$ & $\Delta K_{Acc}\neq0$	$3.6221\cdot10^{-4}$	$1.5654\cdot10^{-4}$	$1.5281\cdot10^{-4}$	11.6629	6.3902	77.6825	0.3929	0.1846	2.5918
$B_{Giro}\neq0$	$6.3875\cdot10^{-4}$	$3.0529\cdot10^{-4}$	$3.8127\cdot10^{-4}$	2.503	4.0711	17.6175	0.1028	0.1981	0.5878
$\Delta K_{Giro}\neq0$	$3.6132\cdot10^{-4}$	$1.5614\cdot10^{-4}$	$1.5281\cdot10^{-4}$	1.0328	2.0788	17.6175	0.0321	0.0984	0.5878
$B_{Giro}\neq0$ & $\Delta K_{Giro}\neq0$	$6.3874\cdot10^{-4}$	$3.0529\cdot10^{-4}$	$3.8127\cdot10^{-4}$	2.503	4.0711	17.6175	0.1028	0.1981	0.5878
All non-null	$6.3964\cdot10^{-4}$	$3.0623\cdot10^{-4}$	$3.8127\cdot10^{-4}$	10.1927	4.3979	77.6825	0.3195	0.0981	2.5918

Table 1. Absolute maximal values of the attitude, position and speed errors for first navigation case.

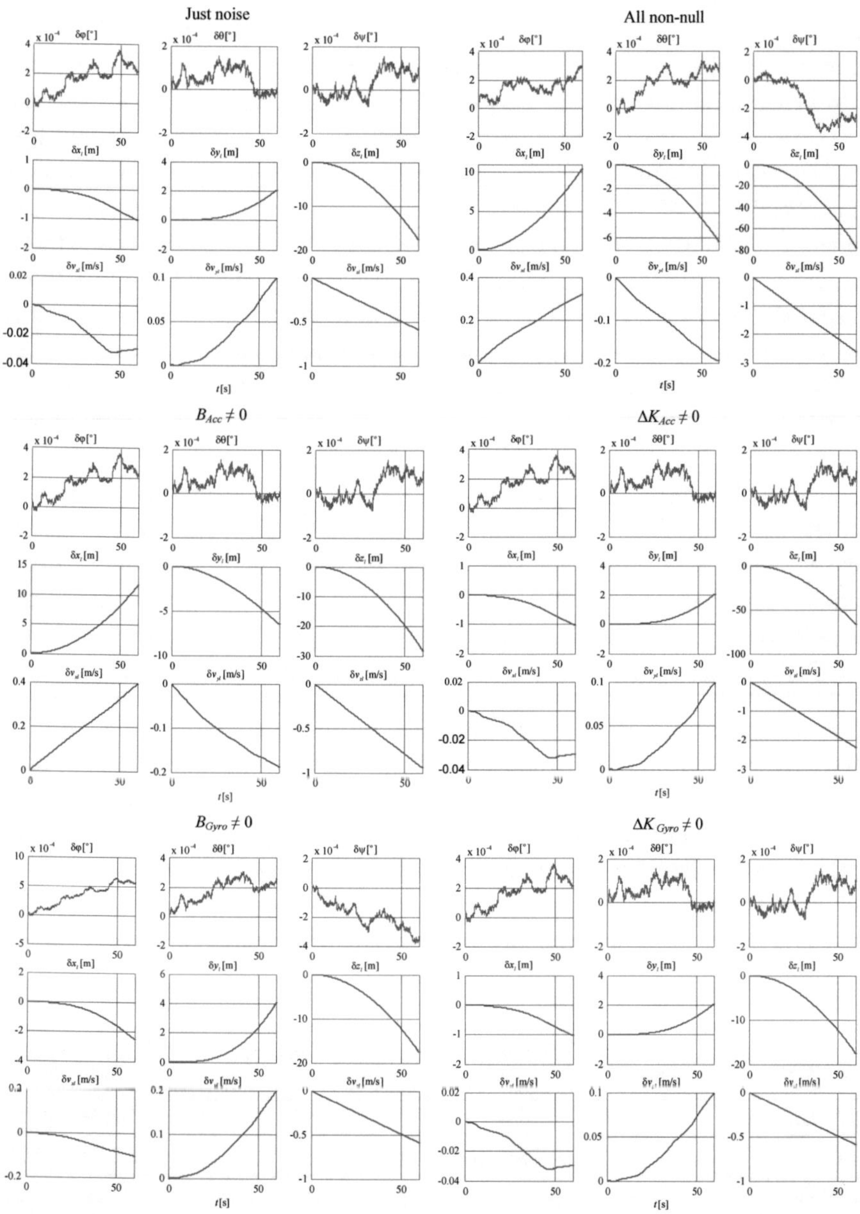

Figure 9. Simulation results for the first navigation case.

Regarding the positioning errors we can observe that: the scale factor error of gyros does not produce any increase in the errors of the three channels; the accelerometers scale factor error influences negligible the errors increase in the horizontal channels (with 0.00968% in x channel and with 0.00962% in y channel) and influences strongly the increase of the vertical channel error (with 280.33%); the accelerometers bias influences strongly the increase of the errors in horizontal channels (with 1031.57% in x channel and with 211.82% in y channel) and with 60.43% in the vertical channel; the gyros bias does not affect the error in vertical channel but has an important influence regarding the increase of the errors in horizontal channels (with 142.32% in x channel and with 94.39% in y channel); the simultaneous considering of the bias and of the scale factor error for the accelerometers has as result an increase of the error with 1029.14% in x channel, with 207.39% in y channel and with 340.93% in vertical channel (it is noted a beneficial effect of the combination of the two errors in the presence of noise, but only in the horizontal channels, in the vertical channel a negative effect is achieved in this regard); the simultaneous considering of the bias and of the scale factor error for the gyros has as result an increase of the error with 142.32% in x channel and with 94.39% in y channel, and does not affect the value of the error in vertical channel; the simultaneous considering of all errors of the inertial sensors in IMU leads to the errors increases with 886.8% in x channel, with 111.55% in y channel and with 340.93% in vertical channel (it is noted a beneficial effect of the combination of all errors in the presence of noise, but only in the horizontal channels, in the vertical channel, keeping the results obtained when all errors of accelerometers were taken into account). Therefore, the positioning errors are negligibly influenced by the scale factor errors of the sensors in IMU, excepting a strong influence on the vertical channel induced by the accelerometers scale factor errors (280.33%), the accelerometers biases have strong influences on all channels (the biggest is on x channel (1031.57%)), and the gyros biases have strong influences on the horizontal channels while in the vertical channel theirs effects are negligible.

For the second navigation case, are considered the taxiing of aircraft in which it is mounted the inertial navigator, starting from the same initial position and the same conditions of speed and attitude as in the first case, with the acceleration of 0.1 g along the x axis. With this case the aim is to study the influence of sensor errors in the navigator errors when on one of the horizontal axis of the accelerometer is applied a non-zero acceleration. By performing numerical simulations for the same cases of influence of sensor errors, the absolute maximal values of the navigator errors in Table 2 and the graphical characteristics in Fig. 10 are obtained.

Sensors errors	Attitude angles errors [°]			Position errors [m]		
	$\delta\varphi$	$\delta\theta$	$\delta\psi$	δx_l	δy_l	δz_l
All null (just noise)	$3.6130\cdot10^{-4}$	$1.5608\cdot10^{-4}$	$1.5284\cdot10^{-4}$	2.7912	2.0834	17.5142
$B_{Acc}\neq0$	$3.6220\cdot10^{-4}$	$1.5649\cdot10^{-4}$	$1.5284\cdot10^{-4}$	9.9327	6.4778	28.1575
$\Delta K_{Acc}\neq0$	$3.6130\cdot10^{-4}$	$1.5619\cdot10^{-4}$	$1.5284\cdot10^{-4}$	0.7522	2.068	66.9016
$B_{Acc}\neq0$ & $\Delta K_{Acc}\neq0$	$3.6220\cdot10^{-4}$	$1.5660\cdot10^{-4}$	$1.5284\cdot10^{-4}$	13.4510	6.4012	77.5747
$B_{Giro}\neq0$	$6.3879\cdot10^{-4}$	$3.0516\cdot10^{-4}$	$3.8113\cdot10^{-4}$	4.2608	4.3299	17.3668
$\Delta K_{Giro}\neq0$	$3.6130\cdot10^{-4}$	$1.5608\cdot10^{-4}$	$1.5284\cdot10^{-4}$	2.7912	2.0834	17.5142
$B_{Giro}\neq0$ & $\Delta K_{Giro}\neq0$	$6.3879\cdot10^{-4}$	$3.0516\cdot10^{-4}$	$3.8113\cdot10^{-4}$	4.2608	4.3299	17.3668
All non-null	$6.3969\cdot10^{-4}$	$3.0636\cdot10^{-4}$	$3.8113\cdot10^{-4}$	11.9814	4.1546	77.4273

Table 2. Absolute maximal values of the attitude and position errors for the second navigation case.

http://dx.doi.org/10.5772/57583

Comparing the numerical results in Table 2 with those in Table 1 it can be seen that the percentage of errors influences are almost the same, the only noticeable change being that of accelerometers and gyros biases effect on the positioning error in x channel.

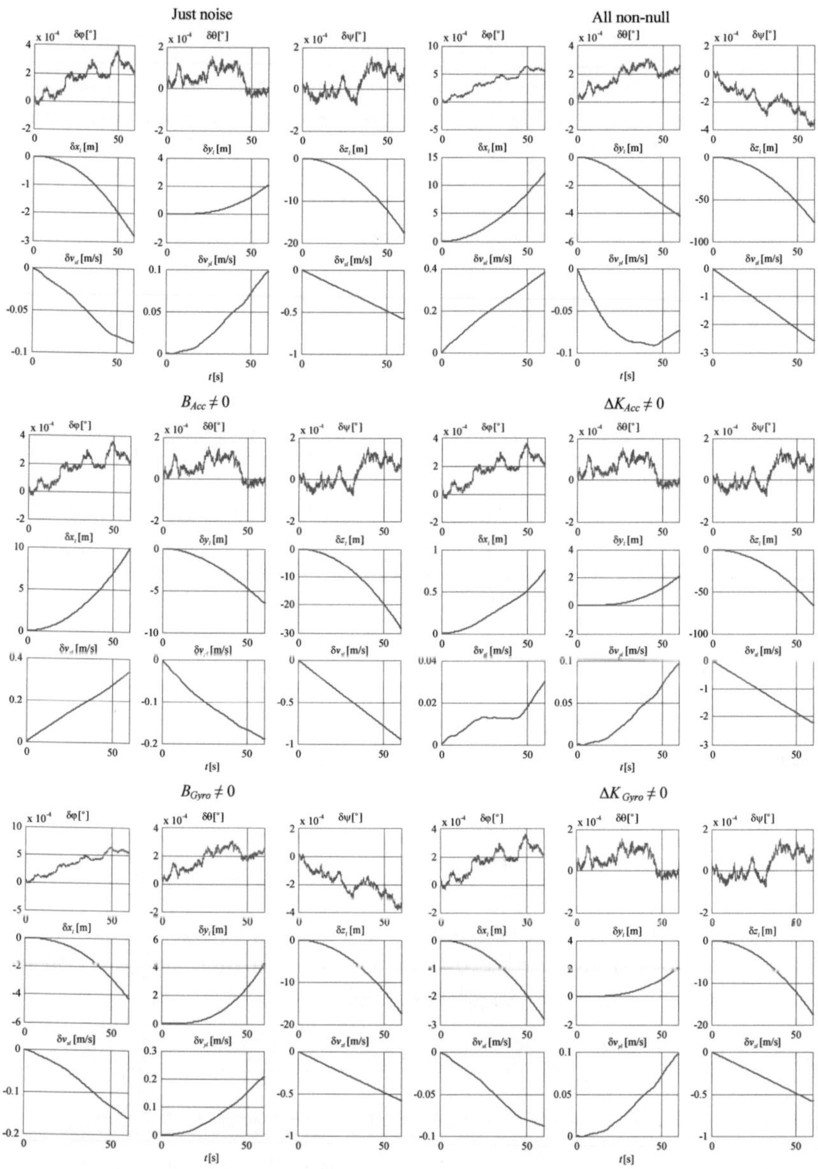

Figure 10. Simulation results for the second navigation case.

It notes, also, the effect of non-zero entry in acceleration, on the x axis of the navigator, on the change of the weights held by the accelerometers scale factor errors in the calculus of the position errors.

Subjecting the vehicle to a gyration angular speed of 0.1°/s, while running on the track with the acceleration 0.1 g along the *x* axis, it has a change of the heading angle of 6 degrees after 1 min and a lateral deviation of 185.4039 m a distance of 1764 m on the East direction. Because the speed is close to the take-off limit, the motion is equivalent to the horizontal movement on a circular arc with a radius of about 16.907 km, which means the sensing of an acceleration of-0.0516 m/s² (-0.0053 g) along the *y* axis of the vehicle. Considering the same initial conditions as in the two previous cases, the graphical characteristics of the errors obtained through the numerical simulation are given in Fig. 11, while the absolute maximal values of the navigator errors are shown in Table 3.

Sensors errors	Attitude angles errors [°]			Position errors [m]		
	$\delta\varphi$	$\delta\theta$	$\delta\psi$	δx_l	δy_l	δz_l
All null (just noise)	$3.6773 \cdot 10^{-4}$	$1.6036 \cdot 10^{-4}$	$1.5284 \cdot 10^{-4}$	2.8475	2.1074	17.4978
$B_{Acc} \neq 0$	$3.6823 \cdot 10^{-4}$	$1.6078 \cdot 10^{-4}$	$1.5284 \cdot 10^{-4}$	10.1635	6.0022	28.1410
$\Delta K_{Acc} \neq 0$	$3.6749 \cdot 10^{-4}$	$1.6048 \cdot 10^{-4}$	$1.5284 \cdot 10^{-4}$	0.7238	1.2121	66.8852
$B_{Acc} \neq 0$ & $\Delta K_{Acc} \neq 0$	$3.6832 \cdot 10^{-4}$	$1.6088 \cdot 10^{-4}$	$1.5284 \cdot 10^{-4}$	13.7066	6.8065	77.5581
$B_{Giro} \neq 0$	$6.3662 \cdot 10^{-4}$	$3.1738 \cdot 10^{-4}$	$3.8113 \cdot 10^{-4}$	4.3550	4.3143	17.3350
$\Delta K_{Giro} \neq 0$	$3.6737 \cdot 10^{-4}$	$1.6036 \cdot 10^{-4}$	$1.4694 \cdot 10^{-4}$	2.8472	2.1125	17.4978
$B_{Giro} \neq 0$ & $\Delta K_{Giro} \neq 0$	$6.3662 \cdot 10^{-4}$	$3.1738 \cdot 10^{-4}$	$3.8955 \cdot 10^{-4}$	4.3547	4.3194	17.335
All non-null	$6.3760 \cdot 10^{-4}$	$3.1860 \cdot 10^{-4}$	$3.8955 \cdot 10^{-4}$	12.1993	4.5943	77.3953

Table 3. Absolute maximal values of the attitude and position errors for the third navigation case.

From the graphic and numeric results, it is found the maintaining approximately constant of the final percentages of influence in the navigator error even if the acceleration is not zero in the all three axes of the vehicle, and the angular speed is non-zero on the *z* axis. Also, can be observed the exercise of a stronger influence on the navigator *y* axis by the scale factor error of accelerometer *y*, even the acceleration applied to this axis is the smallest. The big value of the percent (-42.84%) is due to the higher negative value of the scale factor error of accelerometer *y* (-1.08%) comparatively with the other two accelerometers (-0.2% on *x* axis, and 0.28% on *z* axis) (see Table 4). Having non-zero angular speed on the z axis, can be seen a small influence of gyros scale factor errors in yaw channel.

Sensors	Bias			Scale factor error		
	x Axis	*y* Axis	*z* Axis	*x* Axis	*y* Axis	*z* Axis
Gyros	$5.61 \cdot 10^{-6}$ °/s	$4.2 \cdot 10^{-6}$ °/s	$-7.2 \cdot 10^{-6}$ °/s	$-4.056 \cdot 10^{-4}$%	$-3.12 \cdot 10^{-4}$%	$-1.456 \cdot 10^{-4}$%
Acc.	-0.00709128 m/s²	0.00472752 m/s²	0.0059094 m/s²	−0.2 %	−1.08 %	0.28 %

Table 4. Bias and scale factor error for inertial sensors used in simulations.

Assessing the positioning errors in differences relative to the situation when it is considered only the sensors noise, it is observed that the influence of the sensors errors is approximately the same for the three simulated cases. The errors combining in the general case compared to particular cases, in which are studied the influences of each sensor error, is explained by positive and negative values of the parameters found in Table 4, but also by the crossings in the positive and negative area of the error characteristics in Fig. 9. Also, the high values of position errors in the vertical channel are due largely to the presence of 1g acceleration on the z axis of the navigator, amplifying in this way the errors of the accelerometer in this channel.

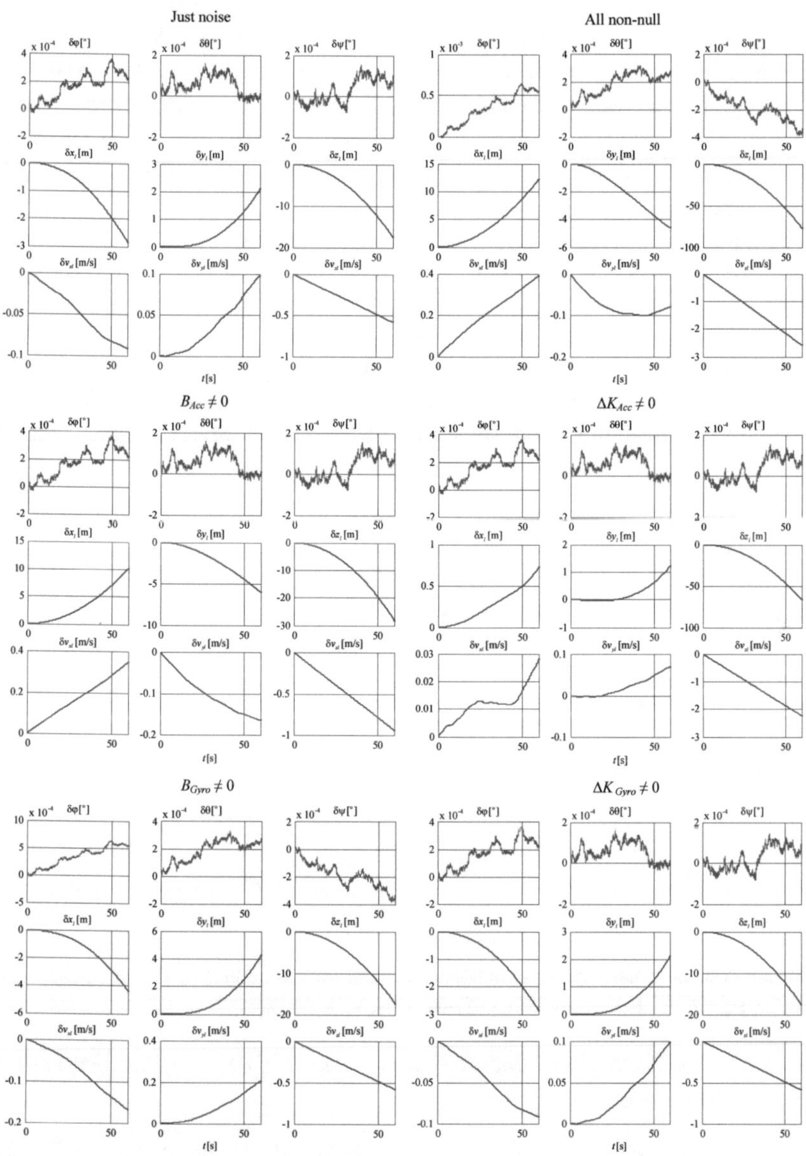

Figure 11. Simulation results for the third navigation case.

5. Conclusions

The numerical simulation of the influences of the inertial sensors errors on the solution of navigation of strap-down inertial navigator was here presented. To perform the simulations some Matlab/Simulink models for the acceleration and rotation sensors based on the sensors data sheets and on the IEEE equivalent models for the inertial sensors were realized. Also, the solving of a navigation problem relative to terrestrial non-inertial reference frames and the development of an error model for the navigator were achieved. The validation of the navigation algorithm and of its error model was realized by building Matlab/Simulink models for them, followed by numerical simulation of these models for several navigation particular cases. Following, a study of the dependence of the inertial navigator outputs errors by the errors of the used inertial sensors was conducted. Simulations were made for three different navigation cases, the vehicle having the same initial position in all three cases: 1) the vehicle is immobile, 2) the vehicle runs at 0.1 g acceleration on the x-axis, 3) The vehicle is subjected to turning with angular velocity 0.1 degree/s, while running on the track with acceleration 0.1 g along x-axis, which means the sensing of an acceleration of-0.0516 m/s2 (-0.0053 g) along y-axis.

The methodology presented here can be used successfully to estimate the effects of the sensors errors on the solution of navigation precision since in the design phase of the inertial navigator, without a prior acquisition of inertial sensors, and based only on their data sheet.

Author details

Teodor Lucian Grigorie[1] and Ruxandra Mihaela Botez[2]

1 University of Craiova, Romania

2 École de Technologie Supérieure, Canada

References

[1] Bekir, E. (2007). *Introduction to Modern Navigation Systems,* World Scientific Publishing Co. Pte. Ltd., ISBN-10: 9812707662, USA, 2007

[2] Bose, P. (2008). *Modern Inertial Sensors and Systems,* Prentice-Hall, ISBN-13: 978-8120333536, India, 2008

[3] Barbour, N., Hopkins, R., Kourepenis, A. & Ward, P. (2010). Inertial MEMS System Applications, NATO RTO Lecture Series, RTO-EN-SET-116, Low-Cost Navigation Sensors and Integration Technology, March 2010

[4] Barbour, N. & Schmidt, G. (2001) Inertial Sensor Technology Trends, *IEEE Sensors Journal*, Vol. 1, No. 4, pp. 332-339, 2001

[5] Barbour, N. (2010). Inertial Navigation Sensors, NATO RTO Lecture Series, RTO-EN-SET-116, Low-Cost Navigation Sensors and Integration Technology, March 2010

[6] Dahia, K. (2005). *Nouveles methodes en filtrage particulaire. Application au recalage de navigation inertielle par mesures altimetriques*, Office National d'Etudes et de Recherches A ´erospatiales (ONERA), Universite Joseph Fourier, These du Doctorat, France, 4 Jan. 2005

[7] Divakaruni, S. & Sanders S. (2006). Fiber optic gyros – a compelling choice for high accuracy applications, 18th International Conference on Optical Fiber Sensors, Cancun, Mexico, October 2006

[8] Dumke, R. & Mueller, T. (2010). Technology with Cold Atoms. *Innovation*, Vol. 9, No. 2, 2010

[9] Edu, I.R., Obreja, R. & Grigorie, T.L. (2011). Current technologies and trends in the development of gyros used in navigation applications – a review, Conference on Communications and Information Technology (CIT-2011), July, 14-16, Corfu, Greece, pp. 63-68, 2011

[10] Farrell, J. (2008). *Aided Navigation: GPS with High Rate Sensors*, McGraw-Hill, ISBN: 978-0-07-149329-1, USA, 2008

[11] Grewal, M. S., Andrews, A. P. & Bartone, C. (2013). *Global navigation satellite systems, inertial navigation, and integration*, John Wiley & Sons, ISBN-13: 978-1118447000, USA, 2013

[12] Grigorie, T. L., Hiliuta, A., Botez, R. M., Aron, I. (2006). Étude numérique et expérimentale d'un algorithme d'attitude pour un système inertiel à composantes liés. *Transactions of the Canadian Society of the Mechanical Engineering (CSME)*, Vol. 30(3), pp. 429-442, ISSN: 0315-8977, 2006

[13] Grigorie, T. L. (2007). *Strap-Down Inertial Navigation Systems. Optimization studies*. Sitech, ISBN: 978-973-746-723-2, Craiova, Romania, 2007

[14] Grigorie, T. L., Lungu, M., Edu, I. R. & Obreja, R. (2010 a). Concepts for error modeling of miniature accelerometers used in inertial navigation systems, *Annals of the University of Craiova, Electrical Engineering series*, Vol. 34, pp. 212-219, ISSN: 1842-4805, 2010

[15] Grigorie, T. L., Lungu, M., Edu, I. R. & Obreja, R. (2010 b). Concepts for error modeling of miniature gyros used in inertial navigation systems, Proceedings of the IEEE International Conference on Mechanical Engineering, Robotics and Aerospace (ICMERA 2010), Bucharest, Romania, December 2-4, 2010

[16] Grigorie, T. L., Lungu, M., Edu, I. R. & Obreja, R. (2010 c). Analysis of the Miniaturized Inertial Sensors Stochastic Errors with the Allan Variance Method: A Review,

Proceedings of the International Conference of Aerospace Sciences "AEROSPATIAL 2010", Section 5, pp. 1-10, ISSN 2067-8622, Bucharest, 20-21 October, 2010

[17] Grigorie, T. L., Botez, R. M., Lungu, M., Edu, I. R. & Obreja, R. (2012 a). MEMS Gyro Performance Improvement through Bias Correction over Temperature using an Adaptive Neural Network trained Fuzzy Inference System, *Proceedings of the Institution of Mechanical Engineers, Part G: Journal of Aerospace Engineering*, September 2012, Vol. 226(9), pp. 1121-1138, ISSN: 0954-4100, 2012

[18] Grigorie, T. L., Obreja, R., Sandu, D. G., Corcau, J. I. (2012 b). Allan variance analysis of the miniaturized sensors in a strap-down inertial measurement unit, 12th International Multidisciplinary Scientific GeoConference - SGEM2012, ISSN 1314-2704, Vol. 3, pp. 443 – 450, June 17-23, 2012

[19] Hopkins, R., Barbour, N., Gustafson, D.E. & Sherman, P. (2010). Miniature Inertial and Augmentation Sensors for Integrated Inertial/GPS Based Navigation Applications, NATO RTO Lecture Series, RTO-EN-SET-116, Low-Cost Navigation Sensors and Integration Technology, March 2010

[20] Kraft, M. (2000). Micromachined inertial sensors: The state-of-the-art and a look into the future, *Meas. Control*, vol. 33, no. 6, pp.164 -168, 2000

[21] KVH Industries Inc. (2007). *An update on KVH fiber optic gyros and their benefits relative to other gyro technologies*, March 2007

[22] Lawrence, A. (1998). *Modern Inertial Technology: Navigation, Guidance and Control* – Second Edition, Springer Verlag, New York, ISBN: 978-1-4612-7258-8, 1998

[23] Pavlath, G. (2006). Fiber Optic Gyros: The Vision Realized, 18th International Conference on Optical Fiber Sensors, Cancun, Mexico, October 2006

[24] Radix, J.C. (1993). *Systemes inertiels a composants lies <<Strap-Down>>, Cepadues-Editions*, Ecole Nationale Superieure de l'Aeronautique et de l'Espace SUP'AERO, Toulouse, France

[25] Salychev, O. S. (1998). *Inertial Systems in Navigation and Geophysics*, Bauman MSTU Press, ISBN: 5703813468, Moscow, Russia, 1998

[26] Savage, P. G. (2000). *Strapdown Analytics, Part 1.* Strapdown Associates, Inc., ISBN: 9780971778603, USA, 2000

[27] Schmidt, G. (2010). INS/GPS Technology Trends, NATO RTO Lecture Series, RTO-EN-SET-116, Low-Cost Navigation Sensors and Integration Technology, March 2010

[28] Tawney, J., et al. (2006). Photonic Crystal Fiber IFOGs, Optical Society of America 18th International Conference on Optical Fiber Sensors, Cancun, Mexico, October 2006

[29] Titterton, D. H. & Weston, J. (2004). *Strapdown inertial navigation technology - 2nd Edition*, Institution of Engineering and Technology, ISBN: 0 863413587, USA, 2004.

Chapter 12

Tool of the Complete Optimal Control for Variable Speed Electrical Drives

Marian Gaiceanu

Additional information is available at the end of the chapter

http://dx.doi.org/10.5772/57521

1. Introduction

The main objective of the chapter is to use Matlab software in order to develop the optimal control knowledge in relation to the biggest worldwide power consumers: electrical machines. These two major components, optimal control and electrical machines form an optimal drive system. The proposed drive system conducts to the energy efficiency increasing during transient regimes (starting, stopping and reversing), therefore reducing the impact upon the environment. Taking into account the world energy policies, the chapter is strategically oriented towards the compatibility with the priority requirements from world research programmes. This chapter will offer an original Matlab tool in order to implement a highly performant control for electrical drives. The optimal solution provided by the optimal problem is obtained by numerical integration of the matrix Riccati differential equation (MRDE). The proposed optimal control, based on energetic criterion, can be implemented on-line by using a real time experimental platform. The solution has three terms: the first term includes the reference state of the electrical drive system, the second term assures a fast compensation of the disturbance (i.e. the load torque in case of the electrical drives) by using feedforward control, and the third is the state feedback component. Therefore, there is a completed optimal control for linear dynamic systems. The simulation and experimental results will be provided. By using knowledge regarding the electrical machines, electrical and mechanical measurements, control theory, digital control, and real time implementation, a high degree of interdisciplinarity is obtained in the developed Matlab tool The optimal problem statement is without constraints; by choosing adequate weighting matrices, the magnitude constraints of control and of state variable are solved.

INTECH
open science | open minds

© 2014 The Author(s). Licensee InTech. This chapter is distributed under the terms of the Creative Commons Attribution License (http://creativecommons.org/licenses/by/3.0), which permits unrestricted use, distribution, and reproduction in any medium, provided the original work is properly cited.

Matlab is a widespread software used both in academia and research centres. The author of this chapter facilitates the easy understanding and implementation of the highly efficient electrical drive systems by using Matlab software. The energy problem is one of the most important aspects related to the sustainable growth of the industrial nations. On the one hand, the industrial systems and the increased quality of life require every year a higher quantity of electrical energy produced; on the other hand, the same quality of life requires the generation and the harnessing of this energy with low pollution.

On the one hand, the electrical machines are the main worldwide energy consumer (Siemens), (Tamimi, *et al.*, 2006). Therefore, the focus of the research on this system type is essential in order to minimize the energetical losses. A seemingly insignificant reduction of electricity consumed by each electrical motor has particularly important consequences at national/international level, primarily by reducing consumption of fossil fuels widely used to generate electricity, therefore contributing also to $CO2$ emissions reduction. Researches in this area are at different levels: I) direct conversion by redesigning the electric motors to obtain high efficiency; II) the power electronic systems by introducing static converters with diminished switching losses; III) control implementation of the conversion process by using the enhanced capabilities of new generation digital signal processor DSP (Veerachary M., 2002).

The efficiency of the motor is high on steady state operation, but very low in transients. On the other hand, the associated equipment for energy conversion purposes, i.e. power converters together with the control subsystem, assures both high static and dynamic performances (related to the settling time, error minimizing and so on), but they are not related to energy expenditure. The analysis of various technical publications shows a yearly increase of energy expenditure of the electrical motors, with a rate of 1,5% in Europe, 2,2% in USA, 3,1% in Japan; these values can even reach the rate of 13%, depending on the development of calculus technology (Matinfar, *et al.*, 2005), (Gattami, *et al.*,2005), (COM, 2006).

Dynamic programming tool is very useful to obtain the optimal solution, but the values of the torque and speed must be known in advance (Mendes, *et al.*, 1996). In machine building industry the operating cycle is well-known (Lorenz, *et al.*, 1992; 1998) therefore, the dynamic programming is an efficient tool only for these type of applications. But the optimization method fails when the conventional electrical drives are taken into account because the load torque could not be known in advance, i.e. at the final time of the process.

The optimal solution (Gaiceanu, 1997) provided in this chapter overcomes this type of scientific barrier (Rosu, 1985), making possible implementation of the optimal solution to any type of application, without knowing the speed and load torque in advance. As it is nonrecursive, determined on the basis of variational methods (by integrating the Matrix Riccati Differential Equation), the optimal solution can be calculated on-line without memorizing it from the final time to the initial time, as in the recursive method. Therefore, the nonrecursive solution can be implemented to any type of electrical motor with any load variation, for any operating dynamical regimes.

On the other hand, the problem of increasing power conversion efficiency in the drive systems is the subject of numerous worldwide studies. The Siemens Automation (Siemens) claims the optimization based on the speed controller which can be optimized in the time or in the frequency range. In the time range, the symmetrical optimum method can be used. In the frequency range, the optimizing is done according to the amplitude and phase margin rules, known from the control theory, but these are the conventional controls that are used in drives.

The interdisciplinarity of the chapter consists of using specific knowledge from the fields of: energy conversion, power converters, Matlab/Simulink simulation software, real time implementation based on dSPACE platform, electrotechnics, and advanced control techniques.

This chapter is focused on mathematical modelling, optimal control development on power inverter, Matlab implementation and analysis of the optimal control solution in order to minimize the electric input energy of the drive system. The Matlab on-line solution can be downloaded in real-time platforms, as dSPACE or dsPIC Digital Signal Controllers (Gaiceanu, *et al.*, 2008).

The practical implication of using the proposed method is the on-line calculation of the optimal control solution. The main lines of the research methodology are:

- The optimal control of the dynamical electrical drives problem formulation;
- The optimal control solution;
- The numerical simulation results;
- The implementation of the optimal control.

The strategy of the optimal control electrical drive system is to use both the conventional control during the steady state and the developed optimal control during the transients. The conventional control is based on the rotor field orientated control using Proportional Integral controllers. If the speed error is different from zero, the software switch will enable the optimal control, else will enable the conventional control. Both types of control are developed in the next Sections.

2. Mathematical model of the variable speed electrical drives (VSED)

There are variable speed DC and AC drives. A DC drive system controlled by armature voltage at constant field is a linear, invariant and controllable dynamic system. Variable speed AC drives are mostly used in connection with induction and synchronous electrical machines. The modern drives contain the energy source, the power converters, the electrical machines, the mechanical power transmission and the load, linked by an adequate control. The well-known mathematical model of the vector controlled AC drive using three phase squirrel cage induction machine in rotor field coordinates supplied from the current inverter, operating at the constant flux (Leonhard, 1996) becomes a linear system (Gaiceanu, 2002). For the electrical drives having the power less than 50 kW, the power loss of the converter could be neglected. In order to compute the optimal solution for synchronous Drive system, the control in rotor field oriented reference frame of surface mounted permanent magnet synchronous motor (PMSM) drives is used. The decoupling of the control loops (torque and flux) is performed in rotor field reference frame. By setting a zero value of direct current stator component, the mathematical model of the PMSM becomes linear. Therefore, there is a common mathematical model of the electrical drives, described by the linear state space standard form representation:

$$\dot{x}(t) = \boldsymbol{A}\boldsymbol{x}(t) + \boldsymbol{B}\boldsymbol{u}(t) + \boldsymbol{G}w(t) \tag{1}$$

where $\boldsymbol{x}(t)$ is the state vector, **u**(t) is the control vector, and the perturbation vector is the load torque w(*t*)=$[T_L\ (t)]$.

Taking into consideration the most used electrical machine, the three-phase squirrel cage induction machine, the electrical drive based on it will be explained as follows. Starting from the nameplate data of the induction machine (Fig.1), the main parameters of the electrical motor can be found (Appendix 1).

```
%Nominal Power (mechanical power)
Pn=750;% kW
%Stator resistance
Rs=1.7;      %[ohmi]
%rotor resistance
Rr=2.55;     %[ohmi]
%stator leakage inductance
Lss=0.00986;  %[H]
%rotor leakage inductance
Lrs=0.01002;  %[H]
%mutual inductance
Lm=0.2680; %[H]
%total equivalent inertia mass
J=0.002;    %[kgm^2]
% number of pole pairs
p=2;
%power factor
cosfi=0.71;
%rated efficiency
etan=0.794;
%rated speed
nn=1480;
%frequency
f1=50;     %[Hz]
```

Figure 1. Nameplate data of the electrical machine (three phase induction motor)

The mathematical model of the three phase squirrel cage induction machine (IM) in rotor field reference system operating at constant flux is (Leonhard, 1996):

http://dx.doi.org/10.5772/57521

$$\begin{cases} T_r \dfrac{\mathrm{d}i_{mr}}{\mathrm{d}t} + i_{mr} = i_{ds} \\ \dfrac{\mathrm{d}q}{\mathrm{d}t} = \dfrac{\omega_{\mathrm{e}}}{p} + \dfrac{i_{qs}}{T_r i_{mr}} \\ \dfrac{J}{p}\dfrac{\mathrm{d}\omega_{\mathrm{e}}}{\mathrm{d}t} = T_{\mathrm{e}} - \dfrac{F}{p}\omega_{\mathrm{e}} - T_L \\ T_{\mathrm{e}} = k_m \cdot i_{mr} \cdot i_{qs}, \end{cases} \qquad \text{(a)}$$

where i_{mr} – rotor magnetizing current; i_{ds}, i_{qs} – flux and torque components of the stator current;
T_e – electromagnetic torque, TL – load torque, p – number of pole pairs, F – viscous force; (2)
Ts, Tr stator and rotor time constants;
q – angle of the magnetizing current vector; w_e, w – electrical and mechanical rotor speed,

$$\omega_{\mathrm{e}} = p\omega \qquad \text{(b)}$$

with L_m – magnetizing inductance, s_r – rotor magnetizing dispersion factor.

$$K_m = \frac{2}{3} p \cdot \frac{L_m}{1+\sigma_r} \qquad \text{(c)}$$

By varying the flux component of the stator current, i_{ds}, the magnetizing current response, $i_{mr}(t)$, can have signifiant delay. By using an adequate control of power inverter (Gaiceanu, 2002), the rotor magnetizing current, i_{mr}, can be maintained at the constant value, and according to the mathematical model of the IM (1a), the flux component of the stator current, i_{ds}, equates the rotor magnetizing current): $i_{mr}=i_{ds}$=ct.. Therefore, the standard state space form of the IM mathematical model can be obtained (Fig.2):

```
%    INITIAL DATA
      isd=Idref;
      imr=isd;
      km=2*Lm*imr/(3*(1+sigmar));
      Fv=0.0006;
%    The matrix of the system
     A=[-Fv/J       0;
           1        0];
%    The control vector
      kq=1/(Tr*imr);
      B=[    km/J;
              kq ];
%    The perturbation vector
     G=[-1/J;
          0  ];
%    The output matrix
     Ct=[1   0];
%    D=[0   0];
```

Figure 2. Standard space state form characterization of the three phase Induction Motor

3. Optimal control problem statement

The common objectives of the optimal control drive systems are: the smooth dynamic response, without oscillations; achieving the desired steady state; the fast compensation of the load torque; energy minimization. Taking into consideration the main objectives of the electrical drive system, the following Section describes the chosen quadratic performance criterion.

3.1. The quadratic performance criterion

The functional cost or the quadratic performance criterion is chosen such that the electrical input power, the energy expended in the stator windings of the electrical machines is minimized, and the cost of the control is weighted. Therefore, the performance functional quadratic criterion (Rosu, 1985), (Gaiceanu, 2002), (Athans, 2006), is as follows:

$$J = \frac{1}{2}\left[x(t_1) - x_1\right]^T S\left[x(t_1) - x_1\right] + \frac{1}{2}\int_{t_0}^{t_1}\left[x^T(t)\,Qx(t) + u^T(t)\,Ru(t)\right]dt \tag{3}$$

in which, taking into consideration a starting of the IM, the initial conditions consists of the initial time t_0=0[s] and the initial state vector $x(t_0)=[\omega(t_0)\ \ q(t_0)]^T=[0\ \ 0]^T$, T-being the transpose symbol of the initial state vector. The final condition is the required final state, $\mathbf{x}_1$. The components of the $\mathbf{x}_1$ are: the desired angular velocity, ω^*_m, and a free rotor magnetizing angle value, q^*=0, i.e $x_1=\begin{bmatrix}\omega^*_m \\ 0\end{bmatrix}$; the final time, t_1=0.9[s]. The value of the final time is established by the feasibility condition, i.e. the value of it is taken from the obtained final time of the starting process with conventional control (Proportional Integral controllers). In order to exist and to obtain a unique optimal solution, the weighting matrices must be chosen according to: $\mathbf{S}\geq 0$, $\mathbf{R}>0$, $\mathbf{Q}\geq 0$. The weighted matrix **S** minimizes the square error between the reached state $x(t_1)$, and the desired state, $\mathbf{x}_1$, in the fixed time t_1, the weighted matrix **R** minimizes the control effort, $u(t)=i_{qs}(t)$, and the weighted matrix **Q** minimizes the expended energy in the motor windings. The optimal control problem taken into account in this chapter is with free-end point, fixed time and unconstrained. The restrictions of the magnitude for the control vector, and state vectors are managed through the design process, by an adequate choice of the weighting matrices.

3.2. The solution of the optimal control problem.

The existence and the unicity of the optimal control problem solution are based on the controllability and observability of the system (1). The system (1) being controllable and completely observable, the weighting matrices are chosen such that $\mathbf{Q}, \mathbf{S}\geq \mathbf{0}$ are positive semidefinite, and matrix $\mathbf{R}>\mathbf{0}$ is positive definite (Gaiceanu, 2002). In this way, the existence and the unicity of the optimal control problem solution are assured.

By using variational method, the Hamiltonian of the optimal control problem is given by

http://dx.doi.org/10.5772/57521

$$H(p,x,u,t)=\frac{1}{2}\left[\boldsymbol{x}^T(\boldsymbol{t})\,\boldsymbol{Q}\boldsymbol{x}(\boldsymbol{t})+\boldsymbol{u}^T(\boldsymbol{t})\boldsymbol{R}\boldsymbol{u}(\boldsymbol{t})+\boldsymbol{y}^T(\boldsymbol{t})\cdot\left(\boldsymbol{A}x(t)+\boldsymbol{B}\boldsymbol{u}(t)+\boldsymbol{G}w(t)\right)\right] \tag{4}$$

in which $\boldsymbol{y}\ (t)\in\Re^2$ is the costate vector.

The condition **R>0** assures the inversability of the eigenvectors and that the optimal solution has a minimum (Gaiceanu, 2002). The optimal control minimizing the Hamiltonian (4) is given by

$$u^*(t)=-\boldsymbol{R}^{-1}\boldsymbol{B}^T\boldsymbol{y}(t) \tag{5}$$

By using the canonical system, the solutions of the costate $\boldsymbol{y}(t)$ and state vectors $\boldsymbol{x}(t)$ can be obtained:

$$\begin{bmatrix}\overset{\circ}{\boldsymbol{x}}\boldsymbol{(t)}\\ \overset{\circ}{\boldsymbol{y}}\boldsymbol{(t)}\end{bmatrix}=\begin{bmatrix}\boldsymbol{A} & -\boldsymbol{B}\boldsymbol{R}^{-1}\boldsymbol{B}^T\\ -\boldsymbol{Q} & -\boldsymbol{A}^T\end{bmatrix}\begin{bmatrix}\boldsymbol{x(t)}\\ \boldsymbol{y(t)}\end{bmatrix}+\begin{bmatrix}\boldsymbol{G}\\ \boldsymbol{0}\end{bmatrix}\boldsymbol{w(t)} \tag{6}$$

The boundary conditions of the canonical system (5) are:

-the initial state $\boldsymbol{x}(\boldsymbol{0})=\boldsymbol{x}_o$;

-the transversality condition of the costate vector:

$$\boldsymbol{y}(\boldsymbol{t}_1)=\left.\frac{\partial\boldsymbol{\lambda}(\boldsymbol{t})}{\partial\boldsymbol{x}}\right|_{t=t_1}=\boldsymbol{S}\left[\boldsymbol{x}(\boldsymbol{t}_1)-\boldsymbol{x}_1\right] \tag{7}$$

$$y(t_1)=S[x(t_1)-x_1]-100\begin{bmatrix}\omega(t_1)\\ q(t_1)\end{bmatrix}-\begin{bmatrix}15707{,}96\\ 0\end{bmatrix},$$

where the weighting matrix $\boldsymbol{S}=\begin{bmatrix}100 & 0\\ 0 & 0\end{bmatrix}$, and q is the angle of the rotor magnetizing flux.

The integration of the canonical system leads to the well-known matrix Riccati differential equation and the associate vectorial equation (Rosu, 1985), (Gaiceanu, 2002), (Athans, *et al.*, 2006). The integration of these two equations is a very difficult task because the Riccati equation is nonlinear, its solution is recursive (which can be calculated backward in time) (Gattami, *et al.*, 2005), (Jianqiang, *et al.*, 2007), (Rosu, 1985). Moreover, the backward computation needs to know a priori the variation of the perturbation vector **w**(t) during the control interval [0, t_1]. In most electrical drives the last condition cannot be accomplished.

A nonrecursive solution of the Riccati equation has been developed by using two linear transformations (Rosu, *et al.*, 1998). *The first transformation* changes actual time t into t_1-t, that is time remaining until the end of the optimal process.

$$\tau = t_1 - t = 0.9 - t, \tag{8}$$

In order to use only the negative eigenvalues for the computation of the fundamental matrix of the system (1), *the second transformation* is made. Therefore, by defining new vectors $\mathbf{p}(\tau)$, $\mathbf{q}(\tau)$, $\mathbf{r}(\tau)$,

$$\begin{bmatrix} \overset{\circ}{p}(\tau) \\ \overset{\circ}{q}(\tau) \end{bmatrix} = \begin{bmatrix} -A & BR^{-1}B^T \\ Q & A^T \end{bmatrix} \begin{bmatrix} p(\tau) \\ q(\tau) \end{bmatrix} - \begin{bmatrix} G \\ 0 \end{bmatrix} r(\tau) \tag{9}$$

and by noting the canonical matrix (4×4) of the system (1) as:

$$\begin{bmatrix} -A & BR^{-1}B^T \\ Q & A^T \end{bmatrix} = M \tag{10}$$

the eigenvalues λ_i, $i = \overline{1, 4}$ of the canonical matrix $\mathbf{M}$ can be computed with:

$$\det\left[\lambda I - M\right] = 0 \tag{11}$$

By using the developed Matlab file from Appendix 3, the appropriate negative eigenvalues position placed on the main diagonal of the eigenvalues matrix, $\mathbf{D}$, with diag(D)=$\{\lambda_1, \lambda_2, \lambda_3, \lambda_4\}$, can be obtained:

$$\begin{bmatrix} \lambda_1 & 0 & 0 & 0 \\ 0 & \lambda_2 & 0 & 0 \\ 0 & 0 & -\lambda_1 & 0 \\ 0 & 0 & 0 & -\lambda_2 \end{bmatrix} = \begin{bmatrix} 5.1663 & 0 & 0 & 0 \\ 0 & 0.7205 & 0 & 0 \\ 0 & 0 & -5.1663 & 0 \\ 0 & 0 & 0 & -0.7205 \end{bmatrix} = \begin{bmatrix} \Lambda & 0 \\ 0 & -\Lambda \end{bmatrix}, \tag{12}$$

in which

$$\Lambda = \begin{bmatrix} \lambda_1 & 0 \\ 0 & \lambda_2 \end{bmatrix} = \begin{bmatrix} 5.1663 & 0 \\ 0 & 0.7205 \end{bmatrix}. \tag{13}$$

http://dx.doi.org/10.5772/57521

In the Appendix 3 the proper position of the eigenvalues and the eigenvectors of the linear system (1) is provided. By using the program sequence from Appendix 3, the stability of the system is assured and the corresponding matrix of the eigenvectors is obtained:

$$W = \begin{bmatrix} 0.9877 & -0.5906 & -0.9740 & -0.5702 \\ -0.1567 & 0.8070 & -0.2268 & -0.8215 \\ 0.0004 & -0.0001 & 0.0004 & 0.0000 \\ -0.0000 & 0.0011 & 0.0000 & 0.0011 \end{bmatrix} \quad (14)$$

By knowing the inverse of the eigenvector matrix $\mathbf{W}^{-1}$

$$W-1 = 1.0e+003 * \begin{bmatrix} 0.0005 & 0.0001 & 1.3542 & 0.3153 \\ 0.0000 & 0.0006 & 0.3158 & 0.4549 \\ -0.0005 & 0.0000 & 1.3732 & -0.2178 \\ 0.0000 & -0.0006 & -0.3271 & 0.4469 \end{bmatrix} \quad (15)$$

the new vectors, $\mathbf{m}(\tau)$, $\mathbf{n}(\tau)$, $\mathbf{p}(\tau)$, $\mathbf{q}(\tau)$ are introduced as follows:

$$\begin{bmatrix} m(\tau) \\ n(\tau) \end{bmatrix} = \mathbf{W}^{-1} \begin{bmatrix} p(\tau) \\ q(\tau) \end{bmatrix}, \quad (16)$$

$$\begin{bmatrix} p(\tau) \\ q(\tau) \end{bmatrix} = \mathbf{W} \begin{bmatrix} m(\tau) \\ n(\tau) \end{bmatrix} \quad (17)$$

By introducing (15) and (16) transformations in (8), the following differential system is obtained:

$$\mathbf{W} \begin{bmatrix} \overset{\circ}{m}(\tau) \\ \overset{\circ}{n}(\tau) \end{bmatrix} = \mathbf{M}\,\mathbf{W} \begin{bmatrix} m(\tau) \\ n(\tau) \end{bmatrix} - \begin{bmatrix} G \\ 0 \end{bmatrix} r(\tau) \quad (18)$$

Therefore, the canonical system can be written in terms of $\mathbf{n}(\tau)$, and $\mathbf{m}(\tau)$ vectors:

$$\begin{bmatrix} \overset{\circ}{m}(\tau) \\ \overset{\circ}{n}(\tau) \end{bmatrix} = \mathbf{W}^{-1}\mathbf{M}\mathbf{W} \begin{bmatrix} m(\tau) \\ n(\tau) \end{bmatrix} - \mathbf{W}^{-1} \begin{bmatrix} G \\ 0 \end{bmatrix} r(\tau) \quad (19)$$

By using the well-known relation

$$W^{-1}MW = \begin{bmatrix} \Lambda & 0 \\ 0 & -\Lambda \end{bmatrix} \tag{20}$$

and by noting the new vector **H** as:

$$W^{-1}\begin{bmatrix} G \\ 0 \end{bmatrix} = H = \begin{bmatrix} -52.6495 \\ -0.2471 \\ -47.8790 \\ 23.0137 \end{bmatrix}, \tag{21}$$

the new form of the canonical system can be obtained:

$$\begin{bmatrix} \overset{\circ}{m}(\tau) \\ \overset{\circ}{n}(\tau) \end{bmatrix} = \begin{bmatrix} \Lambda & 0 \\ 0 & -\Lambda \end{bmatrix}\begin{bmatrix} m(\tau) \\ n(\tau) \end{bmatrix} - H \cdot r(\tau) \tag{22}$$

The solution of the new canonical system (21) can be obtained by using the following equation:

$$\begin{bmatrix} m(\tau) \\ n(\tau) \end{bmatrix} = \begin{bmatrix} e^{\Lambda\tau} & 0 \\ 0 & e^{-\Lambda\tau} \end{bmatrix}\begin{bmatrix} m(0) \\ n(0) \end{bmatrix} - \int_0^{\tau} \begin{bmatrix} e^{\Lambda\beta} & 0 \\ 0 & e^{-\Lambda\beta} \end{bmatrix} Hr(\beta)\mathrm{d}\beta \tag{23}$$

As it can be observed the solution of the canonical system (22) solution contains both the positive, $e^{\Lambda\tau}$, and the negative exponentials, $e^{-\Lambda\tau}$. It is well-known that the positive exponentials produce the instability of the solution. Moreover, in order to obtain the analytical solution of the system (22) the load torque ($r(\tau)$ or $\mathbf{w}(t)$) at the final time, t_1, must be known in advance. For the most used electrical drive system this condition is hardly accomplished because the load torque cannot be known in advance, at the final time.

A numerical solution of the optimal problem is proposed. The advantage of maintaining the sampled signal at the same value during the sampled period is that the zero order hold (ZOH) offers a brilliant solution to know the load torque at the final time. Therefore, under this assumption, the solution **(22)** is computed each sampled time, *T*, and the perturbation vector **r** has constant value during it:

$$\begin{bmatrix} m(\tau) \\ n(\tau) \end{bmatrix} = \begin{bmatrix} e^{\Lambda\tau} & 0 \\ 0 & e^{-\Lambda\tau} \end{bmatrix}\begin{bmatrix} m(0) \\ n(0) \end{bmatrix} + \begin{bmatrix} I - e^{\Lambda\tau} & 0 \\ 0 & I - e^{-\Lambda\tau} \end{bmatrix}\begin{bmatrix} H_1 \\ H_2 \end{bmatrix} r \tag{24}$$

http://dx.doi.org/10.5772/57521

where **I** is the identity matrix.

The obtained solution of the canonical system (23) is:

$$\begin{bmatrix} m_1(\tau) \\ m_2(\tau) \\ n_1(\tau) \\ n_2(\tau) \end{bmatrix} = \begin{bmatrix} e^{(5.1663)\cdot\tau} & 0 & 0 & 0 \\ 0 & e^{(0.7205)\cdot\tau} & 0 & 0 \\ 0 & 0 & e^{-(5.1663)\cdot\tau} & 0 \\ 0 & 0 & 0 & e^{-(0.7205)\cdot\tau} \end{bmatrix} \cdot \begin{bmatrix} m_1(0) \\ m_2(0) \\ n_1(0) \\ n_2(0) \end{bmatrix} + \begin{bmatrix} 1-e^{(5.1663)\cdot\tau} & 0 & 0 & 0 \\ 0 & 1-e^{(0.7205)\cdot\tau} & 0 & 0 \\ 0 & 0 & 1-e^{-(5.1663)\tau} & 0 \\ 0 & 0 & 0 & 1-e^{-(0.7205)\cdot\tau} \end{bmatrix} \cdot \begin{bmatrix} -52.6495 \\ -0.2471 \\ -47.8790 \\ 23.0137 \end{bmatrix} \cdot r. \tag{25}$$

The negative exponentials can be obtained by extracting **m**(0) function on the **m**(τ). In this way, the first equation of the system **(24)** becomes:

$$\begin{bmatrix} \boldsymbol{m}(0) \\ \boldsymbol{n}(\tau) \end{bmatrix} = \begin{bmatrix} e^{-\Lambda\cdot\tau} & 0 \\ 0 & e^{-\Lambda\cdot\tau} \end{bmatrix} \cdot \begin{bmatrix} \boldsymbol{m}(\tau) \\ \boldsymbol{n}(0) \end{bmatrix} + \begin{bmatrix} \boldsymbol{I}_2 - e^{-\Lambda\cdot\tau} & 0 \\ 0 & \boldsymbol{I}_2 - e^{-\Lambda\cdot\tau} \end{bmatrix} \cdot \begin{bmatrix} \boldsymbol{H}_1 \\ \boldsymbol{H}_2 \end{bmatrix} \cdot r \tag{26}$$

where

$$\boldsymbol{I}_2 = \begin{bmatrix} 1 & 0 \\ 0 & 1 \end{bmatrix} \tag{27}$$

The negative exponentials of the system **(25)** guarantee the stability of the system (1).

The transversality condition (6), in terms of **m** and **n** vectors, is as follows:

$$\boldsymbol{n}(0) = \boldsymbol{E}\cdot\boldsymbol{m}(0) + \boldsymbol{F}\cdot\boldsymbol{x}_f \tag{28}$$

where,

$$\boldsymbol{E} = \left[\boldsymbol{SW}_{12} - \boldsymbol{W}_{22}\right]^{-1}\left[\boldsymbol{W}_{21} - \boldsymbol{SW}_{11}\right] = \begin{bmatrix} 1.0215 & -0.0320 \\ -0.0127 & -0.9811 \end{bmatrix} \tag{29}$$

$$F = \left[SW_{12} - W_{22} \right]^{-1} S = \begin{bmatrix} -1.0504 & 0 \\ 0.0404 & 0 \end{bmatrix} \tag{30}$$

By expressing **n**(τ) function on **m**(τ), the following equation can be deducted :

$$n(\tau) = Z(\tau) \cdot m(\tau) + e^{-\Lambda \cdot \tau} \cdot E \cdot \left(I_2 - e^{-\Lambda \cdot \tau} \right) \cdot H_1 \cdot r + e^{-\Lambda \cdot \tau} \cdot F \cdot x_1 + \left(I_2 - e^{-\Lambda \cdot \tau} \right) \cdot H_2 \cdot r \tag{31}$$

where

$$Z(\tau) = e^{-\Lambda \cdot \tau} \cdot E \cdot e^{-\Lambda \cdot \tau} \tag{32}$$

Going back through the reverse transformations from **m**(τ), **n**(τ) vectors to **p**(τ), **q**(τ) vectors, from the used τ time to the current time t, the state **x**(t) and costate **y**(t) expressions can be obtained. The costate vector at current time is as follows:

$$y(t) = P(t_1 - t) \cdot x(t) - K_1(t_1 - t) \cdot x_1 - K_2(t_1 - t) \cdot w \tag{33}$$

where the matrix **P**(t_1–t) is the solution of the matrix Riccati diferential equation, and the matrices**K**$_1$(t_1–t) and **K**$_2$(t_1-t) vector have the form:

$$K_1(t_1 - t) = -v(t_1 - t) \cdot e^{-\Lambda \cdot (t_1 - t)} \cdot F, \tag{34}$$

$$K_2(t_1 - t) = -v(t_1 - t) \cdot \left[e^{-\Lambda \cdot (t_1 - t)} \cdot E \cdot \left(I - e^{-\Lambda \cdot (t_1 - t)} \right) \cdot H_1 + \left(I - e^{-\Lambda \cdot (t_1 - t)} \right) \cdot H_2 \right], \tag{35}$$

The **v** matrix is as follows:

$$v(\tau) = \left[W_{22} - P(\tau) W_{12} \right]. \tag{36}$$

The solution of the optimal control problem has three components (Fig.3):

1. the state feedback $R^{-1} \cdot B^T P(t_1 - t) \cdot x(t)$, in order to assure the stability of the system;
2. the compensating feedforward load torque $R^{-1} \cdot B^T K_2(t_1 - t) \cdot w$, for fast compensation of the main perturbation, i.e. the load torque;
3. the reference component $R^{-1} \cdot B^T K_1(t_1 - t) \cdot x_1$, to track accurately the reference signal.

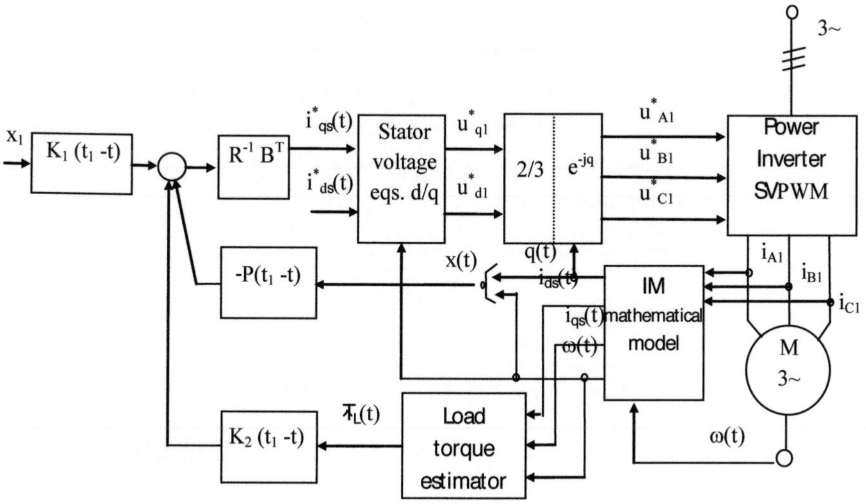

Figure 3. Optimal control (i^*_{sq}) implementation into three phase IM Drive System supplied by the Voltage Power Source Inverter

The optimal control, at any moment *t*, is given by (Gaiceanu, 2002), (Athans, *et al.*, 2006)

$$u^*(t) = -\boldsymbol{R}^{-1}\boldsymbol{B}^T\boldsymbol{P}(t_1 - t)\boldsymbol{x}(t) + \boldsymbol{R}^{-1}\boldsymbol{B}^T\boldsymbol{K}_1(t_1 - t)\boldsymbol{x}_1 + \boldsymbol{R}^{-1}\boldsymbol{B}^T\boldsymbol{K}_2(t_1 - t)\boldsymbol{w}(t) \tag{37}$$

in which $\mathbf{P(t_1\text{-}t)}$ is the solution of the matrix Riccati differential equation, MRDE, and the matrices K_1 and K_2 are calculated via $P(t_1\text{-}t)$ (Rosu, *et al.*, 1998).

The numerical solution supposes the knowledge of the disturbance $\mathbf{w}(t)=T_L(t)$, which could be available by using torque estimator, as in (Rosu, *et al.*, 1998), or with torque sensor (more expensive solution that can produce the faults of the electrical drive system).

4. Simulation and experimental results

In order to implement the optimal control system two electrical drive systems are combined: the conventional vector control and the optimal control drive. Both electrical drive systems operate in parallel. The activation of one of them depends on the speed error: *if* the speed error is zero (steady state operating regime), *then* the *conventional vector control* is active, *else* the *optimal control* drive is active.

4.1. Optimal control implementation

Optimal control implementation consists of loading nine software modules developed by the author: nameplate motor data (Fig.1), determination of the motor parameters (Appendix 1), determination of the six sectors vector components to be used in Space Vector Modulation

(SVM) (Appendix 2), standard space state form characterization of the three phase Induction Motor (Fig.2), the proper arrangement of the eigenvalues and eigenvectors (Appendix 3), optimal control implementation in MATLAB (Appendix 4), the main program (Appendix 5), graphical representation (Appendix 6), Space Vector Modulation –Matlab function **svm_mod** (Appendix 7). By using the Matlab code from Appendix 8 the graphical representation of the simulation results can be obtained (Figures 4-7).

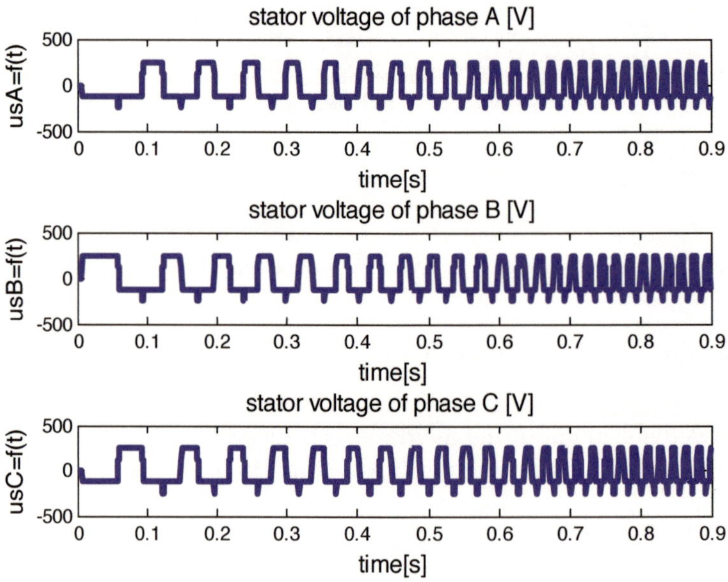

Figure 4. Three phase SVM supply voltages

Remark

The SVM increases the DC-link voltage usage, the maximum output voltage based on the space vector theory is $2/\sqrt{3}$ times higher than conventional sinusoidal modulation (Pulse Width Modulation). The purpose of the SVPWM technique is to approximate the reference voltage vector U_{out} by a combination of the eight switching patterns. The implemented Matlab sequence for obtaining the pulse pattern of the optimal SVM modulator (Appendix 2, Appendix 7) shown above is based on the developed methodology by the author (Gaiceanu, 2002). In optimal control case, there is no speed overshoot, and smoothly state response (speed and angle of the rotor magnetizing current) have been obtained (Fig.5, Fig.7).

http://dx.doi.org/10.5772/57521

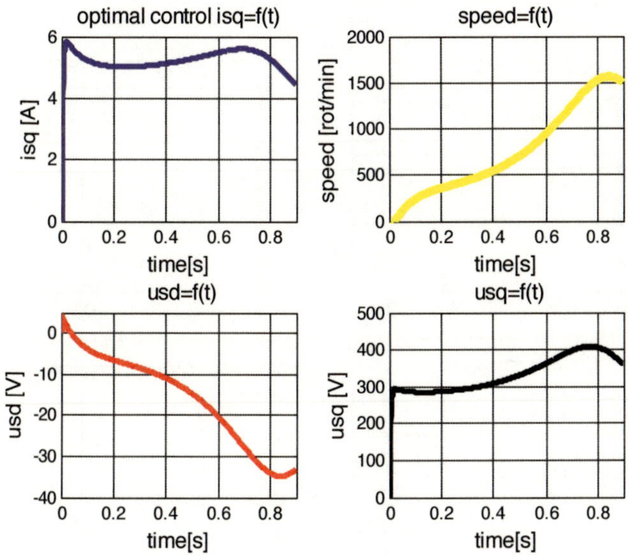

Figure 5. Optimal control, speed, longitudinal and transversal voltage components

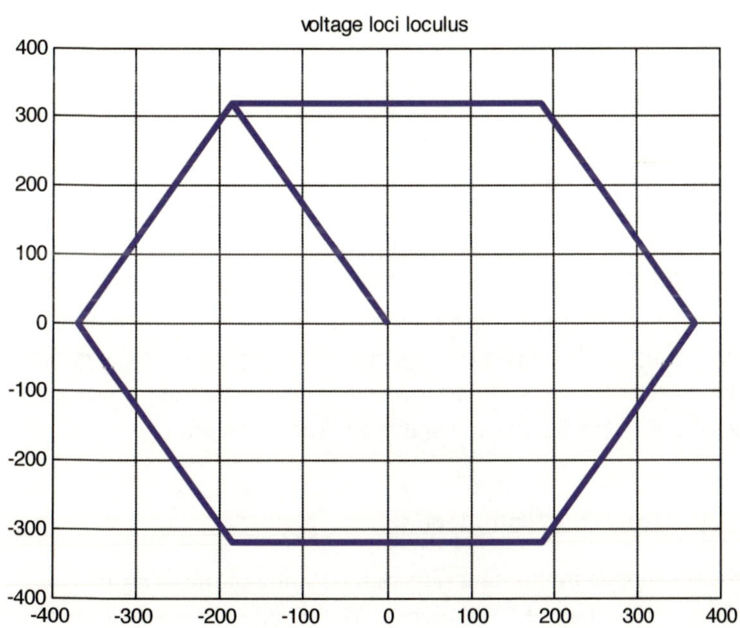

Figure 6. Voltage loci loculus for a starting process

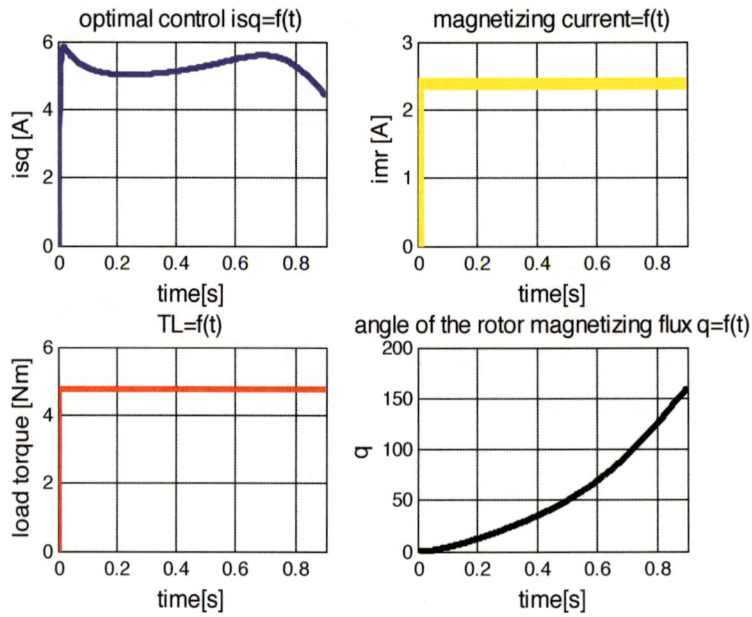

Figure 7. Optimal control i_{qs}=*f*(*t*), current i_{mr}(*t*), load torque T_L(*t*)(elevator), rotor magnetizing angle of the rotor field *q*(*t*) (left to right)

4.2. Conventional vector control

The conventional vector control consists of the rotor flux orientated drive system. The vector control is implemented in Simulink as following. The control system is in cascaded manner and consists of two major loops: the speed loop and the magnetic flux loop. The torque control loop is the minor loop of the speed control one. The references of the control loop are: the desired angular velocity for the speed loop, ω^*, the imposed stator current torque component for the torque loop, i^*_{qs}, and the desired stator current flux component for the magnetization flux loop, i^*_{ds}.

Tuning of the speed and flux controllers

By knowing the nameplate motor data (Fig.1), the tuning of the PI speed and flux controllers parameters can be done (see the developed Matlab file shown in the Appendix 8). The conventional vector control supposes the use of the two independent control axes: *d*-axis, along with the magnetizing flux direction, and *q* axis, in quadrature with *d*-axis. The most used field orientated control is that of the rotor orientated magnetizing flux (Fig.8). The magnetization flux and the torque can be controlled independently.

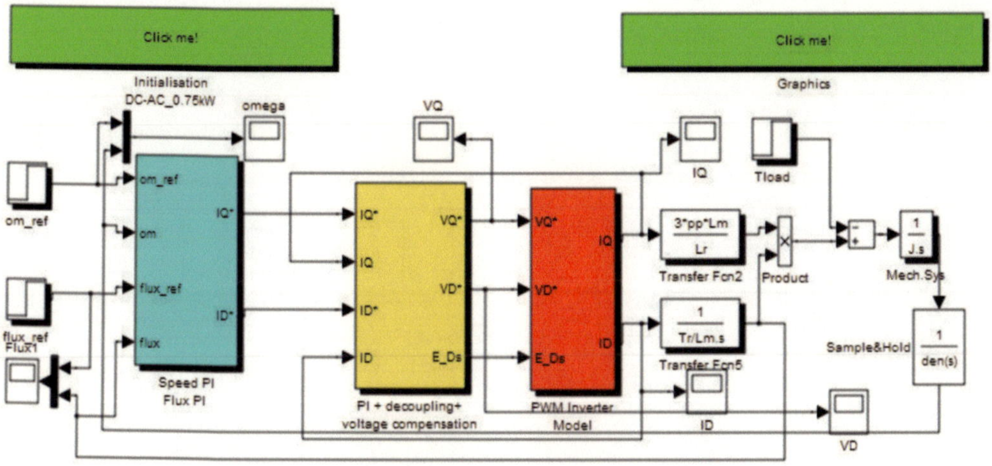

Figure 8. Simulink implementation of the rotor field orientated vector control of the three-phase induction motor

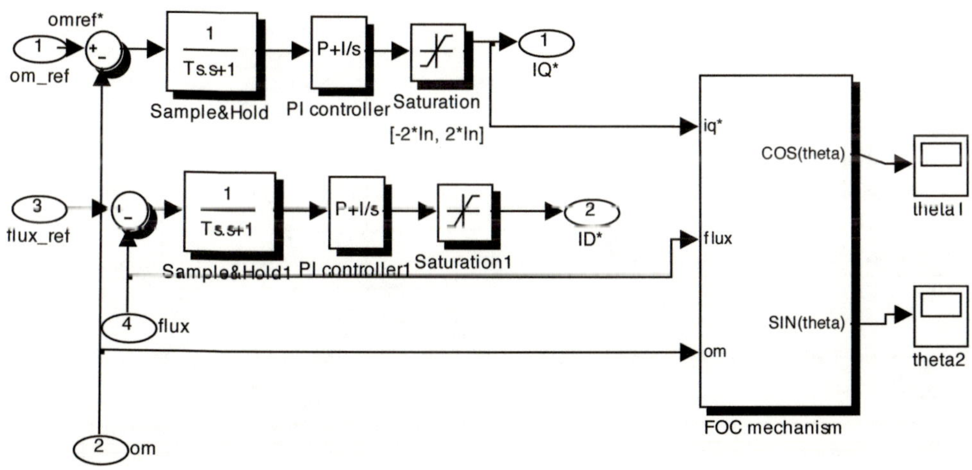

Figure 9. Simulink implementation of the speed and flux Proportional-Integral (PI) regulators

The inputs of the speed and flux regulators Simulink block (Fig.9) are the speed reference and the flux reference; the outputs are the *q*-axis reference current, IQ*, and *d*-axis reference current, ID*(Fig.10). More details can be obtained by using Fig. 10.

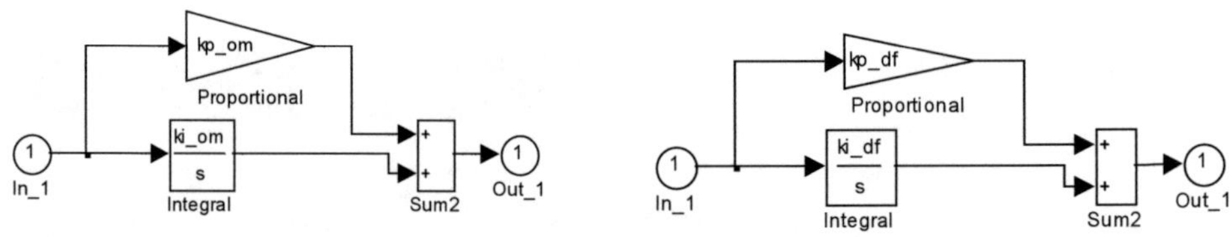

Figure 10. PI Speed regulator of type1 (kp_om+ki_om/s) and Flux regulator of type 3 (kp_df+ki_df/s), according to Matlab file shown in the Appendix 8

By using the field orientated mechanism implemented in Simulink (Fig.11), based on the input signals (IQ*, *flux* and *om*), the frequency of the stator voltage is delivered.

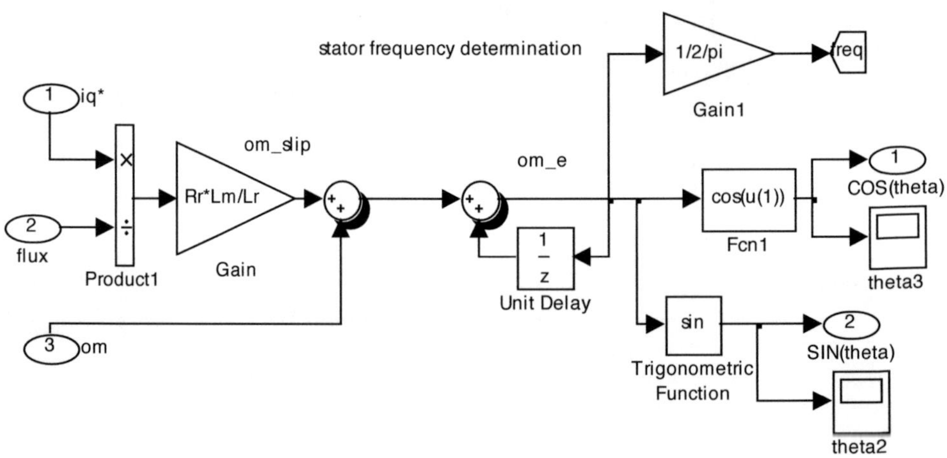

Figure 11. The Field Orientated Control (FOC) mechanism implemented in Simulink

http://dx.doi.org/10.5772/57521

The parameters of the speed and flux regulators are delivered by using the Matlab file developed in the Appendix 8.

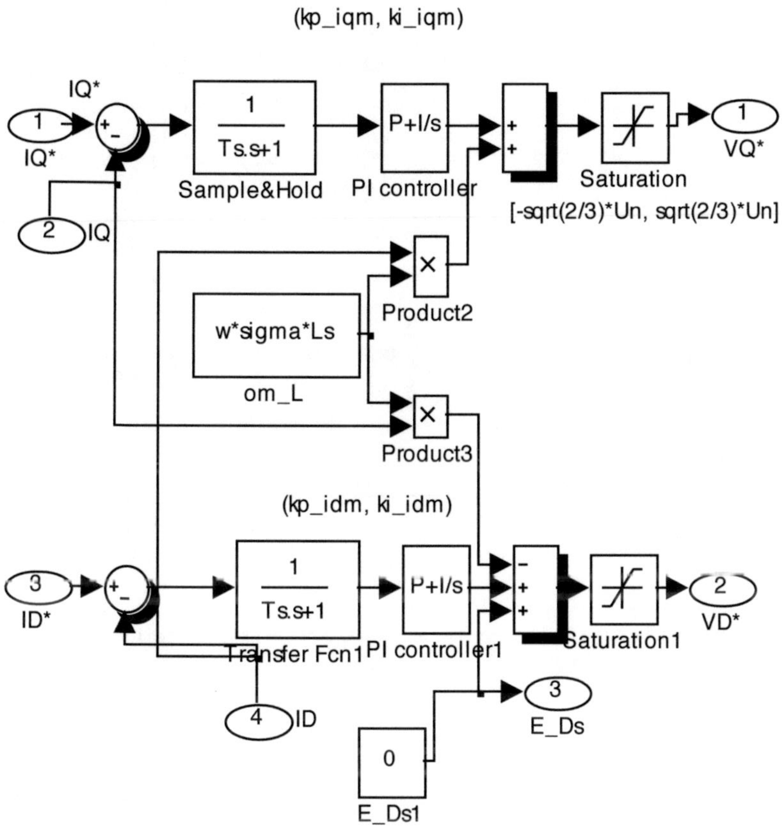

Figure 12. Detailed program of the PI control (torque (IQ*) and flux (ID*) control loops), the decoupling of the *d*, *q* axes, and the voltage compensation Simulink block of Fig.7

In the Fig.12. the detailed decoupling and the voltage compensation between *d*, *q* axes are depicted. In order to control the torque current component (IQ) and the flux current component (ID), the PI controllers are involved. By introducing the compensating voltage components, the independent control of flux and torque is obtained (Fig.12).

The reference voltage components pair (VD*, VQ*) is used as input of the Pulse Width Modulation (PWM) transfer function block, shown in the Fig.13.

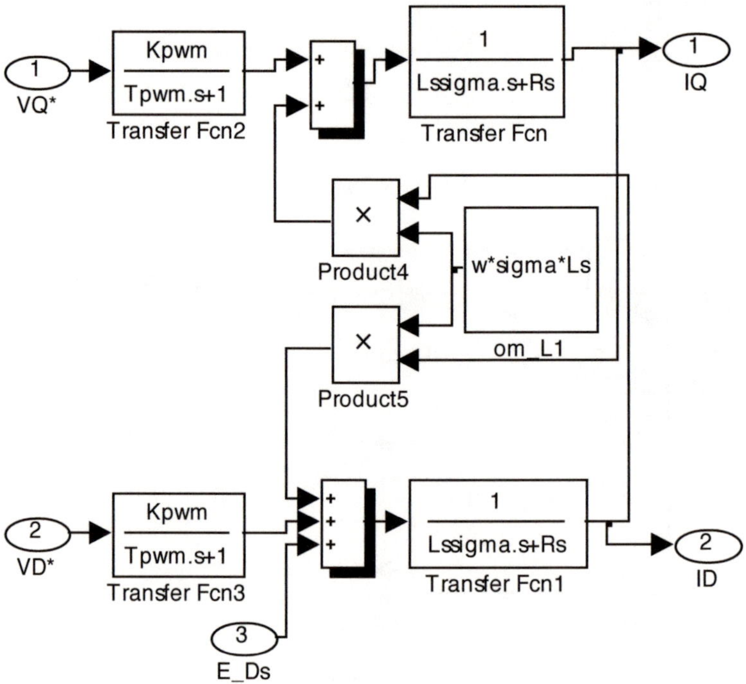

Figure 13. The Simulink models of the PWM modulator and of the equivalent *d*, *q* model of the IM

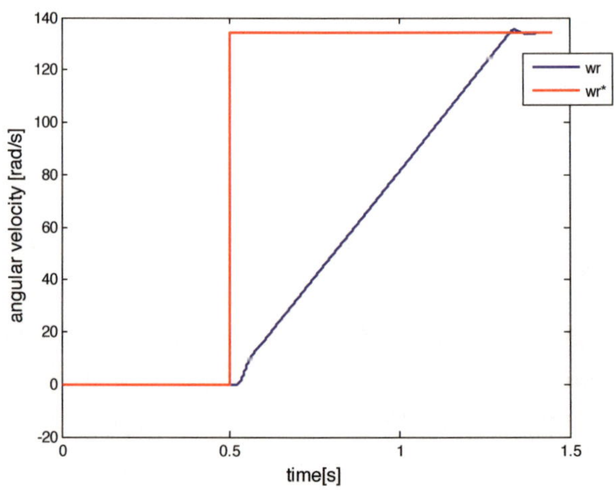

Figure 14. The speed control loop

http://dx.doi.org/10.5772/57521

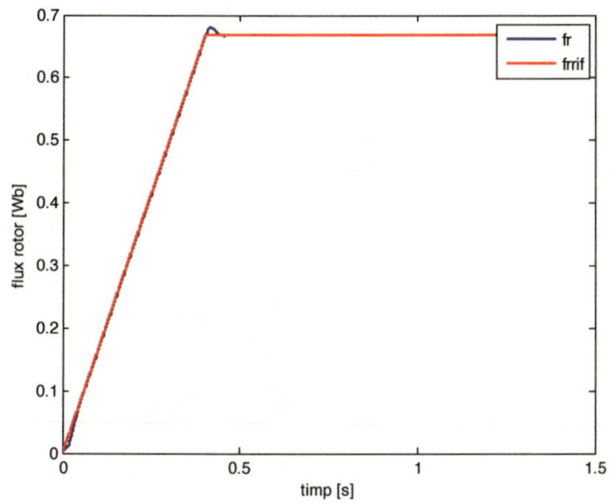

Figure 15. The rotor flux control loop

The performances of the speed control loop are shown in the Fig. 14, in which the step rotor speed reference (om_ref*) is applied and the actual rotor speed (om) follows the reference with zero steady state error. The performances of the implemented flux control loop are shown in the Fig. 15. Small flux overshoot (up to 11%) and zero steady state error are obtained (Fig.15). The IM starts after t=0,5s (Fig.15), when the rated flux of the motor is attained (Fig.15). In order to implement the optimal control for ac drives, a test bench based on the DS1104 platform has been developed (Fig.16).

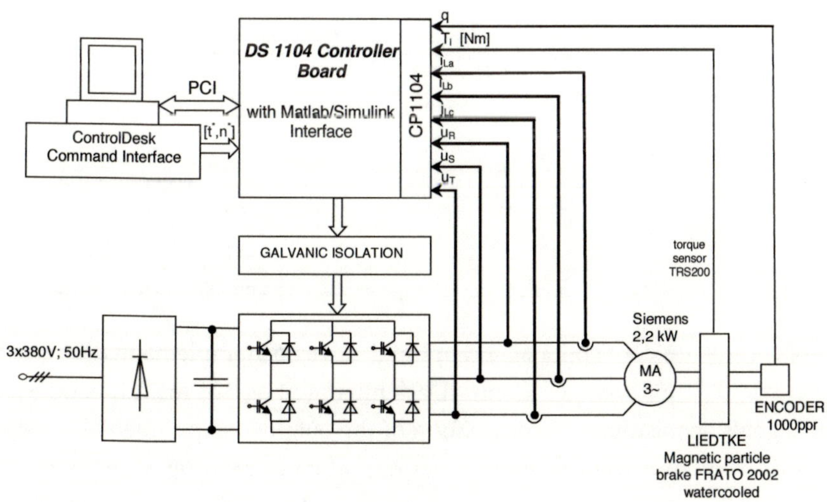

Figure 16. The experimental set-up test bench (Gaiceanu *et al.*, 2008)

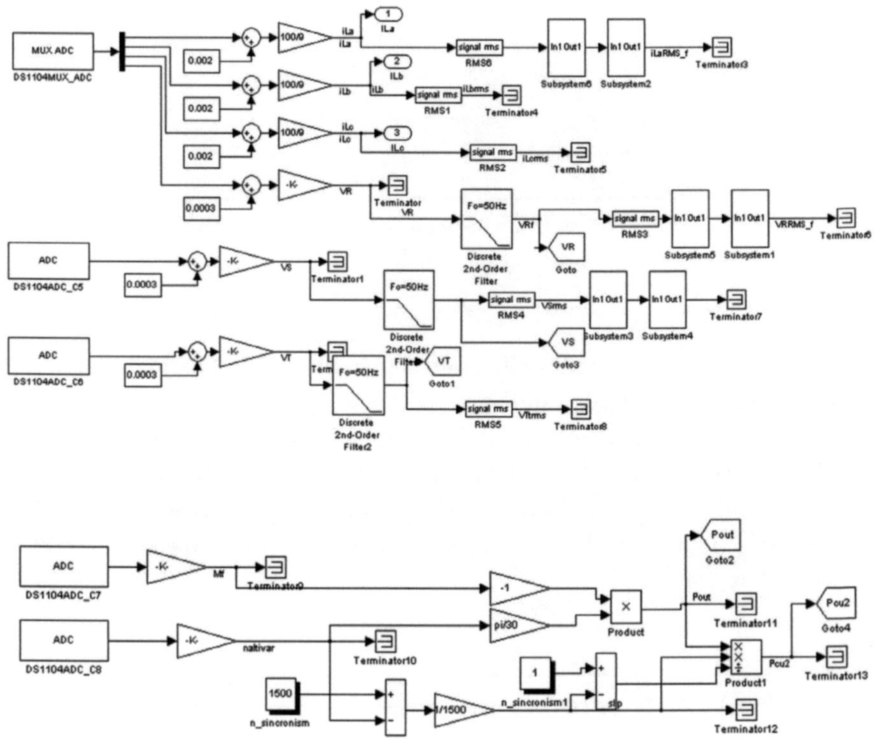

Figure 17. Real time implementation of both electrical drive systems based on the DS1104 real time platform

Both types of control, i.e. conventional and optimal, have been implemented on DS1104 (Fig. 17) controller board. The developed ControlDesk interface has two main functions: real time control and signals acquisition. The evaluation of the obtained experimental results reveals the system efficiency improvement through an important decreasing of the windings dissipation power and input power (Fig.18) in optimal control case. Therefore, the power balance provides an increasing of the system efficiency, thus improved thermal and capacity conditions are obtained.

http://dx.doi.org/10.5772/57521

The optimal control (7) of the electrical drive based on the induction machine (1) has been numerically simulated by using Z transform and zero order hold for a starting of a 0.75 [kW], 1480 [rpm] under a rating load torque of 4.77 [Nm]. The initial conditions of the optimal control problem are: t_o=0[s], $\mathbf{x}_i$=[n_i=0 q=0]. The free final conditions are: t_f=0.9[s], $\mathbf{x}_f$=[n_f=1480 q=0].

5. Conclusions

In order to obtain the optimal control, the nonrecursive solution has been used to avoid the main disadvantages of the recursive solution (that is, the solution can be calculated at the current time, not backward in time; the load torque can have any shape, either linear or nonlinear, in admissible limits, due to the fact that the solution is computed at each sample time).

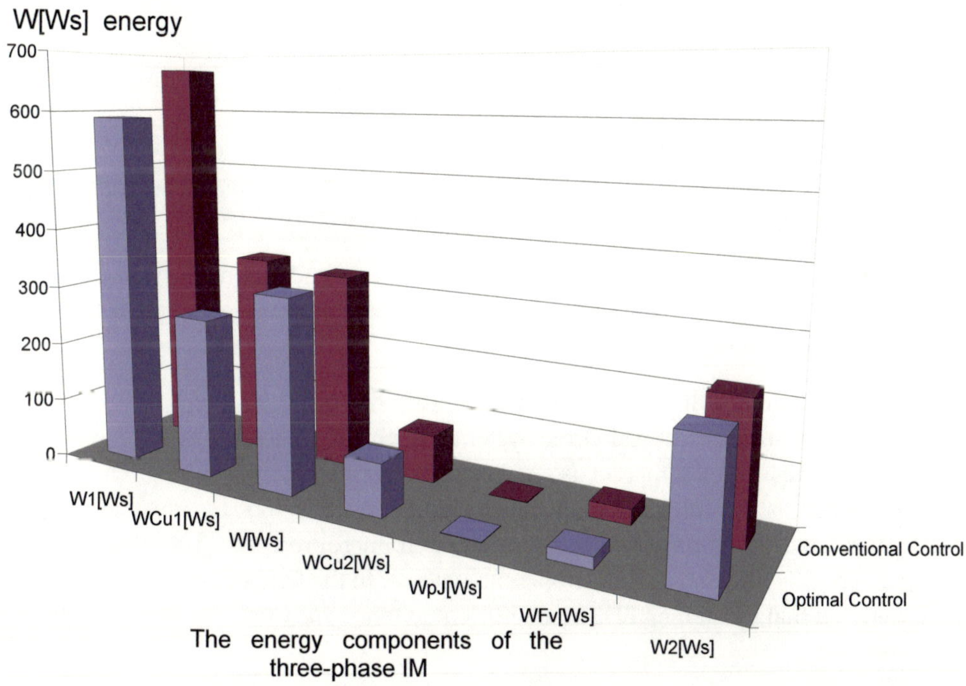

Figure 18. Conventional and optimal control: comparative evaluation of the energy

A simplified solution is proposed by avoiding the constrained optimal control problem type. By using adequate weighting matrices **S**, **R** and **Q**, the magnitude constraints have been solved. In this way the states and the control signals are maintained in admissible limits.

The optimal problem shown in this chapter has been formulated for a starting period. In the Fig.18, the energy evaluation for both control methods, conventional and optimal, is depicted. According to Bellman's theorem of optimality, the optimal problem can be extended also on the braking, or reversing periods. The components of the energy of the three-phase IM (Fig. 20) are: W_1 the input energy, W_2 the output energy, W_{Cu1} the energy expended in the stator windings, W_{Cu2} the energy expended in the rotor windings, W_{Fv} the viscous friction dissipated energy, W_{pJ} the accumulated energy in inertial mass, W the electromagnetic energy.

From the energetic point of view, it could be noticed that the output energy is the same in both controls (conventional and optimal) while the input energy decreases significantly in the optimal control case due to the decreasing of the stator copper losses, even if the rotor losses slightly increase in the optimal control case (Fig.20).

The proposed optimal control conducts to 8% electrical energy reduction, despite of using the conventional control. The conclusion is: decreasing the input energy for the optimal control system at the same time with maintaining the output energy in both systems, classical and optimal, the efficient electric drive system is obtained.

Due to using only the negative exponentials terms, the system is stable.

The optimal control can be applied in the applications with frequent dynamic regimes. The minimization of the consumed energy conducts to an increasing of the operational period of the electrical drives, or to the electrical motor overload allowance.

The optimal control could be extended to the high phase order induction machine applications, in a decoupled *d-q* rotor field oriented reference frame and by using adequate control of the power inverter (Gaiceanu, 2002).

Taking into consideration that this chapter is focused on developing and proving the performances of the optimal Electrical Drive Systems (EDS), an immediate effect is represented by the positive impact on the market as an alternative for electrical efficiency. The key of the proposed chapter is the integration of the developed Matlab tool by means of the high technology, i.e. the development of the systems with microprocessor. The chapter leads to drawing up specific research and development methods in the field of electrical drives. It has been underlined that by making EDS in an efficient manner, the CO2 emission reduction will be also obtained.

The achievement of this chapter is the opportunity to attract young MSc. and PhD students in R&D activities that request both theoretical and practical knowledge. The author will have new opportunities for developing international interdisciplinary research, technological transfer, sharing of experience and cooperation in the framework of the specific Research Programmes.

http://dx.doi.org/10.5772/57521

Appendix 1

```
%%%%%%%%%%%%%%%%%%%%%%%%%%%%%%%%%%%%%%%%%%%%%
% Parameters determination of the three-phase squirrel cage induction motor %
% Developed by Marian Gaiceanu %
%%%%%%%%%%%%%%%%%%%%%%%%%%%%%%%%%%%%%%%%%%%%%
%syncronism speed
n=60*f1/p;    %[rot/min]
%rated electromagnetic torque
Mn=9550*P*10^(-3)/n; %[Nm]
%rated load torque
Mr=Mn;    %[Nm]
%pulsation of the supply voltage
om1=2*pi*f1; %[rad/sec]
%power factor
cosfi=0.71;
%rated efficiency
etan=0.794;
%rated speed
nn=1480;
%syncronism speed
n=60*f1/p;    %[rot/min]
%total inductance
Ls=Lss+Lm;  %[H]
%rotor inductance
Lr=Lrs+Lm;  %[H]
%stator time constant
Ts=Ls/Rs;   %[sec]
%rotor time constant
Tr=Lr/Rr;   %[sec]
%Total leakage factor
sinfi=sqrt(1-cosfi^2);
sigmav=(1-cosfi)/(1+cosfi)
sigma=sigmav
sigmar=Lr/Lm;
%Nominal voltage and nominal frequency of the supply voltage
Un=380;fn=f1;
%rated stator current
In=P/(sqrt(3)*Un*cosfi*etan)
%Nominal magnetizing current
Im=sqrt(sigmav)*In
%Load current Iq=Itorque
It=sqrt(In^2-Im^2)
%Rated flux
lambda_nom=sqrt(1-sigmav)*Un/(sqrt(3)*2*pi*fn) %[Wb]
%number of pole pairs
p=fn*60/n
%nominal slip
sn=n-nn
%Electrical power of the motor
Peln=P/etan
%Torque constant -check point
kt=3*p*lambda_nom/(1+sigmav)%Nm/A
%magnetizing current
Im=lambda_nom/Lm; %A
%inductivitatea de scapari statorica
Lssigma=sigmav*Un/(sqrt(3)*2*pi*fn*Im)
%Rotor approximated inductance
Lr1=(1+sigmav)*Lm  %H
Lrs=Lr1;
%Stator inductance
Lsv=Lssigma/sigmav
Ls1=(1+sigmav)*Lm
Lss=Ls1;
%rotor inductance
Lrv=Lm^2/(Lsv*(1-sigmav))
%d-axis reference stator current
Idref=lambda_nom/Lm
%variable frequency initialization
i=2;%
t0=0.001;%sampling period [s].
t=t0;
q=0; om=0;
tf=0.9;%fixed final time [s] from Fig. 15., conventional control
fi=50; omi=2*pi*fi;
omv=0; tfomv=tf;
imr=Idref;
isd=imr;
```

Appendix 2

```
%%%%%%%%%%%%%%%%%%%%%%%%%%%%%%%%%%%%%%%%%%%%%%%%%%%%%%%%%%%%%%%%%%%%%%%%%%%%%%%%%%%%%%%%%%%%%%%%%%
% vector components of six sectors for using in Space Vector Modulation -SVM (Appendix 6)    %
% Parameters determination of the three-phase squirrel cage induction motor                  %
% Developed by Marian Gaiceanu                                                               %
%%%%%%%%%%%%%%%%%%%%%%%%%%%%%%%%%%%%%%%%%%%%%%%%%%%%%%%%%%%%%%%%%%%%%%%%%%%%%%%%%%%%%%%%%%%%%%%%%%
% Space Vector Modulation PWM: initialization
Tpwm=1/20000; % PWM cycle period
f=50;
oMfaze=2*pi*f;
Tpark=2/3*[1 -1/2 -1/2
           0 sqrt(3)/2 -sqrt(3)/2];
Vd=370; % DC link voltage
% switching/ commutation matrix
Mfaze=[2 -1 -1
   -1 2 -1
   -1 -1 2];
Mfaze=Mfaze*Vd/3;
% 1st vector
global U0_alpha U0_beta
a=1; b=0; c=0;
Vabc=Mfaze*[a b c]';
U0=Tpark*Vabc;
U0_alpha=U0(1,1);
U0_beta=U0(2,1);
% 2nd vector
global U60_alpha U60_beta
a=1; b=1; c=0;
Vabc=Mfaze*[a b c]';
U60=Tpark*Vabc;
U60_alpha=U60(1,1);
U60_beta=U60(2,1);
% 3rd vector
global U120_alpha U120_beta
a=0; b=1; c=0;
Vabc=Mfaze*[a b c]';
U120=Tpark*Vabc;
U120_alpha=U120(1,1);
U120_beta=U120(2,1);
% 4th vector
global U180_alpha U180_beta
a=0; b=1; c=1;
Vabc=Mfaze*[a b c]';
U180=Tpark*Vabc;
U180_alpha=U180(1,1);
U180_beta=U180(2,1);
% 5th vector
global U240_alpha U240_beta
a=0; b=0; c=1;
Vabc=Mfaze*[a b c]';
U240=Tpark*Vabc;
U240_alpha=U240(1,1);
U240_beta=U240(2,1);
% 6th vector
global U300_alpha U300_beta
a=1; b=0; c=1;
Vabc=Mfaze*[a b c]';
U300=Tpark*Vabc;
U300_alpha=U300(1,1);
U300_beta=U300(2,1);
%Fig.2
%State space model
```

http://dx.doi.org/10.5772/57521

Appendix 3

```
%%%%%%%%%%%%%%%%%%%%%%%%%%%%%%%%%%%%%%%%%%%%%%
% The proper arrangement of the eigenvalues and eigenvectors %
% Developed by Marian Gaiceanu                               %
%%%%%%%%%%%%%%%%%%%%%%%%%%%%%%%%%%%%%%%%%%%%%%
% Weighting matrices

  S=[100 0;
     0 0];
  Q=[1*J/1 0;
    0 0.001 ];
  R=[0.08] ;
 % bloc optimal
 % the matrix of the canonical system
M=[-A B*inv(R)*B';
     Q A']
 % eigenvectors and eigenvalues
[v,d]=eig(M);
vecinit=v;
valnit=d;
% the arrangements of the eigenvalues and of the corresponding eigenvectors on the diagonal matrix D
% in order to obtain only the negative eigenvalues
val=[d(1,1) d(2,2) d(3,3) d(4,4)];
x=sort(val);
if x(1,4)==d(2,2),
  aux0=d(2,2);
  d(2,2)=d(1,1);
  d(1,1)=aux0;
  aux9=v(:,2);
  v(:,2)=v(:,1);
  v(:,1)=aux9;
 elseif x(1,4)==d(3,3),
  aux1=d(3,3);
  d(3,3)=d(1,1);
  d(1,1)=aux1;
  aux2=v(:,3);
  v(:,3)=v(:,1);
  v(:,1)=aux2;
 elseif x(1,4)==d(4,4),
  aux3=d(4,4);
  d(4,4)=d(1,1);
  d(1,1)=aux3;
  aux4=v(:,4);
  v(:,4)=v(:,1);
  v(:,1)=aux4;
 end
 if x(1,3)==d(3,3),
  aux5=d(3,3);
  d(3,3)=d(2,2);
  d(2,2)=aux5;
  aux6=v(:,3);
  v(:,3)=v(:,2);
  v(:,2)=aux6;
 elseif x(1,3)==d(4,4),
  aux7=d(4,4);
  d(4,4)=d(2,2);
  d(2,2)=aux7;
  aux8=v(:,4);
  v(:,4)=v(:,2);
  v(:,2)=aux8;
 end
 if x(1,1)==d(4,4),
  aux10=d(4,4);
  d(4,4)=d(3,3);
  d(3,3)=aux10;
  aux11=v(:,4);
  v(:,4)=v(:,3);
  v(:,3)=aux11; end
W=v ; % the eigenvectors
D=d; % the eigenvalues
```

Appendix 4

```
%%%%%%%%%%%%%%%%%%%%%%%%%%%%%
% Optimal control implementation in MATLAB  %
% Developed by Marian Gaiceanu                %
%%%%%%%%%%%%%%%%%%%%%%%%%%%%%
%  checking point of eigenvalues and eigenvectors
  Dv=inv(W)*M*W;
%  the eigenvalues
  lambda=diag(D);
%  Matrix -(lambda)
  mlambda=[D(3,3) D(3,4);
         D(4,3) D(4,4)];
%  submatrices of the eigenvectors
  W11=[W(1,1) W(1,2);
     W(2,1) W(2,2)];
  W12=[W(1,3) W(1,4);
     W(2,3) W(2,4)];
  W21=[W(3,1) W(3,2);
     W(4,1) W(4,2)];
  W22=[W(3,3) W(3,4);
     W(4,3) W(4,4)];
%  the inverse of the eigenvectors matrix
  W1=inv(W);
%  extension of the perturbation vector G
  G1=[G;0;0];
  Gp=W1*G1;
  H= Gp./lambda;
  H1=[H(1,1);
    H(2,1)];
  H2=[H(3,1);
    H(4,1)];
  I1=inv(S*W12-W22);
  E=I1*(W21-S*W11);
  F=I1*S;
 xi=[0;0];    %initial conditions  (state vector) for a starting
 xf=[n;0]; tau=tf; % final conditions for a starting: final state and final time
 Yi3=0;  Yif3=[0;0];% initial value for the filter matrices
 Ii=eye(2);   % [2x2] identity matrix I2
 wp=Mr;       % initial perturbation value
 Ta=0.07;     % filter time constant
 swcu=0;
 kq=1/Tr/imr; % IM torque constant
yc1=exp(-t0/Ta);  yc2=1-yc1; c1=exp(-t0*Fv/J); c3=(1-c1)/Fv;
```

Appendix 5

```
%%%%%%%%%%%%%%%%%%%%%%%%%%%%%%%%%%%%%%%%%%%%%%
% Main Program                                  %
% Developed by Marian Gaiceanu                          %
%%%%%%%%%%%%%%%%%%%%%%%%%%%%%%%%%%%%%%%%%%%%%%
while (t<=tf)&(tau>0),
      tau=tf-t;
      emlamt=expm(mlambda*tau);
      Z=emlamt*E*emlamt;
      P=(W21+W22*Z)*(inv(W11+W12*Z));
      V=W22-P*W12;
      Iie=Ii-emlamt;
      T=V*(emlamt*E*Iie*H1+Iie*H2);
      K=V*emlamt*F;
   %
      Yi1=-inv(R)*B'*(P*xi);
      Yiw=Yi3*exp(-t0/Ta)+wp*(1-exp(-t0/Ta));
      Yi4=-inv(R)*B'*(T*Yiw);
      Yif=Yif3*exp(-t0/Ta)+xf*(1- exp(-t0/Ta));
      Yi2=-inv(R)*B'*(K*Yif);
      %comanda optima
      isq(i)=Yi1+Yi2+Yi4;
      isqo=isq(i-1);%therefore i=2 as initialization;
  %mathematical model
  % d, q supply voltage components
    usd(i)=Rs*isd*(1-sigma*Ts*(om+isqo*kq));
    usq(i)=Rs*(sigma*Ts*isq(i)/t0-isqo*(-1+(sigma-1)*Ts*imr*kq+sigma*Ts*isd*kq)-om*(sigma*Ts*isd+Ts*(sigma-1)*imr));
   Me(i)=p*km*imr*isq(i); %electromagnetic torque
   %electrical speed
   omu(i)=om*exp(-t0*Fv/J)+p*(Me(i)-wp)*(1- exp(-t0*Fv/J))/Fv;
   %rotor (mechanical) speed
   nr(i)=30*omu(i)/pi/p;
   %load torque variation limits
     if t>0,
       wp=1*Mr;
     else
       wp=0*Mr;
     end
   wpr(i)=wp;
  % angle of the rotor magnetization current vector, imr
   qu(i)=q+t0*(omu(i)+isq(i)/(Tr*imr));

   % data refreshing
    xi=[nr(i);qu(i)];
    Yi3=Yiw; Yif3=Yif;
   isalfa=cos(qu(i))*isd-sin(qu(i))*isq(i);
   isbeta=sin(qu(i))*isd+cos(qu(i))*isq(i);
   isa(i)=2*isalfa/3;
   isb(i)=-isalfa/3+isbeta/sqrt(3);
   isc(i)=-isalfa/3-isbeta/sqrt(3);
 %three phase supply stator voltages
usalfa=cos(qu(i))*usd(i)-sin(qu(i))*usq(i);
V_alpha=usalfa;
usbeta=sin(qu(i))*usd(i)+cos(qu(i))*usq(i);
V_beta=usbeta;
ualfas(i)=usalfa;
ubetas(i)=usbeta;
% Space Vector Modulation
[Va Vb Vc]=svm_mod(Vd,V_alpha,V_beta,t,Tpwm);
   usa(i)=2*usalfa/3;
   usb(i)=-usalfa/3+usbeta/sqrt(3);
   usc(i)=-usalfa/3-usbeta/sqrt(3);
   ualfas1(i)=usalfa;
   ubetas1(i)=usbeta;
   V_alfar=Va-(1/2)*Vb-(1/2)*Vc;
   ualfar(i)=V_alfar;
   V_betar=(sqrt(3)/2)*Vb-(sqrt(3)/2)*Vc;
   ubetar(i)=V_betar;
   udr=cos(qu(i))*V_alfar-sin(qu(i))*V_betar;
   uqr=sin(qu(i))*V_alfar+cos(qu(i))*V_betar;
t=t+t0;          tplot(i)=t;          Vaplot(i)=Va;          Vbplot(i)=Vb;          Vcplot(i)=Vc;    imru(i)=imr;    isdu(i)=isd;    isqi(i)=isqo;
q=qu(i);  om=omu(i); i=i+1;
end
```

Appendix 6

```
%%%%%%%%%%%%%%%%%%%%%%%%%%%%%%%%%%%%
% Graphical representation                %
% Developed by Marian Gaiceanu             %
%%%%%%%%%%%%%%%%%%%%%%%%%%%%%%%%%%%%
figure(1)
subplot(3,1,1)
plot(tplot,Vaplot,'LineWidth',3)
ylabel('usA=f(t)','FontSize',12)
    xlabel('time[s]','FontSize',12)
    title('stator voltage of phase A [V]','FontSize',12)
axis([0 .9 -500 500])
subplot(3,1,2)
plot(tplot,Vbplot,'LineWidth',3)
ylabel('usB=f(t)','FontSize',12)
    xlabel('time[s]','FontSize',12)
    title('stator voltage of phase B [V]','FontSize',12)
axis([0 .9 -500 500])
subplot(3,1,3)
plot(tplot,Vcplot,'LineWidth',3)
ylabel('usC=f(t)','FontSize',12)
    xlabel('time[s]','FontSize',12)
    title('stator voltage of phase C [V] ','FontSize',12)
axis([0 .9 -500 500])

figure(2)
    t=0:t0:tf-2*t0;
    i=1:1:length(t);
    subplot(2,2,1);
    plot(t,isq(i),'k','LineWidth',3);
    title('optimal control isq=f(t)','FontSize',12)
    xlabel('time[s]','FontSize',12)
    ylabel('isq [A]','FontSize',12)
    grid
    axis([0 0.9 0 6])
subplot(2,2,2);
    plot(t,nr(i),'k','LineWidth',3);%omu(i)
    title('speed=f(t)','FontSize',12)
    xlabel('time[s]','FontSize',12)
    ylabel('speed [rot/min]','FontSize',12)
    grid
    axis([0 0.9 0 2000])

    subplot(2,2,3);
plot(t,usd(i),'k','LineWidth',3);
    title(' usd=f(t)','FontSize',12)
    xlabel('time[s]','FontSize',12)
    ylabel('usd [V]','FontSize',12)
    grid
    axis([0 0.9 -40 5])
    subplot(2,2,4);
    plot(t,usq(i),'k','LineWidth',3);
    title(' usq=f(t)','FontSize',12)
    xlabel('time[s]','FontSize',12)
    ylabel('usq [V]','FontSize',12)
    grid
    axis([0 0.9 0 400])
figure(3)
     t=0:t0:tf-2*t0;
    i=1:1:length(t);
    plot(ualfas1(i),ubetas1(i),'b','LineWidth',3)
    title('stator voltage loci loculus')
   xlabel('ualfa[V]')
   ylabel('uabeta [V]')
   grid;
figure(4)
     t=0:t0:tf-2*t0;
    i=1:1:length(t);
    plot(ualfar(i),ubetar(i),'b','LineWidth',3);
    title('voltage loci loculus')
   grid;
```

http://dx.doi.org/10.5772/57521

Appendix 7

```
%%%%%%%%%%%%%%%%%%%%%%%%%%%%%%%%%%%%%%%%%%%%%%%%%%%%%%%%%%%
% Space Vector Modulation implemented as a Matlab function %
% Developed by Marian Gaiceanu                            %
% svm_mod (Vd,V_alpha,V_beta,t,Tpwm)                      %
%%%%%%%%%%%%%%%%%%%%%%%%%%%%%%%%%%%%%%%%%%%%%%%%%%%%%%%%%%%
%Implemented Matlab function of the Space Vector Modulation
function [Va,Vb,Vc] = svm_mod (Vd,V_alpha,V_beta,t,Tpwm)

global U0_alpha U0_beta
global U60_alpha U60_beta
global U120_alpha U120_beta
global U180_alpha U180_beta
global U240_alpha U240_beta
global U300_alpha U300_beta

% angle of the space vector
V=sqrt(V_alpha*V_alpha+V_beta*V_beta);
if V_beta >0,
  teta=acos(V_alpha/V);
else
  teta=2*pi-acos(V_alpha/V);
end
teta=teta*180/pi;

% sector selection
if teta>=0 & teta<=60
  s=1;
elseif teta>60 & teta<=120
  s=2;
elseif teta>120 & teta<=180
  s=3;
elseif teta>180 & teta<=240
  s=4;
elseif teta>240 & teta<=300
  s=5;
else
  s=6;
end

% space vector decomposition
switch s
case 1,
  V1_alpha=U0_alpha;
  V1_beta=U0_beta;
  V2_alpha=U60_alpha;
  V2_beta=U60_beta;
case 2,
  V1_alpha=U120_alpha;
  V1_beta=U120_beta;
  V2_alpha=U60_alpha;
  V2_beta=U60_beta;
case 3,
  V1_alpha=U120_alpha;
  V1_beta=U120_beta;
  V2_alpha=U180_alpha;
  V2_beta=U180_beta;
case 4,
  V1_alpha=U240_alpha;
  V1_beta=U240_beta;
  V2_alpha=U180_alpha;
  V2_beta=U180_beta;
case 5,
  V1_alpha=U240_alpha;
  V1_beta=U240_beta;
  V2_alpha=U300_alpha;
  V2_beta=U300_beta;
```

```
case 6,
  V1_alpha=U0_alpha;
  V1_beta=U0_beta;
  V2_alpha=U300_alpha;
  V2_beta=U300_beta;
end
det=V1_alpha*V2_beta-V2_alpha*V1_beta;
T1=Tpwm*(V_alpha*V2_beta-V2_alpha*V_beta)/det;
T2=Tpwm*(V1_alpha*V_beta-V_alpha*V1_beta)/det;
T0=Tpwm-T1-T2;

% switching pulse
tc=rem(t,Tpwm);
C1=0.25*T0;
C2=C1+0.5*T1;
C3=C2+0.5*T2;
patt1 = C1<=tc & tc<=Tpwm-C1;
patt2 = C2<=tc & tc<=Tpwm-C2;
patt3 = C3<=tc & tc<=Tpwm-C3;
switch s
case 1,
  puls_a=patt1;
  puls_b=patt2;
  puls_c=patt3;
case 2,
  puls_a=patt2;
  puls_b=patt1;
  puls_c=patt3;
case 3,
  puls_a=patt3;
  puls_b=patt1;
  puls_c=patt2;
case 4,
  puls_a=patt3;
  puls_b=patt2;
  puls_c=patt1;
case 5,
  puls_a=patt2;
  puls_b=patt3;
  puls_c=patt1;
case 6,
  puls_a=patt1;
  puls_b=patt3;
  puls_c=patt2;
end
Vmatrix=(1/3)*[2 -1 -1
         -1 2 -1
         -1 -1 2]*[puls_a
                 puls_b
                 puls_c]*Vd;
Va=Vmatrix(1,:);
Vb=Vmatrix(2,:);
Vc=Vmatrix(3,:);
```

http://dx.doi.org/10.5772/57521

Appendix 8

The Matlab file for tuning of the PI speed and flux controllers parameters in conventional control

```
%%%%%%%%%%%%%%%%%%%%%%%%%%%%%%%%%%%%%%%%%%%%%%%%%%%%%%%%%%%%%%%%%%%%%%%%%%%%%%%%%%%%
% Tuning of the PI speed and flux controllers parameters: Kessler variant    %
% Developed by Marian Gaiceanu                                              %
%%%%%%%%%%%%%%%%%%%%%%%%%%%%%%%%%%%%%%%%%%%%%%%%%%%%%%%%%%%%%%%%%%%%%%%%%%%%%%%%%%%%
%sampling time
Ts=0.0001; %100us
%PWM
%gain factor
Kpwm=1; %daca nu se considera marimile de la traductoare in sistem unificat de tensiuni: 10V
Tpwm=Ts/2;

%%%%%%%%%%%%%%%%%%%%%%%%%%%%%%%%%%%%
% Current loop: d- axis          %
%%%%%%%%%%%%%%%%%%%%%%%%%%%%%%%%%%%%

%sum of parasite (small) time constant
Teim=Ts+Tpwm;
%controller of type 1: 1+s*tau1/(s*tau2)
tau1=Lssigma/Rs
tau2=2*Teim*Kpwm/Rs
% controller of type 2: kp_idm+ki_idm/s
kp_idm=tau1/tau2
ki_idm=1/tau2 %for Pn<10kW, else:
%for perturbation rejection (Blasko)
% controller of type 3: kp(1+1/sTim)
Tim=10*Teim %Blasko
ki_idm=kp_idm/Tim %assures a damping factor D=0.707 and a bandwidth of fbanda=fs/20

%%%%%%%%%%%%%%%%%%%%%%%%%%%%%%%%%%%%%
%Similarly, Current loop: q- axis%
%%%%%%%%%%%%%%%%%%%%%%%%%%%%%%%%%%%%%
kp_iqm=kp_idm;
ki_iqm=ki_idm;

%%%%%%%%%%%%%%%%%%%%%%%%%%%%
%Speed control loop       %
%%%%%%%%%%%%%%%%%%%%%%%%%%%%
%from the closed loop current transfer function
Ttm=2*Teim
%time delay constant of the sample and hold device
Tdt=Ts;
%sum of the small constant time, speed loop
Tetm=Tdt+Ttm;
%Imposed phase margin:
fimm=45*pi/180;
% a factor
a=(1+cos(fimm))/sin(fimm)

%%%%%%%%%%%%%%%%%%%%%%%%%%%%%%%%%%%%%%%%%%%%%%%%%%%%%%%%%%%%%%%%%%%%%
%Tuning of the speed controller parameters kpt(1+sTit)/sTit %
%%%%%%%%%%%%%%%%%%%%%%%%%%%%%%%%%%%%%%%%%%%%%%%%%%%%%%%%%%%%%%%%%%%%%

kpt=J/(a*Tetm); Tit=a^2*Tetm

%%%%%%%%%%%%%%%%%%%%%%%%%%%%%%%%%%%%%%%%%%%%%%%%%%%%%%%%%%%%
%Speed regulator of type1: kp_om+ki_om/s, Kessler %
%%%%%%%%%%%%%%%%%%%%%%%%%%%%%%%%%%%%%%%%%%%%%%%%%%%%%%%%%%%%

kp_om=kpt; ki_om=kpt/Tit

%%%%%%%%%%%%%%%%%%%%%%%%%%%%%%%%%%%%%%%%%%%%%%%%%%%%%%%%
% Speed regulator of type2: (1+s*tau3)/s*tau4 %
%%%%%%%%%%%%%%%%%%%%%%%%%%%%%%%%%%%%%%%%%%%%%%%%%%%%%%%%

tau3=4*Tetm; tau4=8*Tetm^2/J
%%%%%%%%%%%%%%%%%%%%%%%%%%%%%%%%%%%%%%%%%%%%%%%%%%%%%%%%
```

```
% Speed regulator of type3: kp_omk+ki_omk/s   %
%%%%%%%%%%%%%%%%%%%%%%%%%%%%%%%%%%%%%%%%%%%%%%%
kp_omk=tau3/tau4        %Kessler
ki_omk=1/tau4
%%%%%%%%%%%%%%%%%%%%%%%%%%%%%%%%%%%%%%%%%%%%%%%%%%%%%%%%%%%%%%%%%%%%%%%%%%%%
%Flux loop (d axis)_ approximated mathematical model 1/(s*Tr/Lm): Kessler %
%%%%%%%%%%%%%%%%%%%%%%%%%%%%%%%%%%%%%%%%%%%%%%%%%%%%%%%%%%%%%%%%%%%%%%%%%%%%
% Flux regulator of type1: (1+s*tau3f)/s*tau4f
Tr=Lr/Rr;%rotor time constant
tau3f=4*Tetm
tau4f=8*Tetm^2/(Tr/Lm)
% Flux regulator of type2: kp_dfk+ki_dfk/s
kp_dfk=tau3/tau4
ki_dfk=1/tau4
%%%%%%%%%%%%%%%%%%%%%%%%%%%%%%%%%%%%%%%%%%%%%%%%%%%%%%%%%%%%%%%%%%%%%%%%%%
% Flux loop (d axis) approximated mathematical model 1/(s*Tr/Lm): Blasko%
%%%%%%%%%%%%%%%%%%%%%%%%%%%%%%%%%%%%%%%%%%%%%%%%%%%%%%%%%%%%%%%%%%%%%%%%%%
% from closed loop d axis current transfer function
Tfm=2*Teim   %the same with  Ttm
%delay time constant of the flux loop sample and hold device
Tdf=Ts;
%time delay constant of the sample and hold device
Tefm=Tdt+Tfm;
%Reference of the phase margin:
fimf=60*pi/180;
% af factor
af=(1+cos(fimf))/sin(fimf)

%%%%%%%%%%%%%%%%%%%%%%%%%%%%%%%%%%%%%%%%%%%%%%%
% Speed regulator of type 3:kpf(1+sTif)/sTif  %
%%%%%%%%%%%%%%%%%%%%%%%%%%%%%%%%%%%%%%%%%%%%%%%
kpf=(Tr/Lm)/(a*Tefm)
Tif=a^2*Tefm
%%%%%%%%%%%%%%%%%%%%%%%%%%%%%%%%%%%%%%%%%%%%%%%%
% Flux regulator of type 3: kp_df+ki_df/s      %
%%%%%%%%%%%%%%%%%%%%%%%%%%%%%%%%%%%%%%%%%%%%%%%%
kp_df=kpf; ki_df=kpf/Tif
```

Acknowledgements

This work was supported by a grant of the Romanian National Authority for Scientific Research, CNDI– UEFISCDI, project number PN-II-PT-PCCA-2011-3.2-1680.

Author details

Marian Gaiceanu*

Dunarea de Jos University of Galati, Romania

References

[1] Athans M. & P. L. Falb (2006). Optimal Control: An Introduction to the Theory and Its Applications. ISBN: 0486453286, USA, Dover, 2006

[2] COM(2006). Action Plan for Energy Efficiency: Realising the Potential, Available from

[3] Gaiceanu, M. (1997). "Optimal Control for the Variable Speed Induction Motor"- thesis dissertation Master Degree, Power Electronics and Advanced Control Methods of the Electromechanical Systems, Dunarea de Jos University of Galati, June 1997

[4] Gaiceanu, M. (2002). Ph.D. thesis Optimal Control of the Adjustable Electrical Drive Systems with Induction Motors by using Advanced Methods, Dunarea de Jos University of Galati, April, 2002, Romania

[5] Gaiceanu, M., Rosu E., Paduraru R. & Dache C. (2008). Optimal Control Development System for Electrical Drives, *The Annals of "Dunarea de Jos" University of Galati,* FASCICLE III, Vol.31, No.1, ISSN 1221-454X, pp. 5-10.

[6] Gattami A. & Rantzer A. (2005). Linear Quadratic Performance Criteria for Cascade Control, Proceedings of the 44th IEEE Conference on Decision and Control, and the European Control Conference 2005 Seville, Spain, December 12-15, 2005

[7] http://ec.europa.eu/energy/action_plan_energy_efficiency/doc/com_2006_0545_en.pdf

[8] http://www.automation.siemens.com/

[9] Jianqiang, L., Yang, L., F., Zheng, Z., Trillion., Q. (2007). *Optimal Efficiency Control of Linear Induction Motor Drive for Linear Metro*, 2nd IEEE Conference on Industrial Applications, 2007, ICIEA 2007, 23-25 May 2007, pp. 1981-1985, ISBN 978-1-4244-0737-8, 2007

[10] Leonhard, W.: *Control of Electrical Drives*, Springer-Verlag, Berlin 1996

[11] Lorenz, R. D., Yang S.-M. (1992). "Efficiency-Optimized Flux Trajectories for Closed-Cycle Operation of Field-Orientation Induction Machines Drives", IEEE Trans. Ind. Appl.,Vol. 28, No. 3, May/Jun. 1992, pp. 574-580.

[12] Lorenz, R. D., Yang, S.M. (1998). "Efficiency-Optimized Flux Trajectories for Closed Cycle Operation of Field Oriented Induction Machine Drives", Industry Applications Society Annual Meeting, 1988., Conference Record of the 1988 IEEE, pp 457-462, 1998

[13] Matinfar, M., K.Hashtrudi-Zaad (2005). Optimization-based Robot Compliance Control: Geometric and Linear Quadratic Approaches, International Journal of Robotics Research, ISSN 0278-3649, Sage Publications, Inc., Vol.24, pp. 645-656, August 2005

[14] Mendes, E., A. Baba, A. Razek, (1995). "Losses Minimization of a Field Oriented Controlled Induction Machine", Proceed. of IEE Electrical Machines and Drives Conf., Sep. 1995, pp. 310-314.

[15] Rosu, E. (1985). A Solution of Optimal Problem with Quadratic Performance Criteria, Analele Universitatii "Dunarea de Jos" Galati

[16] Rosu, E., Gaiceanu, M., & Bivol, I. (1998). Optimal Control Strategy for AC Drives, PEMC '98, 8th International Power Electronics & Motion Control Conference, Prague, Czech Republic, pp.4.160-4.165

[17] Rosu, E., Gaiceanu, M., Bivol, I. (1998). "Load Torque Estimation for AC Motors", CNAE '98, The 9th Symposium on Electrical Drives, Craiova, Romania, ISBN 973-9346-68-5, pp. 221-224, 1998

[18] Su, C.T. & Chiang C.L. (2004). Optimal Position/Speed Control of Induction Motor Using Improved Genetic Algorithm and Fuzzy Phase Plane Controller, Journal of Control and Intelligent Systems, ISSN 1480-1752, Vol.32, 2004

[19] Tamimi, J.M.Kh. & Jaddu, H.M. (2006). Optimal vector control of three-phase induction machine, International Association of Science and Technology for Development, Proceedings of the 25th IASTED International Conference on Modeling, Identification and Control, Lanzarote, Spain, Acta Press, CA USA, ISSN 0-88986-549-3, 2006, pp. 92-96

[20] Veerachary M. (2002). Optimal control strategy for a current source inverter fed induction motor, Computers and Electrical Engineering, Vol.28, No.4, July 2002, pp. 255-267

[21] Vukosavic, S.N., Jones, M., Levi, E., and Varga J. (2005). Rotor flux oriented control of a symmetrical six-phase induction machine, Electric Power Systems Research 75 (2005) 142–152

Chapter 13

Modeling of Control Systems

Roger Chiu, Francisco J. Casillas,
Didier López-Mancilla, Francisco G. Peña-Lecona,
Miguel Mora-González and Jesús Muñoz Maciel

Additional information is available at the end of the chapter

http://dx.doi.org/10.5772/58236

1. Introduction

In studying control systems the reader must be able to model dynamical systems in mathematical terms and analyze their dynamic characteristics. This section provides an introduction to basic concepts and methodologies on modeling control systems. It also introduces some fundamentals to solve realistic models used basically in mechanical, electrical, thermal, economic, biological, and so on. A mathematical model is composed by a set of equations that describe a real system accurately, or at least fairly well. However a mathematical model is not unique for a given system, and the system under study can be represented in many different ways, in the same way a mathematical model can be used to represent different systems. Algorithms used to solve the set of equations that represent a control system require a great amount of programming instructions. Matlab is a tool that simplifies and accelerates such algorithms allowing to modeling a great variety of control systems in a very elegant way [1]. There are special Matlab toolbox useful to solve different control systems, in particular Control System Toolbox (included in MATLAB Version 7.8.0.347 (R2009a)): Creating linear models, data extraction, time-domain analysis, frequency-domain analysis, state space models, etc. Some of these are used throughout the chapter to facilitate algorithm development.

This chapter is organized as follows; the section 1 is an introduction to modeling control systems. In section 2, some applications using electrical circuits for series and parallel circuits are given. Section 3, a second order analysis is presented. In section 4, control systems for mechanical vibrations are analyzed. Optical control systems are given in section 5, given a perspective with two basic systems: laser diode, and optical fiber. Some conclusions are presented in section 6.

INTECH
open science | open minds

© 2014 The Author(s). Licensee InTech. This chapter is distributed under the terms of the Creative Commons Attribution License (http://creativecommons.org/licenses/by/3.0), which permits unrestricted use, distribution, and reproduction in any medium, provided the original work is properly cited.

2. Electrical circuits

Undoubtedly, the most classic circuit in literature is the RLC circuit. Due to its great usefulness in the study of linear systems, the model of the RLC circuit helps to understand some of the behaviors of an electrical control system. Thus, the next subsections will address to the modeling of series and parallel RLC circuits. Some behaviors will be analyzed using some tools from Matlab.

Case I: RLC series circuit

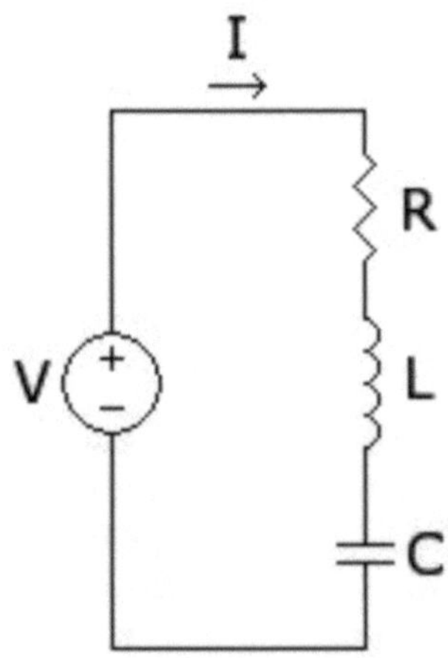

Figure 1. RLC series circuit.

In Figure 1, a RLC series circuit is shown. The modeling consists in to express a number of equations such that all kinds of moves are expressed in those equations. Thus, the input equation is given by

$$v_i(t) = Ri(t) + L\frac{di(t)}{dt} + \frac{1}{C}\int_0^t i(\tau)d\tau. \quad (1)$$

Let be $v_o(t)$ the output in capacitor C. Then, the output equation is represented by

$$v_o(t) = \frac{1}{C}\int_0^t i(\tau)d\tau. \quad (2)$$

In order to find a transfer function, the Laplace transform for both equations is applied obtaining

$$V_i(s) = RI(s) + LsI(s) + \frac{1}{Cs}I(s), \tag{3}$$

and

$$V_o(s) = \frac{1}{Cs}I(s). \tag{4}$$

The transfer function becomes

$$\frac{V_o(s)}{V_i(s)} = \frac{1}{LCs^2 + RCs + 1}. \tag{5}$$

In order to compute a general solution and to analyze the behavior of this RLC series circuit, consider an input constant force $v_i(t) = V_i$. Then $V_i(s) = V_i / s$, therefore the output signal in the Laplace domain is given by

$$V_o(s) = \frac{V_i}{s(LCs^2 + RCs + 1)}, \tag{6}$$

therefore, the output signal results

$$v_o(t) = V_i\left(1 - e^{-\frac{R}{2L}t}\cos\sqrt{\frac{4L + R^2C}{4L^2C}}t - \sqrt{\frac{R^2C}{4L + R^2C}}e^{-\frac{R}{2L}t}\sin\sqrt{\frac{4L + R^2C}{4L^2C}}t\right). \tag{7}$$

Figure 2, shows the block diagram for the RLC series circuit.

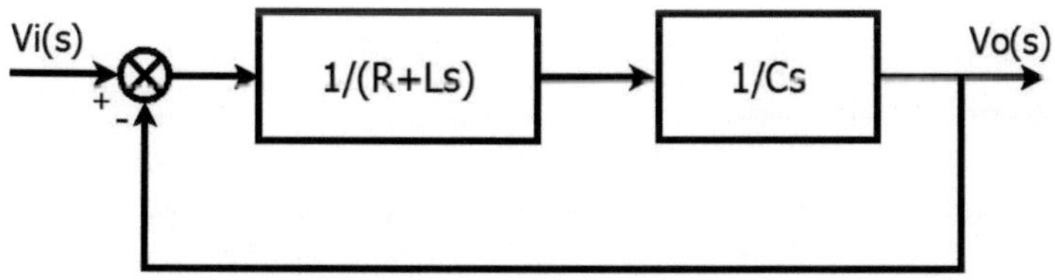

Figure 2. Block diagram for the RLC series circuit.

Suppose a particular case for the block diagram with $R = 2k\Omega$, $L = 1mH$ and $C = 1\mu F$. An easy way to obtain a step response for a RLC series circuit is to draw a block diagram in Simulink, from Matlab, using a source Step and a Scope to observe the response as shown in Figure 3. In Figure 4, the step response for the RLC series circuit is plotted.

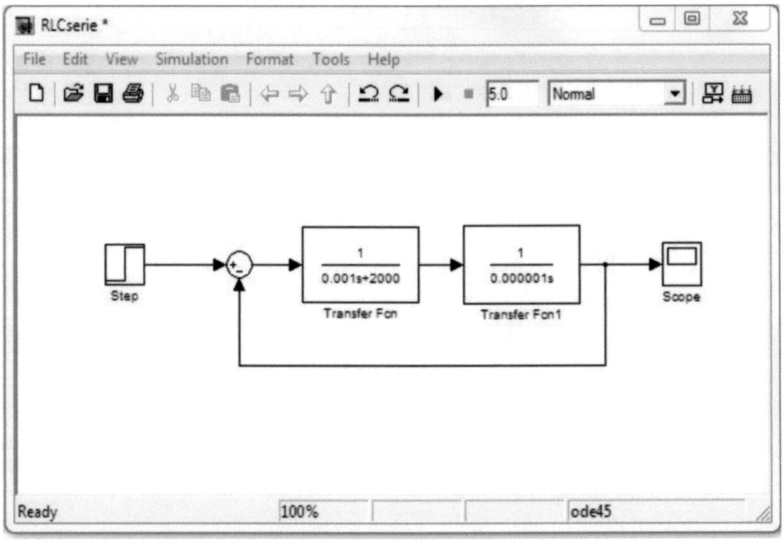

Figure 3. Block diagram using Simulink for a step response.

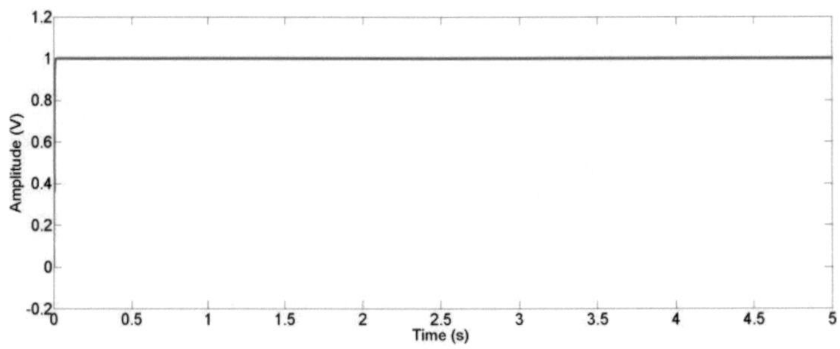

Figure 4. Step response for RLC series circuit using Simulink.

Case 2: RLC Parallel circuit

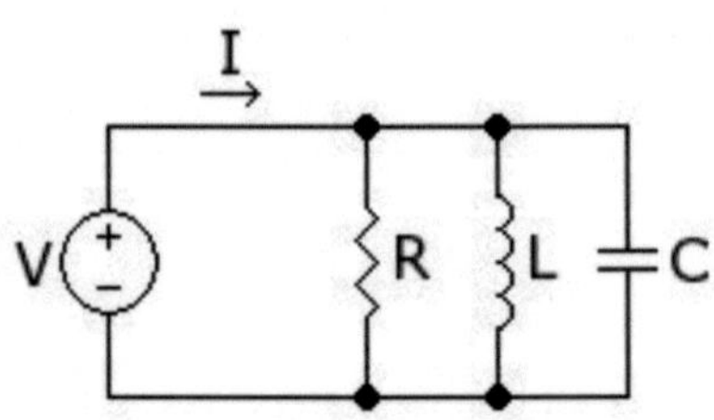

Figure 5. RLC parallel circuit.

http://dx.doi.org/10.5772/58236

In Figure 5, a RLC parallel circuit is shown. The equation of current could be represented by

$$i(t)=\frac{v_R(t)}{R}+\frac{1}{L}\int_0^t v_L(\tau)d\tau+C\frac{dv_C(t)}{dt}. \tag{8}$$

The output voltage through capacitor C, establishes the equalities

$$v_o(t)=v_R(t)=v_L(t)=v_C(t), \tag{9}$$

such that the mathematical model can be written in only one equation

$$i(t)=\frac{v_o(t)}{R}+\frac{1}{L}\int_0^t v_o(\tau)d\tau+C\frac{dv_o(t)}{dt}. \tag{10}$$

In order to find the transfer function, the Laplace transform is

$$I(s)=\frac{V_o(s)}{R}+\frac{1}{Ls}V_o(s)+CsV_o(s). \tag{11}$$

Then, the transfer function results

$$\frac{V_o(s)}{I(s)}=\frac{RLs}{RLCs^2+Ls+R}. \tag{12}$$

To compute a general solution and to analyze the behavior of this RLC parallel circuit, consider an input force of constant current $i(t)=I$. Then $I(s)=I/s$, therefore the output signal in the Laplace domain is given by

$$V_o(s)=\frac{RL}{RLCs^2+Ls+R}I, \tag{13}$$

and the solution signal results

$$v_o(t)=2IR\sqrt{\frac{L}{4R^2C-L}}e^{-\frac{1}{2RC}t}\sin\sqrt{\frac{4R^2C-L}{4R^2L\ C^2}}t. \tag{14}$$

Figure 6, shows the corresponding block diagram for the RLC parallel circuit.

In order to analyze the stability using Matlab, consider a RLC parallel circuit with $R=1k\Omega$, $L=1mH$ and $C=1\mu F$. The aim is to obtain the transfer function, a state space representation, the eigenvalues, and the solution to state space equation.

The coefficients of the transfer function are stored in two vectors *num* and *den* for the numerator and denominator, respectively. The following solution uses the instructions *tf, tf2ss,* from Control Systems Toolbox. Window a) shows this algorithm obtaining the transfer function

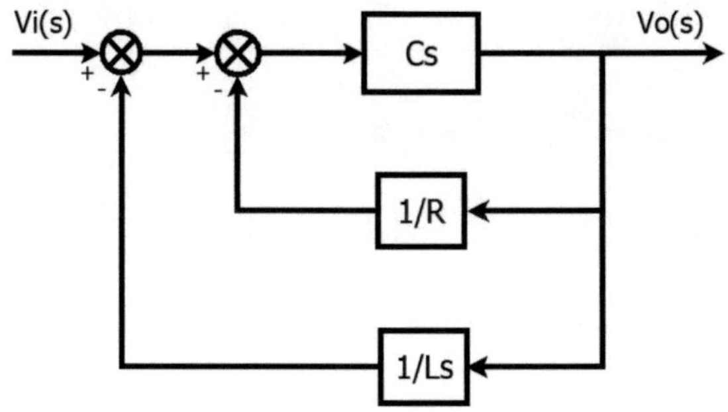

Figure 6. Block diagram for the RLC parallel circuit.

$G(s)$. Window b), uses the instruction *tf2ss* to convert from transfer function to state space, getting arrays A, B, C and D. Window c) illustrate the stability of the system, computing the eigenvalues from array A. Note that the eigenvalues from the system in state space is equivalent to compute the poles of transfer function $G(s)$. Thus, the poles are placed at the negative place of the complex plane, which means that the system is stable.

a)

```
>> num=[1 0];
>> den=[0.000001 0.001
1000];
>> G=tf(num,den)
Transfer function:
 s
----------------------------
```

b)

```
>>
[A,B,C,D]=tf2ss(num,den)
A =
  1.0e+003 *
 -1    -1000000

  0.001     0
B =
    1
 0
C = 1000000          0
D = 0
```

c)

```
>> eig(A)
ans =
  1.0e+004 *
 -0.0500 + 3.1619i
  -0.0500 - 3.1619i
```

http://dx.doi.org/10.5772/58236

To obtain the solution to the state space equation using Matlab, it is necessary to construct an object S, of class '*sym*', from A, using the expression S=*sym*(A), in order of using the instruction *ilaplace*, from Symbolic Math Toolbox. It is well known that the solution to state equation is given by

$$x(t)=\mathrm{L}[(sI - A)^{-1}]x(0). \tag{15}$$

Then, window d) gives a solution using symbolic mathematics and the instruction *ilaplace*, with $x(0)=[1 \quad 1]^T$.

d)

```
>> s=sym('s');
>> f=ilaplace(inv(s*eye(2)-A))
f =
[ (cos(500*3999^(1/2)*t) - (3999^(1/2)*sin(500*3999^(1/2)*t))/3999)/exp(500*t),
-(2000000*3999^(1/2)*sin(500*3999^(1/2)*t))/(3999*exp(500*t))]
[                          (3999^(1/2)*sin(500*3999^(1/2)*t))/(1999500*exp(500*t)),
(cos(500*3999^(1/2)*t) + (3999^(1/2)*sin(500*3999^(1/2)*t))/3999)/exp(500*t)]
```

Note that, all solutions have a negative exponential or they are written explicitly as denominators with positive exponential, which mean that the system is stable. This kind of results could be useful for the next sections for mechanical vibrations and optical control systems.

3. Second order analysis

In the Nature there are many examples that can be modeled with second-degree equations. The general form is represented by a homogeneous linear differential equation with constant coefficients a, b and, c as shown below

$$a\frac{d^2x}{dt^2} + b\frac{dx}{dt} + cx = 0, \tag{16}$$

Laplace transform of the second-order equation is

$$s^2X(s) - sx(0) - \dot{x}(0) + \frac{b}{a}sX(s) - \frac{b}{a}x(0) + \frac{c}{a}X(s) = 0, \tag{17}$$

and solving for the dependent variable

$$X(s) = \frac{sx(0) + \frac{b}{a}x(0) + \dot{x}(0)}{s^2 + \frac{b}{a}s + \frac{c}{a}}. \tag{18}$$

The response for a unitary step input is given by the next equation

$$X(s) = \frac{s^2 x(0) + s\left[\frac{b}{a}x(0) + \dot{x}(0)\right]}{s^2 + \frac{b}{a}s + \frac{c}{a}} \bullet \frac{1}{s}. \tag{19}$$

There are four possible behaviors of equation (19) [2]: overdamped, underdamped, undamped and critically damped. These results can be predicted by analyzing the characteristic equation, as shown below:

$$b^2 - 4ac = \begin{cases} positive, & overdamped \\ negative, & underdamped \\ -4ac, & undamped \\ zero, & critically\ damped \end{cases} \tag{20}$$

Where the initial conditions $x(0)$ and $\dot{x}(0)$ represent the initial state and the point of convergence of the response signal, respectively. The next results uses a step signal as input signal, with the instruction *step*, from Control Systems Toolbox. Thus, the graphical representation of a second-order analysis using Matlab as shown in Figure 7, can be obtained with the next code:

```
clear all;
x0=0.8;
xp0=0.35;
%%%% b*b>4*a*c
a=1;b=5;c=1;
num1=[x0 x0*b/a xp0];den1=[1 b/a c/a];
signal1=step(num1,den1);
%%%% b*b<4*a*c
a=1;b=1;c=1;
num2=[x0 x0*b/a xp0];den2=[1 b/a c/a];
signal2=step(num2,den2);
%%%% b=0
a=1;b=0;c=1;
num3=[x0 x0*b/a xp0];den3=[1 b/a c/a];
signal3=step(num3,den3);
%%%% b*b=4*a*c
a=1;b=5;c=1;
num4=[x0 x0*b/a xp0];den4=[1 b/a c/a];
signal4=step(num4,den4);
subplot(2,2,1);plot(signal1);grid;title('b*b>4*a*c, overdamped');
subplot(2,2,2);plot(signal2);grid;title('b*b<4*a*c, underdamped');
subplot(2,2,3);plot(signal3);grid;title('b=0, undamped');
subplot(2,2,4);plot(signal4);grid;title('b*b=4*a*c, critically damped');
```

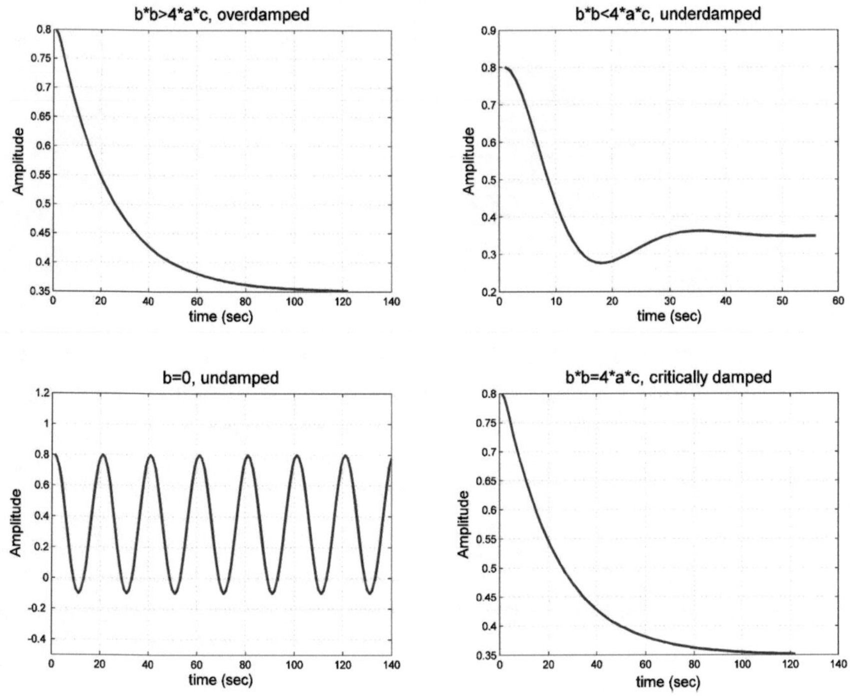

Figure 7. Analysis of second-order system.

4. Mechanical vibrations

Structural vibrations in most cases are undesirable because they can negatively affect the appropriate operation of mechanical systems because of the increasing stresses and energy losses by dissipation especially at resonant frequencies. For these reasons, it is very important the prediction of resonances in the design of mechanical elements to prevent structural failures as fatigue after long period of time [3,4]. The main purpose of this section is to analyze and design a simple mechanical model well known as one-degree of freedom (ODOF) system and calculate with Matlab the frequency response to an external sinusoidal force.

In order to understand the dynamic response, in Figure 8 is illustrated the schematic of a linear damped ODOF system subjected to a harmonic excitation input.

The system consists in a mass m connected to a spring of stiffness k. The other side of the spring is connected to the support. In a damped ODOF system, the coefficient c is the viscous damping

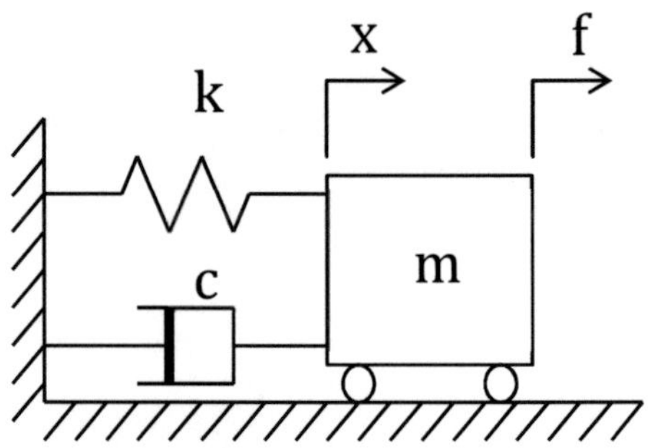

Figure 8. Damped ODOF system

related with the loose of energy in the vibrating system. Considering a force varying harmonically as *f(t)=A sin (ωt);* where *A* is the amplitude oscillating at an angular frequency ω in rad/sec; the equation of motion along the x direction can be written as:

$$m\ddot{x} + c\dot{x} + kx = f(t) \tag{21}$$

With the initial conditions equal to zero, the steady state solution of the differential equation can be obtained applying the Laplace transform of equation 21.

$$ms^2x(s) + csx(s) + kx(s) = F(s) \tag{22}$$

Reordering the terms, the second order transfer function *G(s)* is obtained as:

$$G(s) = \frac{x(s)}{F(s)} = \frac{1}{ms^2 + cs + k} \tag{23}$$

Replacing the terms $\omega_n = \sqrt{\left(k/_m\right)}$ and $\xi = \frac{c}{2\sqrt{(mk)}}$, that represent the natural frequency and the relative damping factor of the system respectively; then *G(s)* can be written as:

$$G(s) = \frac{\frac{1}{m}}{s^2 + 2\xi\omega_n s + \omega_n^2} \tag{24}$$

When a sinusoidal input force is applied to a linear ODOF system, the response is also sinusoidal with the same oscillation frequency but with differences in amplitude and phase. In order to know the frequency response, s is replaced with $j\omega$, where $j = \sqrt{-1}$ is the imaginary unit

$$G(j\omega) = \frac{\frac{1}{m}}{-\omega^2 + j2\xi\omega_n\omega + \omega_n^2}. \tag{25}$$

http://dx.doi.org/10.5772/58236

Defining r as the frequency ratio of the natural frequency ω_n to the angular frequency of the sinusoidal input ω and multiplying numerator and denominator by $1/\omega^2$, the above equation gives:

$$G(j\omega)=\frac{\frac{1}{m\omega^2}}{\left[(r^2-1)+j2\xi r\right]}. \tag{26}$$

Thus, it is clear that the frequency response of a damped ODOF represented by a complex number depends on ω of the sinusoidal input and the damping ratio ξ. Hence, the magnitude ratio and the phase angle of the frequency response can be expressed as:

$$|G(j\omega)|=\frac{1/(m\omega^2)}{\sqrt{(r^2-1)^2+(2\xi r)^2}}, \tag{27}$$

and

$$\varnothing(j\omega)=-\tan^{-1}\frac{2\xi r}{r^2-1}. \tag{28}$$

By inspection of equation 26 we can make some interpretations [5]:

- for $r \approx 0$; that is, when $\omega \ll \omega_n$; the problem can be considered as static, since the frequency of the excitation force is very small in comparison with the natural frequency obtaining also a very small phase shift.
- for $r=1$; namely $\omega=\omega_n$; the system is at resonance, the amplitude of the output increases in function of the damping and the phase shift is 90° for any value of damping.
- for $r > 1$; that is, $\omega \gg \omega_n$ the amplitude of the response approaches to zero and the phase angle to 180°.

Dynamic analysis of a cantilever

The schematic in Figure 9 is cantilever beam with a lumped mass at its free end and is used to detect mechanical resonances; the beam is fixed perpendicular to the support of a machine that can operate at different velocities, generating angular frequencies that move harmonically along the x direction.

Ignoring the mass of the beam, consider the following model to calculate the amplitude and phase angle of the dynamic displacement for angular frequencies of $0<\omega<2$ rad/sec.

$$3\ddot{x}+2\dot{x}+3x=sin(\omega t). \tag{29}$$

The following Matlab code plots the magnitude ratio and the phase angle of the frequency response in function of the angular frequency of the sinusoidal input.

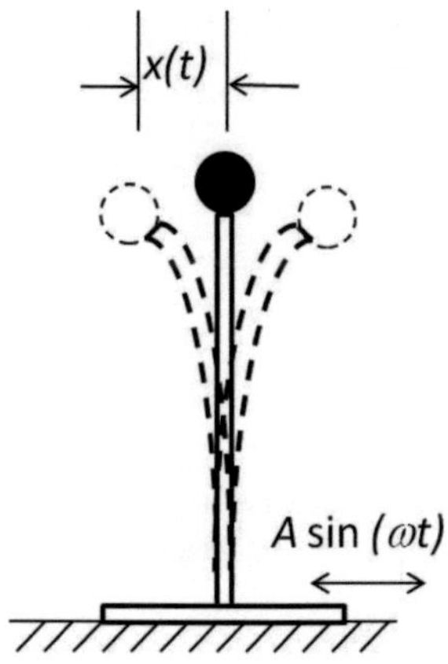

Figure 9. Cantilever beam

```
m=3; c=2; k=3;
wn=sqrt(k/m);
w=[0:0.1:2];
zeta=c/(2*sqrt(m*k));
r=wn./w;
M=abs((1./(m*w.^2))./sqrt((r.^2-1).^2+(2*zeta*r).^2));
phase=-atan2((2*zeta*r),(r.^2-1))*180/pi;
subplot(2,1,1);plot(r,M)
subplot(2,1,2);plot(r,phase)
```

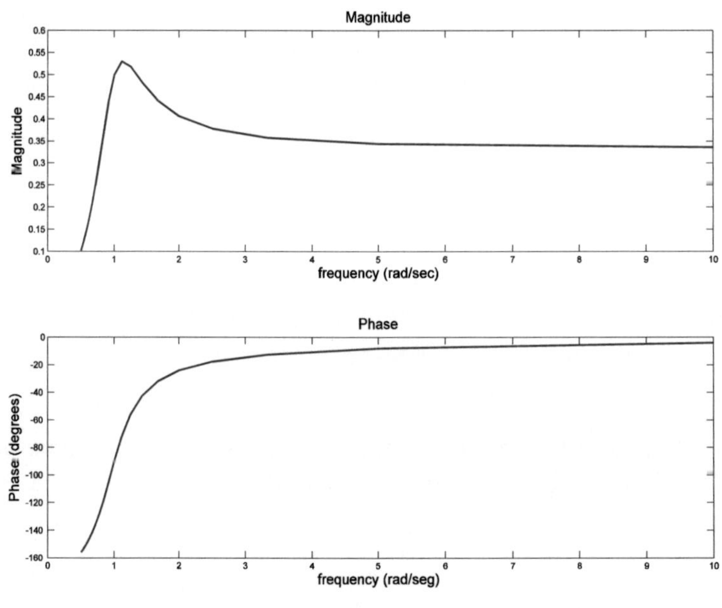

Figure 10. Frequency response.

5. Optical control systems

5.1. Laser diode

Laser diode (LD) are perhaps one of the most used optical systems, in particular for those applications where the high frequency modulation is involved. A LD can be described as a device in which an electric current is converted to photons. The time dependent relation between the input electric current and the output photons are commonly described by the following pair of equations describing the time evolution of photon and carrier densities inside the laser medium.

$$\frac{\partial N_e}{\partial t} = \frac{I}{qad} - A(N_e - N_{om})N_{ph} - \frac{N_e}{\tau_s}, \tag{30}$$

and

$$\frac{\partial N_{ph}}{\partial t} = A(N_e - N_{om})N_{ph} - \frac{N_{ph}}{\tau_{ph}} + \beta\frac{N_e}{\tau_s}, \tag{31}$$

where N_{ph} is the photon density. A is a proportionality constant, N_{om} is the minimum electron density required to obtain a positive gain, and β is the fraction of the spontaneous emission that is coupled the lasing mode, τ_s is the spontaneous carrier life time, τ_{ph} is the photon life time, and N_e is the carrier density, I is the input current, a is the diode area, d is the thickness of the active region, q is the electron charge. These pair of equations can be modeled using the RCL parallel electric model proposed in [6].

Here the LD can be modeled using the parallel circuit whose elements are:

$$R = R_d\left(\frac{I_{th}}{I^0}\right) \tag{32}$$

$$L = \frac{R_d\tau_{ph}}{\left[\left(\frac{I^0}{I_{th}}\right) - 1\right]}, \tag{33}$$

$$C = \frac{\tau_s}{R_d}, \tag{34}$$

and

$$R_d = \frac{2kT}{q}\left(\frac{1}{I_d}\right). \tag{35}$$

If we consider a sinusoidal modulation in small signal around the quiescent point I_p in the form $I = I_p + i_p \sin \omega t$ the equations (30) and (31) can be linearized as follows:

$$Z_0(s) = \frac{V_0(s)}{I_0(s)} = \frac{RLs}{RLCs^2 + Ls + R}, \tag{36}$$

or

$$Z_0(s) = \frac{V_0(s)}{I_0(s)} = \frac{R_d\left(\frac{is}{\tau_s} + \frac{1 + n_{om} - n_e^0}{\tau_s \tau_{ph}}\right)}{-s^2 + i\frac{s}{\tau_s}\left[n_{ph}^0 + 1 + \frac{\tau_s}{\tau_{ph}\left(1 + n_{om} - n_e^0\right)}\right] + \frac{n_{ph}^0 + \beta\left[n_e^0\left(1 + \frac{1}{n_{ph}^0}\right) - n_{om}\right]}{\tau_s \tau_{ph}}}. \tag{37}$$

Figure 11, shows a comparative curve for a sinusoidal input and the photon density output, here; we observe a phase difference between the input and output.

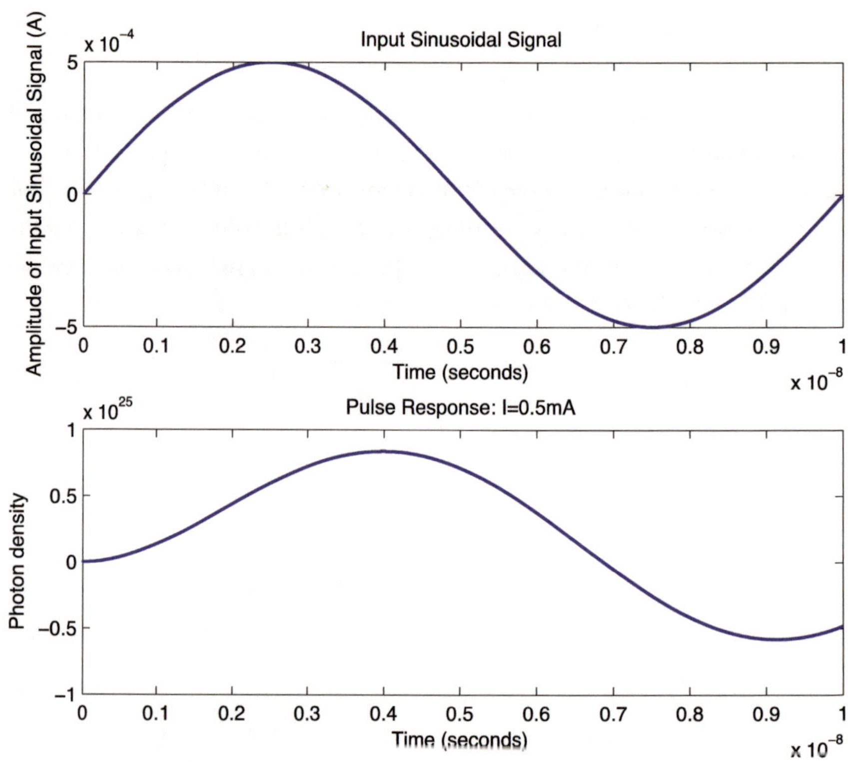

Figure 11. Comparative curve for sinusoidal Input current *vs* photon density.

Figure 12, shows the photon density response for different values of input signal.

http://dx.doi.org/10.5772/58236

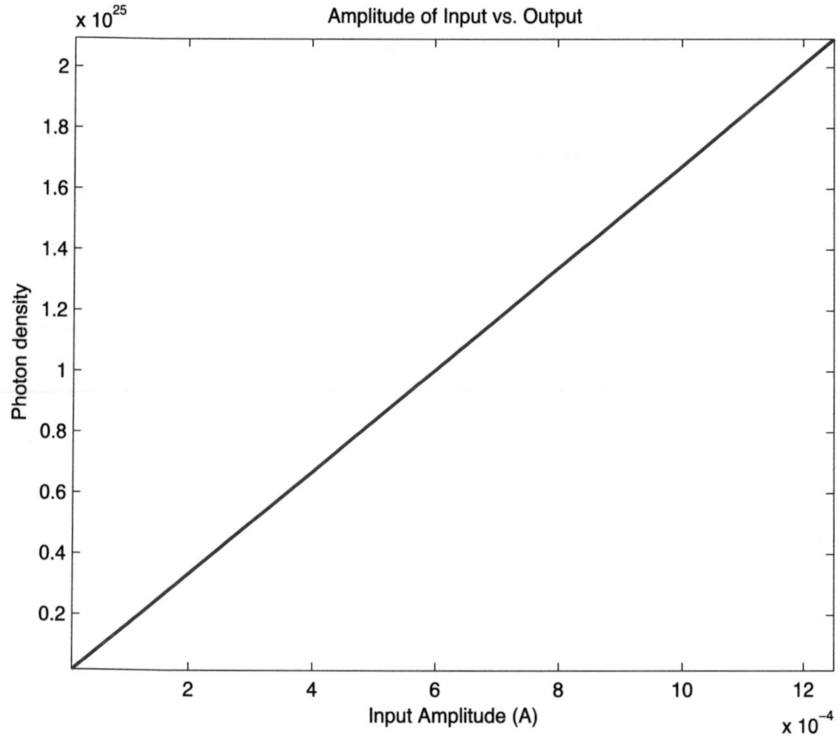

Figure 12. Photon density response for different input values.

The code that was used to generate and plot the curves showed in Figures 11 and 12, is placed in Appendix A.

5.2. Temperature control system for a furnace in a fiber optic drawing process.

The manufacturing process of optical fiber usually requires several control systems, for example, the temperature control system of the furnace for melting the preform, the control system to maintain the fiber diameter constant, the system for deposit control and ultraviolet light curing of the fiber coating system and finally the traction control and fiber winding on the drum (Figure 13).

The problem of modeling a furnace for drawing fiber requires the consideration of variables such as the speed of stretching of the fiber, the rate of purge gas into the furnace, the furnace temperature, the diameter of the preform, etcetera. Moreover, variables such as the flow of gas within the furnace, radiative heat transport between the preform and the interior of the furnace is actually not so simple, this problem has been analyzed for a graphite furnace [7]. However, only for demonstration purposes, we will treat the problem for the linear case and without considering the phenomena mentioned above.

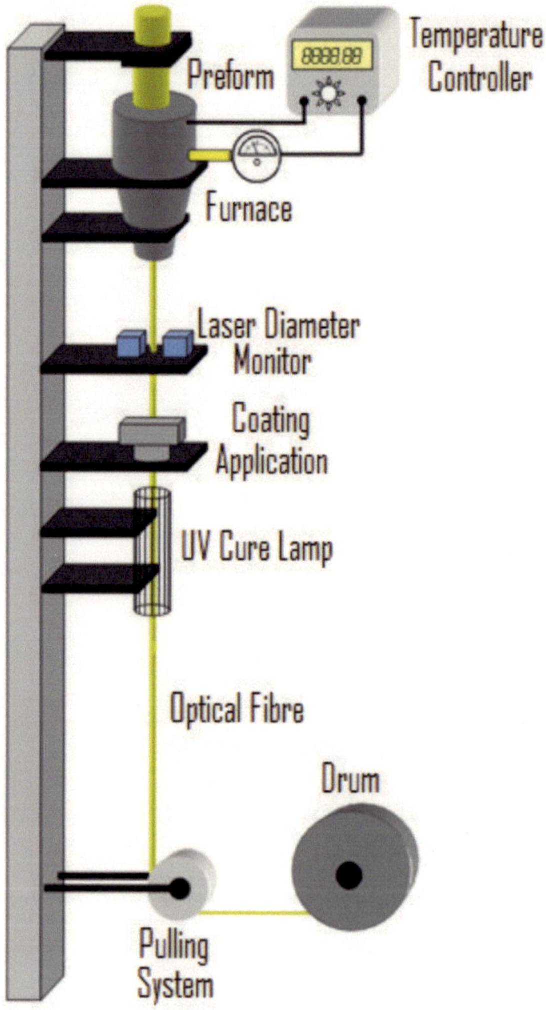

Figure 13. Fiber drawing process system

In the next section, we will demonstrate the use of Simulink of Matlab for modeling a simple temperature control system for a furnace in a fiber optic drawing process.

5.3. Mathematical model

Uniform heating of the preform is due in large part to effective radiative transport inside the furnace and the control of the changes in the temperature distribution. The above with the purpose to achieve fiber softening and stretching at high speed.

Making a simple energy balance of the furnace, we have the variation of energy per unit of time (ΔQ_H) given by

$$\Delta Q_H = Q_C - Q_F = K_T \frac{dT_i}{dt} \tag{38}$$

Where Q_C is the energy provided by the controller, Q_F is the gas heat flow into the furnace, K_T is the thermal capacity and T_i is the internal temperature.

We estimate the thermal capacity K_T for a preform of 100 mm of diameter and 450 mm long. We propose the active cavity of the furnace as a cylindrical shape with 120 mm in diameter and 300 mm long.

Then, knowing the mass of the perform M_P and silicon specific heat C_P, the heat capacity calculated for the silicon preform is

$$K_T = M_P \times Cp = 8.2313[Kg] \times 2.575\left[\frac{Joule}{Kg \bullet {}^\circ C}\right] = 21.19\left[\frac{joule}{{}^\circ C}\right]. \tag{39}$$

Simplifying the heat flux in the furnace to

$$Q_F = \frac{T_i - T_o}{R_{eq}}. \tag{40}$$

Where R_{eq} is the equivalent thermal resistance of the inner walls of the furnace.

The equivalent thermal resistance of the internal cylindrical wall of the furnace made of graphite with a thickness of 5mm is calculated with

$$R_{eq} = 5 \times \frac{10^{-3}[m]}{\left(0.476\left[\frac{W}{m \bullet {}^\circ C}\right] \bullet 0.1131[m^2]\right)} = 92.87 \times 10^{-3}\left[{}^\circ \frac{C}{W}\right]. \tag{41}$$

Then, applying the Laplace transform to Equation 38 we obtain

$$T_i = \frac{Q_C - Q_F}{K_T * s}. \tag{42}$$

Using as reference the Thermo demo of Simulink, the furnace temperature control is sketched in Figure 14

To run the program Fiber_Furnace_System.mdl is necessary to preload the characteristics of the furnace in the file Data_furnace.m (Apendix A). The graph of the system behavior is show in Figure 15.

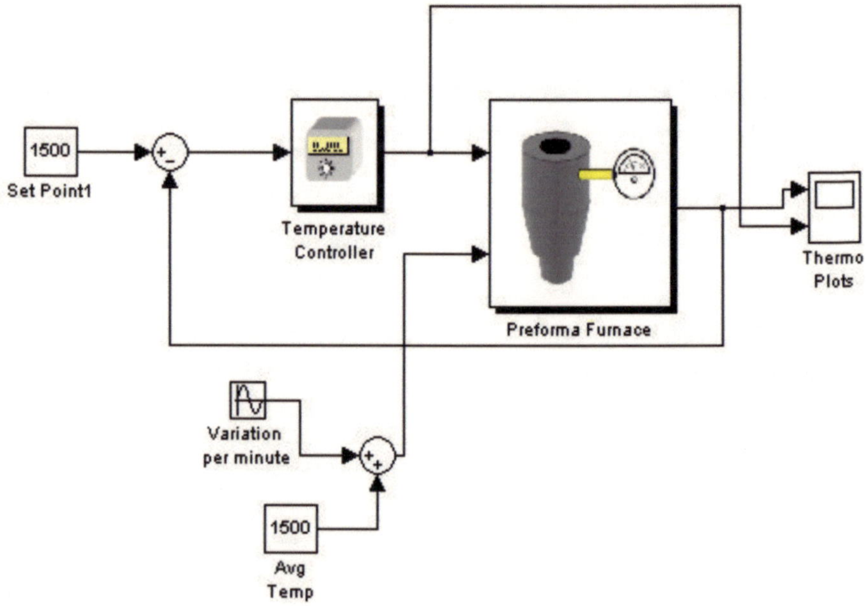

Figure 14. Simulink model of the perform furnace.

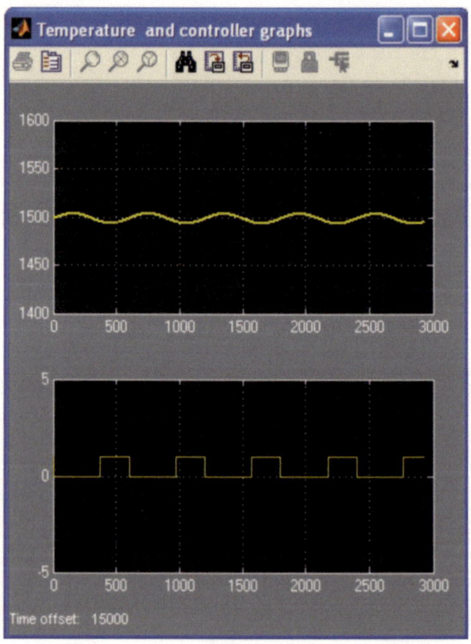

Figure 15. Graph of the system behavior. Upper: Temperature around 1500ºC; Lower Controller activation for each cycle.

http://dx.doi.org/10.5772/58236

6. Conclusions

In order to study and analyze physical systems, along of this chapter, several systems were treated, and different Matlab codes were proposed to solve, analyze and, simulate those systems. Matlab is a powerful tool, and can help to students, engineers and, scientific to develop very simple, elegant and, powerful algorithms, that allows achieving successfully the study and analysis of control systems.

Appendix A

The following Matlab code was used to generate and plot the curves showed in Figures 11 and 12.

```
%program for the simulation of laserdiode system using
%RLC equivalent circuit

FontName = 'arial'; %Define the font type
FontSize = 9;       %define the font size
LineWidth = 1.5;    %define the line width

%parameters
a = 3.5e-3*1.3e-3;%area diode
d =  2000e-6;      %thickness of active region
q = .3e-6;         %Electron charge
Ne=  3e-5;         %DC value for the injectec electron density
Ith = 10e-4;
Io = 10e-5;        %input current
Tau_ph=.23e-6;     %spontaneous photon life time
Tau_s=.25e-9;      %spontaneous carrier life time
T = 77;            %temperature
Id = (Ne/Tau_s)*a*q*d;    %normalized current
k = 8.61e-5;       %Boltzman constant
Rd = ((2*k*T)/q)*(1/Id);


R = Rd*(Ith/Io);
L = Rd*Tau_ph/((Io/Ith)-1);
C = Tau_s/Rd;
[u,t] = gensig('sin',1e-8,1e-8,0.001e-9);
u = u*5e-4;
gs = tf([R*L 0],[R*L*C L R]);
s_10 = 1.9221e13;
y=s_10*lsim(gs,u,t,'zoh');

subplot(2,1,1)
plot(t,u,'linewidth',LineWidth)
set(gca,'fontname',FontName,'fontsize',FontSize)
xlabel('Time (seconds)','fontname',FontName,'fontsize',FontSize);
ylabel('Amplitude of Input Sinusoidal Signal (A)','fontname',FontName,'fontsize',FontSize);
title('Input Sinusoidal Signal','fontname',FontName,'fontsize',FontSize)
subplot(2,1,2)
plot(t,y,'linewidth',LineWidth)
set(gca,'fontname',FontName,'fontsize',FontSize)
xlabel('Time (seconds)','fontname',FontName,'fontsize',FontSize);
ylabel('Photon density','fontname',FontName,'fontsize',FontSize);
title('Pulse Response: I=0.5mA','fontname',FontName,'fontsize',FontSize);
```

```
[u,t] = gensig('sin', 1e-8, 1e-8, 0.001e-9);
count=1;
for i=1:1:125
    I_step = i*1e-5;
    u = u*I_step;
    y = s_10*lsim(gs,u,t);
    u_A(1,count) = max(u);
    y_A(1,count) = max(y);
    ytemp = y(1:round(length(y)/2),1);
    y_P(1,count) = t(find(ytemp==max(ytemp)))-1e-8/4;
    count = count + 1;
    [u,t] = gensig('sin', 1e-8, 1e-8, 0.001e-9);
end
% Plot Amplitude Response
figure
plot(u_A,y_A,'linewidth',LineWidth)
axis tight
set(gca,'fontname',FontName,'fontsize',FontSize)
xlabel('Input Amplitude (A)','fontname',FontName,'fontsize',FontSize);
ylabel('Photon density','fontname',FontName,'fontsize',FontSize);
title('Amplitude of Input vs. Output','fontname',FontName,'fontsize',FontSize);
```

Program Data_furnace.m. The results are showed in Fig. 15.

```
%  DATA_furnace
% This script runs in conjunction with the%"Fiber_Furnace_System"
% Loading images
A= imread('Preforma_Furnace.bmp');
B= imread('Controller.bmp');
% -------------------------------
% Define the furnace geometry
% -------------------------------
% internal furnace height = 0.3 m
inhFurnace = 0.30;
% internal furnace radio = 0.16 m
inrFurnace = 0.16;
% internal wall area
inwallArea = 2*pi*inrFurnace*inhFurnace;
% -------------------------------
% Determine the equivalent thermal
% resistance for graphite wall
% -------------------------------
kg = 0.476;
LWall = .005;
Req = LWall/(kg*inwallArea);
% c = cp of silice = 2.575 J/Kg-C
c = 2.575;
% -------------------------------
% Temperature Set Controller = 1500 deg C = 1773 K
% -------------------------------
TSC = 1773;
% ha = enthalpy of air at 40 deg C = 311400 J/kg
ha = TSC*c;
% Air flow rate Mdot = 0.1 kg/sec
Mdot = 0.1;
% -------------------------------
```

http://dx.doi.org/10.5772/58236

```
% Determine total internal glass mass = M
% ------------------------------
% Density of preforma silice glass = 2329 kg/m^3
densglass = 2329;
Mg = pi*inrFurnace*inhFurnace;
```

Acknowledgements

The authors wish to express their gratitude for financial support of this project to Departamento de Ciencias Exactas y Tecnología, of Centro Universitario de los Lagos, Universidad de Guadalajara.

Author details

Roger Chiu*, Francisco J. Casillas, Didier López-Mancilla, Francisco G. Peña-Lecona, Miguel Mora-González and Jesús Muñoz Maciel

*Address all correspondence to: rchiu@culagos.udg.mx

Department of Exact Sciences and Tecnology, Universitary Center of Los Lagos, University of Guadalajara, Lagos de Moreno, Jalisco, México

References

[1] http://www.mathworks.com/products/matlab/

[2] Nise, N.S. Control Systems Engineering (3rd Ed.). CECSA, ISBN 970-24-0254-9, D.F., Mexico; 2002.

[3] William J. Palm III. Mechanical Vibration. John Wiley & Sons, Inc; 2007.

[4] William Bolton. Control Engineering. Prentice Hall; 1998.

[5] Robert F. Steidel, Jr. An introduction to mechanical vibrations. JohnWiley& Sons, Inc; 1989

[6] Katz J, Margalit S, Herder C, Wilt D, Yariv A. The Intrinsic Electrical Equivalent Circuit of a Laser Diode. IEEE Journal of Quantum Electronics 1981; QE-17(1) 4-7

[7] Zhilong Yin and Y. Jaluria. Thermal Transport and Flow in High-Speed Optical Fiber Drawing; *J. Heat Transfer;* 1998; 120(4) 916-930.

Chapter 14

Advanced Decimator Modeling with a HDL Conversion in Mind

Drago Strle and Dušan Raič

Additional information is available at the end of the chapter

http://dx.doi.org/10.5772/58242

1. Introduction

Today, many systems designers use software tools such as Matlab to model complex, mixed-technology systems prior to physically building and testing the system. These tools, along with their associated toolboxes provide an effective means for the initial modeling and simulation stages in a project. Such software tools also provide the means to extract information in a relevant format to aid the physical realization [see 1-3]. In this chapter we will describe the use of Simulink and its library blocks in conjunction with the HDL Coder tool in order to produce a HDL representation of the model that is, suitable for synthesis into digital logic hardware for implementation on devices such as FPGA and ASICs. We follow the idea of one single model, starting from the system level simulation to the final system integration and hardware implementation, possibly eliminating any designer interventions on the low (RTL) level. This aim can be achieved with the right concept right at the beginning of top level modeling, based on the knowledge of the tool background and its limitations.

Our presentation starts with a simple example, using an existing block from the DSP System Toolbox Library [4]. We then proceed with the redesign of the same block in order to gain more control over the implementation details that will allow fulfilling specific requirements that might be needed for system integration. The presentation is accompanied with practical Simulink and HDL Coder tips that we believe will help the reader to reproduce and possibly upgrade the presented work. The two designs are first compared for equivalence in the Simulink environment, and then again with the circuit simulation of the compiled and synthesized hardware. Finally, some proposals are given to upgrade models with more advanced features targeting the high-precision systems.

INTECH
open science | open minds

© 2014 The Author(s). Licensee InTech. This chapter is distributed under the terms of the Creative Commons Attribution License (http://creativecommons.org/licenses/by/3.0), which permits unrestricted use, distribution, and reproduction in any medium, provided the original work is properly cited.

2. Modeling with a HDL coder in mind

The first surprise that a conventional digital designer is faced with when switching to the Simulink HDL tool is the lack of flip-flops and the associated clock and reset signals. Although there are ways to model the flip-flop functionality (e.g. D Latch, D Flip-Flop and J-K Flip-Flop blocks in the 'Simulink Extras/Flip Flops'library), this is not the right way to go since these models cannot be converted by the HDL coder tool. The answer lies in the high-level modeling approach that is intentionally made free of the low-level circuit details. It must be pointed out that Simulink models are basically graphical interfaces to mathematical operations [5]. Although block diagrams seem to represent connections of physical entities by electric wires, this is not the case since the signals represent mathematical variables. However, a close analogy makes it possible to translate the Simulink models into an equivalent hardware description, where signals turn to wires and blocks turn to library cells.

A HDL coder [6] inserts low-level control signals automatically, e.g. the system clock, the power-on reset, and the clock enable signals are not expected as part of the Simulink model. High-level modeling is released from these details, letting the designer concentrate on system-level considerations. However, the lack of controlling signals at the system model level may introduce some problems. For example, the lack of the output data enable signal on the model level prevents modeling of pipelined structures and data synchronization with other blocks in the system.

2.1. Single-rate vs. multi-rate model implementation

By definition, the CIC decimation filter that we use in our design example is a multi-rate system since it transforms the high-rate input signal into the low-rate output signal so that the decimation rate factor R is a constant, positive integer. The Simulink HDL Coder automatically creates all timing signals to drive the multi-rate system. However, the merging of the compiled code with the rest of the system is much easier and requires less hardware if all system components are based on a common, single base-rate clock. Sharing data between blocks with the appropriate handshaking details may become very complicated if the automatically generated multi-rate clock signals are to be matched with other parts of the system. From a system integration point of view it is therefore advantageous to model our 'demo' design filter as a single-rate system.

In Simulink the multi-rate systems can be easily modeled as enabled, single-rate systems by replacing the Unit Delay block with the Enabled Unit Delay block. By doing so the automatic handling of different sampling times becomes visible and accessible to the designer in the form of various 'enable' signals, added to the block diagrams. There is of course also a drawback with this approach since the block diagram gets more populated with additional signals, prone to design errors, and therefore is more difficult to maintain. Nevertheless, the single-rate modeling brings other advantages, like:

- The possibility to create programmable sample rate,
- Pipeline latency control with base-rate delays,
- Full control over the timing controller.

http://dx.doi.org/10.5772/58242

The automatically generated timing controller (e.g. tc.vhd) of the multi-rate model is built with a number of counters and registers that may be avoided in the centralized, system-wide timing, resulting in lower area and power. In the case of our decimating filter example we will follow the single-rate approach by creating the customized down-sampling block with the integrated down-sampling counter, which will replace the HDL Coder-generated timing controller of the multi-rate version.

Another rather important feature of Simulink models is the fact that pipelining options of the HDL block implementation cannot be simulated. Like timing control signals, the pipelining hardware is generated during the process of HDL compilation, which is separated from the simulation. At this point the Simulink operation is inconsistent; obviously, the pipelined functionality of HDL blocks is present in the data-base, otherwise the testbench generation would not be possible. On the other hand, the simulator ignores the inserted pipelines: the resulting signals cannot be viewed on the Scope or stored to the data file, preventing the application of powerful data analysis tools at the model level. The simulation of pipelined structures is made possible only after the compilation, using other tools in the design loop. From the point of view of consistent Simulink/HDL modeling it is therefore better to bring pipelining into the Simulink model and forget about HDL block implementation options. The latter consideration is one more reason to choose single-rate over multi-rate modeling.

2.2. Using library blocks in the the HDL Coder environment

Only a limited number of blocks from the large Simulink library are supported by HDL Coder. To get an overview of these blocks, enter `hdllib` from the Matlab prompt and create *HDL Demo library;* save the library for later reference and investigation. For example, in Bit Operations we find useful operators like Bit Concat, Bit Reduce, Bit Rotate, Bit Shift, and Bit Slice. Another interesting block is the generic counter model, suitable for HDL coder compilation. It may be investigated with the right-click on the HDL Counter block, selecting the 'Look under the mask' option.

A number of useful operators can be also found in other libraries. However, some blocks that seem to suit the logic design cannot be used with the HDL coder. The Pulse, Multiphase clock, Integer to Bit Converter blocks, for example, cannot be used. The Delay block must be replaced by the Unit Delay block. Some limitations apply in other blocks, e.g.:

- Trigger block: 'Show output port' must be OFF; the Trigger port must be driven by registered logic; outputs of the triggered system must have an initial value of '0'; the trigger type 'either' is not allowed – use 'rising' or 'falling'.
- Divide: use Product block from the Math Operations Library; rounding must be Zero or Simplest; saturation must be ON.
- Data Type Conversion: Double-> Fixed-point conversion is not possible.

Generally, the signed integers should be avoided and operations should be carried out on unsigned integers when logic operations are to be performed on VHDL standard logic vectors.

The key elements for hardware design are logic gates and registers. Registers must be modeled by the Unit Delay block from the 'Discrete' library. The Delay block (with the parameterized number of delay cycles) cannot be used since its data structure is not supported for HDL conversion. Logic gates are modeled with blocks from the 'Logic and Bit operations' library. In the following we present some comments above the library blocks that will be most likely used in designs, intended for the HDL conversion.

To Workspace block: The best way to compare the logic simulation results of a reference design with the Simulink results is to store Simulink signals in the Matlab workspace. The recorded signal must be given a suitable name and the save format should be set to 'Array'. Arbitrary signal values at selected times can be printed out in the workspace using the Matlab expression signame(time_index). Before printouts, do not forget to apply the 'formal long' command to get full precision data.

Extract Bits block: Most frequently only one bit (MSB or LSB) is to be extracted. In such cases the best way is to specify bits to extract from the 'Range starting with MSB' or 'Range ending with LSB' and set 'Number of bits' to 1. The output scaling mode should be set to 'Treat bit field as an integer'. With these settings the output bit will be scaled to ufix1 which is suitable for more logic operations or for the conversion to the Boolean data format. Other bit positions or ranges can be extracted as well.

Rate Transition block is supported for HDL conversion only if both Data Integrity and Deterministic Data Transfer options are ensured. Consequently, the transition from the Downsample output data rate back to the base-rate will introduce additional output delay of one low-rate period. This means that the Downsample block output must be registered with the output-rate clock before being forwarded to any control blocks, like end-of-conversion pulse generation or output data handshaking. Therefore, these procedures can be only performed with considerable delay that may not be acceptable.

Downsample block: The output data rate is equal to its input data rate divided by the down-sample factor K (also frequently referred to as the decimation factor R). The sample offset, D, which must be an integer in the range [0, K–1] allows the definition of output delay. The sample offset is specified in the output data rate period units. Therefore, the downsample output delay cannot be specified in base-rate period units.

CIC Decimation block: This block is based on three parameters: decimation factor (R), differential delay (M) and the number of sections (N). It allows three options for data type specification: user-defined register and/or fraction lengths, maximum precision and register pruning according to the desired output register length. The input word length is automatically determined from the block diagram. The model does not provide an 'output enable' pulse. The timing block is automatically generated (not visible at the model level).

Arithmetic Shift block: Input S in not supported for HDL; you must use the dialog box. The block ignores the Overflow and Rounding modes; it also does not check overflow or underflow. Right shift of unsigned numbers shifts '0' into the MSB position, while in the signed numbers the MSB bit is preserved. The numeric type of output variable is equal to the numeric type of the input variable.

The understanding of the Arithmetic Shift block is important since it can be used for register pruning in CIC Decimation filters. The HDL coder handles arithmetic shifts by automatic adjustment of numeric data types. For example, if the fixed point variable of type sfix23 is pruned by the right shift for 3 bit positions the resulting data type will be set to sfix20_E3.

When dealing with scaled numbers in block diagrams, attention should be paid since shifting is implemented independently from scaling. Let us take as an example the number 162874 represented as fixed point data type fixdt(1,16,-7). The fraction '-7' means that the original value has been pruned by right-shifting for 7 bit positions, i.e. multiplied by 2^(-7) in order to store the approximated magnitude as a 16-bit signed integer. After shifting the stored value is thus equal to bitshift(162874,-7)=1272. The approximated value, reconstructed by the scaling factor 2^7, is therefore equal to 1272*128=162816. If this scaled number is now, for example, shifted right by 6 more bit positions, the stored value would be bitshift(1272,-6)=19, representing the scaled value 19*(2^6)*(2^7)=155648. The result is therefore not equal to 162874 or to 162816 as one might expect.

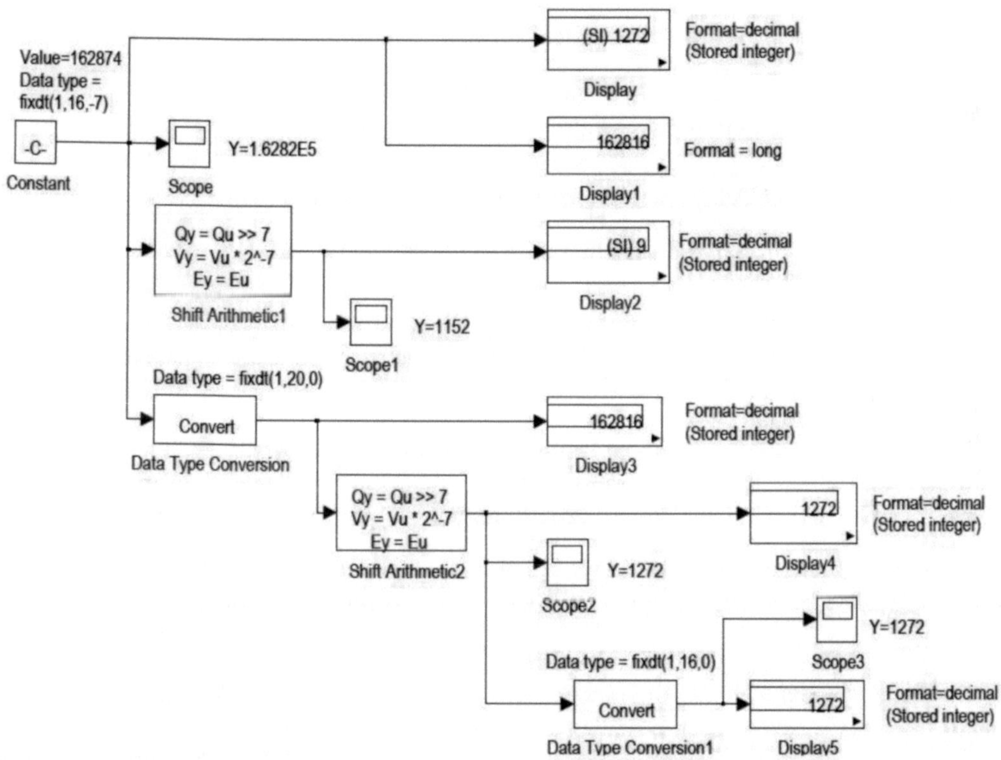

Figure 1. Scaling example.

A number of format options in the Display block allow presenting the signal also as the 'Stored integer' value. Conversely, the Scope block is based on the built-in 5-digit floating decimal point precision without this option, so one has to construct it from the (scaled) input value. Since shifting is independent from scaling we have to remove the scaling before we re-apply it again to display the stored integer value. The Data Conversion block has to convert the input value into integer format without fraction, so the word length must accommodate the largest possible value. If we need the initial word length, one more data conversion to fraction-less data type is needed after shifting. The block diagram in Figure 1 illustrates the wrong (Scope1) and the correct methods (Scope2 and Scope3) to display the stored number of the above example.

2.3. HDL coder tips

General & model-related tips:

- If HDL Coder option is not visible try to run

```
hdlsetup('toplevel_model_name')
```

from the Matlab prompt.

- Use the 'ver' command to verify installed software tool components.
- Minimize sampling time definitions as much as possible; most blocks should use Ts=-1. Limit sampling time definitions to inputs and downsampling blocks. Rate transitions must be specified by Signal Attributes/Rate Transition or Signal Operations blocks (e.g. Downsample). Delay, Unit Delay and Zero-Order Hold blocks cannot change the sample rate.
- Format models to display the sampling time and port data types. HDL conversion requires that model sampling times and data types are consolidated; to display sampling times, use: Format->Sample Time display-> Annotations (colors). To display data types, use Format->Port/Signal Displays->Port Data Types. Finally, use Edit-> Update model to see conflicting definitions.
- Use meaningful signal names. To improve node traceability in the compiled code it is advisable to replace the automatically indexed block names with meaningful node names (e.g. rename the block 'Unit Delay 2' to 'IIR_reg3').

HDL coder keeps Inport names on input signals. User-defined names of signals connected to Inports are ignored. However, signal names of signals connected to Outports may be user-defined.

HDL coder keeps signal names defined in the library blocks (the lowest level); if a number of identical blocks is invocated the names are appended with _x. Toplevel signal names are ignored. In order to allow user-defined signal names in the toplevel block diagram the custom library blocks should not define any signal names.

HDL usage restrictions & implementation details

- The HDL Coder requires Fixed-Point Toolbox
- Maximum word size for fixed-point numbers is 32 bits (Simulink limitation). The maximum number of vector elements is 2^32.

http://dx.doi.org/10.5772/58242

- Multitasking is not supported; the model must be configured for Single-Tasking. Single-rate and multi-rate models are supported within the single-tasking operation.
- The HDL Coder requires equal sampling time between each two blocks. The Rate Transition block (Signal Attributes Library) must be applied when this condition is not met.
- Switch, Manual Switch, and Multiport Switch (Signal Routing Library) cannot select between signals operating at different sample rates. Signals must be brought to (the fastest) common sampling rate, using the Rate Transition block, which may introduce additional registers and timing delay.
- An enabled subsystem may not represent the toplevel for HDL code generation. Outputs in an enabled subsystem are coded so that they come from the bypass selector with the select input connected to the Enable port.

Fixed point arithmetic

Multiplication or division is always performed on fixed-point variables that have zero biases. If an input has a nonzero bias, it is converted to binary-point-only scaling before the operation. If the result is to have a nonzero bias, the operation is first performed with temporary variables that have binary-point-only scaling. The result is then converted to the data type and scaling of the final output.

There are three fixed-point scaling expressions in Simulink:

- Unspecified scaling: fixdt(signed, word_length)
- Slope& bias scaling: fixdt(signed, word_length, slope, bias)
- Bin.point-only scaling: fixdt(signed, word_length, fract_length)

The binary-poin-only scaling should be used for the HDL coder. Matlab uses fixed-point structure coding in the form

- sfix'no.of_bits'_En'negative_fixed_exponent', or
- sfix'no.of_bits'_E'positive_fixed_exponent'.

Attention must be paid when Matlab structure coding is translated into Simulink expressions, since the negative fixed exponent corresponds to the fraction length (shift right to get integer result) and positive fixed exponent corresponds to the negative fraction length (shift left to get integer result). For example:

- fixdt(1,16,8)==sfix16_En8 (signed, 16 bits word length, 8 bits fract. length)
- fixdt(1,52,-25)==sfix52_E25 (signed, 52 bits word,-25 bits fraction length)

(a negative fraction means that the result has to be multiplied by 2^25)

Matlab always works in double precision (unless you are using the Symbolic Math Toolbox), but output display can be changed with the "format" command. This is useful when we are checking testbench results from the Matlab prompt. FORMAT may be used to switch between different output display formats as follows:

```
FORMAT          Default. Same as SHORT.
FORMAT SHORT    Scaled fixed point format with 5 digits.
FORMAT LONG     Scaled fixed point format with 15 digits.
FORMAT SHORT E  Floating point format with 5 digits.
FORMAT LONG E   Floating point format with 15 digits.
FORMAT SHORT G  Best of fixed or floating point with 5 digits.
FORMAT LONG G   Best of fixed or floating point with 15 digits.
FORMAT HEX      Hexadecimal format.
FORMAT RAT      Approximation by ratio of small integers.
FORMAT COMPACT  Suppress extra line-feeds.
```

HDL testbench generation

In order to generate the testbench code we need a toplevel testbench block diagram consisting of the stimulus generator and DUT. The testbench compiler runs the simulation and stores input signals into the appropriate data structure; additionally it generates assertions to check DUT output signals. The HDL Coder/Test Bench option is therefore disabled (gray-out) if the testbench block diagram does not define the DUT input and output signals. The HDL code for DUT is generated separately from the testbench code. Attention must be paid to the Solver Stop time to consider the necessary simulation_cycles; long simulation times generate large input/output data tables that may need prohibitive computer time to be loaded in the logic simulator.

```
sim_cycles=(Stop_time-Start_time)/Simulink_base_rate
simulated_time=sim_cycles * testbench_clock_period
```

The testbench code begins with two packages

```
PACKAGE *_tb_pkg IS... functions & procedures... END *_tb_pkg;
PACKAGE BODY *_tb_pkg IS... END *_tb_pkg;
PACKAGE *_tb_data IS... constants... END *_tb_data;
PACKAGE BODY *_tb_data IS... END *_tb_data;
```

Architecture rtl begins with toplevel component definition, followed by the Component Configuration Statements. Pay attention when compiling the testbench with the DUT synthesized (Verilog) netlist. As Verilog is case sensitive you may get the compilation error

```
Port "x" is declared in component "xx" but is not a formal port in entity "xx"
```

The message is reported because the case sensitive Verilog netlist ports are not found. In this case it might help disabling the Component Configuration Statement of the DUT netlist.

Reset cycles are added automatically to the simulation time (they needn't be considered in the model configuration > solver end time).

Clock, clock-enable, and reset signals are forced. Clock timing is independent from the model; clk_high and clk_low times are defined in the HDL coder/Test Bench Configuration window. A hold time is applied to the reset and input data signals, using the VHDL statements 'WAIT FOR clk_hold' and 'AFTER clk_hold'.

Error detection does not stop the simulation; errors are counted.

Output data are strobed one cycle after the change; each output change is strobed only once. Strobing time is defined by the output signal sampling time. The first check is applied after power-on reset when the output data is in the power-on state to check the reset condition.

Sample time output signals are automatically added on the toplevel as clock enable output ports. The number of clock enable outputs is equal to the number of different sampling times applied to output signals. Details about Output Signal / Clock Enable / Sample Time details are given in the toplevel source code header.

3. Reference design

Let us assume that we need the decimation filter for a typical sigma-delta analog-to-digital converter. For the purpose of this chapter we are more interested in the design flow rather than filter parameters, therefore we decided to choose a small version of the popular CIC filter structure [7-9]. We will assume a low number of stages, a low sampling frequency and will not deal with register pruning to keep the design simple, while devoting more attention to the implementation technique that will allow us to build more advanced features according to specific system requirements. The latter are left to the interested reader as a continuation of this work.

The beauty of Simulink is that we find the answer right away in the DSP System Toolbox Library under Filtering/Multirate filters. The 'CIC Decimation' block does it all for us, we only have to set mask parameters according to given propositions. As we aim at the sigma-delta converter application we assume the signed 2-bit integer data on the filter input, representing the bit-stream data from the sigma-delta modulator. We set the following filter parameters:

- f_{ovs}-the oversampling frequency, equal to f_{clk}; f_{ovs}=512 kHz
- B_{IN}-the input data bit width; B_{IN}=2
- R-the sample rate change implemented by the filter; R=128
- M-the comb filter differential delay; M=1
- N-the number of stages in the filter; N=3

The decimation period of the filter is given by

$$T_{dec} = R/f_{ovs} = 250\text{ us} \tag{1}$$

The gain at the output of the final stage of a CIC decimation filter is calculated as

$$\text{Gain} = (RM)^N = (128)^3 = 2097152 \tag{2}$$

The maximum bit width in a decimation filter occurs at the first integrator register:

$$\text{Bmax} = \text{ceil}\left(\text{N Log}_2\left(\text{RM}\right) + \text{B}_{\text{IN}}\right) = \text{ceil}\,(3\log 2\left(128\right) + 2 = 23\text{ bits} \quad (3)$$

In the full-precision mode all registers following the first register must support the maximum accumulation produced by the first integrator section. According to the known CIC filter properties the overflow in the integrating sections is prevented because

1. The filter is implemented using two's complement arithmetic that wraps around from the most positive to most negative number representations.

2. The range of numbers supported by the bit width of the filter is greater than the maximum value expected at the output of the composite CIC filter.

We start our design by the construction of the testbench model where the reference design (ref_dec) will be simulated and later compared with the demo (demo_dec) design, described in the next section. Both designs are entered as subsystems, the demo_dec being an empty subsystem for the time being. Configuring the designs as subsystems is the best way to select them for the HDL conversion. The testbench presented in Figure 2 applies the unit step input from the Constant block which defines the value (+1) and the sampling rate ($1/f_{ovs}$). The filter base-rate is automatically inherited from the same source.

The verification of the demo filter output is simple: the unit-step input must come out as the integer value representing the Gain, which we check on Scope1. The rest of the testbench is not needed for this initial experiment; we will use it later to verify the demo design by comparing it to the reference design. The simulation time must set to at least $4*T_{dec}$ (in our case ~1 ms) to stabilize the numerical output. The circuit simulation presented in a later section will be run even longer to get an average power consumption value.

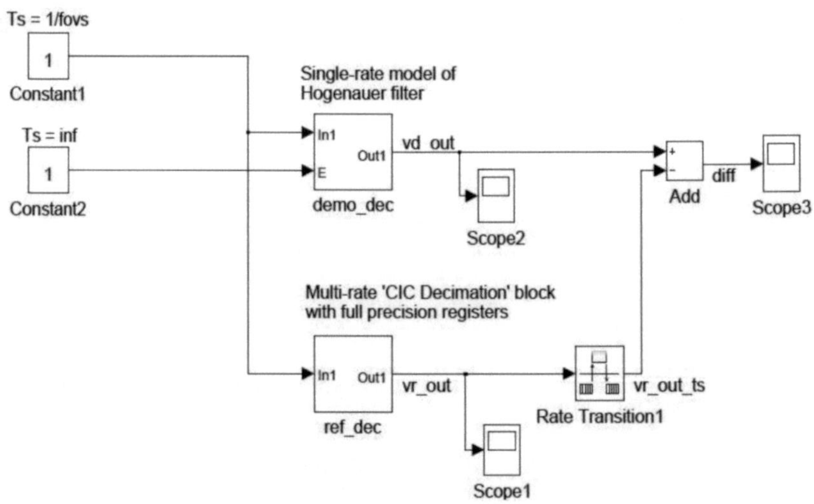

Figure 2. Unit-response testbench

http://dx.doi.org/10.5772/58242

The reference design is presented in Figure 3. It consists of a single masked subsystem (CIC Decimation block) taken from the library and configured for multi-rate operation with dialog parameters R=128, M=1 and N=3.

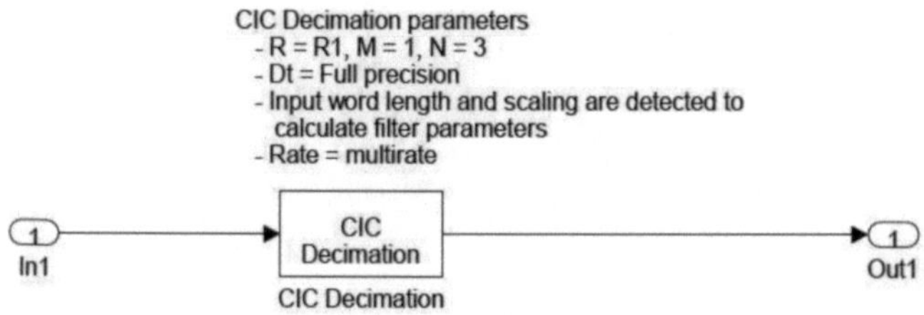

Figure 3. Reference decimator design (ref_dec).

The HDL code generation starts from the Model Explorer by opening the active configuration. Under the HDL Code Generation tab we select 'ref_dec' as the target subsystem and follow the options menu to set the conversion parameters.

There are some mandatory details that must be satisfied to enable the HDL Coder compilation. Under the Solver tag you must set the start time (=0) and stop time, according to the design. Some other settings must be set as follows:

- Solver options: Type=Fixed-step, Solver=discrete, Step size=default (auto).
- Periodic sample time constraint=default (Unconstrained).
- Tasking mode for periodic sample times=Single Tasking.
- Automatically handle rate transition=Off.
- Higher priority value means task priority=Off.
- Diagnostics - Multi-task rate transition=Error.
- Diagnostics – Single task rate transition=Error.

After successful compilation we proceed to the testbench generation which allows us to replicate the testbench simulation with the logic simulation tool.

4. Demo design

If we do some investigation of the HDL code generated for the reference design we can see that the internal structure of our CIC Decimation block puts the down-sampling stage at the end of the last comb section, like the structure presented in Figure 4. This topology spares some hardware. If the system allows additional delay of one base-rate clock cycle at the filter output the down sampler switch can be eliminated so that the down sampler evolves into a simple output register. However, like in the structure presented in Figure 4, this is the worst case solution from the point of view of power consumption because of the direct high-frequency switching data path from the integrating section through all comb section adders to the filter output register.

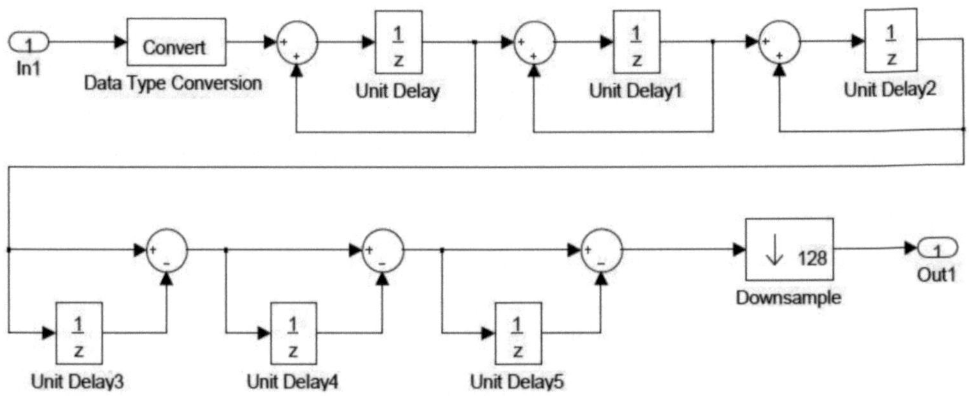

Figure 4. CIC Decimation block internal structure, as used in the reference design.

According to Nobel identity [8] the down sampler can be placed either between the last integrating section and the first comb section, or at the end of the last comb section as in Figure 4. In our demo design we will therefore place the down sampler after the last integrating section, following the Hogenauer filter topology [10] presented in Figure 5. Moreover, we will build our own down sampler block so that it will contain the timing counter and allow single-rate modeling.

The down sampler presented in Figure 6 can be parameterized and put in the user library, using the down sampling factor R as a mask parameter. The remaining parameters are calculated in the mask initialization process:

- CountLen=ceil(log2(R));
- CountLim=R-1;

The decoded zero-state (Ph0) and the last state (Phl) counter signals provide the control for output data synchronization with the rest of the system. Since all signals run with the base-rate clock it is easy to extend the model with the required type of data synchronization on the filter output, using data buffering and/or handshaking protocols. Figure 7 illustrates the down sampler timing with control signals, counter state and filter output at the time when filter output reaches the final unit-response output value.

http://dx.doi.org/10.5772/58242

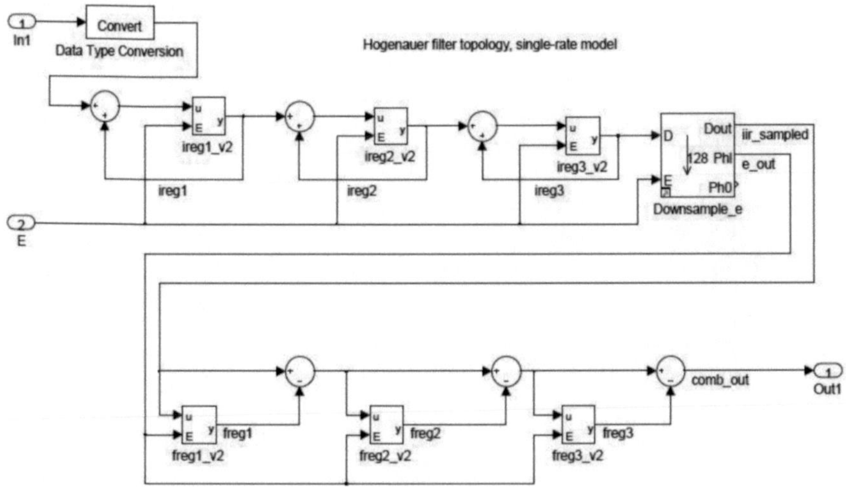

Figure 5. Decimator demo design (demo_dec).

The verification of the demo design is possible by inspecting of the difference between filter outputs. So, the waveform on Scope3 in Figure 2 shows zero difference in the span of the whole simulation time. Since we are comparing waveforms with different time bases we must convert the reference output to the base-rate timing, using the Rate Transition block. The latter must be set with the disabled data integrity checkbox; otherwise the inserted delay prevents the comparison.

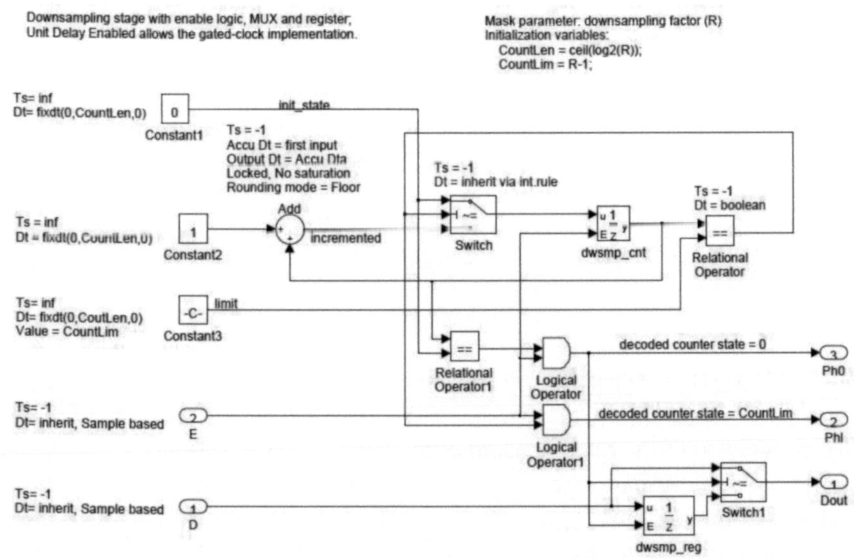

Figure 6. Custom made down-sampling block with built-in counter (Downsample_e).

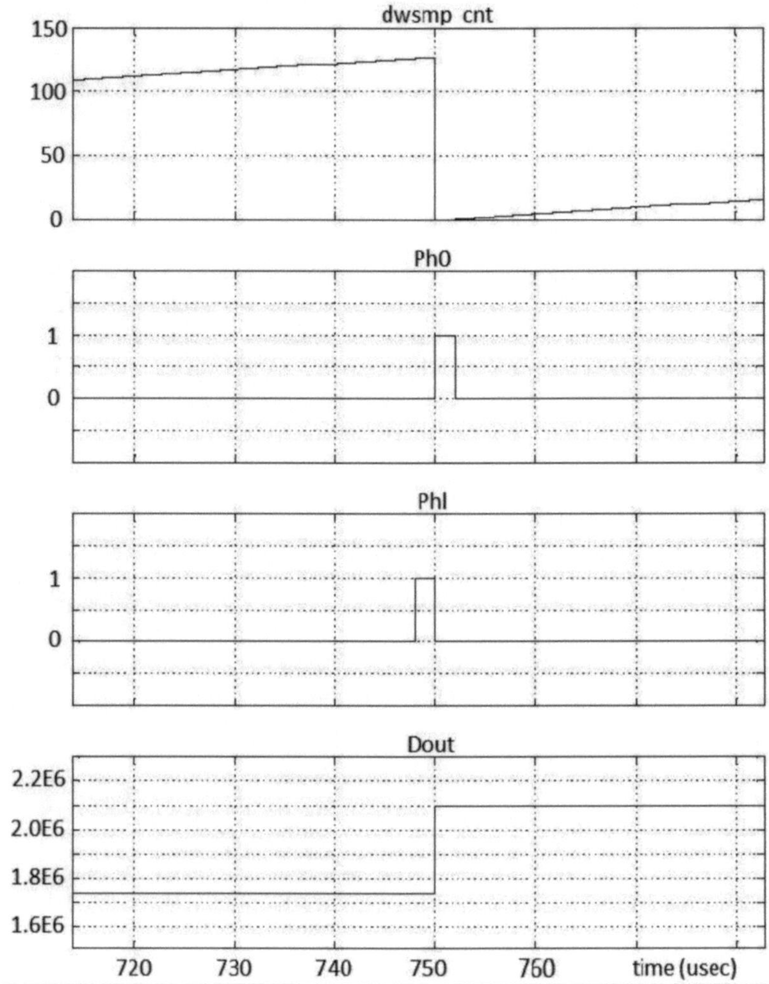

Figure 7. Downsample_e timing detail (vertical axes represent signal integer values).

5. Circuit simulation results

After HDL conversion of the reference and demo designs we proceeded to the synthesis and circuit simulations to compare circuit features. Our synthesis has been based on the TSMC 0.25um CMOS technology, using the ARM standard digital library and Synopsys Design Compiler tool. Gated-clock technology was applied to enable low-power operation. Accordingly, the circuit's physical layout with clock tree synthesis and parasitic extraction has been completed with Cadence tools. Finally, the back-annotated Verilog netlist have been simulated

http://dx.doi.org/10.5772/58242

with the NanoSim tool on the transistor-level to provide realistic circuit parameters. Power consumption was measured for the step-response input, using the setup from Figure 2 with fclk=512 kHz and Vdd=2.5 V. We have applied equal loads of one inverter gate on all output data bits, again to assure realistic circuit application conditions. The simulation time was set to ~16 decimation periods so that the average power supply current reached a practically stable value.

The comparison of the two circuit implementations is presented in Table 1 and in Figure 8. We can see that circuit implementation parameters are very similar, with the exception of power consumption and average supply current, which differ by more than 30%. This is in accordance with initial assumptions, presented at the beginning of the demo design section.

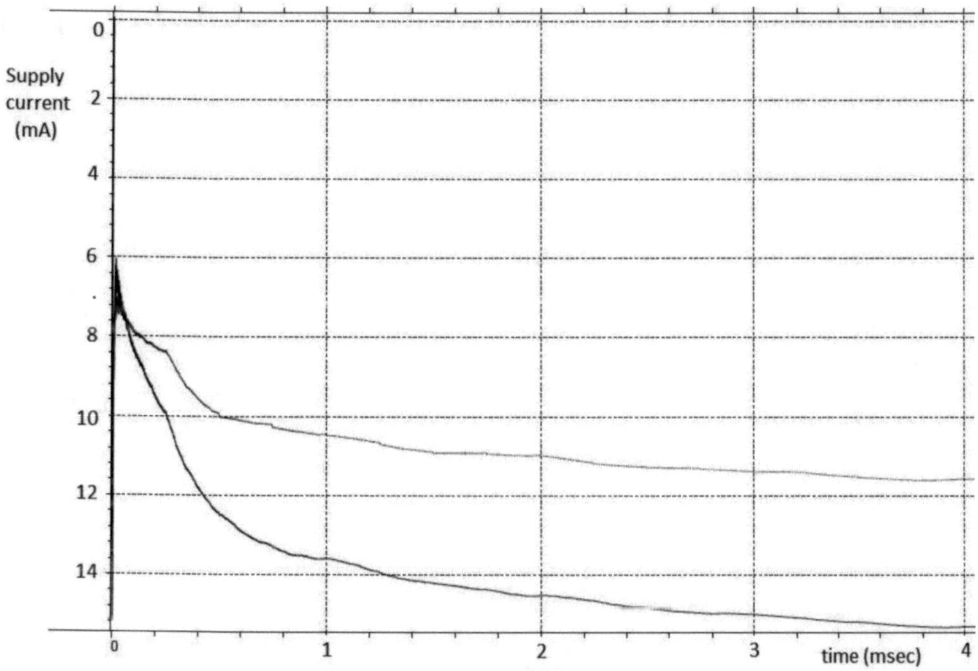

Figure 8. Comparison of the simulated average power supply currents (upper curve: demo design, lower curve: reference design).

Design	Gate-level Leaf cell count	Physical Design area [um]	Circuit power simulation [uW]
reference	487	315 x 315	38.270
demo	466	315 x 315	28.928

Table 1. Comparison of two circuit implementations.

6. Advanced design

6.1. Programmable decimation rate

As we have already mentioned, single-rate modeling gives more control over timing and allows one to model structures that are not available in standard Simulink libraries. One such example is the programmable decimation rate filter, presented in Figure 9. Here we have chosen the very simple architecture of a one-stage decimator in order to have more room to present the concept. The down-sampling stage structure is explained separately in Figure 10. It consists of a counter with selectable last-state signal, implemented by the 'Multiport switch' block from the Simulink Signal Routing library. The 'win' input allows for the selection of deliberate decimation rates in the form R=2^win. The example in Figure 8 assumes 3-bit unsigned integer value on the 'win' input, allowing selecting from seven different down-sampling rates.

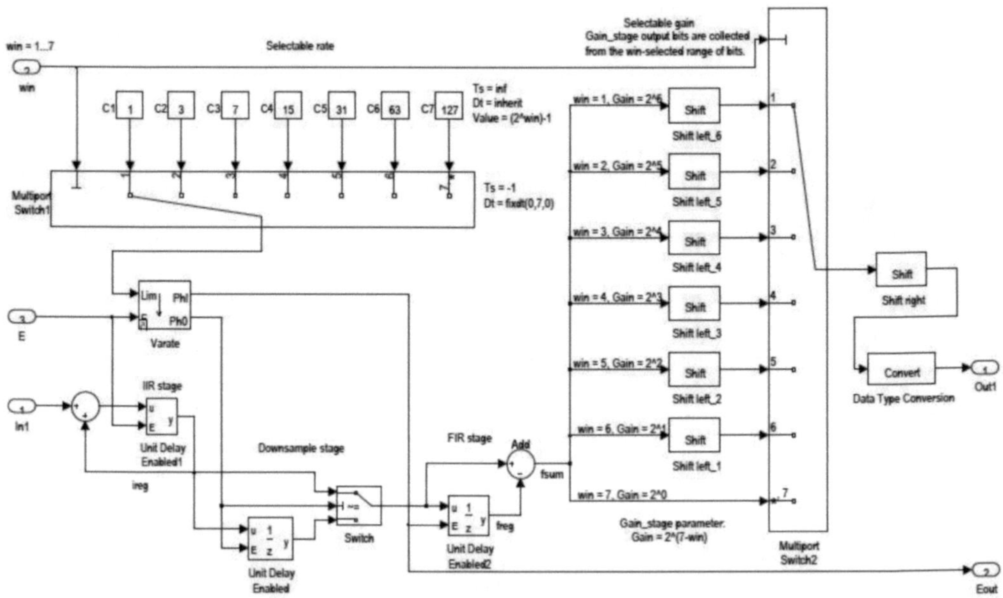

Figure 9. Programmable decimation rate filter.

The trick around the programmable down-sampling stage is that it should be usually followed by the programmable gain stage to compensate the variable decimator gain. In our case this feature is implemented by another Multiport Switch block for the selection of the appropriate gain, implemented by the 'Shift Arithmetic' blocks from the Simulink Logic and Bit Operations library. The final output is then supplemented by another, common gain stage and the conversion to the desired output data type.

http://dx.doi.org/10.5772/58242

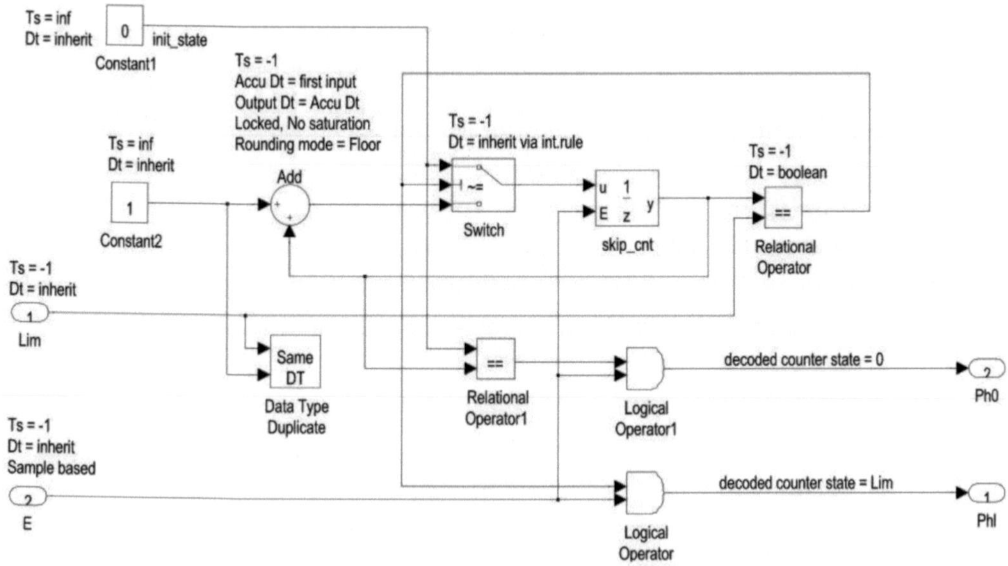

Figure 10. Variable decimation counter block (Varate).

6.2. Unbiased rounding

The results of an arithmetic operation often extend beyond the word length of the data bus and the question arises how to best throw away bits when necessary. Three alternatives are commonly encountered to pare down the result in order to fit the register or bus-width requirements [11].

Truncation of less significant bits systematically underestimates the values; e.g. 1.49 becomes 1.4 when less significant bits are removed.

Rounding pushes a result downwards if the bits to be deleted are less than half of the full-scale LSB, and upward if more than half-scale. For example, 1.44 becomes 1.4 and 1.47 becomes 1.5 when rounded to two digits.

Unbiased rounding rounds up half the time and down the other half. This is usually done by rounding towards an even number and relaying on the random distribution of even and odd numbers.

If only the MSH of a data set is to be kept, rounding is preferable to truncation, and unbiased rounding is preferable to rounding. The uround (unbiased-rounding) algorithm is simple: perform the rounding, and then detect if the LSH is '100…0', signifying that the LSH started out at "half-scale". The uround logic rounds this event up half the time and down half the time. The decision may be based on the evaluation of the LSB of the MSH (for example, add 1 to the LSB of the MSH if it is 1 or 0 if it is 0, respectively).

One possible way to implement the uround algorithm in Simulink is presented in Figure 11. The model can be put in the custom library, using WLin and WLout as mask parameters, while WLstrip is calculated as WLin-WLout in the mask initialization process.

Tables 2 and 3 illustrate paring of the data word y with initial word length WLin and the reduced word length WLout. Four different techniques are compared by calculating the averaged sum S and the mean number value M. To prevent negative results for y=28…31 the uround adder must not be configured for the wrap-around arithmetic. The condition where the uround logic adds MSH(0) to the result is marked with '*'. The sum S is calculated as S=Sum all (y / (2^(WLin-WLout)-1)), while the mean number value M is calculated as M=S/(2^WLin).

Val.	b5	b4	b3	b2	b1	b0				
y		MSH			LSH		Truncate	round with LSH(msb)	uround with MSH(0)	Matlab round (y/8)
0	0	0	0	0	0	0	0	0	0	0
1	0	0	0	0	0	1	0	0	0	0
2	0	0	0	0	1	0	0	0	0	0
3	0	0	0	0	1	1	0	0	0	0
4	0	0	*0	1	0	0	0	1	*0	1
5	0	0	0	1	0	1	0	1	1	1
6	0	0	0	1	1	0	0	1	1	1
7	0	0	0	1	1	1	0	1	1	1
8	0	0	1	0	0	0	1	1	1	1
9	0	0	1	0	0	1	1	1	1	1
10	0	0	1	0	1	0	1	1	1	1
11	0	0	1	0	1	1	1	1	1	1
12	0	0	*1	1	0	0	1	2	*2	2
13	0	0	1	1	0	1	1	2	2	2
…										
…										
28	0	1	*1	1	0	0	3	4	*4	4
29	0	1	1	1	0	1	3	4	4	4
30	0	1	1	1	1	0	3	4	4	4
31	0	1	1	1	1	1	3	4	4	4
S=62							S=48	S=64	S=62	S=64
M=1.9375							M=1.5	M=2.0	M=1.9375	M=2.0

Table 2. Positive numbers example (WLin=6, WLout=3).

http://dx.doi.org/10.5772/58242

Value	b5	b4	b3	b2	b1	b0				
y		MSH			LSH		Truncate	round with LSH(msb)	uround with MSH(0)	Matlab round (y/8)
-32	1	0	0	0	0	0	-4	-4	-4	-4
-31	1	0	0	0	0	1	-4	-4	-4	-4
-30	1	0	0	0	1	0	-4	-4	-4	-4
-29	1	0	0	0	1	1	-4	-4	-4	-4
-28	1	0	*0	1	0	0	-4	-3	-4*	-4
-27	1	0	0	1	0	1	-4	-3	-3	-3
-26	1	0	0	1	1	0	-4	-3	-3	-3
-25	1	0	0	1	1	1	-4	-3	-3	-3
-24	1	0	1	0	0	0	-3	-3	-3	-3
-23	1	0	1	0	0	1	-3	-3	-3	-3
-22	1	0	1	0	1	0	-3	-3	-3	-3
-21	1	0	1	0	1	1	-3	-3	-3	-3
-20	1	0	*1	1	0	0	-3	-2	-2*	-3
-19	1	0	1	1	0	1	-3	-2	-2	-2
-18	1	0	1	1	1	0	-3	-2	-2	-2
-17	1	0	1	1	1	1	-3	-2	-2	-2
-16	1	1	0	0	0	0	-2	-2	-2	-2
-15	1	1	0	0	0	1	-2	-2	-2	-2
-14	1	1	0	0	1	0	-2	-2	-2	-2
-13	1	1	0	0	1	1	-2	-2	-2	-2
-12	1	1	*0	1	0	0	-2	-1	-2*	-2
-11	1	1	0	1	0	1	-2	-1	-1	-1
-10	1	1	0	1	1	0	-2	-1	-1	-1
-9	1	1	0	1	1	1	-2	-1	-1	-1
-8	1	1	1	0	0	0	-1	-1	-1	-1
-7	1	1	1	0	0	1	-1	-1	-1	-1
-6	1	1	1	0	1	0	-1	-1	-1	-1
-5	1	1	1	0	1	1	-1	-1	-1	-1
-4	1	1	*1	1	0	0	-1	0	0*	-1
-3	1	1	1	1	0	1	-1	0	0	0
-2	1	1	1	1	1	0	-1	0	0	0
-1	1	1	1	1	1	1	-1	0	0	0
S=-66							S=-80	S=-64	S=-66	S=-68
M=-2.0625							M=-2.5	M=-2.0	M=-2.0625	M=-2.125

Table 3. Negative numbers example (WLin=6, WLout=3).

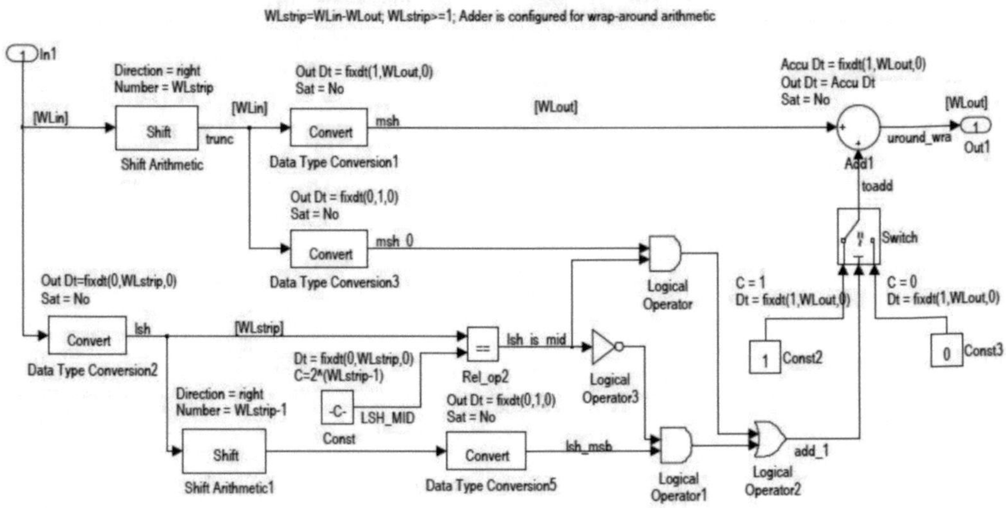

Figure 11. Unbiased rounding block example.

7. Conclusion

This chapter deals with modeling, simulation, and synthesis of a digital module for mixed-signal applications using a high-level Matlab/Simulink model on a high hierarchical level. More specifically, it presents an example design and the modeling details of a 3-stage CIC decimation filter suited for automatic conversion to the synthesizable HDL data base, using the HDL coder tool. The aim was to enable automatic procedures to finish the job, without any designer manipulation of the generated code on the low (HDL) level. Considerable care has been taken to provide practical instructions to cope with some tool-specific requirements. A single-rate modeling approach has been used to enable further modeling of specific operating modes and/or data handshaking procedures. Using the proposed modeling technique, one can speed up the implementation, improve the reliability, assure system integrality, and provide comprehensive documentation by maintaining one single, high-level model throughout the whole design effort.

Appendix A: Glossary of acronyms

ARM	A commercial provider of integrated circuit components
ASIC	Application-specific integrated circuit
Cadence	A commercial provider of the integrated circuit design tools

http://dx.doi.org/10.5772/58242

CIC	Cascaded integrator-comb
CMOS	A specific integrated circuit production technology
DSP	Digital signal processing
DUT	Device under test
FPGA	Field-programmable gate array
HDL	Hardware design language
LSB	Less significant bit
LSH	Less significant half
MSB	Most significant bit
MSH	Most significant half
RTL	Register transfer level
Synopsys	A commercial provider of the integrated circuit design tools
TSMC	A commercial silicon foundry
Verilog	A specific HDL language-
VHDL	A specific HDL language

Acknowledgements

This work was partly supported by the NAMASTE Centre of Excellence.

Author details

Drago Strle* and Dušan Raič

*Address all correspondence to: drago.strle@fe.uni-lj.si

University of Ljubljana, Faculty for Electrical Engineering, Ljubljana, Slovenia

References

[1] Grout, I.A. Modeling, simulation and synthesis: From Simulink to VHDL generated hardware. 5th World Multi-Conference on Systemics, Cybernetics and Informations, SCI 2001.

[2] Mauderer A., Oetjens J.H. System-level design of mixed-signal ASICs using Simulink: Efficient transitions to EDA environments. EETimes; 2012. http://www.eetimes.com/General/PrintView/4373903

[3] Erkkinen T., Breiner S. Automatic Code Generation–Technology Adoption Lessons Learned from Commercial Vehicle Case Studies. The MathWorks; 08AE-22; 2007.

[4] MathWorks. DSP System Toolbox Reference. The MathWorks; 2012.

[5] MathWorks. Simulink User's Guide. The MathWorks; 2012.

[6] MathWorks. HDL Coder User's Guide. The MathWorks; 2012.

[7] Meyer-Baese U. Digital Signal Processing with Field Programmable Gate Arrays. Springer; 2001.

[8] Harris F.J. Multirate Signal Processing for Communication Systems. Prentice Hall; 2004.

[9] Newbold R. Practical applications in digital signal processing. Prentice Hall; 2013.

[10] Hogenauer E.B. An Economical Class of Digital Filters for Decimation and Interpolation. IEEE Transactions on Acoustics, Speech and Signal Processing, ASSP-29(2); 1981. 155–162.

[11] Higgins J.H. Digital signal processing in VLSI. Prentice Hall; 1990.

Chapter 15

Code Generation From MATLAB – Simulink Models

Tiago da Silva Almeida, Ian Andrew Grout and
Alexandre César Rodrigues da Silva

Additional information is available at the end of the chapter

http://dx.doi.org/10.5772/57575

1. Introduction

Nowadays, computational tools are indispensable in the design of electronic circuits due to the increase in complexity of electronic circuits and the need to manage large amounts of related data to design. The development of new methodologies and tools has become a strategic area in the development of new technologies, in particular the development of CAD (Computer Aided Design) tools. CAD tools can be best understood as design information management systems, along with the creation of graphic based input and simulations of the designs are created. These simulations can be used, shared, published, republished and reused in different formats, scales and levels of detail.

But with so many studies involving different methodologies and computational tools, in [1], it was proposed to form a classification model for design and tools at the Electronic System Level (ESL) of design abstraction. This chapter details the characteristics and approaches that differ between computational tools of design, for modeling at level hardware and software. Figure 1 illustrates the design flow in different levels of abstraction. The design flow, called the Double Roof Model, is considered by [1] as an extended version of the Y diagram presented by [2][3]. However, there are still problems of incompatibility between designs the tools and this identifies a number of weaknesses.

Figure 1 shows the process of designing the top-down methodology in an ideal way. The left side corresponds to the process of software creation, while the right side corresponds to the process of hardware creation. Each side is divided into different levels of abstraction, e.g., Task and Instruction (software) or Components and Logic (hardware). There is a common level of abstraction, named ESL. In this level, we cannot distinguish between hardware and software. At each level, we can run a synthesis step (continuous vertical arrow) and the specification is transformed into an implementation. Horizontal dotted arrows indicate the steps which we

INTECH
open science | open minds

© 2014 The Author(s). Licensee InTech. This chapter is distributed under the terms of the Creative Commons Attribution License (http://creativecommons.org/licenses/by/3.0), which permits unrestricted use, distribution, and reproduction in any medium, provided the original work is properly cited.

can change the models of individual elements in the implementation directly to the next level of abstraction (lower level abstraction).

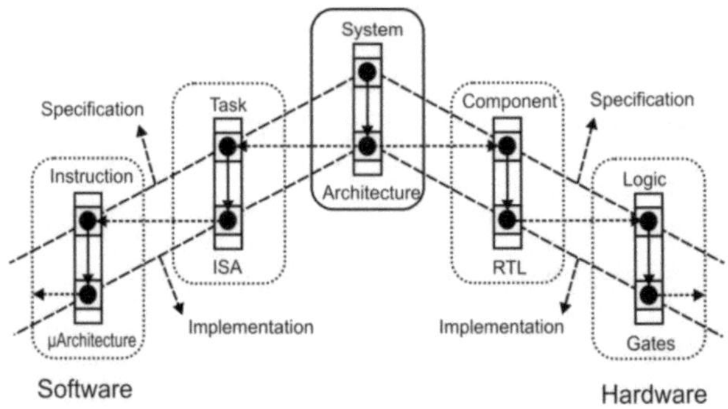

Figure 1. Flow design of electronic systems, also known as Double Roof Model.

In this chapter, we present a methodology for ESL designs based in four computational tools. The first one is the SF²HDL tool (Stateflow to Hardware Description Language or transition states table). The SF²HDL has the ability to convert models of finite state machine (FSM) in Stateflow / Simulink in a corresponding description in VHDL, Verilog or even a text file with a state transition table. The descriptions in the VHDL and Verilog languages are generated at the behavioral abstraction level for the finite state machine. The second computational tool, called MS²SV (MATLAB / Simulink to SystemVision), is able to generate descriptions in VHDL-AMS from models described in Simulink and all of model structure design for simulation in SystemVision environment from Mentor Graphics. The descriptions are generated in VHDL-AMS since even in the standard Simulink toolbox. there are many components with different signal representations of a purely digital representation. The third computational tool developed, called BD²XML (Block Diagram to XML), is able to generate a textual representation of the architecture of this model in XML markup language, also from models described in Simulink. XML was chosen for its applicability and it can be used as object code by other tools. The fourth and last computational tool described works together with BD²XML and it is similar to SF²HDL. The tool, called SF²XML (Stateflow to XML), is able to capture the relevant information in the Stateflow file and generate a corresponding description in XML. The file resulting from the conversion is according to the standard of XML structure called SCXML (StateChart XML) proposed by the W3C [4].

For acceptance in the community of software development, maintainability and practicality, we chose to develop the translation environment using an object-oriented approach. For robustness, the C++language was chosen. With C++ language is possible create linear and nonlinear data structure, and languages like Java, it is not possible do it. In our tools, we used liner lists to store dynamically the data in memory. Thus, C++language is a better choice for programming language. Another reason for this choice, it is the common features between methods were coupled to objects, so there was created a logical interaction with low representational gap.

As case study designs, the digital-to-analog converters (DAC) design was used to explain the MS^2SV and BD^2XML. Data converters are circuits that transform a given representation to another. The ADC (analog to digital converter) is used to convert analog signals to digital data. The digital to analogue converter works in the opposite manner to the ADC, converting digital data input to analogue signal output proportional to value of input digital.

Considering the DAC operation, *n* binary input bits (which can be considered as representing the binary code of a decimal value) are received and there are 2^n possible combinations of binary input. There is also an additional input to the circuit design that is used as a reference signal, represented by V_{ref} and the reference is a voltage level, which is used to determine the maximum value that converter can generate on its output. The analog value is generated by the weighted sum of *n* inputs, multiplied by the reference voltage. Inputs are weighted according to magnitude of each bit, where *n* is the magnitude of input bit, *x* is total number of inputs, and *b* is DAC input value contained in the bit of *n* magnitude, where $b_n \in \{0,1\}$, as described in:

$$V_P = \sum_{n=1}^{x} \frac{1}{2^n} b_n \tag{1}$$

Using Equation (1), the analogue output voltage from the data converter is obtained by multiplying the result of Equation (1) by the reference voltage to obtain:

$$V_{out} = V_P \times V_{ref} \tag{2}$$

There are several methods possible to implement the DAC operation (i.e., there are several different DAC design architectures possible). One common method used is R/2R ladder circuit, where only two values for resistors in circuit are used (R and 2R), and output current depends on positions of switches that are controlled by inputs [5].

To explain the use of SF^2HDL and SF^2XML, we used a HDB3 (High Density Bipolar 3) finite state machine [6]. HDB3 line code, which is a technique for detecting synchronism with bipolar signaling, and it has been used over the years in digital systems. A finite state machine can be represented by state diagrams. State diagrams are used to graphically represent a state transition functions set. Having an input event set, the output event set and the next state set can be determined.

There are also several other forms to represent finite state machine that differ slightly and have different semantic. The State Transition Table and Petri Net are two examples. Figure 2 shows generic schematic of a finite state machine. The circuit has a finite number of inputs, representing all input variable set $\{N_1, N_2, \ldots, N_n\}$. Thus, the circuit has a finite number *m* of outputs, determined by the output set of variables $\{M_1, M_2, \ldots, M_m\}$.

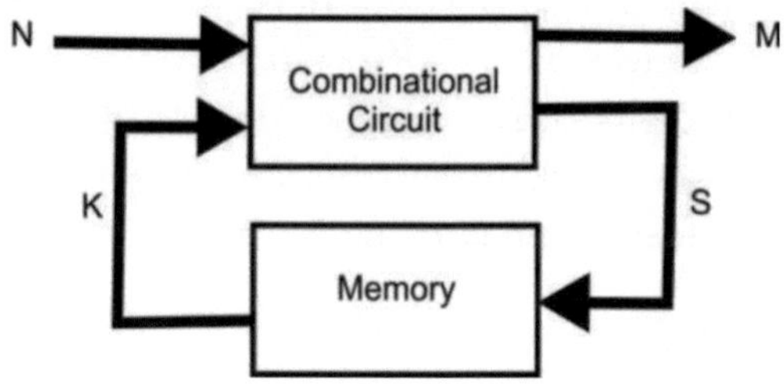

Figure 2. Schematic of a Finite State Machine.

The value in each memory element is called a state variable, and the set denoted by $\{K_1, K_2, \ldots, K_k\}$ form the state variable set. The values contained in *k* memory elements define the internal state of finite state machine. The outputs $\{M_1, M_2 \ldots, M_m\}$ and internal transition functions $\{S_1, S_2, \ldots, S_s\}$ depend on external inputs (input functions) and internal states (state functions) of state machine and they are defined by combinational circuits. The values *S*, which appear in the role of state transitions of machine at time *t*, determine values of state variables at time *t* +*1* and therefore define the next state of machine.

The state transition diagram or the state transition table makes the relationship between present state, next state, input and output.

The finite state machines that determine the next state *K(t+1)* only in the present state *K(t)* and present input *N(t)* are called deterministic machines or Markovian. Deterministic machines can be represented by the following equation:

$$K(t+1) = f[K(t), N(t)] \tag{3}$$

Where, *f* is a state transition function. The value of output M(t) is obtained through of two ways:

$$M(t) = g[K(t)] \tag{4}$$

or,

$$M(t) = g[K(t), N(t)] \tag{5}$$

where, *g* is an output function.

A finite state machine with properties described in Equations (3) and (4) is called Moore model and a machine described by equations (3) and (5) is called Mealy model [7].

To illustrate the state transition diagram, Figure 3 shows a state transition diagram of HDB3 code line, in hexadecimal representation as proposed in [6]. The encoder needed three parts

http://dx.doi.org/10.5772/57575

of memory to store and to identify four successive 0. After this, it was necessary to use a flip-flop to store the polarity of the pulse (0 for+or 1 for-), and finally other flip-flop to store the polarity of the violation. The encoder requests a minimum of 2^5=32 states. The state 00 represents the initial state of the machine, and the two pairs of state 07 and 0F (in the left) and 1F and 17 (in the right) represent the description AMI, what causes the alternate code between +1 and-1 [6].

2. Related research

Project-level electronic systems, also known as ESL (Electronic System Level), require much effort designer. The first work to classify the steps involved in system design at a high level of abstraction [2] subsequently refined to a more current [1] and [3].

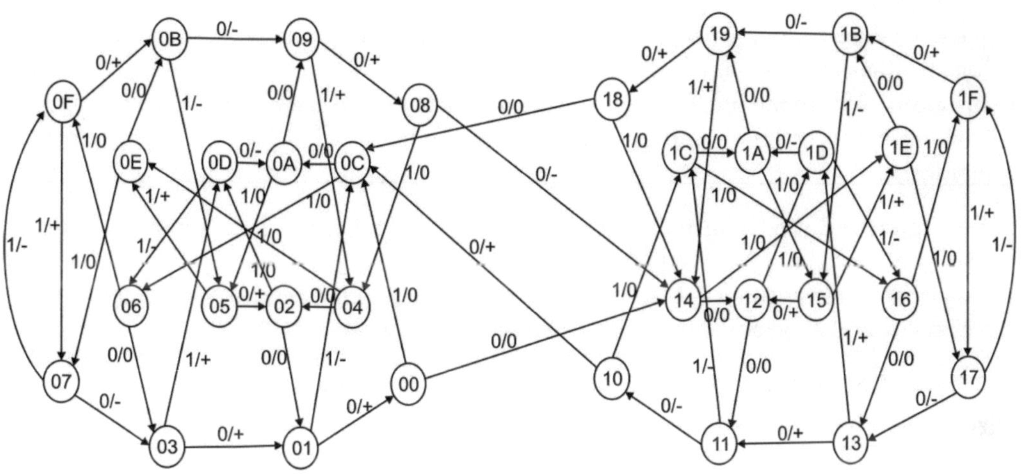

Figure 3. State transition diagram for HDB3 line code.

Some studies deal with design optimization or minimization, for example the work in paper [8]. This work explored the computational complexity of logic minimization problem on two levels for digital circuit designs. In [9] was developed a genetic algorithm for synthesis of multi-core architectures. The target system was an implementation of Petri net. In [10] was presented a method of re-engineering the FSM by rebuilding it with a different topology, but with equivalent functionality. The method is mainly concerned with power consumption of the finite state machine and uses a genetic algorithm to find the best solution. This approach facilitates the process of synthesis for optimal implementations of the system.

The representation of electronic systems by means of the FSM facilitates verification of the system and formal methodologies can be developed to assist in the synthesis process. In [11] was presented a tool capable to translate a FSM described in the VHDL. The focus of the work was modeling and the verification. In [12] was developed a conceptual mathematical model for automatic checking of the FSM by observing the outputs of this particular FSM, allowing checking faulty behavior.

Hardware description languages (HDLs) are widely used in the design of electronic systems and also represent a major means for simulation and project documentation. In [13] was developed an algorithm for automatic generation of analog circuit models for modeling faults in the circuit at a high level. In [14] was developed a methodology for implementing FFT (Fast Fourier Transform) processors in reprogrammable devices using VHDL. In [15] was developed the architecture for implementing a SPICE (Simulation Program with Integrated Circuit Emphasis) simulator using an FPGA (Field Programmable Gate Array)

In [16] the authors proposed a simulator for the VHDL-AMS (Analog and Mixed Signal) language developed in the MATLAB environment. The tool was compared with others simulators available commercially. Another example that can be cited is the tool called SF2VHD, presented in [17]. That tool is capable to translate hierarchical models of finite states machine, modeled in the Stateflow environment, in a code corresponding structural VHDL.

In the work described in [18] was developed a tool called Sim2HDL, which accomplishes the automatic translation of Simulink models in a hardware description language in the attempt to drastically reduce the project time. The generated language can be VHDL or Verilog, at a behavioral level description, and the system can be implemented in FPGAs using commercial synthesizers.

Some commercial modeling tools incorporate the translation need for different forms of modeling. An example is a MATLAB C Compiler tool, developed by Mathworks. That tool translates programs written in MATLAB for a corresponding program in the C language. The functionality and main advantages of these tools are described in [19].

In [20] was proposed an approach to automatic synthesis of additional decoders. The method attempts to find and remove cases where there are no equivalent decoders. To discover all decoders that can exist simultaneously, an algorithm based on functional dependency has also been proposed. To select the correct decoder another algorithm is used to infer formula of each decoder precondition.

In [21] was developed a framework for the synthesis of electronic systems at a high level based on abstract finite state machines. The framework called synASM is capable of generating a CDFG (Control Data Flow Graph) from hardware descriptions based on C language. The authors extended the definitions of abstract state machines to support the parallelism and timing. After generating the CDFG extended, it was possible the automatic generation of optimizable hardware descriptions in VHDL and implementation in a FPGA.

In [22] was presented a complete approach decoder for communication systems. The modelling was based on finite state machines and the method was capable of identifying whether decode exists or not, by observing the input sequence and output of encoder. [23] presented a method of representation and synthesis of Boolean expressions recursively. The method performs a sequence of operations with denial implications using two memristors. With the method, it was proved that it was possible to reduce the number of necessary implications for the expression representation and inference using multiple inputs can reduce the computation of memristor implementation.

In [24] was proposed an algorithm for identifying flowcharts structure. Twelve structures were identified and then the algorithm was used to generate the code flowchart identified using recursion. The technologies and algorithms were used in an integrated development platform. [25] presented an approach of output bit selection based on counter for output response compaction in test systems observable. The hardware implementation requires only a counter and a multiplexer. Thus, the complexity was reduced and the control area was simplified. Furthermore, a change in the ATPG (Automatic Test Pattern Generation) tool was not required. Two output selection algorithms have been developed in several operations which counters can be employed.

In [26] was discussed some work and the importance of developing CAD tools for the synthesis and design of systems and multi-core architectures, highlighting the importance of multi-core optimized and efficient resource allocation. [27] presented revised performance measures of some data type converters ADC (Analog-to-Digital Converter), such as SNR (Signal to Noise Ratio), SINAD (Signal to Noise Ratio and Distortion), SFDR (Spurious free Dynamic Range), THD (Total Harmonic Distortion) and ENOB (Effective Number of Bits). These metrics were analyzed with the case study of an ideal 14-bit converter in MATLAB and a converter with 12-bit commercial manufactured by Analog Devices.

In [28] was presented a methodology for genetic optimization based on VHDL-AMS for Fuzzy Logic controllers. The fuzzy logic controller was used for modeling work in automotive systems in mixed physical domain. A genetic algorithm was developed and simulated in SystemVision environment, is employed in the generation of rough fuzzy sets.

3. Generation code methodology of SF^{2}HDL

The SF^{2}HDL is a computational tool capable to convert a state transition diagram into a hardware description language description. This diagram is described in the Stateflow environment [29]. The Stateflow is toolbox inside Simulink is used to simulate finite state machines in different contexts. The SF^{2}HDL tool is a simplified graphical interface that allows the user to select between generate (i) an input file to be processed by TABELA program and (ii) a.*vhd* file with a behavioral VHDL description obtained directly from state transition diagram.

The TABELA program was developed for synthesize of a finite state machine and was implemented in Pascal language by researchers from UNICAMP [7] (Universidade Estadual de Campinas-Brazil). The program generates combinational functions that implement the finite machine described by state transition table. The transition functions and output functions are minimized and the cost of minimization using minterms and maxterms [7]. The transitions are specified on table form using one line per state transition, so: present state, next state, input, output. The description end is represented by notation "-100". Figure 4 shows the standard file for TABELA program input.

The states, the inputs and outputs must be in decimal notation. The finite state machines can be completely or incompletely specified.

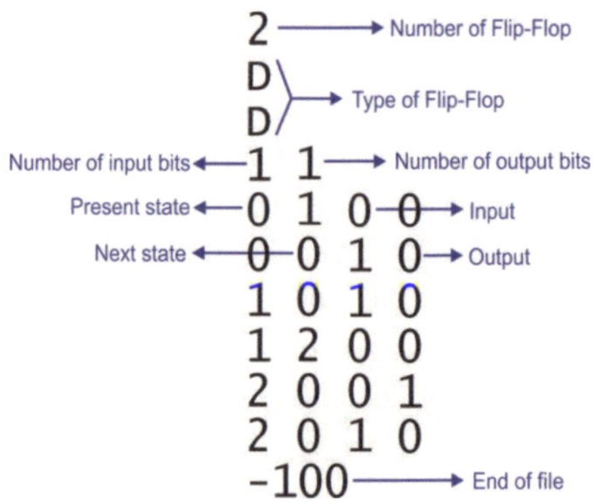

Figure 4. Input file for TABELA program.

The TABELA program assembles a state transition table and stores it in output file. From this table are obtained minterms, maxterms and don't care states of transition functions of all internal flip-flops and circuit output functions. Using Quine-McCluskey algorithm, is made the minimization of Boolean functions.

Figure 5 illustrates the main interface of SF²HDL program. The SF²HDL has a menu called **Ferramentas** (Tools) with the following options: a) **Nova Tradução** (Translation), used to open the file with a finite state machine modeled in Stateflow environment, b) **Traduzir** (Translate), which performs the model translation into one of language was chosen, c) **Sair** (Quit), which terminates the program, and d) **Sobre** (About) option that displays a screen with a brief comment on the tool developed.

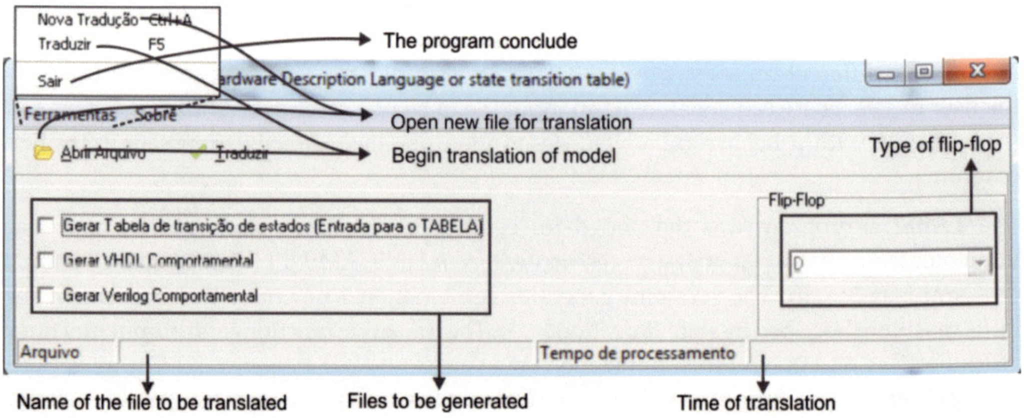

Figure 5. Main interface of SF²HDL program.

http://dx.doi.org/10.5772/57575

Thus, from all the information found in the*.mdl* (Simulink file) file, it is possible to determine the present state, the next state, the input and output of the finite state machine. According to the structure of each file, all the information is grouped and then is generated the input file for TABELA program and/or the corresponding behavioral VHDL. Figure 6 presents the functional diagram of SF²HDL program with all necessary steps to perform the translation, as previously reviewed.

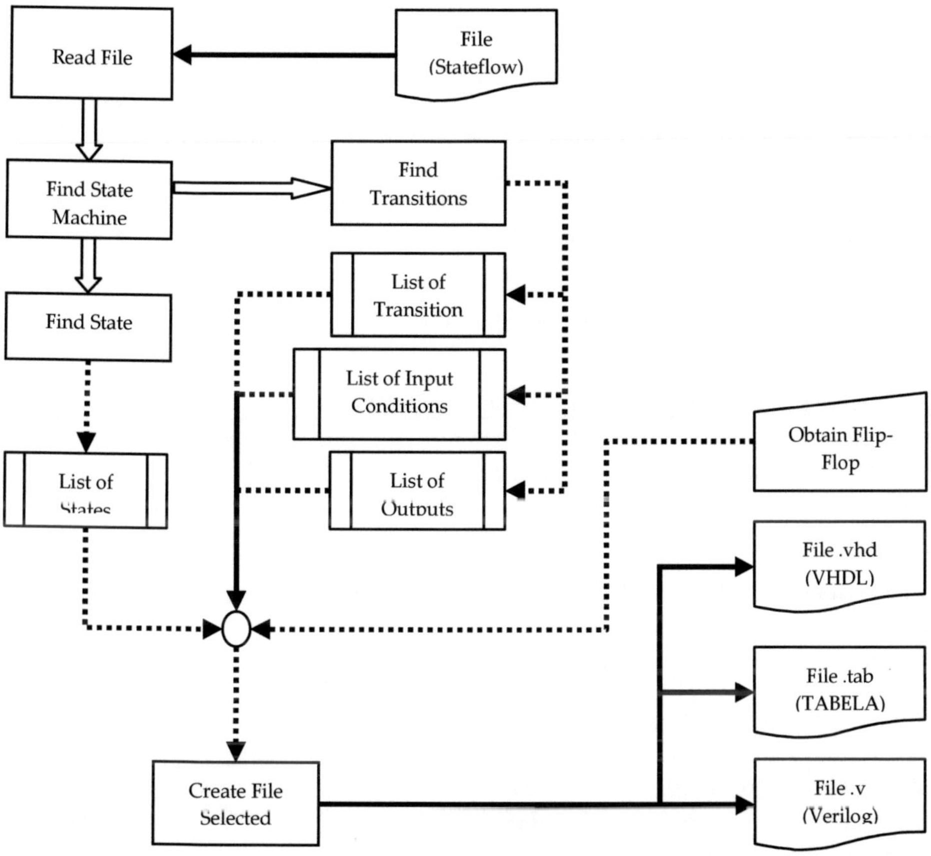

Figure 6. Block diagram of SF²HDL.

SF²HDL initially reads the file containing finite state machine, simulated in the Stateflow environment. Then, the program finds the state machine structure and it makes a temporary storage of this information. After that, the state location list for all states is generated and through the transition locations is generated a transitions list, identifying the conditions for the inputs and outputs. When the user selects to generate the input file for the TABELA program, there is the need to choose what type of memory element (flip-flop) will be used in the generated file. The memory element type must be put manually by the user.

Figure 7 shows the class diagram of SF²HDL. The SF²HDL was built with many inheritances between the classes. There are two objects to store the structure found in the.*mdl* file; the state information and transition information. This distinction is considered because the differences between a Mealy machine and Moore machine described in Equations (3), (4) and (5). SF²HDL is capable of recognizing which machine is used in the model. The **fsm** object is responsible to read the.*mdl* file and to save this information. The **misc** has some operations used many times during running of SF²HDL. The **create_files** object is responsible to create the file that was chosen by user, as illustrate in Figure 7. As SF²HDL can create three files at the same time, the **main** class call the **create_files** more than once, if it is the case.

3.1. Simulation results of HDB3 line code and conversion results

For modeling the state transition diagram on Stateflow environment, some rules must be obeyed, such as the name of the state contained within the symbol should never begin with numeric character (0, 1, 2, 3, 4, 5, 6, 7, 8 or 9), and the condition in the transition to the Mealy model must meet the following syntax:

$$[e[t] == 0]\{s = 0;\} \tag{6}$$

where *e* represents the variable that will receive input value, *t* is a variable that represents a discrete time and *s* is an output variable. The external bracket represents the input condition in the transition from one state to another to obtain an output. The double equal signs (==) represent the verification of a condition and the equal sign alone (=) represents the allocation of value [30].

For proper functionality of the SF²HDL program, is necessary that the values in the transition of model in Stateflow environment, both at input and output, are decimal representations. Figure 8 presents the state diagram of HDB3 code on Stateflow environment.

In simulation are used several words with signs and bits from varying sizes. However, it was standardized in using an input word in the simulation of 24 bits being formed by the following bits: 000100110000110101000100. We used this bit stream because with it we can simulate both characteristics of signal encoder, AMI and HDB3, in a real situation. The result of the simulation is presented in the Figure 9.

The TABELA program creates a new file, containing a description of Boolean functions from the circuit already minimized.

Listing 1 was reduced and is shown only important parts of minimization. Each Boolean function in the finite state machine is minimized. As HDB3 has five flip-flops and two output bits, it is possible to see seven functions in Listing 1 (lines 1, 11, 21, 28, 34, 40 and 51). In each function are described the function minterms in decimal, e.g. line 3. The function prime implicants and essentials are shown too, e.g. lines 4-9. And the function cost is shown in lines 10, 20, 27, 33, 39, 50 and 58. The total cost of the circuit is shown in lie 59, for HDB3 case is 95. It is important to highlight that the cost is expressed like sum of product by TABELA.

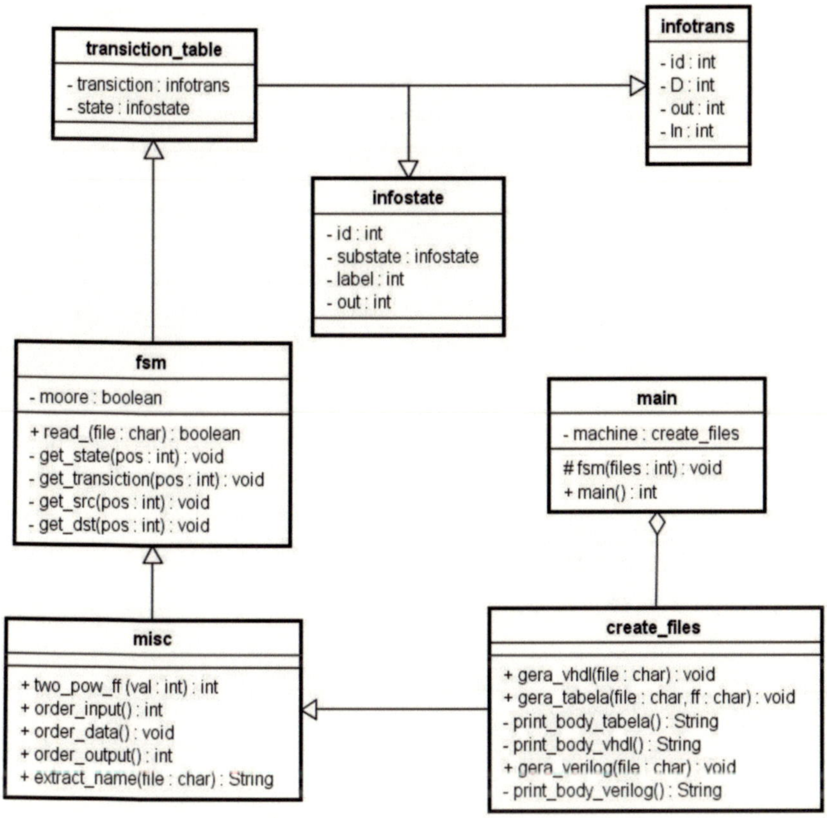

Figure 7. Class diagram of SF²HDL.

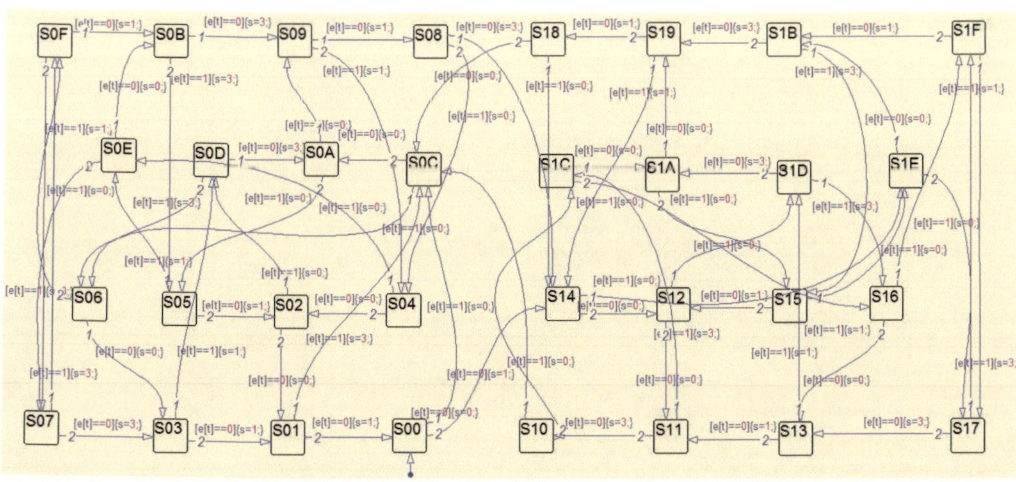

Figure 8. Description of HDB3 code on Stateflow.

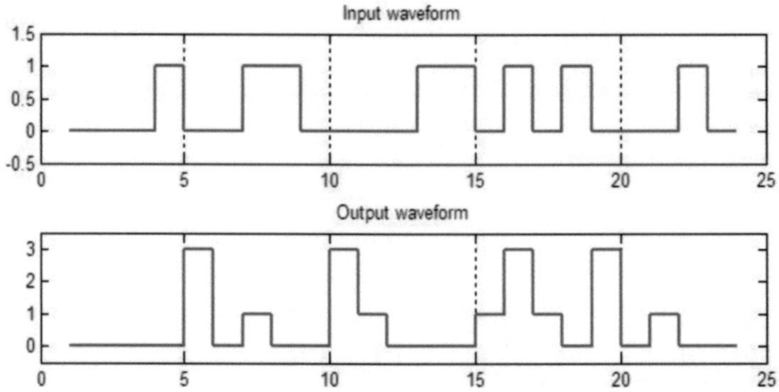

Figure 9. Results of simulation of HDB3on Stateflow.

```
FUNCAO D4
=========
MINTERMOS : 0; 8; 48; 17; 49; 18; 50; 19; 51; 20; 52; 21; 53; 22; 54; 23; 55; 25; 57; 26;
 58; 27; 59; 28; 60; 29; 61; 30; 62; 31; 63;
IMPLICANTES PRIMOS ESSENCIAIS :
ESSENCIAL: 20  REDUNDANCIA:  43 -> x1x1xx
ESSENCIAL: 18  REDUNDANCIA:  45 -> x1xx1x
ESSENCIAL: 17  REDUNDANCIA:  46 -> x1xxx1
ESSENCIAL: 48  REDUNDANCIA:  15 -> 11xxxx
ESSENCIAL: 0  REDUNDANCIA:   8 -> 00x000
CUSTO FINAL DE D4 = 18
FUNCAO D3
=========
MINTERMOS : 32; 33; 34; 35; 36; 37; 38; 39; 9; 10; 11; 12; 13; 14; 15; 48; 16; 49; 50; 51;
 52; 53; 54; 55; 24; 25; 26; 27; 28; 29; 30; 31;
IMPLICANTES PRIMOS ESSENCIAIS :
ESSENCIAL: 16   REDUNDANCIA:    8 -> 01x000
ESSENCIAL: 12   REDUNDANCIA:   19 -> 0x11xx
ESSENCIAL: 10   REDUNDANCIA:   21 -> 0x1x1x
ESSENCIAL: 9   REDUNDANCIA:   22 -> 0x1xx1
ESSENCIAL: 32   REDUNDANCIA:   23 -> 1x0xxx
CUSTO FINAL DE D3 = 21
FUNCAO D2
=========
MINTERMOS : 32; 0; 33; 34; 35; 36; 37; 38; 39; 40; 8; 41; 42; 43; 44; 45; 46; 47; 48; 16;
 49; 50; 51; 52; 53; 54; 55; 56; 24; 57; 58; 59; 60; 61; 62; 63;
IMPLICANTES PRIMOS ESSENCIAIS :
ESSENCIAL: 32   REDUNDANCIA:   31 -> 1xxxxx
ESSENCIAL: 0   REDUNDANCIA:   56 -> xxx000
CUSTO FINAL DE D2 = 6
FUNCAO D1
=========
MINTERMOS : 4; 36; 5; 37; 6; 38; 39; 7; 44; 12; 13; 45; 46; 14; 47; 15; 20; 52; 21; 53; 22;
 54; 55; 23; 60; 28; 61; 29; 62; 30; 63; 31;
IMPLICANTES PRIMOS ESSENCIAIS :
ESSENCIAL: 4   REDUNDANCIA:   59 -> xxx1xx
CUSTO FINAL DE D1 = 1
FUNCAO D0
=========
MINTERMOS : 34; 2; 3; 35; 6; 38; 39; 7; 42; 10; 11; 43; 46; 14; 47; 15; 18; 50; 51; 19; 22;
 54; 55; 23; 26; 58; 59; 27; 62; 30; 63; 31;
IMPLICANTES PRIMOS ESSENCIAIS :
ESSENCIAL: 2   REDUNDANCIA:   61 -> xxxx1x
CUSTO FINAL DE D0 = 1
FUNCAO Z1
=========
MINTERMOS : 33; 39; 7; 8; 11; 43; 13; 45; 17; 49; 55; 23; 59; 27; 61; 29;
IMPLICANTES PRIMOS ESSENCIAIS :
ESSENCIAL: 17   REDUNDANCIA:   32 -> x10001
ESSENCIAL: 13   REDUNDANCIA:   48 -> xx1101
ESSENCIAL: 11   REDUNDANCIA:   48 -> xx1011
ESSENCIAL: 8   REDUNDANCIA:    0 -> 001000
ESSENCIAL: 7   REDUNDANCIA:   48 -> xx0111
ESSENCIAL: 33   REDUNDANCIA:   16 -> 1x0001
CUSTO FINAL DE Z1 = 34
FUNCAO Z0
=========
MINTERMOS : 1; 33; 3; 35; 5; 37; 39; 7; 8; 41; 9; 11; 43; 13; 45; 47; 15; 16; 17; 49; 51;
 19; 21; 53; 55; 23; 57; 25; 59; 27; 61; 29; 63; 31;
IMPLICANTES PRIMOS ESSENCIAIS :
ESSENCIAL: 16   REDUNDANCIA:    1 -> 01000x
ESSENCIAL: 8   REDUNDANCIA:    1 -> 00100x
ESSENCIAL: 1   REDUNDANCIA:   62 -> xxxxx1
CUSTO FINAL DE Z0 = 14
CUSTO TOTAL DAS 7 FUNCOES = 95
```

Listing 1. Minimization generate by TABELA program for HDB3 study case

http://dx.doi.org/10.5772/57575

After the minimization by TABELA was used the TAB2VHDL program [31] which generated VHDL code in RTL (Register Transfer Level) that is shown in Listing 2. The TAB2VHDL is a tool developed by researchers in UNESP (Universidade Estadual Paulista-Brazil) in C language. The only task TAB2VHDL is generated the VHDL code from TABELA output.

```
1.  ENTITY HDB3 IS
2.  PORT(
3.  CLK, CLR: IN BIT;
4.  X0: IN BIT;
5.  Z0, Z1: OUT BIT
6.  );
7.  END HDB3;
8.  ARCHITECTURE RTL OF HDB3 IS
9.  SIGNAL VE0, VE1, VE2, VE3, VE4: BIT;
10. SIGNAL D4, D3, D2, D1, D0: BIT;
11. BEGIN
12. PROCESS (CLK, CLR)
13. BEGIN
14. IF CLR = '0' THEN
15. VE0 <= '0';
16. ELSIF CLK'EVENT and CLK = '1' THEN
17. VE0 <= D0;
18. END IF;
19. END PROCESS;
20. ...
21. ...
22. D4 <= ((VE4) AND (VE2)) OR ((VE4) AND (VE1)) OR ((VE4) AND (VE0)) OR ((X0) AND (VE4)) OR
    (NOT(X0) AND NOT (VE4) AND NOT (VE2) AND NOT (VE1) AND NOT(VE0));
23. D3 <= ( NOT(X0) AND (VE4) AND NOT(VE2) AND NOT(VE1) AND NOT(VE0)) OR (NOT(X0) AND (VE3) AND
    (VE2)) OR (NOT(X0) AND (VE3) AND (VE1)) OR (NOT(X0) AND (VE3) AND (VE0)) OR ((X0) AND
    NOT(VE3));
24. D2 <= ( (X0)) OR (NOT(VE2) AND NOT(VE1) AND NOT(VE0));
25. D1 <= ( (VE2));
26. D0 <= ( (VE1));
27. Z1 <= ( (VE3) AND (VE2) AND NOT(VE1) AND (VE0)) OR ((VE3) AND NOT(VE2) AND (VE1) AND (VE0))
    OR (NOT(X0) AND NOT(VE4) AND (VE3) AND NOT(VE2) AND NOT(VE1) AND NOT(VE0)) OR (NOT(VE3) AND
    (VE2) AND (VE1) AND (VE0)) OR (NOT(VE3) AND NOT(VE2) AND NOT(VE1) AND (VE0));
28. Z0 <= ( (VE3) AND (VE2) AND NOT(VE1) AND (VE0)) OR ((VE3) AND NOT(VE2) AND (VE1) AND (VE0))
    OR (NOT(X0) AND NOT(VE4) AND (VE3) AND NOT(VE2) AND NOT(VE1) AND NOT(VE0)) OR (NOT(VE3) AND
    (VE2) AND (VE1) AND (VE0)) OR (NOT(VE3) AND NOT(VE2) AND NOT(VE1) AND (VE0));
29. END RTL;
```

Listing 2. VHDL code generate by TAB2VHDL program for HDB3 study case.

In Listing 2, there is clear distinction in architecture between the flip-flops and the Boolean function to describe the behavior of HDB3. In lines 15-22 are described the flip-flop used (noting that this listing was reduced to presentation in this chapter). Lines 25-31 show the Boolean function of HDB3. This kind of abstraction has better results for synthesis in order to implement the circuit, e.g. in a FPGA (Field Programming Gate Array).

The other option is to generate the behavioral VHDL directly without using TABELA program. In Listing 3 is shown the file with behavioral VHDL code generated.

This description is different between Listing 2 as it is expressed at a behavioral level of abstraction for HDB3. In lines 3 and 4 in the entity, the signal representation is in decimal instead binary. This is a different way that VHDL can support the representation of input and output signals. Lines 14-41 express the behavior of the finite state machine. The reset signal is shown in line 18 and 19 and lines 21-40 show the transitions of HDB3. SF²HDL does not use the same label used in Stateflow, such as Figure 8. This case study coincidentally is the same (decimal representation instead hexadecimal), but in other cases then this label will be changed. The last process in description, lines 43-47, describes the update of state by clock signal.

The third description language generated by SF²HDL is a behavioral Verilog code [32], which it is shown in Listing 4.

```
ENTITY Mealy_HD IS
PORT(
ent: IN INTEGER RANGE 0 TO 1;
sai: OUT INTEGER RANGE 0 TO 3;
clk, clr: IN BIT
);
END Mealy_HD;
ARCHITECTURE lpssd OF Mealy_HD IS
TYPE tipo_est IS (S0, S1, S2... S31);
SIGNAL est_atual, prox_est: tipo_est;
BEGIN
behavior: PROCESS (reset, input, state)
BEGIN
nxtstate <= state;
output <= 0;
IF reset = '0' THEN
 nxtstate <= S14;
ELSE
 CASE state IS
 WHEN S0 =>
  IF (input = 1) THEN
  output <= 1;
  nxtstate <= S12;
  ELSE
  output <= 1;
  nxtstate <= S2;
  END IF;
 WHEN S1 =>
  IF (input = 1) THEN
  output <= 0;
  nxtstate <= S12;
  ELSE
  output <= 0;
  nxtstate <= S2;
  END IF;
  ...
  ...
 END CASE;
END PROCESS;
clock: PROCESS
BEGIN
WAIT UNTIL clk'EVENT AND clk = '1';
state <= nxtstate;
END PROCESS clock;
END lpssd;
```

Listing 3. Behavioral VHDL code generate by SF²HDL for HDB3 study case.

Listing 4 is very similar to Listing 3, with the difference in the syntax between both languages, VHDL and Verilog. In the same way, lines 18-48 express the behavioral of the finite state machine, the reset signal is shown in line 21 and 23, lines 25-46 is shown the transitions and lines 50-52 describe the update of state by clock signal.

In Figure 10 is shown the simulation of behavioral VHDL code generated by SF²HDL on Quartus II environment [33], using the same word of data in the simulation as that in the Stateflow environment to verify accuracy and violation of HDB3 code too in the Quartus II.

There is a short delay in output least significant in Figure 10. But the delay does not disrupt the behavioral of the HDB3 encoder. The behavioral VHDL, RTL VHDL and behavioral Verilog codes were synthesized and implemented on the Cyclone II EP2C20F484C7 FPGA.

Figure 11 shows the simulation waveform of code generated by TAB2VHDL, i.e., using a RTL VHDL code. This is different from Figure 10 and in Figure 11 is possible to see a stranger behavioral of the code. Possibly this is due to some mistakes in TABELA program as the RTL VHDL is same of the optimization realized by TABELA program. Or even, possibly the results of synthesis of Quartus II. At the moment we do not know the cause of the problem.

Figure 12 illustrates the simulation results for behavioral Verilog code. The simulation waveform of Figure 12 is the same waveform in Figure 10, proving that this representation in behavioral Verilog and VHDL, because the level of abstraction in the same too. The synthesis result in FPGA Cyclone II is another equal result.

http://dx.doi.org/10.5772/57575

```
module Mealy_HD (clk, in, reset, out);
input clk, reset;
input [0:0] in;
output out;
reg [1:0] out;
reg [4:0] state;
reg [4:0] nxtstate;
parameter [4:0]
S0 = 0,
S1 = 1,
...
...
S31 = 31;
always @ (in or reset or state) begin
nxtstate = state;
out = 0;
if (reset) begin
 nxtstate = S14;
end
else begin
 case (state)
 S0:
 if (in == 1) begin
  nxtstate = S12;
  out = 1;
 end
 else begin
  nxtstate = S2;
  out = 1;
 end
 S1:
 if (in == 1) begin
  nxtstate = S12;
  out = 0;
 end
 else begin
  nxtstate = S2;
  out = 0;
 end
 ...
 ...
 endcase
end
end
always @ (posedge clk) begin
state = nxtstate;
end
endmodule
```

Listing 4. Behavioral Verilog code generate by SF²HDL for HDB3 study case.

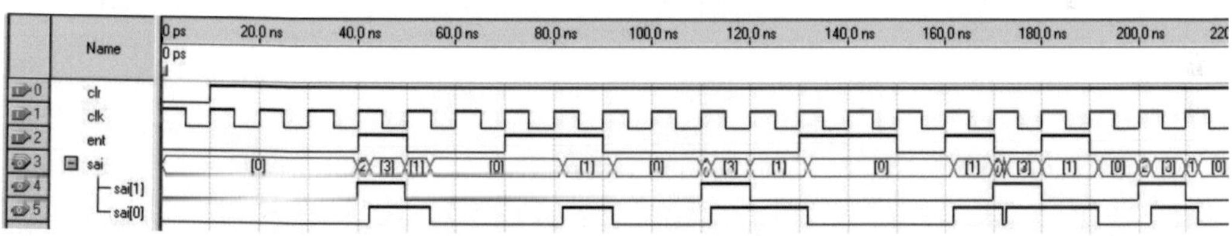

Figure 10. HDB3 line code Simulation in behavioral VHDL.

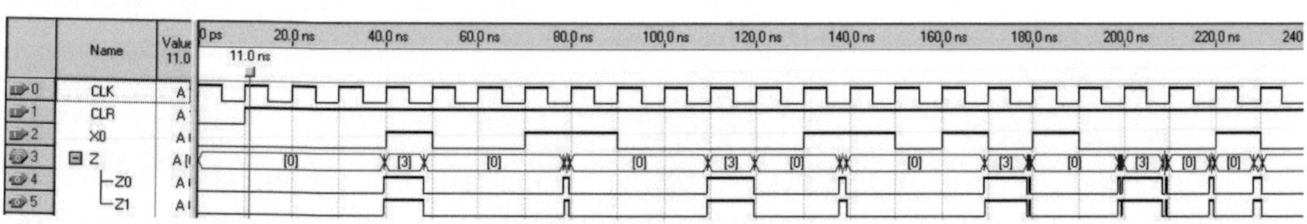

Figure 11. HDB3 line code Simulation in RTL VHDL.

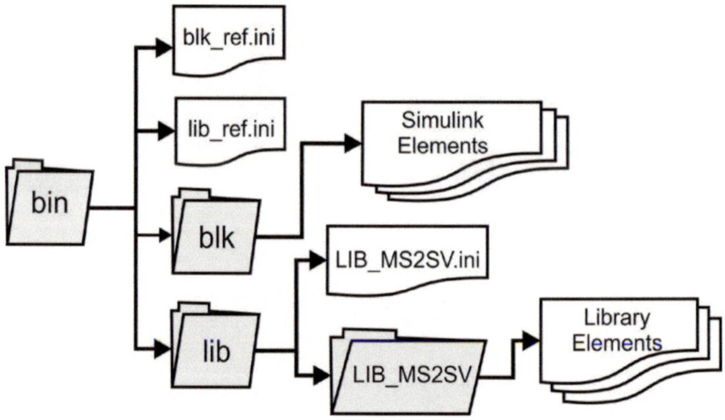

Figure 13. Directory structure and files that are used in configuration and the translation of models in MATLAB / Simulink.

4. Generation code methodology of MS²SV

The MS²SV is capable to convert a simulation model in Simulink to a description in VHDL-AMS [34]. This time, we used a VHDL-AMS description since the models can use different kinds of signals such as electrical, mechanical, hydraulic, etc. MS²SV has two key features:

1. The designer is able to add new components from the Simulink libraries. With this feature, the designer can use different elements previously defined in the standard Simulink libraries.

2. The addition of new Simulink libraries developed by the designer with more complex models, or to change the library named LIB_MS2SV also used in previously paper [36].

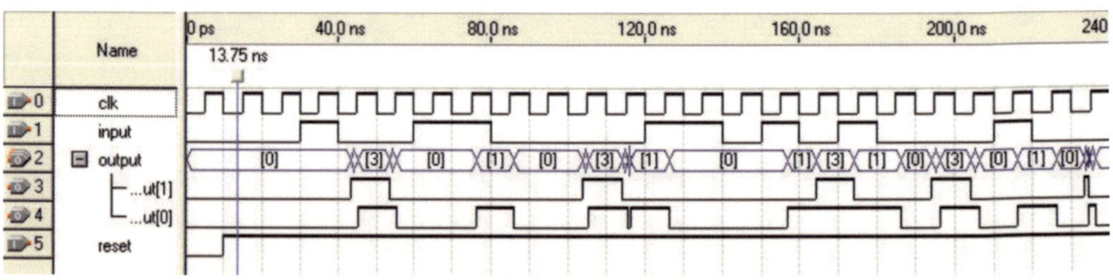

Figure 12. HDB3 line code Simulation in behavioral Verilog.

This added flexibility is made possible by creating a directory structure and configuration as shown Figure 13. From the root directory **bin** configuration files are split between configurations of elements from libraries of MATLAB / Simulink (**lib** directory) and elements of toolbox Simulink (**blk** directory) subject to translation. The pseudo-code concerning the VHDL-AMS models are also arranged between directories.

In the main interface, there is the menu containing the following options: a) **Arquivo** (File): In this option, there are two possible actions. With the first action, the user selects the Simulink model to be translated. When this action is selected, the status bar appears on the file name to be translated. The second action is a button to end execution of the tool, b) **Ferramentas** (Tools): In this option, the user is able to select the project location. The process of translation is then initiated. If there are unknown models that the tool is not able to recognize, it will display a message reporting the fact, c) **Configuração** (Configuration): In this option, there is an action called "Adicionar / Remover Componentes (Add / Remove Components)" and another called "Adicionar / Remover Bibliotecas (Add / Remove Libraries)". These options are used to add / remove elements of toolboxes and Simulink libraries developed by the designer, respectively. If there is not a model configuration to be translated, the tool is not able to recognize it and translate it.

The translation of the model starts with reading a Simulink generated file with an.**mdl** extension. Initially, a check is made of elements and libraries used in model. If there are no unknown libraries or elements, the translation process starts. The tool stores a list of components in model, the list of connections between these components and other important information for generation of circuit netlist. Then, project structure required for simulation and analysis in SystemVision is generated too [35][36]. Finally, all descriptions in VHDL-AMS and files for debugging for project needs are generated. Figure 14 shows the functional diagram of the MS^{2}SV tool.

If subsystems are used, a VHDL-AMS model for each subsystem used is generated. The MS^{2}SV enables the relationship between elements in the same library by creating hierarchical models.

Figure 15 represents the class diagram of tool MS^{2}SV in a software perspective. All interface layers are represented since some aspects do not change the MS^{2}SV functionality. In Figure 15, only the classes **Main**, **Save** and **VHDL** are in the interface layer. The others class makes the translation inference engine. The **SystemFile** class is responsible to generate all project structure to simulate in SytemVision environment. The **TranslateCode** is responsible to generate all VHDL-AMS files. This class inherits the features of **Checking** class, and **Checking** class checks if there is any primitive of Simulink, user libraries or subsystems. **Checking** inherits the features of **Lib** class and **Lib** class is responsible to catch the models into libraries. Last one, **Lib** inherits the features of **ReadMDL**, it responsible to reads the models in MATLAB / Simulink.

The translation process using elements of Simulink toolboxes is started with a verification of elements inside the model using **Checking** class operation. The **Checking** class uses the operation of **ReadMDL** class to read the Simulink file. The reading the Simulink file is done more than once because the interface that controls the inference engine allowing different file being loaded without translation. The process translate of elements inside libraries created by designer is quite similar to elements of Simulink toolboxes, but it includes the Lib class. Lib class copy the descriptions saved into internal libraries in tool MS^{2}SV to represent libraries described by designer.

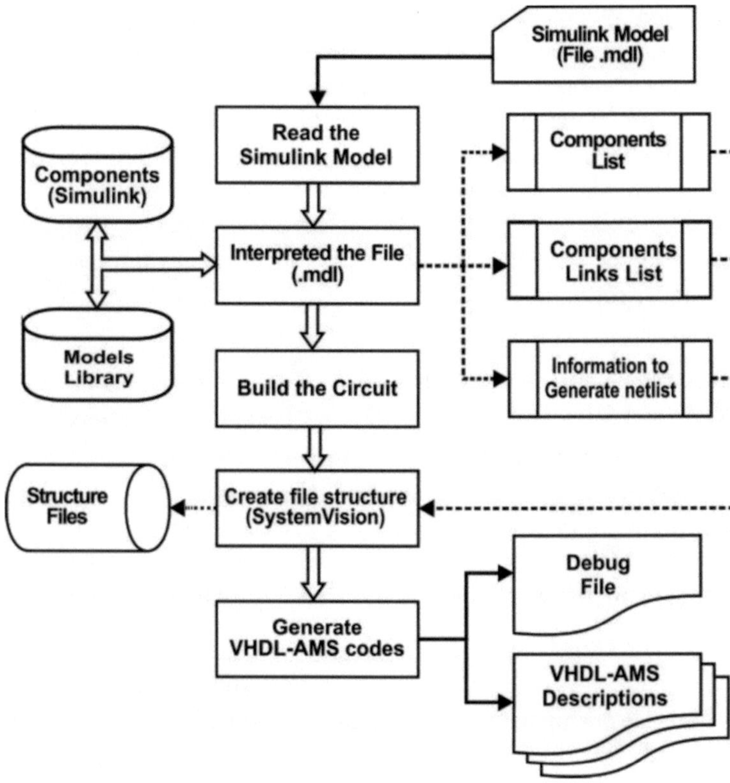

Figure 14. Functional diagram of the MS²SV tool illustrating the steps involved in translating the model to generate input file structure in SystemVision environment.

5. Case study of MS²SV and BD²XML

The DAC08, AD7524 and AD7528 DAC were chosen to model and simulate to evaluate the proposed methodology. All of them are monolithic data converter with 8 bit resolution used in applications such gain control circuit and stereo audio.

5.1. DAC08

DAC08 is a simpler operating model consisting basically of a converter with a resolution of 8 bit parallel input, which performs the digital to analogue conversion. The conversion of digital data into analog is done using the ladder R/2R where the binary inputs control the switching between the current arrival of resistors and current coming directly from the reference voltage.

http://dx.doi.org/10.5772/57575

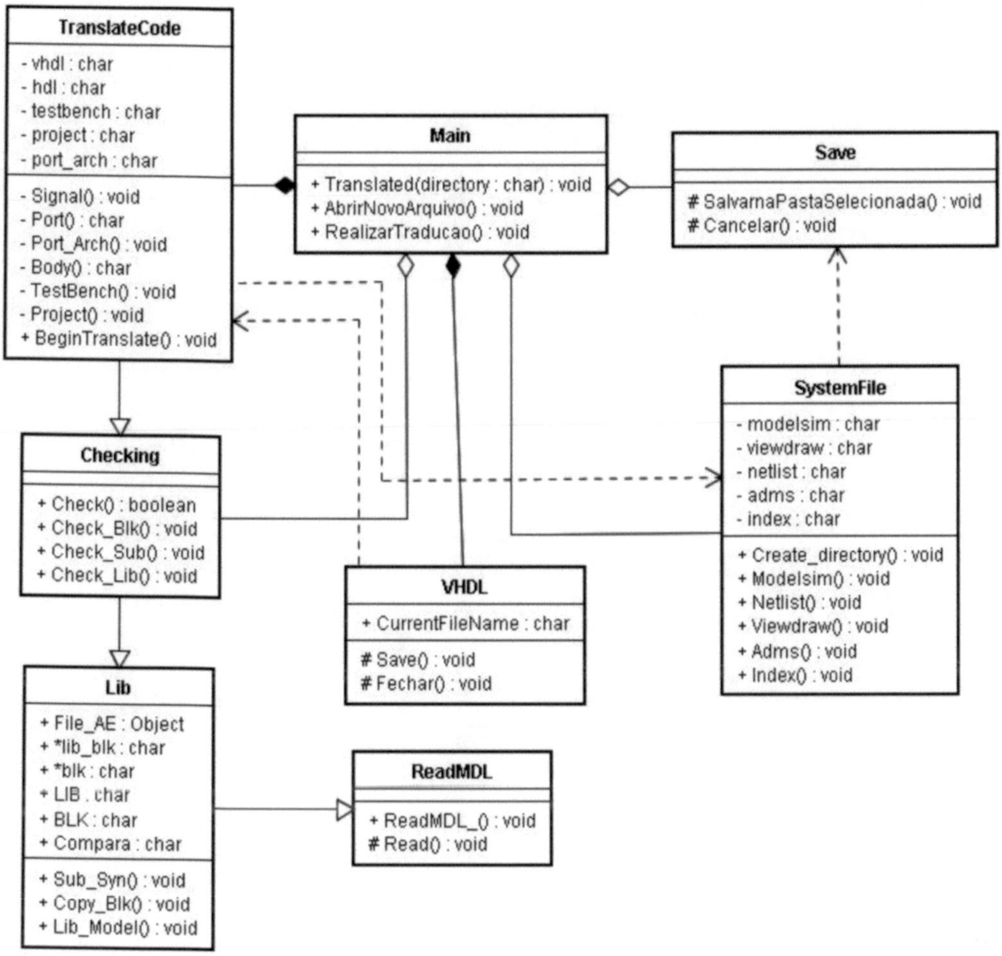

Figure 15. Class diagram of translations rules of MS^2SV.

Based on the specifications found in the datasheet of DAC08 converter [37], it was possible to model it in MATLAB / Simulink. Other details of the implementation on a physical level, such as compatibility with TTL (Transistor-Transistor Logic) and CMOS (Complementary Metal Oxide Semiconductor) technology were not considered since the focus of this work was on modelling at high level of abstraction.

The creation of the R/2R Ladder subsystems involved the use of Equations (1) and (2) in order to adjust the weights of each bit, as shown in Figure 16 [38]. In Figure 16, the Ladder R/2R subsystem was constructed using basic components available in the Simulink libraries. The multiplication between the digital input and weights of each input was made with the "Gain components", the sum with seven "Sum components" of two values and multiplying the result by the reference voltage using "Product component". In this system there are two outputs, the analog signal and the difference between the output and the reference voltage.

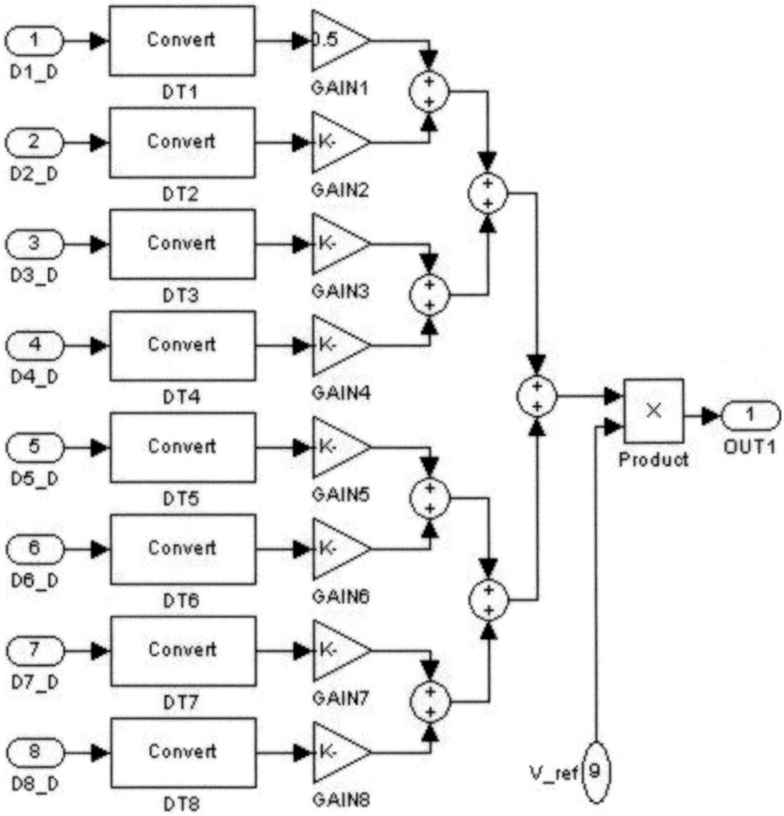

Figure 16. Subsystem in Simulink that represents the R/2R ladder using basic components of the Simulink toolbox, such as Product, Sum, Gain and Data Type Conversion.

An aspect that is important to emphasize in the creation of the R/2R ladder model shown in Figure 16 is that there are "Data Type Conversion components". These components are used to change the way representation of the binary signal (logic 0 or 1) for decimal representation (0 V or 1 V) and subsequent multiplication by weight. In MATLAB / Simulink, this component is not necessary. However, in VHDL-AMS, this component becomes important due to different ways of representing a signal in this language (i.e. the signal types used in VHDL and VHDL-AMS).

5.2. AD7524

The AD7524 has internally flip-flops of a latch type capable of storing last digital input, and a logic interface capable of controlling reading and storing digital input. The mode selection is controlled by CS_B and WR_B inputs. When CS_B and WR_B are at logic low (0) is enabled writing mode, that is, the analog output representing the binary value at input bus DB_0-DB_7. But when CS_B or WR_B assumes a logic high (1), AD7524 is in hold mode, analog output has the value corresponding to last input in DB_0-DB_7 before WR_B or CS_B assume logic high. Table 1 shows the relationship of control inputs and selection mode of AD7524 [39].

CS_B	WR_B	Selection mode	Comments
0	0	Write	The output corresponds to activity on the input bus (DB_0 to DB_7).
1	X	Hold	The output corresponds to the last valid entry, stored in flip-flops.
X	1		

Table 1. Selection mode pins to control the AD7524.

Figure 17 represents the buffers used by the AD7524 to store last valid digital input. This component is basically formed by a set of latches and an input common to all latches to enable the output.

Figure 18 illustrates the circuit capable to represent a selection mode in Table 1. This circuit is minimum using only three logic gates (two NOTs and one AND) and Figure 19 shows a complete AD7524 with a circuit of selection mode, a latch buffer to store last input and Ladder R/2R.

5.3. AD7528

AD7528 is equivalent to two AD7524 converters in a single IC (integrated circuit). The data bus of the AD7528 is also numbered from DB_0 to DB_7. Each internal converter (DAC A and DAC B) has an individual reference pin. Both can vary ± 25 V. The AD7528 has only three control pins called DACA/DACB, CS_B and WR_B. The relationship between control pins is illustrated in the Table 2. At a moment when the AD7528 is in hold mode the last valid input is stored in buffers individually in each internal converter [35].

DACA/DACB	WR_B	CS_B	DAC A	DAC B
0	0	0	Write	Hold
1	0	0	Hold	Write
X	1	X	Hold	Hold
X	X	1	Hold	Hold

Table 2. Selection mode pin to control the AD7528 indicating write mode of the DAC A with all pins active low logic level or in write mode DAC B only with pin in DACA/DACB active-high level, any change in the CS_B pin or WR_B both converters are in hold mode.

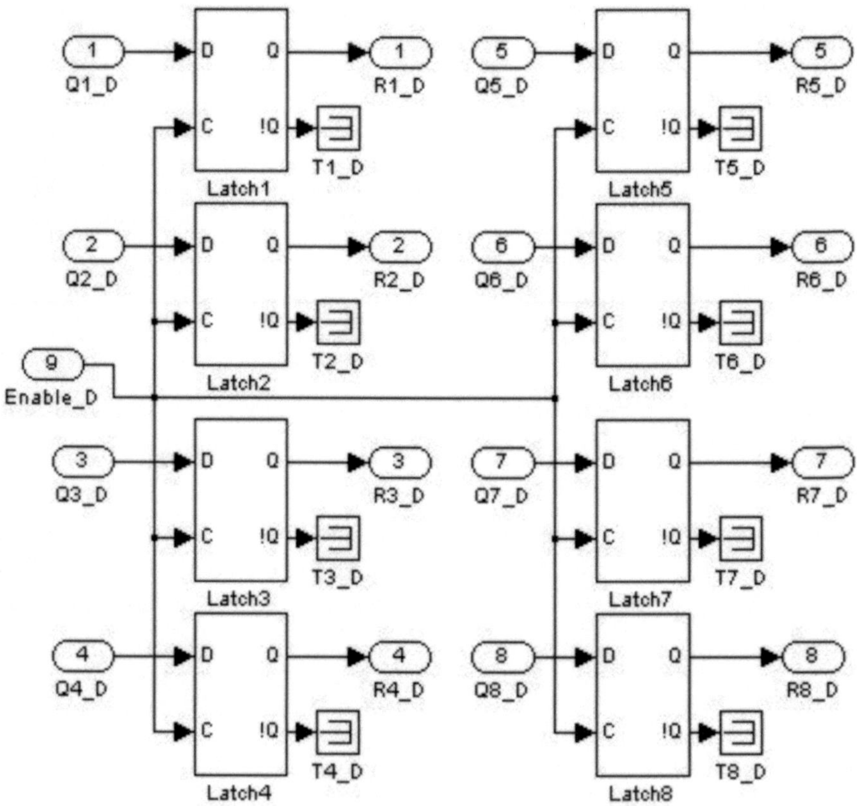

Figure 17. Subsystem that represents internal buffers converter AD7524, being formed by components Terminator and Latch output (the Q_b output from each latch is not used in this work).

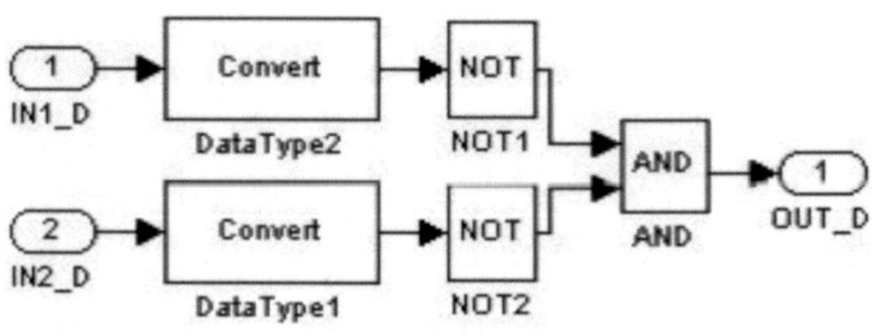

Figure 18. Subsystem that represents the logic controller of AD7524 and formed only by using AND and NOT gates.

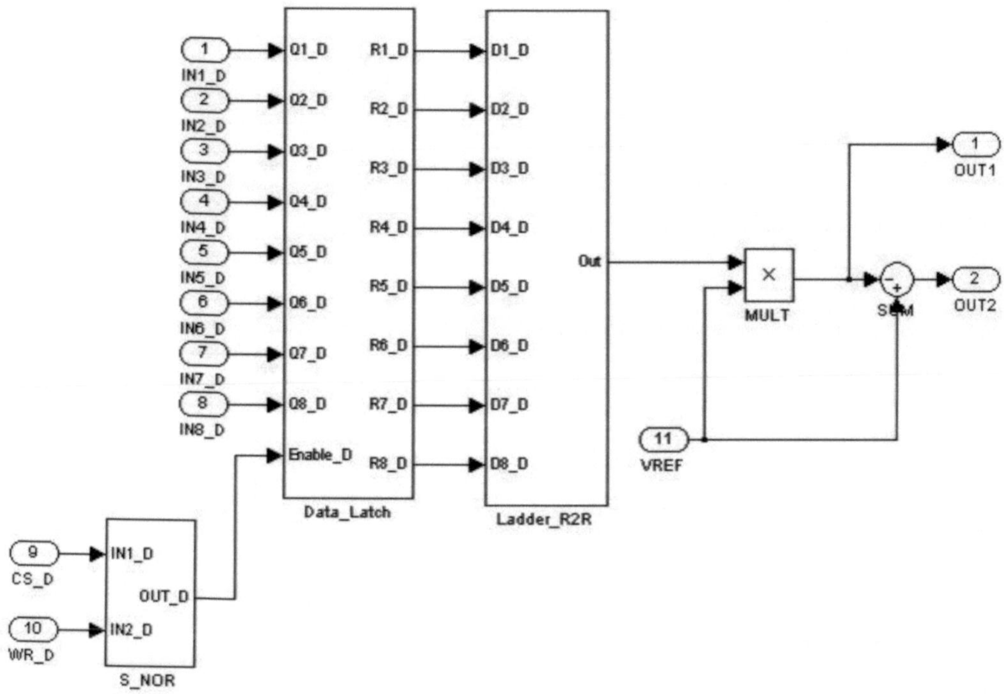

Figure 19. Complete system AD7524 with all subsystems in Figure 16, 17 and 18.

According to the approach described in [40], we created two identical blocks to represent the R/2R ladder, one for the DAC A and one for the DAC B. Similar to the R/2R ladder subsystem of Figure 16, the subsystem of Figure 16 was used twice in the complete system, i.e. one for each block of the AD7528 internal converter (DAC A and DAC B).

Figure 20 represents the logic controller responsible for the selection of which internal drive will be chosen and if converter is in hold or write mode representing behaviour described in Table 2. This subsystem is basically formed by simple logic gates available in toolbox of Simulink as basic primitive [38].

Figure 21 shows the complete AD7528 converter model created in MATLAB / Simulink. In each converter, there are two separate outputs, first one is analog output signal generated by the converter and second one is the difference between analog output and reference voltage. Based on [38] and in order to generate a sine wave signal, MATLAB was able to send the signal to each bit according to its magnitude of the pins of the AD7528 with the "From Workspace" component. Subsequently, the outputs were captured and sent back to MATLAB with the "To Workspace" component to generate the graphic simulation. The reference voltage and the pin configuration for each internal converter were created using "Constant" components (pins DACA/DACB, CS_B and WR_B).

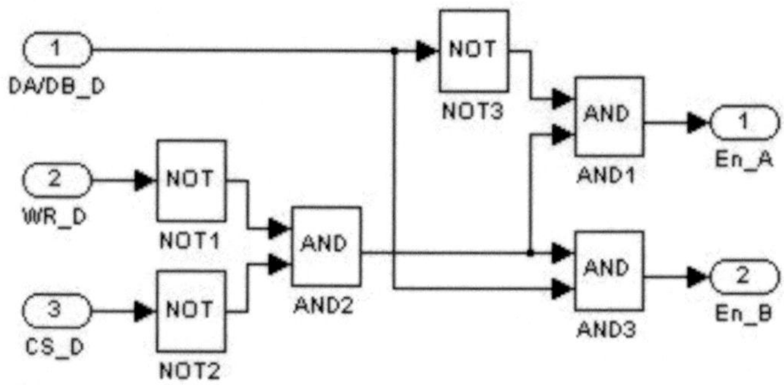

Figure 20. Subsystem that represents logic controller of AD7528 and formed only by using AND and NOT gates.

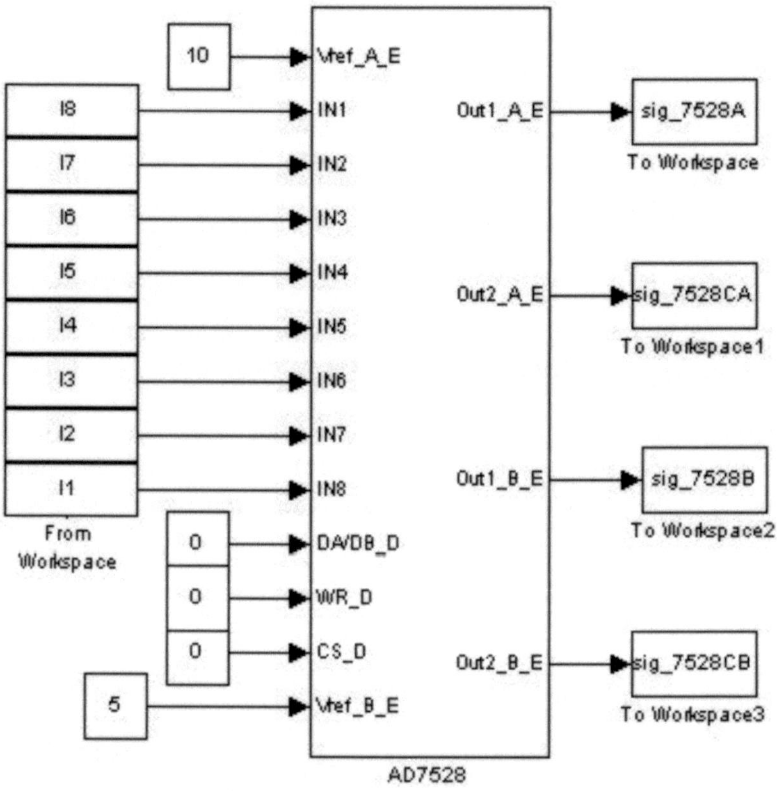

Figure 21. Complete model of AD7528 converter in Simulink with components From Workspace that receive digital signals from MATLAB and sends output back to MATLAB after simulation through To Workspace component.

The DACA/DACB pin could have been used to carry out switching between two converters internally creating two different waveforms from one input. However, as the converters are exactly the same, the kind of simulation does not alter the analysis of signal generated.

http://dx.doi.org/10.5772/57575

5.4. Simulation results of DAC and MS²SV conversion results

After construction and simulation in MATLAB / Simulink, the MS²SV translates model to the SystemVision environment. The hierarchy structure of model in Simulink was maintained in VHDL-AMS codes and MS²SV generated the same configuration of components. The Listing 5 is part of code generated by MS²SV using ladder R/2R in Figure 16. The remains VHDL-AMS description is listed in Appendix A.

```
1.  library IEEE;
2.  use ieee.std_logic_1164.all;
3.  use ieee.electrical_systems.all;
4.  library EduLib;
5.  use WORK.all;
6.  entity Ladder_R2R is
7.  port (
8.  signal D1_D: in std_logic;
9.  signal D2_D: in std_logic;
10. signal D3_D: in std_logic;
11. signal D4_D: in std_logic;
12. signal D5_D: in std_logic;
13. signal D6_D: in std_logic;
14. signal D7_D: in std_logic;
15. signal D8_D: in std_logic;
16. terminal A1: electrical
17. );
18. end entity Ladder_R2R;
19. architecture arch_Ladder_R2R of Ladder_R2R is
20. terminal \1$N0\: electrical;
21. terminal \1$N1\: electrical;
22. ...
23. begin
24. DataType: entity EDULIB.D2A_BIT(IDEAL)
25. generic map ( VHIGH => 1.0,
26. VLOW => 0.0 )
27. port map (
28. D => D1_D,
29. A => \1$N0\
30. );
31. ...
32. E_Gain: entity EDULIB.E_GAIN(BEHAVIORAL)
33. generic map ( K => 0.5 )
34. port map (
35. INPUT => \1$N0\,
36. OUTPUT => \1$N8\
37. );
38. ...
39. E_Sum: entity EDULIB.E_SUM
40. port map (
41. IN1 => \1$N8\,
42. IN2 => \1$N9\,
43. OUTPUT => \1$N16\
44. );
45. ...
46. end architecture arch_Ladder_R2R;
```

Listing 5. Structural VHDL-AMS code generated by MS²SV.

This VHDL-AMS code in Listing 5 has a structural abstraction. It represent the linkage between the components which it has all DAC system, e.g. lines 34-39 represent the ports for Gain block and the linkage between Sum block in lines 41-46 and Data Type Converter block in lines 26-32. The exactly behavior of components are in internal libraries in SystemVision environment named EDULIB (Educational Library).

To perform the simulation, SystemVision was used the same input used in MATLAB / Simulink. Thus was created an input file with the extension*.dat*. It was created to an additional VHDL-AMS code to read this file and send the signal each bit input to the converters, as listed in Listing 6.

```
1.  use std.textio.all;
2.  library IEEE;
3.  use ieee.std_logic_1164.all;
4.  use IEEE.std_logic_textio.all;
5.  entity lerarqp is
6.  port (relogio: in std_logic;
7.     saida: out std_ulogic_vector (8 downto 1));
8.  end entity lerarqp;
9.  architecture behavior of lerarqp is
10. begin
11. testing: process
12.   file f_in: text open READ_MODE is "input.dat";
13.   variable L: LINE;
14.   variable L_BIT: std_ulogic_vector (8 downto 1);
15. begin
16.   while not endfile(f_in) loop
17.     readline (f_in,L);
18.     hread (L,L_BIT);
19.     wait until (relogio'event) and (relogio='1');
20.     saida <= L_BIT;
21.   end loop;
22. end process testing;
23. end architecture behavior;
```

Listing 6. Behavioral VHDL code to read the input simulation file.

In Listing 6 was needed to use a library in order to manipulate files (line 4). It was used for a vector to represent the output which was linked to DAC (line 8). After it was built, a process to read the file and put it into output in lines 13-24 is used.

It was used to save the simulation results in SystemVision in another file with the extension*.dat* so that was possible to analysis the signal generated also in MATLAB, as listed Listing 7.

```
1.  use std.textio.all;
2.  library IEEE;
3.  use IEEE.std_logic_1164.all;
4.  use IEEE.std_logic_textio.all;
5.  entity writewaveform is
6.  port (
7.  signal relogio: in std_logic;
8.  entrada: in real);
9.  end entity writewaveform;
10. architecture behavior of writewaveform is
11. file f_out: text open WRITE_MODE is "C:\Mentor_Projects\DAC08_Test\hdl\output.dat";
12. --quantity escreve_sinal across entrada to ref;
13. begin
14. writying: process
15. variable L: LINE;
16. begin
17.    write(L,REAL'(entrada));
18.    writeline(f_out,L);
19.    wait until (relogio'event) and (relogio='1');
20. end process writying;
21. end architecture behavior;
```

Listing 7. Behavioral VHDL code to write the output simulation file.

Listing 7 follow the same logic in Listing 6, using the library to manipulate file (line 4), a real signal to represent the input which was linked to DAC (line 9) and a process to read from input and write the file in lines 16-22. By space limits, the remains VHDL-AMS description for AD7524 and AD7528 are listed in Appendix B and C, respectively.

For each case study was used a different reference voltage in simulation: 10V, 8V, 6V and 4V, for DAC08, AD7524, AD7528 A and AD7528 B, respectively. Figure 22 shows the simulation results for 1 second. The different voltages were used to create a better view waveform in Figure 21. However in the SystemVision environment, only 10V was used for all converters and only one waveform is plotted in Figure 21 as all converters presented the same simulation results. In MATLAB / Simulink, the AD7524, AD7528 A and AD7528 B presented noise in output because the delays in flip-flop of type latch.

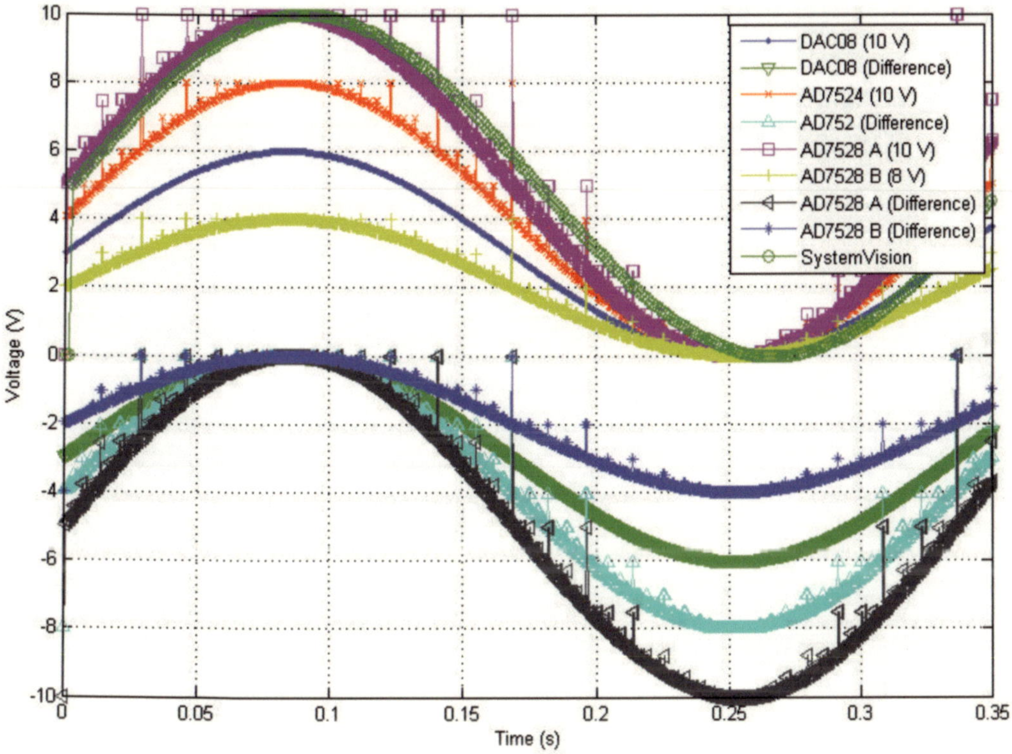

Figure 22. Result of simulation of all case studies in Simulink and signal from SystemVision in simulation total time of 1 second.

Another difference noted in Figure 22 is low simulation time in SystemVision environment compared with simulation MATLAB / Simulink. This was due to the way in which VHDL-AMS sees the frequency inside the SystemVision environment which is different to MATLAB / Simulink.

5.5. Analysis of simulation in MATLAB / Simulink and VHDL-AMS

To verify the quality of signal generated, it was made an analysis of signal obtained through simulation. This analysis was performed through power spectral analysis of the signal obtained from discrete Fourier transform (DFT). Figure 23 illustrates amplitude spectrum of *y(t)* for all case studies, in MATLAB / Simulink and VHDL-AMS. The graph was generated using the discrete Fourier transform described as [41]:

$$X(k)=\sum_{j=1}^{N}x(j)\omega_N^{(j-1)(k-1)} \tag{7}$$

$$x(j)=(1/N)\sum_{k=1}^{N}X(k)\omega_B^{-(j-1)(k-1)} \tag{8}$$

$$\omega_N=e^{(-2\pi i)/N} \tag{9}$$

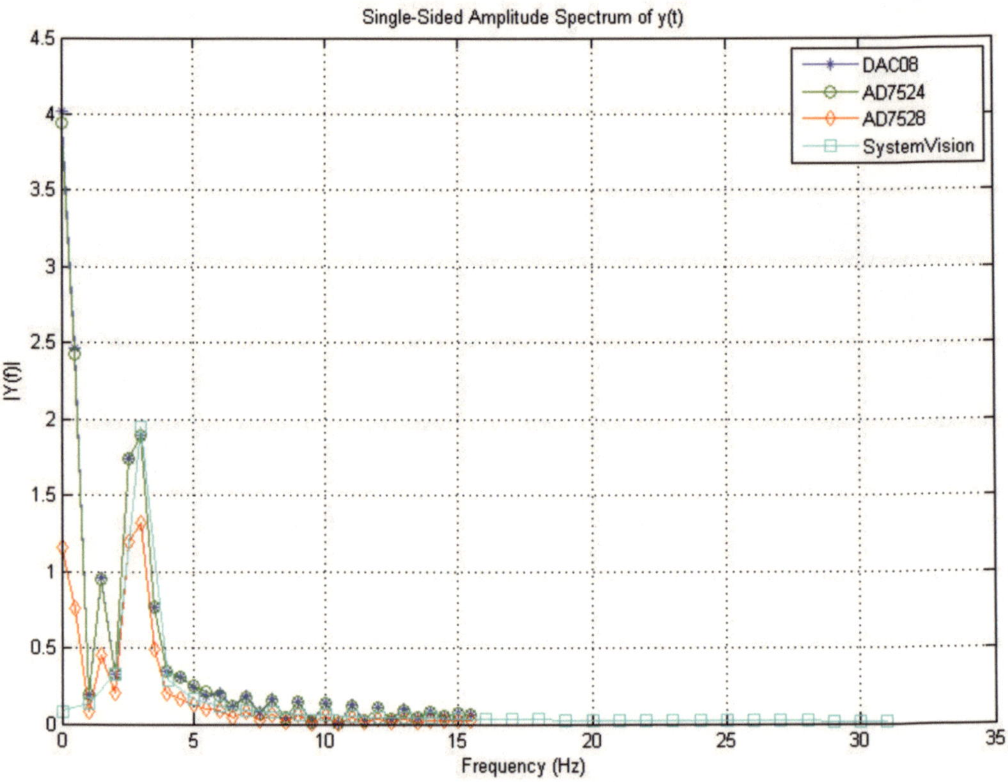

Figure 23. Graph of spectral power all output signals in Simulink and SystemVision with peak in frequency at 2.9297 Hz.

The DC (Direct Current) level of the signal was extracted through shifting the signal along the *y* axis at zero. This resulted in a sine wave signal ranging from-5 to 5 for 10V,-4 to 4 for 8V,-3 to 4 for 6V and-2 to 2 for 4V.

The process of conversion digital to analog represents an interpolation between values of samples provided as inputs, for 20001 points. In this case studies are used linear interpolation, which points of adjacent samples are connected by a straight line. The system output $x_r(t)$ is given by:

$$x_r(t) = \sum_{n=-\infty}^{+\infty} x(nT)h(t - nT) \tag{10}$$

At the same time, the system has unity gain and linear phase. Systems with this frequency response features produce an output that is a shift in the time of input [41]. Importantly, this is a pseudo-conversion to analog, as the conversion happens only while V_{ref} is constant.

In Figure 23, it is possible to note difference in AD7524, AD7528 A and AD7528 B because of noise in signal. The signal from DAC08 and AD7524 presented a distortion in sine wave showed in Figure 23 too. At the end, the most perfect signal presented by amplitude spectral was the signal from SystemVision environment.

6. Generation code methodology of BD²XML

The computational tool, called BD²XML, is able to read a file block diagram in MATLAB / Simulink and generate a corresponding textual description in XML [42]. A key point of the working methodology is to use a configuration file that allows the user to identify MATLAB / Simulink block to use. This file contains all the blocks readable by the BD²XML and the characteristics that are relevant to operation of the blocks. All this information can be extracted by the user from their own MATLAB / Simulink file through the block properties. The file has tokens that are the key point of interpretation. For example, the token **&** is responsible for the identification of a new block, which has characteristics between the tokens **{** and **}**. Since the token # works as a comment in regular language, i.e., every line that has the # is disregarded. If the token # is used before the token **&** all block is disregarded.

Figure 24 illustrates the functional diagram of BD²XML. Initially begins the reading of*.mdl* file in memory. Next is read the configuration file. All of blocks are loaded in memory to compare with the blocks in*.mdl* file. Only afterwards begins the reading of the*.mdl* file. Relevant information is inside*.mdl* file, such as the type of block, values inside the block, linkage between the blocks and some other information is important to create a netlist of circuit. From this point, it is possible to create an XML file with the circuit that can used, and reused in many contexts.

BD²XML was developed according to class diagram showed in Figure 25. The classes responsible for creating a logical structure in memory are inherited by classes responsible for read the configuration file and the block diagram file of the MATLAB / Simulink. The **misc** class with routines common to other classes is also inherited by other classes.

Others instances of classes are composition. This facilitates the creation of threads structure in future to speeding of codes performance for generations of multiple objects codes simultaneously. The designer starts the process specifying the diagram which is the target of BD²XML.

At first, the configuration file is read into a structure and then the block diagram of the MATLAB / Simulink is read into another structure. A comparison is done block by block to check whether the target block is identifiable. Every block of the configuration file has its own characteristics and the default values for these characteristics. In the case of not being identified in some of the characteristics relevant target block are considered the default values of the configuration file to generate the XML. If any block is not identifiable, XML is generated in the same way discarding that particular block.

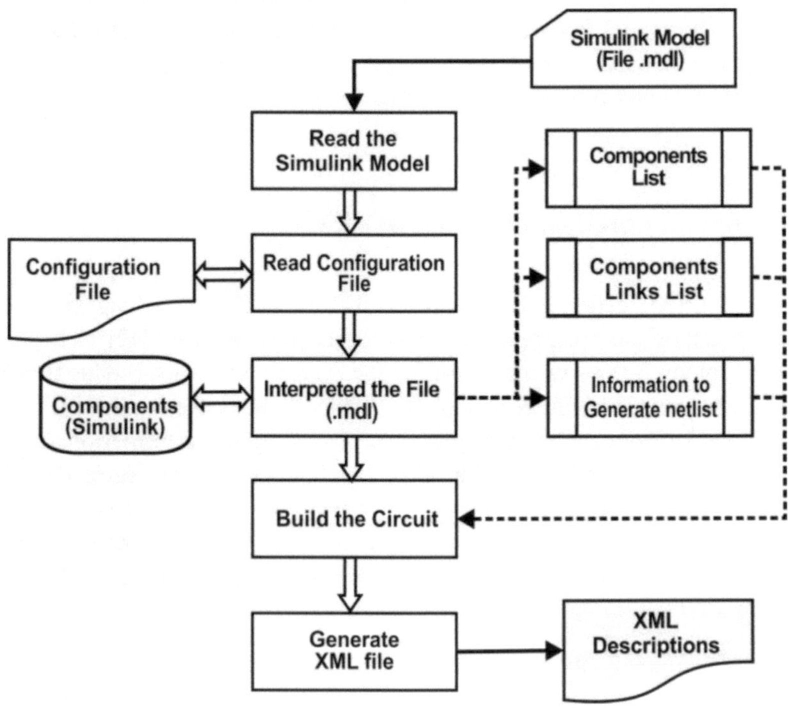

Figure 24. Class diagram of the BD2XML tool.

6.1. Conversion results using AD7528

To demonstrate the BD^{2}XML, we used the Ladder R/2R case study in Figure 16. Listing 8 is shown a partial description in XML generated by the BD^{2}XML from the Ladder R/2R.

The tags **<Diagram>** and **</Diagram>** (lines 2-57) identifying the block diagram. The blocks are identified by tags **<BasicBlock type="..." name="...">** and **</BasicBlock>**, being specified block type and the name used in MATLAB / Simulink, for example, the gain block (lines 30-33).

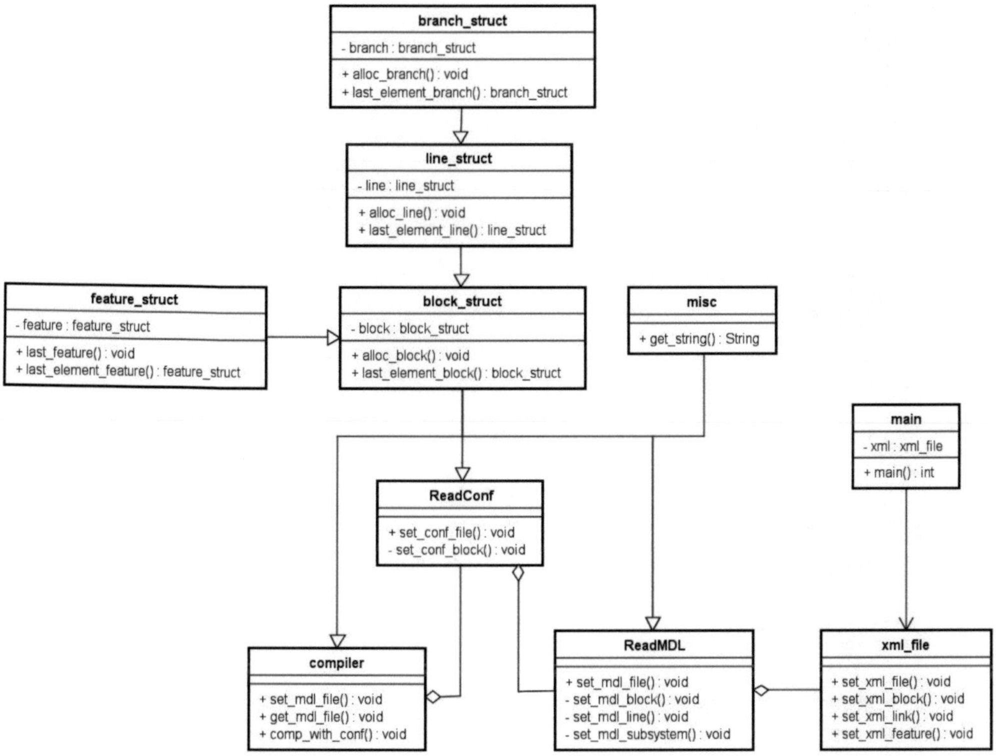

Figure 25. Class diagram of the BD²XML tool.

The data blocks are specified by the tag **<data type="..." value="..." />**. Even in the case of gain, the first tag **data** specifies the kind of signal is used by the block (line 31), e.g., analog. The next type of data (line 32) specifies the gain value that block has.

In the configuration file, the blocks of gain are represented in accordance with the Listing 9 (lines 11-14). The block gain has no specification of input and output ports, because by default a gain always has an input and an output.

The connections between the blocks are made through the tags **<Link>** and **</Link>** (Listing 8, lines 15-20). Inside these tags are two tags named **<OutputPort>** and **</OutputPort>**, that specify the output ports of the block owned by **as="source"** and indicating which is the block output **id="..."**.

The property **id** is understood as the property **name** of the tag **BasicBlock**. Similarly, the entry are specified by the tags **<InputPort>** and **</InputPort>**, and property **as="target"**.

If there are subsystems in the block diagram, they are identified by the tags **<SubSystem name="...">** and **</SubSystem>**, according to the Listing 8 (lines 7-22, 23-40 and 51-55). All configuration of the subsystem is between two tags and their description is the same as already explained.

```
1. <?xml version="1.0" encoding="ISO-8859-1"?>
2. <Diagram>
3. <InBlock name="in1_d">
4. <data type="mixed"/>
5. </InBlock>
6. ...
7. <SubSystem name="datalatch_d">
8. <data type="mixed"/>
9. <data type="ports" value="9, 8"/>
10. ...
11. <OutBlock name="r7_d">
12. <data type="mixed"/>
13. </OutBlock>
14. ...
15. <Link>
16. <OutputPort as="source" id="q1_d"/>
17. </OutputPort>
18. <InputPort as="target" id="latch1"/>
19. </InputPort>
20. </Link>
21. ...
22. </SubSystem>
23. <SubSystem name="ladderr2r">
24. <data type="mixed"/>
25. <data type="ports" value="8, 1"/>
26. <InBlock name="d1_d">
27. <data type="mixed"/>
28. </InBlock>
29. ...
30. <BasicBlock type="gain" name="gain">
31. <data type="analog"/>
32. <data type="gain" value="0.5"/>
33. </BasicBlock>
34. ...
35. <BasicBlock type="sum" name="sum1">
36. <data type="analog"/>
37. <data type="ports" value="2, 1"/>
38. </BasicBlock>
39. ...
40. </SubSystem>
41. <BasicBlock type="product" name="mult">
42. <data type="analog"/>
43. <data type="ports" value="2, 1"/>
44. </BasicBlock>
45. <SubSystem name="snor_d">
46. <data type="mixed"/>
47. <data type="ports" value="2, 1"/>
48. ...
49. <BasicBlock type="logic" name="and1">
50. <data type="digital"/>
51. <data type="ports" value="2, 1"/>
52. <data type="operator" value="and"/>
53. </BasicBlock>
54. ...
55. </SubSystem>
56. ...
57. </Diagram>
```

Listing 8. XML description of Ladder R/2R.

Tags to indicate input and output ports of the block diagram are used most commonly in subsystems and they are in accordance with Listing 8 (lines 3-5, 11-13 and 26-28). Tags to represent input ports are specified by **<InBlock name="...">** and **</InBlock>** (lines 3-5).

Similarly, the output ports are specified by the tags **<OutBlock name="...">** and **</OutBlock>** (Listing 8, lines 11-13). In both the tag property **name** identify the block. Also in either case the tag **<data... />** (Listing 8, lines 4 and 8) are of mixed type, since both blocks can be an input or an output of digital and analog blocks.

All the representation was generated with perfection in one complete file containing all the blocks and subsystems. In this case study AD7528, there are five subsystems representing: the block **Ladder R/2R A**, **Ladder R/2R B**, **Datalatch A**, **Datalatch B** and **Control Logic**.

http://dx.doi.org/10.5772/57575

```
&inport {
mixed;
}
&outport {
mixed;
}
&sum {
analog;
ports   "2,1";
}
&gain {
analog;
gain    "1";
}
&logic {
digital;
ports   "2,1";
operator        "and";
}
&toworkspace {
#
}
&fromworkspace {
#
}
&subsystem {
mixed;
ports   "1,1";
}
```

Listing 9. Representation of the blocks in the configuration file used by BD^2XML.

7. Generation code methodology of SF^2XML

The in this section, the tool called SF^2XML is presented which is capable to capture relevant information in the Stateflow environment and generate a corresponding description in XML [43]. The resulting file conversion is also in accordance with international standards of default file in case the SCXML proposed by W3C [4].

The SF^2XML has four classes of objects, an object that makes up the logical structure of storage memory at runtime, an object of reading the file MATLAB / Simulink and extraction of relevant information, an object to generate the syntactic and semantic file XML and other objects to make interfacing with the user. The class diagram to SF^2XML is shown in Figure 26. In this figure, it is possible to see that the only difference between SF^2XML and SF^2HDL is the highlighted **xml_file** object. Similarly, the functional diagram in Figure 5, is the same to SF^2XM apart from the files generated.

SF^2XML is also able to identify sub-finite state machine, so it has recursive methods for hierarchical finite state machine clustering automatically, which generates a certain economy of code and maintenance. There is this feature inside SF^2HDL too, but a hierarchical FSM can generate instable behavioral in a same file. It could better if SF^2HDL would generate different files for different finite state machines. SF^2XML has the follow algorithm, which can be understood for SF^2HDL:

1. Read the MATLAB / Simulink file and identify the FSM;
2. Store the state or transitions and its information;
    a. If the state has a sub-FSM store the first transition in this sub-FSM, otherwise go to step 2(b).

   b. Verify which type this FSM is (Mealy or Moore);

3. Start write XML file;

   a. a. Seeking relationship between states of the same hierarchical level and which state is the first in highest level;

   b. Write the state tags, the transition related to this states;

   c. If there is a sub-FSM decrease the level hierarchical and go to step 3(a), otherwise go to step 3(d);

   d. While there is a state such that is associated with a transition go to step 3(a).

4. Return the XML file.

7.1. Conversion results of HDB3 line code

The tool was able to accurately generate an XML representation corresponding to the diagram shown in Figure 3. Every XML description is according to SCXML specification. Listing 10 below displays the entire description in XML generated by SF^{2}XML.

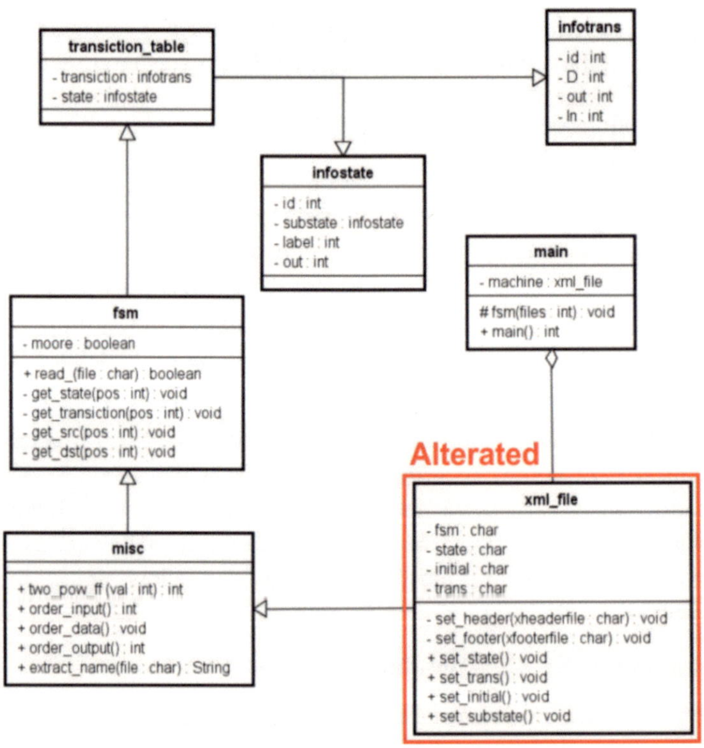

Figure 26. Class diagram of the SF^{2}XML tool.

http://dx.doi.org/10.5772/57575

```
1.  <?xml version="1.0" encoding="ISO-8859-1"?>
2.  <scxml version="1.0" xmlns="http://www.w3.org/2005/07/scxml" initialstate="0">
3.  <state id="0">
4.  <transition event="INPUT=1">
5.  <target next="1" />
6.  <assign expr="OUTPUT=1" />
7.  </transition>
8.  <transition event="INPUT=0">
9.  <target next="0" />
10. <assign expr="OUTPUT=0" />
11. </transition>
12. </state>
13. <state id="1">
14. <transition event="INPUT=0">
15. <target next="2" />
16. <assign expr="OUTPUT=0" />
17. </transition>
18. </state>
19. ...
20. </scxml>
```

Listing 10. XML code representing the finite state machine of HDB3.

It is important to highlight that states assumed a decimal representation continuously, regardless of whether the state is within another state or not.

Line 1 of Listing 10 specifies that it is an XML file, the XML version and encoding used. The tags of lines 2 and 20, specify the start and end of the finite state machine. In line 2 is also specified the version of SCXML used, the name for the XML document (xmlns) and the initial state of the finite state machine (**initialstate="0"**). The tag **<state id="...">** and **</state>** specifies the state and its identifier (lines 3, 12, 13, 18). The tags **<transition event="...">** and **</transition>** to specify a transition that will occur according to a particular event, e.g. " **INPUT=1"** (line 4). If the transition occurs, the tag **<target next="..." />** specifies the next state of the FSM according to its identifier. The tag **<assign expr="OUTPUT=..." />** assigns a new value to the output attribute **expr**. If there are hierarchically nested state, states are chained between the tags **<state id="...">** and **</state>**. However, the initial state is specified by internal tags **<initial>** and **</initial>** within a transition indicating to the initial state.

8. Conclusion

The SF²HDL program makes the translation of finite state machine, but it does not perform circuit optimization. Hence, it also needs a translation into a file that serves as input to TABELA program that is able to perform this work.

The SF²HDL program does not make optimal state assignment to the state machine as well. Thus, it is necessary to use another tool to do that task. In this way circuit synthesis can be really optimize using all the potentialities of developed tools. Future work will extend this tool to also realize the translation of finite state machines for the structural VHDL and Verilog code.

The use of CAD tools and a top-down methodology is a reality that is present in the most electronic circuit design projects, and the development of new computational tools to aid in project implementation is highly desirable, because the range of CAD tools used introduces incompatibilities that can be time consuming and costly in translating between them. Hence, there is the need for suitable tools to be able to translate models between different representations.

The SF^{2}HDL tool was tested in several cases of finite state machines and all have been simulated and synthesized in Quartus II environment and Cyclone II FPGA model EP2C20F484C7, respectively.

For the case study of HDB3 code described in this chapter, SF^{2}HDL program was very effective for translation code modeled on Stateflow, a computational low cost, being accurate in VHDL generation code and the input file for TABELA program corresponding with another programs.

Thus, this research generated a tool that allows to the designers to model a finite state machine at high level of abstraction and obtain a corresponding VHDL model which can be synthesized on synthesis tools available commercially. It is also important to say this new translation tools interact with several other tools developed by research group with TABELA program, creating this way a digital synthesis environment.

The MS^{2}SV tool proved convenient to use as it allows for the creation of multiple libraries for different projects and also recycle the libraries for use in others projects. This allows a significant savings of time and hence costs.

By analysing power spectral of a discrete-time signal, one can say that the output signals in MATLAB / Simulink and VHDL-AMS are almost identical. This fact allows us to change our vision about the abstraction levels and details in modelling. Even in the same environment (MATLAB / Simulink) we have difference in spectral signal. If the system be simulating in another environment, we will also have different simulations.

The conversion to XML (using BD^{2}XML) is convenient because the portability of the language allows a wide applicability of the proposed methodology, e.g., documentation, level synthesis of hardware or software, web publishing, use of XML simulators and as object code for future work. This is the same when using SF^{2}XML, which it use a standardized description in SCXML.

The use of the intermediate code (like XML) is very important since it can be used in frameworks generation and optimization of other types of coding. As an example, hardware description languages like VHDL-AMS, Verilog-AMS, SystemC, etc. Or even reprogrammable devices that have analog and digital blocks and PSoC (Programmable System-on-Chip).

This point highlights the importance to explore more alternatives and standard methodologies of electronic circuit design. Nevertheless, our methodology and tools need further investigation and analysis to consider the need for the development of larger and more complex systems.

http://dx.doi.org/10.5772/57575

Appendix A– DAC08 converter description in structural VHDL-AMS

The complete VHDL-AMS code is listed below for DAC08 case.

```
library IEEE;
use ieee.std_logic_1164.all;
use ieee.electrical_systems.all;
 library EduLib;
 use WORK.all;
 entity DAC08 is
 end entity DAC08;
architecture arch_DAC08 of DAC08 is
    terminal \1$N39\: electrical;
     terminal \1$N41\: electrical;
     signal DIn1_D: std_logic;
     signal DIn2_D: std_logic;
     signal DIn3_D: std_logic;
     signal DIn4_D: std_logic;
     signal DIn5_D: std_logic;
     signal DIn6_D: std_logic;
     signal DIn7_D: std_logic;
     signal DIn8_D: std_logic;
     terminal Vref: electrical;
     terminal Out1: electrical;
 begin
     Ladder_R2R: entity WORK.Ladder_R2R(arch_Ladder_R2R)
         port map (
             D1_D => DIn1_D,
             D2_D => DIn2_D,
             D3_D => DIn3_D,
             D4_D => DIn4_D,
             D5_D => DIn5_D,
             D6_D => DIn6_D,
             D7_D => DIn7_D,
             D8_D => DIn8_D,
             A1 => \1$N39\    );
     E_MULT: entity EDULIB.E_MULT
         port map (
             IN1 => \1$N39\,
             IN2 => Vref,
             OUTPUT => Out1    );
     V_VREF: entity EDULIB.V_CONSTANT(IDEAL)
       generic map ( LEVEL => 10.0 )
       port map ( POS => Vref,
             NEG => ELECTRICAL_REF);
 end architecture arch_DAC08;
```

Appendix B– AD7524 converter descriptions in structural VHDL-AMS

The complete VHDL-AMS code is listed below for Data_Latch subsystem, SNOR subsystem and AD7524 converter.

- Data_Latch

```
library IEEE;
use ieee.std_logic_1164.all;
use ieee.electrical_systems.all;
 library EduLib;
 use WORK.all;
 entity DataLatch_D is
   port (
        signal Q1_D: in std_logic;
    signal Q2_D: in std_logic;
     signal Q3_D: in std_logic;
     signal Q4_D: in std_logic;
     signal Q5_D: in std_logic;
     signal Q6_D: in std_logic;
     signal Q7_D: in std_logic;
     signal Q8_D: in std_logic;
     signal Enable_D: in std_logic;
     signal R1_D: out std_logic;
     signal R2_D: out std_logic;
     signal R3_D: out std_logic;
     signal R4_D: out std_logic;
     signal R5_D: out std_logic;
     signal R6_D: out std_logic;
     signal R7_D: out std_logic;
     signal R8_D: out std_logic );
 end entity DataLatch_D;
 architecture arch_DataLatch_D of DataLatch_D is
     signal \1$N2\: std_logic;
     signal \1$N5\: std_logic;
     signal \1$N8\: std_logic;
     signal \1$N11\: std_logic;
     signal \1$N23\: std_logic;
     signal \1$N16\: std_logic;
     signal \1$N19\: std_logic;
     signal \1$N22\: std_logic;
 begin
     DLatch: entity WORK.DLatch(arch_DLatch)
         port map (
             D => Q1_D,
             CLK => Enable_D,
             Q => R1_D,
             QN => \1$N2\);
     DLatch1: entity WORK.DLatch(arch_DLatch)
         port map (
             D => Q2_D,
```

http://dx.doi.org/10.5772/57575

```
                CLK => Enable_D,
                Q => R2_D,
                QN => \1$N5\);
        DLatch2: entity WORK.DLatch(arch_DLatch)
            port map (
                D => Q3_D,
                CLK => Enable_D,
                Q => R3_D,
                QN => \1$N8\);
        DLatch3: entity WORK.DLatch(arch_DLatch)
            port map (
                D => Q4_D,
                CLK => Enable_D,
                Q => R4_D,
                QN => \1$N11\    );
        DLatch4: entity WORK.DLatch(arch_DLatch)
            port map (
                D => Q5_D,
                CLK => Enable_D,
                Q => R5_D,
                QN => \1$N23\    );
        DLatch5: entity WORK.DLatch(arch_DLatch)
            port map (
                D => Q6_D,
                CLK => Enable_D,
                Q => R6_D,
                QN => \1$N16\);
        DLatch6: entity WORK.DLatch(arch_DLatch)
            port map (
                D => Q7_D,
                CLK => Enable_D,
                Q => R7_D,
                QN => \1$N19\    );
        DLatch7: entity WORK.DLatch(arch_DLatch)
            port map (
                D => Q8_D,
                CLK => Enable_D,
                Q => R8_D,
                QN => \1$N22\    );
    end architecture arch_DataLatch_D;
```

- D Latch

```
LIBRARY IEEE;
USE ieee.std_logic_1164.all;
USE ieee.electrical_systems.all;
 LIBRARY edulib;
 USE work.all;
 entity DLatch is
  port (
    signal D: in std_logic;
  signal CLK: in std_logic;
```

```
     signal Q: out std_logic;
     signal QN: out std_logic );
   end entity DLatch;
   architecture arch_DLatch of DLatch is
   begin
   process(D,CLK)
   begin
    if clk = '1' then
     Q <= D;
     QN <= not D;
    end if;
   end process;
   end architecture arch_DLatch;
```

- SNOR

```
library IEEE;
use ieee.std_logic_1164.all;
use ieee.electrical_systems.all;
library EduLib;
use WORK.all;
entity SNOR_D is
port (
    signal IN1_D: in std_logic;
    signal IN2_D: in std_logic;
     signal OUT_D: out std_logic );
 end entity SNOR_D;
 architecture arch_SNOR_D of SNOR_D is
     signal \1$N63\: std_logic;
     signal \1$N64\: std_logic;
 begin
     G_AND1: entity EDULIB.AND2
         port map (
             IN1 => \1$N63\,
             IN2 => \1$N64\,
             OUTPUT => OUT_D);
     G_NOT1: entity EDULIB.INVERTER
         port map (
             INPUT => IN1_D,
             OUTPUT => \1$N63\);
     G_NOT2: entity EDULIB.INVERTER
         port map (
             INPUT => IN2_D,
             OUTPUT => \1$N64\);
 end architecture arch_SNOR_D;
```

- AD7524

```
library IEEE;
use ieee.std_logic_1164.all;
use ieee.electrical_systems.all;
use ieee.radiant_systems.all;
```

```
library EduLib;
use WORK.all;
entity AD7524 is
end entity AD7524;
architecture arch_AD7524 of AD7524 is
  signal IN1_D: std_logic;
     signal IN2_D: std_logic;
     signal IN3_D: std_logic;
     signal IN4_D: std_logic;
     signal IN5_D: std_logic;
     signal IN6_D: std_logic;
     signal IN7_D: std_logic;
     signal IN8_D: std_logic;
     signal CS_D: std_logic;
     signal WR_D: std_logic;
     terminal VREF: electrical;
     terminal OUT1: electrical;
     terminal OUT2: electrical;
     signal \1$N68\: std_logic;
     signal \1$N69\: std_logic;
     signal \1$N70\: std_logic;
     signal \1$N71\: std_logic;
     signal \1$N72\: std_logic;
     signal \1$N73\: std_logic;
     signal \1$N74\: std_logic;
     signal \1$N75\: std_logic;
     terminal \1$N78\: electrical;
     terminal WR: electrical;
     terminal CS: electrical;
     signal \1$N92\: std_logic;
begin
    DataLatch_D: entity WORK.DataLatch_D(arch_DataLatch_D)
        port map (
            Q1_D => IN1_D,
            Q2_D => IN2_D,
            Q3_D => IN3_D,
            Q4_D => IN4_D,
            Q5_D => IN5_D,
            Q6_D => IN6_D,
            Q7_D => IN7_D,
            Q8_D => IN8_D,
            Enable_D => \1$N92\,
            R1_D => \1$N68\,
            R2_D => \1$N69\,
            R3_D => \1$N70\,
            R4_D => \1$N71\,
            R5_D => \1$N72\,
            R6_D => \1$N73\,
            R7_D => \1$N74\,
            R8_D => \1$N75\);
    LadderR2R: entity WORK.LadderR2R(arch_LadderR2R)
        port map (
```

```
                D1_D => \1$N68\,
                D2_D => \1$N69\,
                D3_D => \1$N70\,
                D4_D => \1$N71\,
                D5_D => \1$N72\,
                D6_D => \1$N73\,
                D7_D => \1$N74\,
                D8_D => \1$N75\,
                Out1 => \1$N78\);
        E_MULT: entity EDULIB.E_MULT
            port map (
                IN1 => \1$N78\,
                IN2 => VREF,
                OUTPUT => OUT1     );
        SNOR_D: entity WORK.SNOR_D(arch_SNOR_D)
            port map (
                IN1_D => CS_D,
                IN2_D => WR_D,
                OUT_D => \1$N92\);
        E_SUM: entity EDULIB.E_SUM
            port map (
                IN1 => \1$N78\,
                IN2 => VREF,
                OUTPUT => OUT2     );
        V_CONT1: entity EDULIB.V_CONSTANT(IDEAL)
          generic map ( LEVEL => 0.0 )
          port map ( POS => CS,
                NEG => ELECTRICAL_REF);

        A2D_BIT1: entity EDULIB.A2D_BIT(IDEAL)
            --generic map ( LEVEL => 1.0 )
            port map (A => CS,
                   D => CS_D);
        V_CONT2: entity EDULIB.V_CONSTANT(IDEAL)
          generic map ( LEVEL => 0.0 )
          port map ( POS => WR,
                NEG => ELECTRICAL_REF);
        A2D_BIT2: entity EDULIB.A2D_BIT(IDEAL)
            --generic map ( LEVEL => 1.0 )
            port map (A => WR,
                   D => WR_D);
        V_REF: entity EDULIB.V_CONSTANT(IDEAL)
          generic map ( LEVEL => 10.0 )
           port map ( POS => VREF,
                 NEG => ELECTRICAL_REF);
    end architecture arch_AD7524;
```

Appendix C– AD7528 converter descriptions in structural VHDL-AMS

The complete VHDL-MAS code is listed for Control_Logic and AD7528 converter.

http://dx.doi.org/10.5772/57575

- Control_Logic

```
library IEEE;
use ieee.std_logic_1164.all;
use ieee.electrical_systems.all;
library EduLib;
use WORK.all;
entity ControlLogic_D is
port (
    signal DADB_D: in std_logic;
    signal WR_D: in std_logic;
     signal CS_D: in std_logic;
     signal EnA_D: out std_logic;
     signal EnB_D: out std_logic );
 end entity ControlLogic_D;
 architecture arch_ControlLogic_D of ControlLogic_D is
     signal \1$N9\: std_logic;
     signal \1$N2\: std_logic;
     signal \1$N3\: std_logic;
     signal \1$N4\: std_logic;
 begin
     G_AND1: entity EDULIB.AND2
         port map (
             IN1 => \1$N2\,
             IN2 => \1$N3\,
             OUTPUT => \1$N9\);
     G_AND2: entity EDULIB.AND2
         port map (
             IN1 => \1$N4\,
             IN2 => \1$N9\,
             OUTPUT => EnA_D);
     G_AND3: entity EDULIB.AND2
         port map (
             IN1 => DADB_D,
             IN2 => \1$N9\,
             OUTPUT => EnB_D);
     G_NOT1: entity EDULIB.INVERTER
         port map (
             INPUT => WR_D,
             OUTPUT => \1$N2\);
     G_NOT2: entity EDULIB.INVERTER
         port map (
             INPUT => CS_D,
             OUTPUT => \1$N3\);
     G_NOT3: entity EDULIB.INVERTER
         port map (
             INPUT => DADB_D,
             OUTPUT => \1$N4\ );
end architecture arch_ControlLogic_D;
```

- AD7528

```
library IEEE;
use ieee.std_logic_1164.all;
use ieee.electrical_systems.all;
library EduLib;
use WORK.all;
entity AD7528 is
end entity AD7528;
architecture arch_AD7528 of AD7528 is
 signal IN1_D: std_logic;
     signal IN2_D: std_logic;
     signal IN3_D: std_logic;
     signal IN4_D: std_logic;
     signal IN5_D: std_logic;
     signal IN6_D: std_logic;
     signal IN7_D: std_logic;
     signal IN8_D: std_logic;
     signal DA_DB_D: std_logic;
     signal WR_D: std_logic;
     signal CS_D: std_logic;
     terminal CS: electrical;
     terminal WR: electrical;
     terminal DA_DB: electrical;
     terminal VrefA: electrical;
     terminal VrefB: electrical;
     terminal Out1A: electrical;
     terminal Out1B: electrical;
     signal \1$N204\: std_logic;
     signal \1$N205\: std_logic;
 begin
     ControlLogic_D: entity WORK.ControlLogic_D(arch_ControlLogic_D)
         port map (
             DADB_D => DA_DB_D,
             WR_D => WR_D,
             CS_D => CS_D,
             EnA_D => \1$N204\,
             EnB_D => \1$N205\    );
     DAC_A: entity WORK.DAC_A(arch_DAC_A)
         port map (
             A1_D => IN1_D,
             A2_D => IN2_D,
             A3_D => IN3_D,
             A4_D => IN4_D,
             A5_D => IN5_D,
             A6_D => IN6_D,
             A7_D => IN7_D,
             A8_D => IN8_D,
             VrefA_I => VrefA,
             EnA_D => \1$N204\,
             OutA => Out1A    );
     DAC_B: entity WORK.DAC_B(arch_DAC_B)
         port map (
             B1_D => IN1_D,
```

http://dx.doi.org/10.5772/57575

```
                   B2_D => IN2_D,
                   B3_D => IN3_D,
                   B4_D => IN4_D,
                   B5_D => IN5_D,
                   B6_D => IN6_D,
                   B7_D => IN7_D,
                   B8_D => IN8_D,
                   VrefB_I => VrefB,
                   EnB_D => \1$N205\,
                   OutB => Out1B );
           V_CONST1: entity EDULIB.V_CONSTANT(IDEAL)
             generic map ( LEVEL => 0.0 )
             port map ( POS => CS,
                   NEG => ELECTRICAL_REF);
           A2D_BIT1: entity EDULIB.A2D_BIT(IDEAL)
               --generic map ( LEVEL => 1.0 )
               port map (A => CS,
                      D => CS_D);
           V_CONST2: entity EDULIB.V_CONSTANT(IDEAL)
             generic map ( LEVEL => 0.0 )
             port map ( POS => WR,
                   NEG => ELECTRICAL_REF);
           A2D_BIT2: entity EDULIB.A2D_BIT(IDEAL)
               --generic map ( LEVEL => 1.0 )
               port map (A => WR,
                      D => WR_D);
           V_CONST3: entity EDULIB.V_CONSTANT(IDEAL)
             generic map ( LEVEL => 0.0 )
             port map ( POS => DA_DB,
                   NEG => ELECTRICAL_REF);
           A2D_BIT3: entity EDULIB.A2D_BIT(IDEAL)
               --generic map ( THRES => 1.0 )
               port map (A => DA_DB,
                      D => DA_DB_D);
           V_REFA: entity EDULIB.V_CONSTANT(IDEAL)
             generic map ( LEVEL => 16.0 )
             port map ( POS => VrefA,
                   NEG => ELECTRICAL_REF);
           V_REFB: entity EDULIB.V_CONSTANT(IDEAL)
             generic map ( LEVEL => 10.0 )
             port map ( POS => VrefB,
                   NEG => ELECTRICAL_REF
    end architecture arch_AD7528;
```


Acknowledgements

The authors would like to thank to National Council for Scientific and Technological Development (CNPq, process: 141744/2010-3 and 309023/2012-2).

Author details

Tiago da Silva Almeida[1], Ian Andrew Grout[2] and Alexandre César Rodrigues da Silva[1]

1 Univ Estadual Paulista, UNESP, Brazil

2 University of Limerik, UL, Ireland

References

[1] Gerstlauer A, Haubelt C, Pimentel A D, Stefanov T P, Gajski D D, Teich J. Electronic System-Level Synthesis Methodologies. Computer-Aided Design of Integrated Circuits and Systems, IEEE Transactions on 2009; 28(10)1517-1530.

[2] Gajski D D, Kuhn R H. Introduction new VLSI tools. IEEE Computer 1983; 16(12) 11-14.

[3] Riesgo T, Torroja Y, Torre E. Design methodologies based on hardware description languages. IEEE Transactions on Industrial Electronics 1999; 46(1) 3-12.

[4] Auburn R, Barnett J, Bodell M, Raman T. State chart XML (SCXML): State machine notation for control abstraction 1.0. http://www.w3.org/TR/2005/WD-scxml-20050705/ (accessed 5 September 2013).

[5] Tocci R J, Widmer N S, Moss G L. Digital Systems: Principles and Applications. New Jersey, USA: Pearson; 2008.

[6] Keogh D B. The State Diagram of HDB3. IEEE Transactions on Communications 1984; 32(11) 1222-1224.

[7] Silva A C R. Contribuição a Minimização e Simulação de Circuitos Lógicos. Master degrees. Universidade Estadual de Campinas, Campinas, Brazil; 1989.

[8] Umans C, Villa T, Sangiovanni-Vicentelli A L. Complexity of two-level logic minimization. IEEE Transactions on Computer-Aided Design of Integrated Circuits and Systems 2006; 25(10) 1230-1246.

[9] Su A P. Application of ESL Synthesis on GSM Edge Algorithm for Base Station. In: Asia And South Pacific Design Automation Conference, 2010, Taipei, Taiwan; 2010.

[10] Yuan L et al. An FSM Reengineering Approach to Sequential Circuit Synthesis by State Splitting. IEEE Transactions on Computer-Aided Design of Integrated Circuits and Systems 2008; 27(6) 1159-1164.

[11] Nehme C, Lundqvist K. A Tool For Translating VHDL to Finite State Machines.In: Digital Avionics Systems Onference, 2003, USA; 2003.

[12] Matrosova A, Ostanin S. Self-cheking FSM design with observing only FSM output. In: IEEE On-Line Testing Workshop, 2000, Palma de Mallorca, Spain; 2000.

[13] Xia L, Bell I M, Wilkison A J. Automated model generation algorithm for high-level fault modeling. IEEE Transaction on Computer-Aided Design of Integrated Circuits and Systems 2010;29(7) 1140-1145.

[14] Correa I S et al. VHDL Implementation of a Flexible and Synthesizable FFT Processor. IEEE Latin America Transaction, São Paulo 2012; 10(1) 1180-1183.

[15] Kapre N, Dehon A. SPICE2: Spatial Processors Interconnected for Concurrent Execution for Accelerating the SPICE Circuit Simulator Using an FPGA. IEEE Transactions On Computer-aided Design of Integrated Circuits and Systems 2012; 31(1) 9-22.

[16] Zorzi M, Franzè F, Speciale N. Construction of VHDL-AMS simulator in MatlabTM. In: Proceedings Of The 2003 International Workshop On Behavioral Modeling, 2003, San Jose, USA, 2002.

[17] Camera K. SF2VHD: A Stateflow to VHDL Translator. Master degrees. University of California, Berkeley, USA; 2001.

[18] Sbarcea B, Nicula D. Automatic Conversion of MATLAB/Simulink Models to HDL Models. http://www.fcd.co.il/doc/optim2004.pdf (accessed 20 September 2012).

[19] Mirotznik M S. Translating MATLAB programs into C code. IEEE Spectrum 1996; 33(1) 63-64.

[20] Shen S et al. Inferring Assertion for Complementary Synthesis. IEEE Transactions on Computer-Aided Design of Integrated Circuits and Systems 2012; 31(8) 1288-1292.

[21] Sinha R, Patel H D. synASM: A High-Level Synthesis Framework With Support for Parallel and Timed Constructs. IEEE Transactions on Computer-Aided Design of Integrated Circuits and Systems 2012; 31(10) 1508-1521.

[22] Liu H et al. Automatic Decoder Synthesis: Methods and Case Studies. IEEE Transactions on Computer-Aided Design of Integrated Circuits and Systems 2001; 31(9) 1319-1331.

[23] Poikonen J H, Lehtonen E, Laiho M. On Synthesis of Boolean Expressions for Memristive Devices Using Sequential Implication Logic. IEEE Transactions on Computer-Aided Design of Integrated Circuits and Systems 2012; 31(7) 1129-1134.

[24] Wu X et al. Research and Application of Code Automatic Generation Algorithm Based on Structured Flowchar. Journal of Software Engineering and Applications 2011; 4(9) 534-545.

[25] Lien W et al. Counter-Based Output Selection for Test Response Compaction. IEEE Transactions on Computer-Aided Design of Integrated Circuits and Systems 2013; 32(1) 152-164.

[26] Marculescu D, Li P. Guest editorial special section on PAR-CAD: parallel CAD algorithms and CAD for parallel architecture / systems. IEEE Transactions on Computer-Aided Design of Integrated Circuits and Systems 2012; 31(1) 7-8.

[27] Meloni L G P, Lenzi K. G. Performance Measurement Simulations for Analog-to-Digital Converters. IEEE Transactions on Latin America 2012; 10(1) 1168-1174.

[28] Wang L, Kazmierski T J. VHDL-AMS based genetic optimization of fuzzy logic controllers. The International Journal for Computation and Mathematics in Electrical and Electronic Engineering 2007; 26(2) 447-460.

[29] Almeida, T. S., Silva, A. C. R., Rossi, S. R. SF2HDL: A Computational Tool of State Transition Diagram Translation. Journal of Mechanical Engineering and Automation., v.3, p.78-86, 2013.

[30] Karris S T. Introduction to Stateflow with applications. United States: Orchard Publications; 2007.

[31] Tancredo L O. TAB2VHDL: Um Ambiente de Síntese Lógica para Máquinas de Estados Finitos. Master degrees. Universidade Estadual Paulista, Ilha Solteira, Brazil; 2002.

[32] 1364-2005-IEEE Standard for Verilog Hardware Description Language. http://standards.ieee.org/findstds/standard/1364-2005.html (accessed 25 December 2013).

[33] Design Entry and Synthesis. http://www.altera.com/products/software/quartus-ii/subscription-edition/design-entry-synthesis/qts-des-ent-syn.html (accessed 25 December 2013).

[34] Almeida, T. S., Silva, A. C. R., Grout, I. A. Acquired Experiences With Computational Tool MS2SV Used in Electronic Circuit Design. Electrical and Electronic Engineering., v.3, p.97-104, 2013.

[35] SystemVision Multi-Discipline Development Environment. http://www.mentor.com/products/sm/system_integration_simulati on_analysis/systemvision/ (accessed 25 December 2013).

[36] Silva A C R, Grout I A, Jeffrey R, O'Shea T, Generating VHDL-AMS Models of Digital-to-Analogue Converters From MATLAB/Simulink. In: Thermal, Mechanical and Multi-Physics Simulation Experiments in Microelectronic and Microsystems, 2007-EUROSIM 2007, 2007, London; 2007.

[37] Analog Devices Inc. CMOS dual 8-bit buffered multiplying DAC: AD7528. http://www. datasheetcatalog.org/datasheet/analogdevices/78586868AD 7528_b.pdf (accessed 5 September 2013).

[38] Tyagi A K. MATLAB and Simulink for Engineers. USA: Oxford University Press; 2012.

http://dx.doi.org/10.5772/57575

[39] Analog Devices Inc. CMOS 8-Bit Buffered Multiplying DAC: AD7524. http://www.datasheet catalog.org/datasheet/analogdevices/888358036ad7524.pdf (accessed 5 September 2013).

[40] Analog Devices Inc. 8-Bit, High-Speed, Multiplying D/A Converter (Universal Digital Logic Interface) DAC: DAC08. http://www.datasheetcata log.org/datasheet/analogdevices/80487346DAC08_b.pdf (accessed 5 September 2013).

[41] Oppenheim A V, Willsky A S, Hamid S. Signals and Systems. USA: Prentice Hall; 1996.

[42] Almeida, Tiago Da Silva, Silva, Alexandre Cesar R. Da, Sampaio, Daniel J. B. S. Computational Tool to Support Design of DAC Converter Model AD7528 with the Object Code in XML In: 2012 IEEE Electronics, Robotics and Automotive Mechanics Conference (CERMA), Cuernavaca. 2012 IEEE Ninth Electronics, Robotics and Automotive Mechanics Conference. IEEE, 2012. v.9. p.327 – 333.

[43] Cruz, E. L., Almeida, T. S., Silva, A. C. R. Metodologia para síntese automática de máquinas de estados finitos baseada em descrição em alto nível de abstração In: VIII International Conference on Engineering and Computer Education, 2013, Luanda. Forming Engineers for a Growing Demand. Santos: Claudio da Rocha Brito, 2013. v. 8. p.371-375

DC/DC Boost-Boost power converter as a didactic system: Experimental results with Matlab/Simulink via current and voltage probes

R. Silva-Ortigoza, M. Antonio-Cruz,
M. Marcelino-Aranda, G. Saldaña-González,
C. A. Merlo-Zapata and P. Pérez-Romero

Additional information is available at the end of the chapter

http://dx.doi.org/10.5772/58243

1. Introduction

Great efforts have been made by undergraduate and postgraduate educators in the field of theory validation through experimentation, with the purpose of students gaining better skills during their academic training, motivating the development of didactic prototypes that contribute to this goal. The importance of using such didactic materials can be seen in papers published in journals indexed in Journal Citation Reports [1], the main intention of which is to spread research of this nature, from engineering [2–6] to physics [7, 8].

Theoretical learning about electric circuit analysis at bachelor level, in specialized engineering (such as electronics, electrical, automatic control, bionics, robotics, mechatronics, etc.) and basic sciences (such as physics and mathematics), can be easily grasped by students if they are able to validate this knowledge experimentally. Herein, this fact represents the main motivation for developing a didactic material where power electronics advances are considered, particularly the ones related to the DC/DC Boost-Boost power converter, due to their importance and multiple applications [9–13].

Educational contributions have been reported in the field of analysis, design, modeling, simulation, construction or control of DC/DC power converters as follows. In 2007, Sandoval-Ibarra *et al.* [14] proposed a DC/DC Boost converter design as well as power electronics definitions associated with simple electrical networks. Additionally, in the same year, Sandoval-Ibarra *et al.* [15] introduced an alternative analysis of switched circuits in order to design square wave generators for DC/DC and DC/AC converters. Dudrik and Bauer in 2008 [16] described techniques in the teaching of power electronics converters and devices for undergraduate students through e-learning methods. In 2010, in the

INTECH
open science | open minds

© 2014 The Author(s). Licensee InTech. This chapter is distributed under the terms of the Creative Commons Attribution License (http://creativecommons.org/licenses/by/3.0), which permits unrestricted use, distribution, and reproduction in any medium, provided the original work is properly cited.

study of Pejović [17], expressions for the discontinuous conduction mode of basic power converters were inferred, relating the output current and output voltage independently to the load type. Likewise, it was mentioned that the method was verified in teaching practice. Campos-Delgado and Espinoza-Trejo in 2010 [18] presented the analysis and construction of the DC/DC Buck, Boost and Buck-Boost power converters. In addition, the design and experimental implementation of proportional integral (PI) controllers for these converters were accomplished. Thus, Altintas in 2011 [19] elaborated an educational graphical user interface (GUI) for the simulation of various topologies of power electronic converters which students can use in order to explore their behavior. The GUI was developed by using Matlab/Simulink, SimPowerSystems, and the GUIDE tool of Matlab, which acts as a front-end that can be used for teaching as well as learning of power converters theory. Also, Abramovitz in 2011 [20] suggested a pedagogical approach to teaching the subject of average modeling of PWM switched-mode power electronics systems through simulation by general-purpose electronic circuit simulators. In 2011, in the work of Deblecker [21] a pre-processing approach was considered. It was based on the $\Sigma - \Delta$ technique for increasing the effective resolution of a digital pulse-width modulator in a voltage-mode controlled Buck converter. Numerical simulations by using Matlab/Simulink allowed the effectiveness of that approach to be verified, and a low-cost development board showed its real behavior. On the other hand, in 2011 Zumel *et al.* [22] designed and implemented, step-by-step, a linear compensator based on a field programmable gate array for a DC/DC Buck power converter. This contribution was oriented to power electronics introductory courses for undergraduate or graduate levels. Recently, in 2012, Liao *et al.* [23] reported a modeling technique for designing switched-mode power supplies (SMPS) aided by Matlab/Simulink. Experimental validation of that technique for the DC/DC Buck power converter, and other SMPS topologies, was realized. Further, in 2012 Lamar *et al.* [24] introduced a problem-based learning method included in a SMPS course, by means of two practical projects: the design and construction of a SMPS prototype (Boost converter), and the static study of a DC/DC power converter topology. Another important contribution that was provided by Silva-Ortigoza *et al.* [25] in 2012 described the model, simulation, construction, and the experimental verifying associated with a DC/DC Boost power converter, as a didactic material intended to support courses on electric circuit analysis. In contrast with this previous work, Choi and Saeedifard [26] in 2012 showed a description of the set of hardware and software tools installed in the power electronics laboratory, constructed at Purdue University, West Lafayette, IN., which was developed primarily to reinforce, experimentally, the fundamental concepts presented in a power electronics course. This facility is used for the design, simulation, control, construction, and verification of power electronic circuits. Finally, work associated with the synthesis or control of DC/DC power converters has been reported [9–11, 27–31].

Having undertaken the educational literature review associated with DC/DC power electronic converters, on the one hand, it was found that the modeling of such converters, generally, was based on equivalent models, validated by specialized software, without deducing the corresponding mathematical models. Also, usually numerical simulations were introduced instead of using experimental implementation. On the other hand, even though the DC/DC power converters, essentially nonlinear, have been controlled via classic control techniques, in the educational literature, generally, modern control techniques have not been proposed for them. For such an aim, the converter models based on state-space representation is more appropriate as the one to be presented for the Boost-Boost converter in this work.

Thus, the main aim of this work is the modeling, design, simulation, and construction of a prototype associated with a DC/DC Boost-Boost converter to validate its mathematical model, using Kirchhoff current and voltage laws, via experimental tests. This, with the intention of enhancing the acquired theoretical knowledge for students in electric circuit analysis courses. Finally, the simulations are performed using Matlab/Simulink as Simulink provides a graphical environment to the user that facilitates the analysis, design and construction of dynamic systems. Several examples of this software's applications have been presented [9, 11, 19, 21, 23, 26]. Also, books associated with theory, real-world examples, and exercises using either MATLAB or Simulink (MathWorks products) can be found in [32]. On the other hand, the experimental results are obtained using some software tools and laboratory equipment, such as: Matlab/Simulink, a dSPACE DS1104 board [33], current and voltage probes, a power supply, and a function generator.

The work is structured as follows. In Section 2 the mathematical model of the DC/DC Boost-Boost power converter is developed. Matlab/Simulink simulations associated with such a converter are presented in Section 3. The construction of the converter prototype is described in Section 4. Moreover, the experimental validation is developed and analyzed in Section 5. Finally, Section 6 is devoted to the conclusions and future research.

2. Modeling and analysis of a DC/DC Boost-Boost power converter

This section is divided into two parts: the first one deals with the mathematical model deduction via Kirchhoff voltage and current laws for the Boost-Boost power converter, and the second part is related to obtaining the properties of such a converter in steady-state using its average model.

2.1. Boost-Boost power converter modeling

On the one hand, the Boost-Boost converter is composed of two DC/DC Boost power converters connected in cascade. As a consequence, the ideal circuit representation of the DC/DC Boost-Boost power converter, that is, the converter synthesized with switches, is the one shown in Figure 1. On the other hand, herein is presented an alternative circuit representation for the converter under study, using MOSFET transistors as switches, as shown in Figure 2.

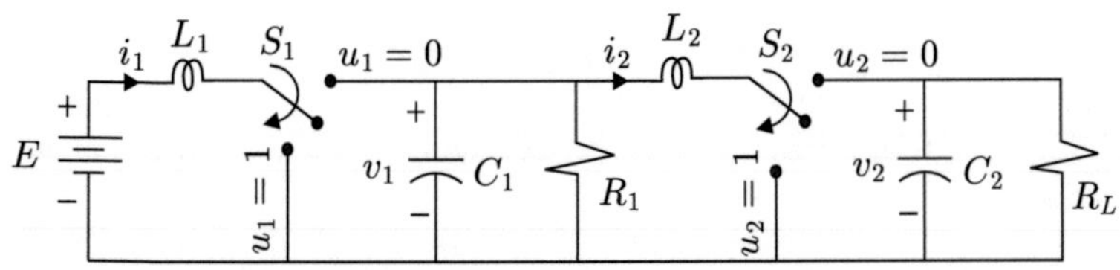

Figure 1. DC/DC Boost-Boost power converter ideal circuit.

In the system shown in Figure 1, inputs u_1 and u_2 can take values in the discrete set $\{0,1\}$, corresponding to the positions of the switches S_1 and S_2, respectively. These positions are set in practice by using transistors (Q_1 and Q_2) in on/off operating mode. The transistors in

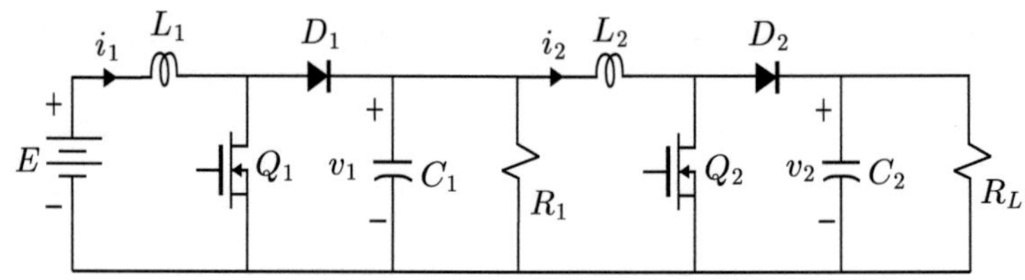

Figure 2. DC/DC Boost-Boost power converter circuit implemented with transistors.

the on-state are equivalent to the positions $u_1 = 1$ and $u_2 = 1$, and the off-states correspond to the positions $u_1 = 0$ and $u_2 = 0$. In the derivation of the mathematical model for the converter it is assumed that the circuit operates in continuous conduction mode, that is, the average value of the inductors currents are never lower than zero [29]. The variables i_1, v_1, i_2, and v_2 correspond to the currents and voltages associated to L_1, C_1, L_2, and C_2, respectively. The loads are represented by R_1 and R_L, which correspond to each output stage of the Boost converters that compose the Boost-Boost converter. Finally, E denotes the power converter primary supply source.

An important feature of the Boost-Boost converter output voltage v_2, is that it satisfies the following condition:

$$v_2 \geq E,$$

which can be shown by analyzing such a converter in steady-state. This is the reason why this converter is also known as a double step-up converter.

From Figure 1 and the Kirchhoff voltage and current laws (abbreviated to KVL and KCL, respectively), the switched model, which describes the Boost-Boost converter dynamic evolution, is obtained as follows.

1/2. –The on/off states of transistors Q_1 and Q_2 are considered to generate the four equivalent circuits shown in Figure 3, each circuit is represented by a fourth-order-differential equations subsystem. Thus, four mathematical subsystems are generated.

2/2. –These four subsystems are integrated only in a system of fourth-order differential equations, which describes the converter's nonlinear dynamics.

The aforementioned process is accomplished as follows:

a) *Equivalent Circuit I* occurs when transistors Q_1 and Q_2 conduct, that is, $u_1 = 1$ and $u_2 = 1$, and diodes D_1 and D_2 are reverse biased. Then, the equivalent circuit is shown in Figure 3(a). Applying KVL to meshes I and II, the following equations for the currents i_1 and i_2, respectively, are obtained:

$$L_1 \frac{di_1}{dt} = E, \tag{1}$$

$$L_2 \frac{di_2}{dt} = v_1. \tag{2}$$

http://dx.doi.org/10.5772/58243

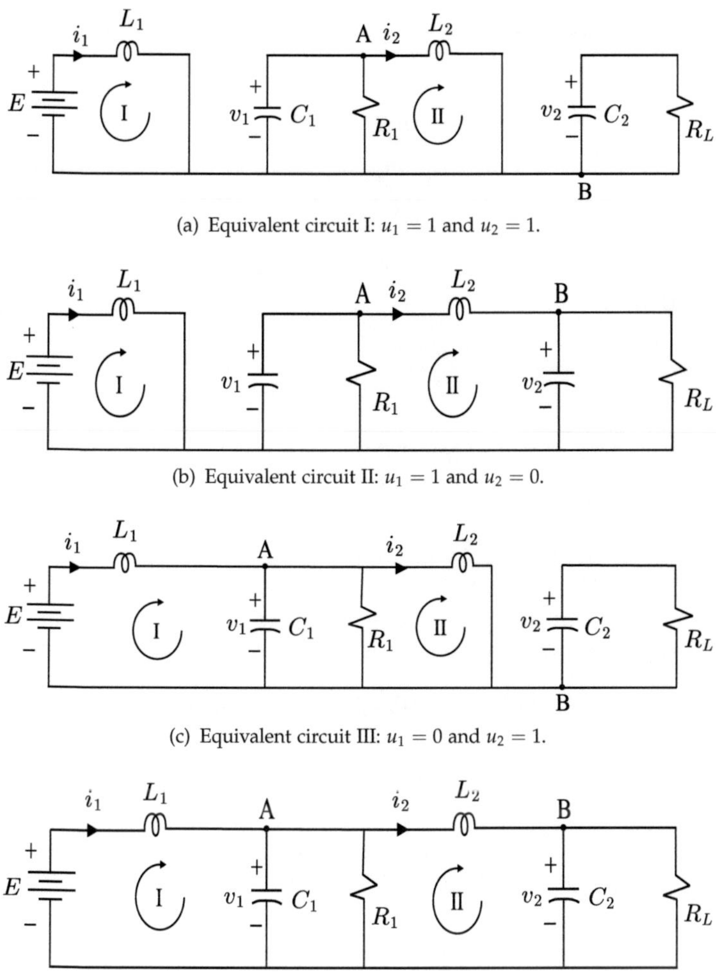

(a) Equivalent circuit I: $u_1 = 1$ and $u_2 = 1$.

(b) Equivalent circuit II: $u_1 = 1$ and $u_2 = 0$.

(c) Equivalent circuit III: $u_1 = 0$ and $u_2 = 1$.

(d) Equivalent circuit IV: $u_1 = 0$ and $u_2 = 0$.

Figure 3. DC/DC Boost-Boost power converter operating modes.

Moreover, applying KCL for nodes A and B in Figure 3(a), the differential equations related to voltages v_1 and v_2 are obtained by

$$C_1 \frac{dv_1}{dt} = -\frac{v_1}{R_1} - i_2, \tag{3}$$

$$C_2 \frac{dv_2}{dt} = -\frac{v_2}{R_L}. \tag{4}$$

b) *Equivalent circuit II* is generated when Q_1 conducts and Q_2 does not conduct, that is, $u_1 = 1$ and $u_2 = 0$, then the diode D_1 is reverse biased and diode D_2 is forward biased. Thus, the corresponding equivalent circuit is shown in Figure 3(b). Applying KVL to meshes I and II the equations for i_1 and i_2, respectively, are obtained:

$$L_1\frac{di_1}{dt} = E, \tag{5}$$

$$L_2\frac{di_2}{dt} = v_1 - v_2. \tag{6}$$

Applying KCL to nodes A and B in Figure 3(b), the dynamics associated to v_1 and v_2, respectively, are obtained:

$$C_1\frac{dv_1}{dt} = -\frac{v_1}{R_1} - i_2, \tag{7}$$

$$C_2\frac{dv_2}{dt} = i_2 - \frac{v_2}{R_L}. \tag{8}$$

c) *Equivalent circuit III* is presented when Q_1 does not conduct and Q_2 conducts, that is, $u_1 = 0$ and $u_2 = 1$, D_1 is forward biased and D_2 is reverse biased. Then, the resultant circuit is as shown in Figure 3(c). Applying KVL to meshes I and II, and the KCL to nodes A and B in Figure 3(c), the equations for i_1, i_2, v_1, and v_2, respectively, are obtained:

$$L_1\frac{di_1}{dt} = -v_1 + E, \tag{9}$$

$$L_2\frac{di_2}{dt} = v_1, \tag{10}$$

$$C_1\frac{dv_1}{dt} = i_1 - \frac{v_1}{R_1} - i_2, \tag{11}$$

$$C_2\frac{dv_2}{dt} = -\frac{v_2}{R_L}. \tag{12}$$

d) *Equivalent circuit IV* occurs when transistors Q_1 and Q_2 do not conduct, that is, $u_1 = 0$ and $u_2 = 0$, D_1 and D_2 are forward biased. The equivalent circuit is shown in Figure 3(d). In order to achieve the equations that govern i_1, i_2, v_1, and v_2, KVL and KCL are applied, obtaining the following:

$$L_1\frac{di_1}{dt} = -v_1 + E, \tag{13}$$

$$L_2\frac{di_2}{dt} = v_1 - v_2, \tag{14}$$

$$C_1\frac{dv_1}{dt} = i_1 - \frac{v_1}{R_1} - i_2, \tag{15}$$

$$C_2\frac{dv_2}{dt} = i_2 - \frac{v_2}{R_L}. \tag{16}$$

Equations related to i_1, (1), (5), (9), and (13), can be associated, using u_1, producing (17). The dynamics associated with v_1 is obtained from a combination of (3), (7), (11), and (15) through u_1, generating (18). The unification of (2), (6), (10), and (14) through u_2, produces the dynamics associated to i_2, determined by (19). Following a similar process for v_2, associating (4), (8), (12), and (16), (20) is produced. Thus, the Boost-Boost converter dynamics is determined by the following nonlinear differential equations system:

$$L_1 \frac{di_1}{dt} = -(1-u_1)\, v_1 + E, \tag{17}$$

$$C_1 \frac{dv_1}{dt} = (1-u_1)\, i_1 - \frac{v_1}{R_1} - i_2, \tag{18}$$

$$L_2 \frac{di_2}{dt} = v_1 - (1-u_2)\, v_2, \tag{19}$$

$$C_2 \frac{dv_2}{dt} = (1-u_2)\, i_2 - \frac{v_2}{R_L}. \tag{20}$$

This is called the converter *switched model* referring to the binary values associated with the switches positions, that is, $u_1 \in \{0,1\}$ and $u_2 \in \{0,1\}$.

2.2. Converter steady-state analysis

In order to know the Boost-Boost converter properties in steady-state its average model is used [11], which is determined by

$$L_1 \frac{di_1}{dt} = -(1-u_{1av})\, v_1 + E, \tag{21}$$

$$C_1 \frac{dv_1}{dt} = (1-u_{1av})\, i_1 - \frac{v_1}{R_1} - i_2, \tag{22}$$

$$L_2 \frac{di_2}{dt} = v_1 - (1-u_{2av})\, v_2, \tag{23}$$

$$C_2 \frac{dv_2}{dt} = (1-u_{2av})\, i_2 - \frac{v_2}{R_L}, \tag{24}$$

where i_1, v_1, i_2, and v_2 now denote average currents and voltages associated with L_1, C_1, L_2, and C_2, respectively, whereas u_{1av} and u_{2av} represent average position functions of the switches or duty cycles [9, 29], taking values in the interval $[0,1)$.

No distinction is made between the variables of the average model (21)–(24) and the switched model (17)–(20). However, in order to distinguish one model from the other, the inputs to the average model are denoted by u_{1av} and u_{2av}, and the inputs of the switched model are denoted by u_1 and u_2. This difference is used in the rest of the work. Furthermore, it is important to note that theoretical justification of the average models has been extensively dealt with since the beginning of power electronics [27].

Based on the average model (21)–(24), the evaluation of the converter equilibrium point proceeded, denoted by $(\bar{i}_1, \bar{v}_1, \bar{i}_2, \bar{v}_2)$, that is, the values of i_1, v_1, i_2, and v_2 in steady-state as a response to the constant average inputs $\bar{u}_{1av}$ and $\bar{u}_{2av}$. Thus, (21)–(24) in equilibrium satisfies the following algebraic equations system:

$$0 = -(1 - \bar{u}_{1av})\bar{v}_1 + E, \tag{25}$$

$$0 = (1 - \bar{u}_{1av})\bar{i}_1 - \frac{\bar{v}_1}{R_1} - \bar{i}_2, \tag{26}$$

$$0 = \bar{v}_1 - (1 - \bar{u}_{2av})\bar{v}_2, \tag{27}$$

$$0 = (1 - \bar{u}_{2av})\bar{i}_2 - \frac{\bar{v}_2}{R_L}, \tag{28}$$

which is represented as a matrix equation by

$$\begin{bmatrix} 0 & -(1-\bar{u}_{1av}) & 0 & 0 \\ (1-\bar{u}_{1av}) & -\frac{1}{R_1} & -1 & 0 \\ 0 & 1 & 0 & -(1-\bar{u}_{2av}) \\ 0 & 0 & (1-\bar{u}_{2av}) & -\frac{1}{R_L} \end{bmatrix} \begin{bmatrix} \bar{i}_1 \\ \bar{v}_1 \\ \bar{i}_2 \\ \bar{v}_2 \end{bmatrix} = \begin{bmatrix} -E \\ 0 \\ 0 \\ 0 \end{bmatrix}. \tag{29}$$

By solving (29) for $\bar{i}_1$, $\bar{v}_1$, $\bar{i}_2$, and $\bar{v}_2$ the following is obtained:

$$\begin{bmatrix} \bar{i}_1 \\ \bar{v}_1 \\ \bar{i}_2 \\ \bar{v}_2 \end{bmatrix} = \begin{bmatrix} \frac{E}{R_1 R_L} \frac{R_1 + R_L(1-\bar{u}_{2av})^2}{(1-\bar{u}_{1av})^2(1-\bar{u}_{2av})^2} \\ \frac{E}{1-\bar{u}_{1av}} \\ \frac{E}{R_L} \frac{1}{(1-\bar{u}_{1av})(1-\bar{u}_{2av})^2} \\ \frac{E}{(1-\bar{u}_{1av})(1-\bar{u}_{2av})} \end{bmatrix}. \tag{30}$$

Therefore, (30) provides the average value of the variables i_1, v_1, i_2, and v_2 in steady-state. Furthermore, from the relation of $\bar{v}_2$ with $\bar{u}_{1av}$ and $\bar{u}_{2av}$ it can be seen that the output of this converter satisfies the inequality $\bar{v}_2 \geq E$, as initially stated, since $\bar{u}_{1av}$ and $\bar{u}_{2av} \in [0, 1)$.

3. Converter numerical simulations with Matlab/Simulink

In this section, numerical simulations of the Boost-Boost converter switched model (17)–(20) are performed, by using Matlab/Simulink. This will enable the dynamic evolution of the system variables i_1, v_1, i_2, and v_2 to be known in response to different switched inputs u_1 and u_2, generated via the constant average inputs $\bar{u}_{1av}$ and $\bar{u}_{2av}$ belonging to the interval $[0, 1)$.

3.1. Simulink blocks for simulations

The developed diagram for the converter's numerical simulations consists of three blocks, namely, *inputs*, *Boost-Boost system*, and *outputs*, (see Figure 4). The description associated with the block diagram shown in the Figure 4 is as follows:

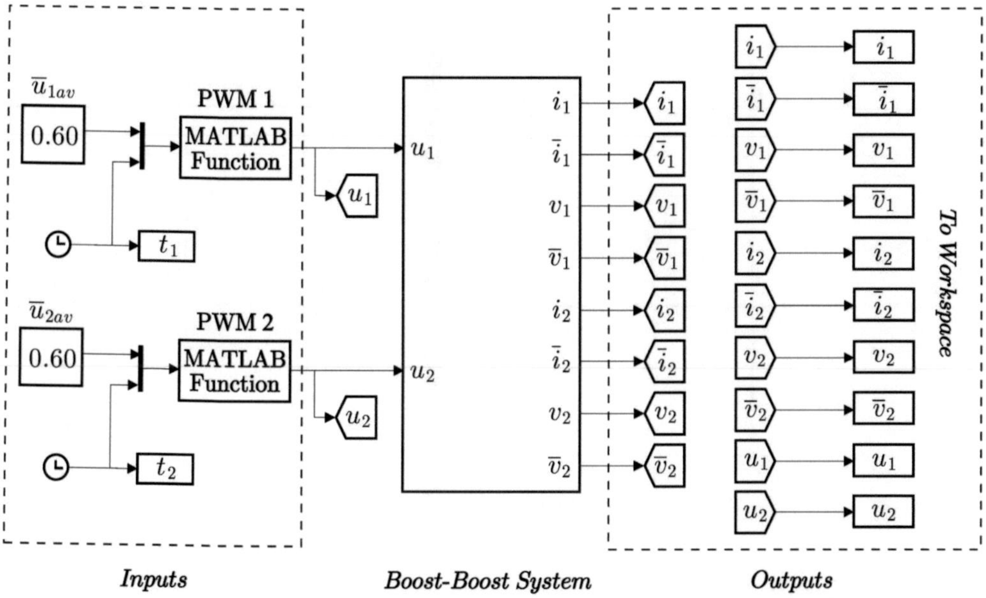

Figure 4. Diagram developed in Matlab/Simulink to perform simulations.

- *Inputs.* The inputs associated with this block correspond to the constant average values $\overline{u}_{1av}$ and $\overline{u}_{2av}$, which represent the inputs to blocks PWM1 and PWM2. Each PWM block is constructed with a Matlab embedded function [34], the outputs of which deliver the switched signals u_1 and u_2, respectively. The code associated with the block PWM1 or block PWM2 is shown in Table 1.

```
function sal=DUTY_CYCLE(uav1)
ciclo=uav1(1);
t=uav1(2);
A=1;
fp=50000;
u1=A*((square(2*pi*fp*t,ciclo)+1)/2;
sal=u1;
```

Table 1. Code for the block PWM1 or block PWM2.

- *Boost-Boost system.* In this block the switched model (17)–(20) is programmed. For this purpose an embedded function of Matlab is used (see Figure 5), whereas, the code associated with this function is presented in Table 2.
- *Outputs.* This block delivers the dynamic evolution of the variables i_1, v_1, i_2, and v_2 and the values in steady-state $\overline{i}_1$, $\overline{v}_1$, $\overline{i}_2$, and $\overline{v}_2$, respectively, obtained via simulation.

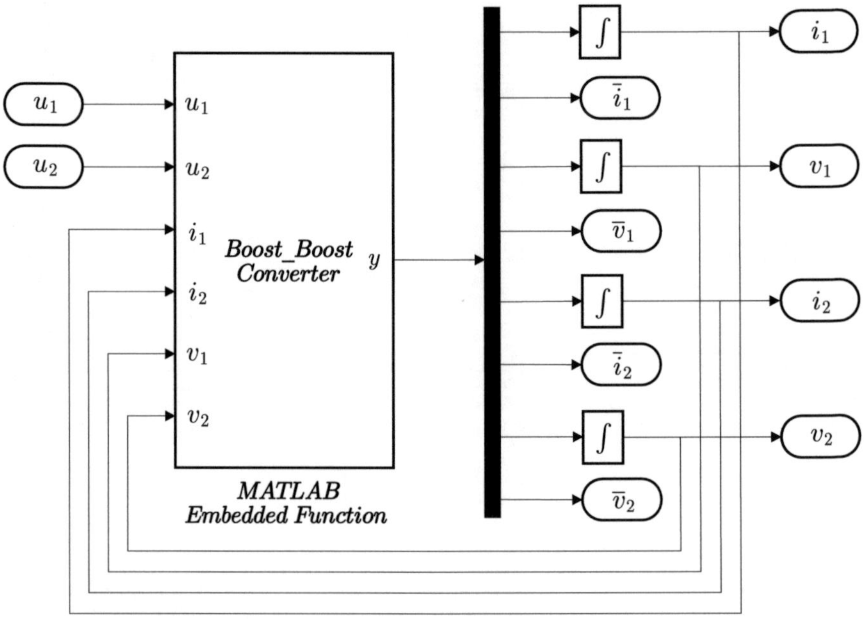

Figure 5. Block *Boost-Boost system.*

```
function y=Boost_Boost(u1,u2,i1,i2,v1,v2)
E=12;L1=4.94e-3;C1=12.2e-6;L2=3e-3;C2=12.2e-6;R1=474;
RL=275;a1=0.55;a2=0.55;
di1=(-(1-u1)*(v1/L1))+(E/L1);
dv1=((1-u1)*(i1/C1))-(v1/(R1*C1))-(i2/C1);
di2=(v1/L2)-((1-u2)*(v2/L2));
dv2=((1-u2)*(i2/C2))-(v2/(RL*C2));
v1d=(E/(1-a1));
i1d=((E/(R1*RL))*((R1+((RL)*((1-a2)^2)))/(((1-a1)^2)*((1-a2)^2))));
v2d=(E/((1-a1)*(1-a2)));
i2d=((E/RL)*(1/((1-a1)*((1-a2)^2))));
y=[di1;dv1;di2;dv2];
```

Table 2. *Boost-Boost system* code.

3.2. Simulation results

In the numerical simulations implementation, the following values for the parameters associated with (17)–(20) were considered:

$$L_1 = 4.94 \text{ mH}, \; C_1 = 12.2 \; \mu\text{F}, \; L_2 = 3 \text{ mH}, \; C_2 = 12.2 \; \mu\text{F}, \; R_1 = 474 \; \Omega, \; R_L = 275 \; \Omega,$$

for the cases in which E takes values of 6 V and 12 V, respectively. The justification of the parameters is shown in next section, whereas, the simulation results associated with the converter under study are presented as follows:

- *Simulation I* considers that $E = 6$ V and the system inputs take the average values $\overline{u}_{1av} = 0.60$ and $\overline{u}_{2av} = 0.60$. In steady-state, according to (30), $(\overline{i}_1, \overline{v}_1, \overline{i}_2, \overline{v}_2) = (931$ mA, 15 V, 340 mA, 37.5 V$)$. For this case, the simulation results are shown in Figure 6.
- *Simulation II* considers that $E = 12$ V and the inputs are $\overline{u}_{1av} = 0.55$ and $\overline{u}_{2av} = 0.55$. According to (30) it is found that $(\overline{i}_1, \overline{v}_1, \overline{i}_2, \overline{v}_2) = (1.19$ A, 26.67 V, 480 mA, 59.26 V$)$. The corresponding simulation results can be seen in Figure 7.

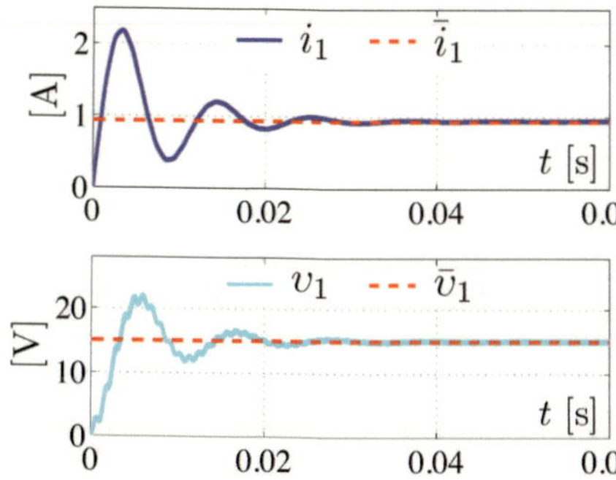

(a) Current through the inductor L_1 and voltage at capacitor C_1.

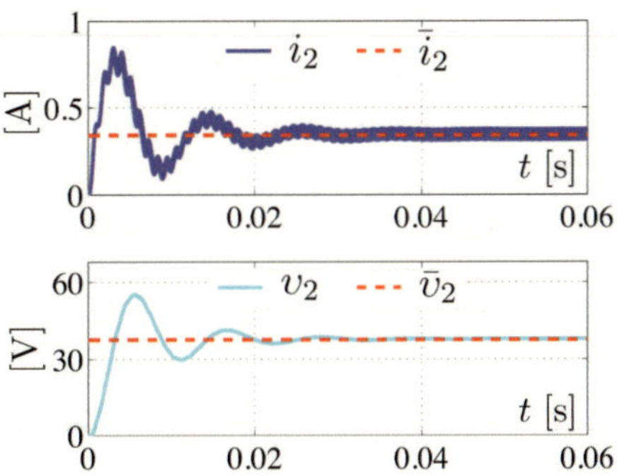

(b) Current through the inductor L_2 and voltage at capacitor C_2.

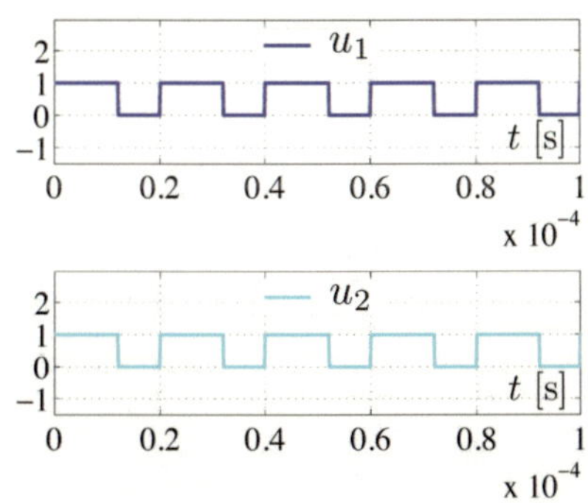

(c) Inputs $u_1 = 60\%$ and $u_2 = 60\%$.

Figure 6. Dynamic response obtained from *simulation I*.

It can be observed that the simulation results validate the converter mathematical model and that the steady-state values of the system variables behave according to (30). Also, it was verified that this converter operates as a voltage amplifier with respect to E, when $u_{1av} \in (0, 1)$ and $u_{2av} \in (0, 1)$.

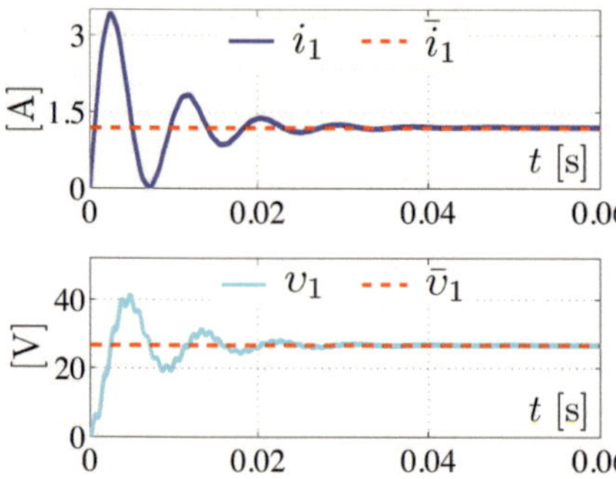

(a) Current through the inductor L_1 and voltage at capacitor C_1.

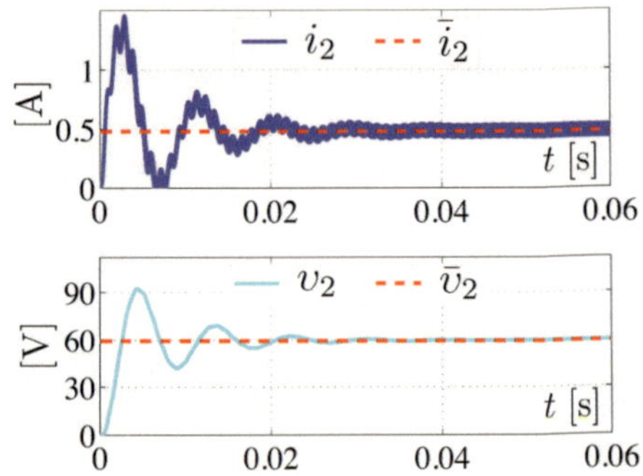

(b) Current through the inductor L_2 and voltage at capacitor C_2.

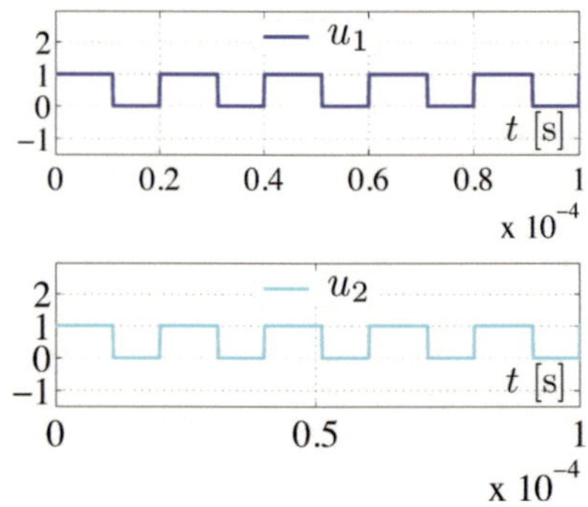

(c) Inputs $u_1 = 55\%$ and $u_2 = 55\%$.

Figure 7. Dynamic response obtained from *simulation II*.

4. Boost-Boost power converter construction

In this section, first the process followed to obtain the design parameters of the DC/DC Boost-Boost power converter is described. Subsequently, the construction of such a converter is presented.

4.1. Boost-Boost power converter design

Table 3 shows the design specifications for the converter construction. Two cases are considered: the first refers to $E = 6$ V and the second to $E = 12$ V.

Here, calculations corresponding to the first case are presented. According to (30) and the converter design specification, the average inputs $\overline{u}_{1av}$ and $\overline{u}_{2av}$ are defined by

$$\overline{u}_{1av} = 1 - \frac{E}{\overline{v}_1} = 1 - \frac{6\text{ V}}{20\text{ V}} = 0.70,$$

$$\overline{u}_{2av} = 1 - \frac{E}{(1-\overline{u}_{1av})\overline{v}_2} = 1 - \frac{6\text{ V}}{(1-0.70)(66.67)\text{ V}} \approx 0.70.$$

http://dx.doi.org/10.5772/58243

	Case 1	*Case 2*
Input voltage (E)	6 V	12 V
Output voltages ($\overline{\upsilon}_1$ and $\overline{\upsilon}_2$)	$\overline{\upsilon}_1 = 20$ V $\overline{\upsilon}_2 = 66.67$ V	$\overline{\upsilon}_1 = 26.67$ V $\overline{\upsilon}_2 = 59.26$ V
Output power associated to R_1 (P_{R_1}) and R_L (P_{R_L})	$P_{R_1} = 0.85$ W $P_{R_L} = 16$ W	$P_{R_1} = 1.48$ W $P_{R_L} = 12.19$ W
Switching frequency (f)	50 kHz	50 kHz
Current ripple ($\Delta\overline{i}_1$ and $\Delta\overline{i}_2$)	5% of nominal value for $\overline{i}_1$, and 12% of nominal value for $\overline{i}_2$	
Voltage ripple ($\Delta\overline{\upsilon}_1$ and $\Delta\overline{\upsilon}_2$)	5% of nominal value for $\overline{\upsilon}_1$ and $\overline{\upsilon}_1$	

Table 3. Design specifications for the Boost-Boost converter.

Since the desired power in load resistance R_1 is 0.85 W, with a voltage of 20 V, then R_1 is calculated using the expression $R_1 = \frac{\overline{\upsilon}_1^2}{P_{R_1}}$, which produces $R_1 \approx 470.59\ \Omega$. Similarly, if $P_{R_L} = 16$ W and $\overline{\upsilon}_2 = 66.67$ V, then the load resistance $R_L \approx 277.81\ \Omega$. On the other hand, the current $\overline{i}_{R_1}$ flowing through R_1 is calculated from the expression $\overline{i}_{R_1} = \frac{P_{R_1}}{\overline{\upsilon}_1} = 42.5$ mA, whereas the current through R_L is defined by $\overline{i}_{R_L} = \frac{P_{R_L}}{\overline{\upsilon}_2} \approx 240$ mA. Moreover, according to (30) the currents through the inductors, L_1 and L_2, are $\overline{i}_1 \approx 2.81$ A and $\overline{i}_2 \approx 800$ mA, respectively.

In the calculations of the inductance and capacitance minimum values associated with the first stage, in order to satisfy the converter design specifications, the following relations are employed [35]:

$$L_{1\,\mathrm{min}} = \frac{E\overline{u}_{1av}}{f\Delta\overline{i}_1} = \frac{(6\ \mathrm{V})\,(0.70)}{(50\ \mathrm{kHz})\,(0.05)\,(2.81\ \mathrm{A})} \approx 0.60\ \mathrm{mH}, \tag{31}$$

$$C_{1\,\mathrm{min}} = \frac{\overline{u}_{1av}}{R_1 f\Delta\overline{\upsilon}_1}\upsilon_1 = \frac{(0.70)}{(470.59\ \Omega)\,(50\ \mathrm{kHz})\,(0.05)\,(20\ \mathrm{V})}(20\ \mathrm{V}) \approx 0.59\ \mu\mathrm{F}. \tag{32}$$

Furthermore, according to [35] the condition $T << 2R_1C_1$ must be satisfied, where $T = 1/f$, which is achieved when $C_{1\,\mathrm{min}}$ is multiplied by 20, generating that C_1 is determined by

$$C_1 = 11.8\ \mu F.$$

Now, the minimum values for inductance and capacitance of the second stage can be calculated as follows:

$$L_{2\,\mathrm{min}} = \frac{\overline{\upsilon}_1\overline{u}_{2av}}{f\Delta\overline{i}_2} = \frac{(20\ \mathrm{V})\,(0.70)}{(50\ \mathrm{kHz})\,(0.12)\,(0.80\ \mathrm{A})} \approx 2.92\ \mathrm{mH}, \tag{33}$$

$$C_{2\min} = \frac{\overline{u}_{2av}}{R_L f \Delta\overline{v}_2}\overline{v}_2 = \frac{(0.70)}{(277.81\ \Omega)\,(50\ \text{kHz})\,(0.05)\,(66.67\ \text{V})}(66.67\ \text{V}) \approx 1.01\ \mu\text{F}. \quad (34)$$

Condition $T << 2R_2C_2$, can be satisfied multiplying $C_{2\min}$ by 12 generating the following:

$$C_2 = 12.12\ \mu F.$$

Finally, the commercial values employed for the converter components were the following:

$$\begin{aligned} L_1 = 4.94\ \text{mH},\ C_1 = 12.2\ \mu F,\ L_2 = 3\ \text{mH}, \\ C_2 = 12.2\ \mu F,\ R_1 = 474\ \Omega/50\ \text{W},\ R_L = 275\ \Omega/50\ \text{W}. \end{aligned} \quad (35)$$

The inductors were built on a ETD49/25/16 core with 3C85 material from Ferroxcube. They were used 110 and 69 turns of 18.5 AWG Litz wire for L_1 and L_2, respectively, with 175 strands. The L_1 internal series resistance, R_{s1}, has associated 10.5 Ω, while the L_2 internal series resistance, R_{s2}, 6.6 Ω. Furthermore, the C_1 and C_2 values were obtained by connecting two MKP capacitors from Kemet in parallel: one of 10 μF and another one of 2 μF, both rated at 275 V.

Following a similar procedure as the one aforementioned, we have found that approach values for L_1, C_1, L_2, C_2, R_1, and R_L, as they are shown in (35), are required for *Case* 2 presented in Table 3.

4.2. Experimental prototype

Figure 8 shows the electronic diagram proposed for the Boost-Boost converter, which is composed of two blocks, namely, *Boost-Boost converter* and *function generator*. The description associated with these blocks is presented as follows:

- *Boost-Boost converter*. Figure 8 shows how the variables i_1, v_1, i_2, and v_2, are measured. In order to visualize the converter dynamic response Matlab/Simulink and a DS1104 electronic board from dSPACE are employed, along with two Tektronix A622 AC/DC current probes (for i_1 and i_2), and two Tektronix P6139A voltage probes (for v_1 and v_2), whereas, a BK Precision 1795 DC power supply is used to provide E.
- *Function generator*. This block is implemented using an HP 8111A function generator, which possesses an option to set the pulse width, to produce the input signals u_1 and u_2 with a 5 V amplitude, which is an appropriate voltage level to trigger the NTE2984 transistors. These transistors have a logic level gate and operate at high speed. Some important parameters of this device are the following: drain–source breakdown voltage $BV_{DSS} = 60$ V, absolute maximum drain current $I_D = 17$ A with continuous $V_{GS} = 5$ V to 25 °C, rise time $t_r = 110$ ns, fall time $t_f = 41$ ns, turn-on delay time $t_{d(on)} = 11$ ns, turn-off delay time $t_{d(off)} = 23$ ns, static drain–source on resistance $R_{DS(on)} = 0.14\ \Omega$ and the maximum operating temperature is 175 °C. The visualizing of u_1 and u_2 are accomplished with a Tektronic TDS 3034B oscilloscope.

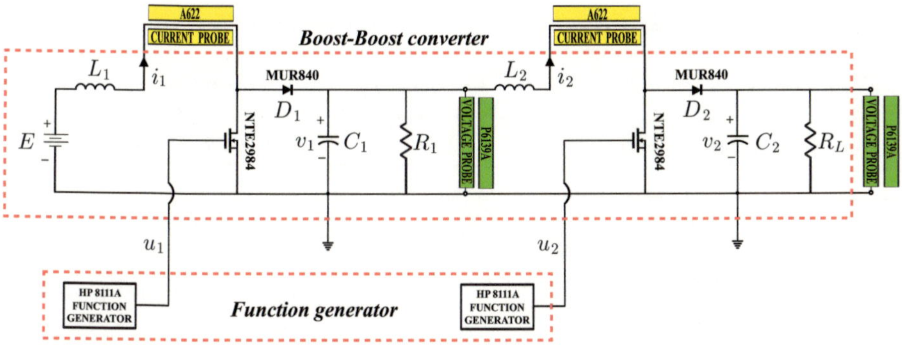

Figure 8. Electronic diagram of the Boost-Boost converter.

Since the Boost-Boost converter is integrated by two Boost converters connected in cascade, they were developed two identical printed circuit boards (PCBs) of a Boost converter that later were interconnected. The PCBs were designed by using a specialized software. In the PCBs design the inductors, transistors, and resistors were replaced by terminal blocks, this with the intent of replacing easily the components associated with the converter whenever necessary. The prototype built is shown in Figure 9.

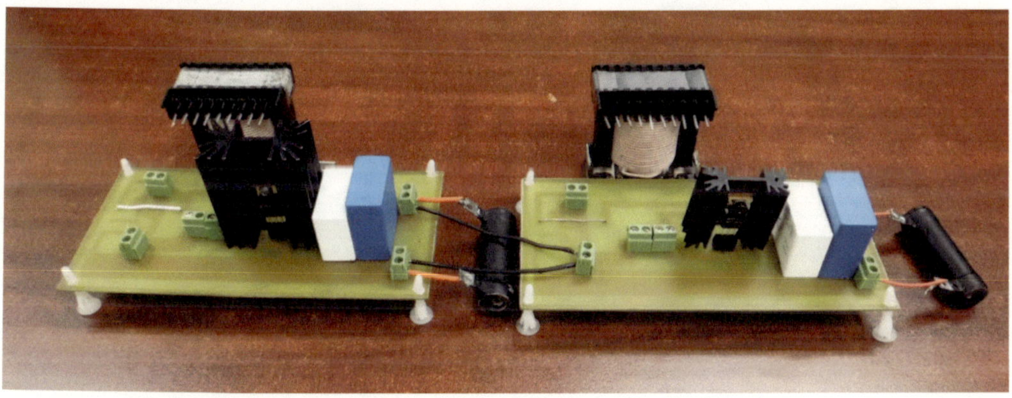

Figure 9. Boost-Boost power converter built.

5. Experimental results

In this section the experimental results related to the dynamic responses of the converter are provided, in order to compare them with the simulation results presented in Section 3. All experiments were performed using the Boost-Boost converter described in Section 4. In order to visualize the system dynamic response Matlab/Simulink and a DS1104 electronic board from dSPACE, along with commercial current and voltage probes are employed.

5.1. Dynamic response of the converter

The converter dynamic response was tested experimentally for the cases indicated in Subsection 3.2.

- *Experiment I.* The experimental results associated with the *simulation I* are presented in Figure 10. These results show the dynamic response of i_1, v_1, i_2, and v_2 as well as the steady-state values $\bar{i}_1$, $\bar{v}_1$, $\bar{i}_2$, and $\bar{v}_2$, respectively. Also, Figure 10 presents the input signals $u_1 = 60\%$ and $u_2 = 60\%$. The corresponding experimental numerical values measured in steady-state are $(\bar{i}_{1m}, \bar{v}_{1m}, \bar{i}_{2m}, \bar{v}_{2m}) = (930\text{ mA}, 13.96\text{ V}, 330\text{ mA}, 36.95\text{ V})$.

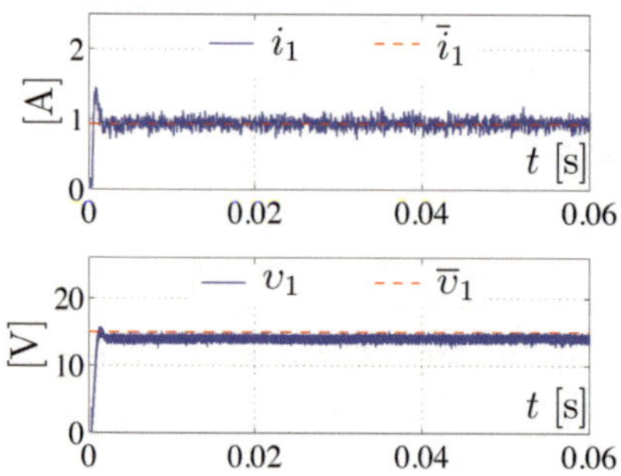

(a) Current through the inductor L_1 and voltage at capacitor C_1.

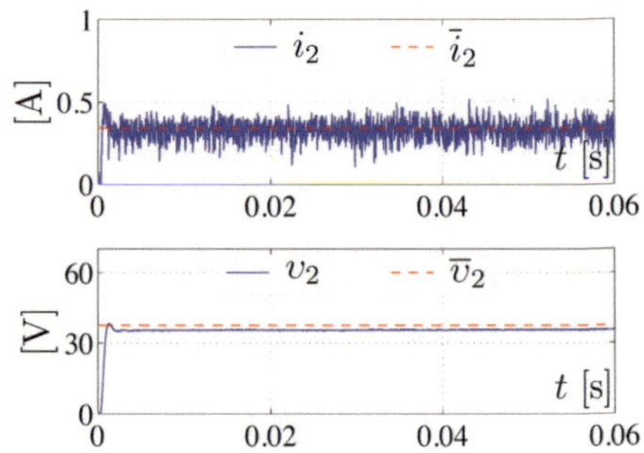

(b) Current through the inductor L_2 and voltage at capacitor C_2.

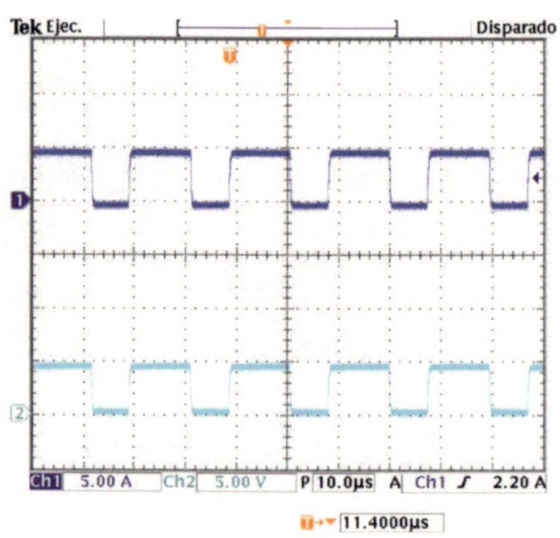

(c) Inputs $u_1 = 60\%$ (upper line) and $u_2 = 60\%$ (bottom line).

Figure 10. Dynamic response obtained from *experiment I*.

- *Experiment II.* Experimental results corresponding to *simulation II* are presented in Figure 11. Here, the experimental numerical values measured in steady-state are $(\bar{i}_{1m}, \bar{v}_{1m}, \bar{i}_{2m}, \bar{v}_{2m}) = (1.35\text{ A}, 25.63\text{ V}, 500\text{ mA}, 58.5\text{ V})$.

5.2. Discussion

The visualization of the converter dynamic response was accomplished via Matlab/Simulink and a DS1104 electronic board, along with current and voltage probes. The experimental results herein obtained are similar to the ones that can be obtained through the use of an oscilloscope. Although the process employed for the acquisition of the signals seems more

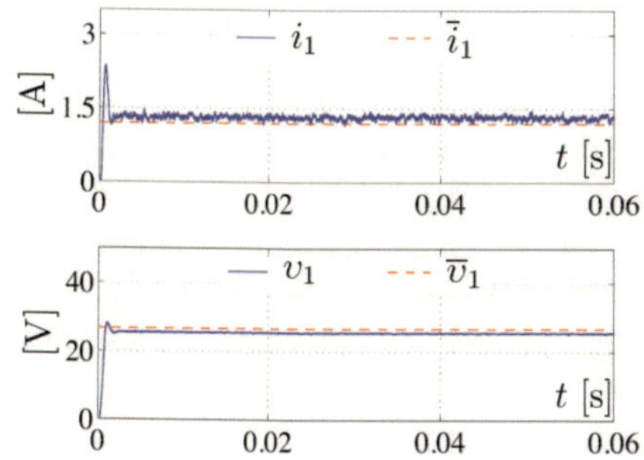

(a) Current through the inductor L_1 and voltage at capacitor C_1.

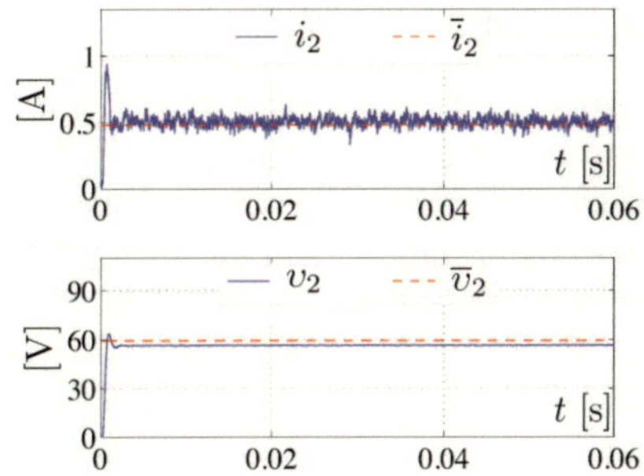

(b) Current through the inductor L_2 and voltage at capacitor C_2.

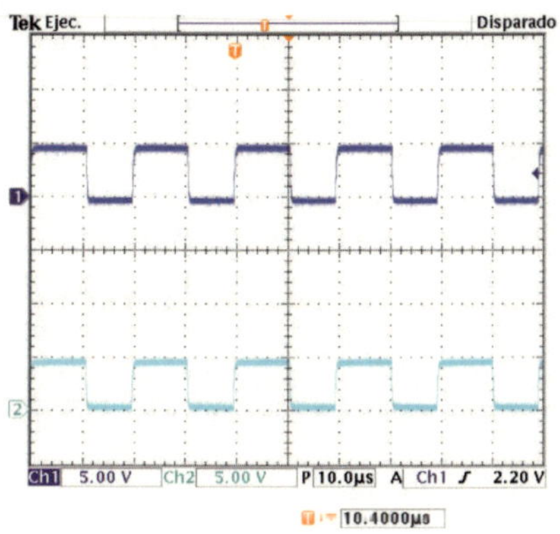

(c) Inputs $u_1 = 55\%$ (upper line) and $u_2 = 55\%$ (bottom line).

Figure 11. Dynamic response obtained from *experiment II*.

complex, the tools herein used could help in the speedy implementation of controllers in real time, in future research works, as Matlab/Simulink provides a GUI for their fast building.

Differences between simulations and experiments in the dynamic responses presented in Figures 6 and 10, on the one hand, and Figures 7 and 11, on the other, are due to the fact that the energy losses are not considered in simulations. This means that the inductors internal resistance is considered to be zero, and the semiconductor devices are assumed to be infinitely fast. Moreover, it has been shown [36] for the DC/DC Boost converter, that oscillations decrease considerably when the simulation model takes into account that the converter components are non-ideal, that is, using the Shockley diode model [37] and the Ebers-Moll transistor model [38], and taking into account the inductors internal resistance. However, it is a challenge to find a fair trade-off between complexity and accuracy; this is because to obtain better accuracy it is necessary to develop a more complex converter model. The advantage of the model used in the simulations presented in this work is simplicity and, at the same time, relatively good accuracy, which is enough for educational proposes.

6. Conclusions

In this work, a DC/DC Boost-Boost power converter was presented as a didactic material, which can be used to verify, experimentally, some theoretical concepts about electric circuit analysis studied in undergraduate courses. This work is intended to teach students how to model a practical circuit, how to design and construct, step-by-step, an experimental setup, and how use it in order to verify, experimentally, some features predicted by the model. Also, we have performed some experimental tests whose results are in accordance with predictions of the converter dynamic model. Furthermore, an additional advantage of the experimental setup is that only low-cost electronic components are employed.

Regarding the measurement and visualization of the variables involved in the converter, Matlab/Simulink, a DS1104 board, and current and voltage probes were used. These tools were employed as together they allow the system variables to be obtained easily and quickly. Moreover, Matlab/Simulink provides a graphical environment that facilitated the analysis, design and construction of the converter under study.

In future works, the Boost-Boost converter model representation based on state-space, as the one herein presented, and the acquired data in real time can be used to develop, step-by-step, different control laws. Such a procedure will be presented from design to experimental implementation, in order to accomplish the tasks of regulation and trajectory tracking associated with the converter output voltage. These tasks will be intended to teach different modern control techniques, which are generally taught at theoretical level, in the areas of electronics, electrical, automatic control, bionics, robotics, mechatronics, and so on.

Acknowledgments

R. Silva-Ortigoza and M. Marcelino-Aranda acknowledge the financial support from Secretaría de Investigación y Posgrado del Instituto Politécnico Nacional (SIP–IPN), SNI–Mexico, and the programs EDI and COFAA of IPN. The work of M. Antonio-Cruz and C. A. Merlo-Zapata was supported by CONACYT and BEIFI scholarships. Finally, G. Saldaña-González acknowledges to the Fondo Mixto CONACYT, since the publication of this work was partially supported with resources from the Fondo Mixto de Fomento a la Investigación Científica y Tecnológica CONACYT-Gobierno del Estado de Puebla.

Author details

R. Silva-Ortigoza[1], M. Antonio-Cruz[1], M. Marcelino-Aranda[2], G. Saldaña-González[3], C. A. Merlo-Zapata[1] and P. Pérez-Romero[1]

1 Instituto Politécnico Nacional. CIDETEC, Área de Mecatrónica. Unidad Profesional Adolfo López Mateos, 07700 México, DF, Mexico

2 Instituto Politécnico Nacional. UPIICSA, Sección de Estudios de Posgrado e Investigación. México, DF, Mexico

3 Universidad Tecnológica de Puebla, División de Mecatrónica, Puebla, PUE, Mexico

References

[1] Journal Citation Reports. JCR. http://www.webofknowledge.com/(accessed 15 October 2013).

[2] International Journal of Electrical Engineering Education. IJEEE. http://www.manchesteruniversitypress.co.uk/cgi-bin/scribe?showinfo=ip023 (accessed 15 October 2013).

[3] International Journal of Engineering Education. IJEE. http://www.ijee.ie/ (accessed 15 October 2013).

[4] IEEE Transactions on Education. http://ieeexplore.ieee.org/xpl/RecentIssue.jsp?punumber=13 (accessed 15 October 2013).

[5] Computer Applications in Engineering Education. http://onlinelibrary.wiley.com/journal/10.1002/(ISSN)1099-0542 (accessed 15 October 2013).

[6] IEEE Transactions on Learning Technologies. http://ieeexplore.ieee.org/xpl/RecentIssue.jsp?punumber=4620076 (accessed 15 October 2013).

[7] European Journal of Physics. EJP. http://iopscience.iop.org/0143-0807 (accessed 15 October 2013).

[8] American Journal of Physics. AJP. http://ajp.aapt.org/ (accessed 15 October 2013).

[9] Rashid MH., editor. Power Electronics Handbook. Burlington: Butterworth-Heinemann; 2011.

[10] Mohan N., Undeland TM., Robbins WP. Power Electronics: Converters, Applications, and Design. New York: Wiley; 2003.

[11] Sira-Ramírez H., Silva-Ortigoza R. Control Design Techniques in Power Electronics Devices. London: Springer; 2006.

[12] Bingöl O., Paçaci S. A virtual laboratory for neural network controlled DC motors based on a DC-DC buck converter. International Journal of Engineering Education 2012;28(3) 713-723.

[13] Silva-Ortigoza R., García-Sánchez JR., Alba-Martínez JM., Hernández-Guzmán VM., Marcelino-Aranda M., Taud H., Bautista-Quintero R. Two-Stage control design of a Buck converter/DC motor system without velocity measurements via a $\Sigma - \Delta$ modulator. Mathematical Problems in Engineering 2013; 1-11. http://dx.doi.org/10.1155/2013/929316 (accessed 20 January 2014).

[14] Sandoval-Ibarra F., Mercado-Moreno JR., Urióstegui-Vázquez LH. Basic circuits to design switched-based DC-DC converters. Revista Mexicana de Física 2007;53(2) 128-133.

[15] Sandoval-Ibarra F., Mercado-Moreno JR., López A., Martínez-Rivera R., Alba-García T. Analyzing switched circuits to design DC-DC and DC-AC converters. Revista Mexicana de Física 2007;53(1) 1-4.

[16] Dudrik J., Bauer P. New methods in teaching of power electronics converters and devices. International Journal of Engineering Education 2008;24(5) 1040-1048.

[17] Peyović P. A new approach to the discontinuous conduction mode in switching power converters. International Journal of Electrical Engineering Education 2010;47(2) 168-176.

[18] Campos-Delgado DU., Espinoza-Trejo DR. Educational experiments in power electronics and control theory: d.c. switched power supplies. International Journal of Electrical Engineering Education 2010;47(4) 430-447.

[19] Altintas A. A GUI-based education toolbox for power electronics converters using MATLAB/Simulink and SimPowerSystems. International Journal of Electrical Engineering Education 2011;48(1) 53-65.

[20] Abramovitz A. An approach to average modeling and simulation of switch-mode systems. IEEE Transactions on Education 2011;54(3) 509-517.

[21] Deblecker O. High-resolution DPWM using sigma-delta modulator implemented on a low-cost Buck development board. International Journal of Electrical Engineering Education 2011;48(4) 391-404.

[22] Zumel P., Fernández C., Sanz M., Lázaro A., Barrado A. Step-by-step design of an FPGA-based digital compensator for DC/DC converters oriented to an introductory course. IEEE Transactions on Education 2011;54(4) 599-609.

[23] Liao WH., Wang SC., Liu YH. Generalized simulation model for a switched-mode power supply design course using Matlab/Simulink. IEEE Transactions on Education 2012;55(1) 36-47.

[24] Lamar DG., Miaja PF., Arias M., Rodríguez A., Rodríguez M., Vázquez A., Hernando MM., Sebastián J. Experiences in the application of project-based learning in a switching-mode power supplies course. IEEE Transactions on Education 2012;55(1) 69-77.

[25] Silva-Ortigoza R., Silva-Ortigoza G., Hernández-Guzmán VM., Saldaña-González G., Marcelino-Aranda M., Marciano-Melchor M. Modelling, simulation and construction of a dc/dc boost power converter: a school experimental system. European Journal of Physics 2012;33(3) 647-655.

[26] Choi S., Saeedifard M. An educational laboratory for digital control and rapid prototyping of power electronic circuits. IEEE Transactions on Education 2012;55(2) 263-270.

[27] Middlebrook RD., Ćuk S. A general unified approach to modeling switching-converter power stages. International Journal of Electronics 1977;42(6) 521-550.

[28] Severns RP., Bloom GE. Modern dc-to-dc Switchmode Power Converter Circuits. New York: Van Nostrand-Reinhold; 1985.

[29] Batarseh I. Power Electronics Circuits. New York: Wiley; 2004.

[30] Ortega R., Loría A., Nicklasson PJ., Sira-Ramírez H. Passivity-based Control of Euler-Lagrange Systems. London: Springer-Verlag; 1998.

[31] Hernández-Guzmán VM., Silva-Ortigoza R., Carrillo-Serrano RV. Control Automático: Teoría de Diseño, Construcción de Prototipos, Modelado, Identificación y Pruebas Experimentales. México D.F.: Colección CIDETEC–IPN; 2013. http://controlautomatico.com.mx (accessed 20 January 2014).

[32] MathWorks. http://www.mathworks.com/support/books/ (accessed 14 January 2014).

[33] DS1104R&D Controller Board.
http://www.dspace.com/en/pub/home/products/hw/singbord/ds1104.cfm
(accessed 14 January 2014).

[34] Karris ST. Introduction to Simulink® with Engineering Applications. Fremont: Orchard Pubications; 2011.

[35] Cortés-Rodríguez DJ. Generación de voltajes de CA mediante convertidores de alta frecuencia de conmutación. PhD Thesis. CICESE; 2004.

[36] Spinetti-Rivera M. Síntesis de controladores para convertidores de potencia utilizando realimentación de la salida pasiva de la dinámica exacta del error de seguimiento: teoría y práctica. PhD thesis. Universidad Politécnica de Cataluña; 2010.

[37] Shockley W. The theory of p-n junctions in semiconductors and p-n junction transistors. Bell System Technical Journal 1949; 28(3) 435-489.

[38] Ebers JJ., Moll JL. Large-signal behavior of junction transistors. Institute of Radio Engineers 1954;42(12) 1761-1772.

Using Matlab and Simulink for High – Level Modeling in Biosystems

Cristina-Maria Dabu

Additional information is available at the end of the chapter

http://dx.doi.org/10.5772/58369

1. Introduction

The advances in biology, bioinformatics, programming technologies and computer systems made possible to store and analyze large amount of biological data with the possibility of global exploration and visualization of this data with sequence browsers (the possibility to select features for genomic and proteomic data, the possibility to identifying the transcription factors; to analyze RNA-Sequences data in order to identify specific expressed genes and common bioinformatics workflows, identify copy number variants and SNPs in microarray data). All these advances in bioinformatics are opening the possibility to elaborate different categories of models, with applicability both in deeper understanding of biological phenomena (analyzing, interpreting, and even predicting the genotype–phenotype relationship), and in the practical application of research results.

Beyond the storage and retrieval of biological data, it is important to study and understand the biochemical processes underlying the existence of living organisms, studies that are extremely difficult to achieve due to the high cost of experiments and uniqueness of the phenomena that characterize living organisms.

Living systems are characterized through thousands of simultaneous crossover high integrated threads of information computation, biochemical reactions and mass transfer processes (metabolic networks, gene regulatory networks, signaling pathways).

High-Level modeling of biological systems allows a better understanding of informational workflows, a deeper understanding of control and regulatory mechanisms generated by the biochemical processes involved in the metabolic and signaling pathways of living systems.

MATLAB® and SIMULINK® are perfect tools for describing and modeling existing control processes within biosystems. Therefore, unlike software systems made using programming

INTECH
open science | open minds

© 2014 The Author(s). Licensee InTech. This chapter is distributed under the terms of the Creative Commons Attribution License (http://creativecommons.org/licenses/by/3.0), which permits unrestricted use, distribution, and reproduction in any medium, provided the original work is properly cited.

languages such as Python, Pearl, or SBLM that are targeted more on pattern matching in the large databases containing genomic information and static representation of the components of a signaling pathway, identify transcription factors and proteins implied in signaling pathways MATLAB® and SIMULINK® offer the possibility to study the dynamic behavior of regulatory mechanisms involved in signaling pathways of living systems through computer simulation.

2. High – Level modeling in biosystems

High level modeling in biology is more complex as modeling in other fields of science and technology.

First reason of that complexity is the indeterminacy and uniqueness of biological systems. Another reason, a specificity of biological systems, is the high level of integration for the biochemical processes and signaling pathways.

Signaling pathways are not operating in isolation. The main characteristic of cellular control mechanisms, that make more difficult high - level modeling in biosystems is the extensive cross-talk between signalling pathways. These highly integrated signaling mechanisms act through different effectors (e.g. muscle proteins, secretory vesicles, transcription factors, ion channels and metabolic pathways) in order to control the activity of cellular processes such as development, proliferation, neural signaling, stress responses and apoptosis [1].

Another particularity of biological systems, difficult to quantify and to represent in modeling metabolic and signaling pathways is that one and the same signaling pathway may control different processes in young cells and mature cells (for example the extracellular signal-regulated kinase 1 and 2 (ERK1 and 2) cascade regulates a number of processes in different cellular evolution stages: proliferation, differentiation, survival, migration, stress responses and apoptosis) [2].

3. Control systems theory and high level modeling in biosystems

There are a multitude of worldwide databases that store information about signaling pathways and factors involved in biochemical processes, but the results of research in this field highlights that mechanisms underlying the bioprocesses are not still fully elucidated.

Control systems theory may provide an engineering approach of bioprocess that characterizes the living systems.

Control systems theory applied in systems biology made possible the study of the dynamic behavior of biological systems pathways (metabolic pathways, cell signaling pathways) and informational workflows defined by biochemical reactions.

http://dx.doi.org/10.5772/58369

Depending on how there are expressed the evolution laws describing the biological system, and the applied methodolgy, there are many types of models used for modeling biological systems:

- Differential models
- Models defined by autonomous differential equations
- Models defined by differential equations with restrictions
- Models defined by differential equations with delay (dead time)
- Integrodiferenţiale models that include the effects of delay
- Models defined by partial differential equations
- Mixed models containing all of the above equations
- Formalism point transformations
- Models using automata theory
- Models described by universal modeling language (Matlab, Simulink)
- Models described by bioinformatics specific modeling languages [3]

On the other hand, in order to be a valid model one must fulfill the following requirements

1. The biological behavior of the modeled system must be in deep understood, based on observations and experimental data.
2. Deep knowledge of the properties of various equations that constitute the model.
3. The problem must be formulated correctly in Hadamarad sense, ie to verify the following restrictions:
   - The solution should exist
   - The solution should be unique
   - The solution should be continuous with respect to restrictions boundary conditions or in relation to initial conditions

Developing systemic models in the case of bioprocesses shows some particularities compared to other areas of science and technology. Building models in classical branches of science and technology starts from basic concepts, definitions and laws. For example, in physico-chemical sciences, for modeling chemical reactions one starts with basic concepts such as chemical potential, fundamental rate equations such as the diffusion equation, and the basics of electrochemistry such as the Nernst equations. These equations are based on fundamental physical theories and concepts, and contain a defined number of parameters, most of which can be individually measured.

In biosciences, there are no very stringent concepts, definitions and laws due to the indeterminacy, uniqueness, complexity and specificity that characterize biological processes. As a result, the parameters or factors which are involved in signaling pathways are difficult to be measured due to the fact that experiments on living systems are expensive and they cannot be reproduced by an infinite number of times, as it is possible in other areas of science (physics, mechanics, chemistry, etc.).

On the other hand, biological systems are characterized by uniqueness, that means in identical experimental conditions, two experiments is not absolutely identical due to different behaviors of living systems.

Another aspect that makes difficult to develop high - level models for biosystems is the high degree of undetermination of living systems and that the biological mechanisms underlying the processes of regulating and control are not yet fully elucidated.

In biosciences, the computer assisted models for the complex living organisms must have information both on the properties of each component in the system as well as on their interconnectivity and interdependency.

The results of research in the life sciences field, demonstrates that, in spite of impressive bioinformatic databases, all of the information needed to build a computer model of a whole cell at subcellular detailed level of description is not available yet. Moreover, the introduction of the whole information characterizing a cell in a model, in order to get a model that integrates all the cellular mechanisms requires a computational effort impossible to achieve and to manage at this moment.

4. Signaling pathways in biosystems

Biological systems are complex systems with hierarchical structure, characterized by a high degree of robustness. The stability and adaptability of living systems to environmental changes is provided by control mechanisms, feedback loops, coordinated by complex genetic programs.

The genetic programs and algorithms that control entire cell evolution and activity are expressed through the metabolic and signaling pathways. The metabolic and signaling pathways are determining all cell processes: cell profilation, cell differentiation into specific cell types, cell functions and cell apoptosis [1].

The inter- and intra-cellular signaling mechanism, through biochemical signals (biochemical components), represent the most common signaling method in living systems.

The biochemical signal released by a cell is captured by the membrane receptors from the target cell and converted into specific second messengers. The second messengers are triggering specific processes at nucleus level, cytoplasma level and endoplasmaticum reticullum level for DNA transcription and specific protein synthesis.

Proteins are macromolecular organic substances with an essential role both in the cell and the entire body. In the cell, proteins are classified as:

http://dx.doi.org/10.5772/58369

- Structural proteins - involved in setting up structures resistant cells
- Functional proteins - are divided into:
  - permanent functional protein
  - temporary functional protein

Permanent functional proteins are fulfilling different roles inside the cell in which they were synthesized: for example proteins-enzymes with biocatalytic role, nucleoprotein, located in genome constitution and involved in the synthesis and cellular functions, and the transmission of hereditary characters [3].

Temporary functional proteins are present for a limited time interval in the cell in which they were synthesized. Temporary functional proteins are eliminated in the extracellular environment and they are treveling through the body, and fulfilling their function in the target organs or cellular structures. In this category of proteins are hormones, which can be classified into:

- Classical hormones: pituitary hormones, thyroid, etc, produced by certain specialized bodies and which, circulating through the body are acting at great distances.
- Neurotransmitters: acetylcholine, norepinephrine, dopamine, and so on, are released at the synapses and provide local nerve transmission.
- Local Hormones: histamine, plasmakinine, etc, released by cells of various tissues, ensure tissue homeostasis and organ.

Intensive research have shown that certain substances, being considered for long time as only local hormones also play the role of neurotransmitters with important implications on the evolution of the human body. In this category enter, for example, serotonin and histamine [3]. It was also shown that a number of classic hormones, such as insulin and adrenaline fulfill specialized roles as synaptic neurotransmitters and found that in many synapses, nerve crossing, are released simultaneously two or more active substances some fulfilling, besides local neurotransmitter function, and other roles in the body. Also, research in the field have revealed the existence of a genuine diffuse endocrine system, consisting of nerve cells scattered throughout the body and able to secrete a variety of substances, involved in work many tissues and organs (central and peripheral nervous system, digestive system, etc.).

Once these biochemical signals reach their targets they use a various number of cell signaling pathways to control the cellular activity (fig.1)

Some biochemical components of signaling pathways are packaged into vesicles where they are stored before being released by exocytosis (hormones with role in neuronal transmission). These stimuli then have different modes of action (juxtacrine, autocrine, paracrine and endocrine), which may be defined based on the distance they travel in order to reach their cellular receptor targets.

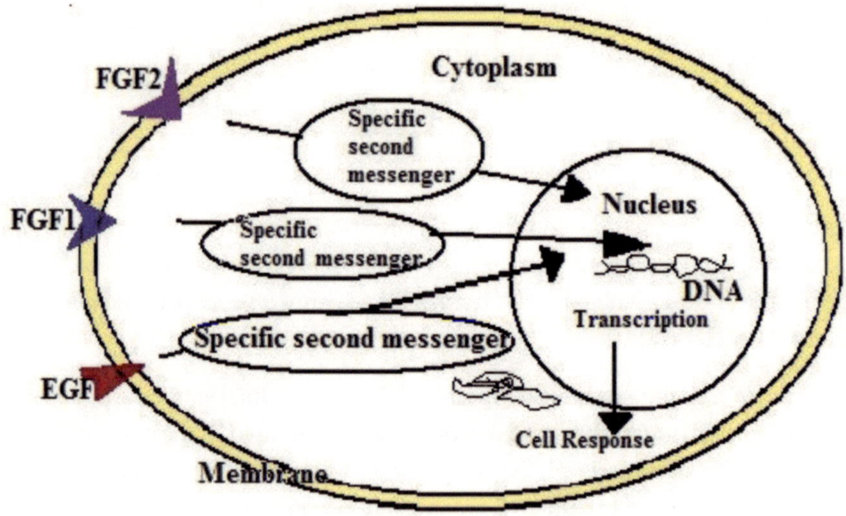

Figure 1. Cell processes

Taking into account the biological processes presented above, one may consider the Systemic approach for cell processes (fig 2)

The information transfer mechanisms implied in cell signaling pathways differ according to physiological function and messenger biochemical structure. Experimental studies have highlighted the following mechanisms for inter- and intra-cellular information transfer: diffusion, direct protein-protein interactions, covalent modifications (protein phosphorylation, acetylation, nitrosylation) [1].

Experimental studies revealed also that each cell type has a unique repertoire of cell signaling components, signalsome, determined by the cell phenotype, expressed during the final stages of cell development, in order to control cell particular physiology. The signalsomes are characterized by a high degree of plasticity being constantly remodeled in order to adjust cell responses to environmental changes. The signalsomes high degree of plasticity provides robust regulatory mechanisms of the cell and for the entire organism to the environment. On other hand, abnormal remodeling of cellular signalsomes creates signaling defects that have great significance for the onset of many diseases [1].

More, linear signaling cascades are involving progressive signal amplification initiated by ligands and governed by phosphorylation, proteins associated with other pathways and an array of modifications fine tune the signal. Cells are using also scaffolding proteins, phosphatases, and second messengers to refine complex signaling programs connecting extracellular stimuli to intracellular responses [2].

A way to describe this diversity is to consider the nature of the stimuli that feed into different cell signaling pathways. Some signaling mechanisms are used by many different signaling pathways, whereas other pathways respond to a specific set of stimuli [2].

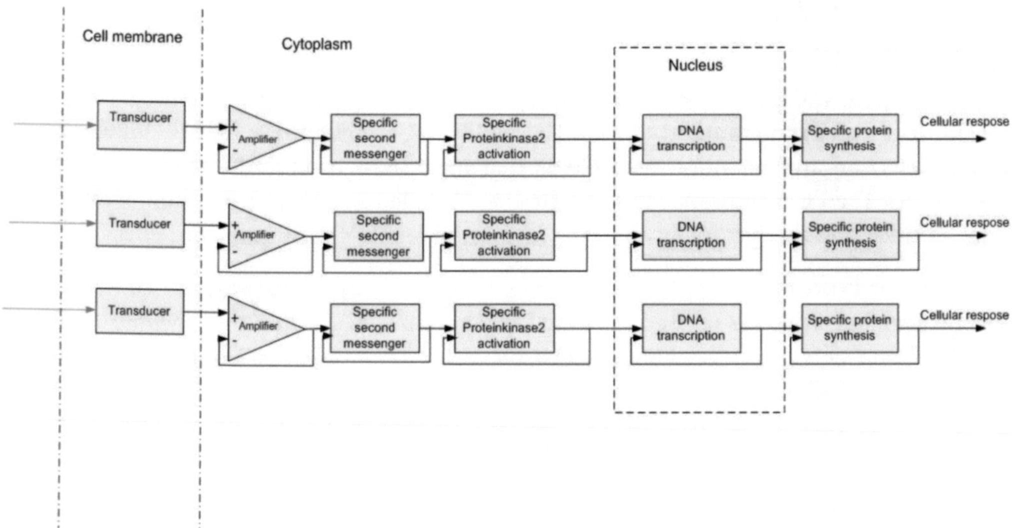

Figure 2. Cell processes-Block diagram

5. Signaling pathways and cellular regulating mechanisms

We have mentioned above that the cell is characterized by a multitude of control mechanisms. Signaling pathways does not operate in isolation, and a key element of cellular control mechanisms is the extensive cross-talk between signaling pathways.

The role of control mechanisms is to maintain the cell inside the normal operating parameters. In the following we will present some of them:

5.1. The (ERQC) control mechanism

How it was mentioned above, abnormal remodeling of cellular signalsomes creates signaling defects that have great significance for the onset of many diseases. The Endoplasmic Reticulum–mediated Quality Control (ERQC) control mechanism is a protein quality control mechanism, integrated with an adaptive stress response. The role of the ERQC control mechanism is to assure that the cell synthetized proteins have the correct three-dimensional structure, essential for normal function of the cell [4]. In essence, cellular response and cellular activity lies in synthesis of a specific protein required to fulfill various physiological functions of the cell.

Biochemical structure and spatial geometry of the protein components are those that cause active or inactive state of the protein, and the impact that will have on other protein-specific mechanisms of cellular metabolism. Sometimes, during to the synthesis process, some parts of functional proteins may remain unfolded or may be misfolded. Scientific studies reveals that failures to fold into native structure generally produces inactive proteins, or, in some instances, may generate modified or toxic functionality.

The ERQC pathway is characterzed by a number of factors located into the endoplasmaticum reticulum lumen membrane and cytosol. The role of ERQC factors located in ER lumen consist in the detection and retention of proteins that have been produced by cell with folding aberrations. The ER membrane located factors are implied in retrotranslocation of misfolded polypeptides, and the cytosol located enzymes degrade retrotranslocated proteins.

The integrated stress response (termed ER stress or unfolded protein response, UPR) contains several signaling branches elicited from the ER membrane, which fine-tune the rate of protein synthesis and entry into the ER to match the ER folding capacity ER-associated protein degradation (ERAD)

Elimination of misfolded proteins from the ER by the ERQC program counteracts the production of aberrant proteins from various folding mishaps. Misfolded proteins are exported from the ER and subsequently destroyed by the ubiquitin-proteasome system in the cytosol by a process called retrotranslocation or ER-associated protein degradation (ERAD) [5]. In Fig 3. is presented the ERQC pathway systemic model.

5.2. Cellular mechanisms for protein degradation

Protein synthesis processes are subject of interference from both intracellular and extracellular environment. The effects of intracellular and extracellular disturbances are materialized in aberrations of structure and folding of proteins

There are two mechanisms used to eliminate nonfunctional proteins or proteins with aberrations of the structure, as well as other subcellular components: the proteosome degradation and the autophagy.

5.2.1. Proteasomal degradation

The 26S proteasome is the major degradation machinery in the cell for dysfunctional or damaged proteins [5].

Proteasomal degradation also regulates a variety of cellular process such as cell cycle progression. The proteasome is a large multi-subunit enzyme that is comprised of two sub-complexes, the 19S regulatory complex and the 20S proteolytic complex [5].

5.2.2. Autophagy

Autophagy is a lysosomal degradation pathway that degrades damaged or superfluous cell components into basic biomolecules, which are then recycled back into the cytosol. In this respect, autophagy drives a flow of biomolecules in a continuous degradation-regeneration cycle. Autophagy is a non-selective, bulk degradation pathway and it is generally considered a pro-survival mechanism protecting cells under stress or poor nutrient conditions. Current research clearly shows that autophagy fulfills numerous functions in vital biological processes.

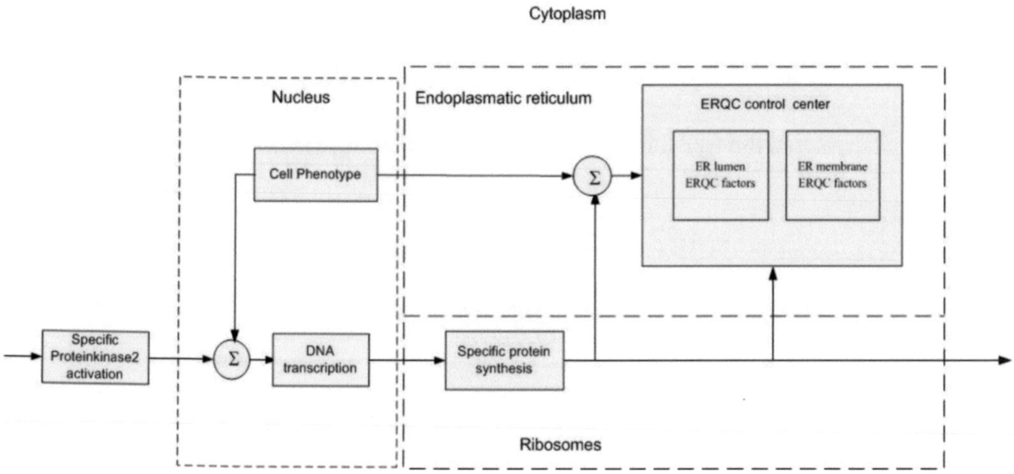

Figure 3. ERQC pathway systemic model

It is implicated in development, differentiation, innate and adaptive immunity, ageing and cell death [5].

Research in the field have identified Three types of autophagy mechanisms have been in mammalian cells:

- chaperone-mediated autophagy,
- microautophagy and
- macroautophagy [6]

They were identified the main mechanisms involved in autophagy:

- mitophagy,
- pexophagy,
- reticulophagy,
- nucleophagy,
- lipophagy
- xenophagy,

but the mechanisms through which the autophagic machinery regulates these diverse processes are not entirely understood [6].

If it is noted with $Z_i^{'}$, each individual perturbation wich act on an signalling pathway, where i=1-n, their cumulative effect will be

$$Z(s) = \sum_{i=1}^{n} Z_i^{'}(s) H_{D_{Z_i}}(s) \tag{1}$$

where $H_{D_{Z_i}}$ represents the transfer function of each perturbing factor

$$Y(s) = Z(s) + \left[I(s) - Y(s) \right] H_C(s) H_{SP}(s) \tag{2}$$

where $I(s)$ represents the input biochemical signal.

$$Y(s) = \frac{1}{1 + H_C(s) H_{SP}(s)} Z(s) + \frac{H_C(s) H_{SP}(s)}{1 + H_C(s) H_{SP}(s)} I(s) \tag{3}$$

The perturbation transfer function will be

$$H_Z(s) = \frac{Y(s)}{Z(s)} = \frac{1}{1 + H_C(s) H_{SP}(s)} \tag{4}$$

6. Actual state of the art in high level modeling of biosystems

Presently there are available a variety of software systems for high level modeling of biosystems, developed in miscellaneous programming languages: Python, Mathematica, Pearl, SBML (Systems Biology Markup Language), Matlab®. The vast majority of these systems are oriented towards pattern recognition processes of large volumes of data in in the field of and proteoemic genomic the identification transcription factors, RNA sequence analysis, modeling biochemical factors involved in the generation and transmission of information in case of signaling pathways, such as and other similar activities that can be divided into static modeling bioprocesses.

Mathematica (Wolfram Mathematica) [7] is a dedicated software system; a multi-paradigm programming language; with a huge built-in library of both general-purpose and highly specialized functions. Programming in Mathematica consist in finding the right combination of primitives. It works with Element Data, Chemical Data, Particle Data, Genetic Data and Protein Data [8]. In contrast to Matlab, Mathematica does not offer similar features to the other module in Matlab Simulink module.

Python is a programming language interpreter based [9], with a good numerical support, provided by Numerical Python (numpy) package, which also provides the possibility to define specific bioinformatics functions for tasks as data management, file parsing, string processing, and interaction with databases. Models designed in Python find their applicability in pattern

http://dx.doi.org/10.5772/58369

matching or pattern identification in genomic and proteomic data. Python makes a distinction between *matching* and *searching*, which other languages do not. Matching looks only at the *start* of the target string, whereas searching looks for the pattern *anywhere* in the target [10].

6.1. Using MATLAB®and Simulink® for high – Level modeling in biosystems

In contrast to the biosystems models developed using programming languages such as Python, Pearl, or SBML that are targeted more on pattern matching in the large databases containing genomic information and static representation of the components of a signaling pathway, identification of transcription factors and proteins involved in signaling pathways, MATLAB® and SIMULINK® provide the possibility to study the dynamic behavior of the regulatory mechanisms involved in signaling pathways of living systems through computer simulation.

During the last decade the use of MATLAB® has increased consistently in scientific and academic institutions as well as in several branches of industry that deal with topics ranging from economics to spacecraft orbit simulations and bioinformatics.

The MATLAB® and SIMULINK® software package and the additional specific toolboxes have been proven to be very efficient and robust for numerical data analysis, modeling, programming, simulation and computer graphic visualization.

The main features of MATLAB® and SIMULINK® are:

- High-level language for technical computing
- Aditional toolboxes, dedicated to solve particular classes of problems
- The possibility integrate the MATLAB® code with other languages and applications (C, C++, Java)
- A wide range of integrated mathematical and statistical functions.
- The possibility of automated generating code from SIMULINK® models to MATLAB® code files
- User-friendly interfaces

Due to the extended capabilities of Simulink module in the analysis and modeling of automatic control systems, MATLAB® became the standard in the area of simulation and modeling and it is used by the researchers and students at universities mainly in the areas of Control Engineering, Power Plant Systems, Aerospace, Bioinformatics, Economics and Statistics. Its open architecture enables sharing all source code among the user community and several different areas are solved and the solution appears usually as a new toolbox.

SIMULINK® is the important MATLAB® enlargement which simplifies very much the computation and model building process. SIMULINK® is a modeling environment in which systems are represented as block diagrams, which are most often a convenient way to show process actions and interactions. SIMULINK® provides a set of predefined blocks that can combined in order to create a detailed block diagram of the studied biological process/system/ sub-system. The dynamic model for a biological system may be created dragging and dropping the blocks from the block libraries to the new window and connect them and run the model. In order to implement complex mathematical functions or algorithms for describing the dynamic behavior of the modeled biological system, SIMULINK® can interface with C, Fortran, and MATLAB® m-file scripts, Java™ applications, deploy the developed algorithms and custom interfaces as standalone applications, convert MATLAB® algorithms into Microsoft®.NET or COM components that can be accessed from any COM-based application, and create Microsoft Excel® add-ins [11].

The computation underlying Simulink models is handled by the set of solvers included in the MATLAB® package. The "From Workspace" block can be used to input MATLAB® data to a SIMULINK® model.

Main Features of the Bioinformatics Toolbox:

- Next Generation Sequencing analysis and browser Sequence analysis and visualization, including pairwise and multiple sequence alignment and peak detection
- Microarray data analysis, including reading, filtering, normalizing, and visualization
- Mass spectrometry analysis, including preprocessing, classification, and marker identification
- Phylogenetic tree analysis
- Graph theory functions, including interaction maps, hierarchy plots, and pathways
- Data import from genomic, proteomic, and gene expression files, including SAM, FASTA, CEL, and CDF, and from databases such as NCBI and GenBank [12]

Matlab Bioinformatics Toolbox ™ library of functions and algorithms dedicated to the analysis and processing of data in the bioinformatics provides algorithms and specific applications for analizing and explore and visualize this data with sequence browsers, analyze whole genomes while performing calculations at a base pair level of resolution, spatial heatmaps, and clustergrams, imputing values for missing data, selecting features for genomic and proteomic data, identify transcription factors; analyze RNA-Seq data to identify differentially expressed genes; common bioinformatics workflows, identify copy number variants and SNPs in microarray data; use several methods for normalizing microarray data, including lowess, global mean, median absolute deviation (MAD), and quantile normalization and classify protein profiles using mass spectrometry. [11]

The toolbox provides also the possibility to manipulate and analyze DNA or RNA sequences. One may be converted DNA or RNA sequences to amino acid sequences using the genetic code, Perform statistical analysis on the sequences and search for specific patterns within a sequence. The toolbox provides also protein sequence analysis techniques, including routines for calculating properties of a peptide sequence such as atomic composition, isoelectric point, and molecular weight. It can be determined the amino acid composition of protein sequences, cleave a protein with an enzyme, and create backbone plots and Ramachandran plots of PDB data.

http://dx.doi.org/10.5772/58369

7. Using MATLAB® and SIMULINK® for modeling the dynamical behavior of signaling pathways

In contrast with other systems dedicated for analysis, data processing and modeling in the field of bioinformatics, MATLAB® and SIMULINK® offers not only the possibility of genome-wide data analysis, protein databases, protein pattern recognition, identification and classification of genes and DNA sequences, highlighting signaling pathways and factors involved, but also offers the possibility of analyzing inter- and intra– cellular processes from the of engineering systems theory and automatic regulation points of view. MATLAB® and SIMULINK® enable researchers understanding the dynamic behavior of the signaling pathways in specific regulatory mechanisms bioprocesses.

Because biological systems are highly complex structures and the mechanisms that control signaling pathways are not very well known, the multilevel hierarchical models built using MATLAB® and SIMULINK® can be developed in order to describe only certain categories of functions or biological processes, as well as on the whole system or subsystem, using the black box model for the processes or sub-processes there are not very well known.

Considering the above issues, it is imperative in the model design for the biological system, to make the block diagrams resemble the logical flow of information through the biological system.

Additionally, biological systems are characterized by extremely rapid adjustment and response mechanisms to disturbing factors from the environment, and from this point of view, SIMULINK® offers enhanced capabilities to capture time-based events with high fidelity, essential for the study of processes ensuring the stability and adaptability over time of biological systems

The overall goal in designing a high level model for biosystems is to use the principle of feedback loops to adjust the controlled variable to follow a desired command variable accurately regardless of the command variables path and to minimize the effect of any external disturbances or changes in the dynamics of the system. The standard structure of is a relatively complex task if one must meet the basic requirements listed below:

- The minimum requirement is that the closed loop is stable.
- The disturbances should be rejected or they must have a small influence on the controlled variable
- The controlled variable should track the command input as precisely and as fast as possible.
- The closed loop should be as insensitive as possible with respect to changes in the plant parameters.

Based on the model system shown in Figure 1, using MATLAB® and SIMULINK® to build the next model for studying intracellular processes regulating the dynamic behavior.

In the model there are detailed the membrane receptors and it highlights how specific biochemical binding of a compound to the membrane receptor generates dynamic response of intracellular effectors and regulatory mechanisms.

Delay elements are corresponding to bioprocesses occurring in the membrane when the biochemical signaling structure (biochemical factor) is binding on the specific receptor (specific factor receptor) existing in the target cell membrane.

Feedback control loops correspond to recognition processes of aberrant protein structures and folding aberrations and their destruction processes in the mitochondria.

The results of different parameters simulations are presented in figures 5 a,b,c,d.

In simulations where used Runge Kutta 5th order method (fig 5 a,c) and Runge Kutta 3th order method (fig 5 b,d).

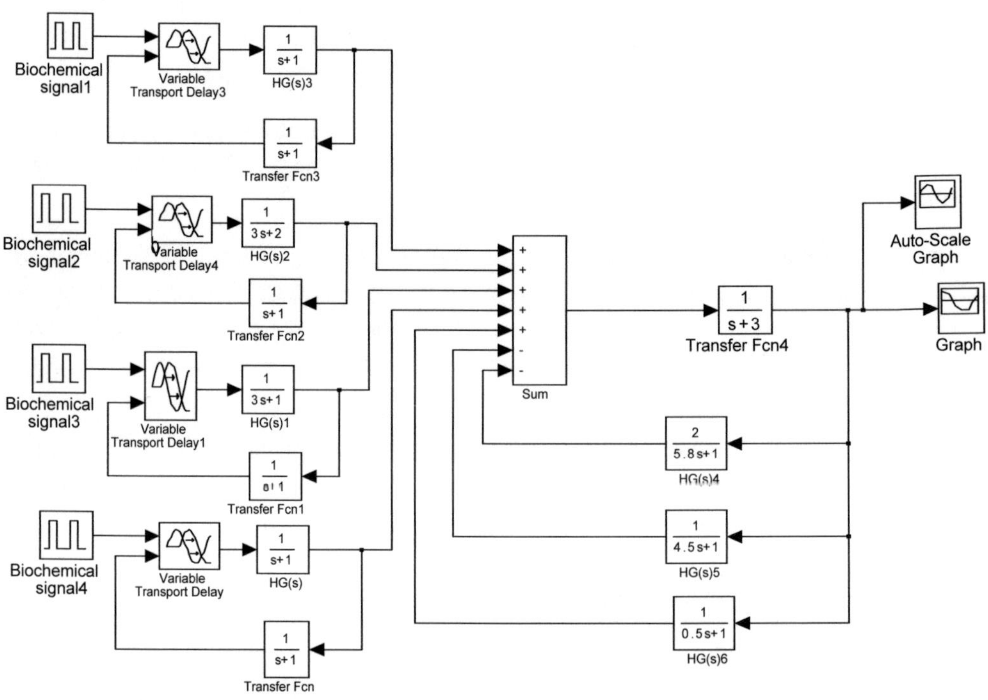

Figure 4. Simulink model for membrane receptors signalling pathways

Adjusting the transfer functions patameters, entire dynamic behavior of the model may be adjusted.

From the point of view of the dynamic behavior of the model, the simulation results revealed that after overcoming the transitional regime, the model shows a stable behavior, similary to the living systems behavior observed from experimental data (pSOS, pJAK2).

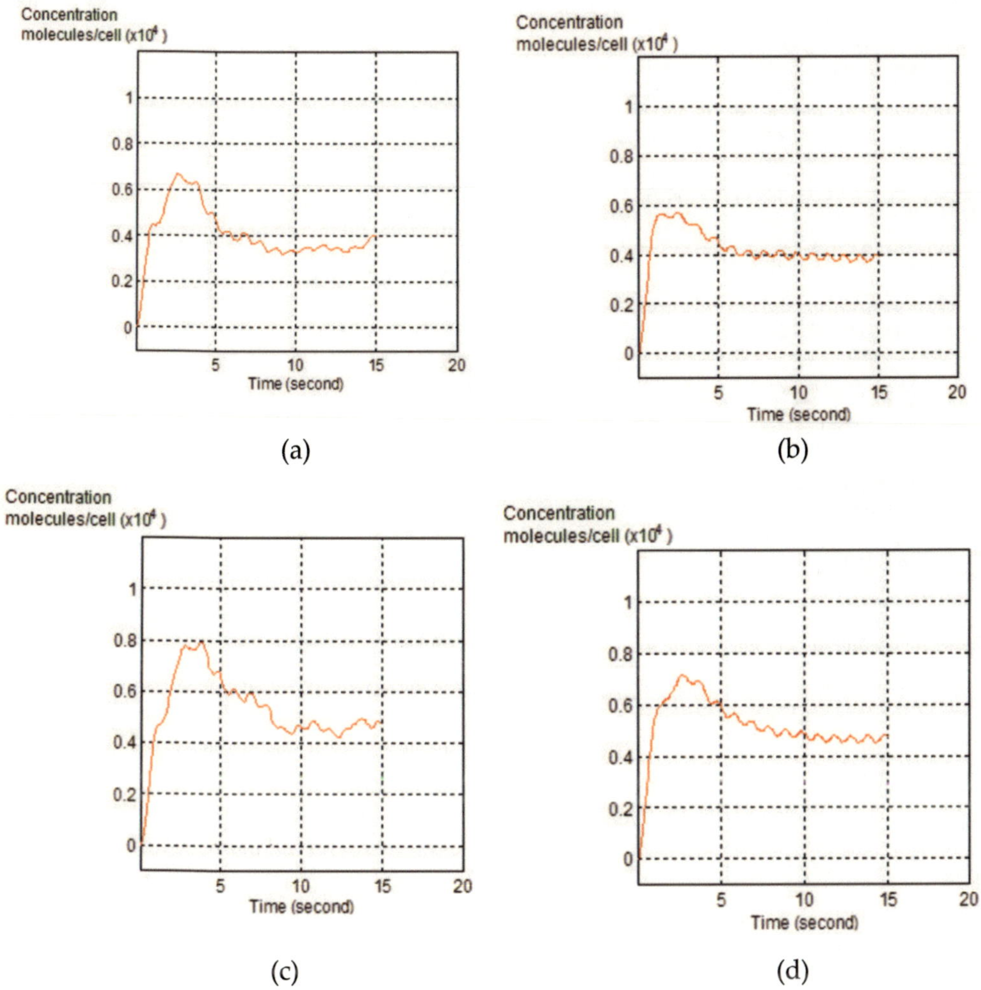

Figure 5. The system response (intracellular messenger/protein) concentration using the runge kutta order method. (a), (c) The result of the simulation using the runqe kutta 5th order method; (b), (d) The result of the simulation using the runge kutta 3th order method

In fig. 6 it is presented the hierarchical Simulink model for the cellular signaling pathways.

There were detalied the Nucleus regulating processes and Mithocondria control mechanisms. The outputs of simulations are presented in figures 7 (a,b).

The differences between Figures 5 (a, b,c,d) and 7 (a, b) representing the shape of the output signal of the model shows that the model detailed at subcellular level and proper adjustment of transfer functions that describe each subcellular component ensure high accuracy of the model.

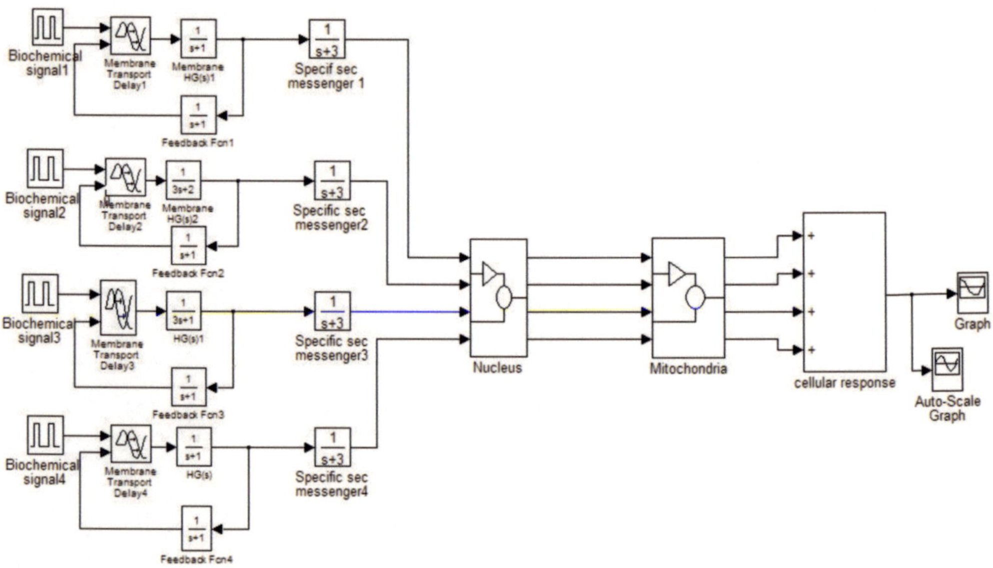

Figure 6. Simulink model for hierarchical control structures in cellular signalling pathways

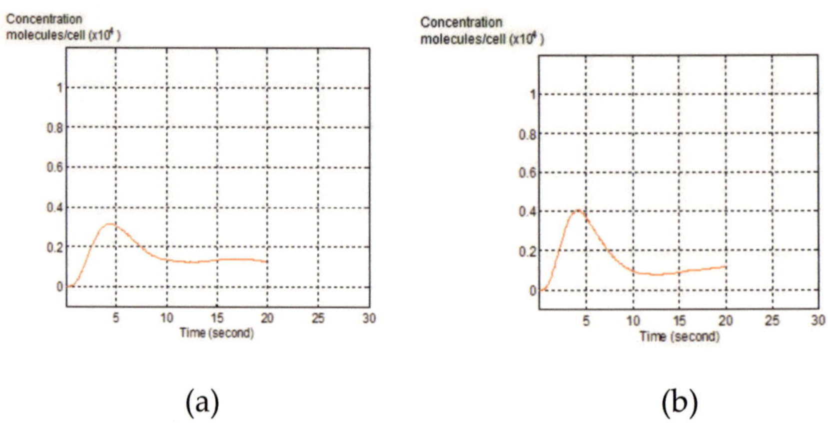

Figure 7. Model responses – System dynamic behavior. (a), (b) The output of the system with amplification factor inserted

Attenuation or amplification factors may be adjusted from control loops according to the real behavior of the modeled signaling pathway. For example, in the case of signaling pathway that that activates Janus2 protein tyrosine kinase (JAK2) or phosphorylated EPOR attenuation factors are recommended, while the signaling pathways corresponding to double phosphorylated ERK1 and 2 or double phosphorylated MEK1 and 2 are recommended amplification factors.

8. Conclusions

Living systems are complex systems, characterized by a multitude of control mechanisms. Signaling pathways do not operate in isolation, and a key element of living systems control mechanisms is the extensive cross-talk between signaling pathways that control all biological regulating mechanisms.

High level modeling in biosystems, consist in modeling the signaling pathways.

Experimental studies revealed that each cell type has a unique repertoire of cell signaling components, signalsome, determined by the cell phenotype, expressed during the final stages of cell development, in order to control cell particular physiology. The signalsomes are characterized by a high degree of plasticity being constantly remodeled to in order to adjust cell responses to environmetal changes.

High level modeling in biosystems is a laborious process due a number of facts: the uniqueness of living systems behavior, insufficient knowledge of bioprocesses, high costs of experiments and the impossibility to repeat them in absolutely identical conditions, the large number of unknowns involved in the models, the extensive cross-talk between signaling pathways.

MATLAB® and SIMULINK® provide the possibility to study the dynamic behavior of the regulatory mechanisms involved in signaling pathways of living systems through computer simulation.

Author details

Cristina-Maria Dabu

CRIFST, Romanian Academy, Romania

References

[1] Berridge, M.J. (2012) Cell Signalling Biology;doi:10.1042/csb0001001, visited 01.09.2013

[2] Jihan K Osborne, Elma Zaganjor, Melanie H Cobb, Signal control through Raf: in sickness and in health, *Cell Research* (2012) 22:14-22. doi:10.1038/cr.2011.193; published online 6 December 2011

[3] Cristina-Maria Dabu, M. D. Nicu, *Calculatoare în Biotehnici – Note de curs pentru uzul studentilor*, Universitatea "Politehnica" Bucureşti, 1997

[4] Jeremy M. Berg, John L. Tymoczko, Lubert Stryer; Web content by Neil D. Clarke (2002). "Protein Structure and Function". Biochemistry. San Francisco: W. H. Freeman. ISBN 0-7167-4684-0.

[5] Yanfen Liu, Yihong Ye, Proteostasis regulation at the endoplasmic reticulum: a new perturbation site for targeted cancer therapy, Cell Research (2011) 21:867-883, http://www.nature.com/cr, visited 02.09.2013

[6] Ellen Wirawan and colab, Autophagy: for better or for worse, *Cell Research* (2012) 22:43-61. doi:10.1038/cr.2011.152

[7] www.wolfram.com visited Nov, 2013

[8] Sal Mangano, Mathematica Cookbook, O'Reilly Media, Inc USA, 2010

[9] www.python.org visited Nov, 2013

[10] Mitchel L. Model, Bioinformatics programmind using Python, O'Reilly Media, Inc., USA, 2009

[11] Matlab, www.mathworks.com, visited 0ct. 2013

[12] http://www.mathworks.com/products/bioinfo/, visited 0ct. 2013

Chapter 18

Eigenvalue Analysis in Mode Domain Considering a Three-Phase System with two Ground Wires

R. C. Monzani, A. J. Prado, L.S. Lessa and L. F. Bovolato

Additional information is available at the end of the chapter

http://dx.doi.org/10.5772/58383

1. Introduction

The analysis of a transmission line allows a complex study that can be used to measure losses in line, to understand the behavior of them in case of a voltage surge and other kinds of phenomena.

This chapter presents the development of a routine that evaluates a method for determining real transformation matrices in three-phase systems considering the presence of ground-wires. Thus, for Z (longitudinal impedance) and Y (transversal admittance) matrices that represent the transmission line, the ground wires are considered not implicit in the values of the phases. This routine was developed using the mathematical tool Matlab™.

As a proposal, the routine uses a real transformation matrix throughout the frequency range of analysis. This transformation matrix is an approximation of the exact transformation matrix. For elements related to the phase of the system considered, the transformation matrix is composed from the elements of the Clarke's matrix [18].

In parts related to ground wires, the elements of the transformation matrix must establish a relationship with the elements of the phases considering the establishment of a unique, single homopolar reference in mode domain.

In case of three-phase transmission lines with the presence of two ground wires, it is not possible to obtain the complete diagonalization of Y and Z matrices in mode domain. Finally, a correction routine is applied with the goal of minimizing errors obtained for the eigenvalues.

INTECH
open science | open minds

© 2014 The Author(s). Licensee InTech. This chapter is distributed under the terms of the Creative Commons Attribution License (http://creativecommons.org/licenses/by/3.0), which permits unrestricted use, distribution, and reproduction in any medium, provided the original work is properly cited.

2. Background

Different methods can be used in order to analyze electromagnetic transient phenomena in transmission lines. Many mathematical tools can be used. The main tools are: circuit analysis using Laplace transform and Fourier transform, state variables and also differential equations. These tools can be included in a numerical routine in order to obtain the values of voltage and current in electromagnetic transient simulation for any point in the circuit.

The EMTP (ElectroMagnetic Transient Program) identifies a type of program, considering its various versions, which performs simulations of transients in electrical networks [1]. The prototype was developed in the 1960s by professionals in power systems, led by Dr. Hermann Dommel (University of British Columbia, Vancouver, BC, Canada), and Dr. Scott Meyer (Bonneville Power Administration in Portland, Oregon, USA). Currently, the EMTP is the basis of simulations of electromagnetic transients in power systems.

With EMTP-type programs, the following tests may be performed: simulation by switching and lightning surges, transient and temporary overvoltages, transients in electric machines, resonance phenomena, harmonics, power quality and power electronics applications. The most popular type programs are EMTP: MicroTran, PSCAD and ATP.

In analysis of transmission systems, there are simulators that represent different types of systems, from generation, transmission and distribution.

Because it is practically impossible to perform the simulation of electromagnetic transients on real transmission lines, simulations by digital models become useful tools. However, these tools do not provide satisfactory performance as regards the correct representation of the electrical line parameters, as these are dependent on the frequency.

In modal domain, it's possible to represent the transmission line circuits using simple circuits and easily entering frequency dependence of longitudinal parameters.

In general, a system composed of n-phases can be transformed into independent modes using a real and unique transformation matrix, if transposition applies to all phases for the frequency range used (ideal transposition). If the analyzed system is not transposed, a mode is obtained for each phase using the frequency dependent phase-mode transformation matrix.

Applying real and unique transformation matrix for the nontransposed lines, approximate results can be obtained. Thus, there is an approximate representation of frequency dependence using a real phase-mode transformation matrix [2]-[3]. One possible simplification is to consider the transformation matrix frequency independent, obtaining insignificant errors related to the eigenvalues that represent the line. Using the mentioned simplification, the obtained numerical routine may be faster because it avoids using a convolution method [4]-[28].

The objective of this chapter is to analyze the application of a real transformation matrix that is frequency independent in three-phase lines considering the presence of two ground wires. Errors are presented in relation to the exact values obtained from the matrix of eigenvalues.

http://dx.doi.org/10.5772/58383

The proposed model is based on an approximate modal transformation performed by a single real phase-mode transformation matrix, and frequency independent. This matrix is obtained by linear combination of Clarke's matrix elements. With the implementation of the transformation matrix frequency independent, it's obtained a diagonal matrix for transposed lines. In case of a three-phase transmission line not transposed the line parameters matrix can't be diagonalized, with application of a single real phase-mode transformation matrix mentioned. For these cases, the goal is to analyze the relative errors obtained by the establishment circumstances to use a transformation matrix frequency independent.

For the proposed method in this chapter, a similar mathematical basis is used to homopolar hypothesis of a single reference for all phases of the system regardless of the geometrical distribution and organization of the three-phase circuit. Thus, the development is based on the analysis of eigenvectors and eigenvalues, using a linear combination of Clarke's matrix elements, and assuming a unique homopolar reference.

It's presented two different proposals for real matrices and frequency independent in order to replace the modal transformation matrix of a typical three-phase transmission line in the presence of two ground-wires.

3. Mathematical model

A transmission line is represented by a longitudinal impedance Z and the transversal admittance Y matrices, the characteristics of ground wires are not implied in the values related to the phases. Thus, for a line with two ground wires, the Z and Y matrices are 5-order ones.

For the mentioned systems, the three-phase circuit configurations are considered and the transposed case can be described by a system where each three-phase circuit is ideally transposed and there are coupling impedances and admittances among the three-phase circuits. For EMTP type programs, if each three-phase circuit is considered independently, the transformation matrix is frequency dependent for general cases. For the method proposed in this chapter, a similar mathematical base is used for all considered cases: the assumption of unique ground reference for all phases of the system independently of the geometrical distribution and the organization of the three-phase circuits. The unique ground reference leads to a unique homopolar mode in mode domain.

The relationships between transversal voltages u_F and the longitudinal currents i_F can be expressed by the following equations, where Z is the longitudinal impedance matrix per unit length and Y is the transversal admittance matrix per unit length in phase domain.

$$-\frac{du_F}{dx} = Z \cdot i_F \text{ and } -\frac{di_F}{dx} = Y \cdot u_F \qquad (1)$$

Applying the eigenvector and eigenvalue analyses for YZ and ZY product matrices, the λ diagonal eigenvalue matrix and the eigenvector matrices are determined. The eigenvector matrices, T_V and T_I, correspond to voltage and current mathematical relationships, respectively. The T_V and T_I matrices are related to λ based on the following equation:

$$\lambda = T_V \cdot Z \cdot Y \cdot T_V^{-1} = T_I \cdot Y \cdot Z \cdot T_I^{-1} \tag{2}$$

If the T_V and T_I transformation matrices are used, the eigenvalues can be obtained in mode domain using (1). The per unit length longitudinal impedance matrix (Z_{MD}) and transversal admittance matrix (Y_{MD}) are:

$$Z_{MD} = T_V \cdot Z \cdot T_I^{-1} \text{ and } Y_{MD} = T_I \cdot Y \cdot T_V^{-1} \tag{3}$$

In general, these frequency dependent transformation matrices (T_V and T_I) are different and have complex elements. Using the proposed methodology, the transformation matrices are changed into a single real transformation matrix (T_{SR}). The T_{SR} matrix is determined from linear combinations of the Clarke's matrix elements [4]-[7]. The determination of exact eigenvalues is approximated and changed into the following:

$$\lambda_{SR} = T_{SR} \cdot Z \cdot Y \cdot T_{SR}^{-1} = T_{SR} \cdot Y \cdot Z \cdot T_{SR}^{-1} \tag{4}$$

In case of the EMTP type programs, the transformation matrices are real, if the system is ideally transposed. For this, there is only one self-impedance value for all phase interactions. Considering the admittance values, a similar structure to the impedance values is obtained. Applying the EMTP type programs, a system composed by three-phase circuits is analyzed as a non-transposed case, if the each three-phase circuit is considered transposed independently of the ground wires.

Using a single homopolar mode reference, the λ_{SR} matrix is equal to the exact eigenvalue matrix (λ) [8] as well as T_V and T_I being equal to a single real transformation matrix for transposed cases [9]-[11]. So, with a single homopolar mode reference, there is a link between the three-phase circuit and the ground wires of the system. With this technique, a transformation matrix (T_{SR}) is obtained which has interesting characteristics: single, real, frequency independent, line parameter independent and identical to voltages and currents. With these characteristics, phase-mode transformations are carried out using only one matrix multiplication.

The homopolar or zero sequence components (V_{a0}, V_{b0} and V_{c0}) for a three-phase system are equal and they make the unique ground reference for the three-order phasor system. Using the homopolar reference phasor concept, the application of a single mode reference to the single real phase-mode transformation matrix is proposed. So, the homopolar mode is used as the only mode reference for the analyzed transmission line systems. To compose the T_{SR} matrix, each mode must have a unitary modulus. Because of this, each homopolar mode element value depends on the number of phase conductors. If this number is identified by n, the homopolar mode elements are described by (6).

$$T_{SR\text{-}n} = \frac{1}{\sqrt{n}} \tag{5}$$

4. Ground wires in three-phase transmission line

Considering two ground wires in a three-phase lines system, these matrices are 5-order ones. Therefore, the single real phase-mode transformation matrix has the following structure presented in (6).

$$T_{SR5} = \begin{bmatrix} -\frac{1}{\sqrt{6}} & \frac{2}{\sqrt{6}} & -\frac{1}{\sqrt{6}} & 0 & 0 \\ \frac{1}{\sqrt{2}} & 0 & -\frac{1}{\sqrt{2}} & 0 & 0 \\ \frac{1}{\sqrt{5}} & \frac{1}{\sqrt{5}} & \frac{1}{\sqrt{5}} & \frac{1}{\sqrt{5}} & \frac{1}{\sqrt{5}} \\ \frac{1}{\sqrt{5}} & \frac{1}{\sqrt{5}} & \frac{1}{\sqrt{5}} & -\frac{1}{\sqrt{5}} & -\frac{1}{\sqrt{5}} \\ 0 & 0 & 0 & \frac{1}{\sqrt{2}} & -\frac{1}{\sqrt{2}} \end{bmatrix} \tag{6}$$

In case of a three-phase lines system is ideally transposed, it creates only one coupling impedance between the lines. The average self-phase impedance value is represented by A. The average coupling impedances are represented by B, within a circuit, and C, between the line and ground wires or other circuits. The average ground wires impedance value is represented by D. The average coupling impedance between the both ground wires is represented by E. For the case of a single three-phase line in the presence of two ground wires (Fig. 1), the structure of the impedance matrix is shown in (7).

$$Z_5 = \begin{bmatrix} A & B & B & C & C \\ B & A & B & C & C \\ B & B & A & C & C \\ C & C & C & D & E \\ C & C & C & E & D \end{bmatrix} \tag{7}$$

The three-phase transmission line circuit tower (Fig. 2) has a height of 36.0 m and is the structure used in this chapter. This is a 400 km length line that operates in 440 kV. It is a system whose conductors are disposed in such way that there is a vertical symmetry plane.

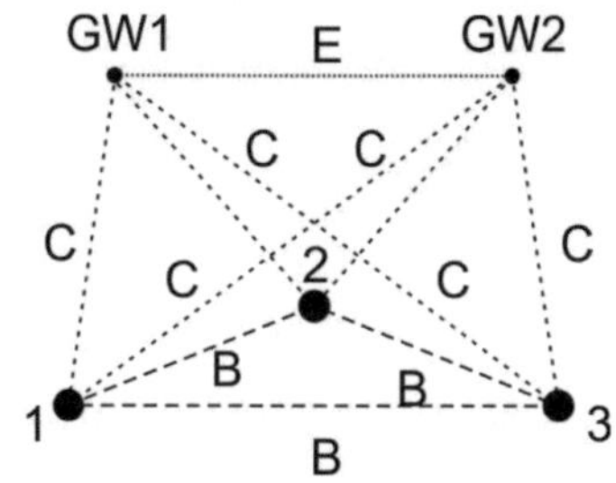

Figure 1. Coupling impedances for a three-phase transmission line with two ground wires for transposed cases.

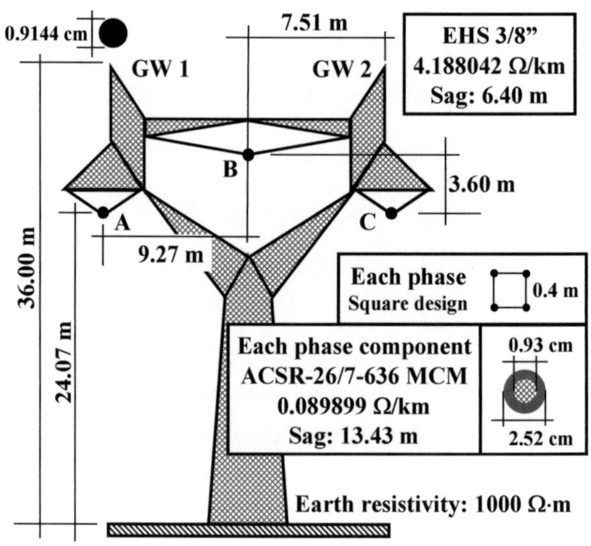

Figure 2. Three phase line tower with two ground wires

The result determined through (4) is a diagonal matrix and the matrix elements are the exact eigenvalues, for the cases where the ground wires are implicit in the phase values and the line is transposed. The impedance matrix in mode domain (Z_M) can be calculated as:

$$Z_M = T_{SR} \cdot Z \cdot T_{SR}^{-1} \tag{8}$$

Considering ground wires, the single real phase-mode transformation matrix does not perfectly diagonalize the impedance matrix.

http://dx.doi.org/10.5772/58383

$$\lambda_{SR5}=\begin{bmatrix} A-B & 0 & 0 & 0 & 0 \\ 0 & A-B & 0 & 0 & 0 \\ 0 & 0 & \frac{3A+6B-12C+2D+2E}{5} & \frac{3A+6B-2D-2E}{5} & 0 \\ 0 & 0 & \frac{3A+6B-2D-2E}{5} & \frac{3A+6B+12C+2D+2E}{5} & 0 \\ 0 & 0 & 0 & 0 & D-E \end{bmatrix} \tag{9}$$

5. Initial configuration routine

A routine with initial configuration was developed in order to set parameters that would be used for other routines. This routine was developed using Matlab and is presented below:

```
initial_conf.m
%Three-phase line with vertical symmetry
ntpc = 1; %three-phase circuit amount
ngw = 2; %ground wires amount
ncond = ntpc*3+ngw;  %conductors amount
frequency     %subroutine to call an array of frequencies from 0 to 1 GHz
%Conductors' position in x axis (in meters)
xc(1)=   0;
xc(2)=   9.27;
xc(3)=   18.54;
xc(4)=   1.76;    %ground wire 1
xc(5)=   16.78;   %ground wire 2
%Conductors' position in y axis (in meters)
yc(1)=  24.07-0.7*13.43; %the subtracted value is the sag of each wire
yc(2)=  27.67-0.7*13.43;
yc(3)=  24.07-0.7*13.43;
yc(4)=  36.00-0.7*6.40;
yc(5)=  36.00-0.7*6.40;
%Radius (in meters)
rc   = 2.52e-2;  %total radius
rin   = 0.93e-2;  %internal radius
r_dist = 0.4;    %distance between conductors
nph = 4;   %number of conductors per phase
Arg   = rc*r_dist^3*sqrt(2); %argument of root
GMR   = power(Arg,1/nph);  %geometric mean radius
radius   = GMR;
sk_radius = rc-rin;  %for skin effect procedure
gw_radius = 0.9144e-2;  %ground wire radius
resist = 1000;               %Earth resistance (ohms x meters)
mizero = 4*pi*1e-7;          %magnetic permeability (H/m)
epszero = 8.8542*1e-9; %dielectric permittivity (F/km)
sigma= 3.82*1e7;             %conductor's conductivity (mho/m)
```

6. Eigenvalue analyses for non-transposed three-phase transmission line

Considering the three-phase line tower with two ground wires shown in Fig. 2, the total longitudinal impedance value is composed by earth effect, calculated by Carson`s method [28], external effects and skin effect. For phase 1, the longitudinal resistance is shown in Fig. 3 (a), the longitudinal inductance in Fig. 3 (b) and capacitance in Fig. 3 (c).

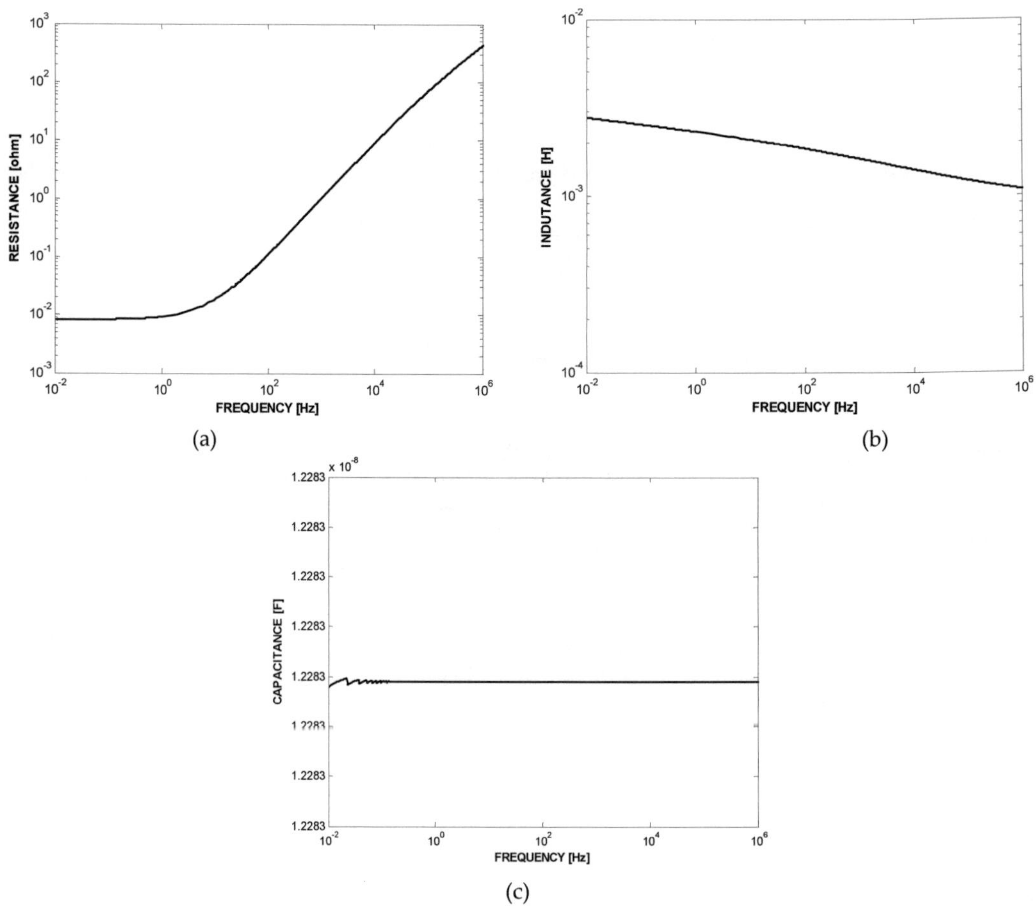

Figure 3. (a) Longitudinal Resistance, (b) Longitudinal inductance, (c) Capacitance : phase 1.

The longitudinal resistance and inductance and the capacitance of phase 1 were obtained using a routine developed in MatLab, which is commented and shown below:

```
external_impedance.m
clear all
'Calculating Z due to external effect'
%File Reading (calling subroutine of initial configuration)
```

```
initial_conf

for j = 1:ncond,
xi(j) = xc(j);
yi(j) = -yc(j);
for k = j:ncond
  str = ['Zext' int2str(j) '_' int2str(k) '.m'];
  fid(j,k) = fopen(str,'w');
  if j==k
 str = ['%% External impedance of phase ' int2str(j) ' \n clear x\n x = [\n'];
 fprintf(fid(j,k),str);
  else
 str = ['%% External impedance between phase ' int2str(j) ' and ' int2str(k) '
\n clear x\n x = [\n'];
 fprintf(fid(j,k),str);
 end
end
end

%Image conductor coordinates
for j = 1: ncond,
   xi(j) =  xc(j);
 yi(j) = -yc(j);
end

%External inductance (H/km)
for j = 1:ncond,
   for k = j:ncond,
      if j == k
         if j < ntpc*3+1
 ld = radius;
 else
 ld = gw_radius;
 end
      else
         dx = xc(j) - xc(k);
 dy = yc(j) - yc(k);
 ld = sqrt(dx^2 + dy^2);
      end
      dx = xcondut(j) - xi(k);
 dy = ycondut(j) - yi(k);
 bd = sqrt(dx^2 + dy^2);
      induct(j,k) = 1000*(1/(2*pi))*mizero*log(dezao/dezinho);
 end
end
for j = 1:length(freq),
    for k = 1:ncond
        for m = k:ncond
            z = i*2*pi*freq(j)*induct(k,m);
 fprintf(fid(k,m), '%30.20f  %30.20f\n',real(z),imag(z));
        end
    end
```

```
end
for j = 1:ncond
    for k = j:ncond
 fprintf(fid(j,k), ']; \n');
 str = ['ze' int2str(j) '_' int2str(k) ' = x(:,1) + i*x(:,2);'];
 fprintf(fid(j,k), str);
    end
end
fclose('all');

z_skins.m
%Internal impedance (skin effect)
clear all
'Calculatin Z due to skin effect'
%File reading
initial_conf

fid10 = fopen('zskin.m','w');
fprintf(fid10, '%% Internal impedance \n clear x\n x = [\n');

%============================================================
%Bessel Formula
%===========================================================

%mi  = mizero/1000 ;
%radiuso = raio/1000  ;

for j = 1:length(freq),
   m  = sqrt(i*2*pi*freq(j)*mizero*sigma);
 mr = sk_radius * sqrt(i*2*pi*freq(j)*mizero*sigma);
 I0 = BESSELI(0,(mr),1);
   I1 = BESSELI(1,(mr),1);
   %Impedance calculus (number 4 appears because there are 4 subconctors)
 z = (1/4)*1000*((1/sigma)*m)/(2*pi*sk_radius)*(I0/I1);
  fprintf(fid10, '%30.20f  %30.20f\n',real(z),imag(z));
end

fprintf(fid10, ']; \n');
fprintf(fid10, 'zskin = x(:,1) + x(:,2)*i;');
fclose('all');

z_carson.m
%Impedance due to earth effect (Carson's method)
clear all
'Calculating Z due to earth effect   Carson's method
%File reading
initial_conf

nt = 120; %amount of terms to be used (number multiple of 4)
v = -1;   %variable used for signal

%Image conductors coordinates
```

http://dx.doi.org/10.5772/58383

```
for j = 1:ncond,
   xi(j) = xc(j);
 yi(j) = -yc(j);

    for k = j:ncond
 str = ['Zcarson' int2str(j) '_' int2str(k) '.m'];
       fid(j,k) = fopen(str,'w');
 if j==k
 str = ['%% Phase impedance ' int2str(j) ' due to earth effect \n clear x\n x
= [\n'];
 fprintf(fid(j,k),str);
 else
 str = ['%% Impedance between phases ' int2str(j) ' and ' int2str(k) ' due to
Earth effect \n clear x\n x = [\n'];
 fprintf(fid(j,k),str);
       end
   end
end

for j = 1:ncond,
   for k = j:ncond,
      dx  = xc(j) - xi(k);
 dy  = yc(j) - yi(k);
 bd(j,k)  = sqrt(dx^2 + dy^2);
      cat  = yc(j) + yc(k);
 cossine  = cat/bd(j,k);
 ang(j,k) = acos(cossine);
 end
end

%**************************************************************************
% Calculus of terms b, c and d of Carson's series
%**************************************************************************
%signal change each 4 terms
n = 0;
for j = 1:nt/4,
   v = -v;
   for k = 1:4,
 n = n+1;
 signal_b(n) = v;
   end
end

%Calculus of bi element
b(1) = sqrt(2)/6;
b(2) = 1/16;
for j = 3:nt,
   b(j) = abs(b(j-2))*(1/(j*(j+2)))*signal_b(j);
end

%Calculus of ci element
c(2) = 1.3659315;
```

```
for j = 4:nt,
   c(j) = c(j-2) + (1/j) + (1/(j+2));
end

%Calculus of di element
d = (pi/4)*b;
%*****************************************************************************
for f = 1:length(freq),
   for j = 1:ncond,
      for k = j:ncond,
         phi = ang(j,k);
 a = sqrt(mizero*2*pi*freq(f)/resist)*bd(j,k);
         subrotine_carson_delta_r;
         subrotine_carson_delta_x;
         fprintf(fid(j,k), '%30.20f  %30.20f\n',delta_r(j,k), delta_x(j,k));
  end
   end
end

for j = 1:ncond,
    for k = j:ncond,
 fprintf(fid(j,k), ']; \n');
  fprintf(fid(j,k), ['zsolo' int2str(j) '_' int2str(k) ' = x(:,1) + i*x(:,
2);']);
    end
end
fclose('all');

subrotine_carson_delta_r.m
if a < 5,
%'ok'
  r1 = b(1)*a*cos(phi);
  for nj = 1:(nt/4) -1,
    term1 = b(4*nj +1)*(a^(4*nj +1))*cos((4*nj + 1)*phi);
 r1 = term1 + r1;
 end
  parc1 = (c(2) - log(a))*(a^2)*cos(2*phi);
 parc2 = (phi*(a^2)*sin(2*phi));
 r2 = b(2)*(parc1 + parc2);
  for nj = 1:(nt/4) -1,
    parc1 = (c(4*nj +2) - log(a))*(a^(4*nj +2))*cos((4*nj +2)*phi);
 parc2 = (phi*(a^(4*nj +2))*sin((4*nj +2)*phi));
 r2 = r2 + b(4*nj +2)*(parc1 + parc2);
 end
  r3 = b(3)*(a^3)*cos(3*phi);
  for nj = 1:(nt/4) -1,
    term3 = b(4*nj + 3)*(a^(4*nj + 3))*cos((4*nj + 3)*phi);
 r3 = r3 + term3;
  end
 r4 = d(4)*(a^4)*cos(4*phi);
 for nj = 1:(nt/4) -1,
    term4 = d(4*nj + 4)*(a^(4*nj + 4))*cos((4*nj + 4)*phi);
```

```
  r4 = r4 + term4;
  end
   delta_r(j,k) = 4*2*pi*freq(f)*(1e-4)*((pi/8) - r1 + r2 + r3 - r4);
 else
   t1 = cos(phi)/a;
   t2 = sqrt(2)*cos(2*phi)/(a^2);
  t3 = cos(3*phi)/(a^3);
   t4 = 3*cos(5*phi)/(a^5);
   t5 = 5*cos(7*phi)/(a^7);
   delta_r(j,k) = (4*2*pi*freq(f)*(1e-4)/sqrt(2))*(t1 -t2 + t3 +t4 +t5);
 end

 subrotine_carson_delta_r.m
 %Carson's series to calculate reactance of conductors due to Earth effect
 if a < 5,
   x1 = b(1)*a*cos(phi);
   for nj = 1:(nt/4) -1,
     term1 = b(4*nj +1)*(a^(4*nj +1))*cos((4*nj + 1)*phi);
  x1 = term1 + x1;
   end
   x2 = d(2)*(a^2)*cos(2*phi);
   for nj = 1:(nt/4) -1,
     term2 = d(4*nj + 2)*(a^(4*nj + 2))*cos((4*nj + 2)*phi);
     x2 = x2 + term2;
   end
   x3 = b(3)*(a^3)*cos(3*phi);
   for nj = 1:(nt/4) -1,
     term3 = b(4*nj + 3)*(a^(4*nj + 3))*cos((4*nj + 3)*phi);
  x3 = x3 + term3;
   end
   term4 = (c(4) - log(a))*(a^4)*cos(4*phi) + (phi)*(a^4)*sin(4*phi);
   x4 = b(4)*term4;
   for nj = 1:(nt/4) -1,
       term4 = (c(4*nj + 4) - log(a))*(a^(4*nj + 4))*cos((4*nj + 4)*phi) +
 (phi)*(a^(4*nj + 4))*sin((4*nj + 4)*phi);
     x4 = x4 +  b(4*nj + 4)*term4;
   end
  delta_x(j,k) = 4*2*pi*freq(f)*(1e-4)*(0.5*(0.6159315 - log(a)) + x1 - x2 + x3
 - x4);
 else
   t1 = cos(phi)/a;
   t2 = sqrt(2)*cos(2*phi)/(a^2);
   t3 = cos(3*phi)/(a^3);
   t4 = 3*cos(5*phi)/(a^5);
   t5 = 5*cos(7*phi)/(a^7);
   delta_x(j,k) = (4*2*pi*freq(f)*(1e-4)/sqrt(2))*(t1 - t3 + t4 + t5);
 end
```

The theoretical procedure of routines presented above can be fully found in [29]-[30]. The above routines show how useful Matlab is in order to perform calculus and link routines. It's easy to note that the routines are simple to implement and to understand.

The principal point to be observed is that all the data generated by the routines are stored into m-files to be used by other routines. To perform this action, first it's necessary to open a file (if doesn't exist, it'll be automatically created) and link with a variable, for this operation, function *fopen* shall be used, the arguments of this function are the name of file and the kind of action to be performed by the file, in this case, *w* was used in order to *write* in the file. To write in the file, the function *fprintf* must be used, the arguments are the name of file, the text (which can be variables of decimal point (%d), float point (%f), and so forth, followed by the variables name. Finally, it's necessary to close the file, with the function *fclose*. In this case the argument *all* is used in order to close all opened files.

As the procedure for calculus in all impedances cases shown above are the same, a lasso function can be used in order to make the routine shorter. Thus, structure *for* is implemented together structure *if* in order to make a loop and to decide what kind of operation shall be performed.

In the *z_skins.m* file it's noted the use of Bessel function; this is a special function which can be found in any advanced mathematical calculus. This function is used in order to calculate the impedance due to skin effect, as described in [29].

```
calc_capacitance.m
clear all
'Calculating capacitances'
%File reading
initial_conf
fid10 = fopen('capacitance.m','w');
fprintf(fid10, '%% Capacitances \n clear x\n cap = [\n');
%Image conductors coordinates
for j = 1: ncond,
   xi(j) =  xc(j);
 yi(j) = -yc(j);
end
%Potential matrix coefficients
for j = 1:ncond,
   for k = j:ncond,
      if j == k
          if j < ntpc*3+1
 ld = radius;
          else
 ld = gw_radius;
 end
      else
         dx = xc(j) - xc(k);
 dy = yc(j) - yc(k);
 ld = sqrt(dx^2 + dy^2);
      end
      dx = xc(j) - xi(k);
 dy = yc(j) - yi(k);
 bd = sqrt(dx^2 + dy^2);
      pot(j,k) = log(bd/ld);
```

http://dx.doi.org/10.5772/58383

```
        pot(k,j) = pot(j,k);
      end
    end
    cap = 2*pi*epslonzero*(inv(pot));
    for j = 1:ncond,
     for k = 1:ncond,
     fprintf(fid10, '%30.20f  ',cap(j,k));
        end
     fprintf(fid10, '\n');
    end
    fprintf(fid10, ']; \n');
    fclose('all');
```

Evaluation of proposed real transformation matrix

A first analysis is based on Eq. (9). Through iterative process the exact eigenvectors and eigenvalues, and also the eigenvectors and eigenvalues, from Clark`s matrix are calculated. At the end of process the relative difference is calculated for each mode with Eq. (10).

$$err(\%)=\frac{\lambda_{cl}-\lambda_{ex}}{\lambda_{ex}}\cdot 100 \tag{10}$$

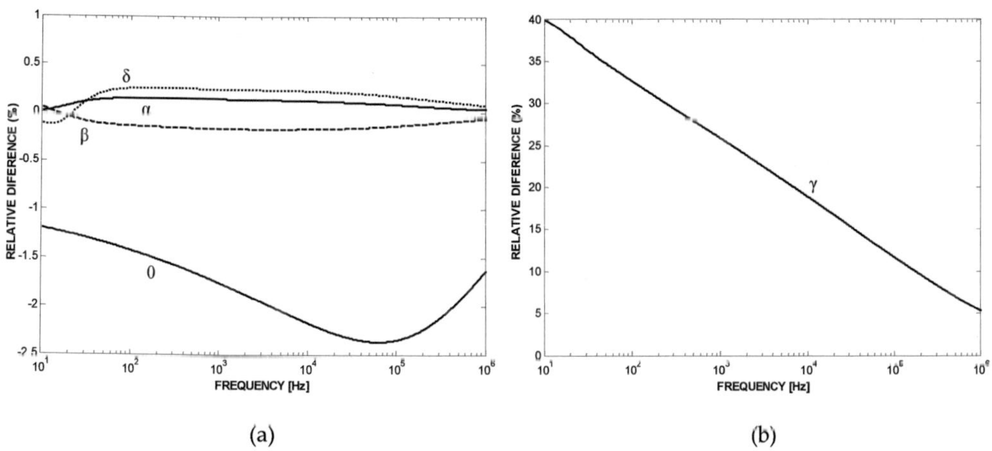

Figure 4. Relative differences between the exact modes and the quasi-modes.

The relative difference between modes α, β, 0 and δ is relatively low (Fig. 4 (a)), however, the relative difference of mode γ is high (Fig. 4 (b)). To minimize the error shown for mode 4, a correction procedure for non-transposed three-phase transmission line cases [31]-[35] shall be used in a future work.

In order to verify the limits of this method, a frequency range from 10 $[Hz]$ to 1 $[GHz]$ was applied, from the results of resistance, inductance and capacitance obtained, it was verified that the method could converge until 1 $[MHz]$, after this range the method is not valid and need a new approach will be requested.

The numeric routine used to obtain the results shown above was developed with Matlab and is described below in details:

```
external_impedance.m
clear all
'Calculating Z due to external effect'
%File Reading (calling subroutine of initial configuration)
initial_conf

for j = 1:ncond,
xi(j) = xc(j);
yi(j) = -yc(j);
for k = j:ncond
  str = ['Zext' int2str(j) '_' int2str(k) '.m'];
  fid(j,k) = fopen(str,'w');
  if j==k
 str = ['%% External impedance of phase ' int2str(j) ' \n clear x\n x = [\n'];
 fprintf(fid(j,k),str);
  else
 str = ['%% External impedance between phase ' int2str(j) ' and ' int2str(k) '
\n clear x\n x = [\n'];
 fprintf(fid(j,k),str);
 end
end
end

%Image conductor coordinates
for j = 1: ncond,
   xi(j) =  xc(j);
 yi(j) = -yc(j);
end

%External inductance (H/km)
for j = 1:ncond,
   for k = j:ncond,
      if j == k
         if j < ntpc*3+1
 ld = radius;
 else
 ld = gw_radius;
 end
      else
         dx = xc(j) - xc(k);
 dy = yc(j) - yc(k);
 ld = sqrt(dx^2 + dy^2);
      end
      dx = xcondut(j) - xi(k);
 dy = ycondut(j) - yi(k);
 bd = sqrt(dx^2 + dy^2);
      induct(j,k) = 1000*(1/(2*pi))*mizero*log(dezao/dezinho);
 end
```

http://dx.doi.org/10.5772/58383

```
end
for j = 1:length(freq),
    for k = 1:ncond
        for m = k:ncond
            z = i*2*pi*freq(j)*induct(k,m);
 fprintf(fid(k,m), '%30.20f  %30.20f\n',real(z),imag(z));
        end
    end
end
for j = 1:ncond
    for k = j:ncond
 fprintf(fid(j,k), ']; \n');
 str = ['ze' int2str(j) '_' int2str(k) ' = x(:,1) + i*x(:,2);'];
 fprintf(fid(j,k), str);
    end
end
fclose('all');

z_skins.m
%Internal impedance (skin effect)
clear all
'Calculatin Z due to skin effect'
%File reading
initial_conf

fid10 = fopen('zskin.m','w');
fprintf(fid10, '%% Internal impedance \n clear x\n x = [\n');

%============================================================
%Bessel Formula
%============================================================

%mi  = mizero/1000 ;
%radiuso = raio/1000  ;

for j = 1:length(freq),
   m  = sqrt(i*2*pi*freq(j)*mizero*sigma);
 mr = sk_radius * sqrt(i*2*pi*freq(j)*mizero*sigma);
 I0 = BESSELI(0,(mr),1);
   I1 = BESSELI(1,(mr),1);
   %Impedance calculus (number 4 appears because there are 4 subconctors)
 z = (1/4)*1000*((1/sigma)*m)/(2*pi*sk_radius)*(I0/I1);
  fprintf(fid10, '%30.20f  %30.20f\n',real(z),imag(z));
end

fprintf(fid10, ']; \n');
fprintf(fid10, 'zskin = x(:,1) + x(:,2)*i;');
fclose('all');

z_carson.m
%Impedance due to earth effect (Carson's method)
clear all
```

```
'Calculating Z due to earth effect - Carson's method
%File reading
initial_conf

nt = 120; %amount of terms to be used (number multiple of 4)
v = -1;   %variable used for signal

%Image conductors coordinates
for j = 1:ncond,
   xi(j) = xc(j);
 yi(j) = -yc(j);

    for k = j:ncond
 str = ['Zcarson' int2str(j) '_' int2str(k) '.m'];
       fid(j,k) = fopen(str,'w');
 if j==k
 str = ['%% Phase impedance ' int2str(j) ' due to earth effect \n clear x\n x
= [\n'];
 fprintf(fid(j,k),str);
 else
 str = ['%% Impedance between phases ' int2str(j) ' and ' int2str(k) ' due to
Earth effect \n clear x\n x = [\n'];
 fprintf(fid(j,k),str);
       end
   end
end

for j = 1:ncond,
   for k = j:ncond,
      dx  = xc(j) - xi(k);
 dy  = yc(j) - yi(k);
 bd(j,k)  = sqrt(dx^2 + dy^2);
      cat  = yc(j) + yc(k);
 cossine  = cat/bd(j,k);
 ang(j,k) = acos(cossine);
 end
end

%*****************************************************************************
% Calculus of terms b, c and d of Carson's series
%*****************************************************************************
%signal change each 4 terms
n = 0;
for j = 1:nt/4,
   v = -v;
   for k = 1:4,
 n = n+1;
 signal_b(n) = v;
   end
end

%Calculus of bi element
```

```
b(1) = sqrt(2)/6;
b(2) = 1/16;
for j = 3:nt,
   b(j) = abs(b(j-2))*(1/(j*(j+2)))*signal_b(j);
end

%Calculus of ci element
c(2) = 1.3659315;
for j = 4:nt,
   c(j) = c(j-2) + (1/j) + (1/(j+2));
end

%Calculus of di element
d = (pi/4)*b;
%*****************************************************************************
for f = 1:length(freq),
   for j = 1:ncond,
      for k = j:ncond,
         phi = ang(j,k);
 a = sqrt(mizero*2*pi*freq(f)/resist)*bd(j,k);
         subrotine_carson_delta_r;
         subrotine_carson_delta_x;
         fprintf(fid(j,k), '%30.20f  %30.20f\n',delta_r(j,k), delta_x(j,k));
  end
   end
end

for j = 1:ncond,
    for k = j:ncond,
 fprintf(fid(j,k), ']; \n');
  fprintf(fid(j,k), ['zsolo' int2str(j) '_' int2str(k) ' = x(:,1) + i*x(:,
2);']);
    end
end
fclose('all');

subrotine_carson_delta_r.m
if a < 5,
%'ok'
  r1 = b(1)*a*cos(phi);
  for nj = 1:(nt/4) -1,
    term1 = b(4*nj +1)*(a^(4*nj +1))*cos((4*nj + 1)*phi);
 r1 = term1 + r1;
 end
  parc1 = (c(2) - log(a))*(a^2)*cos(2*phi);
 parc2 = (phi*(a^2)*sin(2*phi));
 r2 = b(2)*(parc1 + parc2);
  for nj = 1:(nt/4) -1,
    parc1 = (c(4*nj +2) - log(a))*(a^(4*nj +2))*cos((4*nj +2)*phi);
 parc2 = (phi*(a^(4*nj +2))*sin((4*nj +2)*phi));
 r2 = r2 + b(4*nj +2)*(parc1 + parc2);
 end
```

```
  r3 = b(3)*(a^3)*cos(3*phi);
  for nj = 1:(nt/4) -1,
    term3 = b(4*nj + 3)*(a^(4*nj + 3))*cos((4*nj + 3)*phi);
 r3 = r3 + term3;
  end
 r4 = d(4)*(a^4)*cos(4*phi);
 for nj = 1:(nt/4) -1,
    term4 = d(4*nj + 4)*(a^(4*nj + 4))*cos((4*nj + 4)*phi);
 r4 = r4 + term4;
 end
  delta_r(j,k) = 4*2*pi*freq(f)*(1e-4)*((pi/8) - r1 + r2 + r3 - r4);
else
  t1 = cos(phi)/a;
  t2 = sqrt(2)*cos(2*phi)/(a^2);
 t3 = cos(3*phi)/(a^3);
  t4 = 3*cos(5*phi)/(a^5);
  t5 = 5*cos(7*phi)/(a^7);
  delta_r(j,k) = (4*2*pi*freq(f)*(1e-4)/sqrt(2))*(t1 -t2 + t3 +t4 +t5);
end

subrotine_carson_delta_r.m
%Carson's series to calculate reactance of conductors due to Earth effect
if a < 5,
  x1 = b(1)*a*cos(phi);
  for nj = 1:(nt/4) -1,
    term1 = b(4*nj +1)*(a^(4*nj +1))*cos((4*nj + 1)*phi);
 x1 = term1 + x1;
  end
  x2 = d(2)*(a^2)*cos(2*phi);
  for nj = 1:(nt/4) -1,
    term2 = d(4*nj + 2)*(a^(4*nj + 2))*cos((4*nj + 2)*phi);
    x2 = x2 + term2;
  end
  x3 = b(3)*(a^3)*cos(3*phi);
  for nj = 1:(nt/4) -1,
    term3 = b(4*nj + 3)*(a^(4*nj + 3))*cos((4*nj + 3)*phi);
 x3 = x3 + term3;
  end
  term4 = (c(4) - log(a))*(a^4)*cos(4*phi) + (phi)*(a^4)*sin(4*phi);
  x4 = b(4)*term4;
  for nj = 1:(nt/4) -1,
      term4 = (c(4*nj + 4) - log(a))*(a^(4*nj + 4))*cos((4*nj + 4)*phi) +
(phi)*(a^(4*nj + 4))*sin((4*nj + 4)*phi);
    x4 = x4 +  b(4*nj + 4)*term4;
  end
 delta_x(j,k) = 4*2*pi*freq(f)*(1e-4)*(0.5*(0.6159315 - log(a)) + x1 - x2 + x3
- x4);
else
  t1 = cos(phi)/a;
  t2 = sqrt(2)*cos(2*phi)/(a^2);
  t3 = cos(3*phi)/(a^3);
  t4 = 3*cos(5*phi)/(a^5);
```

```
    t5 = 5*cos(7*phi)/(a^7);
    delta_x(j,k) = (4*2*pi*freq(f)*(1e-4)/sqrt(2))*(t1 - t3 + t4 + t5);
  end
```

The above routines show the procedure to calculate the correct and proposed method values. The first routine call subroutines capacitance and Zfull (which is the sum of impedances shown before), thus for the correct value it uses the eigenvalue function (*eig*) and for the proposed method it performs calculus as shown before.

The second routine gets all processed data and plot the information considering the relative difference between the correct value and the proposed one as could be seen in Fig. 4.

7. Conclusion

The objective of this project was to analyze the application of modal transformation matrix that is independent of frequency in analyses of three-phase lines considering the presence of 2 ground wires. Through analysis, both the limits of this approach and the possible errors in relation to the exact values obtained from eigenvalues and eigenvectors.

The model proposed in this project uses approximate modal transformation, accomplished through a transformation matrix independent of frequency. This matrix is obtained by linear combination of elements of Clarke's matrix. With application of this transformation matrix independent of frequency, it obtains diagonal matrices for the cases of transposed three-phase lines. For non-transposed three-phase lines, matrices of parameters are not diagonal with the application of the transformation matrix mentioned. For those cases not implemented, the proposal is to analyze the relative errors obtained by establishing circumstances in which one can use a transformation matrix independent of frequency.

This chapter presented a method that can be used for analyzing electromagnetic transients using real transformation matrices in three-phase systems considering the presence of ground wires. This method was implemented using Matlab, and then the routines used to develop it were presented and commented. The proposal analyzed used a real transformation matrix for the entire frequency range considered in this case. For those elements related to the phases of the considered system, the transformation matrix was composed of the elements of Clarke's matrix. In part related to the ground wires, the elements of the transformation matrix had to establish a relationship with the elements of the phases considering the establishment of a single homopolar reference in the mode domain. In the case of three-phase lines with the presence of two ground wires, it was unable to get the full diagonalization of the matrices Z and Y in the mode domain. The relative errors between the proposed routine and the correct values of eigenvalues were shown by graphs plotted using Matlab. Thus, for a future work, a correction routine will be used for non-transposed three-phase transmission line cases for the transformation matrix presented.

Acknowledgements

This work was supported by FAPESP.

Author details

R. C. Monzani[2], A. J. Prado[1], L.S. Lessa[2] and L. F. Bovolato[2]

1 Departamento de Sistemas e Energia (DSE) – Faculdade de Engenharia Elétrica e Computação (FEEC) – Campinas State University (UNICAMP), Brazil

2 Departamento de Engenharia Elétrica (DEE) – Faculdade de Engenharia de Ilha Solteira (FEIS) – Paulista State University (UNESP) , Brazil

References

[1] Microtran Power System Analysis Corporation. Transients analysis program reference manual. Vancouver: MPSAC, 1994.

[2] Semlyen, A.; Dabuleanu, A. Fast and accurate switching transient calculations on transmission lines with ground return using recursive convolutions. IEEE Transaction on Power Apparatus and Systems Pas-94, New York, v. 94, n. 2, p. 561-571, 1975.

[3] Marti, J. R. Accurate modeling of frequency-dependent transmission lines in electromagnetic transients simulations. IEEE Transaction on Power Apparatus and Systems, New York, v. 101, n. 1, p. 147 – 155, 1982.

[4] Tavares, M. C.; Pissolato, J.; Portela, C. M. Mode domain multiphase transmission line model-use in transient studies. IEEE Transactions on Power Delivery, New York, v. 14, p. 1533-1544, 1999.

[5] Tavares, M. C.; Pissolato, J.; Portela, C. M. Quasi-modes three-phase transmission line model-transformation matrix equations. International Journal of Electrical Power & Energy Systems, Oxford, v. 23, n. 4, p. 325-334, 2001.

[6] Kurokawa, S.; Tavares, M. C.; Pissolato, J.; Portela, C. M. Applying a new methodology to verify transmission line model performance – the equivalent impedance test. in: Power Engineering Society Summer Meeting, 2001, Montreal. Conference of the… Montreal: IEEE, 2001. p. 1766-1771.

[7] Morched, A.; Gustavsen, B.; Tartibi, M. A universal model for accurate calculations of electromagnetic transients on overhead lines and underground cables. IEEE Transactions on Power Delivery, New York, v. 14, n. 3, 1999, p. 1032-1035.

[8] Nguyen, H. V.; Dommel, H. W.; Marti, J. R. Direct phase-domain modeling of frequency-dependent overhead transmission lines. IEEE Transactions on Power Delivery, New York, v. 12, n. 3, p. 1335-1344, 1997.

[9] Noda, T.; Gagaoka, N.; Ametani, A. Phase domain modeling of frequency dependent transmission lines by means of an ARMA model. IEEE Transactions on Power Delivery, New York, v. 11, n. 1, p. 401-411, 1996.

[10] Tavares, M. C.; Pissolato, J.; Portela, C. M. Six-Phase transmission line propagation characteristics and new three-phase representation. IEEE Transactions on Power, New York, v. 8, n. 3, p. 1470-1483, 1993.

[11] Semlyen, M. H.; Abdel-Rahman, M. H. State equation modeling of untransposed three phase lines. IEEE Transaction on Power Apparatus and Systems Pas, New York, v. 103, n. 11, p. 3402-3405, 1984.

[12] Bhatt, N. B.; Venkata, S. S. Venkata; Guyker, W. C.; Booth, W. H., Sixphase (multiphase) power transmission systems: fault analysis, IEEE Transactions on Power Apparatus and Systems Pas, Morgantown, v. 96, n. 3, p. 758-765, 1977.

[13] Ryan, H. M. High voltage engineering and testing. London: Peter Peregrinus on behalf of the Institution of Electrical Engineers, 1994. 447 p.

[14] Dommel, H. W. Electromagnetic transients program. Oregon: Rule Book, 1984.

[15] Brandão, J. A.; Faria, J. Overhead three-phase transmission lines – nondiagonalizable situations. IEEE Transactions on Power Delivery, New York, v. 3, n. 4, p. 1348–1355, 1988.

[16] Brandão, J. A. F.; Briceño Mendez, J. H. Modal analysis of unstransposed bilateral three-phase lines – a perturbation approach. IEEE Transactions on Power Delivery, New York, v. 12, n. 1, p. 497 – 504, 1997.

[17] Brandão, J. A. F.; Briceño Mendez, J. H. On the modal analysis of asymmetrical three-phase transmission lines using standard transformation matrices. IEEE Transaction on Power Delivery, New York, v. 12, n. 4, p. 1760 – 1765, 1997.

[18] Clarke, E. Circuit analysis of A-C power systems. New York: J. Wiley, 1950. v.1.

[19] Prado, A. J.; Pissolato Filho, J.; Kurokawa, S.; Bovolato, L. F. Eigenvalue analyses of two parallel lines using a single real transformation matrix, in: IEEE/Power Engineering Society General Meeting, 2005, San Francisco. Conference of the… San Francisco: IEEE, 2005.

[20] Prado, A. J.; Pissolato Filho, J.; Kurokawa, S.; Bovolato, L. F. Nontransposed three-phase line analyses with a single real transformation matrix. in: IEEE/Power Engineering Society General Meeting, 2005, San Francisco. Conference of the… San Francisco: IEEE, 2005.

[21] Wedepohl, L. M.; Nguyen, H. V.; Irwin, G. D. Frequency-dependent transformation matrices for untransposed transmission lines using Newton-Raphson method. IEEE Transactions on Power Systems, New York, v. 11, n. 3, p. 15381546, 1996.

[22] Nguyen, T. T.; Chan, H. Y. Evaluation of modal transformation matrices for overhead transmission lines and underground cables by optimization method. IEEE Transactions on Power Delivery, New York, v. 17, n. 1, p. 200-209, 2002.

[23] Nobre, D. M.; Boaventura, W. C.; Neves, W. L. A. Phase-domain network equivalents for electromagnetic transient studies. in: IEEE Power Engineering Society General Meeting, 2005, San Francisco. Conference of the… San Francisco: IEEE, 2005.

[24] Budner, A. Introduction of frequency dependent transmission line parameters into an electromagnetic transients program. IEEE Transactions on Power Apparatus and Systems PAS, New York, v. 89, p. 88-97, 1970.

[25] Carneiro JR., S.; Martí, J. R.; Dommel, H. W.; BARROS, H. M. Na Efficient procedure for the implementation of corona models in electromagnetic transients programs. IEEE Transactions on Power Delivery, New York, v. 9, n. 2, p. 849-855, 1994.

[26] Martins, T. F. R. D.; Lima, A. C. S.; Carneiro Jr., S. Effect of impedance approximate formulae on frequency dependence realization. In: IEEE Power Engineering Society General Meeting, 2005, San Francisco. Conference of the… San Francisco: IEEE, 2005.

[27] Wedepohl, L. M.; Wilcox, D. J. Transient analysis of underground power transmission system – system model and wave propagation characteristics. in: Proceedings of Institution Electrical Engineers, Michigan, v. 120, n. 2, p. 253260,1973.

[28] Fuchs, R. D.; Almeida, M. T. Projetos mecânicos das linhas aéreas de transmissão. São Paulo: Edgard Blücher, 1984. 360 p.

[29] Stevenson, W. D. Elementos de análise de sistemas de potência. São Paulo: McGraw-Hill do Brasil, 1977.

[30] Grainger, J.J.; Stevenson, W.D. Power System Analysis. New York, p. 271-274, 1994.

[31] Prado, A. J.; Pissolato Filho, J.; Kurokawa, S.; Bovolato, L. F. Modal transformation analyses for Double three-phase transmission lines. IEEE Transactions on Power Delivery, New York, v. 22, n. 3, p.1926 – 1936, 2007.

[32] Prado, A. J.; Pissolato Filho, J.; Kurokawa, S.; Bovolato, L. F. Correction procedure applied to a single real transformation matrix – untransposed three-phase transmission line cases. In: IEEE/PES Transmission & Distribution Latin America, 2006, Caracas. Proceedings of the… Caracas: IEEE, 2006.

[33] Prado, A. J.; Kurokawa, S.; Pissolato Filho, J.; Bovolato, L. F. Step by step analyses of Clarke's matrix correction procedure for untransposed threephase transmission line cases. In: IEEE/PES General Meeting, 2010, Minneapolis. Proceedings of the… Minneapolis: IEEE, 2010.

[34] Prado, A. J.; Kurokawa, S.; Pissolato Filho, J.; Bovolato, L. F. Voltage and current mode vector analyses of correction procedure application to Clarke's matrix-symmetrical three-phase cases. Journal of Electromagnetic Analysis and Applications, v. 2, n. 1, p. 7-17, 2010.

[35] Prado, A. J.; Kurokawa, S.; Pissolato Filho, J.; Bovolato, L. F.; Costa, E. C. M. Phase-mode transformation matrix application for transmission line and electromagnetic transient analyses. New York: New Science Publishers, 2011. 102 p.

Chapter 19

Analysis of Balancing of Unbalanced Rotors and Long Shafts using GUI MATLAB

Viliam Fedák, Pavel Záskalický and Zoltán Gelvanič

Additional information is available at the end of the chapter

http://dx.doi.org/10.5772/58378

1. Introduction

Rotating machinery is commonly used in mechanical and electromechanical systems that include rotors of motors and engines, machining tools, industrial turbomachinery, etc. In case of unbalanced distribution of rotating masses around an axis of rotation the rotor unbalance arises. This presents a serious engineering problem because it is a major cause of excessive vibrations, esp. at higher speeds. Arising large centrifugal unbalanced forces can lead to damage of bearings and finally to destruction of machines. This is the reason why solving of the unbalance is a basic concern in design and operation of the machinery.

Vibration of the rotating machinery is suppressed by eliminating the root cause of vibration – the system unbalance. Practically, vibrations cannot reach zero values but usually it is acceptable to decrease them to a value lower than that one prescribed for a certain quality class of the machinery [1]. Balancing of the rotor increases the bearing life, minimizes vibrations, audible noise, power losses, and finally it results in increased quality of products.

The problems arising when dealing with unbalanced rotating bodies have been analyzed in many references. The exceptional positions among them hold two references [1, 2]. Due to its importance, numerous references have dealt with vibrations and their eliminations, e.g. [3] – [6] and also serious companies are facing the vibrations, just to mention few of them – [7, 8]. If the vibrations are below a normal level, they may indicate only normal wear but when they are increasing, it may signal the need to take an immediate maintenance action. A level of unbalance that is acceptable at low speeds is completely unacceptable at a higher speed. This is because the unbalance condition produces centrifugal force, which increases with square of the speed [9] – if the speed doubles, the force quadruples; etc. For this reason it is important to determine the critical speed at which excessive oscillations present a direct serious danger.

INTECH
open science | open minds

© 2014 The Author(s). Licensee InTech. This chapter is distributed under the terms of the Creative Commons Attribution License (http://creativecommons.org/licenses/by/3.0), which permits unrestricted use, distribution, and reproduction in any medium, provided the original work is properly cited.

Unbalancing of the rotating body is evaluated by the ISO standards that specify Balance Quality Grade [10]. The ISO standards (ISO 1940-2 and ISO 11342) contain detailed methods of calculating different unbalance tolerances. Balance Quality Grade is a term used to define the limits of residual unbalance. It represents the product of the eccentricity e (in mm) multiplied by the operating frequency f (in Hz). The standards contain guidelines with regard to a number of varieties of devices. Tab.1 shows an example of standard guidelines with regard to different devices (it is an indicative example only, more details are in [7, 8]).

The main goal of our simulation study consists in off-line analysis of influence of rotating body eccentricity to its vibrations, their following elimination by calculation of position and value of additional masses removing vibrations.

Class G of unbalancing	Magnitude $e \times f$ [mm/s]	Examples of machines
G 4000	4000	Slow diesel engines.
G 630	630	Drives of rigidly mounted large two-cycle engines.
G 250	250	Rigidly mounted fast four-cylinder diesel engines.
G 100	100	Diesel and petrol combustion engines (for cars, trucks, locomotives).
G 40	40	Wheels for car and motorcycles, drive shafts.
G 16	16	Components of agriculture machines: crankshaft drives, grinders, connecting shafts.
G 6,3	6.3	Parts of process plant machines, gas turbines, centrifuges, small electrical motors (max. diameter of shaft Ø 80 mm and max. 950 rev/min), machine tools, pumping devices, fans, water turbines, flywheels, paper machinery rolls.
G 2,5	2.5	Gas and steam turbines, turbo-compressors, drives in computers, large electrical motors (more than Ø 80 mm and 950 rev/min), gas turbines, machine tools, parts of textile machines.
G 1	1	Video, audio and tape recorder and phonograph drives.
G 0,4	0.4	Spindles, discs, shafts of machines with high precision, gyroscopes.

Table 1. Balance quality grades and representatives of various groups of rotating machines

2. Analysis of forces caused by unbalanced rotating body

Considered in this study are two cases of cylindrical rotating bodies: a rotor and a long shaft. Their drawings and parameters used for later simulation are shown in Fig. 1. Both rotating bodies are similar, what concerns their dynamical properties and calculation of possible vibrations. Fig. 1 also shows parameters of rotating bodies. Here, the rotor is considered to be fixed, resting on massless shaft that is supported on bearings and the shaft is circular and solid.

http://dx.doi.org/10.5772/58378

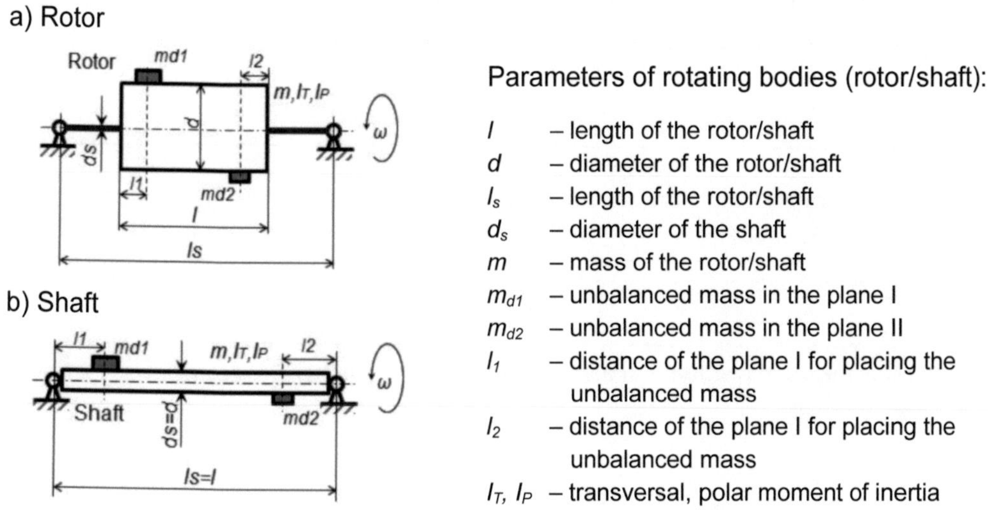

Figure 1. Parameters of rotating bodies: rotor and shaft

The unbalanced rotating body can move in radial direction horizontally and vertically and it can also rotate around axes *x*, *y*, that are in the plane perpendicular to the axis *z* of rotation.

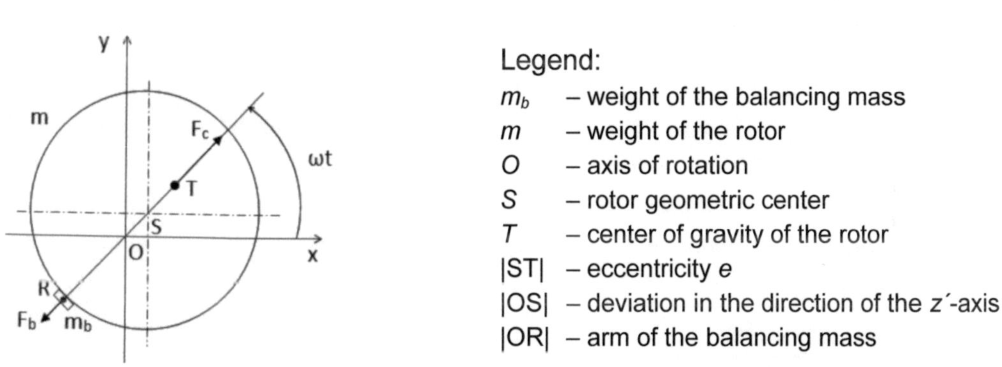

Figure 2. Analysis of forces in an unbalanced rotor

Analysis of arising radial forces in case of the unbalanced rotor and principle of its balancing by adding a balanced mass results from the drawing in Fig. 2. Due to the unevenly distributed mass around the axis of rotation, the center of gravity is shifted from its geometric center by the eccentricity e (given by the distance $\overline{ST}$). The centrifugal force F_c during rotation causes that the rotor is deviated from its direction, what leads to the increase of the distance between the center of gravity and axis of rotation. It is obvious that to eliminate the eccentricity e a small balancing mass must be placed in opposite direction so that its centrifugal force F_b would also act in this direction – against the force F_c. From the Newton's Third Law of Motion it is obvious that at rotation, the centrifugal force caused by the mass m_n on the radius r is equal to the centrifugal force activated by mass m rotating on the radius e:

$$m_n\, r = m\, e \tag{1}$$

from which we can calculate the eccentricity:

$$e = \frac{m_n\, r}{m} \tag{2}$$

For tolerable maximal residual unbalance e in the certain class G one gets:

$$e = \frac{v}{w} = \frac{v}{2\pi f} = \frac{v}{2\pi \frac{n}{60}} \tag{3}$$

where v is equal to the class of unbalancing G (because the classification is based on circumferential speed v and on the radius e around the rotor center of gravity).

Other possibility to eliminate the unbalance consists in removing a part of material (e.g. by drilling it off) from determined position on the rotor in direction of the centrifugal force F_c.

According to position of unevenly distributed mass of the rotating body round and along the axis of rotation we distinguish a static unbalance and the dynamic one (Tab. 2). To activate an unbalance of the rotating body two balancing masses having different value of the mass m_1 and m_2 are placed into two different planes that are mutually placed at farther distance and in radial direction they are shifted by the angle 180 °. The mass activating the static unbalance of the originally uniformly rotating body is given by the difference of both masses:

$$m_s = m_{d1} - m_{d2} \tag{4}$$

a) Balanced rotating system	b) Static unbalanced rotating system
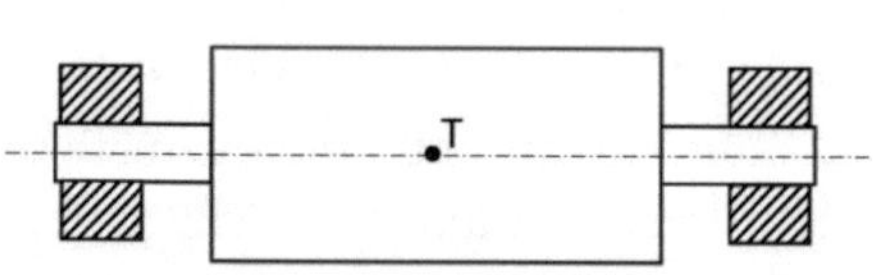	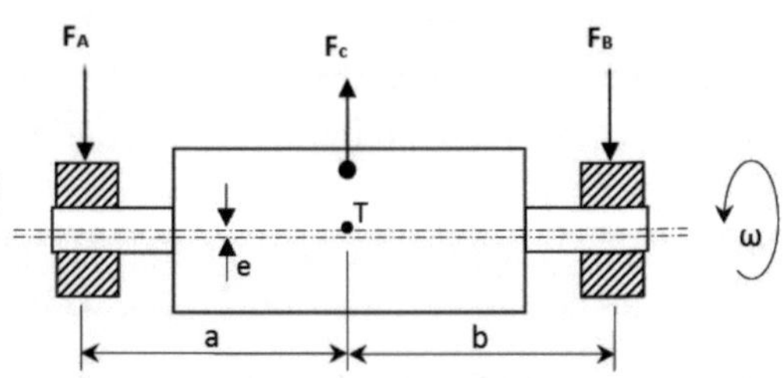

c) Torque unbalanced rotating system	d) Dynamic unbalanced rotating system
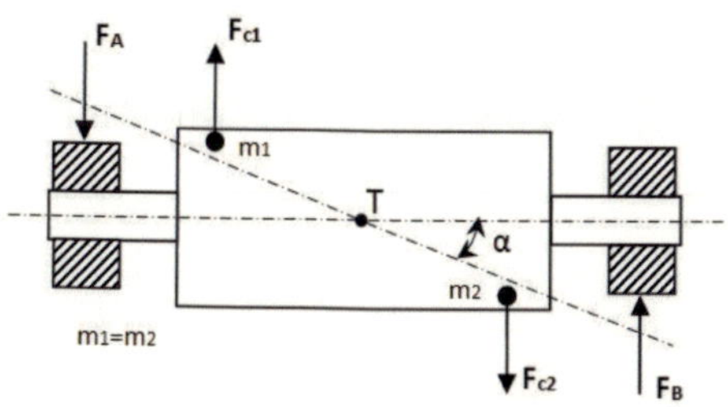	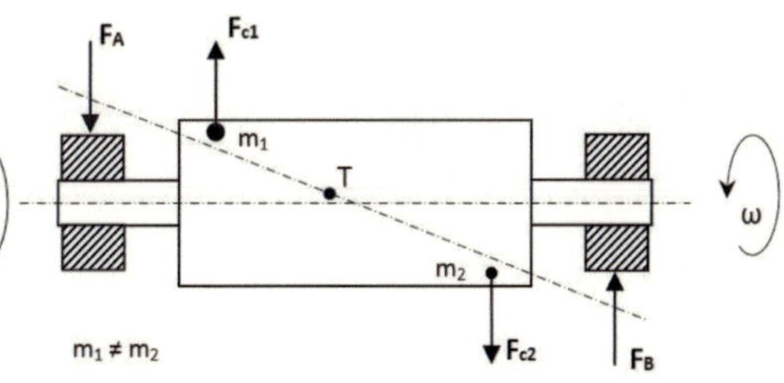

Table 2. Explanation of types of rotating systems unbalance

In case that two equal balancing masses are placed in two planes, the static unbalance is not activated, but a dynamic unbalance arises. It is graphically displayed in Tab. 2.

Let's consider a console (Fig. 3) that is supported by two rigid bearings and is loaded by force F. This causes console bending y which is directly proportional to force F. The console reacts by force F_D having the same value but opposite orientation. If a mass m is placed on the console, it will behave similarly like being placed on a spiral spring, [12].

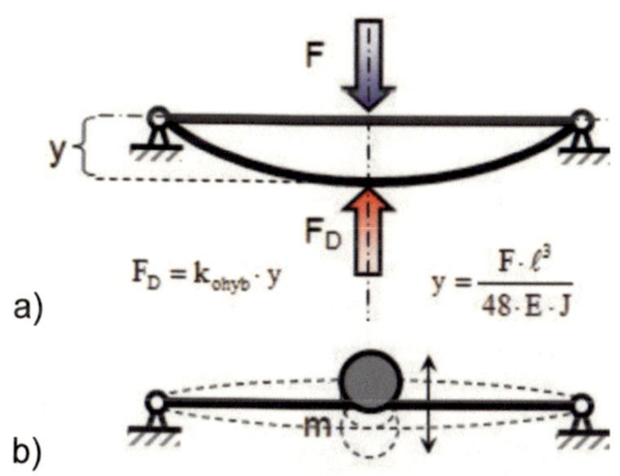

Legend:

l – length of the member
E – Young modulus of elasticity (steel: 2,1.10^{11} Pa)
J – Moment of Inertia of a body with a solid circular cross section

Figure 3. Calculation of stiffness of a console supported by two rigid bearings, [12]

For calculation of the mathematical model several further formulas are necessary (with the nomenclature listed in Fig. 1 and Fig. 3):

- The **torque stiffness** of symmetrical isotropic rotor is given by the equation, [3]:

$$K = k\, l^2 \tag{5}$$

- The **transversal moment of inertia**, presents the moment of inertia round the axis that is perpendicular to the axis of rotation, [5]:

$$I_T = \frac{1}{4} m_c \, r^2 \tag{6}$$

- The **polar moment of inertia** of the same rotating body presents the main moment of inertia round the main axis of rotation and is given by formula [5]:

$$I_P = \frac{1}{2} m_c \, r^2 \tag{7}$$

- The **bending rigidity** of a console fixed in rigid bearings is [5]:

$$k = \frac{48 \, E \, J}{l^3} \tag{8}$$

- where for the **quadratic moment of inertia** of the cross-section it holds that:

$$J = \frac{\pi \, d^4}{64} \tag{9}$$

3. Mathematical model of an unbalanced rotor

The most frequently used model of unbalanced rotating body is based on the so called *Jeffcott model* of an unbalanced rotor (developed by H. H. Jeffcott in 1919, [2]). It presents a linear model and consists of a substantial unbalanced disc that is located in center of unsubstantial elastic shaft bedded in two rigid bearings (Fig. 4a). The Jeffcott model has four degrees of freedom that are described by four differential equations of the second order. Considering a disc with the mass m as a mass point, the rotor has only two degrees of freedom and it can move only in radial direction in horizontal and vertical axes. During rotation, the center of gravity moves along a trajectory called the orbit, [5].

A simplified dynamical model of the rotor from Fig. 4a is shown in Fig. 4b. The model also contains flexural rigidity and damping of the bearing what can be considered as a spring and damper rotating synchronously with the rotor. In this way, the rotor is connected with the ground through linear springs and dampers and the movement in x-and y-directions is actuated by time-variable radial components of the rotating vector of the force. It is a consequence of the rotating unbalanced rotor (Fig. 4b). Motion equations for the described substitute model are derived from the Newton's Second Law: $F = ma = m\ddot{x}$, [11]:

http://dx.doi.org/10.5772/58378

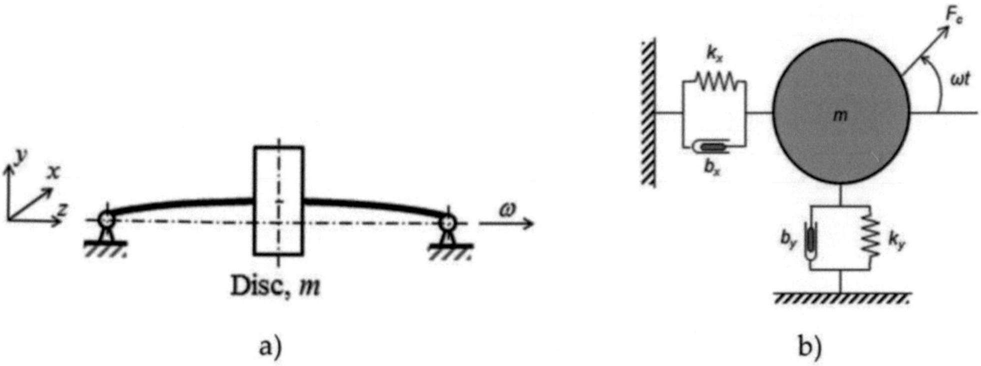

Figure 4. Jeffcott model of a rotor (*a*) and its simplified model with dampers and springs (*b*), [2]

$$m\ddot{x} + b_x\dot{x} + k_x x = F_c\cos(\omega t) \tag{10}$$

$$m\ddot{y} + b_y\dot{y} + k_y y = F_c\sin(\omega t) \tag{11}$$

where b_x, b_y– damping in the x-axis and y-axis, respectively

k_x, k_y– stiffness in the x-axis and y-axis, respectively

If $b_x = b_y$ and $k_x = k_y$, the model presenting the static unbalance of the rotor is considered to be isotropic one and the equations are mutually independent – i.e. they are decoupled. This means that damping and elasticity in the directions of the x-axis and y-axis are equal and the reference frame can rotate in the plane without any change in the motion equations, [5]. The mathematical model is then described in the coordinates $\{x, y\}$ by the following motion equations:

a. motion equations for the static unbalance:

$$m_c\ddot{x} + b\dot{x} + kx = F_c\cos(\omega t) \tag{12}$$

$$m_c\ddot{y} + b\dot{y} + ky = F_c\sin(\omega t) \tag{13}$$

b. motion equations for the dynamic unbalance:

$$I_T\ddot{\theta}_x + \omega\, I_P\dot{\theta}_y + K\theta_x = M\cos(\omega t) \tag{14}$$

$$I_T\ddot{\theta}_y - \omega\, I_P\dot{\theta}_x + K\theta_y = M\sin(\omega t) \tag{15}$$

where for the centrifugal force F_c and torque M, caused by unbalance, we can derive:

$$F_c = m_s(r + z')\ \omega^2 \tag{16}$$

$$M = \left(m_{d1} + m_{d2}\right)\ \left(l - l_1 - l_2\right)\ r\ \omega^2 \tag{17}$$

The value of eccentricity can be determined by inserting equation (4) into equation (2). The value of $\left(r + z'\right)$ presents an instantaneous value of the arm of unbalancing and z' is total deviation presenting the amplitude of total vibration of the rotor:

$$z' = \sqrt{x^2 + y^2} \tag{18}$$

Let's just remind that for calculation of longitudinal vibration a similar formula is valid like in the previous case. Total twist angle γ consists of two components, [4]:

$$\gamma = \sqrt{\theta_x{}^2 + \theta_y{}^2} \tag{19}$$

To eliminate the centrifugal force F_c and resulting torque M caused by the rotor unbalance it is necessary to add or remove (e.g. be drilling-off) a certain mass in both planes. We obtain it mathematically by summing or subtracting the centrifugal force from the balancing mass the angle of which is shifted from the force F_c by angle φ.

For balancing we can derive the motion equations having the final form:

a. Adding of the balancing mass:

Static balancing:

$$m_c\ddot{x} + b\dot{x} + kx = m_s(r + z')\ \omega^2\cos(\omega t) + m_b(r_b - z')\ \omega^2\cos(\omega t + \phi) \tag{20}$$

$$m_c\ddot{y} + b\dot{y} + ky = m_s(r + z')\ \omega^2\sin(\omega t) + m_b(r_b - z')\ \omega^2\sin(\omega t + \phi) \tag{21}$$

http://dx.doi.org/10.5772/58378

Dynamic balancing:

$$I_T\ddot{\theta}_x + \omega\, I_P\dot{\theta}_y + K\theta_x = M\cos(\omega t) + \left(m_{b1} + m_{b2}\right)\,\left(l - l_1 - l_2\right)\, r_b\;\omega^2\cos(\omega t + \phi) \tag{22}$$

$$I_T\ddot{\theta}_y - \omega\, I_P\dot{\theta}_x + K\theta_y = M\sin(\omega t) + \left(m_{b1} + m_{b2}\right)\,\left(l - l_1 - l_2\right)\, r_b\;\omega^2\sin(\omega t + \phi) \tag{23}$$

where $\phi = 180\ °$

b. Removing mass (e.g. by drilling off):

Static balancing:

$$m_c\ddot{x} + b\dot{x} + kx = m_s(r + z')\;\omega^2\cos(\omega t) - m_b(r_b + z')\;\omega^2\cos(\omega t + \phi) \tag{24}$$

$$m_c\ddot{y} + b\dot{y} + ky = m_s(r + z')\;\omega^2\sin(\omega t) - m_b(r_b + z')\;\omega^2\sin(\omega t + \phi) \tag{25}$$

Dynamic balancing:

$$I_T\ddot{\theta}_x + \omega\, I_P\dot{\theta}_y + K\theta_x = M\cos(\omega t) - \left(m_{b1} + m_{b2}\right)\,\left(l - l_1 - l_2\right)\, r_b\;\omega^2\cos(\omega t + \phi) \tag{26}$$

$$I_T\ddot{\theta}_y - \omega\, I_P\dot{\theta}_\chi + K\theta_y = M\sin(\omega t) - (m_{b1} + m_{b2})\;(l - l_1 - l_2)\; r_b\;\omega^2\sin(\omega t + \phi) \tag{27}$$

where $\phi = 0\ °$

4. Simulation model of unbalanced rotor

Based on the mathematical model the simulation model was designed in MATLAB/Simulink program. The simulation model corresponding to the mathematical model of unbalanced rotor is shown in Fig. 5. At the input there is a start-up block presenting linear increasing of the rotor speed to the working revolutions n in steady-state (the blocks Ramp, Ramp1 and Subtract).

Fig. 6 shows the *Static balancing* subsystem from Fig. 5. It was derived from the motion equations and contains the following blocks (that are equal both for x-and y-axes).

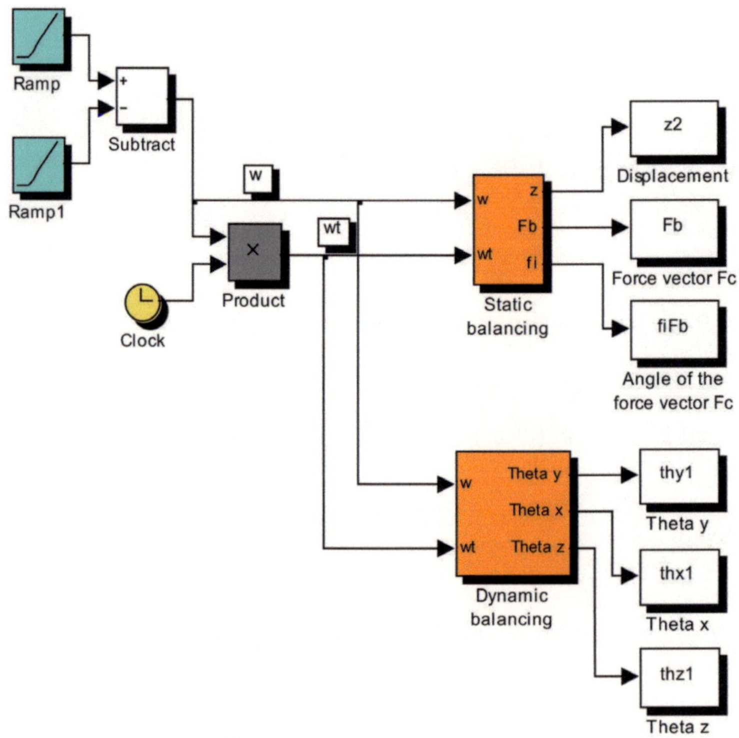

Figure 5. Simulation model of the unbalanced rotor

Description of the blocks:

- **Centrifugal force Fc** – the block calculates centrifugal force causing an unbalance and deviation of the rotor in the x-and y-axes.
- **Centrifugal force of the balancing mass** – the block calculates value of the centrifugal force caused by the added mass (or the removed one) m_b across the radius r_b. The force is shifted by the angle φ towards to that one causing the unbalance.
- **Sum of forces** – giving sum of all forces acting in the system. At the output there is a total force acting in the direction of the x-axis and y-axis.
- **Stiffness** – presents bending rigidity of the shaft according to the equation (8).

http://dx.doi.org/10.5772/58378

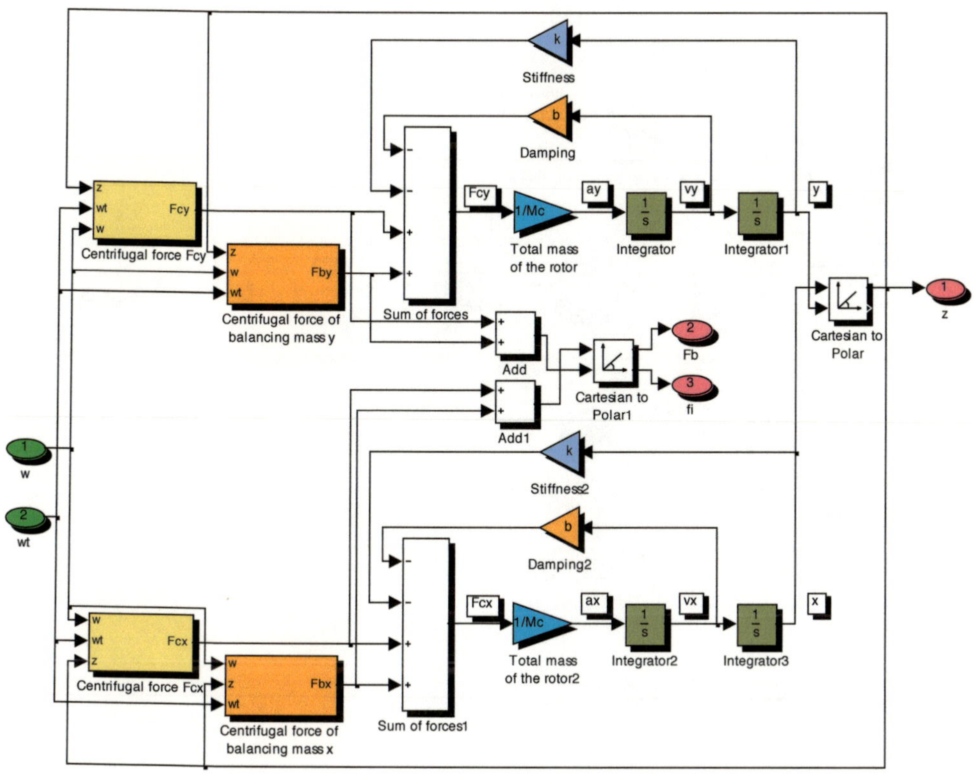

Figure 6. Subsystem *Static balancing*

- **Damping** – presents damping of the bearings (set by the user).
- **Cartesian to Polar** – this block calculates the deviation in the z'-axis that presents radial vibrations of rotating body. The value is re-calculated from Cartesian coordinate system into the polar one.
- **Rotor total mass** – it is a block gaining the input signal by inverted value of the total rotor mass. Its output presents acceleration of the rotor gravity center. During process of balancing the mass of the rotor can be enlarged or decreased according to the choice (of adding or removing the balancing mass).

The block diagrams of subsystems for calculation of the centrifugal forces of unbalanced masses in the x-and y-axes are shown in Figs. 7 and 8. The constant fi1 presents the angle chosen by the user at which the balancing mass should be placed. For purpose of simulation this value in degrees is transformed changed to radians (the block **Degrees to Radians**).

Fig. 9 shows a subsystem for calculation of the centrifugal force of balancing masses in direction of the y-axis and illustrated in Fig. 10 is the same one in direction of the x-axis.

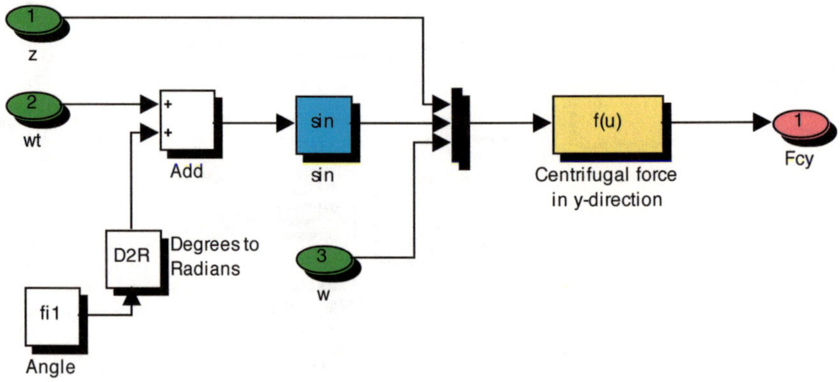

Figure 7. Calculation of the centrifugal force Fcy of the unbalancing mass

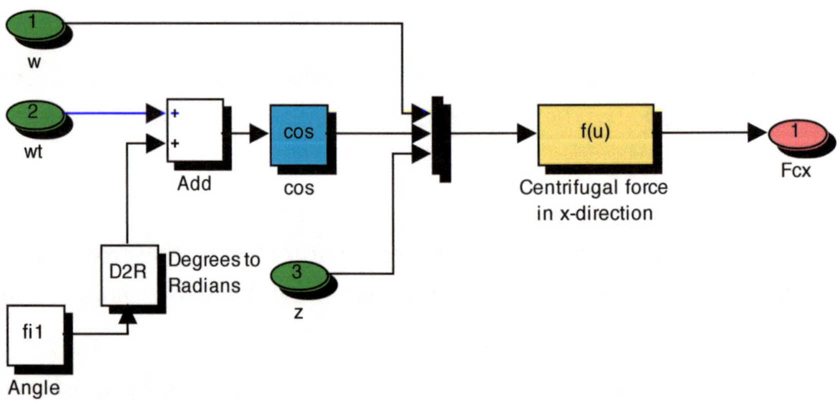

Figure 8. Calculation of the centrifugal force Fcx of the unbalancing mass

http://dx.doi.org/10.5772/58378

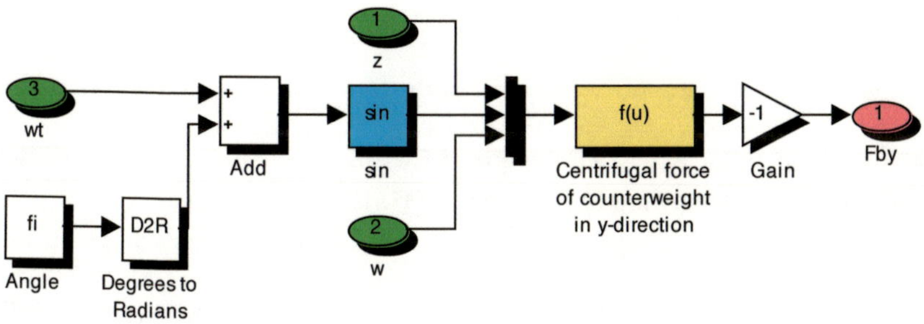

Figure 9. Calculation of centrifugal force Fby for the balancing mass

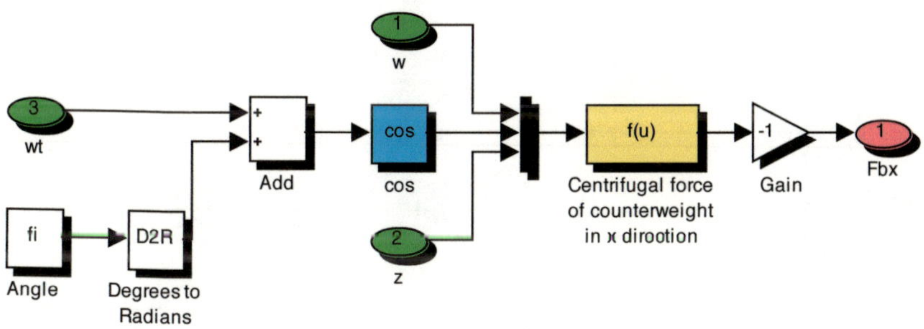

Figure 10. Calculation of Fbx centrifugal force for the balancing mass

Fig. 11 shows the second part of the simulation model from Fig. 5 – the subsystem *Dynamic balancing*. The scheme contains the following blocks for the coordinate system $\{x, y\}$:

- **Torque from unbalanced masses Mx, My** – using the input parameters, the value of the torque that is excited by the rotor dynamic unbalance is calculated here.
- **Torque from balancing masses Mx, My** – calculates the torque from added or removed balancing masses m_{b1} and m_{b1} across radius r_b. The balancing masses are placed in the position given by angle φ that is chosen by the user.
- **Sum of torques** – presents sums all torques acting in the system. At the output it gives total torque acting in the direction of the x-and y-axes.
- **Torque stiffness** – presents a torque stiffness of the shaft - the equation (5).

- **Transverse inertia** – the block calculates transversal moment of inertia according to equation (6).
- **Polar moment** – presents the polar moment of the body inertia-equation (7).
- **Total torsion angle** – it calculates the angle of the rotor torsion that presents longitudinal vibrations of the rotor according to the equation (18).

The subsystem for calculation of the torque acting on the rotor/shaft in the direction of the x- and y-axes is shown in Figs. 12 and 13. The constant fi1 presents the angle of the balancing mass placement that is chosen by the user (it is the same angle like at static balancing).

Figures 14 and 15 show subsystems for calculation of torque components.

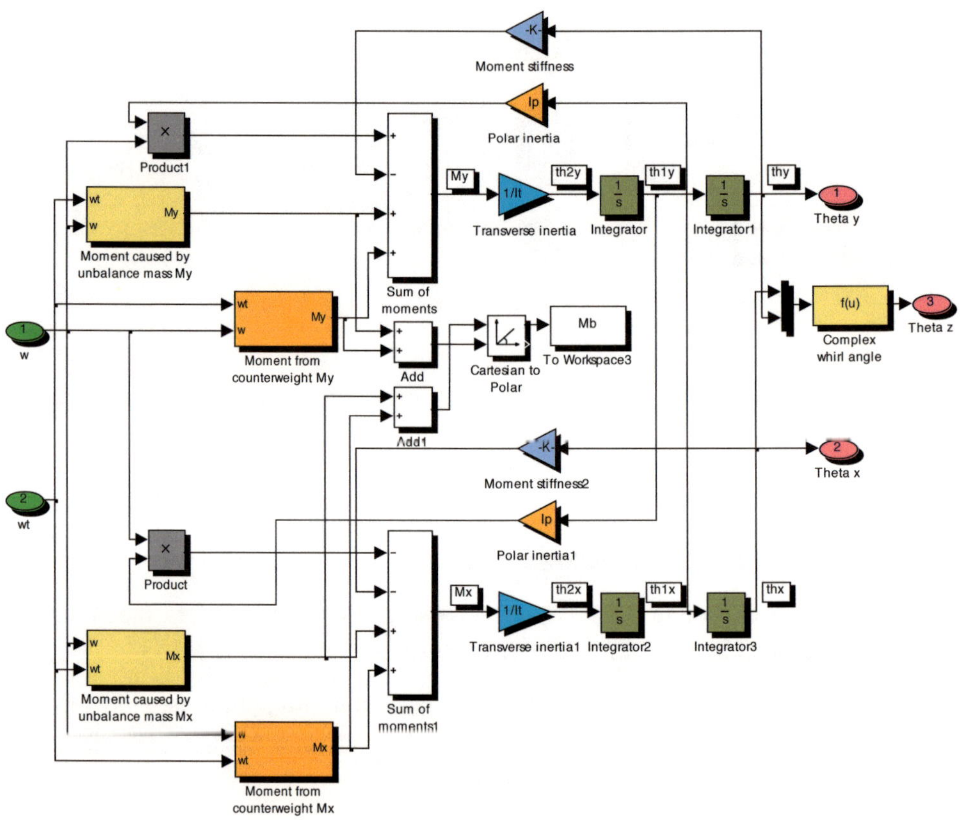

Figure 11. Subsystem *Dynamic balancing*

http://dx.doi.org/10.5772/58378

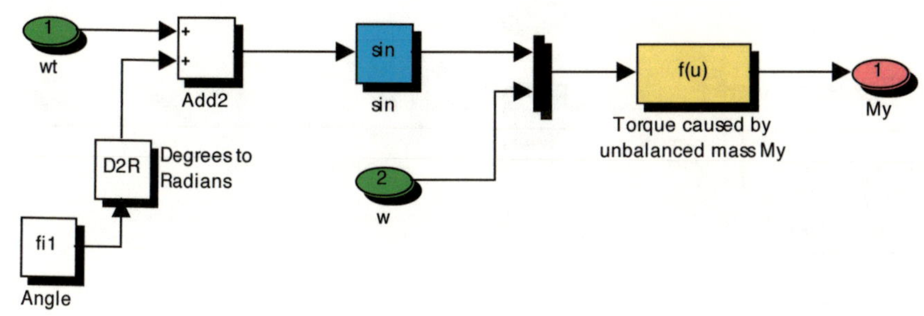

Figure 12. The torque in the *y*-axis direction that is generated by balancing masses

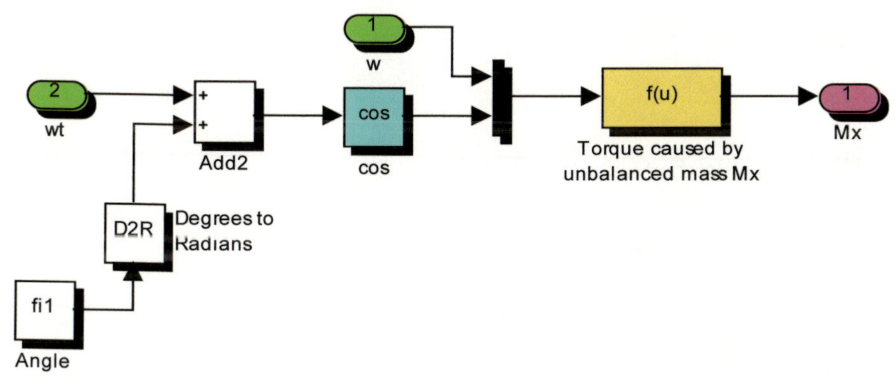

Figure 13. The torque in the *x*-axis direction that is generated by balancing masses

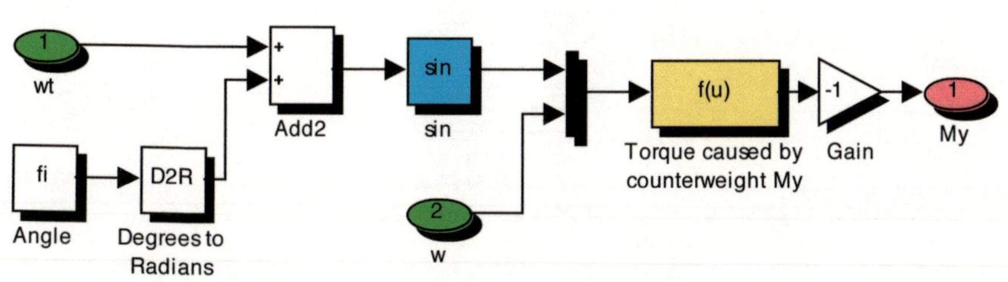

Figure 14. The torque from the balancing masses in the *y*-axis direction

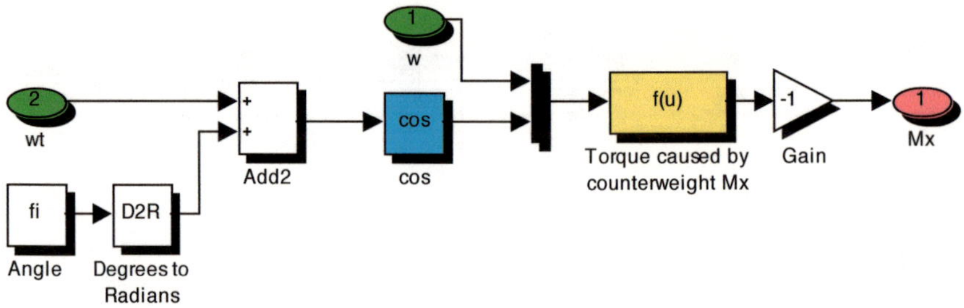

Figure 15. The torque from the balancing masses in the *x*-axis direction

Similarly, in the case of static balancing, the gain equaling to - 1 of the signal presents a drilling-off a part of the rotor mass; the gain value+1 corresponds with adding of the balancing mass. Also, the constant fi presents the angle where the balancing mass (or a drilled whole) should be placed (it is the same, like in the case of static balancing).

5. Simulation results

5.1. Parameters of the simulation models

For virtual experimentation of changes at balancing the rotating body we have performed simulation experiments both for the rotor and shaft. Basic mechanical and dimensional parameters of both rotating bodies are listed in Tab. 3.

Parameter of the rotor/shaft	Rotor	Shaft
Length l [mm]	200	150
Diameter d [mm]	50	20
Length of the shaft l_s [mm]	240	150
Diameter of the shaft d_s [mm]	10	20
Damping of the material b [Nm/s]	0	0
Working revolutions n [rev./min]	800	1000
Diameter of placing unbalancing masses r [mm]	25	10
Mass of the unbalanced mass in the plane I: m_{d1} [g]	20	30
Mass of the unbalanced mass in the plane II: m_{d2} [g]	10	10
Distance of the plane I from the left border l_1 [mm]	10	10
Distance of the plane II from the right border l_2 [mm]	10	10

Table 3. Parameters for simulation of unbalanced rotor/shaft

http://dx.doi.org/10.5772/58378

Tab. 4 shows parameters of the rotor/shaft that are calculated from parameters given in Tab. 3 and finally, in Tab. 5 listed are the parameters determining the place for adding or removing the balancing mass for balancing of the rotating body.

Parameter of the rotor/shaft	Rotor	Shaft
Stiffness k [N/m]	3.58 10^5	2,34 10^7
Mass of the rotor m [kg]	3.08	0.37
Torque stiffness K [Nm]	7.15 10^3	2.63 10^5
Transversal moment of inertia I_T [kgm^2]	0.0195	0.0011
Polar moment of inertia I_P [kgm^2]	0.0389	0.0023

Table 4. Calculated parameters from the parameters in Table 3

Parameter of the rotor/shaft	Rotor (recommended / chosen)	Shaft (recommended / chosen)
Diameter of balancing masses r_b [mm]	25 / 25	10 / 10
Mass of the balancing mass in the plane I m_{b1} [g]	20 / 20	31.667 / 31.6
Mass of the balancing mass in the plane II m_{b2} [g]	10 / 10	11.667 / 11.5
Distance of the plane I from the left border l_{1b} [mm]	10 / 10	15 / 15
Distance of the plane II from the left border l_{2b} [mm]	10 / 10	15 / 15

Table 5. Recommended and chosen parameters for simulation of balanced rotor and shaft

To compare the results, in case of balancing of rotor we have used the calculated masses, but in case of the shaft for the balancing masses we used a little smaller mass than recommended. Simulations were performed for unbalanced and balanced rotor and various forms of graphs were obtained, which are analyzed in the following. The basic graph types are: time-dependence, orbital trajectory of the center of gravity and logarithmic Bode frequency characteristics.

5.2. Run-up of the rotating body to working revolutions

The unbalancing of the rotating body becomes evident during its rotation. To reach the steady-state speed, the simulation model is actuated from the starting block giving a linear increasing signal during pre-set time (Fig. 16, the rising time of 0.1 s was chosen). The steady-state angular speed for the rotor is equal to 83.78 rad/s and for the shaft 104.72 rad/s.

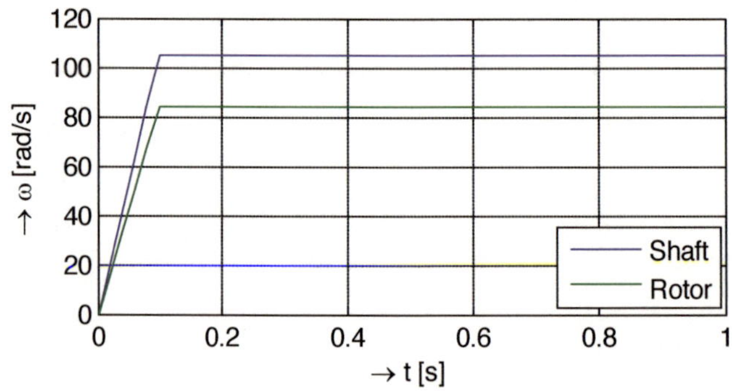

Figure 16. The graph showing angular speed course at starting of the rotor and shaft. In time of 0.1 s they reach the operating speed.

5.3. Simulation results for unbalanced and balanced rotor

The deviations present vibrations that are caused by static unbalance (Fig. 17). Resulting vibrations are permanent-undamped. When comparing outputs from simulations – the vibrations of unbalanced rotor (Fig. 17a) – with the vibrations of the balanced rotor (Fig. 17b), one can see approximately several orders lower amplitude of vibrations after balancing (compare the scaling factor of both graphs in each figure – they are different for the unbalanced and balanced rotor).

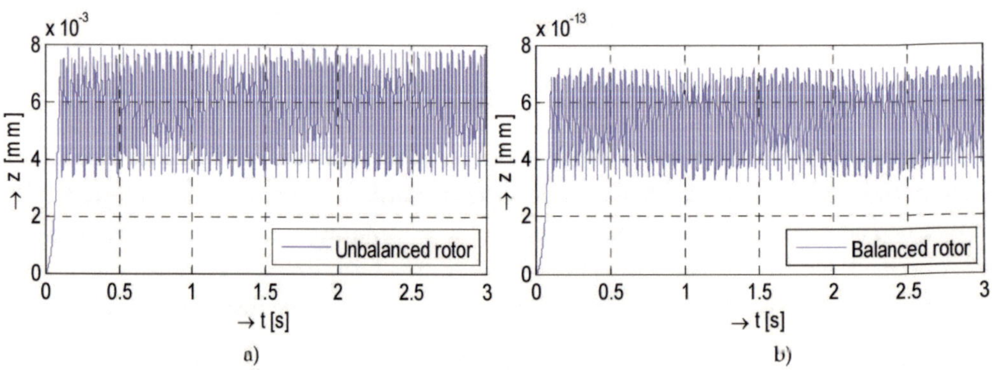

Figure 17. Bending vibrations of the rotor: a) unbalanced, b) balanced one

During start-up, the diameter of trajectory gradually grows and finally its orbit circulates in a certain range (Fig. 18). The analyzed system presents the 4th order system, which means that the resulting time course consists of mixing two harmonic courses of various frequencies. After

http://dx.doi.org/10.5772/58378

balancing (Fig. 18b), the orbital trajectory turns round a considerably lower diameter (note different scales in y-axes in the figures prior and after balancing).

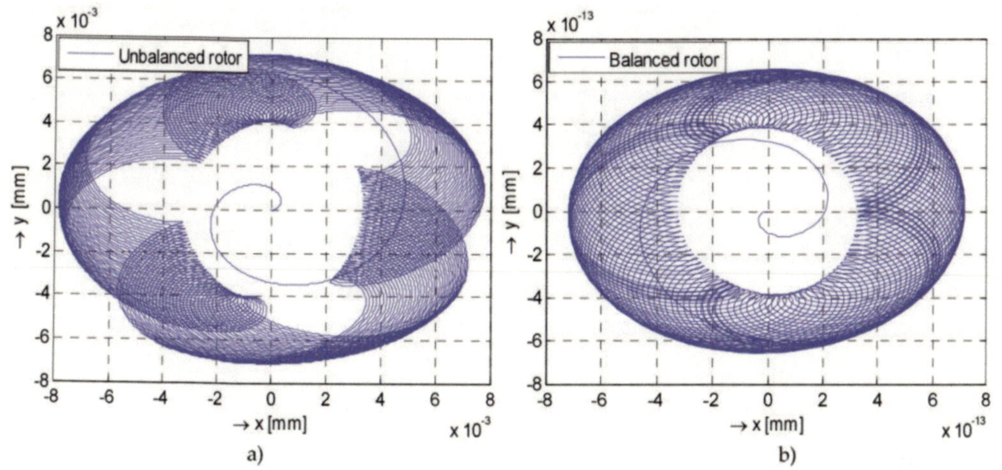

Figure 18. Orbital trajectory of the rotor: a) unbalanced, b) balanced one

Fig. 19a shows amplitude of the force acting on bearings due to a static unbalance. This is a total force; in case of asymmetrical rotor the force acting on a bearing is equal to one half of the total force. After balancing (Fig. 19b), the force from the unbalance masses is negligible.

Fig. 20 shows rotating vectors of the centrifugal force in case of the unbalanced rotor (Fig. 20a) and the balanced one (Fig. 20b). Let's note that in Fig. 20b the scaling factor is much lower in comparison with that one shown in Fig. 20a.

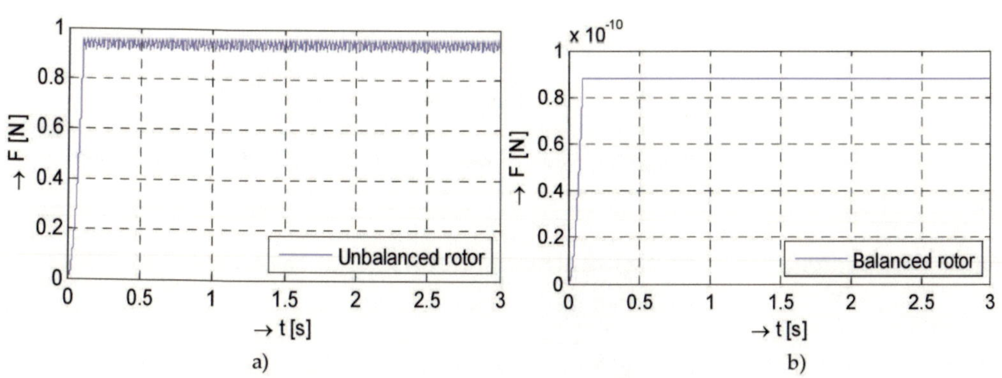

Figure 19. Force acting on bearings: a) prior to and b) after the rotor balancing

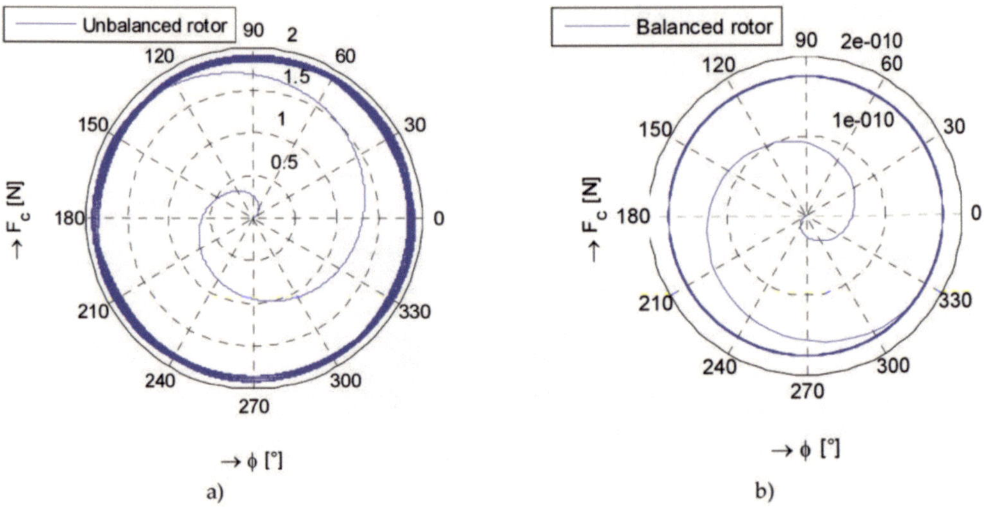

Figure 20. Rotating vector of rotor centrifugal force: a) unbalanced, b) balanced rotor

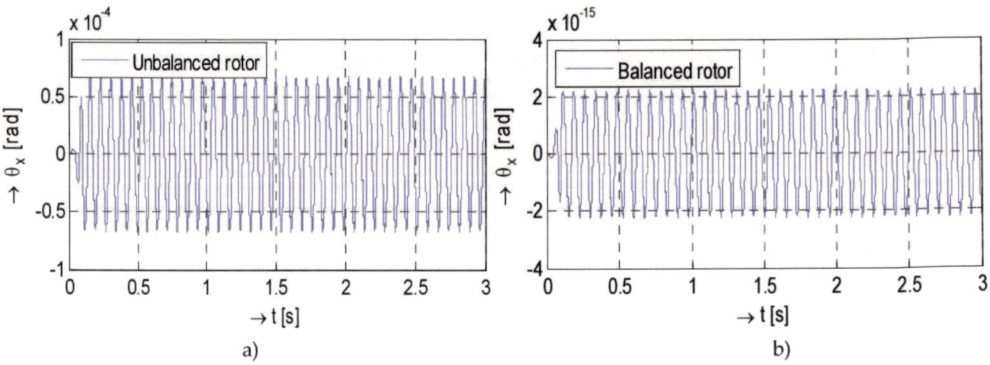

Figure 21. Twist angle of the rotor round the *x* axis for: a) unbalanced and b) balanced rotor

Fig. 22 shows time courses of complex twist of the rotor that present longitudinal vibrations prior to and after the balancing.

Fig. 23 shows torque acting on the unbalanced rotor (Fig. 23a) or on the balanced one (Fig. 23b). The amplitude of the unbalanced torque remains constant, of course.

Fig. 24 shows Bode logarithmic frequency characteristics depicting critical resonance frequency of investigated unbalanced rotor (its value is 339 rad/s). The steep overshoot at the resonance frequency is caused by zero damping of the model (a theoretical case only).

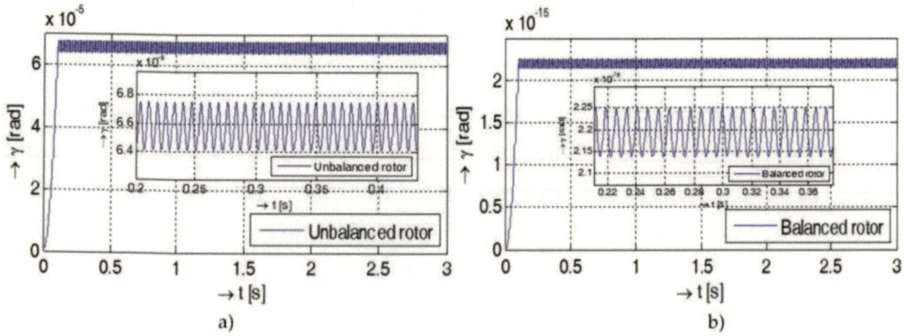

Figure 22. Complex twist of the rotor: a) the unbalanced one, b) the balanced rotor with the detailed course

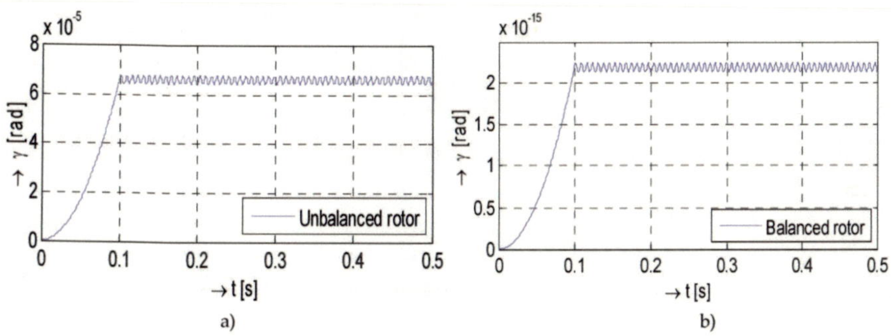

Figure 23. Torque acting on the rotor in case of: a) unbalanced rotor, b) the balanced one

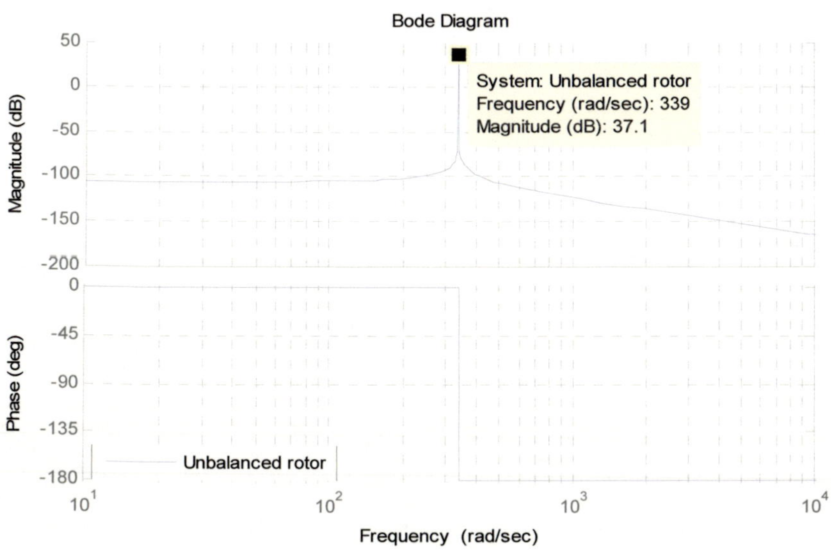

Figure 24. Bode logarithmic frequency characterictics of the unbalanced rotor

5.4. Simulation results for the unbalanced and balanced shaft

Dynamic behavior of an unbalanced and balanced circular solid shaft is very similar to the behavior of the unbalanced and balanced rotors. The deviations have origin in a smaller diameter and larger length of the shaft that leads to higher resonance frequencies and larger angle of twist. The following simulation results show these similarities and differences that are comparable to those in the previous subchapter so we are not going to comment them. Note: let's remark, that the graphs for the balanced shaft are in different scale.

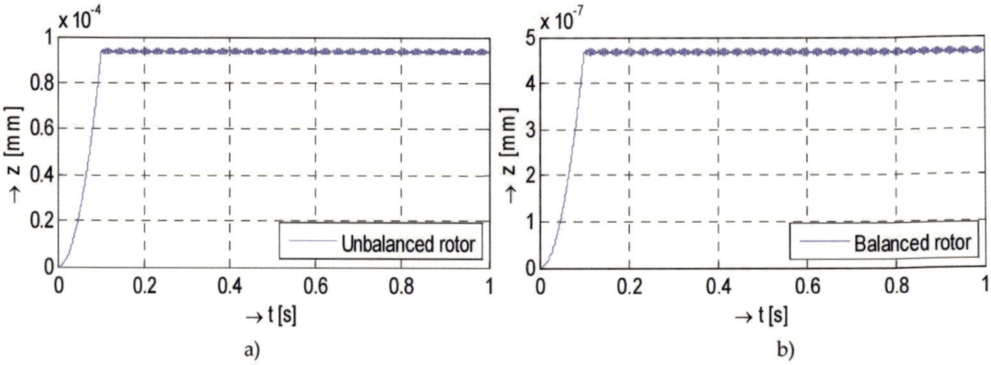

Figure 25. Bending vibration of the shaft: a) unbalanced, b) balanced shaft

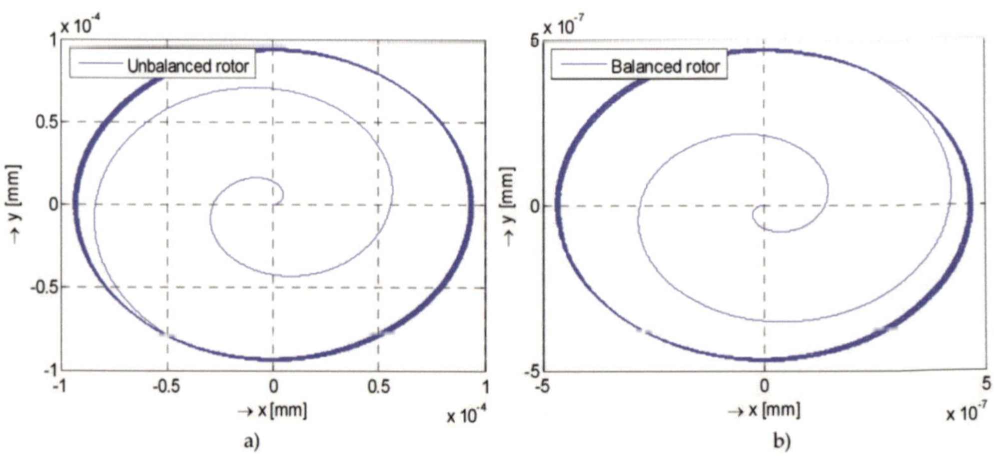

Figure 26. Orbital trajectory of the shaft: a) the unbalanced, b) the balanced one

http://dx.doi.org/10.5772/58378

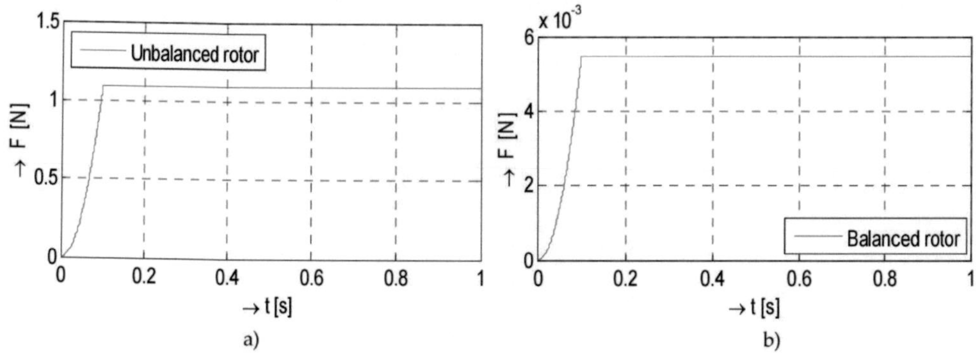

Figure 27. Force acting on the bearings: a) prior balancing, b) after balancing the shaft

From logarithmic characteristics (Fig. 30) it is obvious that the resonance frequency is higher than in case of the rotor of a similar length, material constants and unbalancing masses.

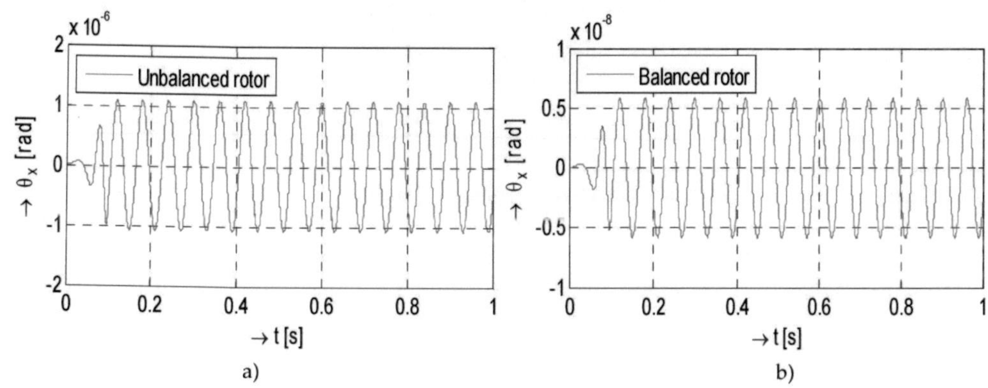

Figure 28. Twist angle of the shaft around the *x*-axis in case of: a) the unbalanced shaft, b) the balanced one

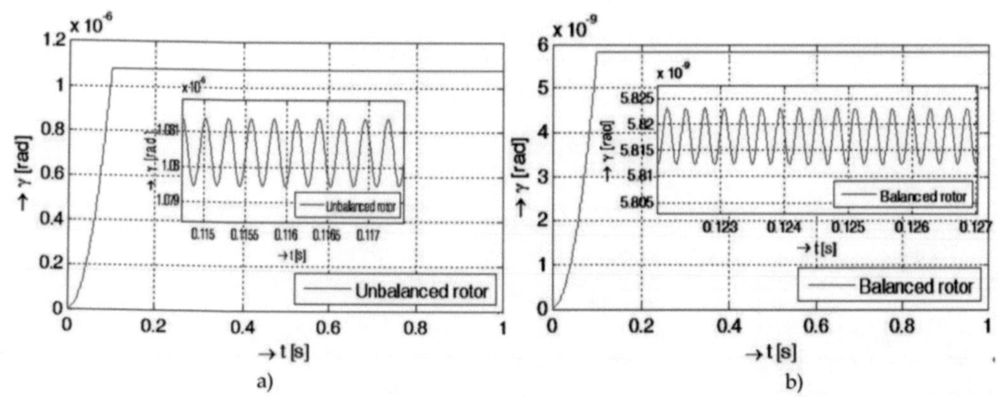

Figure 29. Complex twist angle with detail of the time course of: a) the unbalanced shaft, b) the balanced one

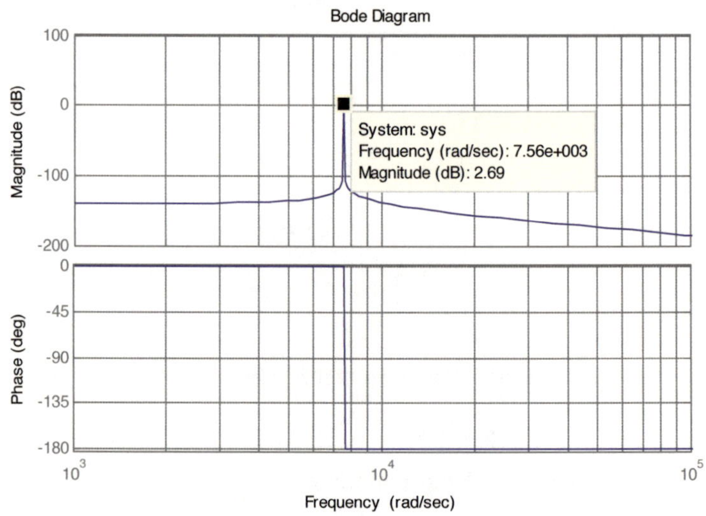

Figure 30. Bode logarithmic frequency characteristics of the unbalanced shaft

6. Numerical evaluation of simulation results

The following tables show numerical results obtained from the simulation of the rotor and prior to and after balancing (Tab. 6) and the same for the shaft (Tab. 7).

Parameters of the rotor	prior	after
Eccentricity e [mm]	0.0803	0
Own vibration frequency f [Hz]	53.97	53.712
Vibration cycle T [s]	$18.5\ 10^{-3}$	$18.61\ 10^{-3}$
Critical frequency ω_n [rad/s]	339.1	337.48
Max. amplitude of vibrations [mm]	$7.9\ 10^{-3}$	$3.2\ 10^{-16}$
Class of quality of balancing G	16	0.4

Table 6. Values of basic mechanical parameters of the rotor prior to and after balancing

http://dx.doi.org/10.5772/58378

Parameters of the rotor	prior	After
Eccentricity e [mm]	0.488	0.0027
Own vibration frequency f [Hz]	1203.9	1145.2
Vibration cycle T [s]	$0.83\ 10^{-3}$	$0.87\ 10^{-3}$
Critical frequency ω_n [rad/s]	7564.6	7195.8
Max. amplitude of vibrations [mm]	$9.4\ 10^{-5}$	$4{,}7.10^{-7}$
Class of quality of balancing G	40	0.4

Table 7. Values of basic mechanical parameters of the shaft prior to and after the balancing

When comparing the results in both tables one can see that balancing considerably decreased the rotating body vibration, which is observable esp. in case of the rotor. When balancing the rotor, the weights of balancing masses are much smaller in comparison with the weight of the rotor, so they do not influence value of the critical frequency. On the other hand, in case of the shaft, the weight of balancing masses is comparable with the weight of the shaft, so they considerably influence the critical frequency. By balancing also the class of balancing quality was improved, which means that the balancing rotating bodies fell into the best class – G 0,4.

7. Virtual model for unbalancing analysis and the balancing procedure

For easier interpretation of results and observation of influence of changeable parameters to unbalanced rotating body behavior a graphic user interface (GUI) in the MATLAB environment has been developed. The GUI has been developed for experimental observing of behavior of rotating unbalanced and balanced bodies – it enables to observe and evaluate influence of changing parameters of the rotor to mechanical oscillations.

The main screen of GUI is shown in Fig. 31. The graphical interface allows to input parameters of the mechanical systems by sliders and numerical values. Both rotating bodies (the rotor and the shaft) differ in their dimensions; further processing is the same. The screen displays the system arrangement (rotor/shaft) where the picture is interchanged with displaying its mathematical model (i.e. the equations). After inputting masses for static/dynamic unbalance and based on given class G of balancing the computer calculates masses for balancing and their placement (radius, mass, plane). Further it is possible to change simulation time, time of starting (increasing the revolutions) possibly time of loading the rotating body and also it is possible to choose a detail form the displayed graph. Based on chosen modes of graphs displaying the user can get the results in a required form.

The described functionalities make the designed GUI enough complex. To have a better overview and easier operating, the controlling buttons and sliders are grouped and the groups are framed. Functions of individual parts are briefly described here:

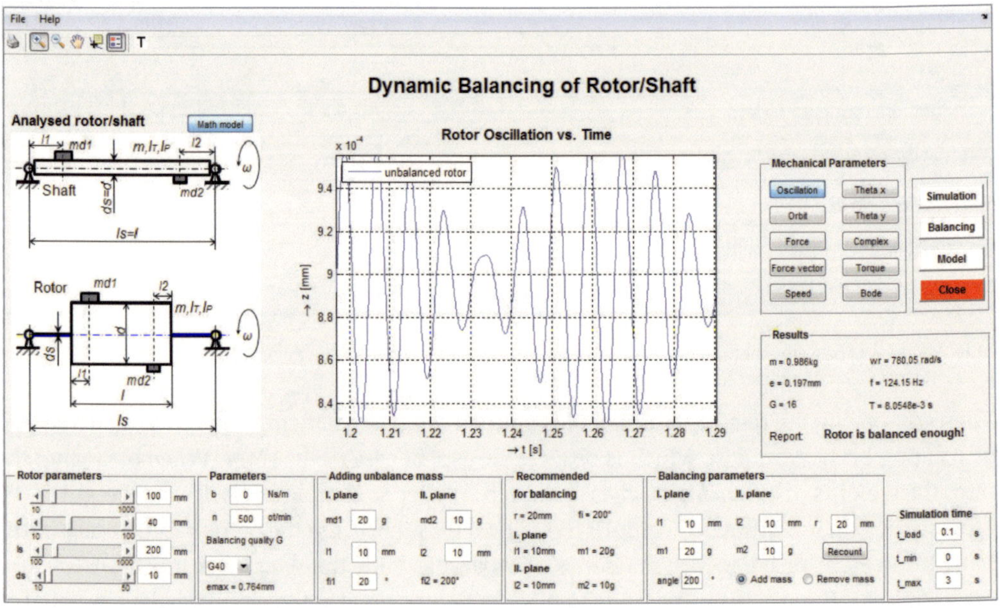

Figure 31. Graphical user interface for static and dynamic balancing of the rotor and shaft

Analyzed rotor/shaft – the picture shows a model of analyzed rotor/shaft. The rotor itself presents a rotating body placed in center of an immaterial shaft. The rotating system is supported by two rigid bearings.

Mathematical model – contains equations of the chosen system that is based on a simplified Jeffcott model of the rotor using differential equation of the second order. It is shown after pushing the *Math model* button that is shown over the picture of the analyzed rotor. On the left side of the equation there are forces acting against the sense of rotation containing damping, bending stiffness, polar and transverse moment of inertia. The right side of the equation presents input into the system, i.e., centrifugal force f and torque T that have excited the motion. At simulation of balancing the centrifugal force and corresponding torque from the added (removed) balanced masses are also considered.

Rotor Oscillation vs. Time – the graph presents a dependence of bending vibrations vs time and shows deviation $\omega_n$of the rotor during its starting. The user defines time of the rotor run-up up to the working revolutions f, that are kept constant by end of the simulation. Here we can also observe influence of parameters like bending stiffness, damping, and eccentricity. The visualized deviations present rotor vibrations.

Rotor parameters – the panel contains basic parameters of the rotor selected by the user: length of the rotor T, diameter ω_n, length F_c and diameter M of the immaterial shaft. In case of the shaft that is supported by two stiff bearings, the length and diameters are equal z' and n.

Other parameters – the panel allows to set revolutions l, the original class of balancing G, and a damping d.

http://dx.doi.org/10.5772/58378

Adding unbalance mass – two counterbalances with masses l_s and d_s can be added by the user onto two planes in the distance $l_s=l$ and $d_s=d$, respectively, measured from planes of the bearings. The angle for the second counterbalance is not important as the final unbalanced torque consists of the sum of forces acting on bearings.

Recommended balancing parameters – here are the main recommended parameters calculated by the program for the process of rotating body balancing: the radius r_b and amount of correcting masses - counterbalances m_{b1} and m_{b2} that are necessary for adding or removing the mass (e.g. by drilling). The value of the balancing masses corresponds to the mass that is necessary for total removal of the eccentricity.

Balancing parameters – the user decides whether to add or remove the balancing mass. The parameters are chosen by the user who decides value of radius for adding/removing mass and its amount (the program calculates precise value of balancing mass but the user can decide on using a different mass and radius of its fixing). If he chooses a smaller radius than recommended by the program, he must use a larger mass than recommended, of course. The procedure of adding masses can be repeated several times for various arrangements (push the *Recount button*).

Balancing – for balancing the unbalanced rotor/shaft the user has to choose parameters of the rotating body on the panel **Balancing parameters**. The results of balancing can be observed on time responses and/or on the orbits.

Results – the panel displays information before and after balancing. This is valid for critical resonance frequency n for amplitude of eccentricity b and class of quality of balancing G. Also, the resonance frequency m_{d1} and the period of vibration m_{d2} is displayed. The course can be zoomed. Displayed here is also the value of maximal acceptable unbalancing l_1 that is calculated on the basis of given quality of balancing G and revolutions l_2. If the value of eccentricity ω_n is larger than e, the rotor must be balanced. After balancing, the rotor can reach the better class than it was in before balancing.

Mechanical parameters here are the buttons to select mode of displaying graphs obtained as results of simulation of unbalanced and balanced rotating body. Pre-set types of the graphs are follows:

- Rotor oscillations in radial direction (vibrations of the force in bearings).
- Forces acting on the bearing.
- Rotating vector of the centrifugal force caused by the unbalancing.
- Orbit showing orbital trajectory of the center of the gravity during rotation.
- The torsional angle of rotor around axes x and y.
- Complex angular displacement of the rotor.
- Total torque acting on the rotor.
- Bode logarithmic frequency characteristics.

Menu Help – description of classes of balancing, quality of the balancing and a procedure for using the GUI. The File is used in the case the user wants to save the graphical outputs.

Toolbar – it contains the classical MATLAB function for interactive work with graphical output. The user can print the graph, perform graph zooming, offset. Here is a tool for processing the legend and a possibility to show or hide the grid.

Simulation – Starting the simulation. The result – dependence of bending vibrations vs. time and recommended parameters for rotor balancing are shown on the panel *Recommended balancing* parameters. *Simulation time* can be changed as well.

Simulation time – three parameters: f, T a e_{max} can be changed here. The user sets min and max time for displaying the results and time n determining the time when the rotating body reaches operational (final) revolutions.

Close – Closes all open windows and the graphical interface.

8. Conclusion

A simulation model for analyzing vibrations of both static and dynamic unbalanced rotating bodies has been developed. It is based on principle of a Jeffcott rotor model characterized by 4 dynamic differential equations describing 4 degrees of freedom in two perpendicular axes. The angular velocity ω presents input for the model and movement of the center of gravity in the plane perpendicular to the axis of rotation presents an output from the model. The model has been verified by comparing simulation results with those reported in the references.

All calculations and simulations were performed in the MATLAB/Simulink environment and the simulation model was involved into the GUI. The MATLAB GUIDE (GUI Development Environment) offers a comfortable work with the model: it enables simply to change parameters of the mechanical system, to observe behavior of unbalanced rotating body and finally – to solve its balancing by calculation of balancing masses and finding their proper position for their fixing. The solution is interactive and enables user to perform repetitive experiments and to find optimal balancing of the unbalanced body based on required class G of balancing quality. As the outputs from simulation show, vibrations of the rotating body were considerably decreased by adding the balancing masses on the place determined by the program. For a deeper analysis of the system, the GUI also displays logarithmic frequency characteristics. Further we observed influence of bending stiffness and damping to steady running of the rotating body as dependent on the rotating speed. In case of increasing the speed, the rotations of the rotor reaches instability region and increased vibrations of longitudinal and transverse occurs there. They are caused by the fact the rotor speed approaches to the resonance frequency. The GUI was verified by a series of experiments and comparing the obtained results with those published in the references. A significant advantage of developed GUI dwells in the possibility of detailed studying of rotating body vibration problems. The graphical interface can be used also in case of other shapes of bodies by simple exchange of the simulation model preserving the inputs, outputs and variables notation in the simulation scheme. The

http://dx.doi.org/10.5772/58378

GUI is extremely suitable for students in Bc., MSc., and PhD. courses in mechanical and mechatronic engineering studying appropriate subjects dealing with rotating bodies.

Further research will cover investigation of vibration of rotating bodies with other cross section than circular, investigation of influence of non-homogenous rotating magnetic field in case of rotors of electrical motors to vibrations of the rotor as well as practical measurements on the laboratory set-up.

Acknowledgements

The financial support of the Slovak Research and Development Agency under the contract No: APVV-0138-10 is acknowledged.

Author details

Viliam Fedák, Pavel Záskalický and Zoltán Gelvanič

*Address all correspondence to: Viliam.Fedak@tuke.sk

Department of Electrical Engineering and Mechatronics, FEEaI, Technical University of Košice, Slovakia

References

[1] BRÜEL and KJAER Static and Dynamic Balancing of Rigid Rotors. Application notes. Germany: Naerum Offset; 1989.

[2] Muszyńska A,. Rotordynamics. Taylor & Francis Group, LLC, U.S.A.; 2005.

[3] Rieger F.N. Balancing of Rigid and Flexible Rotors. New York: Rochester, Stress Technology, Inc.; 1986.

[4] Fox R.L., Dynamic Balancing. Houston, Texas: IRD Mechanalysis, Inc.; 1980.

[5] Adams M.L. Rotating Machinery Vibration from Analysis to Troubleshooting. New York, Basel: Marcel Dekker, Inc.; 2001.

[6] Shiyu Zhou, Jianjun Shi, Active Balancing and Vibration Control of Rotating Machinery: A Survey. The Shock and Vibration Digest 2011;33(4) 361-371.

[7] Rotating Machinery Rotor Balancing. Lifetime Reliability, Solutions Co. http://www.lifetime-reliability.com/free-articles/precision-maintenance/Rotating_Machinery_Rotor_Balancing.pdf (accessed 15 February 2014)

[8] Balancing Standards (example). Precision Balancing Co. http://www.precisionbalancing.com.au/industrial-balancing-standards.html (accessed 15 February 2014).

[9] Grim G. K., Haidler J. W., Mitchell Jr. B. J., The Basics of Balancing. BTI, Precision Measuring and Testing Equipment and Services. Balance Technology Inc. (accessed 15 February 2014) http://www.balancetechnology.com/pdf/balancing_basics202.pdf

[10] ISO 1940-1:2003 Mechanical vibration--Balance quality requirements for rotors in a constant (rigid) state – Part 1: Specification and verification of balance tolerances. http://www.iso.org/iso/home/store/catalogue_tc/catalogue_detail.htm?csnumber=27092

[11] Lamár K. and Kocsis A. G., Implementation of Speed Measurement for Electrical Drives Equipped with Quadrature Encoder in LabVIEW FPGA. Acta Technica Corviniensis – Bulletin of Engineering 2013; 6(4) 123-6.

[12] Vibrations. Department of Mechanics, VŠB TU – Ostrava, 2005. http://www.337.vsb.cz/materialy/dynamika_zaklady_mechaniky_Jirka_e_learning/dynamika/kapitola_11/D11_kmitani_vlastni.ppt (accessed 15 February 2014), (in Czech).

[13] Mahmoud al-Wedyan, H. et al. The Behaviour of the Jeffcott Rotor ander a Vibrating Base of Fluid Film Bearing. Suranaree Journal of Science and Technology 2008;15(3) 167-176.

[14] Tuma J., Bilosova A, Simek J., Svoboda R. A., Simulation Study of the Rotor Vibration in a Journal Bearing. Engineering Mechanics 2008;15(6) 461–470.

[15] Gelvanic Z. Analysis of Rotor Excentricity Influence to Rotor Vibration and its Decreasing. BSc. thesis. FEEaI-Technical University Kosice; 2013; (in Slovak).

Chapter 20

Analysis of Robotic System Motion in SimMechanics and MATLAB GUI Environment

Viliam Fedák, František Ďurovský and Róbert Üveges

Additional information is available at the end of the chapter

http://dx.doi.org/10.5772/58371

1. Introduction

Robots present considerably complicated electromechanical systems with mutual interactions of robot mechanics and drives, at design of which the mechatronic approach should be taken into consideration. The computer modeling presents such basic tool for mentioned mechatronic approach. When designing control of a robot, we need to know necessary torque and angle of rotation of each motor, to visualize behavior of the robot, and to obtain mathematical model of each part. Generally, this inverse kinematic task is not solvable analytically and the numerical calculation often entails difficulties. The design of a control law for the drive system is also connected with the need of transfer function derivation and with simulation of dynamical properties of the robot mechanical system as a whole.

The physical modeling in the SimMechanics environment [1] considerably facilitates simulation efforts of complex mechanical systems regardless of their complication by elastic and damping elements and by number of degrees of freedoms. The SimMechanics program scheme having the form of interconnected blocks shows how the physical components with geometric and kinematic relationships of the robot are mutually interconnected. The SimMechanics program enables one to model mechanical systems by bodies and joints, to simulate their motion, to change easily the structure, to optimize system parameters, and to analyze results all within the Simulink environment. This approach does not require cumbersome deriving differential equations of the system and presents an easy and fast way to obtain the dynamic model of the system and saves time and effort.

INTECH
open science | open minds

© 2014 The Author(s). Licensee InTech. This chapter is distributed under the terms of the Creative Commons Attribution License (http://creativecommons.org/licenses/by/3.0), which permits unrestricted use, distribution, and reproduction in any medium, provided the original work is properly cited.

Several approaches for the robot model development in the SimMechanics environment that appeared in last years are known worldwide, e.g. [3]-[7]. The robot models were developed on basis of the robot configuration. To simplify the development task we have used a special feature announced by The MathWorks in 2003 which integrates SimMechanics with The SolidWorks CAD Assemblies. [2]. Mathworks collaboration with Solidworks Corporation extended the engineering analysis capabilities of SimMechanics by allowing seamless integration of Solidworks CAD Assemblies into the SimMechanics simulation and design environment. This means that the SolidWorks models can be simulated in the Simulink environment in order to analyze forces and torques in mechanical joints, plot accelerations and displacements of each part of the system, to visualize motion of the CAD assembly, while taking into consideration masses of individual objects. This facility is enabled by installing an appropriate plug-in in SimMechanics which imports the 3D CAD model of the full system with bodies, joints, couplings, and masses from the SolidWorks program into the SimMechanics for further work with the model.

The objective of the proposed chapter is to present an application of effective way of the robot mechanics modeling and its dynamic simulation using add-on modules of the MATLAB advanced environment: SimMechanics and Graphical User Interface (GUI) MATLAB.

A complete description of the procedure is presented on example of a SEF-ROBOTER SR 25 type welding robot [1] weighing 480 kg with payload of 25 kg. Calculations were performed in the MATLAB/SimMechanics environment that enables a simple physical modeling of mechanical systems without any necessity of motion equations derivation. After this a 3D CAD model of the robot mechanics was developed using SolidWorks program. This procedure also enables verification of the model-whether it corresponds to the reality and whether it behaves according to the presumptions and requirements. By importing the 3D CAD model into SimMechanics a basic simulation scheme is obtained. After completing it by few blocks the simulation scheme is utilized for analysis in both direct and inverse kinematics tasks. Finally, a GUI model of the robot system has been developed that enables one to perform various virtual experiments and to obtain required outputs: position (angles), forces and torques. The GUI also solves analyzing of the inverse and direct kinematics tasks.

2. Employed SimMechanics blocks

SimMechanics contains a set of block libraries and special simulation interfaces (Sensor and Actuator blocks) for interconnection of the SimMechanics scheme with the Simulink environment. The SimMechanics blocks present elements enabling to model mechanical systems consisting of rigid bodies connected by joints that represent translational and rotational degrees of freedom. SimMechanics automatically sets up a single absolute inertial reference frame and coordinate system (CS) called World, [9]. For easier interpretation of the following block diagrams, the function of used SimMechanics blocks is shown in Table 1.

http://dx.doi.org/10.5772/58371

Group	Block	Name	Description
Bodies	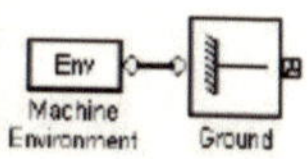	Env	The block *Machine Environment* defines environment for calculation of the scheme. Each SimMechanics model contains one such block that is connected with the block *Ground*. Except of inputting the precision of calculation and parameters of the environment, the required analysis type can be set up: • *Forward Dynamics* – based on initial values and forces in the system the program calculates values of positions and speeds. • *Linearization* – this mode calculates the system linear model. • *Trimming* – finds the machine steady states. • *Inverse Dynamics* for open loop In this mode the SimMechanics calculates forces necessary for performing the motion forced by kinematic excitation. • *Kinematics* does the same for closed loop systems by including extra internal invisible constraints arising from those structures.
		Ground	The *Ground* block represents a fixed point having infinite mass. At least one block *Ground* connected with the *Machine Environment* must be involved.
	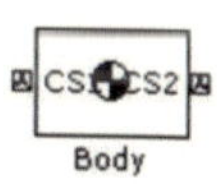	Body	The block *Body* in SimMechanics replaces all fixed rigid bodies among which the degrees of freedom are added. The bodies are defined by their final and non-zero masses, inertia, positions, directions, and by coordinate systems that are connected to them.
Joints	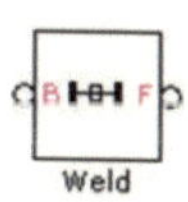	Weld	The blocks *Joints* interconnect blocks of the *Body* type and they are added degrees of freedom. The blocks determine direction and type of motion. In difference to the physical joints, in SimMechanics they present massless bodies and a physical connection of the bodies is not required. In the block there are shown ports: *B-Base* and *F-Follower* what means, the *Follower* performs a motion regarding to the *Base*. The block *Weld* – means a body without any degree of freedom.
	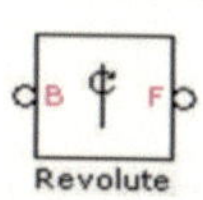	Revolute	The *Revolute* block from the *Joints* group represents one degree of freedom (rotation).
		Custom Joint	The *Custom Joint* is developed by the user using so called primitives (*Joint Primitives*) that create degrees of freedom. The motion performed by the *Custom Joint* is done in the order prescribed by the list of primitives.

Drivers & Constraints	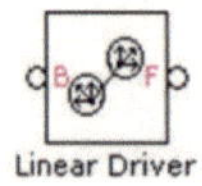	Linear Driver	Linear Driver – is used to define the distance between *Base* and *Follower* following x, y or z axis of the *World*.
	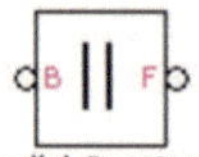	Parallel Constraint	The *Parallel Constraint* block ensures that vectors of axes of two bodies are parallel.
Sensors & Actuators		Driver Actuator	*Sensors and Actuators* are the blocks used as interfaces between non-SimMechanics Simulink blocks and SimMechanics blocks. By the *Actuators* it is possible to transform a Simulink signal into physical one actuating the bodies in SimMechanics diagram. The *Sensors* preform reverse functions – they transform signal from SimMechanics into Simulink environment. These blocks can be connected to *Joints*, *Drivers* and *Constraints* (only *Sensors*) into special purpose- oriented ports. In *Bodies* they are connected directly to the chosen CS. Outputs from the sensors are: positions, speeds, accelerations, reaction forces, etc.

Table 1. Description of functions of the used blocks in the SimMechanics program

3. Robot model development

3.1. 3D model of the robot

Development of dynamic model of a robot starts by identifying its parameters: based on technical specifications from the producer and completing them by own measurement of dimensions and distribution of masses depending on form of robot arms. Some missing data were estimated and approximated and the complex geometric forms were replaced by equivalent and simpler ones. Thus we gradually increased the model precision, position of centers of gravity and masses and where not possible, we used approximated data. In every case, the precise identification of model parameters is a laborious and trial-and error process, [2].

Fig. 1 shows the analyzed robot – both its picture and sketch showing possible movements of the robot joints. Based on measured and estimated data of the robot mechanical subsystem a precise technical drawing (compare the 2D sketch in Fig. 1b) create a basis for 3D modeling of the robot. By use of the SolidWorks program a 3D CAD model has been developed (Fig. 2).

Modeling of separate bodies and joints in the SolidWorks is much more advantageous because based on animation in the SolidWorks one can simultaneously verify correctness of kinematics of the mechanical model. The imported model also contains masses of the bodies, centers of inertia, tensors of the inertia and graphics that will be used at visualization. Of course, the forms of the bodies have been simplified but the time responses of such electromechanical system (i.e. the mechanical system completed by the drive subsystem) lie within acceptable boundaries.

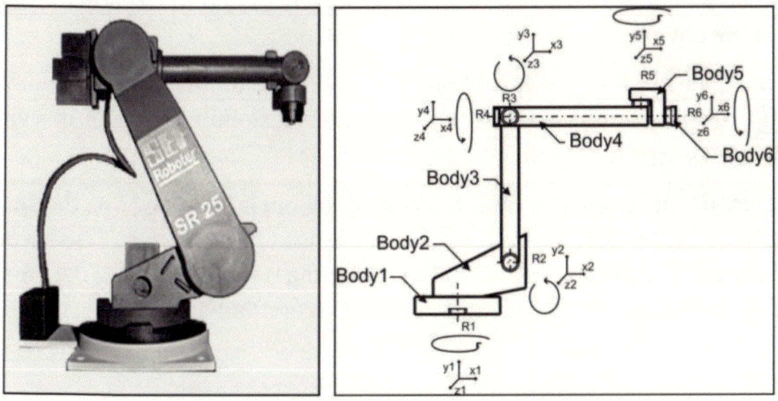

a) b)

Figure 1. Picture of the analyzed robot (a); and its 2D sketch (b)

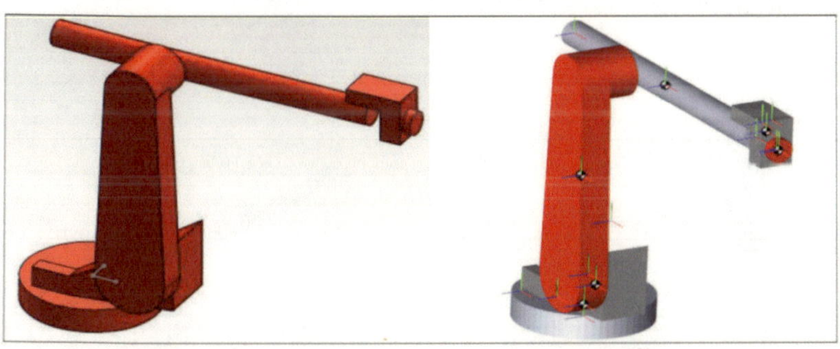

c) d)

Figure 2. Visualization of the robot imported from the 3D model into the SolidWorks program

3.2. Development of the program scheme in SimMechanics

The model in SimMechanics is built in the following steps:

1. Specification of body inertial properties, degrees of freedom, and constraints, along with coordinate systems attached to bodies to measure positions and velocities.
2. Applying forces/torques and completing the model by sensors and actuators to initiate and record body motions.
3. Starting the simulation, calling the Simulink solvers to find motions of the system, while maintaining any imposed constraints.
4. Visualizing the machine while building the model and animation of the running simulation, applying the Graphical User Interface (i.e. using Handle Graphics) or a virtual reality visualization tool.

The 3D CAD model developed in the SolidWorks program is imported into the SimMechanics suitable format using the SimMechanics link that creates a basic mechanic chain completed by system parameters. The program scheme after importing is shown in Fig. 3. For a better relation with the robot parts also sketches of particular bodies are shown.

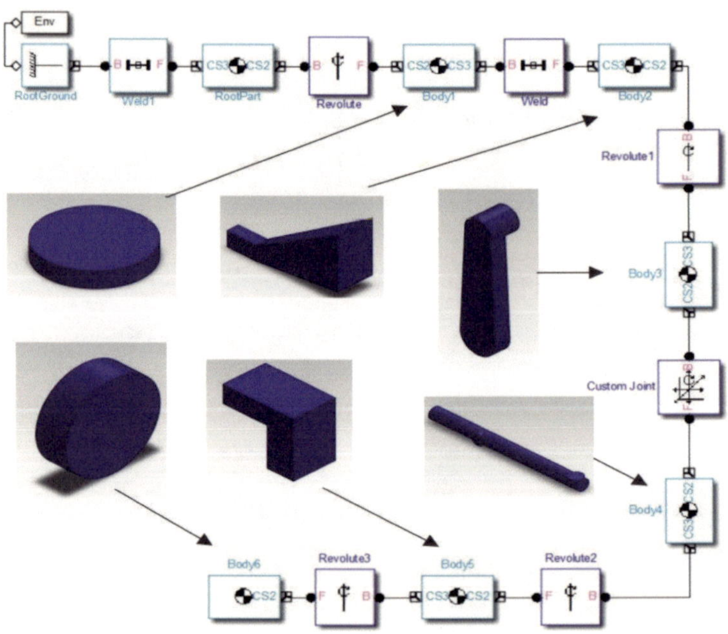

Figure 3. Program scheme of the 6-DOF robot in SimMechanics with appropriate bodies (mechanical parts - arms of the robot) and their corresponding blocks.

This basic SimMechanics scheme is completed by couplings, joints, sensors, connections and further blocks for the inverse kinematic task. The completed scheme is shown in Fig. 4.

http://dx.doi.org/10.5772/58371

4. Robot inverse kinematics

In inverse kinematic task the angles of joints (corresponding to angles of rotation of the driving motors) are calculated, [9]. In case of the robot they are necessary for obtaining a required trajectory (position, orientation and trajectory of the effector reference point). Due to nonlinearities of the mechanical system the analytic solution of the inverse kinematic task presents a quite difficult and complex problem, solution of which cannot be usually obtained in a closed mathematic formula. Although the solution with help of SimMechanics considerably facilitates the task, the problems with existence of solution and ambiguity still persist.

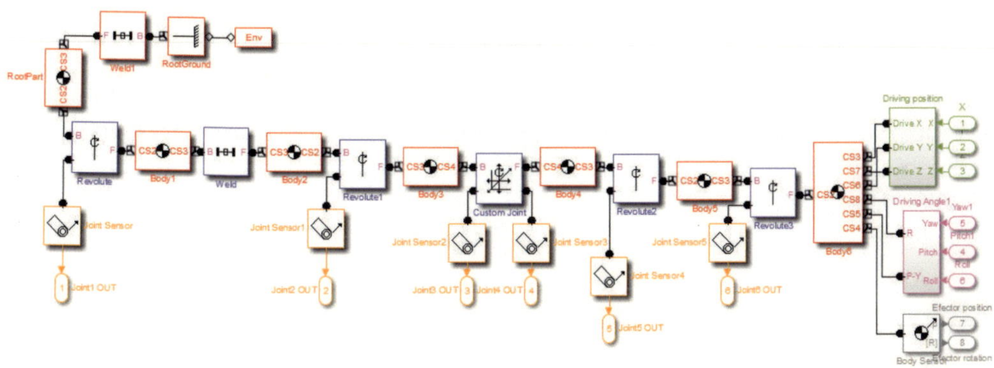

Figure 4. Program scheme – inverse kinematics of the analyzed robot mechanics

4.1. Solution of inverse kinematic task

In this case the block Joint Actuator is not connected to the joints because the system is completely and exactly defined by position and orientation of the effector. This assumption enables us to change calculation mode in the block Machine Environment to the "Kinematics". The choice also increases speed of simulation.

Position of the effector is defined in relation to the base point using the constraint *Linear Driver* (Fig. 5). It defines the distance along each axis of the {x, y, z} coordinate system (the vector basis).

Orientation of the effector is defined by a reference body and the *Parallel Constraint* of the x_e-axis to the x_b-axis of the reference body. Defined here are:

- *Pitch* (turning round z_b-axis) and
- *Yaw* (round y_b-axis).

The y_e-axis of the effector runs parallel with y_b-axis of the reference body where defined is the:

- *Roll* (turning round the x_b-axis).

4.2. Completing the program scheme

Position of the vector is defined by the *Driving position* subsystem (Fig. 5), determining effector coordinates towards its initial (baser) point.

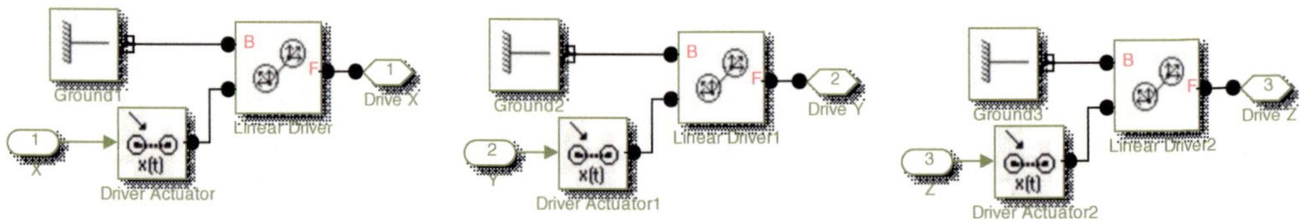

Figure 5. Subsystem Driving position

Orientation of the coordinate system of the effector terminal point is determined by the *Driving angle* subsystem. Its outputs are angles of the effector swinging in x-y-z axes in respect of initial conditions. Let's remind that the *effector axes* (Body 6 in Fig. 3) are in parallel with the *reference body axes* (Body 2, Fig. 6).

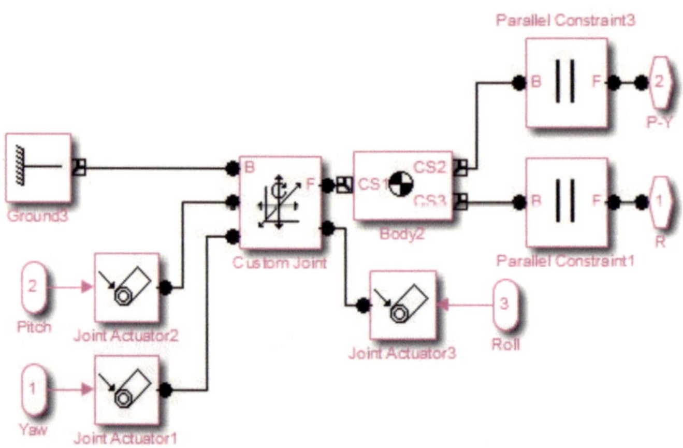

Figure 6. Driving angle" Subsystem

The inputs and outputs of the complete model of robot mechanical part in SimMechanics is shown in Fig. 7.

http://dx.doi.org/10.5772/58371

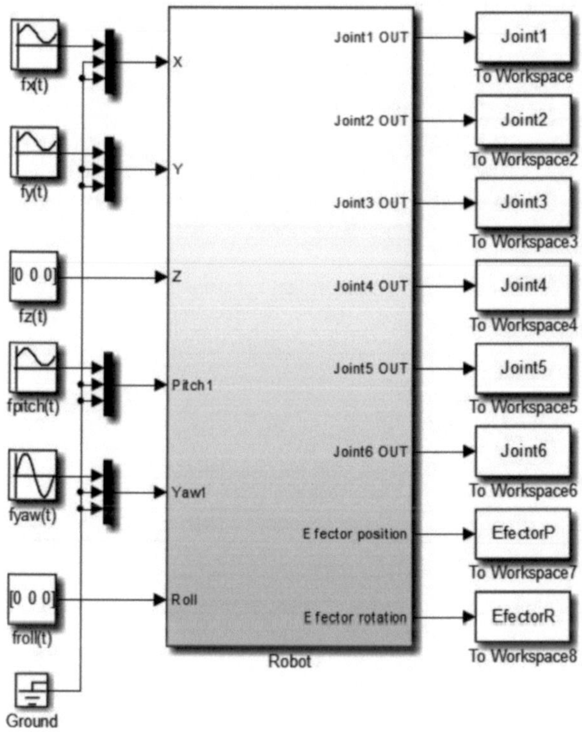

Figure 7. Robot model input and output signals

4.3. Simulation results

As an example for verification of the model properties an effector trajectory was programmed as a circle in the x-y plane with the period of 2π. In this case, the trajectory is easily described by simple mathematical functions which task is unambiguous and solvable:

$$f_x(t)=0.2\sin\left(t+\frac{\pi}{2}\right)-2,\ f_y(t)=0.2\sin(t)-1,\ f_z(t)=0$$

$$f_{pitch}(t)=10\sin(t+\pi)+85,\ f_{yaw}(t)=10sin\left(t+\frac{\pi}{2}\right),\ f_{roll}(t)=0$$

Its trajectory is shown in Figs. 8 and 9. Final time courses of turning the joints 1-6 obtained from the inverse kinematics scheme are shown in Fig. 10 (from top to bottom the courses belong to joints 6, 5, etc.). Several experiments have shown that the obtained results can be utilized in the forward kinematics.

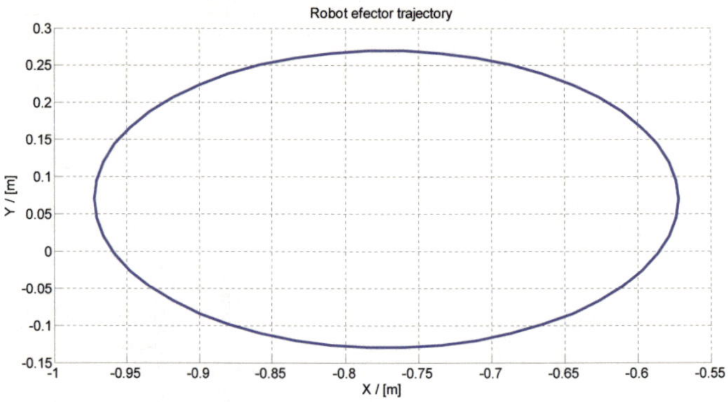

Figure 8. Desired effector trajectory in the x-y plane

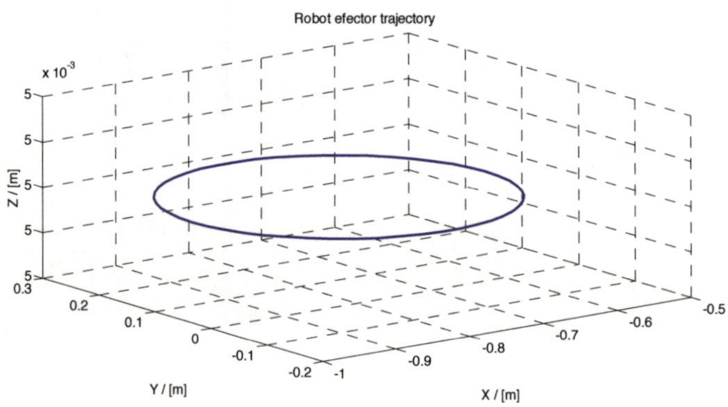

Figure 9. Desired trajectory of the effector reference point in 3D space

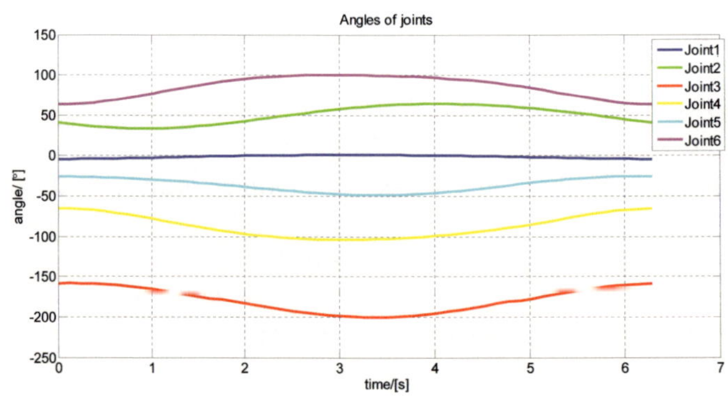

Figure 10. Time courses of angles of the joints to get the desired trajectory according to Fig. 9

http://dx.doi.org/10.5772/58371

5. Forward kinematics and inverse dynamics of the robot

The *Forward Kinematics* presents a basic problem at robot motion solving. Its result consists of geometric calculation of position of coordinates and orientation of the robot effector towards the basic coordinate system when rotating the joints by certain angles. In the *Forward Dynamics* mode, the SimMechanics uses the Simulink suite of ordinary differential equation (ODE) solvers to solve the mechanical ODEs (i.e. Newton's equations). The *Forward Kinematics Task* is simpler than the *Inverse Kinematics Task* but here, in the paper, it is described in the second place because the calculated values from the previous task can be easily used and verified.

5.1. Program scheme for forward kinematics

In this case, controlled are the angles of joints and the position and sensed is orientation of the effector. The blocks *Joint Actuator* will operate in the mode of kinematic excitation (Motion). The mode of calculation in the block *Machine Environment* is set to the *Inverse Dynamics*. The *Kinematics* mode can be used only in case of closed kinematic chain.

By connecting sensors to particular joints it is possible to determine the torques of the motors which are necessary for performing a defined trajectory of the effector. This scheme can be used also at solution of the system dynamics.

Note: During simulation an abnormal situation can occur: some parts of the block scheme behave abnormally. It is caused by the *Joint Sensor* block that senses angles of the joints within the range of $\langle -180°; 180° \rangle$. After crossing these values there appears a step change of the sensor output value from one marginal value to the other. This phenomenon can be avoided by employing the *unwrap* instruction adapting the step change signal into a smooth continuous form.

5.2. Simulation results

The trajectory in Fig. 12 calculated by the *Forward Kinematic* analysis corresponds to the trajectory of the effector from the Inverse Kinematic task presented above. Time responses of the torques in the robot joints 1 – 6 that are necessary for development of the effector trajectory are shown by graph in Fig. 13.

Graphs of the torques of the motors (Fig. 13) are as follows: the joints 5 – 6 on the top; 4 – 3 in the middle; joints 2 – 1 at the bottom (the coordinate systems are referred to Fig. 1b).

The torques in Fig. 13 depend strongly on the system parameters – masses, friction in the joints, moments of inertia of the motors. Eventual discrepancies between the simulated time responses and the real system may have their roots just here.

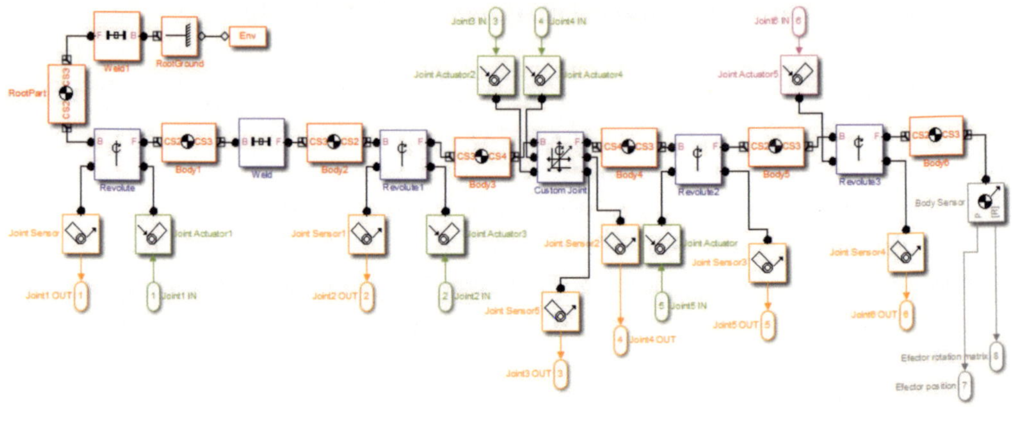

Figure 11. Program scheme – forward kinematics for the analyzed robot

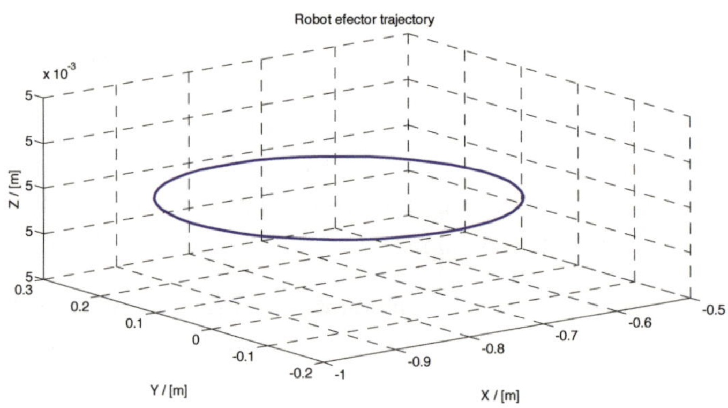

Figure 12. Robot effector trajectory in 3D space calculated by the direct kinematic task

6. Design of graphical user interface

To simplify experimentation work and to obtain a better view of the system behavior a *Graphical User Interface* (GUI) was developed in the MATLAB environment using MATLAB's *Graphical User Interface Development Environment* (GUIDE) tool. For a chosen set of parameters the GUI performs simulation showing time responses of the angles of joints, torques in joints and position of the robot effector. Various possibilities of the GUI modes and the appropriate screens are shown in Fig. 14 and Fig. 15.

Using switches in the **Mode group** the user chooses the required task type:

- Forward Kinematics,
- Inverse Kinematics,

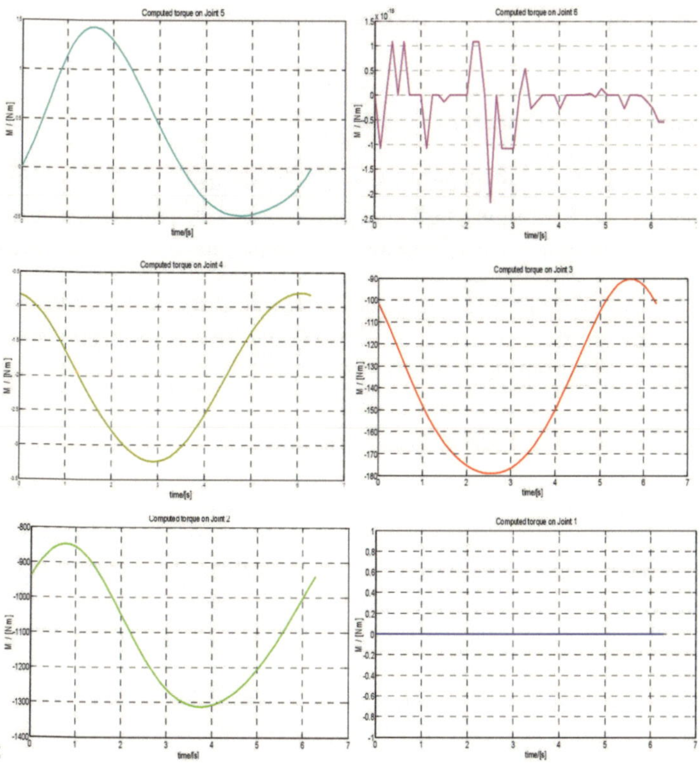

Figure 13. The torques in the robot particular joints

- Forward Dynamics,
- Inverse Dynamics.

7. Program in the inverse kinematics mode

In this mode the user defines trajectory of the effector motion. Choices include a possibility of entering position and orientation or eventually their derivations, both by entering mathematical functions into the text boxes *Effector rotation* and *Effector position*, including variable of the time, denoted as "t". This way of entering the required trajectory is impractical for the use and here it serves for demonstration purposes only.

For practical solution the program was modified by adding a possibility of importing the set of coordinates and speeds of the effector from a table developed in an Excel file. Based on the points of the trajectory the program calculates the trajectory of the effector movement. The speed among the points is considered to be constant. The results of the described simulations are shown in Fig. 14 (the right window). In the **Effector position window** displayed is the chosen trajectory consisting of sections of straight lines and in the right **Angles of joints**

window there are joint angles that are necessary to generate the prescribed trajectory of the effector in the 3D space.

7.1. Program in the forward kinematics mode

In this mode the user defines joint variables as mathematical functions written into the text boxes that are shown in the frame **Angles of Joints** (Fig. 15). The angles of the joints can be defined by the angle, angular velocity and angular acceleration (a choice there).

Based on given functions the program calculates the trajectory of the effector in the 3D space (shown in the window on the left side of the screen) and time responses of required angles of joints 1 – 6 in the graphs on the right side there.

7.2. Program in the inverse and direct dynamics mode

SimMechanics can solve the reverse of the forward dynamics problems: instead of starting with given forces/torques and finding the resulting motions, the Inverse Dynamics mode determines the forces/torques needed to produce a given set of motions that you apply to the machine. This mode only works with open topology systems (model diagrams without closed loops).

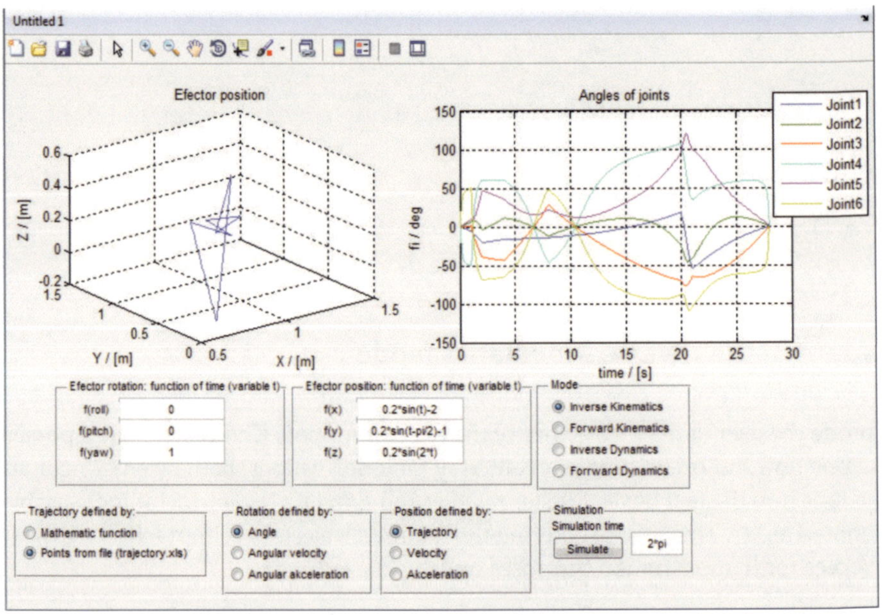

Figure 14. GUI for the inverse kinematics of the robot

When switching the program into the **Inverse Dynamics mode** the interface environment remains unchanged. The only change is that after simulation the time course of each torque is displayed on display in the right window.

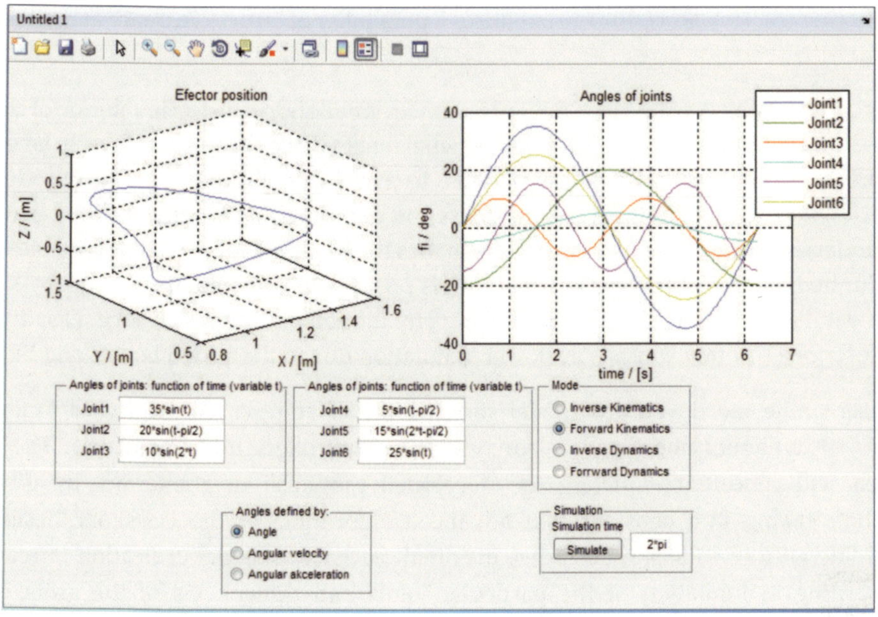

Figure 15. GUI for the direct kinematics of the robot

In the **Direct Dynamics mode** there are entered time courses of the torques acting on the particular joints. The required values of the torques are displayed in the left window and the calculated time responses of the angles appear in the right window.

8. Conclusion

SimMechanics presents a powerful tool for modeling mechanics of rigid bodies. It is suitable for modeling of dynamics and kinematics of considerably complicated systems with many joints without using any mathematical description. For these advantageous properties it is often used in the first phase of designing robotic systems, esp. due to simplicity of changing parameters and dimensions of particular bodies without necessity to repeat design of new model.

To get a dynamical model for the systems with more complex bodies of various shapes and connections connected through joints it is advantageous to model them in a compactible 3D CAD software and then to import the model from the program into the SimMechanics program. This solution enables us to avoid analytical calculations, esp. in case of the of moment of inertia tensor of an irregular body. The CAD software automatically calculates this tensor and moreover it adds visualization to the developed model.

The described development of the 3D CAD space model of the robot in the SolidWorks program and its import into the SimMechanics facilitates the work at developing the model of robot mechanics. This procedure also reduces a possibility of error occurrence at modeling the system.

A drawback in using the SimMechanics program for simulation consists in solution of collision of bodies and in limitation of angles of joints (what makes difficulties esp. at inverse kinematics task). In the mode of dynamics it is possible to avoid this disadvantage by introducing a feedback with a spring having a high stiffness and damping that is activated after exceeding set boundaries. In the mode of forward kinematics the required value of joint variables can be easily limited. In case of inverse kinematics it is possible to complete the scheme by suitably chosen parallel kinematic chains not allowing any motion out of preset range. Disadvantage of all described solution consists in slower simulation due to the added bodies and blocks.

At present time the developed model serves for further research – forward kinematics, analysis of dynamics and finally - for design of controllers for joint drives. The future research will concern completing the developed graphical user interface by advanced algorithms taking into consideration advanced algorithms of the trajectory design, e.g. curved line with considering obstacles, maximal reachable speed, verification of reachability according to limitation of the particular joints and dimensions of the arms. Within framework of the planned Hardware in the Loop system we plan to interconnect the master computer the SimMechanics program with a real robot of the SF25 type where on the first computer will run the SimMechanics program serving together with Simulink as a generator of controlling signals in the mode of inverse dynamics together with RT-LAB (a real time digital simulation software from Opal Technologies). Through a CAN bus the second computer will control frequency converters (of the SINAMICS CU 320 type from SIEMENS) supplying electrical drives of the robot.

Acknowledgements

The work was supported by Slovak Cultural and Educational Agency of the Ministry of Education of Slovak Republic under the contract KEGA 042TUKE-4/2012 "Teaching Innovation in Control of Mechatronic Systems".

Author details

Viliam Fedák*, František Ďurovský and Róbert Üveges

*Address all correspondence to: Viliam.Fedak@tuke.sk

Department of Electrical Engineering and Mechatronics, FEEaI, Technical University of Kosice, Slovakia

http://dx.doi.org/10.5772/58371

References

[1] SimMechanics-Model and Simulate Multibody Mechanical Systems. http://www.mathworks.com/products/simmechanics/ (accessed 15 February 2014).

[2] The MathWorks Integrates SimMechanics with SolidWorks CAD Assemblies. http://www.embeddedstar.com/press/content/2003/5/embed ded8871.html (Accessed 15 February 2014).

[3] Shanoiqiang Y., Zhong L., Xingshan L., Modeling and Simulation of Robot Based on Matlab/SimMechanics. In: The 27th Chinese Control Conference, 16-18 July 2008, Kunming, Yunnan, China, pp. 161-165.

[4] Vavrinčíková V., Hroncová D., Modeling of Robot Dynamics in the SimMechanics Environment. ATP Journal PLUS, "Intelligent Motion Systems", 2009, 60-64, ISSN 1336-5010. (in Slovak)

[5] Hanchen L., Xinhua Z., Haoliang X., Modeling and Simulation of 3-RRRT Parallel Manipulator Based on MATLAB with SimMechanics. In: Proceedings of 2009 IEEE Int. Forum for Information Technology and Applications IFITA '09, 15-17 May 2009, Chengdu, China, pp. 290-293.

[6] Dung Le Tien, Kang Hee-Jung, Ro Young-Shick, Robot Manipulator Modeling in Matlab-SimMechanics with PD Control and Online Gravity Compensation. In: Proceedings of the 5th IEEE International Forum on Strategic Technology, IFOST 2010, 13-15 Oct. 2010, 4p.

[7] Boros T., Lamár K., Six-axis Educational Robot Workcell with Integrated Vision System. In: Proc. of 4th IEEE International Symposium on Logistics and Industrial Informatics "LINDI 2012", Smolenice, Slovakia, 2012, pp.239-244. ISBN 978-1-4673-4518-7.

[8] SEF Roboter SR 25. http://www.youtube.com/watch?v=disu_RAoBAY. (Accessed 15 February 2014)

[9] Grepl R., Modeling of Mechatronic Systems. Praha, BEN, 2007, ISBN 978-80-7300-226-8. (in Czech).

Chapter 21

Vibration Analysis of Laminated Composite Variable Thickness Plate Using Finite Strip Transition Matrix Technique and MATLAB Verifications

Wael A. Al-Tabey

Additional information is available at the end of the chapter

http://dx.doi.org/10.5772/57384

1. Introduction

In the past, the model of thin plate on the elastic foundation was mainly used in structural applications. Currently, thin films of metal, ceramic or synthetic materials deposited on the surface of the structural parts of the electronic devices are used to improve their mechanical, thermal, electrical and tribological properties. These thin films of material are considered as thin plates and in these applications, the substrate of thin film can be simulated as an elastic foundation [1-2].

The laminated composite rectangular plate is very common in many engineering fields such as aerospace industries, civil engineering and marine engineering. The ability to conduct an accurate free vibration analysis of plates with variable thickness is absolutely essential if the designer is concerned with possible resonance between the plate and driving force [3].

Ungbhakorn and Singhatanadgid [4] investigated the buckling problem of rectangular laminated composite plates with various edge supports by using an extended Kantorovich method is employed.

Setoodeh, Karami [5] investigated A three-dimensional elasticity approach to develop a general free vibration and buckling analysis of composite plates with elastic restrained edges.

Luura and Gutierrez [6] studied the vibration of rectangular plates by a non-homogenous elastic foundation using the Rayleigh-Ritz method.

Ashour [7] investigated the vibration analysis of variable thickness plates in one direction with edges elastically restrained against both rotation and translation using the finite strip transition matrix technique.

INTECH
open science | open minds

© 2014 The Author(s). Licensee InTech. This chapter is distributed under the terms of the Creative Commons Attribution License (http://creativecommons.org/licenses/by/3.0), which permits unrestricted use, distribution, and reproduction in any medium, provided the original work is properly cited.

Grossi, Nallim [8] investigated the free vibration of anisotropic plates of different geometrical shapes and generally restrained boundaries. An analytical formulation, based on the Ritz method and polynomial expressions as approximate functions for analyzing the free vibrations of laminated plates with smooth and non-smooth boundary with non classical edge supports is presented.

LU, et al [9] presented the exact analysis for free vibration of long-span continuous rectangular plates based on the classical Kirchhoff plate theory, using state space approach associated with joint coupling matrices.

Chopra [10] studied the free vibration of stepped plates by analytical method. Using the solutions to the differential equations for each region of the plate with uniform thickness, he formulated the overall Eigen value problem by introducing the boundary conditions and continuity conditions at the location of abrupt change of thickness. However this method suffers from the drawback of excessive continuity, as in theory the second and third derivatives of the deflection function at the locations of abrupt change of thickness should not be continuous.

Cortinez and Laura [11] computed the natural frequencies of stepped rectangular plates by means of the Kantorovich extended method, whereby the accuracy was improved by inclusion of an exponential optimization parameter in the formulation.

Bambill et al. [12] subsequently obtained the fundamental frequencies of simply supported stepped rectangular plates by the Rayleigh–Ritz method using a truncated double Fourier expansion.

Laura and Gutierrez [13] studied the free vibration problem of uniform rectangular plates supported on a non-homogeneous elastic foundation based on the Rayleigh–Ritz method using polynomial coordinate functions which identically satisfy the governing boundary conditions.

Harik and Andrade [14] used the "analytical strip method" to the stability analysis of unidirectionally stepped plates. In essence, the stepped plate is divided into rectangular regions of uniform thickness. The differential equations of stability for each region are solved and the continuity conditions at the junction lines as well as the boundary conditions are then imposed.

1.1. The chapter aims

This chapter presents the finite strip transition matrix technique (FSTM) and a semi-analytical method to obtain the natural frequencies and mode shapes of symmetric angle-ply laminated composite rectangular plate with classical boundary conditions (S-S-F-F). The plate has a uniform thickness in x direction and varying thickness h(y) in y direction, as shown in Figure 1. The boundary conditions in the variable thickness direction are simply supported and they are satisfied identically and the boundary conditions in the other direction are free and are approximated. Numerical results for simple-free (S-S-F-F) boundary conditions at the plate edges are presented. The illustrated results are in excellent agreement compared with solutions

http://dx.doi.org/10.5772/57384

available in the literature, which validates the accuracy and reliability of the proposed technique.

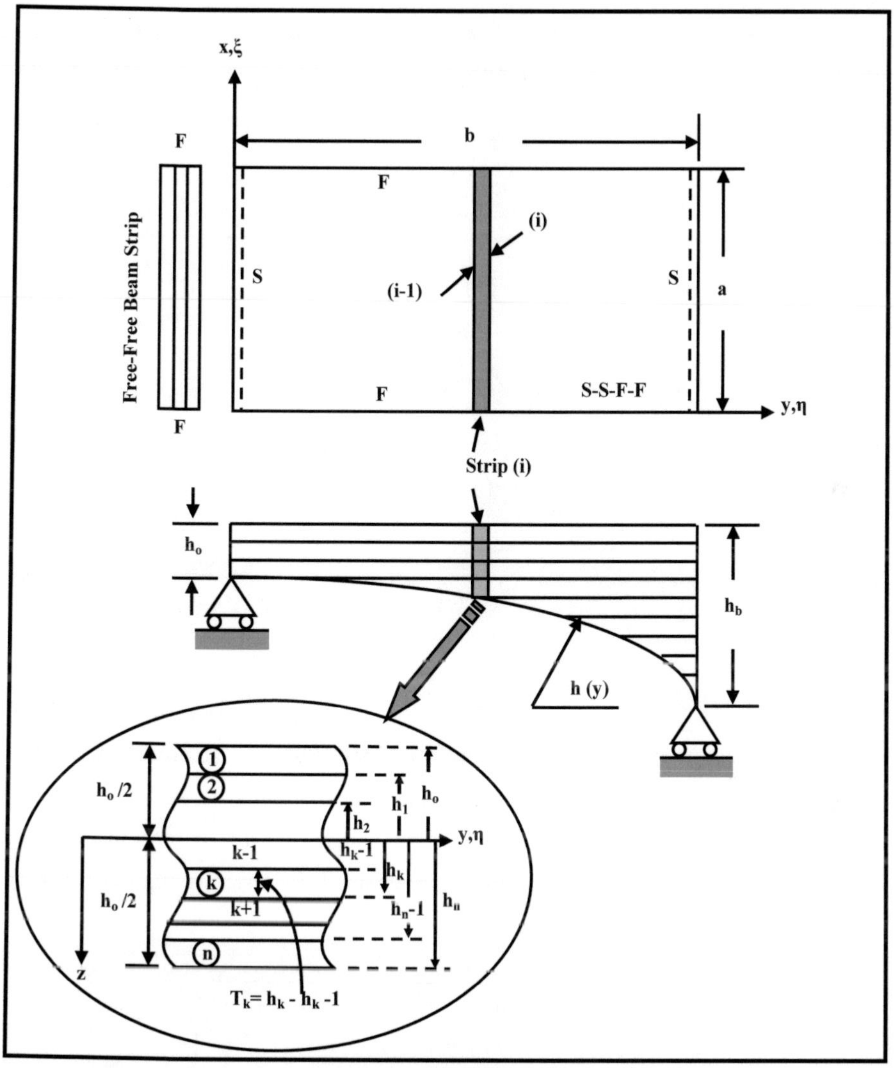

Figure 1. A rectangular laminated plate with variable thickness

2. Formulation

The equation of motion governing the vibration of rectangular plate under the assumption of the classical deformation theory in terms of the plate deflection W(x, y, t) is given by:

$$\frac{\partial^2 M_X}{\partial x^2} - 2\frac{\partial^2 M_{XY}}{\partial x \partial y} + \frac{\partial^2 M_Y}{\partial y^2} = -\rho\ h(y)\frac{\partial^2 w_o}{\partial t^2} \tag{1}$$

Where W is the transverse deflection, ρ = the density per unit area of the plate and h(y) is the plate thickness at any point. The bending and the twisting moments in terms of displacements are given by:

$$\left.\begin{aligned} M_X &= -D_{11}\frac{\partial^2 w_o}{\partial x^2} - D_{12}\frac{\partial^2 w_o}{\partial y^2} - 2D_{16}\frac{\partial^2 w_o}{\partial x \partial y} \\ M_Y &= -D_{12}\frac{\partial^2 w_o}{\partial x^2} - D_{22}\frac{\partial^2 w_o}{\partial y^2} - 2D_{26}\frac{\partial^2 w_o}{\partial x \partial y} \\ M_{XY} &= -D_{16}\frac{\partial^2 w_o}{\partial x^2} - D_{26}\frac{\partial^2 w_o}{\partial y^2} - 2D_{66}\frac{\partial^2 w_o}{\partial x \partial y} \end{aligned}\right\} \tag{2}$$

The flexural rigidities D_{ij} of the plate are given by:

$$D_{ij} = \frac{1}{3}\frac{h^3(y)}{h_o^3}\sum_{k=1}^{n}\left[(\overline{Q}_{ij})\right]_k (h_{ok}^3 - h_{ok-1}^3), \qquad i,j = 1,2,3,\ldots\ldots\ldots \tag{3}$$

Where h_{ok} is the distance from the middle-plane of the plate according to h_o to the bottom of the h_{oth} layer as shown in Figure 1. And $\overline{Q_{ij}^k}$ are the plane stress transformed reduced stiffness coefficients of the lamina in the laminate Cartesian coordinate system. They are related to reduced stiffness coefficients of the lamina in the material axes of lamina Q_{ij}^k by proper coordinate relationships they can be expressed in terms of the engineering notations as:

$$Q_{ij} = \begin{bmatrix} Q_{11} & Q_{12} & Q_{13} \\ Q_{12} & Q_{22} & Q_{23} \\ Q_{13} & Q_{23} & Q_{66} \end{bmatrix} = \begin{bmatrix} \dfrac{E_{11}}{(1-\upsilon_{12}\upsilon_{21})} & \dfrac{\upsilon_{21}E_{11}}{(1-\upsilon_{12}\upsilon_{21})} & 0 \\ \dfrac{\upsilon_{21}E_{11}}{(1-\upsilon_{12}\upsilon_{21})} & \dfrac{E_{22}}{(1-\upsilon_{21}\upsilon_{12})} & 0 \\ 0 & 0 & G_{12} \end{bmatrix} \tag{4}$$

Where E_{11}, E_{22} are the longitudinal and transverse young's moduli parallel and perpendicular to the fiber orientation, respectively and G_{12} is the plane shear modulus of elasticity, υ_{12} and υ_{21} are the poisson's ratios. Thus, the governing partial differential equation of laminated composite rectangular plate with variable thickness as shown in Figure 1 is reduced to:

$$D_{11}\frac{\partial^4 w_o}{\partial x^4}+4D_{16}\frac{\partial^4 w_o}{\partial x^3\partial y}+2(D_{12}+2D_{66})\frac{\partial^4 w_o}{\partial x^2\partial y^2}+4D_{26}\frac{\partial^4 w_o}{\partial x\partial y^3}+D_{22}\frac{\partial^4 w_o}{\partial y^4}=-\rho\ h(y)\frac{\partial^2 w_o}{\partial t^2} \tag{5}$$

Or in contraction form:

$$D_{11}W_{xxxx}+4D_{16}W_{xxxy}+2(D_{12}+2D_{66})W_{xxyy}+4D_{26}W_{xyyy}+D_{22}W_{yyyy}=-\rho\ h(y)W_{tt} \tag{6}$$

The substitution of equation (3) into equation (6) given the governing Partial differential equation:

$$\begin{aligned}&D_{11}\left\{\frac{\partial^2}{\partial x^2}\left(\frac{h^3(y)}{h_o^3}W_{,xx}\right)\right\}+2(D_{12}+2D_{66})\left\{\frac{\partial^2}{\partial x\partial y}\left(\frac{h^3(y)}{h_o^3}W_{,xy}\right)\right\}+D_{16}\left\{\frac{\partial^2}{\partial x^2}\left(\frac{h^3(y)}{h_o^3}W_{,xy}\right)\right\}\\&+4D_{26}\left\{\frac{\partial^2}{\partial y^2}\left(\frac{h^3(y)}{h_o^3}W_{,xy}\right)\right\}+D_{22}\left\{\frac{\partial^2}{\partial y^2}\left(\frac{h^3(y)}{h_o^3}W_{,yy}\right)\right\}=-m_o\frac{h(y)}{h_o}W_{tt}\end{aligned} \tag{7}$$

Equation (7) may be written as:

$$\begin{aligned}&D_{11}\frac{h^3(y)}{h_o^3}W_{xxxx}+\left(\frac{2(D_{12}+2D_{66})}{h_o^3}\right)\frac{\partial h^3(y)}{\partial y}W_{xxy}+\left(\frac{2(D_{12}+2D_{66})}{h_o^3}\right)h^3(y)W_{xxyy}+D_{16}\frac{h^3(y)}{h_o^3}W_{xxxy}\\&+\left(\frac{4D_{26}}{h_o^3}\frac{\partial^2 h^3(y)}{\partial y^2}\right)W_{xy}+\frac{4D_{26}}{h_o^3}h^3(y)W_{xyyy}+\frac{8D_{26}}{h_o^3}\frac{\partial h^3(y)}{\partial y}W_{xyy}+\left(\frac{D_{22}}{h_o^3}\frac{\partial^2 h^3(y)}{\partial y^2}\right)W_{yy}\\&+\frac{D_{22}}{h_o^3}h^3(y)W_{yyyy}+\frac{2D_{22}}{h_o^3}\frac{\partial h^3(y)}{\partial y}W_{yyy}=-m_o\frac{h(y)}{h_o}W_{tt}\end{aligned} \tag{8}$$

The equation of motion (8) can be normalized using the non-Dimensional variables ξ and η as follows :

$$\begin{aligned}&\psi_1\frac{1}{a^4}W_{\xi\xi\xi\xi}+\frac{2\psi_2}{h^3(\eta)}\frac{1}{a^2b}\frac{\partial h^3(\eta)}{\partial\eta}W_{\xi\xi\eta}+2\psi_2\frac{1}{a^2b^2}W_{\xi\xi\eta\eta}+\psi_3\frac{1}{a^3b}W_{\xi\xi\xi\eta}+4\psi_4\frac{1}{ab^3}W_{\xi\eta\eta\eta}\\&+\frac{1}{ab}\frac{4\psi_4}{h^3(\eta)}\frac{\partial^2 h^3(\eta)}{\partial\eta^2}W_{\xi\eta}+\frac{8\psi_4}{h^3(\eta)}\frac{1}{ab^2}\frac{\partial h^3(\eta)}{\partial\eta}W_{\xi\eta\eta}+\frac{1}{b^2}\frac{1}{h^3(\eta)}\frac{\partial^2 h^3(\eta)}{\partial\eta^2}W_{\eta\eta}\\&+\frac{1}{b^4}W_{\eta\eta\eta\eta}+\frac{2}{h^3(\eta)}\frac{1}{b^3}\frac{\partial h^3(\eta)}{\partial\eta}W_{\eta\eta\eta}=-\frac{m_o}{D_{22}}\frac{h_o^2}{h^2(\eta)}W_{tt}\end{aligned} \tag{9}$$

Where $\beta=\frac{a}{b}$ is the aspect ratio, $\xi=\frac{x}{a}$, $\eta=\frac{y}{b}$, $\psi_1=\frac{D_{11}}{D_{22}}$, $\psi_2=\frac{(D_{12}+2D_{66})}{D_{22}}$, $\psi_3=\frac{D_{16}}{D_{22}}$ and $\psi_4=\frac{D_{26}}{D_{22}}$.

3. Method of solution

The displacement $W(\xi, \eta, t)=W(\xi, \eta)e^{i\omega t}$ can be expressed in terms of the shape function $X_i(\xi)$, chosen a prior; and the unknown function $Y_i(\eta)$as:

$$W(\xi,\eta,t) = \sum_{i=0}^{N} X_i(\xi) Y_i(\eta)\; e^{i\omega\, t} \tag{10}$$

The most commonly used is the Eigen function obtained from the solution of beam free vibration under the prescribed boundary conditions at ξ=0 and ξ=1.

The free vibration of a beam of length a can be described by the non-Dimensional differential equation:

$$\left(\frac{2F_{T1}\mu_i\left(F_{R1}F_{R2} - \mu_i^2\right)}{\left(\mu_i^4 + F_{R1}F_{T1}\right)} \sin\mu_i + \frac{2F_{T1}\mu_i\left(F_{R1} + F_{R2}\right)}{\left(\mu_i^4 + F_{R1}F_{T1}\right)} \mu_i \cos\mu_i \right) A_3 \tag{11}$$

Where EI is the flexural rigidity of the beam. The boundary conditions for free edges beam as shown in Fig. 2 are:

at ξ=0 and ξ=1

$$\left. \begin{array}{l} \dfrac{\partial^2 X_i(\xi)}{\partial \xi^2} = 0 \\ \dfrac{\partial^3 X_i(\xi)}{\partial \xi^3} = 0 \end{array} \right\} \tag{12}$$

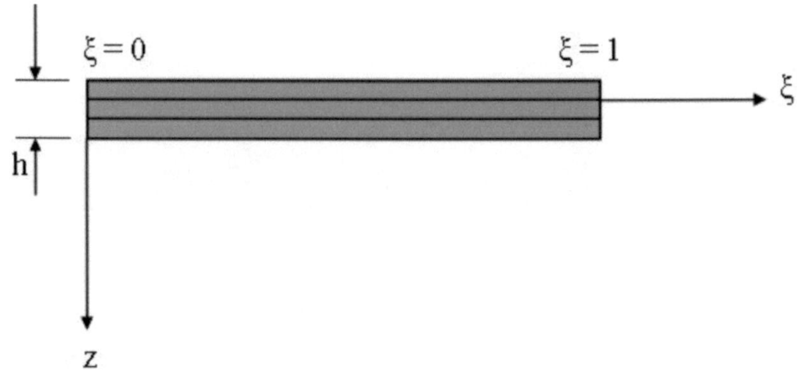

Figure 2. The two free edges beam strip in ξ-direction

In this paper, the beam shape function in ξ-direction is considered as a strip element of the plate and the flexural rigidity EI of the beam can replaced by $(1-\upsilon^2)D_{22}$ and for $\upsilon=0.3$, it can be just approximated by $E \approx D_{22}$. The solution of the beam equation is given as:

$$X_i(\xi) = A_1 \sin(\mu_i \xi) + A_2 \cos(\mu_i \xi) + A_3 \sinh(\mu_i \xi) + A_4 \cosh(\mu_i \xi) \tag{13}$$

One can obtain the following system of homogenous linear equations by satisfying the boundary conditions (12) at ξ=0 and ξ=1.

$$\left.\begin{aligned} \Phi_i &= \frac{-\sinh \mu_i + \sin \mu_i}{\cosh \mu_i - \cos \mu_i} \\ X_i(\xi) &= \sin(\mu_i \xi) - \sinh(\mu_i \xi) + \frac{1}{\Phi_i}\left(\cos(\mu_i \xi) - \cosh(\mu_i \xi)\right) \end{aligned}\right\} \tag{14}$$

The different value of μ_i are the roots of equation:

$$\frac{-2\cos(\mu_i)\cosh(\mu_i) + \cos^2(\mu_i) + \sin^2(\mu_i) - \sinh^2(\mu_i) + \cosh^2(\mu_i)}{\sinh(\mu_i)\cosh(\mu_i) + \sin(\mu_i)\cosh(\mu_i) - \sinh(\mu_i)\cos(\mu_i) - \sin(\mu_i)\cos(\mu_i)} = 0 \tag{15}$$

The roots of equation (15) are represented in the recurrence form:

$$\mu_i = (i + 0.5)\pi, \qquad i = 0, 1, 2, 3, \dots\dots\dots \tag{16}$$

The substitution of equation (10) into equation (9), multiplying both sides by $X_j(x)$ and after some manipulation, we can find:

$$\begin{aligned} &\sum_{i=0}^{N}\sum_{j=0}^{M} \frac{\beta^4}{f_3(\eta)} Y_{i,\eta\eta\eta\eta} + 2\beta^3 a \frac{f_1(\eta)}{f_3(\eta)} Y_{i,\eta\eta\eta} + \left(\frac{2\psi_2\beta^2}{f_3(\eta)}\frac{c_{ij}}{a_{ij}} + 8\psi_4\beta^2 a \frac{f_1(\eta)}{f_3(\eta)}\frac{b_{ij}}{a_{ij}} + \beta^2 a^2 \frac{f_2(\eta)}{f_3(\eta)}\right) Y_{i,\eta\eta} \\ &+ \left(2\psi_2\beta a \frac{f_1(\eta)}{f_3(\eta)}\frac{c_{ij}}{a_{ij}} + \frac{\psi_3\beta}{f_3(\eta)}\frac{d_{ij}}{a_{ij}} + 4\psi_4\beta a^2 \frac{f_2(\eta)}{f_3(\eta)}\frac{b_{ij}}{a_{ij}} + \frac{4\psi_4\beta^3}{f_3(\eta)}\frac{b_{ij}}{a_{ij}}\right) Y_{i,\eta} \\ &+ \left(\frac{\psi_1}{f_3(\eta)}\frac{e_{ij}}{a_{ij}} - \lambda^2\right) Y_i = 0 \end{aligned} \tag{17}$$

Where $\lambda^2 = \frac{m_o \omega^2 a^4}{D_{22}}$, $f_1(\eta) = \frac{1}{h^3(\eta)}\frac{\partial h^3(\eta)}{\partial \eta}$, $f_2(\eta) = \frac{1}{h^3(\eta)}\frac{\partial^2 h^3(\eta)}{\partial \eta^2}$, $f_3(\eta) = \frac{h_o^2}{h^2(\eta)}$,

$$a_{ij}=\int_0^1 X_i X_j d\xi,$$

$$b_{ij}=\int_0^1 X_j X_{i,\xi} d\xi,$$

$$c_{ij}=\int_0^1 X_j X_{i,\xi\xi} d\xi,$$

$$d_{ij}=\int_0^1 X_j X_{i,\xi\xi\xi} d\xi$$

and $e_{ij}=\int_0^1 X_j X_{i,\xi\xi\xi\xi} d\xi.$

From the orthogonality of the beam Eigen function, $a_{ij}=e_{ij}=0$ for $i\neq j$, this is true for all boundary conditions except for plates having free edges in the ξ-direction.

The system of fourth order partial differential equations in equation (17) can be reduced to a system of first order homogeneous ordinary differential equations:

$$\frac{d}{d\eta}\{Y_k\}_{ij}=[A_i]_k\{Y_k\}_{ij} \tag{18}$$

And after some manipulation, the governing differential equation (17) will become:

$$\sum_{i=0}^{N}\sum_{j=0}^{M} E_{ij}Y_i^{////}+\frac{(O_1)_{ij}}{(O_0)_{ij}}Y_i^{///}+\frac{(O_2)_{ij}}{(O_0)_{ij}}Y_i^{//}+\frac{(O_3)_{ij}}{(O_0)_{ij}}Y_i^{/}+\frac{(O_4)_{ij}-\lambda^2}{(O_0)_{ij}}Y_i=0 \tag{19}$$

Where the frame denotes differentiation with respect to η.

Where: $(O_0)_{ij}=\beta^4 t_1(\eta)E_{ij}$, $(O_1)_{ij}=2\beta^3 a t_2(\eta)E_{ij}$, $(O_2)_{ij}=(2\psi_2\beta^2 t_1(\eta)\frac{c_{ij}}{a_{ij}}+8\psi_4\beta^2 a t_2(\eta)\frac{b_{ij}}{a_{ij}}+\beta^2 a^2 t_3(\eta))$

$(O_3)_{ij}=(2\psi_2\beta a t_2(\eta)\frac{c_{ij}}{a_{ij}}+\psi_3\beta\, t_1(\eta)\frac{d_{ij}}{a_{ij}}+4\psi_4\beta a^2 t_3(\eta)\frac{b_{ij}}{a_{ij}}+4\psi_4\beta^3 t_1(\eta)\frac{b_{ij}}{a_{ij}})$, $(O_4)_{ij}=\psi_1 t_1(\eta)\frac{e_{ij}}{a_{ij}}$,

$[E_{ij}]=i\times j$ Unit matrix,

i= 0, 1, 2, 3, ……….,N, j= 0, 1, 2, 3, ……….,M

where the coefficients of the matrix $[A_i]_k$ in equation (18), in general, are functions of η and the Eigen value parameter λ. The vector Y_k is given by:

$$Y_k = \begin{bmatrix} \overline{Y}_1 & \overline{Y}_2 & \mathrm{K} & \overline{Y}_i & \mathrm{K} & \overline{Y}_N \end{bmatrix} \tag{20}$$

Where:

$$\overline{Y}_i = \begin{bmatrix} Y_i & Y_i^{/} & Y_i^{//} & Y_i^{///} \end{bmatrix} \tag{21}$$

Solving the above system of first order ordinary differential equations using the transition matrix technique yields, at any strip element (i) with boundaries (i-1) and (i) to,

$$\{Y_i\}_j = [B_i]_j \{Y_{i-1}\}_j \tag{22}$$

Where $[B_i]_j$ is called the transition matrix of the strip element (i), which can be obtained using the method of system linear differential equations of the strip element (i) in equation (18) (the exact solution of (ODE)).

Following the same procedure, the above boundary conditions (equations (12)) can be written. The simple boundary conditions at η=0 and η=1 as shown in Figure 3 are:

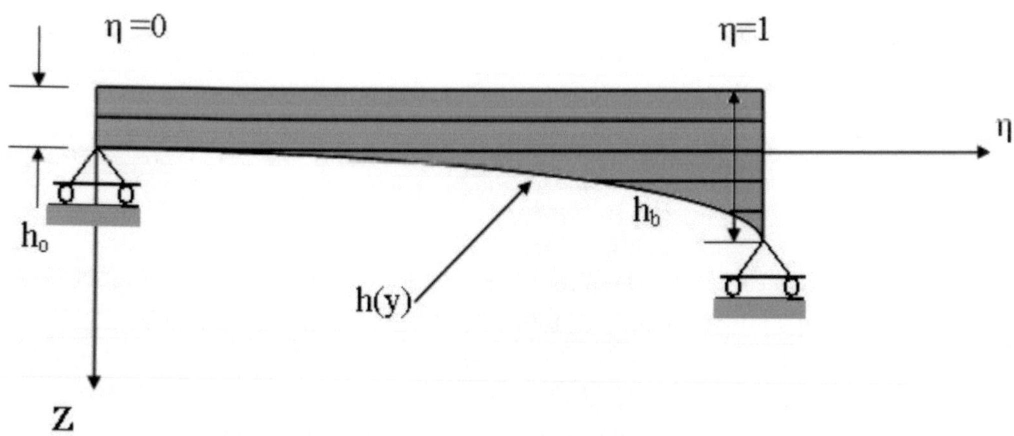

Figure 3. The two edges clamped variable thickness beam strip in η-direction

The boundary conditions at η=0 and η=1 can be expressed as:

$$\left.\begin{aligned} w_o &= 0 \\ -\frac{D_{12}}{a^2}\frac{\partial^2 w_o}{\partial \xi^2} - \frac{D_{22}}{b^2}\frac{\partial^2 w_o}{\partial \eta^2} - \frac{2D_{26}}{ab}\frac{\partial^2 w_o}{\partial \xi \partial \eta} &= 0 \end{aligned}\right\} \tag{23}$$

Using the assumed solution, equation (10) the boundary conditions can be given by the following equations:

At η=0 and η=1

$$\left.\begin{aligned} Y_i &= 0 \\ \frac{\partial^2 Y_i}{\partial \eta^2} &= \sum_{i=0}^{N} -\frac{2\psi_4 b_{ij}}{\beta a_{ij}}\frac{\partial Y_i}{\partial \eta} - \frac{\psi_5 c_{ij}}{\beta^2 a_{ij}} Y_i \end{aligned}\right\} \tag{24}$$

Or in contraction form:

$$\left.\begin{aligned} Y_i &= 0 \\ Y_i^{//} &= \sum_{i=0}^{N} -CF_1 \frac{b_{ij}}{a_{ij}} Y_i^{/} - CF_2 \frac{c_{ij}}{a_{ij}} Y_i \end{aligned}\right\} \tag{25}$$

Where $CF_1 = \frac{2\psi_4}{\beta}$, $CF_2 = \frac{\psi_5}{\beta^2}$, $\psi_5 = \frac{D_{12}}{D_{22}}$

The solution is found using 2N initial vectors Y_0 at η=0. Equation (22) is applied across the stripped plate until the final end at η=1 is reached. Thus, 2N solutions S_i, where i= 0, 1, 2, 3, ……….,N, can be obtained. The true solutions $[S]$ can be written as a linear combination of these solutions [7]:

$$[S] = \sum_{i=1}^{2N} C_i S_i \tag{26}$$

Where C_i are arbitrary constants. These constants can be determined by satisfying 2N boundary conditions at η=1 [7]. The matrix $[S]$ forms a standard Eigen value problem.

4. Numerical results and discussion

In this section, some numerical results are presented for symmetrically laminated, angle-ply variable thickness rectangular plate with simple support in the variable thickness direction

http://dx.doi.org/10.5772/57384

and free in the other direction. The designation (S-S-F-F) means that the edges x=0, x=a, y=0, y=b are free, free, simple supported and simple supported respectively. The plates are made up of five laminates with the fiber orientations [θ, - θ, θ, - θ, θ] and the composite material is Graphite/Epoxy, of which mechanical properties are given in Table 1. The Eigen frequencies obtained are expressed in terms of non-dimensional frequency parameter $\lambda = (\rho h_o \omega^2 a^4 / D_{22})^{1/2}$. To illustrate the solution, a plate with linear variable thickness, $h(y)$is used (see Appendix A).

$$h(\eta) = 1 + \Delta\eta \tag{27}$$

Where Δ is the tapered ratio of plate given by $\Delta = (h_b - h_0) / h_0$, (h_0) is the thickness of the plate at η=0 and (h_b) is the thickness of the plate at η=1. A convergence investigation is carried out for a uniform plate and for plate of variable thickness (Δ =0.5) with aspect ratio β=(0.5, 1.0). By varying the harmonic numbers of the series solution in equation (10). The results are shown in Table 2. It is found that excellent agreement and stable and fast convergence can be achieved with only a few terms of series solution (N= 3 to 5).

Material	E1, (GPa)	E2, (GPa)	G12, (GPa)	υ12	E2/ E1	G12/ E1
Graphite/Epoxy	138	8.96	7.1	0.3	25	0.8

Table 1. Material properties of unidirectional composite

In order to validate the proposed technique, a comparison of the results with some results available for other numerical methods [15] for uniform laminated plates with simple support in the y-direction and free in the other direction. The first six natural frequencies of such uniform laminated plates are depicted in Table 2.

			Δ = 0.0			
N	λ1	λ2	λ3	λ4	λ5	λ6
1	70.4212	70.7012	140.4421	173.5211	180.6231	235.6753
2	70.4212	70.7012	140.4421	173.5211	180.6231	235.6753
3	70.2882	70.5827	140.2496	173.2098	180.2833	235.3197
4	70.2882	70.5827	140.2496	173.2098	180.2833	235.3197
5	70.2882	70.5827	140.2496	173.2098	180.2833	235.3197
Ref*	70.302	70.604	140.255	173.218	180.287	235.322

*Y.K. Cheung and D. Zhou [15].

Table 2. Comparison of the first six natural frequencies of symmetric angle-ply uniform laminated square plates (θ=45°), (β=1.0)

Table 3 and Table 4 shows a convergence analysis of the first six frequencies parameters of symmetrically angle-ply five laminates [45/-45/45/-45/45] variable thickness plate with tapered ratio (Δ =0.5) and with aspect ratio β=(0.5, 1.0) with simple support in the y-direction and free in the other direction (S-S-F-F).

Figure 4 and Figure 5 show the mode shapes of the first six fundamental frequencies of the above plate. Figure 4 and Figure 5 both are divided into two graphics. The first one shows the mode shapes of the plate in surface form and the other shows the mode shapes of the plate in surface contour form. All simulation results and graphics were obtained using MATLAB software.

			Δ = 0.5			
			β = 0.5			
N	**λ1**	**λ2**	**λ3**	**λ4**	**λ5**	**λ6**
1	80.2177	82.5621	155.9665	188.6633	194.6253	251.7333
2	80.2177	82.5621	155.9665	188.6633	194.6253	251.7333
3	79.8625	82.0025	155.3232	188.1111	194.1002	251.2035
4	79.8625	82.0025	155.3232	188.1111	194.1002	251.2035
5	79.8625	82.0025	155.3232	188.1111	194.1002	251.2035

Table 3. The first six frequencies parameter of S-S-F-F symmetrically angle-ply laminated [45/-45/45/-45/45] variable thickness plate (Δ =0.5), (β=0.5).

			Δ = 0.5			
			β = 1.0			
N	**λ1**	**λ2**	**λ3**	**λ4**	**λ5**	**λ6**
1	72.7575	73.8666	143.3334	175.4963	183.7825	240.7621
2	72.7575	73.8666	143.3334	175.4963	183.7825	240.7621
3	72.1199	73.4444	142.9019	175.0024	183.1121	240.0159
4	72.1199	73.4444	142.9019	175.0024	183.1121	240.0159
5	72.1199	73.4444	142.9019	175.0024	183.1121	240.0159

Table 4. The first six frequencies parameter of S-S-F-F symmetrically angle-ply laminated [45/-45/45/-45/45] variable thickness plate (Δ =0.5), (β=1.0)

http://dx.doi.org/10.5772/57384

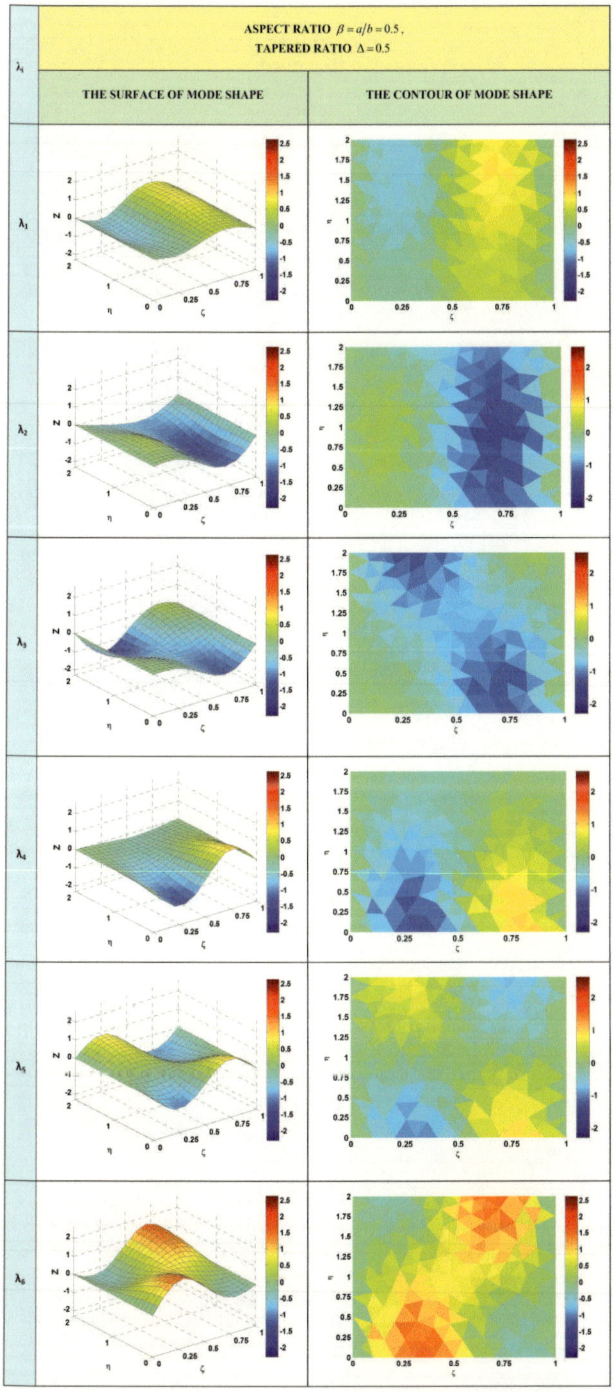

Figure 4. The mode shapes of the first six fundamental frequencies of the angle-ply symmetrically [45/-45/45/-45/45] laminated variable thickness rectangular plate with S-S-F-F edges, aspect ratio$\beta = a / b = 0.5$, tapered ratio $\Delta = 0.5$

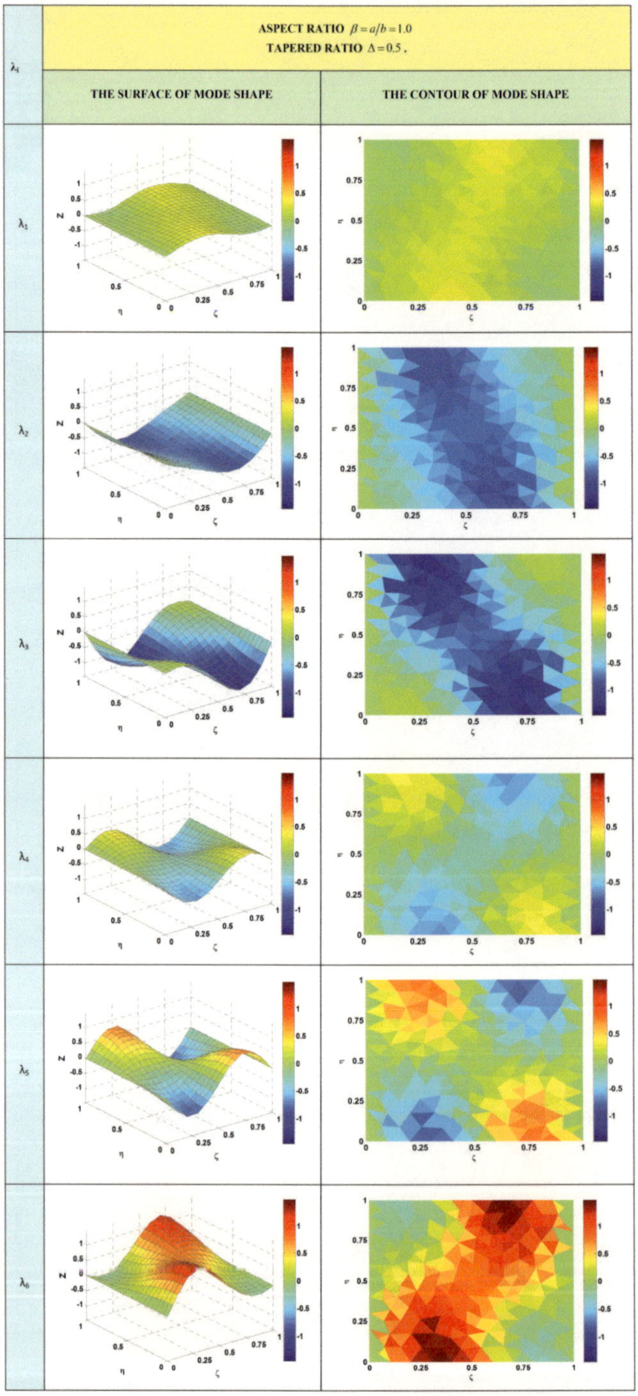

Figure 5. The mode shapes of the first six fundamental frequencies of the angle-ply symmetrically [45/-45/45/-45/45] laminated variable thickness rectangular plate with S-S-F-F edges, aspect ratio $\beta = a / b = 1.0$, tapered ratio $\Delta = 0.5$.

5. Concluding remarks

A semi-analytical solution of the free vibration of angle-ply symmetrically laminated variable thickness rectangular plate with classical boundary condition (S-S-F-F) is investigated using the finite strip transition matrix technique (FSTM). The numerical results for uniform angle-ply symmetrically square plate with classical boundary condition (S-S-F-F) is presented and compared with some available results. The results agree very closely with other results available in the literature. It can be observed from Tables 2 and 3 that rapid convergence is achieved with small numbers of N in the series solution. Comparing to other techniques, the finite strip transition matrix (FSTM) proves to be valid enough in this kind of application. In all cases the FSTM method is easily implemented in a computer program a yields a fast convergence and reliable results. Also, the effect of the tapered ratio (Δ) and aspect ratio (β) on the fundamental natural frequencies and the mode shapes for five layers angle-ply symmetrically laminated variable thickness plates has been investigated for two cases of tapered ratio (uniform and variable thickness) and two cases of aspect ratio (square and rectangular). In fact the varying of the thickness and the increase the length (b) about a length (a) tend to increase the natural frequencies and the mode shapes of the laminated plate. The results from this investigation have been illustrated in the three dimensional surface contours for two different aspect ratios.

Appendix (A)

Plate thickness function

In this appendix the derivation of the relation of the plate thickness h(y) in y-direction as shown in the Figure 6 is given.

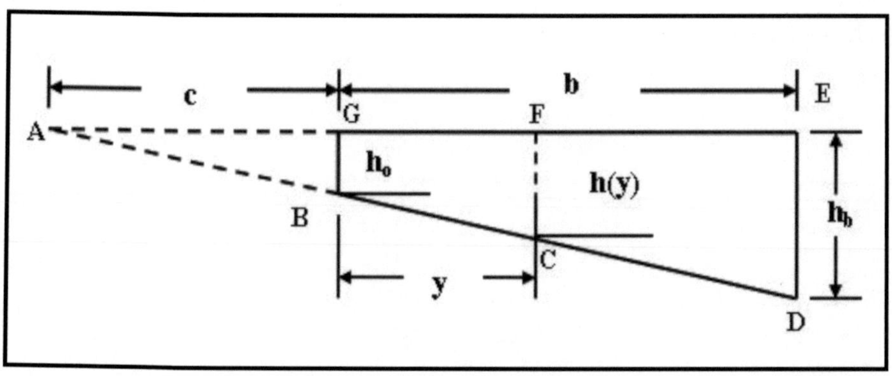

Figure 6. The relation of the plate thickness h(y) in y-direction

By similarity between the triangles (ABG) and (ACF):

$$h(y) = h_o(1 + \frac{y}{c}) \tag{28}$$

By similarity between the triangles (ABG) and (ADE):

$$\frac{h_o}{c} = \frac{h_b}{c+b} \tag{29}$$

From equations (28) and (29) the plate thickness relation is:

$$h(y) = h_o + \frac{(h_b - h_o)}{b} y \tag{30}$$

Where $h(y)=h_o$ at $y=0$,

$h(y)=h_b$ at $y=b$,

$h(y)=h_o+\frac{(h_b-h_o)}{b}y$ at $y=y$,

and $h(y)=h$ at $h_o=h_b$

Using the assumed solution, equation (10) The relation between the thickness of the plate h(y) can be given by the following equation:

$$h(\eta) = h_o + (h_b - h_o)\eta \tag{31}$$

Appendix (B)

MATLAB code

Composite coefficients (function programs)

http://dx.doi.org/10.5772/57384

Appendix (B)

MATLAB Code

Composite Coefficients (function programs)

```
%*********************************************************************************************************************************************
function yEx = Ex(E1,E2,NU12,G12,theta)
%Ex This function returns the elastic modulus
% along the x-direction in the global
% coordinate system. It has five arguments:
% E1 - longitudinal elastic modulus
% E2 - transverse elastic modulus
% NU12 - Poisson's ratio
% G12 - shear modulus
% theta - fiber orientation angle
% The angle "theta" must be given in degrees.
% Ex is returned as a scalar
m = cos(theta*pi/180);
n = sin(theta*pi/180);
denom = m^4 + (E1/G12 - 2*NU12)*n*n*m*m + (E1/E2)*n^4;
yEx = E1/denom;
%***************************************************************THE end**********************************************************************
%*********************************************CREATED BY WAEL A. AL-TABEY****************************************************
%*********************************************************************************************************************************************
function yEy = Ey(E1,E2,NU21,G12,theta)
%Ey This function returns the elastic modulus
% along the y-direction in the global
% coordinate system. It has five arguments:
% E1 - longitudinal elastic modulus
% E2 - transverse elastic modulus
% NU21 - Poisson's ratio
% G12 - shear modulus
% theta - fiber orientation angle
% The angle "theta" must be given in degrees.
% Ey is returned as a scalar
m = cos(theta*pi/180);
n = sin(theta*pi/180);
denom = m^4 + (E2/G12 - 2*NU21)*n*n*m*m + (E2/E1)*n^4;
yEy = E2/denom;
%***************************************************************THE end**********************************************************************
%*********************************************CREATED BY WAEL A. AL-TABEY****************************************************
%*********************************************************************************************************************************************
function yGxy = Gxy(E1,E2,NU12,G12,theta)
%Gxy This function returns the shear modulus
% Gxy in the global
% coordinate system. It has five arguments:
% E1 - longitudinal elastic modulus
% E2 - transverse elastic modulus
% NU12 - Poisson's ratio
% G12 - shear modulus
% theta - fiber orientation angle
% The angle "theta" must be given in degrees.
% Gxy is returned as a scalar
m = cos(theta*pi/180);
n = sin(theta*pi/180);
denom = n^4 + m^4 + 2*(2*G12*(1 + 2*NU12)/E1 + 2*G12/E2 - 1)*n*n*m*m;
yGxy = G12/denom;
%***************************************************************THE end**********************************************************************
%*********************************************CREATED BY WAEL A. AL-TABEY****************************************************
%*********************************************************************************************************************************************
function yNUxy = NUxy(E1,E2,NU12,G12,theta)
```

```
%NUxy This function returns Poisson's ratio
% NUxy in the global
% coordinate system. It has five arguments:
% E1 - longitudinal elastic modulus
% E2 - transverse elastic modulus
% NU12 - Poisson's ratio
% G12 - shear modulus
% theta - fiber orientation angle
% The angle "theta" must be given in degrees.
% NUxy is returned as a scalar
m = cos(theta*pi/180);
n = sin(theta*pi/180);
denom = m^4 + (E1/G12 - 2*NU12)*n*n*m*m + (E1/E2)*n*n;
numer = NU12*(n^4 + m^4) - (1 + E1/E2 - E1/G12)*n*n*m*m;
yNUxy = numer/denom;
%*************************************************************THE end**********************************************************************
%*********************************************CREATED BY WAEL A. AL-TABEY******************************************************
%********************************************************************************************************************************************
function yNUyx = NUyx(E1,E2,NU21,G12,theta)
%NUyx This function returns Poisson's ratio
% NUyx in the global
% coordinate system. It has five arguments:
% E1 - longitudinal elastic modulus
% E2 - transverse elastic modulus
% NU21 - Poisson's ratio
% G12 - shear modulus
% theta - fiber orientation angle
% The angle "theta" must be given in degrees.
% NUyx is returned as a scalar
m = cos(theta*pi/180);
n = sin(theta*pi/180);
denom = m^4 + (E2/G12 - 2*NU21)*n*n*m*m + (E2/E1)*n*n;
numer = NU21*(n^4 + m^4) - (1 + E2/E1 - E2/G12)*n*n*m*m;
yNUyx = numer/denom;
%*************************************************************THE end**********************************************************************
%*********************************************CREATED BY WAEL A. AL-TABEY******************************************************
%********************************************************************************************************************************************
function y = OrthotropicCompliance(E1,E2,E3,NU12,NU23,NU13,G12,G23,G13)
%OrthotropicCompliance This function returns the compliance matrix
% for orthotropic materials. There are nine
% arguments representing the nine independent
% material constants. The size of the compliance
% matrix is 6 x 6.
y = [1/E1 -NU12/E1 -NU13/E1 0 0 0 ; -NU12/E1 1/E2 -NU23/E2 0 0 0 ;-NU13/E1 -...
NU23/E2 1/E3 0 0 0 ; 0 0 0 1/G23 0 0 ; 0 0 0 0 1/G13 0 ;0 0 0 0 0 1/G12];
%*************************************************************THE end**********************************************************************
%*********************************************CREATED BY WAEL A. AL-TABEY******************************************************
%********************************************************************************************************************************************
function C = OrthotropicStiffness(E1,E2,E3,NU12,NU23,NU13,G12,G23,G13)
%OrthotropicStiffness This function returns the stiffness matrix
% for orthotropic materials. There are nine
% arguments representing the nine independent
% material constants. The size of the stiffness
% matrix is 6 x 6.
x = [1/E1 -NU12/E1 -NU13/E1 0 0 0 ; -NU12/E1 1/E2 -NU23/E2 0 0 0 ;-NU13/E1 -...
 NU23/E2 1/E3 0 0 0 ; 0 0 0 1/G23 0 0 ; 0 0 0 0 1/G13 0 ;0 0 0 0 0 1/G12];
C = inv(x);
%*************************************************************THE end**********************************************************************
%*********************************************CREATED BY WAEL A. AL-TABEY******************************************************
%********************************************************************************************************************************************
function S = ReducedCompliance(E1,E2,NU12,G12)
```

```
%ReducedCompliance This function returns the reduced compliance
% matrix for fiber-reinforced materials.
% There are four arguments representing four
% material constants. The size of the reduced
% compliance matrix is 3 x 3.
S = [1/E1 -NU12/E1 0 ; -NU12/E1 1/E2 0 ; 0 0 1/G12];
%************************************************************THE end************************************************************
%********************************************CREATED BY WAEL A. AL-TABEY**************************************************
%*******************************************************************************************************************************
function Q = ReducedStiffness(E1,E2,NU12,G12)
%ReducedStiffness This function returns the reduced stiffness
% matrix for fiber-reinforced materials.
% There are four arguments representing four
% material constants. The size of the reduced
% stiffness matrix is 3 x 3.
NU21 = NU12*E2/E1;
Q = [E1/(1-NU12*NU21) NU12*E2/(1-NU12*NU21) 0 ;NU12*E2/(1-NU12*NU21) E2/(1-...
NU12*NU21) 0 ; 0 0 G12];
%************************************************************THE end************************************************************
%********************************************CREATED BY WAEL A. AL-TABEY**************************************************
%*******************************************************************************************************************************
function SBar = Sbar(S,theta)
%Sbar This function returns the transformed reduced
% compliance matrix "Sbar" given the reduced
% compliance matrix S and the orientation
% angle "theta".
% There are two arguments representing S and "theta"
% The size of the matrix is 3 x 3.
% The angle "theta" must be given in degrees.
R=[1 0 0;0 1 0;0 0 2];
Rinv=inv(R);
m = cos(theta*pi/180);
n = sin(theta*pi/180);
T = [m*m n*n 2*m*n ; n*n m*m -2*m*n ; -m*n m*n m*m-n*n];
Tinv = [m*m n*n -2*m*n ; n*n m*m 2*m*n ; m*n -m*n m*m-n*n];
SBar = Tinv*S*R*T*Rinv;
%************************************************************THE end************************************************************
%********************************************CREATED BY WAEL A. AL-TABEY**************************************************
%*******************************************************************************************************************************
function QBar = Qbar(Q,theta)
%Qbar This function returns the transformed reduced
% stiffness matrix "Qbar" given the reduced
% stiffness matrix Q and the orientation
% angle "theta".
% There are two arguments representing Q and "theta"
% The size of the matrix is 3 x 3.
% The angle "theta" must be given in degrees.
R=[1 0 0;0 1 0;0 0 2];
Rinv=inv(R);
m = cos(theta*pi/180);
n = sin(theta*pi/180);
T = [m*m n*n 2*m*n ; n*n m*m -2*m*n ; -m*n m*n m*m-n*n];
Tinv = [m*m n*n -2*m*n ; n*n m*m 2*m*n ; m*n -m*n m*m-n*n];
QBar = Tinv*Q*R*T*Rinv;
%************************************************************THE end************************************************************
%********************************************CREATED BY WAEL A. AL-TABEY**************************************************
%*******************************************************************************************************************************
function y = Amatrix(A,QBar,z1,z2)
%Amatrix This function returns the [A] matrix
% after the layer k with stiffness [Qbar]
% is assembled.
```

```
% A - [A] matrix after layer k
% is assembled.
% Qbar - [Qbar] matrix for layer k
% z1 - z(k-1) for layer k
% z2 - z(k) for layer k
for i = 1 : 3
for j = 1 : 3
A(i,j) = A(i,j) + QBar(i,j)*(z2-z1);
end
end
y = A;
%*******************************************************THE end*********************************************************************
%*****************************************CREATED BY WAEL A. AL-TABEY*********************************************************
%****************************************************************************************************************************************
function y = Bmatrix(B,QBar,z1,z2)
%Bmatrix This function returns the [B] matrix
% after the layer k with stiffness [Qbar]
% is assembled.
% B - [B] matrix after layer k
% is assembled.
% Qbar - [Qbar] matrix for layer k
% z1 - z(k-1) for layer k
% z2 - z(k) for layer k
for i = 1 : 3
for j = 1 : 3
B(i,j) = B(i,j) + QBar(i,j)*(z2^2 -z1^2);
end
end
y = B;
%*******************************************************THE end*********************************************************************
%*****************************************CREATED BY WAEL A. AL-TABEY*********************************************************
%****************************************************************************************************************************************
function y = Dmatrix(D,QBar,z1,z2)
%Dmatrix This function returns the [D] matrix
% after the layer k with stiffness [Qbar]
% is assembled.
% D - [D] matrix after layer k
% is assembled.
% Qbar - [Qbar] matrix for layer k
% z1 - z(k-1) for layer k
% z2 - z(k) for layer k
for i = 1 : 3
for j = 1 : 3
D(i,j) = D(i,j) + QBar(i,j)*(z2^3 -z1^3);
end
end
y = D;
%*******************************************************THE end*********************************************************************
%*****************************************CREATED BY WAEL A. AL-TABEY*********************************************************
%****************************************************************************************************************************************
%****************************************************************************************************************************************
%**********The Function MATLAB code for Laminate Analysis*****************
%*************calculate [A],[B]&[D] matrix for Laminate******************
%*****************Using Orthotropic Qbar function**********************
%****************************************************************************************************************************************
function [A,B,D]=ABDmatrix(E11,E22,NU12,G12,ho,n);
%****************************************************************************************************************************************
% The reduced stiffness [Q] in GPa is calculated for this material
Q=ReducedStiffness(E11,E22,NU12,G12);
%****************************************************************************************************************************************
A=zeros(3,3);
```

http://dx.doi.org/10.5772/57384

```
B=zeros(3,3);
D=zeros(3,3);
for i=1:n
z=-(ho/2):(ho/n):(ho/2);
theta(i)=input('The angle of the layer laminate (degree)=');
%The transformed reduced stiffnesses [¯Q] in GPa for the two layers are now calculated
QBar=Qbar(Q,theta(i));
%The [A] matrix is calculated
A=Amatrix(A,QBar,z(i),z(i+1));
%The [B] matrix is calculated
B=Bmatrix(B,QBar,z(i),z(i+1));
%The [D] matrix is calculated
D=Dmatrix(D,QBar,z(i),z(i+1));
end
A=A;
B=B/2;
D=D/3;
%************************************************************THE end**********************************************************************
%********************************************CREATED BY WAEL A. AL-TABEY****************************************************
%*****************************************************************************************************************************************
%*****************************************************************************************************************************************
%********The Function MATLAB code for Laminate Coefficients****************
%********calculate Epsy-Alfa-beta Coefficients for Laminate****************
%********************Using Orthotropic Qbar function************************
%*****************************************************************************************************************************************
function
[epsy1,epsy2,epsy3,epsy4,epsy5,epsy6,beta,alfa1,alfa2,alfa3]=EpsyAlfa(E11,E22,NU12,G12,ho,n,Nxbar,Nybar,Nxybar,a,)
%*****************************************************************************************************************************************
%The [A],[B]&[D] matrix is calculated
[A,B,D]=ABDmatrix(E11,E22,NU12,G12,ho,n)
%*****************************************************************************************************************************************
epsy1=D(1,1)/D(2,2)              %D11/D22
epsy2=(D(1,2)+(2*D(3,3)))/D(2,2)  %(D12+2D66)/D22
epsy3=D(1,3)/D(2,2)              %D16/D22
epsy4=D(2,3)/D(2,2)              %D26/D22
epsy5=D(1,2)/D(2,2)              %D12/D22
epsy6=(D(1,2)+(4*D(3,3)))/D(2,2)  %(D12+4D66)/D22
beta=a/b
alfa1=Nxbar/D(2,2)               %Nx/D22
alfa2=Nybar/D(2,2)               %Ny/D22
alfa3=Nxybar/D(2,2)              %Nxy/D22
%************************************************************THE end**********************************************************************
%********************************************CREATED BY WAEL A. AL-TABEY****************************************************
%*****************************************************************************************************************************************
%*****************************************************************************************************************************************
%********The Function MATLAB code for Laminate Coefficients****************
%**calculate D03,Cf2,FR3,FR4,FT3,FT4 Coefficients for Boundary Conditions**
%*****************************************************************************************************************************************
function [EI,FR1,FR2,FR3,FR4,FT1,FT2,FT3,FT4]=CoeffBC(E11,E22,NU12,G12,ho,n,a,b,R1,R2,R3,R4,T1,T2,T3,T4)
%*****************************************************************************************************************************************
%The [A],[B]&[D] matrix is calculated
[A,B,D]=ABDmatrix(E11,E22,NU12,G12,ho,n);
%*****************************************************************************************************************************************
EI=(1-(NU12^2))*D(1,1)            %(1-NU12^2)*D11
FR1=(R1*a)/EI                     %R1*a/EI
FR2=(R2*a)/EI                     %R2*a/EI
FR3=(R3*b)/D(2,2)                 %R3*b/D22
FR4=(R4*b)/D(2,2)                 %R4*b/D22
FT1=(T1*(a^3))/EI                 %T1*a^3/EI
FT2=(T2*(a^3))/EI                 %T2*a^3/EI
FT3=(T3*(b^3))/D(2,2)             %T3*b^3/D22
```

```
FT4=(T4*(b^3))/D(2,2)              %T4*b^3/D22
%****************************************************************THE end**********************************************************************************
%***********************************************CREATED BY WAEL A. AL-TABEY************************************************************
%*************************************************************************************************************************************************************
```

The main program (Call program)

```
%*************************************************************************************************************************************************************
%**********************Laminate Coefficients*********************************
%****epsy1,epsy2,epsy3,epsy4,beta,alfa1,alfa2,alfa3,Pbar,f1,f2,f3,f4*******
%******************lambda,D03,Cf2,FR3,FR4,FT3,FT4***************************
%*************************************************************************************************************************************************************
clc;
close all; clear all;
syms y ho hb b Eta hy
%*************************************************************************************************************************************************************
hy=input('The Thickness Equation of Layer Laminate as Function of y h(y)=');
%*************************************************************************************************************************************************************
 [t1,t2,t3,t4]=VThecknis s(y,ho,hb,b,Eta,hy);
%*************************************************************************************************************************************************************
E11=input('The Modulus of Elasticity E11(GPa)=');
E22=input('The Modulus of Elasticity E22(GPa)=');
NU12=input('The Poisson Coefficient NU12=');
G12=input('The Shear Modulus G12(GPa)=');
ho=input('The Inetial thickness of Layer Laminate at y = 0.0 ho (mm)=');
hb=input('The Final thickness of Layer Laminate at y = 0.0 ho (mm)=');
a=input('The Dimensions of Laminate at x Direction a(mm)=');
b=input('The Dimensions of Laminate at y Direction b(mm)=');
n=input('The Total Number of Laminate Layer n=');
Nxbar=input('The In-Plane Load in X Direction Nxbar(N)=');
Nybar=input('The In-Plane Load in Y Direction Nybar(N)=');
Nxybar=input('The In-Plane Load in XY Plane Nxybar(N)=');
R1=input('The Rotational Stiffness of support at x=0 R1 (N.m/rad)=');
R2=input('The Rotational Stiffness of support at x=a R2 (N.m/rad)=');
R3=input('The Rotational Stiffness of support at y=0 R3 (N.m/rad)=');
R4=input('The Rotational Stiffness of support at y=b R4 (N.m/rad)=');
T1=input('The Translation Stiffness of support at x=0 T1 (N/m)=');
T2=input('The Translation Stiffness of support at x=a T2 (N/m)=');
T3=input('The Translation Stiffness of support at y=0 T3 (N/m)=');
T4=input('The Translation Stiffness of support at y=b T4 (N/m)=');
%*************************************************************************************************************************************************************
t1=eval(t1)
t2=eval(t2)
t3=eval(t3)
t4=eval(t4)
%*************************************************************************************************************************************************************
[epsy1,epsy2,epsy3,epsy4,epsy5,epsy6,beta,alfa1,alfa2,alfa3]=EpsyAlfa(E11,E22,NU12,G12,ho,n,Nxbar,Nybar,Nxybar,a,);
%*************************************************************************************************************************************************************
 [EI,FR1,FR2,FR3,FR4,FT1,FT2,FT3,FT4]=CoeffBC(E11,E22,NU12,G12,ho,n,a,b,R1,R2,R3,R4,T1,T2,T3,T4);
%****************************************************************THE end**********************************************************************************
%***********************************************CREATED BY WAEL A. AL-TABEY************************************************************
```

http://dx.doi.org/10.5772/57384

The Beam Equations

```
%*************************************************************************************************************************************
echo off;
clc;
clear all;
echo on;
%*************************************************************************************************************************************
%*The MATLAB code for Calculate Constants Of The Equation of X of The Beam*
%*************************A1, A2, A3, A4************************************
%****Using Normalizatio of FR1 FR2 FT1 FT2 For Each Case Separately********
%****************And Estimated The Constant Fay in (C.22)******************
%**********************And Beam Equation X (C.39)**************************
%*************************************************************************************************************************************
echo off;
syms m A1 A2 A3 A4 FR1 FR2 FT1 FT2 zeta
a11=FR1;
a12= -m;
a13= FR1;
a14= m;
a21= m^3;
a22= FT1;
a23= -m^3;
a24= FT1;
a31= FR2*m*cosh(m)+(sinh(m))*m^2;
a32= FR2*m*sinh(m)+(cosh(m))*m^2;
a33=FR2*m*cos(m)-(sin(m))*m^2;
a34= -FR2*m*sin(m)-(cos(m))*m^2;
a41= FT2*sinh(m)-cosh(m)*m^3;
a42= FT2*cosh(m)-sinh(m)*m^3;
a43= FT2*sin(m)+cos(m)*m^3;
a44= FT2*cos(m)-sin(m)*m^3;
a=[a11,a12,a13,a14;a21,a22,a23,a24;a31,a32,a33,a34;a41,a42,a43,a44];%(C.9)
b=[A4;A3;A2;A1];
E=a*b;
A11=solve(E(1),A1);%(C.11)
A12=solve(E(2),A1);%(C.10)
A13=A11-A12;%(C.12)
A14=solve(A13,A2);%(C.14)
A15=subs(E(3),A11,A1);%(C.15)
A16=simplify(A15);%(C.16)
A17=subs(A16,A14,A2);%(C.17)
A18=simplify(A17);%(C.18)
A19=solve(A18,A3);%(C.21)
fay=subs(A19,A4,1)%(C.22)
A21=subs(E(4),A11,A1);%(C.23)
A22=simplify(A21);%(C.24)
A23=subs(A22,A14,A2);%(C.25)
A24=simplify(A23);%(C.26)
A25=solve(A24,A3);%(C.29)
fay1=subs(A25,A4,1)%(C.30)
MUEQ=fay-fay1%(C.31)
Ax1=solve(E(1),A2);%(C.32)
Ax2=subs(E(2),Ax1,A2);%(C.33)
Ax3=subs(Ax2,A19,A3);
Ax4=solve(Ax3,A4);%(C.35)*A4=**A1
Ax5=subs(A14,A19,A3);
Ax6=subs(Ax5,Ax4,A4);%(C.36)*A2=**A1
syms fay
Ax7=Ax6*fay;%(C.37)*A3=**A1
A=1;%A1 Assumption
```

```
B=subs(Ax6,A1,1);%A2
C=subs(Ax7,A1,1);%A3
D=subs(Ax4,A1,1);%A3
X=A*cos(m*zeta)+B*sin(m*zeta)+C*cosh(m*zeta)+D*sinh(m*zeta)
%*************************************************************THE end***********************************************************************
%**********************************************CREATED BY WAEL A. AL-TABEY*******************************************************
%****************************************************************************************************************************************
echo off;
clc;
clear all;
echo on;
%****************************************************************************************************************************************
%*The MATLAB code for Calculate Constants Of The Equation of X of The Beam*
%**************************A1, A2, A3, A4**************************************
%****Using Normalizatio of FR1 FR2 FT1 FT2 For Each Case Separately********
%*****************And Estimated The Constant Fay in (C.22)******************
%***********************And Beam Equation X (C.39)***************************
%****************************************************************************************************************************************
echo off;
syms m A1 A2 A3 A4 FR1 FR2 FT1 FT2 zeta
BC=input('The Type of The Boundary Condition ( SS, CC, FF, CF, FR, FT, SC, TT, RR, RT, RS, TS, CR, CT, ES, CE, FE, EE)=','s');
if BC=='SS'
K1=0;
K2=0;
K3=1;
K4=1;
else if BC=='CC'
K1=1;
K2=1;
K3=1;
K4=1;
else if BC=='FF'
K1=0;
K2=0;
K3=0;
K4=0;
else if BC=='CF'
K1=1;
K2=0;
K3=1;
K4=0;
else if BC=='FR'
K1=0;
K2=1;
K3=0;
K4=1;
else if BC=='FT'
K1=0;
K2=0;
K3=0;
K4=1;
else if BC=='SC'
K1=0;
K2=1;
K3=1;
K4=1;
else if BC=='TT'
K1=0;
K2=0;
K3=1;
```

```
K4=1;
else if BC=='RR'
K1=1;
K2=1;
K3=1;
K4=1;
else if BC=='RT'
K1=1;
K2=0;
K3=1;
K4=1;
else if BC=='RS'
K1=1;
K2=0;
K3=1;
K4=1;
else if BC=='TS'
K1=0;
K2=0;
K3=1;
K4=1;
else if BC=='CR'
K1=1;
K2=1;
K3=1;
K4=1;
else if BC=='CT'
K1=1;
K2=0;
K3=1;
K4=1;
else if BC=='ES'%RTS
K1=1;
K2=0;
K3=1;
K4=1;
else if BC=='CE'%CRT
K1=1;
K2=1;
K3=1;
K4=1;
else if BC=='FE'%FRT
K1=0;
K2=1;
K3=0;
K4=1;
else if BC=='EE'%RTRT
K1=1;
K2=1;
K3=1;
K4=1;
end
if K1==1
a11=FR1;
a12= -m;
a13= FR1;
a14= m;
else
a11=1.0;
a12= -m/FR1;
a13= 1.0;
```

```
a14= m/FR1;
end
if K3==1
a21= m^3;
a22= FT1;
a23= -m^3;
a24= FT1;
else
a21= m^3/FT1;
a22= 1.0;
a23= -m^3/FT1;
a24= 1.0;
end
if K2==1
a31= FR2*m*cosh(m)+(sinh(m))*m^2;
a32= FR2*m*sinh(m)+(cosh(m))*m^2;
a33=FR2*m*cos(m)-(sin(m))*m^2;
a34= -FR2*m*sin(m)-(cos(m))*m^2;
else
a31= cosh(m)+(m/FR2)*sinh(m);
a32= sinh(m)+(m/FR2)*cosh(m);
a33= cos(m)-(m/FR2)*sin(m);
a34= -sin(m)-(m/FR2)*cos(m);
end
if K4==1
a41= FT2*sinh(m)-cosh(m)*m^3;
a42= FT2*cosh(m)-sinh(m)*m^3;
a43= FT2*sin(m)+cos(m)*m^3;
a44= FT2*cos(m)-sin(m)*m^3;
else
a41= sinh(m)-cosh(m)*m^3/FT2;
a42= cosh(m)-sinh(m)*m^3/FT2;
a43= sin(m)+cos(m)*m^3/FT2;
a44= cos(m)-sin(m)*m^3/FT2;
end
a=[a11,a12,a13,a14;a21,a22,a23,a24;a31,a32,a33,a34;a41,a42,a43,a44];%(C.9)
b=[A4;A3;A2;A1];
E=a*b;
A11=solve(E(1),A1);%(C.11)
A12=solve(E(2),A1);%(C.10)
A13=A11-A12;%(C.12)
A14=solve(A13,A2);%(C.14)
A15=subs(E(3),A11,A1);%(C.15)
A16=simplify(A15);%(C.16)
A17=subs(A16,A14,A2);%(C.17)
A18=simplify(A17);%(C.18)
A19=solve(A18,A3);%(C.21)
fay=subs(A19,A4,1)%(C.22)
A21=subs(E(4),A11,A1);%(C.23)
A22=simplify(A21);%(C.24)
A23=subs(A22,A14,A2);%(C.25)
A24=simplify(A23);%(C.26)
A25=solve(A24,A3);%(C.29)
fay1=subs(A25,A4,1)%(C.30)
MUEQ=fay-fay1%(C.31)
Ax1=solve(E(1),A2);%(C.32)
Ax2=subs(E(2),Ax1,A2);%(C.33)
Ax3=subs(Ax2,A19,A3);
Ax4=solve(Ax3,A4);%(C.35)*A4=**A1
Ax5=subs(A14,A19,A3);
Ax6=subs(Ax5,Ax4,A4);%(C.36)*A2=**A1
```

http://dx.doi.org/10.5772/57384

```
Ax7=Ax6*fay;%(C.37)*A3=**A1
A=1;%A1 Assumption
B=subs(Ax6,A1,1);%A2
C=subs(Ax7,A1,1);%A3
D=subs(Ax4,A1,1);%A3
X=A*cos(m*zeta)+B*sin(m*zeta)+C*cosh(m*zeta)+D*sinh(m*zeta)
%************************************************************THE end**********************************************************************
%********************************************CREATED BY WAEL A. AL-TABEY******************************************************
%*****************************************************************************************************************************************
echo off;
clc;
clear all;
echo on;
%*****************************************************************************************************************************************
%****The MATLAB code for Calculate The Equation of Fay of The Beam********
%***************For All Cases Of Boundary Condations************************
%******Using The Value of FR1 FR2 FT1 FT2 For Each Case Separately*********
%*************To Used The Equation of Fay in BeamSrip Programe*************
%*******************Using One Equation of Fay (C.34)*************************
%*****************************************************************************************************************************************
echo off;
syms FR1 FR2 FT1 FT2 m zeta
fay1=-(m^5*sinh(m)+sin(m)*m*FT1*FR1+m^4*FR2*cosh(m)+FR2*m^4*cos(m)+2*cos(m)*m^4*FR1-
sin(m)*m^5+FR2*cosh(m)*FR1*FT1+m*sinh(m)*FR1*FT1-FR2*cos(m)*FT1*FR1+2*FR2*sin(m)*FR1*m^3)/(-
2*sin(m)*m^2*FT1+m^5*cosh(m)-cos(m)*m^5+FR2*sinh(m)*FR1*FT1+m*cosh(m)*FR1*FT1-
FR2*sin(m)*m^4+2*FR2*m*cos(m)*FT1+m^4*FR2*sinh(m)+FR2*sin(m)*FR1*FT1+cos(m)*m*FR1*FT1);
BC=input('The Type of The Boundary Condition ( SS, CC, FF, CF, FR, FT, SC, TT, RR, RT, RS, TS, CR, CT, SE, CE,
FE)=','s');
if BC=='SS'
fay2=limit(fay1,FR1,0);
fay3=limit(fay2,FR2,0);
fay4=limit(fay3,FT1,inf);
fay=limit(fay4,FT2,inf)
else if BC=='CC'
fay2=limit(fay1,FR1,inf);
fay3=limit(fay2,FR2,inf);
fay4=limit(fay3,FT1,inf);
fay=limit(fay4,FT2,inf)
else if BC=='FF'
fay2=limit(fay1,FR1,0);
fay3=limit(fay2,FR2,0);
fay4=limit(fay3,FT1,0);
fay=limit(fay4,FT2,0)
else if BC=='FR'
fay2=limit(fay1,FR1,0);
fay3=limit(fay2,FT1,0);
fay=limit(fay3,FT2,inf)
else if BC=='FT'
fay2=limit(fay1,FR1,0);
fay3=limit(fay2,FR2,0);
fay=limit(fay3,FT1,0);
else if BC=='SC'
fay2=limit(fay1,FR1,0);
fay3=limit(fay2,FR2,inf);
fay4=limit(fay3,FT1,inf);
fay=limit(fay4,FT2,inf)
else if BC=='CF'
fay2=limit(fay1,FR1,inf);
fay3=limit(fay2,FR2,0);
fay4=limit(fay3,FT1,inf);
fay=limit(fay4,FT2,0)
```

```
else if BC=='TT'
fay2=limit(fay1,FR1,0);
fay=limit(fay2,FR2,0)
else if BC=='RR'
fay2=limit(fay1,FT1,inf);
fay=limit(fay2,FT2,inf)
else if BC=='RT'
fay2=limit(fay1,FR2,0);
fay=limit(fay2,FT1,inf)
else if BC=='RS'
fay2=limit(fay1,FR2,0);
fay3=limit(fay2,FT1,inf);
fay=limit(fay3,FT2,inf)
else if BC=='TS'
fay2=limit(fay1,FR1,0);
fay3=limit(fay2,FR2,0);
fay=limit(fay3,FT2,inf)
else if BC=='CR'
fay2=limit(fay1,FR1,inf);
fay3=limit(fay2,FT1,inf);
fay=limit(fay3,FT2,inf)
else if BC=='CT'
fay2=limit(fay1,FR1,inf);
fay3=limit(fay2,FR2,inf);
fay=limit(fay3,FT1,inf)
else if BC=='SE'
fay2=limit(fay1,FR1,0);
fay=limit(fay2,FT1,inf)
else if BC=='CE'
fay2=limit(fay1,FR1,inf);
fay=limit(fay2,FT1,inf)
else if BC=='FE'%FRT
fay2=limit(fay1,FR1,0);
fay=limit(fay2,FT1,0)
end
pretty(fay)
%************************************************************THE end**********************************************************************
%*********************************************CREATED BY WAEL A. AL-TABEY*******************************************************
%**************************************************************************************************************************************************
echo off;
clc;
clear all;
echo on;
%**************************************************************************************************************************************************
%*****The  MATLAB code for Calculate The Equation of MU of The Beam********
%***************For All Cases Of Boundary Condations***********************
%******Using The Value of FR1 FR2 FT1 FT2 For Each Case Separately*********
%*******************Using One Equation of MU (C.31)************************
%**************************************************************************************************************************************************
echo off;
syms FR1 FR2 FT1 FT2 m
eMU1=-(m^5*sinh(m)-
sin(m)*m^5+m^4*FR2*cosh(m)+FR2*m^4*cos(m)+2*cos(m)*m^4*FR1+FR2*cosh(m)*FR1*FT1+m*sinh(m)*FR1*FT1-
FR2*cos(m)*FT1*FR1+sin(m)*m*FT1*FR1+2*FR2*sin(m)*FR1*m^3)/(-FR2*sin(m)*m^4-
2*sin(m)*m^2*FT1+FR2*sinh(m)*FR1*FT1+m^4*FR2*sinh(m)+m^5*cosh(m)+2*FR2*m*cos(m)*FT1-
cos(m)*m^5+m*cosh(m)*FR1*FT1+FR2*sin(m)*FR1*FT1+cos(m)*m*FR1*FT1)+(m^7*cosh(m)-m^7*cos(m)-
m^4*FT2*sinh(m)-m^4*FT2*sin(m)-2*sin(m)*FR1*m^6-
FT2*sinh(m)*FR1*FT1+m^3*cosh(m)*FR1*FT1+FT2*sin(m)*FT1*FR1+m^3*cos(m)*FT1*FR1+2*FT2*cos(m)*FR1*m^3)/(m
^7*sinh(m)-FT2*cos(m)*m^4-2*m^4*cos(m)*FT1-FT2*cosh(m)*FR1*FT1-m^4*FT2*cosh(m)-
2*m*FT2*sin(m)*FT1+sin(m)*m^7+m^3*sinh(m)*FR1*FT1+FT2*cos(m)*FR1*FT1-sin(m)*m^3*FR1*FT1);
```

```
BC=input('The Type of The Boundary Condition ( SS, CC, FF, CF, FR, FT, SC, TT, RR, RT, RS, TS, CR, CT, SE, CE,
FE)=','s');
if BC=='SS'
eMU2=limit(eMU1,FR1,0);
eMU3=limit(eMU2,FR2,0);
eMU4=limit(eMU3,FT1,inf);
eMU=limit(eMU4,FT2,inf)
else if BC=='CC'
eMU2=limit(eMU1,FR1,inf);
eMU3=limit(eMU2,FR2,inf);
eMU4=limit(eMU3,FT1,inf);
eMU=limit(eMU4,FT2,inf)
else if BC=='FF'
eMU2=limit(eMU1,FR1,0);
eMU3=limit(eMU2,FR2,0);
eMU4=limit(eMU3,FT1,0);
eMU=limit(eMU4,FT2,0)
else if BC=='FR'
eMU2=limit(eMU1,FR1,0);
eMU3=limit(eMU2,FT1,0);
eMU=limit(eMU3,FT2,inf)
else if BC=='FT'
eMU2=limit(eMU1,FR1,0);
eMU3=limit(eMU2,FR2,0);
eMU=limit(eMU3,FT1,0);
else if BC=='SC'
eMU2=limit(eMU1,FR1,0);
eMU3=limit(eMU2,FR2,inf);
eMU4=limit(eMU3,FT1,inf);
eMU=limit(eMU4,FT2,inf)
else if BC=='CF'
eMU2=limit(eMU1,FR1,inf);
eMU3=limit(eMU2,FR2,0);
eMU4=limit(eMU3,FT1,inf);
eMU=limit(eMU4,FT2,0)
else if BC=='TT'
eMU2=limit(eMU1,FR1,0);
eMU=limit(eMU2,FR2,0)
else if BC=='RR'
eMU2=limit(eMU1,FT1,inf);
eMU=limit(eMU2,FT2,inf)
else if BC=='RT'
eMU2=limit(eMU1,FR2,0);
eMU=limit(eMU2,FT1,inf)
else if BC=='RS'
eMU2=limit(eMU1,FR2,0);
eMU3=limit(eMU2,FT1,inf);
eMU=limit(eMU3,FT2,inf)
else if BC=='TS'
eMU2=limit(eMU1,FR1,0);
eMU3=limit(eMU2,FR2,0);
eMU=limit(eMU3,FT2,inf)
else if BC=='CR'
eMU2=limit(eMU1,FR1,inf);
eMU3=limit(eMU2,FT1,inf);
eMU=limit(eMU3,FT2,inf)
else if BC=='CT'
eMU2=limit(eMU1,FR1,inf);
eMU3=limit(eMU2,FR2,inf);
eMU=limit(eMU3,FT1,inf)
else if BC=='SE'
```

```
eMU2=limit(eMU1,FR1,0);
eMU=limit(eMU2,FT1,inf)
else if BC=='CE'
eMU2=limit(eMU1,FR1,inf);
eMU=limit(eMU2,FT1,inf)
else if BC=='FE'%FRT
eMU2=limit(eMU1,FR1,0);
eMU=limit(eMU2,FT1,0)
end
pretty(eMU)
%*************************************************************THE end*********************************************************************
%*********************************************CREATED BY WAEL A. AL-TABEY*******************************************************
%*******************************************************************************************************************************************
echo off;
clc;
clear all;
echo on;
%*******************************************************************************************************************************************
%****The  MATLAB code for Calculate The Equation of X of The Beam********
%***************For All Cases Of Boundary Condations***********************
%******Using The Value of FR1 FR2 FT1 FT2 For Each Case Separately*********
%*************To Used The Equation of Fay in BeamSrip Programe*************
%*******************Using One Equation of X (C.39)************************
%*******************************************************************************************************************************************
echo off;
syms FR1 FR2 FT1 FT2 m zeta fay
x1=sin(m*zeta)-((2*FR1*m*fay+FR1*FT1*(m^4)-1)/(fay-FR1*FT1*(m^4)*fay+2*FT1*(m^3)))*cos(m*zeta)-
((1+FR1*FT1*(m^4))/(fay-FR1*FT1*(m^4)*fay+2*FT1*(m^3)))*(fay*sinh(m*zeta)+cosh(m*zeta));
BC=input('The Type of The Boundary Condition ( SS, CC, FF, CF, FR, FT, SC, TT, RR, RT, RS, TS, CR, CT, SE, CE,
FE)=','s');
if BC=='SS'
x2=limit(x1,FR1,0);
x3=limit(x2,FR2,0);
x4=limit(x3,FT1,inf);
x=limit(x4,FT2,inf)
else if BC=='CC'
x2=limit(x1,FR1,inf);
x3=limit(x2,FR2,inf);
x4=limit(x3,FT1,inf);
x=limit(x4,FT2,inf)
else if BC=='FF'
x2=limit(x1,FR1,0);
x3=limit(x2,FR2,0);
x4=limit(x3,FT1,0);
x=limit(x4,FT2,0)
else if BC=='FR'
x2=limit(x1,FR1,0);
x3=limit(x2,FT1,0);
x=limit(x3,FT2,inf)
else if BC=='FT'
x2=limit(x1,FR1,0);
x3=limit(x2,FR2,0);
x=limit(x3,FT1,0);
else if BC=='SC'
x2=limit(x1,FR1,0);
x3=limit(x2,FR2,inf);
x4=limit(x3,FT1,inf);
x=limit(x4,FT2,inf)
else if BC=='CF'
x2=limit(x1,FR1,inf);
x3=limit(x2,FR2,0);
```

http://dx.doi.org/10.5772/57384

```
x4=limit(x3,FT1,inf);
x=limit(x4,FT2,0)
else if BC=='TT'
x2=limit(x1,FR1,0);
x=limit(x2,FR2,0)
else if BC=='RR'
x2=limit(x1,FT1,inf);
x=limit(x2,FT2,inf)
else if BC=='RT'
x2=limit(x1,FR2,0);
x=limit(x2,FT1,inf)
else if BC=='RS'
x2=limit(x1,FR2,0);
x3=limit(x2,FT1,inf);
x=limit(x3,FT2,inf)
else if BC=='TS'
x2=limit(x1,FR1,0);
x3=limit(x2,FR2,0);
x=limit(x3,FT2,inf)
else if BC=='CR'
x2=limit(x1,FR1,inf);
x3=limit(x2,FT1,inf);
x=limit(x3,FT2,inf)
else if BC=='CT'
x2=limit(x1,FR1,inf);
x3=limit(x2,FR2,inf);
x=limit(x3,FT1,inf)
else if BC=='SE'
x2=limit(x1,FR1,0);
x=limit(x2,FT1,inf)
else if BC=='CE'
x2=limit(x1,FR1,inf);
x=limit(x2,FT1,inf)
else if BC=='FE'%FRT
x2=limit(x1,FR1,0);
x=limit(x2,FT1,0)
end
pretty(x)
%*****************************************************************THE end**********************************************************************
%**********************************************CREATED BY WAEL A. AL-TABEY***********************************************************
%*****************************************************************************************************************************************
echo off;
clc;
clear all;
echo on;
%*****************************************************************************************************************************************
%*************The MATLAB code for Plot The Beam Mode Shape****************
%******************For All Cases Of Boundary Condations********************
%*****************************************************************************************************************************************
%FOR SS (FR1=0, FR2=0, FT1=inf, FT2=inf)**
%*****************************************************************************************************************************************
%FOR CC (FR1=inf, FR2=inf, FT1=inf, FT2=inf)
%*****************************************************************************************************************************************
%FOR FF (FR1=0, FR2=0, FT1=0, FT2=0)**
%*****************************************************************************************************************************************
%FOR CF (FR1=inf, FR2=0, FT1=inf, FT2=0)**
%*****************************************************************************************************************************************
%FOR FR (FR1=0, FR2=FR, FT1=0, FT2=inf)**
%*****************************************************************************************************************************************
%FOR FT (FR1=0, FR2=0, FT1=0, FT2=FT)**
%*****************************************************************************************************************************************
```

```
%FOR SC (FR1=0,  FR2=inf,  FT1=inf,  FT2=inf)**
%*******************************************************************************************************
%FOR TT (FR1=0,  FR2=0,  FT1=FT2=FT)**
%*******************************************************************************************************
%FOR RR (FR1=FR2=FR,  FT1=inf,  FT2=inf)**
%*******************************************************************************************************
%FOR RT (FR1=FR,  FR2=0,  FT1=inf,  FT2=FT)**
%*******************************************************************************************************
%FOR RS (FR1=FR,  FR2=0,  FT1=inf,  FT2=inf)**
%*******************************************************************************************************
%FOR TS (FR1=0,  FR2=0,  FT1=FT,  FT2=inf)**
%*******************************************************************************************************
%FOR CR (FR1=inf,  FR2=FR,  FT1=inf,  FT2=inf)
%*******************************************************************************************************
%FOR CT (FR1=inf,  FR2=0,  FT1=inf,  FT2=FT)
%*******************************************************************************************************
%FOR ES (FR1=FR,  FR2=0,  FT1=FT,  FT2=inf)**
%*******************************************************************************************************
%FOR CE (FR1=inf,  FR2=FR,  FT1=inf,  FT2=FT)**
%*******************************************************************************************************
%FOR FE (FR1=0,  FR2=FR,  FT1=0,  FT2=FT)**
%*******************************************************************************************************
%FOR EE (FR1=FR2=FR,  FT1=FT2=FT)**
%*******************************************************************************************************
echo off;
format long
syms m
BC=input('The Type of The Boundary Condition ( SS, CC, FF, CF, FR, FT, SC, TT, RR, RT, RS, TS, CR, CT, ES, CE, FE,
EE)=','s');
if BC=='SS'
FR1=0.00000000001;
FR2=0.00000000001;
FT1=10000000000;
FT2=10000000000;
else if BC=='CC'
FR1=10000000000;
FR2=10000000000;
FT1=10000000000;
FT2=10000000000;
else if BC=='FF'
FR1=0.00000000001;
FR2=0.00000000001;
FT1=0.00000000001;
FT2=0.00000000001;
else if BC=='CF'
FR1=10000000000;
FR2=0.00000000001;
FT1=10000000000;
FT2=0.00000000001;
else if BC=='FR'
FR1=0.00000000001;
FR2=input('The Rotational Stiffness of support at x=a R2 (N.m/rad)=');
FT1=0.00000000001;
FT2=10000000000;
else if BC=='FT'
FR1=0.00000000001;
FR2=0.00000000001;
FT1=0.00000000001;
FT2=input('The Translation Stiffness of support at x=a T2 (N/m)=');
else if BC=='SC'
FR1=0.00000000001;
```

```
FR2=10000000000;
FT1=10000000000;
FT2=10000000000;
else if BC=='TT'
FR1=0.00000000001;
FR2=0.00000000001;
FT1=input('The Translation Stiffness of support at x=0 T1(N/m)=');
FT2=input('The Translation Stiffness of support at x=a T2(N/m)=');
else if BC=='RR'
FR1=input('The Rotational Stiffness of support at x=0 R1 (N.m/rad)=');
FR2=input('The Rotational Stiffness of support at x=a R2 (N.m/rad)=');
FT1=10000000000;
FT2=10000000000;
else if BC=='RT'
FR1=input('The Rotational Stiffness of support at x=0 R1 (N.m/rad)=');
FR2=0.00000000001;
FT1=10000000000;
FT2=input('The Translation Stiffness of support at x=a T2(N/m)=');
else if BC=='RS'
FR1=input('The Rotational Stiffness of support at x=0 R1 (N.m/rad)=');
FR2=0.00000000001;
FT1=10000000000;
FT2=10000000000;
else if BC=='TS'
FR1=0.00000000001;
FR2=0.00000000001;
FT1=input('The Translation Stiffness of support at x=0 T1(N/m)=');
FT2=10000000000;
else if BC=='CR'
FR1=10000000000;
FR2=input('The Rotational Stiffness of support at x=a R2 (N.m/rad)=');
FT1=10000000000;
FT2=10000000000;
else if BC=='CT'
FR1=10000000000;
FR2=0.00000000001;
FT1=10000000000;
FT2=input('The Translation Stiffness of support at x=a T2(N/m)=');
else if BC=='ES'%RTS
FR1=input('The Rotational Stiffness of support at x=0 R1(N.m/rad)=');
FR2=0.00000000001;
FT1=input('The Translation Stiffness of support at x=0 T1(N/m)=');
FT2=10000000000;
else if BC=='CE'%CRT
FR1=10000000000;
FR2=input('The Rotational Stiffness of support at x=a R2 (N.m/rad)=');
FT1=10000000000;
FT2=input('The Translation Stiffness of support at x=a T2(N/m)=');
else if BC=='FE'%FRT
FR1=0.00000000001;
FR2=input('The Rotational Stiffness of support at x=a R2 (N.m/rad)=');
FT1=0.00000000001;
FT2=input('The Translation Stiffness of support at x=a T2(N/m)=');
else if BC=='EE'%RTRT
FR1=input('The Rotational Stiffness of support at x=0 R1 (N.m/rad)=');
FR2=input('The Rotational Stiffness of support at x=a R2 (N.m/rad)=');
FT1=input('The Translation Stiffness of support at x=0 T1(N/m)=');
FT2=input('The Translation Stiffness of support at x=a T2(N/m)=');
end
syms m
zeta=1;
```

```
syms zeta
N=input('The Number of Plate Strips N=');
R1=input('The Rotational Stiffness of support at x=0 R1 (N.m/rad)=');
R2=input('The Rotational Stiffness of support at x=a R2 (N.m/rad)=');
T1=input('The Translation Stiffness of support at x=0 T1 (N/m)=');
T2=input('The Translation Stiffness of support at x=a T2 (N/m)=');
NU12=input('The Poisson Coefficient NU12=');
a=input('The Dimensions of Laminate at x Direction a(mm)=');
D=input('enter D(1,1)=');
EI=(1-(NU12^2))*D;
FR1=(R1*a)/EI;                    %R1*a/EI
FR2=(R2*a)/EI;                    %R2*a/EI
FT1=(T1*(a^3))/EI;                 %T1*a^3/EI
FT2=(T2*(a^3))/EI;                  %T2*a^3/EI
for i=1:N
for j=1:N
m(i)=i*pi;
m(j)=j*pi;
fay(i)=((((2*FR1*FR2*(m(i).^4))-(m(i).^6)+(FR1*FT1*(m(i).^2))).*sin(m(i)))+(((2*FR1*(m(i).^5))+(FR2*(m(i).^5))-
(FR1*FR2*FT1*m(i))).*cos(m(i)))+(((m(i).^6)+(FR1*FT1*(m(i).^2))).*sinh(m(i)))+((((m(i).^5)*FR2)+(FR1*FR2*FT1*m(i))).*co
sh(m(i))))./((((FR1*FR2*FT1*m(i))-(2*FT1*(m(i).^3))-
(FR2*(m(i).^5))).*sin(m(i)))+((((FR1*FT1*(m(i).^2))+(2*FR2*FT1*(m(i).^2))-
(m(i).^6))).*cos(m(i)))+(((FR2*(m(i).^5))+(FR1*FR2*FT1)).*sinh(m(i)))+(((m(i).^6)+(FR1*FT1*(m(i).^2))).*cosh(m(i))))
fay(j)=((((2*FR1*FR2*(m(j).^4))-(m(j).^6)+(FR1*FT1*(m(j).^2))).*sin(m(j)))+(((2*FR1*(m(j).^5))+(FR2*(m(j).^5))-
(FR1*FR2*FT1*m(j))).*cos(m(j)))+(((m(j).^6)+(FR1*FT1*(m(j).^2))).*sinh(m(j)))+((((m(j).^5)*FR2)+(FR1*FR2*FT1*m(j))).*cos
h(m(j))))./((((FR1*FR2*FT1*m(j))-(2*FT1*(m(j).^3))-
(FR2*(m(j).^5))).*sin(m(j)))+((((FR1*FT1*(m(j).^2))+(2*FR2*FT1*(m(j).^2))-
(m(i).^6))).*cos(m(j)))+(((FR2*(m(j).^5))+(FR1*FR2*FT1)).*sinh(m(j)))+(((m(j).^6)+(FR1*FT1*(m(j).^2))).*cosh(m(j))))
x(i)=cos(m(i)*zeta)+((((-2*m(i).*FT1*fay(i)).*((m(i).^4)-(FT1*FR1)))-(((m(i).^4)-(FT1*FR1))^2))./((((m(i).^8)-
((FT1*FR1)^2)).*fay(i))-((2*(m(i)^3)*FR1).*((m(i)^4)+(FR1*FT1)))))).*sin(m(i)*zeta)-((((m(i).^4)-
(FT1*FR1))).*fay(i))./((((m(i).^4)-(FT1*FR1)))-((2*(m(i)^3)*FR1))).*(sinh(m(i)*zeta)+(fay(i).*cosh(m(i)*zeta)))
dx(i)=diff(x(i),zeta)
ddx(i)=diff(dx(i),zeta)
dddx(i)=diff(ddx(i),zeta)
ddddx(i)=diff(dddx(i),zeta)
x(j)=cos(m(j)*zeta)+((((-2*m(j).*FT1*fay(j)).*((m(j).^4)-(FT1*FR1)))-(((m(j).^4)-(FT1*FR1))^2))./((((m(j).^8)-
((FT1*FR1)^2)).*fay(j))-((2*(m(j)^3)*FR1).*((m(j)^4)+(FR1*FT1)))))).*sin(m(j)*zeta)-((((m(j).^4)-
(FT1*FR1))).*fay(j))./((((m(j).^4)-(FT1*FR1)))-((2*(m(j)^3)*FR1))).*(sinh(m(j)*zeta)+(fay(j).*cosh(m(j)*zeta)))
f1(i,j)=x(i)*x(j)
f2(i,j)=dx(i)*x(j)
f3(i,j)=ddx(i)*x(j)
f4(i,j)=dddx(i)*x(j)
f5(i,j)=ddddx(i)*x(j)
f6(i,j)=x(j)
a=int(f1,zeta,0,1)
b=int(f2,zeta,0,1)
c=int(f3,zeta,0,1)
d=int(f4,zeta,0,1)
e=int(f5,zeta,0,1)
p=int(f6,zeta,0,1)
end
end
a=eval(a)
b=eval(b)
c=eval(c)
d=eval(d)
e=eval(e)
p=eval(p)
%*****************************************************************************THE end*******************************************************************************
%******************************************************CREATED BY WAEL A. AL-TABEY*********************************************************************
%************************************************************************************************************************************************************
```

http://dx.doi.org/10.5772/57384

```
%******************************************************************************************************
%********The programe to calculate the initial value **********************
%***********************BOUNDARY CONDITIONS*********************************
%******************************************************************************************************
clc;
clear all;
%******************************************************************************************************
for i=1:m
  mi=4*i-2
  j=i
  yyi(mi,j)=1
end
%******************************************************************************************************
for i=1:m
  for j=1:m
    j=i
     mi=4*i
    yyi(mi,j)=-a24*(CK(i,j)/AK(i,j))
  end
end
%******************************************************************************************************
%*********************New for B.C.against rotation***************************
%******************************************************************************************************
for i=1:m
  j=i
  mi=4*i-1
  yyi(mi,j)=1/R3
end
%******************************************************************************************************
for i=1:m
  jj=i+m
  mii=4*i-3
  yyi(mii,jj)=1
end
%******************************************************************************************************
for i=1:m
  for j=1:m
    j=i
    mii=4*i-1
    jj=j+m
    yyi(mii,jj)=-C13*(CK(i,j)/AK(i,j))
  end
end
%******************************************************************************************************
for i=1:m
  mii=4*i
  jj=i+m
  yyi(mii,jj)=-1/T3
end
%***************************************************************THE end*******************************************************************
%*********************************************CREATED BY WAEL A. AL-TABEY*******************************************************
%******************************************************************************************************
%*******The programe to calculate the eigenvalue and eigenvvector**********
%******************************************************************************************************
clc;
clear all;
%*****************************The eigenvalue********************************
syms k1 k3
Ak=[0 1 0 0;0 0 1 0;0 0 0 1;-k1 0 -k3 0]
Lampda=eig(Ak)
%******************************************************************************************************
```

The Plate Mode Shape

```
%**********************************************************************************************************************
%********************** The Plate Mode Shape ****************************
%**********************************************************************************************************************
echo on
clc;
clear all;
pause % Strike any key to continue.
clc
%*********************Problem definition************************************
g='squareg'; % The unit square
b='squareb3'; % 0 on the left and right boundaries and
%**********0 normal derivative on the top and bottom boundaries************
c=1;
a=0;
f=0;
d=1;
%*********************************Mesh***************************************
[p,e,t]=initmesh('squareg');
pause % Strike any key to continue.
clc
%*****************************************************************************
x=p(1,:)';
y=p(2,:)';
%*****************************************************************************
u0=atan(cos(pi/2*x));
ut0=3*sin(pi*x).*exp(sin(pi/2*y));
pause % Strike any key to continue.
clc
%*******We want the solution at 31 points in time between 0 and 5**********
n=31;
tlist=linspace(0,5,n);

%*************************Solve PDE problem of Plate***********************
uu=hyperbolic(u0,ut0,tlist,b,p,e,t,c,a,f,d);
pause % Strike any key to continue.
clc
%*****To speed up the plotting, we interpolate to a rectangular grid*******
delta=-1:0.1:1;
[uxy,tn,a2,a3]=tri2grid(p,t,uu(:,1),delta,delta);
gp=[tn;a2;a3];
%***************************Make the animation*****************************
newplot;
M=moviein(n);
umax=max(max(uu));
umin=min(min(uu));
for i=1:n,
 if rem(i,10)==0,
  fprintf('%d ',i);
 end
 pdeplot(p,e,t,'xydata',uu(:,i),'zdata',uu(:,i),'zstyle','continuous','mesh','on','xygrid','on','gridparam',gp,'colorbar','on');
 grid on
 colormap
 axis([-1 1 -1 1 umin umax]); caxis([umin umax]);
 title('Plate mode shape')
 xlabel('X')
 ylabel('Y')
 zlabel('Z')
 M(:,i)=getframe;
 if i==n;
```

```
  fprintf('done\n');
 end
end
%******************************Show movie**********************************
nfps=5;
movie(M,10,nfps);
pause % Strike any key to end.
echo off
%**********************************************************THE end**********************************************************************
%******************************************CREATED BY WAEL A. AL-TABEY****************************************************
%***********************************************************************************************************************************
```

Author details

Wael A. Al-Tabey

Department of Mechanical Engineering Faculty of Engineering, Alexandria University, Alexandria, Egypt

References

[1] Utku M., Citipitioglu E. and Inceleme I, 2000, Circular plate on elastic foundation modeled with annular plates, J. Computinal Structures, 74, 78-365.

[2] Chadrashekhara K. and Antony J., 1997, Elastic analysis of an annular slab-soil interaction problem using hybrid method. Compt. Geotech, 76, 20-161.

[3] Ng SF, Araar Y, 1989, Free vibration and buckling analysis of clamped rectangular plates of variable thickness by Galerkin Method. J. Sound Vibration, 135(2):263-74.

[4] Ungbhakorn V and Singhatanadgid P, 2006, Buckling analysis of symmetrically laminated composite plates by the extended Kantorovich method, J. composite Structures, 73, 120-123.

[5] Setoodeh A.R, Karami G, 2003, A solution for the vibration and buckling of composite laminates with elastically restrained edges, J. composite Structures, 60, 245-253.

[6] Laura P. and Gutierrez R., 1985, Vibrating non uniform plates on elastic foundation. J. Mechanical Engineering. ASCE, 96 111-1185.

[7] Ashour A.S, 2004, vibration of variable thickness plates with edges elastically restrained against rotational and translation, Thin-Walled Structures, 42, 1-24.

[8] Grossi R.O, Nallim L.G, 2008, On the existence of weak solutions of anisotropic generally restrained plates, J. Applied Mathematical Modelling, 32, 2254-2273.

[9] LU C.F, Lee Y.Y, Lim C.W and Chen W.Q, 2006, free vibration of long-span contagious rectangular Kirchhoff plates with internal rigid line supports, J. Sound and Vibration, 297, 351-364.

[10] Chopra I. 1974, Vibration of stepped thickness plates. International Journal of Mechanical Science; 16:337–44.

[11] Cortinez VH, Laura PAA. 1990, Analysis of vibrating rectangular plates of discontinuously varying thickness by means of the Kantorovich extended method. J. of Sound and Vibration; 137(3):457–61.

[12] Bambill DV, Laura PAA, Bergmann A, Carnicer R. 1991, Fundamental frequency of transverse vibration of symmetrically stepped simply supported rectangular plates. J. of Sound and Vibration; 150(1):167–9.

[13] Laura PAA, Gutierrez RH. 1985, Transverse vibrations of rectangular plates on inhomogeneous foundations, Part I: Rayleigh-Ritz method. J. of Sound and Vibration; 101(3):307–15.

[14] Harik IE, Andrade MG. 1989, Stability of plates with step variation in thickness. J. Computers and Structures; 33(1):257–63.

[15] Cheung Y.K and Zhou D 2001, Vibration analysis of symmetrically laminated rectangular plates with intermediate line-supports, J. Thin-walled Structures, 79, 33-41.

Section 4

Image Processing

Chapter 22

Image Processing with MATLAB and GPU

Antonios Georgantzoglou, Joakim da Silva and
Rajesh Jena

Additional information is available at the end of the chapter

http://dx.doi.org/10.5772/58300

1. Introduction

MATLAB® (The MathWorks, Natick, MA, USA) is a software package for numerical computing that can be used in various scientific disciplines such as mathematics, physics, electronics, engineering and biology. More than 40 toolboxes are available in the current release (R2013b released in September 2013), which include numerous built-in functions enhanced by access to a high-level programming language.

Since images can be represented by 2D or 3D matrices and the MATLAB processing engine relies on matrix representation of all entities, MATLAB is particularly suitable for implementation and testing of image processing workflows. The Image Processing Toolbox™ (IPT) includes all the necessary tools for general-purpose image processing incorporating more than 300 functions which have been optimised to offer good accuracy and high speed of processing. Moreover, the built-in Parallel Computing Toolbox™ (PCT) has recently been expanded and now supports graphics processing unit (GPU) acceleration for some functions of the IPT. However, for many image processing applications we still need to write our own code, either in MATLAB or, in the case of GPU-accelerated applications requiring specific control over GPU resources, in CUDA (Nvidia Corporation, Santa Clara, CA, USA).

In this chapter, the first part is dedicated to some essential tools of the IPT that can be used in image analysis and assessment as well as in extraction of useful information for further processing and assessment. These include retrieving information about digital images, image adjustment and processing as well as feature extraction and video handling. The second part is dedicated to GPU acceleration of image processing techniques either by using the built-in PCT functions or through writing our own functions. Each section is accompanied by MATLAB example code. The functions and code provided in this chapter are adopted from the MATLAB documentation [1], [2] unless otherwise stated.

INTECH
open science | open minds

© 2014 The Author(s). Licensee InTech. This chapter is distributed under the terms of the Creative Commons Attribution License (http://creativecommons.org/licenses/by/3.0), which permits unrestricted use, distribution, and reproduction in any medium, provided the original work is properly cited.

2. Image processing on CPU

2.1. Basic image concepts

2.1.1. Pixel representation

A digital image is a visual representation of a scene that can be obtained using a digital optical device. It is composed of a number of picture elements, pixels, and it can be either two-dimensional (2D) or three-dimensional (3D). Different bit-depth images can be found but the most common ones in scientific image processing are the 1-bit binary images (pixel values 0 or 1), the 8-bit grey-scale images (pixel range 0-255) and the 16-bit colour images (pixel range 0-65535) [3]. Figure 1 shows the grey-scale variation, from black to white, for an 8-bit image.

Figure 1. Variation of grey-scale intensities for an 8-bit image.

2.1.2. MATLAB pixel convention

MATLAB uses one-based indexing, where the first pixel along any dimension has index1, whereas many other platforms are zero-based and consider the first index to be 0. By convention, counting of pixel indices starts from the top-left corner of an image with the first and second indices increasing down and towards the right, respectively. Figure 2 visualises the way that MATLAB indexes a 512×512 pixel image. This information is particularly important when the user intends to apply a transformation to a specific pixel or a neighbourhood of pixels.

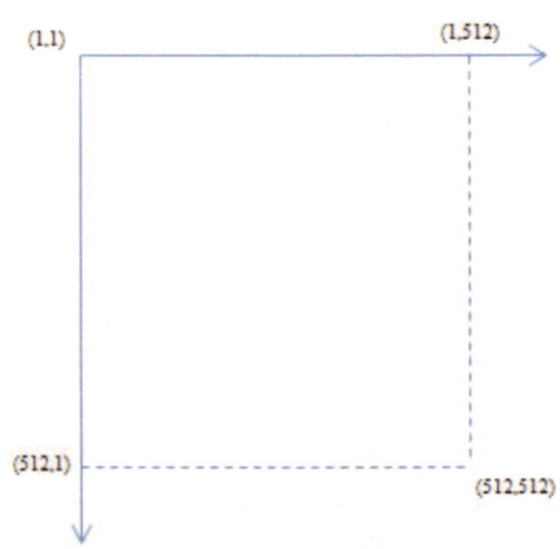

Figure 2. MATLAB's pixel indexing convention.

http://dx.doi.org/10.5772/58300

2.1.3. *Image formats*

Various image formats are supported by MATLAB including the most commonly used ones, such as JPEG, TIFF, BMP, GIF and PNG. Images can be read, processed and then saved in a format other than their initial one. Various parameters such as the resolution, the bit-depth, the compression level or the colour-space can be adjusted according to the user's preferences.

2.1.4. *Digital image processing*

Digital image processing refers to the modification of a digital image using a computer in order to emphasise relevant information. This can be achieved by both revealing latent details and suppressing unwanted noise. The process is usually designed according to the desired final outcome which can include simple image enhancement; object detection, segmentation or tracking; parameter estimation; or condition classification. Moreover, when dealing with images intended for inspection by people, the structure and function of the human visual system may be a critical factor in designing any such technique as this determines what can be perceived as an easily distinguishable feature.

2.2. Image pre-processing

Image pre-processing is a procedure that gives initial information about the digital condition of a candidate image. In order to receive such information, we need to load the image on the software platform and examine its type and pixel values.

2.2.1. *Image input and output*

Just as any other data set in MATLAB, images are represented by a variable. If we consider an image file with name 'image' and format 'tiff', using the function *imread*, the image can be loaded as a 2D or 3D matrix, depending on the image type. Image visualisation is achieved using the function *imshow*; to produce a new figure, a call to *imshow* has to be preceded by a call to *figure*. If, instead, *imshow* is used on its own, the new image replaces the last one in the last open figure window. Saving an image can be achieved using the function *imwrite* where the desired image (i.e. variable), the format and the final name have to be specified. Although the name of the saved image can be chosen freely, when building a large pipeline, it is suggested that the name of each resulting image be representative of the processing step in order to maintain process coherence. The following example represents how this sequence can be achieved.

```
% Image import as variable
im=imread('image.tif');
% Image visualisation
figure; imshow(im);
% Application of image processing
im_proc=...
% Export processed image as file
imwrite(im_proc, 'im_processed.tif', 'tif');
```

The function *imshow* can also be accompanied by a two-element vector *[low high]* with which the user specifies the display range of the grey-scale image. If this vector is left empty *[]*, the minimum and maximum grey-scale values of the image are displayed as black and white pixels, respectively, with the intermediate values as various shades of grey.

```
% Image visualisation with automatically and manually selected
% intensity ranges, respectively
figure; imshow(im, []);
figure; imshow(im, [low high]);
```

2.2.2. *Image type conversions*

Image type conversion is a useful tool as the user can convert the input image into any desired type. A special and often useful conversion is the transformation of an unsigned integer into a double-precision representation. Any image processing algorithm may thus result in more accurate outcomes since this conversion increases the dynamic range of intensities. The range of the resulting image is 0.0 to 1.0 with MATLAB maintaining up to 15 decimal digits. The following commands are examples of image conversions.

```
% Conversion to double-precision and 8-bit unsigned integer, respectively
im_double=im2double(im);
im_ui8=im2uint8(im);
```

2.2.3. *Pixel information*

A histogram is a useful intensity representation as it reveals the pixels' intensity distribution. It can be obtained using the function *imhist*. This information can, for example, be used for selecting an appropriate threshold value. Apart from this, a profile of intensities can also reveal information about local intensity variations which can be used to model small details. The function *improfile* can either be applied on pre-selected pixels or as a command prompt function for the user in order to manually select the desired area. Example of code for such processes follows [1], [3].

```
% Histogram presentation: output is the number of pixels (pixel_count)
% distributed at each grey-scale intensity (grey_levels)
[pixel_count grey_levels]=imhist(im);
% Visualisation of histogram with manual limit in grey levels
figure; bar(pixel_count, 'r');
set(gca, 'XLim', [0 grey_levels(end)]);
% Normalisation of histogram
pixel_count_norm=pixel_count / numel(im);
figure; bar(pixel_count_norm, 'b');
set(gca, 'XLim', [0 grey_levels(end)]);
% Profiling of specific pixels
x=[1 205 150 35];
y=[105 230 25 15];
figure; improfile(im, x, y);
```

http://dx.doi.org/10.5772/58300

2.2.4. Contrast adjustment

One of the main pre-processing techniques is contrast adjustment since this process can enhance desired features whilst suppressing other, unwanted ones. MATLAB has various tools for varying the image contrast. The function *imcontrast* supplies a manual adjustment tool through which the user can experiment and find the optimal contrast. The resulting parameters can then be adopted, saved and applied to a stack of images taken under the same conditions. The function *imadjust* can be used to specify an intensity range when the user knows the optimal values or has found them using the *imcontrast* tool. The same function also provides input for the gamma factor of the power-law non-linear contrast adjustment. Besides, a custom-made logarithmic transformation can be applied [3].

```
% Contrast adjustment
im_adj=imadjust(im, [low_in hign_in], [low_out high_out], gamma);
% Example of contrast adjustment
im_adj=imadjust(im, [0.2 0.8], [0.1 0.9], 1.0);
```

Figure 3 presents an original grey-scale image and its contrast adjusted counterpart using the parameters specified in the previous example.

Figure 3. Original image (left, 1296×1936 pixels) and contrast adjusted outcome (right).

```
% Custom logarithmic transformation
im_log=a*log(b+im);
im_log=a+b*log(c – im);
```

Parameters *a, b* and *c* can be defined and adjusted by the user meaning any such custom-made logarithmic transformation can be introduced according to specific needs.

Other techniques that can affect contrast are histogram-based ones. A histogram represents an image's grey-level intensity distribution or probability density function. Such knowledge can assist in further processing by helping the user choose the right tools [4]. Histogram stretching can be performed through the *imadjust* function while histogram equalisation can be performed through the function *histeq*. Adaptive histogram equalization can also be applied using the function *adapthisteq* which considers small image neighbourhoods instead of the whole image as an input.

```
% Histogram equalisation and adaptive equalisation, respectively
im_eq=histeq(im);
im_adeq=adapthisteq(im, 'NumTiles', NumTilesValue);
```

The parameter *NumTilesValue* takes the form of a vector that specifies the number of tiles in each direction. Other parameters can also be specified in the *adapthisteq* function such as the dynamic range of the output data or the histogram shape. Figure 4 shows examples of histogram equalisation and adaptive histogram equalisation, respectively.

Figure 4. Histogram equalisation transformation (left) and adaptive histogram equalization transformation (right) of the original image in Figure 3. Notice the enhanced details in the right-hand image.

2.2.5. *Arithmetic operations*

Arithmetic operations refer to addition, subtraction, multiplication and division of two images or an image and a constant. Images subject to arithmetic operations need to have the same dimensions and grey-scale representation. The resulting image will have the same dimensions as the input. When a constant value is added or subtracted (instead of a second image), this constant is added or subtracted to each pixel's intensity, increasing or reducing the image luminosity. Most often, such operations are used for detail enhancement or suppression of unnecessary information.

```
% Addition, subtraction, multiplication and division of two images,
% respectively
im_add=imadd(im1, im2);
im_sub=imsubtract(im1, im2);
im_mult=immultiply(im1, im2);
im_div=imdivide(im1, im2);
```

In the code above, the second input parameter (*im2*) can be replaced by a scalar constant.

2.2.6. *Miscellaneous transformations*

Other useful image transformations include cropping, resizing and rotation. Cropping can be used if the user is interested only in one particular part of the input image. The user can define a specific region of interest and apply any transformation only to this part. Resizing can be applied in order either to expand or reduce the image size. Image size reduction can be especially useful in speeding up a process in case of larger images or large data sets. Rotation can be particularly useful when an image includes features of a particular directionality. The user can specify the applied interpolation method out of nearest neighbour, bilinear and bicubic. Inversion of grey-scale intensities can be useful when the interesting objects have intensities lower than the background. The following functions perform these processes.

```
% Image cropping, resizing, rotation and inversion, respectively
im_crop=imcrop(im, [x y size_x size_y]);
im_res=imresize(im, scale);
im_rot=imrotate(im, angle, method);
im_com=imcomplement(im);
```

2.3. Image processing

2.3.1. *Thresholding*

Thresholding is one of the most important concepts in image processing as it finds application in almost all projects. Thresholding can be manual or automatic, global or local. In manual mode, the user defines a threshold value, usually depending on the conception of the image (several trials may be needed). In automatic mode, a more detailed understanding of the image is required in order to select the correct method. The IPT provides the function *graythresh* which is based on Otsu's method and the bimodal character of an image [5]. This global threshold will create a black-and-white image where pixels with intensities above this threshold will become white (value 1) and pixels with intensities below this threshold will become black (value 0).

This method can be easily extended to multi-thresholding by using the IPT function *multithresh*. Using this function, the user specifies a suitable number of threshold levels (k) for the image. If this parameter is not supplied, it has the same functionality as the original *graythresh* function. The IPT can visualise the result of the *multithresh* function by using the *imquantize* function. The latter labels the various areas of the image according to the number of thresholds previously specified. The labelled image can then be transformed into an RGB image, preserving the type (e.g. uint8) of the original input. The following code can be used in these processes.

```
% Single threshold application and binarisation, respectively
thresh=graythresh(im);
im_bin=im2bw(im, thresh);
% Multiple threshold application and visualisation of thresholded
% areas as colours of image, respectively
```

```
mult_th=multithresh(im, k);
im_th=imquantize(im, mult_th);
im_rgb=label2rgb(im_th);
```

Figure 5 provides an example of single- and multi-threshold application on the original image of Figure 3.

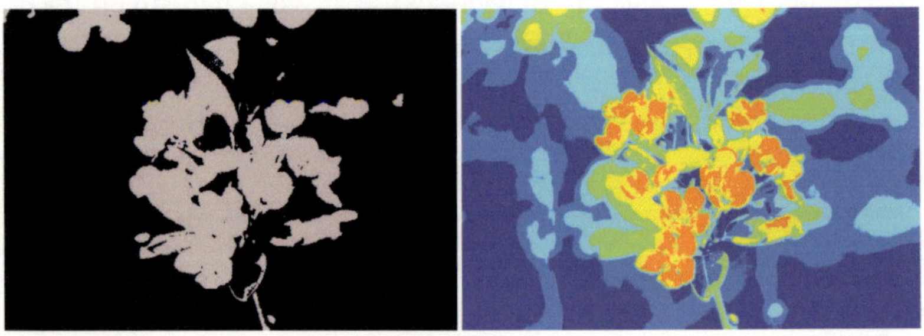

Figure 5. Single-thresholded image (left) and multi-thresholded image using 5 threshold values (right).

2.3.2. *Edge detection*

Edge detection is an essential part of image processing as it usually emphasises objects' outline or internal structure. An edge is a representation of discontinuity in an image and may characterise a surface that separates two objects or an object from the image background [4]. Boundaries can be characterized by single pixels or connected sequences of pixels. Such a feature can assist in further object recognition and, thus, edge detection is applied in many image processing sequences. The outcome of edge detection is a binary image with edges presented by white pixels.

2.3.3. *First-order edge detection operators*

The IPT includes the standard first-order edge detectors such as the Roberts, Sobel and Prewitt. Roberts edge detector relies on 2×2 masks whereas the other two rely on 3×3 masks. An optional *threshold* can be specified in order to define the minimum gradient magnitude. Useful code for such detectors follows.

```
% First-order edge detection
im_bin=edge(im, 'roberts', threshold);
im_bin=edge(im, 'sobel', threshold);
im_bin=edge(im, 'prewitt', threshold);
```

Other first-order edge-detectors can also be designed. Examples are the Kirsch and the Robinson masks which are not included in the IPT but are easy to design. They are examples of directional edge detectors which scan the image from different directions in order to detect edges with various orientations. A single kernel is used which, through rotations from 0° to

http://dx.doi.org/10.5772/58300

315° in steps of 45°, creates eight different masks. The image is convolved with each mask and the pixels in the final image are assigned the highest edge detection magnitude obtained from any of the masks [4] The following code presents these two edge-detectors, respectively [6], [4].

```
% Kirsch edge detector
K(:,:,1)=[-5 3 3; -5 0 3; -5 3 3];
K(:,:,2)=[-5 -5 3; -5 0 3; 3 3 3];
K(:,:,3)=[-5 -5 -5; 3 0 0; 3 3 3];
K(:,:,4)=[3 -5 -5; 3 0 -5; 3 3 3];
K(:,:,5)=[3 3 -5; 3 0-5; 3 3 -5];
K(:,:,6)=[3 3 3; 3 0 -5; 3 -5 -5];
K(:,:,7)=[3 3 3; 3 0 3; -5 -5 -5];
K(:,:,8)=[3 3 3; -5 0 3; -5 -5 3];
% Robinson edge detector
R(:,:,1)=[-1 0 1; -2 0 2; -1 0 1];
R(:,:,2)=[0 1 2; -1 0 1; -2 -2 0];
R(:,:,3)=[1 2 1; 0 0 0; -1 -2 -1];
R(:,:,4)=[2 1 0; 1 0 -1; 0 -1 -2];
R(:,:,5)=[1 0 -1; 2 0 -2; 1 0 -1];
R(:,:,6)=[0 -1 -2; 1 0 -1; 2 1 0];
R(:,:,7)=[-1 -2 -1; 0 0 0; 1 2 1];
R(:,:,8)=[-2 -1 0; -1 0 1; 0 1 2];
```

The point detector, another example of an edge detector, detects bright points based on the intensity difference between a central pixel and its neighbours. A point detector can be specified by the following code [7].

```
% Point edge detector
P=[-1 -1 -1; -1 8 -1; -1 -1 -1];
```

2.3.4. Second-order edge detection operators

In addition to first-order edge detectors, second-order edge detectors can find wide application. Such detectors are for example the Canny, zero-cross and Laplacian-of-Gaussian (LoG; also called Marr-Hildreth). The Canny method uses the derivative of a Gaussian filter for finding the gradient of the original image after which it relies on local maxima of the resulting image. [3] The zero-cross method searches for zero crossings after an arbitrary filter has been applied. Finally, the LoG method searches for zero crossings after the LoG transformation has been applied. Useful code for such detectors follows.

```
% Second-order edge detection
im_bin=edge(im, 'log', threshold, sigma);
im_bin=edge(im, 'canny', threshold, sigma);
im_bin=edge(im, 'zero-cross', threshold, filter);
```

In this case, *threshold* refers to the strength of an edge; *sigma* refers to the standard deviation of the Gaussian filter while *filter* refers to any filter that the user applies prior to the edge detection. In LoG and Canny methods, threshold and sigma can be left unspecified but in the case of the zero-cross method the user has to define a filter. Figure 6 presents the resulting images after application of 'Roberts' and 'Canny' edge detectors, respectively.

Figure 6. Application of 'Roberts' edge detector (left) and 'Canny' edge detector with a threshold value of 0.05 (right).

2.3.5. *Image filtering*

Spatial filtering is one of the most important processes in image processing as it can extract and process specific frequencies from an image while other frequencies can be removed or transformed. Usually, filtering is used for image enhancement or noise removal. IPT includes the standard tools needed for image filtering. The function *fspecial* can be used for filter design. Mean, average, Gaussian, Laplacian, Laplacian-of-Gaussian, motion, Prewitt-edge and Sobel-edge filters can be introduced. The designed filter is applied to the image by using the function *imfilter*. Typical examples of code follow.

```
% Filter design
filt_av=fspecial('average', hsize);
filt_gaus=fspecial('gaussian', hsize, sigma);
```

The parameter *hsize* is a vector that represents the number of rows and columns of the neighbourhood that is used when applying the filter. The parameter *sigma* is the standard deviation of the applied Gaussian filter.

```
% Filter application
im_filt_av=imfilter(im, filt_av);
im_filt_gaus=imfilter(im, filt_gaus);
```

Edge detectors can also be applied by filtering the image with the edge operator. An example follows with the application of the previously mentioned point edge detector.

```
% Filter with point edge detector
im_filt_p=imfilter(im, P);
```

Apart from user designed filters, IPT includes filters that can be directly applied to the image. Such examples are the median filter (*medfilt2*), the Wiener filter (*wiener2*) or the 2D order-statistics filter (*ordfilt2*).

```
% Filter application
im_filt_med=medfilt2(im, neighbourhood);
im_filt_ord=ordfilt2(im, order, domain);
im_filt_win=wiener2(im);
```

The *neighbourhood* in the *medfilt2* function specifies the dimensions of the area in which the median value of the pixel will be found. The *ordfilt2* function is a generalised version of the median filter. A neighbourhood is defined by the non-zero pixels of *domain*, and each pixel in the image is replaced by the *order*-th smallest of its neighbours within this domain [1]. An example could be the following command, where each pixel is replaced by the 6th smallest value found in its 3×3 neighbourhood.

```
% Order-statistics filter example
im_filt_ord=ordfilt2(im, 6, ones(3));
```

Figure 7 shows examples of Gaussian and order statistics filtered images.

Figure 7. Images filtered using a Gaussian filter (left – hsize [9 9] and sigma 1) and a 6th order statistics filter (right).

2.3.6. *Morphological image processing*

Morphological image processing refers to the extraction of descriptors which describe objects of interest and, thus, their morphology determines the tools that are used [8]. Structuring elements are used to probe the image [3]. The function *bwmorph* performs all morphological operations with the addition of suitable parameters. Since the processing time of this function may increase significantly with image complexity, it is supported by the PCT for increased speed of processing. Morphological processing includes dilation, erosion, opening, closing, top-hat and bottom-hat transformation, hit-or-miss transformation as well as other processes that perform pixel-specific changes.

```
% Morphological processing
im_bin=bwmorph(im, operation, n);
```

The parameter *operation* accounts for the type of morphological operator while *n* is the number of times that this process should be repeated. If *n* is not defined, the process is applied only once. Processes such as dilation and erosion can also be applied using individual functions when a custom-made structuring element is to be used. Examples of individual processes follow.

```
% Definition of flat and non-flat structuring element, respectively
se=strel('disk', 5);
se=strel('ball', 10, 5);
% Dilation, erosion and top-hat transformation
im_mor=imdilate(im, se);
im_mor=imerode(im, se);
im_mor=imtophat(im, se);
```

Figure 8 presents examples of dilation and top-hat transformation with a 'disk' structuring element of radius 10.

Figure 8. Dilated image (left) and a top-hat transformed image using a 'disk' structuring element of radius 10 (right).

The distance transform is usually applied to binary images and represents the distance between a white pixel and its closest zero pixel. Pixels in the new image obtain higher values with larger distance from a zero pixel. This transformation can act as a segmentation function and it is often used in the segmentation of overlapping disks [1], [8].

```
% Distance transform
im_dist=bwdist(im_bin);
```

2.3.7. Colour image processing

Colour images are subject to processing in many scientific fields, as different colours can represent different features. The most commonly used colour representation is RGB (Red-Green-Blue). Transformation of RGB images into grey-scale intensity or extraction of a specific colour can be done using the following code:

http://dx.doi.org/10.5772/58300

```
% RGB image to grey-scale intensity image
im_grey=im_rgb=rgb2gray(im);
% Extraction of each colour
im_r=im_rgb(:,:,1);
im_g=im_rgb(:,:,2);
im_b=im_rgb(:,:,3);
```

2.4. Feature extraction

Feature extraction is the process through which recognised objects are assessed according to some geometrical criteria. The first step of this process is to 'label' the objects of a binary image *im_bin* using the function *bwlabel*. The resulting image is referred to as labelled image (*im_lab*). The function scans the image from top to bottom and from left to right attributing a number to each pixel indicating to which object it belongs. Additionally, the IPT has the function *regionprops* which measures features of labelled objects such as area, equivalent diameter, eccentricity, perimeter, and major and minor axis lengths. This function operates on labelled images which contains *n* labelled objects. A full list of the features that can be calculated using *regionprops* can be found in the MATLAB IPT documentation [1].

Apart from the standard features that are included in the IPT, custom-defined features can be measured either by using already calculated features or by introducing completely new measurements. An example could be the measurement of an object's standard geometric characteristics as well as the thinness ratio and compactness (or irregularity) using a *for* loop for assessment of all *n* objects. Since the user may have to handle numerous measurements for many objects, it is usually useful to pre-allocate memory in order to reduce the processing time. The following code can be used to label image objects, measure the features and store them as a table of variables [1], [3].

```
% Labelling and measurement of geometrical features
[im_lab, n] = bwlabel(im_bin);
% Measurement of geometrical features
stats = regionprops(im_lab, 'Area', 'Perimeter', 'Eccentricity', ...
 'MinorAxisLength', 'MajorAxisLength', 'EquivDiameter');
% Memory pre-allocation for new features
[stats(1:n).Roundness] = deal(0);
[stats(1:n).Compactness] = deal(0);
% Measurement of new features Thinesss Ratio and Compactness
for k = 1:n
    [stats(k).ThinessRatio] = ...
        4*pi*[stats(k).Area]/([stats(k).Perimeter].^2);
    [stats(k).Compactness] = 1 / [stats(k).ThinessRatio];
end
```

Measured features are stored in structure arrays. Usually, further processing of features requires transforming structure arrays into matrices. MATLAB cannot perform such transformations without the application of an intermediate step: the structure arrays have first to be transformed into cell arrays which in turn can be converted into matrices.

```
% Conversion of a structure array into a cell array and then into a matrix
cell_features=struct2cell(stats);
features=cell2mat(cell_features');
save('features.mat', 'features');
```

Notice that the transpose of the cell array *cell_features* has been used in order to allocate features to matrix columns rather than rows. For performance reasons it is usually best to orient the data in such a way that they are processed column by column rather than row by row; in this case we are expecting to go through the data feature by feature rather than image by image.

2.5. Processing series of images

In many cases, handling of multiple images can be a laborious task unless an automated process can be established. Assuming we have a batch of 100 images that we would like to process, using a *for* loop and defining the path to the image directory, we can load, process and save the images one at a time. After saving the first image, the next one in the directory is automatically loaded, processed and saved. The procedure continues until the last image has been saved. The following code performs this operation.

```
% Find the images in the current directory with the expected name
% The symbol * indicates that the name 'image' can be followed by any
% additional characters
filelist = dir('image*.tif');
% Find the number of files to be processed
numImages = length(filelist);
% Loop to read, process and save each image
for k = 1:numImages
    myfilename=filelist(k).name;
    im = imread(myfilename);
    im_proc = ... (processing)
    imwrite(im_proc, ['image', num2str(k), '_new.tif'], 'tif');
end
```

2.6. Video handling

2.6.1. Video to frames

An interesting application for image processing is handling video data. In this case, the video file has to be divided into single frames. The function *VideoReader* can be used in order to input the file as a variable. For *n* frames, each frame is then saved as a separate image in any format. The following code reads a video (called *movie*) to a MATLAB structure and saves the frames one by one into 'tiff' format. [9]

```
% Initialisation and frames characteristics
video = VideoReader('movie.avi');
n = video.NumberOfFrames;
height = video.Height;
```

http://dx.doi.org/10.5772/58300

```
width = video.Width;
% Preallocate movie structure
movie(1:n) = struct('cdata', zeros(height, width, 3, 'uint8'));
% Reading video and saving frames
for k = 1:n
    movie(k).cdata = read(video, k);
    imwrite(movie(k).cdata, ...
         strcat('frame_', (strcat(int2str(k), '.tif'))));
end
```

2.6.2. Frames to video

Since every frame is stored as a single image it can be processed accordingly, either one by one or in batch mode. A possible next step in this process can be to combine the processed images into a single video again. If a new movie (called *movie_new*) is to be created from frames (called *frame#*), then the following code supplies the backbone for such a process [9].

```
% Specify video name and frame rate
video = VideoWriter('movie_new.avi');
video.FrameRate = 1;
% Open video recorder to add frames
open(video);
% Find the images in the current directory with the expected name
% The symbol * indicates that the name 'frame' can be followed by any
% additional characters
filelist = dir('frame*.tif');

% List the files and find the number of frames to be added
fileNames = {filelist.name}';
numImages = length(filelist);
% Loop over all images to read, and write to movie file
for k=1:numImages
    myfilemane = strcat('frame', num2str(k), '.tif');
    frame = imread(myfilemane);
    writeVideo(video, frame);
end
% Close video file recorder and play the new video
close(video);
implay('movie_new.avi');
```

3. Image processing on GPU in MATLAB

Large amounts of image data are produced in many technical and experimental situations, in particular where images are repeatedly acquired over time or when dealing with images of higher dimensionality than two. Time-lapse imaging and video recording can be mentioned as examples of the former, whereas the latter can be represented by any of the many tomographic imaging modalities present. 4D computed tomography (CT), where 3D CT images are acquired at regular intervals to monitor internal patient motion, is an example of an application pertaining to both categories. It is often desirable or even critical to speed up the analysis and processing of such large image data sets, especially for applications running in or near real-time. Due to the inherently parallel nature of many image processing algorithms, they are well suited for implementation on a graphics processing unit (GPU), and consequently we can expect a substantial speedup from such an implementation over code running on a CPU. However, despite the fact that GPUs are nowadays ubiquitous in desktop computers, only 34 out of the several hundred functions of the IPT are GPU-enabled by the PCT in the current MATLAB release (2013b). In this sub-chapter we will explore the possibilities available for someone either wanting to harness the computing power of the GPU directly from MATLAB or to incorporate external GPU code into MATLAB programs. The focus will be on image processing applications, but the techniques presented can with little or no effort be adapted to other applications.

In the first part of this part we look at how to use the built-in, GPU-enabled image processing functions of the PCT. Following this, we explain how pixel-wise manipulations can be carried out using the GPU-enabled version of `arrayfun` and how we can write our own image processing functions making use of over one hundred elementary MATLAB functions that have been implemented to run on GPUs. In the second part of this section, we show how the PCT can be used to call kernel functions written in the CUDA programming language directly from MATLAB. This allows us to make use of existing kernel functions in our MATLAB applications. Further, for those with knowledge of CUDA, it makes more of the GPU's potential available from MATLAB and also provides an easy way of testing kernel functions under development. The third and final part is dedicated to more advanced users who might want to make use of one of the CUDA libraries provided by NVIDIA, who prefer to write their code in a language different from CUDA, who lack access to the Parallel Computing Toolbox, or who have access to an existing GPU code library that they would like to call from MATLAB. We look at how CUDA code can be compiled directly into MEX functions using the PCT, followed by a description of how GPU code written in either CUDA or OpenCL can be accessed from MATLAB by compiling it into a library and creating a MEX wrapper function around it. Finally, we show how the code for a MEX wrapper function can be built directly in our external compiler and, for example, included in an existing Visual Studio (Microsoft Corporation, Redmond, WA, USA) solution so that this is done automatically when building the solution.

3.1. *gpuArray* and built-in GPU-enabled functions

For the examples in this part to work, we need a computer equipped with an NVIDIA GPU of CUDA compute capability 1.3 or greater which is properly set up and recognised by the PCT [10]. The functions `gpuDeviceCount` and `gpuDevice` can be used to identify and select a GPU as described in the PCT documentation [11].

To be able to process an image on the GPU, the corresponding data first have to be copied from main CPU memory over the PCI bus to GPU memory. In MATLAB, data on the GPU are accessed through objects of type `gpuArray`. The command

http://dx.doi.org/10.5772/58300

```
imGpu=gpuArray(im);
```

creates a new `gpuArray` object called `imGpu` and assigns to it a copy of the image data in `im`. `imGpu` will be of the same type as `im` (e.g. `double`, `single`, `int32`, etc.), which might affect the performance of the GPU computation as discussed below. Let us for now assume that `im` is a 3072×3072 array of single precision floating point numbers (`single`). Correspondingly, when we have executed all our GPU calculations, we call the function `gather` to retrieve the result. For example,

```
result=gather(resultGpu);
```

copies the data in the `gpuArray` object `resultGpu` back to `result` in CPU memory. In general, copying data over the PCI bus is relatively slow, meaning that when working with large data sets we should try to avoid unnecessary copies between CPU and GPU memory. When possible, it might therefore be faster to create filters, masks or intermediates directly on the GPU. To do this, `gpuArray` has several static constructors corresponding to standard MATLAB functions, currently `eye`, `false`, `inf`, `nan`, `ones`, `true`, `zeros`, `linspace`, `logspace`, `rand`, `randi` and `randn`, to pre-allocate and initialise GPU memory. These can be invoked by calling `gpuArray.`*`constructor`* where *`constructor`* is replaced by the function call. For example,

```
noiseGpu=gpuArray.randn(3072, 'single');
```

creates a 3072 × 3072 array of normally distributed pseudorandom numbers with zero mean and standard deviation one. As with the corresponding standard MATLAB functions, the last function argument specifies the array element type (in this case `single`), and if omitted it defaults to `double`. While this is normally not a problem when working on modern CPUs, it is worth bearing in mind that NVIDIAs consumer GPUs are often several times faster at processing single precision floating point numbers (`single`), compared to double precision (`double`) or integers (`int32`). This means that where double precision is not crucial, it is a good habit to declare arrays on the GPU as single precision. As an alternative, the first seven static constructors listed above can be called through their corresponding MATLAB function by appending the argument list with `'gpuArray'`. E.g.

```
zerosGpu=zeros(3072, 'int32', 'gpuArray');
```

creates a `gpuArray` object containing 3072×3072 32-bit integers (`int32`) initialised to zero. When calling these functions, an alternative to explicitly specifying the type is using the `'like'` argument. This creates an array of the same type as the argument following the `'like'` argument, i.e.

```
onesGpu=ones(3072, 'like', zerosGpu);
```

creates a `gpuArray` object of `int32` values initialised to one, whereas

```
onesWsp=ones(3072, 'like', im);
```

creates a standard MATLAB array of `single` values initialised to one. This can be useful when creating new variables in functions that are meant to run both on the CPU and the GPU where we have no *a priori* knowledge of the input type. For a `gpuArray` object to be able to hold complex numbers, this has to be explicitly specified upon construction, either by using the `'complex'` argument when creating it directly on the GPU or by explicit casting when copying non-complex data, e.g. `gpuArray(complex(im))`. To inspect the properties of a GPU array we can use the standard MATLAB functions such as `size`, `length`, `isreal` etc. In addition to these, the function `classUnderlying` returns the class underlying the GPU array (since `class` will just return `gpuArray`) while `existsOnGPU` returns true if the argument is a GPU array that exists on the GPU and is accessible.

Once our image data are in GPU memory, we have two options for manipulating them: either we can use the sub-set of the built-in MATLAB functions (including some functions available in toolboxes) that run on the GPU, or we can write our own functions using only element-wise operations and launch them through `arrayfun` or `bsxfun`. In the first case, we use normal MATLAB syntax with the knowledge that any of these functions are automatically executed on the GPU as long as at least one argument is of type `gpuArray`. Using `imGpu` and `rand-NoiseGpu` defined above we can create a new, noisy image on the GPU by typing:

```
noisyImGpu=imGpu+0.2+0.3*noiseGpu;
```

A list of the GPU-enabled MATLAB functions available on the current system, together with all static constructors of `gpuArray`, can be displayed by typing `methods('gpuArray')`. For MATLAB 2013b, the list comprises around 200 standard functions plus any additional functions in installed toolboxes [2]. For example, using the GPU-enabled function `imnoise` from the IPT, the same result as above can be obtained through:

```
noisyImGpu2=imnoise(imGpu, 'gaussian', 0.2, 0.09);
```

(where a variance of 0.09 equals a standard deviation of 0.3). Another, potentially more useful, GPU-enabled function from the IPT is `imfilter`. Using `imGpu` from earlier

```
sobelFilter=fspecial('sobel');
filteredImGpu=imfilter(imGpu, sobelFilter);
```

filters the image using a horizontal Sobel filter. Note that `sobelFilter` is an ordinary 2D MATLAB array, `[1 2 1; 0 0 0; -1 -2 -1]`, but since `imGpu` is a GPU array, the GPU-

http://dx.doi.org/10.5772/58300

enabled version of `imfilter` is automatically called and the output, `filteredImGpu`, will be a GPU array.

The second option for manipulating GPU arrays directly from MATLAB is by calling our own functions through the built-in `bsxfun` or `arrayfun` functions. As before, if any of the input arguments to the function is a GPU array, the calculation will automatically be carried out on the selected GPU. Thus, a third way of producing a noisy version of `imGpu` would be to first create the function `addAndOffset` that performs an element-wise addition of two images and adds a constant offset:

```
function result=addAndOffset(im1, im2, offset)
result=im1+im2+offset; end
```

and then calling

```
noisyImGpu3=arrayfun(@addAndOffset, imGpu, 0.3*noiseGpu, 0.2);
```

The benefit of writing functions and launching them through `bsxfun` or `arrayfun` compared to calling MATLAB functions directly on GPU arrays is a potential speedup for large functions. This is because in the former case, the whole function can automatically be compiled to a GPU function, called CUDA kernel, resulting in a single launch of GPU code (although the overhead for compiling the function will be added to the first call). In contrast, in the latter case, each operation has to be launched in sequence using the precompiled kernel functions available in MATLAB. However, when running on a GPU, `arrayfun` and `bsxfun` are limited to element-wise operations. In a typical image processing application, this means that each pixel is unaware of its neighbours, which limits the use to functions where pixels are processed independently of one another. As a result, many image filters cannot be implemented in this way, in which case we are left either to use built-in functions as described earlier, or to write our own kernel functions as described in the next part. Further, since we are constrained to element-wise manipulations, the number of built-in functions at our disposal inside our function is somewhat limited. For a complete list of the available built-in functions, as well as some further limitations when using `bsxfun` and `arrayfun` with GPU arrays, see the PCT documentation [12].

Before moving on to the next part we should stress that since GPUs are built to process large amounts of data in parallel, there is no guarantee that running code on a GPU instead of a CPU will always result in a speedup. Although image processing algorithms provide good candidates for substantial speedups, this characteristic of the GPU means that vectorisation of code and simultaneous processing of large amounts of data (i.e. avoiding loops wherever possible) becomes even more crucial than in ordinary MATLAB programs. Further, GPU memory latency and bandwidth often limit the performance of GPU code. This can be alleviated by ensuring that, as far as possible, data that are operated on at the same time are stored nearby in memory. Since arrays are stored in a sequential column-major order in MATLAB, this means avoiding random memory-access patterns where possible and organising our data so that we mostly operate on columns rather than on rows. Finally, when evaluating the performance of our GPU code we should use the function `gputimeit`. It is called in the same manner as the regular MATLAB function `timeit`, i.e. it takes as argument a function, which itself does not take any arguments, and times it, but is guaranteed to return the accurate execution time for GPU code (which `timeit` is not). If this is not feasible, the code section we want to time can be sandwiched between a `tic` and a `toc`, as long as we add a call to `wait(gpuDevice)` just before the `toc`. This ensures that the time is measured only after execution on the currently selected GPU has finished. (Otherwise MATLAB continues to execute ensuing lines of GPU-independent code, like `toc`, asynchronously without waiting for the GPU calculation to finish). Since the MATLAB profiler only measures CPU time, we need to employ a similar trick to get accurate GPU timings when profiling: if we sandwich the lines or blocks of GPU code we want to time between two calls to `wait(gpuDevice)`, the execution time reported for the desired line or block plus the time taken by the second call to `wait` gives the correct timing.

3.2. Calling CUDA kernel functions from MATLAB

By using the techniques described in the previous part we can use MATLAB to perform many of our standard image processing routines on the GPU. However, it does not allow us to test our own CUDA-implemented algorithms or use existing ones in our MATLAB programs, nor does it provide a means to explicitly control GPU resources, such as global and shared memory. In this part we demonstrate how this can be remedied by creating a `CUDAKernel` object from a kernel function written in CUDA. Instructions on how to write CUDA code is well beyond the scope of this chapter, and therefore this part assumes some previous basic knowledge of this language.

A `CUDAKernel` object required to launch a CUDA kernel function from MATLAB is constructed by calling the static constructor `parallel.gpu.CUDAKernel`. The constructor takes three MATLAB string arguments: the path to a .`ptx` file containing the kernel code, the interface of the kernel function, and the name of the desired entry point. For the first argument, a .`ptx` file with the same name as the source file, containing the corresponding code compiled into pseudo-assembly language, is automatically generated when using the NVIDIA CUDA Compiler (NVCC) with the flag `--ptx` to compile a .`cu` file (if it contains one or more kernel functions). (Note that if using an integrated development environment, you might have to instruct it not to delete .`ptx` files when finishing the build; for example Visual Studio 2010 requires that the flag`--keep` is used.) The second argument can be either the .`cu` file corresponding to the .`ptx` file specified in the first argument, from which the argument list of the desired kernel function can be derived, or the explicit argument list itself. The latter is useful when the .`cu` file is not available, or when the argument list contains standard data types that have been renamed through the use of the `typedef` keyword. The third argument specifies which kernel function in the .`ptx` file to use, and although NVCC mangles function names similar to a C++ compiler, the names in the .`ptx` file are guaranteed to contain the original function name. MATLAB uses substring matching when searching for the entry point and it is therefore often enough to provide the name of the original kernel function (see exceptions

http://dx.doi.org/10.5772/58300

below). Let us assume that we have access to `myFilters.cu` containing several kernel functions named `myFilter1`, `myFilter2`, etc., and its corresponding `myFilters.ptx`. Then

```
gpuFilter1=parallel.gpu.CUDAKernel('myFilters.ptx', myFilters.cu',
 'myFilter1');
```

creates a `CUDAKernel` object called `gpuFilter1` that can be used to launch the CUDA kernel function `myFilter1` from MATLAB. If we further assume that `myFilter1` is declared as

```
__global__ void myFilter1(const float *imIn, float *imOut, float parameter)
```

the second argument above, `'myFilters.cu'`, could equally be replaced by the string `'const float *, float *, float'`. In some cases, care has to be taken when specifying the entry point. For example, if `myFilter2` is a templated function instantiated for more than one template argument, each instance of the resulting function will have a name containing the string `'myFilter2'`. Likewise, if another kernel function called `myFilter1_v2` is declared in the same .cu file, specifying `'myFilter1'` as the third argument of `parallel.gpu.CUDAKernel` becomes ambiguous. In these cases, we should provide the mangled function names, which are given during compilation with NVCC in verbose mode, i.e. with--`ptxas-options=-v` specified. The full mangled name of the kernel used by a `CUDAKernel` object is stored in the object property `EntryPoint`, and can be obtained by e.g. `gpuFilter1.EntryPoint`.

Once a `CUDAKernel` object has been created, we need to specify its launch parameters which is done through the `ThreadBlockSize`, `GridSize` and `SharedMemorySize` object properties. Thus,

```
gpuFilter1.ThreadBlockSize=[32 8 1];
gpuFilter1.GridSize=[96 384 1];
gpuFilter1.SharedMemorySize=4*32*8;
```

sets the block size to 32×8 threads, the grid size to 96×384 blocks and the shared memory size per block to 4×32×8=1024 bytes, enough to hold 256 `single` or `int32` values, or 128 `double` values. In total this will launch 3072×3072 threads, one per pixel of our sample image. A fourth, read-only property called `MaxThreadsPerBlock` holds the upper limit for the total number of threads per block that we can use for the kernel function. If the kernel function is dependent on constant GPU memory, this can be set by calling `setConstantMemeory`, taking as the first parameter the `CUDAKerner` object, as the second parameter the name of the constant memory symbol and as the third parameter a MATLAB array containing the desired data. For example, we can set the constant memory declared as `__constant__ float myConstData [128]` in `myFilters.cu` and needed in `myFilter1` by calling:

```
setConstantMemory(myFilter1, myConstData, sqrt(single(0:127)));
```

To execute our kernel function we call `feval` with our `GPUKernel` object as the first parameter, followed by the input parameters for our kernel. For input parameters corresponding to arguments passed by value in the CUDA kernel (here: scalars), MATLAB scalars are normally used (although single element GPU arrays also work), whereas for pointer type arguments, either GPU arrays or MATLAB arrays can be used. In the latter case, these are automatically copied to the GPU. A list of supported data types for the kernel arguments can be found in the PCT documentation [13]. In general these are the C/C++ standard types (along with their corresponding pointers) that have MATLAB counterparts, with the addition of `float2` and `double2` that map to MATLAB's complex `single` and `double` types, respectively. `CUDAKernel` objects have three additional, read-only properties related to input and output. `NumRHSArguments` and `MaxNumLHSArguments` respectively hold the expected number of input arguments and the maximum number of output arguments that the objects accepts, and `ArgumentTypes` holds a cell of strings naming the expected MATLAB input types. Each type is prefixed with either `in` or `inout` to signal whether it is input only (corresponding to an argument passed by value or a constant pointer in CUDA) or combined input/output (corresponding to a non-constant pointer in CUDA).

To function in a MATLAB context, a call to a CUDA kernel through a `GPUKernel` object must support output variables. Therefore, pointer arguments that are not declared `const` in the kernel declaration are seen as output variables and, if there is more than one, they are numbered according to their order of appearance in the declaration. This means that calling `gpuFilter1` above produces one output, whereas `gpuFilter2` created from

```
__global__ void myFilter2(const float *imIn, int *imInterm, float *imOut)
```

produces two outputs. With this information we can now call the `myFilter1` kernel function through

```
gpuRes1=gpuArray.zeros(3072, 'single');
gpuRes1=feval(gpuFilter1, gpuIm, gpuRes1, sqrt(2));
```

Similarly, we can call `myFilter2` through

```
gpuInterm=gpuArray.zeros(3072, 'int32');
gpuRes2=gpuArray.zeros(3072, 'single');
[gpuInterm, gpuRes2]=feval(gpuFilter2, gpuIm, gpuInterm, gpuRes2);
```

The output from a `CUDAKernel` object is always a GPU array, which means that if the corresponding input is a MATLAB array it will be created automatically. Consider the kernel

```
__global__ void myFilter3(float *imInOut, float parameter)
```

with its corresponding `CUDAKernel` object `gpuFilter3`. Since `im` from our previous examples a MATLAB array, calling

```
gpuRes3=feval(gpuFilter3, im, 3.14);
```

automatically copies `im` to the GPU and creates a new `gpuArray` object called `gpuRes3` to hold the result.

3.3. MEX functions and GPU programming

In the previous part we saw how, by running our own CUDA kernels directly from MATLAB, we can overcome some of the limitations present when working only with built-in MATLAB functionality. However, we are still (in release 2013b) limited to using kernel functions that take only standard type arguments, and we can access neither external libraries, such as the NVIDIA Performance Primitives, the NVIDIA CUDA Fast Fourier Transform or the NVIDIA CUDA Random Number Generation libraries, nor the GPU's texture memory with its spatial optimised layout and hardware interpolation features. Further, we need to have an NVIDIA GPU, be writing our code in CUDA and have access to the PCT to use the GPU in our MATLAB code. In this section we look at how we can use MEX functions to partly or fully circumnavigate these limitations. This again assumes previous experience of GPU programming and some knowledge of how to write and use MEX functions. A good overview of the latter can be found in the MATLAB documentation [14].

The first option, which removes the technical restrictions but still requires access to the PCT (running on a 64-bit platform) and a GPU from NVIDIA, is to write MEX functions directly containing CUDA code. The CUDA code itself is written exactly as it would be in any other application, and can either be included in the file containing the MEX function entry point or in a separate file. Although this process is well documented in the PCT documentation [15] and through the PCT examples [16], we briefly describe it here for consistency. The main advantage of this approach over the one described later is that it enables us to write MEX functions that use GPU arrays as input and output through the underlying C/C++ object `mxGPUArray`. As all MEX input and output, GPU arrays are passed to MEX functions as pointers to `mxArray` objects. The first step is therefore to call either `mxGPUCreateFromMxArray` or `mxGPUCopyFromMxArray` on the pointer to the `mxArray` containing the GPU data, in order to obtain a pointer to an `mxGPUArray`. In the former case, the `mxGPUArray` becomes read-only, whereas in the latter case the data is copied so that the returned `mxGPUArray` can be modified. (`mxGPUCreateFromMxArray` and `mxGPUCopyFromMxArray` also accept pointers to `mxArray` objects containing CPU data, in which case the data is copied to the GPU regardless of the function used.) We can now obtain a raw pointer to device memory that can be passed to CUDA kernels by calling `mxGPUGetDataReadOnly` (in the case of read-only data) or `mxGPUGetData` (otherwise) and explicitly casting the returned pointer to the correct type. Information about the number of dimensions, dimension sizes, total number of elements, type and complexity of the underlying data of an `mxGPUArray` object can be further obtained through the functions `mxGPUGetNumberOfDimensions`, `mxGPUGetDimensions`, `mxGPUGetNumberOfElements`, `mxGPUGetClassID`, and `mxGPUGetComplexity`. We can also create a new `mxGPUArray` object through `mxGPUCreateGPUArray`, which allocates and, if we want, initialises memory on the GPU for our return data. With this we are in a position where we can treat input from MATLAB just as any other data on the GPU and perform our desired calculations. Once we are ready to return our results to MATLAB we call either `mxGPUCreateMxArrayOnCPU` or `mxGPUCreateMxArrayOnGPU` to obtain a pointer to an `mxArray` object that can be returned to MATLAB through `plhs`. The former copies the data back to the CPU making the MEX function return a standard MATLAB array whereas in the latter case the data stays on the GPU and a GPU array is returned. Finally, we should call `mxGPUDestroyGPUArray` on any `mxGPUArray` objects that we have created. This deletes them from the CPU and, unless they are referenced by another `mxArray` object (as will be the case if they are returned through `plhs`), frees the corresponding GPU memory. Note that there are several other functions in the `mxGPU` family to examine, duplicate, create and copy `mxGPUArray` objects, and in particular for working with complex arrays, that work in a similar way and which are described in the PCT documentation [17].

For the above to work, we need to include `mxGPUArray.h`, in addition to `mex.h`, in our source file. The source file has to have the extension .cu and it should contain a call to the function `mxInitGPU` before launching any GPU code in order to initialise the MATLAB GPU library. Provided that the environment variable `MW_NVCC_PATH` is set to the NVCC folder path and that a copy of the PCT version of `mexopts.bat` or `mexopts.sh` (`*matlabroot*\toolbox\distcomp\gpu\extern\src\mex\*xxx*64\`) is located in the same folder as the source code, we can compile our CUDA containing MEX functions from MATLAB in the usual way using the mex command. If using external libraries, these also have to be provided, which can normally be done by passing the full library path, including file name, to the mex command after the `.c`, `.cpp` or `.cu` file path.

A bare-bone MEX function calling the kernel function `myFilter1` from earlier, which takes into account the considerations above but is stripped of any boundary or argument checking, follows:

```
#include "mex.h"
#include "gpu\mxGPUArray.h"

__global__ void myFilter1(const float *imIn, float *imOut, float parameter)
{
    // Kernel code
}

void mexFunction(int nlhs, mxArray *plhs[], int nrhs, mxArray const *prhs[]) {
    mxGPUArray const *gpuArrayIn;
    mxGPUArray *gpuArrayOut;
    float const *devIn;
```

```
        float *devOut;

        mxInitGPU();
        gpuArrayIn = mxGPUCreateFromMxArray(prhs[0]);
        devIn = (float const *)(mxGPUGetDataReadOnly(gpuArrayIn));
        gpuArrayOut =
            mxGPUCreateGPUArray(mxGPUGetNumberOfDimensions(gpuArrayIn),
            mxGPUGetDimensions(gpuArrayIn), mxGPUGetClassID(gpuArrayIn),
            mxGPUGetComplexity(gpuArrayIn), MX_GPU_DO_NOT_INITIALIZE);
        devOut = (float *)(mxGPUGetData(gpuArrayOut));

        const mwSize *dim = mxGPUGetDimensions(gpuArrayIn);
        int height = (int)(dim[0]);
        int width = (int)(dim[1]);
        dim3 block(32, 8, 1);
        dim3 grid((height+block.x-1)/block.x, (width+block.y-1)/block.y, 1);

        float param = *(float *)(mxGetData(prhs[1]));

        myFilter1<<<grid, block>>> (devIn, devOut, param);

        plhs[0] = mxGPUCreateMxArrayOnGPU(gpuArrayOut);
        mxGPUDestroyGPUArray(gpuArrayIn);
        mxGPUDestroyGPUArray(gpuArrayOut);
}
```

After compilation, assuming the above code is found in `mexFilter1.cu`, we can call the MEX function like this:

```
gpuRes3=mexFilter1(imGpu, single(2.72));
```

Note the explicit type conversion necessary to convert the second argument to `single` to match the input type. Note also that, depending on the compiler and system settings, in order to have `mwSize` correctly identified as a 64-bit type, we might need to use the `–largeArraysDims` flag when compiling using the `mex` command.

The rest of this part will be dedicated to describing how we can call GPU code from MATLAB even if we do not have access to the PCT or write our code in CUDA. Since without the PCT, the `mex` command is not set up to compile anything except standard C/C++ code, we have two alternatives to achieve what we want. The only drawback with these, compared to when using `mxGPUArray` from the PCT is that it is harder to have data in GPU memory persist when returning to MATLAB between calls to MEX functions. (This can still be achieved by explicitly casting a GPU memory pointer to an integer type of correct length which is returned to MATLAB. The integer is then passed to the next MEX function which casts it back to the correct pointer type. However, the problem with this approach lies in eliminating the risk of memory leaks; although solutions for this exist, they are beyond the scope of this chapter.) This means that unless we go through any extra effort, we are left either to perform all our GPU calculations from the same MEX function before returning control to MATLAB or suffer the penalty associated with copying our data back and forth between each call. In many cases, however, this may provide less of a limitation than one might initially think, especially when using MATLAB to test GPU code under development or using MATLAB as a front-end to existing code libraries.

The first alternative is to compile our GPU code, regardless of in which language it is written, into a static library using our external compiler, and then to call this library from a MEX function that we compile using the `mex` command. Since our MEX function cannot call GPU functions directly, a small C/C++ wrapper function has to be written around our GPU code. A wrapper for the `myFilter1` CUDA kernel, which we can place either in the same file as the CUDA code or in a separate .cu file, could look like this (again, error checking has been omitted for brevity):

```
void callMyFilter1(const float *imIn, float *imOut, float param, int height,
int width)
{
    float *devIn;
    cudaMalloc((void**)&devIn, height*width*sizeof(float));
    cudaMemcpy(devIn, imIn, height*width*sizeof(float),
        cudaMemcpyHostToDevice);
    float *devOut;
    cudaMalloc((void**)&devOut, height*width*sizeof(float));

    dim3 block(32, 8, 1);
    dim3 grid((height+block.x-1)/block.x, (width+block.y-1)/block.y, 1);

    myFilter1<<<grid, block>>> (devIn, devOut, param);

    cudaMemcpy(imOut, devOut, height*width*sizeof(float),
        cudaMemcpyDeviceToHost);
    cudaFree(devIn);
    cudaFree(devOut);
}
```

Once the static library, normally a `.lib` file under Windows or a .a file under Linux and Mac OS, has been created, we can write a MEX function calling the wrapper:

```
#include "mex.h"

void callMyFilter1(const float *, float *, float, int, int);

void mexFunction(int nlhs, mxArray *plhs[], int nrhs, mxArray const *prhs[]) {
    int height = mxGetM(prhs[0]);
    int width = mxGetN(prhs[0]);
    const float *imIn = (float *)(mxGetData(prhs[0]));
    float param = (float)(mxGetScalar(prhs[1]);
    plhs[0] = mxCreateNumericMatrix(height, width, mxSINGLE_CLASS, mxREAL);
```

```
        float *imOut = (float *)(mxGetData(plhs[0]));
        callMyFilter1(imIn, imOut, param, height, width);
    }
```

Note that it is normally better, especially if using a pre-existing library, to use `#include` to include the corresponding header files rather than, as in the example above, to manually enter the function prototype. We should now be able to compile this wrapper using the `mex` command, remembering to pass the path to our own library as well as to the necessary GPU runtime library. For CUDA, this is `cudart.lib` on Windows, `libcuda.so` on Linux, or `libcuda.dylib` on Mac OS. Thus, assuming that the code above is found in `myFilter1Mex.cpp` and that the library is called `myLibrary.lib`, on Windows the call would look like:

```
mex myFilter1Mex.cpp 'library_path\myLibrary.lib' 'cuda_path\cudart.lib'
```

The second alternative is to build the MEX function directly in our external compiler, without going through the `mex` command. By doing this, the whole process can be carried out in one step and, if we wish, we are free to keep all our code in a single file. The main advantage of this approach occurs if we are developing or using an existing GPU library which we would like to call from MATLAB, for example for testing purposes. In such a case we can add the MEX file to our normal build routine so that every time we rebuild our library we automatically get the MEX function to call it from MATLAB.

A MEX function is a dynamically linked shared library which exports a single entry point called `mexFunction`. Hence, by mimicking the steps carried out by the `mex` command (found in `mexopts.bat` or `mexopts.sh`) when calling the external compiler, we can replicate this from outside MATLAB. We can view the exact steps carried out on a particular system by calling the `mex` command in verbose mode, i.e. using the –v flag. Detailed information on how to build MEX functions for Windows and UNIX-like systems (Linux and Mac OS) can be also found in the MATLAB documentation [18]. Here we look at a minimal example from a Windows-centric point of view, although the procedure should be similar on other systems. First, we need to specify that we want to build a dynamically linked shared library, called a dynamic-link library on Windows, and give it the correct file extension, e.g. .`mexw64`; second, we have to provide the compiler with the path to our MEX header files, normally `mex.h`; third, we have to pass the libraries needed to build our MEX function, called `libmx.lib`, `libmex.lib` and `libmat.lib` on Windows, to the linker together with their path; and finally, as mentioned above, we need to export the function named `mexFunction`. In Visual Studio 2010, all of the above steps are done in the Project Properties page of the project in question. Under `Configuration properties-> General`, we set the `Target Extension` to .`mexw64` and the `Configutation Type` to `Dynamic Library (.dll)`. For the header files we add `$(MATLAB_ROOT)\extern\include;` to `Include Directories` under `Configuration Properties-> VC++Directories`. For the libraries, we add `libmx.lib;libmex.lib;libmat.lib;` to `Additional Dependencies` under Configuration Properties-> Linker-> Input and $(MATLAB_ROOT)\extern\lib \win64\microsoft; to Additional Library Directories under Configuration properties-> Linker-> General. Finally, we add /export:mexFunction to Additional Options under Configuration Properties-> Linker-> Command Line. In the above steps it is assumed that the variable MATLAB_ROOT is set to the path of the MATLAB root, otherwise we have to change $(MATLAB_ROOT) to, for example, C:\Program Files\MATLAB\2013b. The code for the MEX example, finally, would look something like this:

```
#include <cuda.h>
#include "mex.h"

__global__ void myFilter1(const float *imIn, float *imOut, float parameter)
{
    // Kernel code
}

void mexFunction(int nlhs, mxArray *plhs[], int nrhs, mxArray const *prhs[])
{
    int height = mxGetM(prhs[0]);
    int width = mxGetN(prhs[0]);
    const float *imIn = (float *)(mxGetData(prhs[0]));
    float param = (float)(mxGetScalar(prhs[1]));
    plhs[0] = mxCreateNumericMatrix(height, width, mxSINGLE_CLASS, mxREAL);
    float *imOut = (float *)(mxGetData(plhs[0]));

    float *devIn;
    cudaMalloc((void**)&devIn, height*width*sizeof(float));
    cudaMemcpy(devIn, imIn, height*width*sizeof(float),
        cudaMemcpyHostToDevice);
    float *devOut;
    cudaMalloc((void**)&devOut, height*width*sizeof(float));

    dim3 block(32, 8, 1);
    dim3 grid((height+block.x-1)/block.x, (width+block.y-1)/block.y, 1);

    myFilter1<<<grid, block>>> (devIn, devOut, param);

    cudaMemcpy(imOut, devOut, height*width*sizeof(float),
        cudaMemcpyDeviceToHost);
    cudaFree(devIn);
    cudaFree(devOut);
}
```

In the case of an existing code library, we can add a new component (such as a new project to an existing solution in Visual Studio) containing a MEX function calling our desired GPU functions so that it is built directly with the original library without any additional steps.

http://dx.doi.org/10.5772/58300

4. Conclusion

In conclusion, MATLAB is a useful tool for prototyping, developing and testing image processing algorithms and pipelines. It provides the user with the option of either using the functions of the IPT or leveraging the capabilities of a high-level programming language combined with many built-in standard functions to create their own algorithms. When high performance or processing of large amounts of data is required, the computational power of a GPU can be exploited. At this point, there are three main options for image processing on GPU in MATLAB: i) we can stick entirely to MATALB code, making use of the built-in, GPU-enabled functions in the IPT and the PCT as well as our own GPU functions built from element-wise operations only; ii) we can use the framework provided by the PCT to call our own CUDA kernel functions directly from MATLAB; iii) we can write a MEX function in C/C++ that can be called from MATLAB and which in turn calls the GPU code of our choice.

Acknowledgements

The authors would like to acknowledge the European Commission FP7 ENTERVISION programme, grant agreement no.: 264552

Author details

Antonios Georgantzoglou*, Joakim da Silva and Rajesh Jena

*Address all correspondence to: ag718@cam.ac.uk

Department of Oncology, University of Cambridge, Cambridge, UK

References

[1] The MathWorks, Inc., "Image Processing Toolbox Documentation," The MathWorks, Inc., 2013. [Online]. Available: http://www.mathworks.co.uk/help/images/. [Accessed 25 October 2013].

[2] The MathWorks, Inc., "Parallel Computing Toolbox Documentation," The MathWorks, Inc., 2013. [Online]. Available: http://www.mathworks.co.uk/help/distcomp/. [Accessed 25 October 2013].

[3] O. Marques, Practical Image and Video Processing, Hoboken, NJ: John Wiley & Sons, Inc., 2011.

[4] S. Sridhar, Digital Image Processing, New Delhi: Oxford University Press, 2011.

[5] N. Otsu, "A Threshold Selection Method from Gray-Level Histograms," *IEEE Transactions on Systems, Man, and Cybernetics,* Vols. SMC-9, no. 1, pp. 62-66, 1979.

[6] W. Burger and M. J. Burge, Principles of Digital Image Processing: Fundamental Techniques, London: Springer, 2009.

[7] K. Najarian and R. Splinter, Biomedical Signal and Image Processing, Boca Raton, FL; London: CRC Press / Taylor & Francis Group, 2006.

[8] C. Solomon and T. Breckon, Fundamentals of Digital Image Processing: A Practical Approach with Examples in MATLAB, Chichester: John Wiley & Sons, Ltd, 2011.

[9] The MathWorks, Inc., "Data and File Management > Data Import and Export > Audio and Video," The MathWorks, Inc., 2014. [Online]. Available: http://www.mathworks.co.uk/help/matlab/audio-and-video.html. [Accessed 25 January 2014].

[10] The MathWorks, Inc., "Discovery > MATLAB GPU Compurting > MATLAB GPU Computing Support for NVIDIA CUDA-Enabled GPUs," The MathWorks, Inc., 2014. [Online]. Available: http://www.mathworks.co.uk/discovery/matlab-gpu.html. [Accessed 25 January 2014].

[11] The MathWorks, Inc., "Parallel Computing Toolbox Documentation (Parallel Computing Toolbox > GPU Computing > Identify and Select a GPU Device)," The MathWorks, Inc., 2013. [Online]. Available: http://www.mathworks.co.uk/help/distcomp/. [Accessed 25 October 2013].

[12] The MathWorks, Inc., "Parallel Computing Toolbox Documentation (Parallel Computing Toolbox > GPU Computing > Run Element-wise MATLAB Code on a GPU)," The MathWorks, Inc., 2013. [Online]. Available: http://www.mathworks.co.uk/help/distcomp/. [Accessed 25 October 2013].

[13] The MathWorks, Inc., "Parallel Computing Toolbox Documentation (Parallel Computing Toolbox > GPU Computing > Run CUDA or PTX Code on GPU)," The MathWorks, Inc., 2013. [Online]. Available: http://www.mathworks.co.uk/help/distcomp/. [Accessed 25 October 2013].

[14] The MathWorks, Inc., "MATLAB Documentation (MATLAB > Advanced Software Development > External Programming Language Interfaces > Application Programming Interfaces to MATLAB > Use and Create MEX-Files)," The MathWorks, Inc., 2013. [Online]. Available: http://www.mathworks.co.uk/help/matlab/. [Accessed 25 October 2013].

[15] The MathWorks, Inc., "Parallel Computing Toolbox Documentation (Parallel Computing Toolbox > GPU Computing > Run MEX-Functions Containing CUDA Code)," The MathWorks, Inc., 2013. [Online]. Available: http://www.mathworks.co.uk/help/distcomp/. [Accessed 25 October 2013].

http://dx.doi.org/10.5772/58300

[16] The MathWorks, Inc., "Parallel Computing Toolbox Documentation (Parallel Computing Toolbox > Parallel Computing Toolbox Examples)," The MathWorks, Inc., 2013. [Online]. Available: http://www.mathworks.co.uk/help/distcomp/. [Accessed 25 October 2013].

[17] The MathWorks, Inc., "Parallel Computing Toolbox Documentation (Parallel Computing Toolbox > GPU Computing > C Functions)," The MathWorks, Inc., 2013. [Online]. Available: http://www.mathworks.co.uk/help/distcomp/. [Accessed 25 October 2013].

[18] The MathWorks, Inc., "MATLAB Documentation (MATLAB > Advanced Software Development > External Programming Language Interfaces > Application Programming Interfaces to MATLAB > Use and Create MEX-Files > Build C/C++ MEX-Files > Custom Building MEX-Files)," The MathWorks, Inc., 2013. [Online]. Available: http://www.mathworks.co.uk/help/matlab/. [Accessed 25 October 2013].